face! — You don't w
our ~~~~~ (confidence), a
on others gaze.

the face! — You don't understand the
~~into~~ out of the single assumption
— that somebody's watching.
we ~~saw~~ caught sight of ourselves,
and pouring ourselves down a

~~it~~ demented children mincing about
rhymed couplets, ~~and~~ killing each other
as no man ever spoke, protestations
after promises of vengeance, even
the thin unpopulated air. We
uncomprehending ~~birds~~ listened —
we're the opposite of people!

Tom Stoppard

Tom Stoppard

A Life

Hermione Lee

faber

First published in 2020
by Faber & Faber Limited
Bloomsbury House, 74–77 Great Russell Street
London WC1B 3DA

Typeset by Ian Bahrami
Printed and bound in the UK by TJ International Ltd, Padstow, Cornwall

A CIP record for this book
is available from the British Library

ISBN 978–0–571–31443–0

10 9 8 7 6 5 4 3 2 1

For John Barnard

It's wanting to know that makes us matter. Otherwise we're going out the way we came in.

Contents

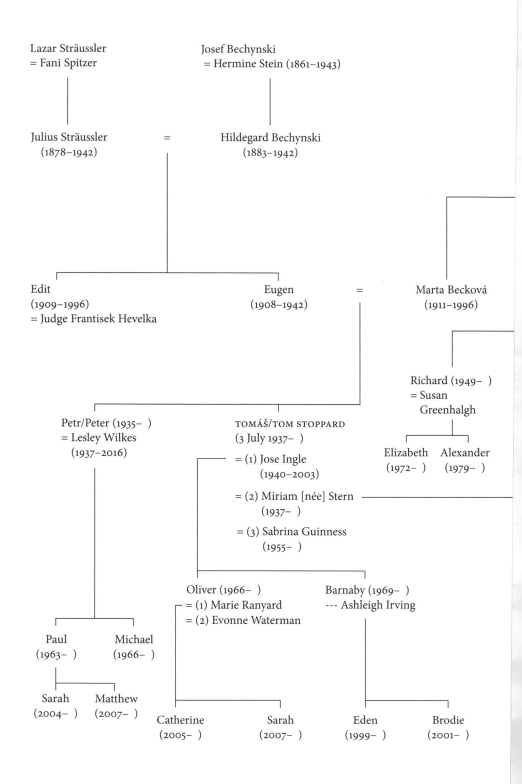

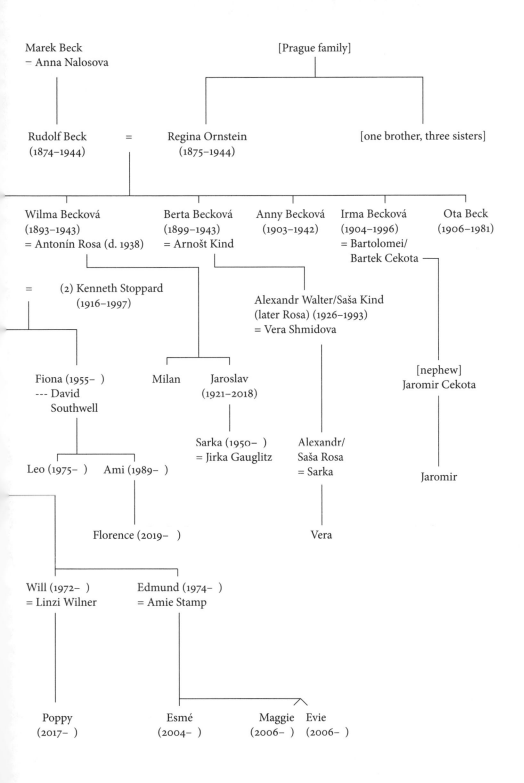

Marek Beck
– Anna Nalosova

[Prague family]

Rudolf Beck   =   Regina Ornstein   [one brother, three sisters]
(1874–1944)   (1875–1944)

Wilma Becková   Berta Becková   Anny Becková   Irma Becková   Ota Beck
(1893–1943)   (1899–1943)   (1903–1942)   (1904–1996)   (1906–1981)
= Antonín Rosa (d. 1938)   = Arnošt Kind   = Bartolomei/
                                                                     Bartek Cekota

=   (2) Kenneth Stoppard
         (1916–1997)

                                              Alexandr Walter/Saša Kind
                                              (later Rosa) (1926–1993)
                                              = Vera Shmidova

Fiona (1955–)   Milan   Jaroslav   [nephew]
--- David   (1921–2018)   Jaromir Cekota
    Southwell

                                       Sarka (1950–)   Alexandr/
                                       = Jirka Gauglitz   Saša Rosa
Leo (1975–)   Ami (1989–)   = Sarka   Jaromir

                                                                Vera
             Florence (2019–)

Will (1972–)   Edmund (1974–)
= Linzi Wilner   = Amie Stamp

Poppy   Esmé   Maggie   Evie
(2017–)   (2004–)   (2006–)   (2006–)

PART ONE

1

First Acts

G: What's the first thing you remember?

R: Oh, let's see . . . The first thing that comes into my head, you
mean?

G: No – the first thing you remember.

R: Ah. (*Pause.*) No, it's no good, it's gone. It was a long time ago.

G (*patient but edged*): You don't get my meaning. What is the first
thing after all the things you've forgotten?

R: Oh I see. (*Pause.*) I've forgotten the question.

The first thing he remembers, he thinks, comes from the winter of 1940
or 1941, when he was three or four. There was a man dressed up as a
devil with a forked tail, who was making the children frightened. They
had to promise to be good, and all the children received a present: a tin
boat, was it? This would have been St Nicholas's Eve, 5 December, when
the Czech Santa Claus, Svatý Mikuláš, appears with two figures, an angel
who rewards every good boy with favours and a devil who frightens the
bad children to make them be good. He was Tomáš, or Tomik, Sträussler.
His baby words would have been in his natal language, which he would
soon forget. These children were not in Czechoslovakia. They were a
little group of exiles, war refugees and survivors, in transit. They were in
Singapore; and this is one of his very few memories of being in Singapore.
Another was of being on a beach with his family. His father must have
been there. But he couldn't remember his father. He had disappeared
from memory.

Children like these from Czechoslovakia were being scattered all
over the world – to India, Kenya, Canada, Argentina, the USA, England.
History seized them and chucked them about. Their lives would be shaped
out of random acts of fate. Language, family, home, histories, would survive, or be lost and erased, and sometimes eventually re-found, on the
throw of a coin.

When asked, all his life, about his 'Czech-ness', Tom Stoppard's answers have varied. When he suddenly became famous in the late 1960s, and all the interviewers asked him about his past, he said he was a 'bounced Czech'. He told them he couldn't speak Czech and he'd been speaking English for almost as long as he could remember. When the USSR invaded Czechoslovakia in 1968, and his first wife thought he should be taking it more personally, he said that he 'used to be Czech' but he didn't feel Czech. When he went to Prague in 1977 to 'do his bit for Charter 77', he 'felt no identification at all'. From then onwards, though, his friendship with Václav Havel, his involvement with human rights causes in Russia and Eastern Europe, his plays on those subjects, and, in the 1990s, his discoveries about his family, and his mother's death, altered the way he talked about being Czech. In the 2000s, receiving an honorary doctorate at the University of Brno, and reminiscing with pride about his parents, he spoke with tender feeling about his origins: 'I grew up far away, knowing that Moravia was where I come from and where my mother and father came from.' In a speech on the stage of the Czech National Theatre, when the Czech Republic entered the European Union in 2004, he talked about his 'patriotic pride' in the Czech flag 'when I and my elder brother and our mother were still a Czech family far from home'. And he ended the speech: 'Some things are ineradicable.' Among these things, too, was his Jewishness, which, he came late to recognise, was also ineradicable.

As with the world histories that encircle and forge the destinies of characters in his plays, plays such as *The Coast of Utopia*, *Rock 'n' Roll* and *Leopoldstadt*, behind his English life stands the history of Central and Eastern Europe: two hundred years of war, national conflicts, pogroms, exile and shifting borders. The ideological and national forces at work in the course of these centuries – imperialism, Nazism, Communism – also shaped the lives of his ancestors and his family, and composed his 'ineradicable' origins.

The story goes back to territories right in the heart of Europe, the ancient lands of Bohemia (capital, Prague) and Moravia (capital, Brno), bordered by Poland, Germany, Austria, Hungary and Silesia. It goes back to a mixed ancestry of Czechs, Austrians and Germans, with Czech and German speakers living in the same towns, Jews and Catholics often linked in families by marriage. It goes back to generations of hard-working, bourgeois professionals, bringing up their families, keeping the peace, none of them artists or actors or musicians or philosophers, but earning their living on the railways or in shoe factories or in hospitals or schools, moving across borders between Vienna and Prague, Brno and Zlín, the city of Tomáš Sträussler's birth in 1937.

Tomáš Sträussler's name would change, and all the names have changed. Bohemia and Moravia were part of the Austro-Hungarian Empire in the nineteenth century and into the twentieth, until its demise at the end of the First World War. In 1918, Czechoslovakia became an independent nation under its first president, Tomáš Masaryk. The Austro–Czech borders shifted. Part of Austria became Czech; place names were changed all along the border. When Nazi Germany invaded Czechoslovakia in 1939, it was renamed 'The Protectorate of Bohemia and Moravia'. Germany annexed the Sudetenland, the German-speaking borderlands of Bohemia and Moravia. When the Communists 'liberated' the region at the end of the Second World War, in 1945 – and expelled the minority German population – it became the Czechoslovak Republic. The town of Zlín, in Moravia, was renamed 'Gottwaldov', after the first Communist president of the Republic. Zlín stayed that way until 1990, after the Velvet Revolution in Czechoslovakia and the fall of Communism in much of Eastern Europe. In 1993, Czechoslovakia split into the Czech Republic and Slovakia.

Tom Stoppard's father, Eugen Sträussler, born in 1908, had a quite common Austrian surname. A well-known early-twentieth-century Austrian neuropathologist, for instance, called Ernst Sträussler (no relation), was born in Moravia and worked in Prague and in Vienna. Eugen's family, who were all Jewish, similarly crossed borders. His paternal grandparents, Lazar Sträussler and Fani (née Spitzer), and his maternal grandparents, Josef Bechynski and Hermine (née Stein), had a mix of Austrian and Moravian surnames.

Eugen's father, Julius Sträussler, the son of Lazar and Fani, was born in 1878 in Březové, an ore-mining town in south-eastern Moravia. He worked on the rapidly expanding Austro-Hungarian railway network, and rose to be superintendent. He was, according to his future daughter-in-law, an autocratic and bossy character. He married twice, the second time to Eugen's mother Hildegard, daughter of Josef and Hermine Bechynski. They moved between Prague and Podmokly, in the northwest of Bohemia, on the Austrian border, where Eugen was born, and Vienna, where Eugen grew up and where his sister Edit was born. Julius Sträussler did his military service for the cause of the Austro-Hungarian Empire, from 1914 to 1918. (The future president, Masaryk, saw his people 'answering the call-up in horror, as if going to the slaughter'.) Julius survived the war and took his family back to the newly independent Czechoslovakia in 1918, to live in Brno, on Francouzská Street, and take up the lucrative position of head of the Czechoslovak State Railways. In Brno, Eugen was a student in the newly established Medical Faculty of Masaryk University, and his sister Edit met and married Frantisek Hevelka, a law student who, decades later, would become a 'Judge of the People's Court' in Communist-ruled Brno. She worked in an office and had no children. The young Sträusslers were Czechs of the new, post-imperial, post-war world, full of aspiration and energy.

While Eugen was still a medical student, he took holiday jobs as a trainee doctor in the hospital at Zlín, about seventy kilometres away. There, on a skiing trip with some fellow students, he met a beautiful, dark, lively young woman called Marta (or Martha) Becková, who was training as a nurse and doing secretarial work for what she, and everyone else, called 'The Firm'. They were both in their twenties; she was three years younger than him.

The Becks were less well established and comfortably off than the Sträusslers. Like the Sträusslers, they were Jewish Czechs, but they came from a different part of the country, and they made marriages, like many Czechs of the time, which intermixed Jewish and Catholic families. Marta's father, Rudolf Beck, was a teacher, so the family had to move whenever he was appointed to another school. His parents, Marek and Anna, came from northern Bohemia, on the Sudeten–Czech border, near the town of Ústí, which when the Germans annexed the Sudetenland was renamed Aussig (and was infamous for a massacre of native Germans in 1945, at the end of the war). Rudolf Beck was born in 1874 in a town in the Sudetenland called Lovosice. Both parents died young, and he was brought up by an aunt and had to make his own way. His daughter Marta remembered him as a hard-working, kind and decent man, bringing 'stacks of marking' home every day, smoking his pipe and doing the crossword for relaxation.

His wife, Regina Ornstein, came from a Bohemian family. Her three sisters lived in Prague and after her marriage she would visit them once a year; Marta remembered being told, as a regular item of family gossip, that 'two of them did not speak to each other for years; they had a cat and spoke to each other via the cat'. But the eccentric Prague aunts were living in another world; the Becks hardly ever went there. Between 1898 and 1911, moving between small towns in the heart of Czechoslovakia, they had six children – one son, Ota (or Otto), and five daughters. Marta, born on 11 July 1911 in Rosice, near Brno, was the baby. When Marta was a teenager, the family moved to Zlín. Her mother Regina, a much more demanding character than Rudolf, dominated the household; she was jealous of her husband, somewhat fussy and over-protective and given to making occasional scenes. By her sixties she was an invalid, suffering from heart disease. But for as long as she could, she worked non-stop, bringing up the children, doing the housework, cooking, and in her spare time reading the papers cover to cover – as her youngest daughter would, all her life.

Marta led a sheltered life, going to a bilingual and then a Czech school before starting work, and always accompanied by her mother as chaperone when she went out to a dance. The expectation was that the girls would live at home and then get married. The eldest, Wilma (or Vilemina), married a country doctor, Antonín, who died young. Berta married a German, Arnošt Kind, but the marriage did not last. Irma married Bartolomei Cekota, who would move his family to Argentina before the war, where he worked for Bata and became an extremely wealthy man. Only Anny, the middle daughter, stayed single.

Eugen kept coming over from Brno to Zlín to see Marta, on free first-class rail tickets provided by his father – who withdrew the favour when he found out his son was going to visit a girlfriend rather than for his medical education. But Marta was accepted by the Sträusslers – Hildegard,

Eugen's mother, was very kind to her. By the time Eugen graduated from Brno, in 1933, they had decided to get married. The custom was that the bride and her family paid for the wedding. Marta and her family were saving like mad, but Eugen knew there would be no dowry. A photograph of Marta in 1927, shown to her younger son many years later, made him understand what her standard of living had been: 'The fact that my mother was beautiful had escaped me and the realisation was shocking, and then touching when I saw that the dress had obviously been run up at home, and the coat was a poor girl's best.' Unlike many young Czech men of the time, Eugen was marrying for love, not for money. Looking back, she would consider this 'heroic'.

Somehow her parents managed to provide them, as the custom was, with a furnished house, 'carpets, curtains, everything from the first day, all table and bed-linen hand-embroidered'. Eugen got a job with 'The Firm', as a doctor in the hospital at Zlín, with the aim of becoming a heart and lung specialist. On 23 June 1934, he and Marta were married in Zlín. An enchanting photograph shows a warmly smiling, dark-eyed Marta looking joyously at the camera, wearing a lacy cream suit and jauntily tilted hat, with her husband gazing at her adoringly. He is wearing thick black spectacles and a formal suit, and has dark receding hair, a big toothy smile and huge ears. He looks very young, very intelligent and very much in love.

They settled down to a life in Zlín, living near the river Dřevnice on a pretty, leafy street called Zálešnà III, one of a grid of twelve identical, numbered Zálešnà streets, in a small square redbrick house (number 2619), with a flagstone path running through a little front garden, very like its neighbours, 'with exactly 193 square feet for a living room, a bathroom and a kitchenette, and upstairs another 193 square feet for the bedroom'. There were minor variations – slightly larger houses for the doctors or managers, houses placed at an angle to each other for privacy and to break up the straight lines. But in each one there was a cellar for storage, a tiny kitchen and living room, two or three small bedrooms on the upper floor, and a garden. The houses were called *batovky*, because, like almost everything else in Zlín, they belonged to 'The Firm'.

The Firm was the shoe-making company Bata, which owned, built, designed and managed the house, the street, the hospital and the town, and controlled the employment, income and lives of most of Zlín's inhabitants. The Firm's policies and administrative decisions dominated the life of the young Sträusslers and would play a part in their children's journeys into the world, like those two children setting out on their long path in the advertisement of Bata's English rivals, Start-Rite, with the motto: 'Children's Shoes Have Far to Go'.

Zlín, since the turn of the century, *was* Bata. This otherwise unremarkable Moravian town, 250 kilometres south-east of Prague (about four hours on the train), nestled in a deep valley between high hills, with a river running through it, surrounded by farmlands, mountains and forests, and once known mainly for its plum brandy, *slivovitz*, became the site of a social and industrial project with a global reach, a project which was, in its own way, as ambitious and unremitting as any empire or ideological movement.

The Bata shoe factory began as a cobbler's workshop in Zlín in the 1880s. Through the next generations of the Bata family, it became a global enterprise and, in its home town of Zlín, a highly controlled community. 'Bata-isation' became, after 1918, a symbol of the new independent Czechoslovakia. Amazingly, it survived two world wars, family feuds, the German occupation and the Communist regime. Tomáš Bata, the cobbler's son who founded the Bata empire, modelled it on Henry Ford's assembly-line theory. Everything was geared to speed, productivity, profit and competition. His factory survived the Great War by supplying thousands of boots to the Austro-Hungarian army. His half-brother Jan Antonín, who took over the business in 1932 after Tomáš's death in an air crash (flying in his own aeroplane from Bata's own airport), expanded the enterprise to Africa, Canada, France, South America, Singapore, Malaysia and India – where a city called Batanagar was founded. 'Bata shoes conquer the world', was the message. These Bata outposts would be crucial way-marks in the Stoppard story.

The Bata family ruled with a controlling hand over their workforce. (A satirical account of their Orwellian control is given in Mariusz Szczygieł's book *Gottland*, while more hagiographical accounts emphasise the family's benevolent paternalism.) The town was structured in functional sections: workplace, management, leisure, domestic accommodation, health-care. As well as providing residential housing for all its employees, much admired by Le Corbusier, it founded schools to train up 'Batamen' and built an eight-storey Community Centre (now the Hotel Moskva), with facilities for sport, chess, dancing and eating, but no alcohol. The kitchens in the Bata houses were designed small, so as to encourage the employees to eat in the communal canteen. There were signs on the walls and fences of Zlín reading: 'OUR CUSTOMER – OUR MASTER'. There were also Bata department stores, a movie theatre, the first Czech skyscraper office block, the first Czech escalator, a company savings bank and a hospital. This opened in 1932 under the direction of the enlightened and pioneering Dr Bohuslav Albert, with 320 beds and jobs for twenty-six doctors. Dr Albert hired a large number of Jewish doctors, including Eugen Sträussler and his friend Alexander 'Sanyi' Gellert.

Dr Albert noticed the young Dr Sträussler's exceptional qualities, and within four years promoted him as assistant to the head consultant. Others noticed him too. He was a writer and a public speaker as well as a promising doctor. Because he could speak German, he was chosen to give lectures to German-speaking doctors around the country. Between 1934 and 1936, he wrote a number of pieces for the local newspaper, on tuberculosis and its treatment, on visiting the ill, on the workings of the Bata hospital, on sunburn and on sleep. The articles are interested in changing medical practices, and in the way everyday behaviour affects illness. They are commonsensical rather than theoretical, clear-headed and morally sound. On sleep, for instance: 'It is important that we realize that the *sine qua non* of good sleep is good work and that only good work makes good sleep possible . . . It is not healthy to sleep in underwear worn during the day. Bodily hygiene is a condition of sound sleep . . . insomnia is relieved by appropriate life-styles . . . the best therapy for insomnia is orderliness, good will and self-discipline.'

He looked after children and delivered babies. (Quite possibly one of these was John Tusa, broadcaster and arts administrator, who was born in the hospital at Zlín in 1936.) He was the doctor the youngest patients asked for when they had measles or such childhood illnesses. He always made them feel that everything would be all right, and he was well remembered by his patients. He brought 'jollity' into the room with him. In his spare time, he relaxed by playing billiards at the hotel in the centre of town, owned by a fellow doctor's father, Mr Bájaja. Marta described Eugen, many years later, as 'not handsome in the conventional way' but very charming (she was 'always fighting off the nurses'). He had a 'first class brain', great modesty and total integrity.

The Sträusslers and the Gellerts were next-door neighbours. Nelly Gellert was Marta's best friend. They were always dropping in on each other. They went as a foursome to the movies and to dances and Red Cross functions in the Community Centre; their friends would drop in and 'stay up half the night talking'. Another friend of the Gellerts at the hospital, Dr Friedmann, remembered Marta as a charming woman with a 'slightly mischievous smile', a melodious voice and a willingness to join in with his schemes for abolishing some of the strict Bata social rules.

The Sträusslers were well off enough to have a car, and went on local excursions with Sanyi and Nelly. Once, Eugen was driving when they had an accident, and Nelly was hurt. As an apology, Eugen and Marta gave Nelly a ring with a pale-blue, local spinel stone, set with clasps. She wore it all her life – and her daughter wears it still.

Marta had two children during these years. Petr Sträussler was born on 21 August 1935. Tomáš Sträussler was born, two years later, on 3 July 1937. Tomáš was circumcised; Petr wasn't. Nelly had had her daughter Vera two months before. Marta couldn't breastfeed her second baby, so Nelly acted as a wet nurse and fed him. Tomik and Vera, almost exact contemporaries, were milk-brother and sister, and friends in the cradle: their mothers thought they should get married when they grew up. Marta had a girl who lived in to help and to babysit. She was enjoying her life as a wife and mother in her twenties; she remembered those times as 'blissful'.

For the Sträusslers and the Gellerts, for the other Jewish doctors working in the Bata hospital, and for hundreds of thousands of other

Czechoslovakians, those agreeable, domestic, steady patterns of life were now to be wiped out. There had been anti-Semitism in Czechoslovakia, and anxiety in Bata about Hitler's rise to power for some time, but life had gone on as normal for many people. Then, on 12 March 1938, the *Anschluss* took place: Nazi Germany invaded Austria. On 29 September 1938, the Munich Agreement permitted the Third Reich's annexation of parts of Czechoslovakia. On 1 November, German troops occupied the Sudetenland. Large-scale displacements and flights into exile, and the persecution of Jews and Romanis, began. On 15 March 1939, Germany invaded the rest of Czechoslovakia. Two days before that, Jan Antonín Bata left for America; his nephew, Thomas Bata, was already in Canada, from where he would continue to run the business.

Dr Albert had seen what was coming. He got a phone call early on the morning of 14 March telling him that the Germans had crossed the border. He immediately called in all the Jewish doctors to his house, and told them they had to get out. His wife was there, and she saw the doctors, all smoking, all sweating with fear. Dr Albert set himself to save as many of them as he could, making contact with Bata branches all over the world and arranging for a number of his employees to be offered jobs there. On 23 March, Jewish doctors were suspended from practising. Eugen and Sanyi discharged themselves from the hospital. Dr Albert offered them the chance of a refuge in Singapore or a refuge in Kenya. Who chose which destination first became a matter of family legend. The Gellerts remembered that Eugen didn't want to go to Kenya, and that Dr Gellert said that it was all the same to him, he didn't mind where he went; so he took the Kenya offer, and Eugen took Singapore. The Stoppard family would remember it the other way round, that it was Gellert who definitely didn't want to go to Singapore, so Eugen agreed to swap with him. In any case – it was a matter of chance.

With the job offers in hand, Alexander Gellert went every day to the Gestapo office in Zlín, to get permission to travel. Visas were required for them to get out of the country. The Gestapo office kept telling him to come back the next day. In despair, he gave it up, telling Nelly it was no use. Nelly Gellert got dressed up, went to the office and told the Gestapo officer that she wouldn't leave until he gave her the permits. The story she would tell her children in the years to come was that the officer was charmed by her and 'didn't believe that she could be Jewish'; that she told him she was proud to be Jewish, and that she was doing this for the sake of her two-year-old daughter; and that he said it might cost him his job, but he would give her the permits. And then – the heroic story continues – she said that she wouldn't leave without two more permits, for her friends the Sträusslers and their little boys.

The Gellerts, equipped with their green visas, stamped 5 April 1939 and valid for a month, got out on 19 April and set out for Nairobi. The Sträusslers, leaving behind their family, friends, employment and lifelong habits, like millions of other wartime refugees desperately fleeing Europe, set out on their enormous journey to Singapore – probably via Hungary and Yugoslavia and thence to Genoa. Petr was three and a half; Tomik was eighteen months old. In all, about fifteen of the Bata doctors got out. The others did not.

Rock 'n' Roll, staged in 2006, nearly seventy years after that journey, has as its central character a young man called Jan, who was born in Zlín and whose family left Czechoslovakia before the German occupation because they were Jewish, but returned – to what was then Gottwaldov – in 1948. In the 1960s, Jan has the chance of staying in Cambridge as a student but chooses to go back to Prague under Communism. The play has the vestigial trace of something Stoppard has often thought of writing, an 'autobiography in a parallel world', in which his family has returned 'home' after the war and he has grown up in Communist Czechoslovakia, through the middle of the twentieth century. In the first draft of the play, 'Jan' was called 'Tomas', 'my given name', Stoppard writes, adding, a little doubtfully, 'which, I suppose, is still my name'.

2

In Transit

Did you ever feel like a refugee?
I don't think one thinks like that at that age. One accepts one's fate.

I wouldn't have known the word 'refugee' when I was one . . . It was just
my childhood.

The Czechs from Bata reached the British colony of Singapore in the
spring of 1939. A branch of Bata had been set up there in 1930, and a Bata
factory was being built. They were housed in the city of Singapore, temporarily, in a semicircular ring of fifteen or so small block-houses, where
there were about five other Czech families. In the early days, Marta found
it pleasant. Their first experience of the tropical climate, the intense warm
heat and greenery of the island, was exciting; the locals were friendly;
the food – especially the fruit – was exotic. They had a car, and a daily
cleaner from the Bata office, and a kind Malayan ayah who pushed the
little boys around in a double cane pushchair and tried to speak Czech to
them: 'Don't cry!' 'Hurry up, bath-time!' After a while the boys went to a
nearby English convent kindergarten, travelling by rickshaw. Some letters came through from the families left behind. Marta and Eugen spoke
Czech at home, so that was the language the two-to-four-year-old Tomáš
first heard and spoke, but she started to pick up some English. The first
film he ever saw, Disney's newly released *Pinocchio*, was in English. He
would always remember Pinocchio's nose growing like a branch 'for telling lies', and a bird's nest on the end of it. There was an English family,
the Smiths, living next door, and they went to the open-air swimming
club on Sundays together. When Mrs Smith dropped in, Petr would call
out, 'Mama! Pani Smithova!' Eugen had a harder time: the situation at the
hospital was difficult, he didn't like the heat and food, and a stomach ulcer
he'd had as a student flared up. But they settled in, and started to look for
a house nearer the sea.

In Stoppard's screenplay for the 1987 film of J. G. Ballard's *Empire of the Sun*, when Shanghai is falling to the Japanese in 1937, an Englishman at the club advises Jim's father to get him out somewhere safe: 'Singapore.' The irony was not lost on the screenwriter. The fall of Shanghai was rapidly followed by the invasion of the eastern seaboard of China and of Indo-China, and the relentless advance southward of the Japanese by air, land and sea. On 7 December 1941, the Japanese bombed Pearl Harbor. The following day they launched air attacks on British airfields in Malaya and Singapore, and Britain and the United States declared war on Japan. On 11 December, Germany and Italy declared war on the US. By the end of 1941, Hong Kong had fallen to the Japanese, the campaign in Burma had begun and Japanese troops were fighting their way down through the jungles of Malaya towards Singapore. In January 1942 the British forces withdrew from Malaya to Singapore, which was heavily bombarded by the Japanese. Every night, the Sträussler family went to a friend's shelter. The boys would remember hiding under a table covered with blankets while bombs were falling, and the smell of sandbags.

On 8 and 9 February, the Japanese army crossed the Johore straits from the Malayan mainland. The big British naval defences, the long-range guns all pointing out to sea, from where the attack had been envisaged, could not be moved. The airfields and the water reservoirs were taken within days. Many people were killed, many taken prisoner. By the end of the week, on 15 February 1942, Singapore fell and the British general surrendered. The island would be occupied by the Japanese until the dropping of the bombs on Hiroshima and Nagasaki in August 1945, and the end of the war.

The official evacuation had got underway in January, in terror and con-fusion. Most of the women and children had left by the middle of January – and many of the ships they were on, heading for Australia, were bombed – but Marta stayed on as long as she could, hoping they would all be able to leave together. She did not want to travel alone to Australia. But by the end of the month she had to take the children and go. Eugen, who like some other Czechs enlisted in a British volunteer Defence Corps, would follow when he could. She got onto a ship with the children, and he spent about two hours with them and then had to leave.

had taken over an estate belonging to the Lebong Tea Company, a group of solid grey buildings built four-square around a quadrangle, at North Point on the Lebong Road, on the outskirts of Darjeeling. From the windows was the view of Kanchenjunga. One of the day girls who went there in the 1950s would remember her mother telling her to be home before the mountains turned pink.

They were boarders, and slept in the small boys' dormitory, nearest to the Matron. (As the boys at Mount Hermon got older, their dormitories got further away from the girls'.) The iron beds had stretched interlocking springs and the boys used to bounce up and down on them like trampolines. One boy kept them awake with nightly stories of his secret life as a fighter pilot with the American Air Force. But this was not Tomáš. He was a well-behaved little boy, eager to learn, not 'interestingly naughty' or extrovert, though talkative, with curly hair, big eyes, a Czech accent, an enormous smile and an affectionate nature. He was 'besotted' with the Matron's daughter:

> We smallest boys lived in two dormitories at the end of the corridor, and on hair-wash nights we congregated in the larger one to have our hair dried by Matron or by her daughter. The smell of damp hair cooking in the blast of an electric dryer is still a Proustian trigger for pleasurable and disturbing emotions. I received a letter from the Matron's daughter a few years ago – 'You won't remember me but,' etc – and I wrote back, 'Not only do I remember you, I was madly in love with you', and never heard from her again.

The school motto was *Non Scholae Sed Vitae Discimus*: 'We do not learn for school, but for life'. Round the buildings were engraved the words 'Character', 'Faithfulness', 'Godliness', 'Trust' and 'Loyalty'. The day started early, with a six-thirty breakfast, and religious assembly taken by the chaplain. The younger boys had a break in the morning, with milk, and a rest upstairs in the dormitories after lunch. They wore a blue school uniform with a striped tie. Discipline was firm – no running or shouting in the corridors – but not harsh. The smaller children got away with sliding down the banisters. There was no corporal punishment. Many of the children were far from home or separated from their parents (though quite a few of the parents lived in Darjeeling), and the school's aim was to be a home from home and to make them feel safe.

Most weekends, Marta would come to see them, walking down the zig-zagging Lebong Road from the centre of Darjeeling, bringing food parcels and treats. On Sunday afternoons, the boys would sit on a bench under a large and particularly splendid fir tree, looking up the long track down which their mother would eventually be seen coming to visit them. In the distance they couldn't tell if it was her; 'but it was always her in the end', and they would run to meet her, bring her back to the bench and unpack the packages she had brought. While they were waiting, they carved their initials in the tree. For many years Stoppard wanted to go back to see if the bench, the tree and his initials were still there. When he did return, in 1991, he found that the tree had been chopped down long ago.

It was a comfort to Marta that both the boys were doing well at school. T. Sträussler's school report, aged seven, in November 1944, put him tenth in a class of thirty and marked him as Good, Very Good or Excellent in all topics: Excellent in Literature, and Very Good in Dictation and Arithmetic. He played the triangle in the school band. He liked books, and he and his mother had a shared fantasy of opening a bookshop together – a rival to the famous Oxford Book Store on Chowrasta.

Their home was Minto Villa, on Auckland Road, a grey house with pillars. (Later they moved to a big solid apricot-coloured mansion called Struan Lodge.) At home, Tomáš used to hang around outside the gateway of Minto Villa, hoping to see American soldiers go by. They seemed to him debonair, romantic and stylish, and they dominated his memories of Darjeeling: meeting with 'easy manners' his request for 'Any gum, chum?', coming into the school sports ground to play baseball, showing him how to aim his toy revolver or getting out of the train to make a snowball for him when, on their very first journey to Darjeeling, the train broke down above the snow-line – the first sight of snow he would remember. Writing a screenplay for a film about an American bodyguard in the early 1980s, he noted: 'When I was a boy in India, Americans were glamorous.'

In retrospect, life at Minto Villa and Mount Hermon seemed 'familiar and safe', 'a lost domain of uninterrupted happiness'. That generalised memory of happiness centred on a particular remembered moment, 'a day when I was walking along the corridor which led from the door to the playground, trailing a finger along a raised edge on the wall, and it suddenly came upon me that *everything was all right*, and would always be all right'.

'All right', that was, in comparison with their life before Darjeeling, a turmoil of uprootings, and of dimly remembered chaos and fear. He was six, seven, eight; he was being looked after; he felt secure; he took every day as it came. He had no imaginary idea of another possible life, and he was not worrying about what had happened to his father, or what would happen to them next. But on one of his returns to India, in old age, asked about that vividly remembered moment, he supposed there must also have been some underlying anxiety.

For Marta, nothing was stable, anything could happen to them, and the worrying never stopped. Quite soon after they moved to Darjeeling, she was advised to go to the Czech Consul in Calcutta to get what information they had. She was told that as many civilian Czechs as possible had been accounted for, and that Eugen Sträussler was amongst those missing, presumed lost. She knew no details then of how he died, but may have learned them later from survivors from Singapore, though she never passed them on to the boys. She returned to Darjeeling the next day, but said nothing to them, feeling that they had enough to cope with. A habit of protecting them through her silence had begun. Some time later, perhaps fearing that she would upset the boys with her own emotions, perhaps unable to bear to give them the final news, she asked a woman friend to tell them (in English) that their father was dead. They were taken for a walk, carefully given the information, and on their return found their mother waiting 'teary-eyed and anxious' to see how they had taken it. Tomáš took it well: that is, he felt almost nothing. 'I felt the significance of the occasion', he would recall, 'but not the loss.'

In the school holidays, there were visits to other places in Northern India like Lucknow or Cawnpore (now Kanpur). Marta once took them to a rajah's palace. An attractive young widow in her thirties, she made friends, and wanted to enjoy herself if she could, even though her life felt, to her, uncertain and provisional. For a while she was seeing someone called Rudi, a Czech or a German, who ran Pliva's, a Darjeeling restaurant (later renamed Glenary's). Then a Czech girlfriend came to stay, who had a contact with a Chinese-American woman whose husband was in the army. Marta and this woman became friends, and she invited Marta to a celebratory dinner in the Mount Everest Hotel when her husband came home on leave. One of the other guests was Major Kenneth Stoppard, who was in service with the army in New Delhi and was on leave in Darjeeling for a fortnight.

After the dinner party, in those two weeks, he came to the Bata shop every day and took Marta out to lunch, and he bombarded her with flowers and chocolates. It sounds like love at first sight. He went with her on one of her Sunday visits to the school, and thought her sons were decent boys. The rapid courtship went on 'at a crazy pace', she remembered, for some months, while Major Stoppard shuttled back and forth between New Delhi and Darjeeling. A lieutenant-commander who also used the Jodhpur Officers' Mess in New Delhi in 1944 and 1945 remembered how Ken would often talk of a young woman, whom he referred to affectionately as 'Bobby', living in Darjeeling with two sons. He said that after the war was over he hoped they would get married.

Stoppard was a handsome, clean-cut Englishman, with a passion for fly-fishing and a strong commitment to King and Country. His family – a mother and a sister – were based in Nottinghamshire; his father had died when he was young. His mother ran a dressmaker's business in Retford. Before the war he had been a sales rep for a steel company. Early on in the war he had been in China, and had plans to get into reconstruction work when the war ended, either with the construction company Balfour Beattie in China or with Firth-Brown steel agents in Bombay.

Ken Stoppard rushed Marta off her feet, with a forceful set of moves which set the terms of their future life together. From Delhi, he sent her a telegram asking her to marry him. He was due to go back to China, but he went to his colonel and asked for forty-eight hours' leave to get married. Then he followed up his telegram with a phone call, telling Marta he had got the weekend leave so they could be married. According to her, she said, 'No, we're not, what are you talking about?' He told her he would be court-martialled if he went back unmarried. She had no time to think and no one to consult. 'I had to decide on my own what I thought would be best for us.' It was wartime, a time of rapid changes and choices, her fortune was completely uncertain, she was widowed, she had lost her family. Here, out of the blue, was a good-looking, fit, competent Englishman with prospects, an army officer, who had fallen for her and who liked her boys, and seemed to have the decisiveness and energy to take care of them all. Without telling the boys, or anyone in the shop, and missing her Sunday visit to the school, she got on the train from Darjeeling and travelled all day (a six-hundred-kilometre journey) to marry Major Stoppard in St Andrew's Church, Calcutta, on 25 November 1945.

For years afterwards, she would feel guilty about not having told the boys in advance. But they took it just as the next thing in their lives. They had a new stepfather, who played games and ran races with them and whom they called Daddy or Father. Eventually his younger stepson settled for 'Dad' in his letters home, though Peter remembered that Ken thought 'Dad' was vulgar. Ken decided that he wouldn't stay abroad but would take them all to England. Perhaps Marta had asked him to do this; perhaps it was a condition of the marriage. England was the ultimate desirable place, 'the place everybody would want to go to if only they were allowed to'. They left Darjeeling for Delhi. Next they went to the army transit camp of Deolali (where the long wait to embark could drive you 'doolally'), and then boarded ship for England.

After he was grown up, Peter found it hard to understand why Kenneth Stoppard had married his mother. Peter and his brother both came to see their stepfather as a bitter, disappointed man, bigoted, xenophobic and anti-Semitic. He became the sales manager of a company manufacturing machine tools. He bullied their mother, was often bad-tempered and had to be placated. Peter thought that Ken's father's early death, and his poorly rewarded army service, had blighted him, and that he spent the rest of his life feeling that he should have been treated better by the world. Why would such a man marry a Jewish widow with two small children? As adults, their sense of him did not take into account what he might have felt for her, and what he might have been like when he first met her.

Why she married him, though, was not hard to understand. He represented safety and control. From now on he would make the decisions. And because of his overriding Englishness, from now on she would speak only English, play down her Czech history, discount her Jewishness and keep quiet about the past. If she knew, by the time she left India, what had happened to her family, she said nothing.

While Eugen and Marta were together in Singapore, Eugen's parents, Julius and Hildegard Sträussler, both in their sixties, were evicted from their house in Brno and, early in 1941, were put on the transport of Moravian Jews to the Theresienstadt concentration camp at Terezin. On 9 January 1942, a month before their son Eugen's death, they were transported to the ghetto in Riga, in Latvia, where they died. The following year, Eugen's grandmother, Hildegard's mother Hermine Bechynski, died at Terezin, aged eighty-two. Eugen's married sister Edit was transported to Terezin in 1945, but survived and returned to Brno. In 1944, Marta's parents, Rudolf Beck, aged seventy, and Regina, a chronic invalid at sixty-nine, died at Auschwitz. So did two of her four sisters, Wilma and Berta. They had married Gentiles, but 'that had not saved them'. Berta Kindová's son Sascha (Saša) was sixteen, a Bata apprentice, when the Germans came. She wrote instructions for whoever could look after him, went into a church and approached two strangers, a married couple. She asked them to take her son; and they did so. A few days later, she was put on the transport. Saša survived the war. Anny, the unmarried sister, died in Riga. Marta's brother Ota survived and lived on in Brno; her sister Irma, with her husband Bartolomei Cekota, had gone to Argentina. It is not certain when Marta learned of the fate of her parents, her three sisters and her in-laws. She was certainly told at some time; Berta's fostered son and Wilma's children knew the facts, and so did Irma. But she never told her sons, either that she was Jewish or that most of her family had perished in the Holocaust. They would find out, very much later.

*

The Stoppards left India at the beginning of 1946. Marta – now Mrs 'Bobby' Stoppard – was thirty-five, Peter was ten, Tom was eight. It was their third marathon sea journey in seven years. Just as they had narrowly escaped the Nazi atrocities in Czechoslovakia and the Japanese atrocities in Singapore, they left India before the violence, mass displacement and loss of life which accompanied independence and Partition, they avoided a post-war return to Czechoslovakia under Communism and they arrived in England after the end of the wartime bombing. With good reason did Stoppard come to think of himself, in this historical context, as a lucky man, leading a charmed life. The luck of the draw, the road not taken, the alternative possible path to the one chosen, was not something he thought about as a child. But it came to haunt him as an adult. What would that other Tom have been, the one who didn't become an Englishman?

Soon after they arrived, deed polls authorising a change of name were made out. Petr became Peter Stoppard; Tomáš, or Tomik, became Thomas, or Tom, Stoppard. (His mother went on calling him Tommy.) They were from now on to be English schoolboys. Ken, their legal guardian, would say to Tom, in later moments of hostility: 'Don't you realise I made you British?' The boys weren't naturalised as British subjects, though, perhaps through an oversight. Peter was surprised when, years later, in the late 1950s or early '60s, the local policeman came to see him where he was living in Bristol to inform him that he was an 'alien'. He was shocked to discover he was still Czech, and organised his naturalisation papers at once. Tom Stoppard's own naturalisation certificate wasn't issued until 22 February 1960, when he was registered as 'from Czechoslovakia, living in Bristol'. Neither of them had a birth certificate, but Marta's Czech passport, with their names and dates of birth, was accepted in lieu when their names were changed and, much later, when their naturalisation was formalised.

Their long journey to England, unlike their journey from Singapore to India, was made without disturbance or confusion, on a British troopship. Peter vividly remembered going through the Suez Canal, the passage-way to the West. They arrived in England, docking at Southampton, on 14 February 1946, the same day they had reached India four years before. It was freezing; Tom's feet were so cold that he cried. Bomb damage was everywhere. They were going to Nottinghamshire by train. Peter was amazed to be on a train with no bunk-bed, where you sat up. Their destination was Retford, where they were to stay with Ken's widowed mother Alice and his sister Muriel. Always he would remember, with a kind of nostalgia and intensity, the strangeness of those first weeks in England. Marta was extremely apprehensive, but the Stoppard family was kind to her. The war was over. She had brought her boys to a safe haven.

3

Englishness

Jenkins (*to Gale*): . . . And it was all pasture land then, you know. On
long summer evenings when we were all in bed and almost asleep,
we'd hear the farmer's boy on the hill, calling the cattle home. Singing
them home . . . God, yes.

Marks (*loudly, independently*): Happiest days of my life, to coin a phrase!

The Stoppard boys were sent to boarding school soon after they arrived in
England. Kenneth used a contact in Retford, who knew the headmaster, to
get them into the Dolphin School. This was a boys' preparatory school run
by Charles Roach, a South African Rhodes Scholar, son of the Bishop of
Natal, and later by his son Peter. The school had moved during the war, for
safety, from just outside Newark to Okeover Hall, near Ashbourne, on the
border of Staffordshire and Derbyshire. Bobby, let alone the boys, had no
say in the matter, it was all settled for them. But, as she said to them, much
later: 'How could I have asked you if you wanted to go there, knowing that
there was no alternative? Luckily it worked out all right.'

The school did work out all right. It was a humane, easy-going, though
not outstanding, English prep school. This was what it advertised:

The Dolphin School, C. G. Roach, Head. Prepares boys for the Public
Schools and the Royal Navy. Boys go to bed in relays starting at 7 p.m.
The youngest boys sleep in a dormitory next door to the Matron.
Domestic and feeding arrangements are under the direct control of
Mrs Roach . . . a well balanced diet . . . The milk is TB tested. All boys
are given some nourishment between games and afternoon school.

Stoppard Two, with his brother, Stoppard One, settled into the routine
of classes and games, in what he would describe as a 'somewhat decay-
ing' stately home. Okeover Hall was a splendid mid-eighteenth-century
Palladian house with three wings (a fourth had been demolished), an

imposing stable block, an ivy-covered church and landscaped grounds sloping away to farmland beyond. This landscape immediately became, and would always be, at the heart of Stoppard's strong feeling for England. It provided a romantic introduction to his new country. In that first summer and in the legendarily cold, snowy winter of 1946–7 that followed, Okeover Hall 'was just paradise'. The small boys went to bed when it was still light, and out of the dormitory window on the first floor was the rather unkempt garden, leading to a ha-ha, and beyond that the farmer's fields. In the long, long summer evenings, as the light was dimming outside the windows, the farmer's boy would yodel – half-sing, half-call – the herd of cows home, and the small boys would lie in bed listening to the sound.

In the daytime, in their breaks, they would run free in the grounds, where there were wild paths and a hidden pond. They would make insecure rafts and navigate the pond – even though some of them, like Stoppard, couldn't swim. They would build dens in the woods out of branches and sacking. There was great excitement when the ivy covering the church caught fire. When the big winter came, they would toboggan down the slope through the fields.

Again and again, in his memory and his imagination, Stoppard would return to this scene, where, as he would say, he put on Englishness like a coat. 'At the age of eight I fell in love with England almost at first glance, never considering that the England I loved was, in the first place, only a corner of Derbyshire, and, in the second place, perishable.' Sidley Park, the eighteenth-century house with its hermit and its English country landscape, the setting for *Arcadia*, is firmly sited in Derbyshire. In 1947, the school relocated to Langford Hall in Nottinghamshire, another grand 1740s house in an equally tranquil pastoral setting. But Okeover was always, for Stoppard, the primal English scene.

At the Dolphin School, where he stayed for four years, till he was thirteen, he became a reader, a writer, a cricketer, a boy scout, and as English as he could be. His 'foreignness' came out in his pronunciation of 's' and 'th' and his rolling 'r', which he retained. He was slightly teased for this, though not so much as to make him feel alien: 'I was foreign, but I did not know it.' He traded a little on his exotic Indian history. But, just after the war, there were plenty of other dramatic stories to be heard at the school. The headmaster's son Peter Roach had just come back from a heroic war. An adventurous, unconventional man, he taught the boys English, sitting at a big Edwardian oak table with a fire burning in winter. He thought Tom was very bright. His father, the headmaster, said: 'That boy will go far.'

There were no books to speak of at home – Ken's collection was mainly of fishing books and the odd Nevil Shute, later on some Alistair MacLean and Winston Churchill's *The Second World War*. There were some visits from home to the local library. But it wasn't a literary household. It was a long time, for instance, before he realised that a play could also be a published object. Nevertheless, he rapidly became a voracious reader, the kind of child 'who read the sauce bottle and the cornflake packet if there was nothing else to hand', and who later would never dream of getting on a bus without something to read. The first real book he picked up, soon after getting to England, was Arthur Ransome's *Peter Duck*, the third in the 'Swallows and Amazons' series, a 1930s epic of Atlantic Ocean travel, shipwreck, hostile pursuit and secret treasure. He spotted on the jacket that Ransome had written some other books too. 'My method of searching for these books had a sort of pathos about it: I simply went around picking up any book I saw lying about to see if it was called *Swallows and Amazons*. But it never was.' At school, though, there were 'sets' of Ransome, Richmal Crompton (*Just William*) and Captain W. E. Johns (Biggles). He read the usual classics, *The Wind in the Willows*, *Treasure Island*, *The Coral Island*, *Stalky & Co*.

The other big passion, for both boys, was cricket. Their school reports noted that they were 'precocious and good at sport'. Stoppard One was more of an all-rounder; Stoppard Two was mainly a wicket-keeper – though as a bowler he developed a nice left-arm finger spin delivery. He enjoyed the feeling of having the hands 'protected by thick armoured gloves made of leather and rubber', the satisfaction of catching the ball and of the quick strategic understanding there has to be between wicket-keeper and bowler – even though, as a rapidly growing, tall, thin boy, he wasn't the ideal shape and size: 'Great wicket-keepers are small men with the sort of energy contained in those rubber balls that come back up into your hand when you drop them on a stone floor.' His hero was England's legendary wicket-keeper, Godfrey Evans, who had 'the reflexes of a mousetrap'. 'At the age of ten, I felt I understood him completely.' For his tenth birthday, he was given Evans's book, *Behind the Stumps*, and at the 1948 Test Match against Australia at Trent Bridge in Nottingham (not too far from home and school), he witnessed one of Evans's most astonishing catches, made while running backwards at great speed, still written of with awe in histories of the Test Match, which left him, thinking of his own cricketing skills, 'chastened'. Peter Roach taught the little boys their cricket, and would yell at them (in Stoppard's later paraphrase) at every other stroke: 'Suffering cats, what the hell was that supposed to be, you raving nit – you look like a carthorse on roller skates trying to dance *Swan Lake*.' They all adored him.

Other school obligations were less compelling, but had to be done, like rugby on Wednesdays – where he played full-back, and found it rough – or praying on Sundays. (If you were English, you were Christian, it seemed then.) In class, he was good at reading, Latin, geometry, algebra, arithmetic and English, where he was one of the best at writing essays, though marked as 'careless' in his history and 'only fair' in music. He got mildly involved with school theatricals. There was a tradition of a production every Guy Fawkes Night. In 1948 he and his fellow actors were told they had done very well. On 5 November 1949, he played a puppet, Francisco, in a one-acter called 'The Puppet Show', set in Old Maffeo's Caravan.

The only blot on the landscape was the corporal punishment, standard practice at the time. The boys would be cuffed round the ear and shouted at for misdemeanours – 'all very frightening if you were a small child'. There was one particular red-faced bully, who had to be propitiated and flattered in case he turned on you. His repressed sexuality would not have been recognised, and he was a good teacher; but the boys found him intimidating. Once, when Tom was sick and couldn't go to lessons, he asked his brother to lend him a book, because he was so anxious about keeping up with that teacher's classes. When, in the English lesson, Peter was found to be without the book, he was beaten. Having landed his brother in this situation was a terrible feeling, not to be forgotten. Years later he would say, of the 'bastard' who terrified him, I hope his soul is already damned. The fear and guilt fed into a lifelong distaste for coercion, and is given to one of the reminiscing characters at the school reunion in the radio play of 1970, *Where Are They Now?*:

> Gale: We walked into French like condemned men. We were too afraid to *learn*. All our energy went into ingratiating ourselves and deflecting his sadism on to our friends . . . Once when I was ill – itself an admission of some obscure failure, you will remember – I spent my time in the San feverishly keeping up with the French I had missed, using my brother's exercise book – he used to lend me it. One day he forgot to pick it up and found himself in a French lesson without any prep to hand in. Jenkins slapped him around for five minutes . . . What a *stupid* man!

Half-terms were often spent by the Stoppard boys at school, rather than at home – perhaps this was Ken's preference, or perhaps Bobby didn't understand that most English boys went home for half-term. They would be taken to Ashbourne by Matron, who would provide a bag of plums, or other goodies. One of these outings was to see the 1948 film of Laurence Olivier's *Hamlet*: 'God, it was boring!' (There was no reason for him to notice that Olivier had cut out the characters of Rosencrantz and Guildenstern.) Much better was a 1942 film called *The First of the Few*, in which Leslie Howard played R. J. Mitchell, the designer of the Spitfire.

While they were at school, their mother sent them regular parcels of 'tuck', symbols of her affection – and her displacement. There were 'plum dumplings powdered with cinnamon, and delicious jam-filled buns called *buchti* . . . Her tuck parcels were misshapen triple-wrapped double-trussed Kellogg boxes overstuffed with things she thought were good for you, like glucose tablets and dried fruit, to offset the quantity of things which were definitely not.'

They were fifty miles away from home, which seemed far. The first Stoppard house, after Retford, was an unexceptional pebble-dash semi called Rosegarth in the Derbyshire village of Calver Sough, just off the main through road, with woods beyond the narrow garden. It was about two miles from Baslow and the great Devonshire estate of Chatsworth. When Stoppard, in much later life, met the Duke of Devonshire, he said to him, 'I used to live in a house near Baslow.' Delightedly, the Duke replied, '*I* live in a house near Baslow!' Stoppard became a regular visitor at Chatsworth and a friend of Debo, Duchess of Devonshire. He reworked that joke about class, when writing a tribute to her in 2001: 'Our first house in England was a boy's bicycling ride from Chatsworth, and we went picnicking there in the immediate post-war years before the house (Chatsworth, that is, not our semi in Calver Sough) was re-opened to the public.'

There were no trips from home to the cinema or the theatre, but there were plenty of holiday jaunts in their pre-war Riley, with packed sandwiches and a Thermos flask, for instance to the river Dove, where Ken taught Tom to fly-fish. This, like cricket, became a lifelong passion. Most of his adult communications with Ken were on this subject, and he would go into technical detail about their only shared interest. Fly-fishing is a patient, stealthy, addictive pastime, which can be either sociable or solitary, a day of slow, pleasurable concentration spent on an English river. It was part of his induction into Englishness. Ken taught him 'to fish, to love the countryside, to speak properly, to respect the Monarchy'.

Rosegarth was their first English home, but not for long. Ken was working, for a time, for Firth Brown, the Sheffield-based stainless steel and machine-tool manufacturers, and, following the work, he and Bobby moved house several times in quick succession, buying and selling again, to Dore near Sheffield, to a vicarage in Borrowash, near Nottingham, and then, for a decade or so, back to Bristol. They started another family: their son Richard was born in 1949, when Tom was twelve. Typically, while she was expecting Richard, Bobby sent her boys at boarding school the government's gift of orange juice for pregnant women, having scrubbed the label off the bottle. The boys could see they were medicine bottles, and one of their schoolmates said, 'Oh, that's orange juice for mothers.' And it didn't taste right either, Tom noticed, not like normal orange juice. Then his time at the Dolphin School came to an end, and, in the same year that their parents moved to Providence Lane in Long Ashton, in the leafy, hilly

suburbs of Bristol, he followed Peter to a direct grant independent boarding school in Pocklington, North Yorkshire.

Bobby's life, with her sons mostly away at boarding school, a succession
of moves which made it hard to make permanent friends anywhere, and
then a new baby, now revolved around Ken. This often wasn't easy. Peter,
in retrospect, summed it up as an unhappy marriage; his brother was more
lenient, and didn't think that their mother ever fantasised an alternative life.
Ken's chippiness, Peter thought, arose from class resentment. Ken's mother's
clients at her dressmaker's business in Retford were the local squirearchy,
and Ken would have liked to be one of them. He dressed as if he was always
paying impeccable attention, army style, to his blazers and his cuffs and
his shiny shoes. His field sports – fishing, shooting – contributed to that
self-image. But in reality he was trying not very successfully or lucratively
to make his way in the machine-tool business (which he later gave up),
feeling that five years in the army ought to have earned him a better life, and
becoming increasingly curmudgeonly. His prejudices – against foreigners,
non-whites, Jews, Irish, Yanks, homosexuals, the urban working class and
'arty' types – got more and more entrenched, and his patriotic opinions
ever more emphatic: 'He believed with Cecil Rhodes that to be born an
Englishman was to have drawn first prize in the lottery of life . . . his utopia
would have been populated by landed gentry, honest yeomen and Gurkhas.'
(Later in life, Stoppard would reclaim Rhodes's much-mocked phrase to
describe his own feelings about England.) Something of that domineering, chauvinistic, dissatisfied personality, profoundly dependent on a long-
suffering wife, gets into the character of George Riley in Stoppard's early
play *A Walk on the Water*, of 1960, later transformed into *Enter a Free Man*
(1968), where the curtain goes up to the strains of 'Rule Britannia', and Riley
laments 'the country going to the dogs': 'No pride, no patriotism. The ero-
sion of standards, the spread of mediocrity.'

Bobby's upbringing, her wartime experiences, and her second marriage, combined to make her anxious, compliant and dependent. She never
learned to drive. Peter always noticed that if, on a journey, she wanted to
go half a mile out of their way, perhaps to look at a shop, Ken would be
irritable and reluctant – but that he would make a twenty-mile diversion if

he wanted to look at a trout stream. He was the head of the family, the one who went out to work and ruled the roost, and he expected to be waited on hand and foot and everyone to be grateful to him. So Bobby became 'a kind of skivvy housekeeper'. But (as she once said to Tom in her old age), at least Ken didn't get drunk, he didn't chase women and he didn't gamble.

They were not poor – the houses they lived in were comfortable, there were sofas and decent meals and hot water coming out of the taps, and they kept a family pet, a spaniel. But there was no money to spare, and it was a tight-run ship. The boys were given tasks when they were at home. As Peter put it: 'He wasn't going to paint the window ledges with us looking on, we'd have to help.' Bobby had a housekeeping allowance, but would never spend anything on herself, only on the boys and the home. Her idea of shopping for herself was window shopping. Tom got in the habit, if he needed a new shirt for school, of persuading her that the cheapest shirt would do: 'That's *fine*, Mum, don't . . .'. At his second school, all the boys wore detachable stiff collars, and as long as the stiff white collars were clean, the state of the shirt didn't matter too much. A wealthy farmer's son, who was acting in an end-of-term skit, said to him: 'I'm playing a tramp on a bench with fleas, could I borrow your shirt?' Far from being mortified, Tom was pleased to think that by having that kind of a shirt, he had saved his mother a couple of pounds.

He was his mother's favourite. They were, always, very close; he was, as he would put it, very 'mother-conscious'. From the time he was at school at Pocklington, he wrote regular letters home, addressed sometimes, in the early years after he'd left home, to 'Dear all' or 'Dear family', mostly, as a courtesy, to 'Dear Mum and Dad', and occasionally just to 'Dear Mum'. But they were intended for her (apart from the bits about fishing). The habit of writing was a leftover from the obligation of the weekly boarding-school letter; and it was also in response to her regular letters to him. But if it was a duty, it was a loving one. Over nearly fifty years, his regular phone calls home never displaced these weekly or twice-weekly letters, which kept her in touch with him all through her life. They were not, on the whole, intimate or self-exposing: this was a family wary of intimacy. They avoided subjects he thought would worry her. But otherwise they were a continuing diary

be living in a country where there were no bombs, no starvation and no oppressive regime. She was one of the lucky ones, grateful to the country that had taken them in. But she didn't think that kind of security should entitle people to wax indignant about the horrors of Communism. She thought of that as a form of self-indulgence. Ordinary people living under Communism – in Zlín, for example – were getting on with their lives and making do. They had roofs over their head, in state-subsidised housing. If they didn't have a car, they went by bus. If they didn't have lavatory paper, they used newspapers. It was a ridiculous luxury, actually, to throw away newspapers and buy lavatory paper. People made do with what they had, under the circumstances they lived in; and those more privileged, the lucky ones, should not be too quick to be outraged on others' behalf. This philosophy of stoical acceptance had a strong influence on her writer son, who respected her views, even if he would come to disagree with some of them.

She need not have worried about protecting her sons from prejudice at their next school. Pocklington, a boarding school set in a small market town in rather bleak Yorkshire countryside, on the edge of the Wolds, was rule-bound, austere, physically uncomfortable and exam-centred, in ways that the Dolphin School hadn't been, but it was not an intolerant community, there was some good teaching, and, of course, lots of sport. There were no girls, so not much scope for early teenage heterosexual fantasies, and no conspicuous scandals, though one boy did get expelled for unmentionable reasons. Tom, who spent four long years of teenage life there, from 1950 to 1954, did not like the school. Peter did. Up till then the brothers had been close, now they started to diverge. Peter was the short, unremarkable-looking, jovial, hard-working, law-abiding brother, who did GCE O Levels (introduced in 1951) and then stayed on to do A Levels and the exams needed to qualify as a chartered accountant. Tom, the taller and more good-looking younger brother, was also more impatient, less biddable, more stylish and more independent-minded. He went on being a good student and a good cricketer, encouraged by the fact that his English teacher, Mr Thornton, was also the cricket coach. The *Pocklingtonian* for summer 1953 recorded that T. Stoppard, in the First Eleven, was 'a keen and lively wicket-keeper who has improved steadily, but must learn to take the ball more cleanly. A useful bat.' Later reports described him as sound in defence and 'a good close fielder'. 'Je suis vice-captain of the Wilberforce junior cricket team,' he wrote home. He was also a member of the Senior Scout troop, wearing a red beret, getting a badge for tying knots, and doing very long weekend hikes, where the boys would be sent off in pairs, with map references and a compass, sleep out, climb some hills ('Don't worry yourself', he told his mother, 'I can take care of myself and I have enough sense not to take risks') and cook their own dinner. It was the sort of thing Ken would have approved of as part of an English education. Senior Scout T. Stoppard went along with it, but was not wildly enthusiastic, and retained a gloomy memory of going to a Scout camp where it rained a lot and he felt woebegone.

In academic subjects, he had one term of physics when he first got to the school, no chemistry, and biology lessons only memorable for the smell of cutting up dogfish ('he has hardly done justice to his abilities'; 'could do much better with a more serious attitude'; 'work is still messy'). So the future author of *Arcadia* and *The Hard Problem* left school with very little science. In maths, he came in for some criticism: 'Does not know his geometry theorems'. In the humanities subjects, he was always in the upper half of the class. He showed 'an intelligent interest' in divinity, was good at French, won a 'Use of English Prize', addressed the Sixth Form Society on the theme of 'A Day in the Life of a Mediaeval Student', and was treasurer of the Antiquarian Society. He liked debating – as in: 'This House considers a banana skin a more efficacious weapon than a Tommy-gun.' His English essays, however, didn't always find favour: 'He writes a very pleasant boyish style. It is time he was maturing a little both in style and in selection of models. He should read the better weeklies.' He enjoyed Latin and Greek – very few boys did Greek – and got the same kind of pleasure out of writing Greek verse and getting it to scan as he would have out of doing Lego. He liked it for the mathematical challenge, not for any poetical or emotional possibilities. 'I came top in Greek,' he told his parents proudly. 'Definite ability', wrote his Greek teacher.

Drama didn't much interest him. They were taken on trips, for instance to see a Greek play at Cambridge, but this did not inspire a desire either to write plays, or go to Cambridge. Shakespeare made no great impression either. The academic study of a Shakespeare play, as a text, left him cold:

> My first conscious response to Shakespeare's work – we were studying
> *The Merchant of Venice* at school – was one of bewilderment and
> bafflement and keen disappointment at the crudeness and naïvety, as I
> thought it, of the mechanics of the plot. At the age of fifteen you know
> everything. The business of the pound of flesh, and the literal-minded
> pedantry which enabled Portia to get Antonio off the hook, all that
> was a collapsed soufflé as far as I was concerned.

When they were reading the play in class, he was cast as an embarrassing (and embarrassed) Nerissa. Literary set texts, like *David Copperfield*, bored him. His private reading, dominated by a passion for Dornford Yates and, a bit later, Damon Runyon, was avid, unintellectual and undirected. Once he saw a boy laughing, absorbed in a book, and asked him what it was. It was *Vile Bodies* by Evelyn Waugh, a writer he had never heard of. At fifteen he was as innocent about literature as he was about sex. Instead of reading Waugh (that came later), he read *England, Their England*, by A. G. Macdonell. He loved his ironical, facetious Scottish view of inter-war English habits and traditions (fox hunting, country-house weekends, village cricket) and it had a lasting and, he thought, probably unfortunate influence on him. That was what the tone of light reportage ought to be, he felt. The juvenile comical style he was practising, not entirely to his English teacher's taste, got into his letters, as when his parents are moving house and he hopes it will have the word 'Hall' in it:

> Suits of armour? And a marble staircase that looks like a monument?
> An attic? Cellar? Windows like an observatory? Fireplace like a spare
> room? . . . Oh, I nearly forgot. How big is the swimming pool? And
> the stables? How much are you going to pay the man who lives at the
> end of the drive and opens the gates?

Another letter anticipates his return home:

Beware! You have precisely five days from now . . . Be warned . . . the
'enfant terrible' will cause chaos and destruction by . . . demands
of immediate production of fabulous yet unproduceable
drinks . . . refusing to go to bed till a disgusting hour . . . refusing to
pack at the long awaited conclusion of the 4 weeks until the very last
moment . . . YOU HAVE BEEN WARNED.

His housemaster cannily noted, of this cheerful, well-mannered,
engaging and 'effervescent' schoolboy, in the autumn of 1951, that 'there is
more to him than meets the eye'. A year later, the school was slightly less
enthusiastic about him: 'He is far too abstract, but pleasant enough with
it.' 'His work is unreliable at present . . . He must always set himself high
standards.' He took his O Levels in 1954, and had already started A Level
Ancient History, though with criticisms for carelessness and lack of 'single-
mindedness'. In January 1954, his friend A. J. Wood had bet T. Stoppard
two shillings and sixpence that he would go to university directly from
Pocklington School, not counting National Service. But that was not his
plan. He wanted to stop doing class-work and taking exams, he wanted
to earn his living and explore the world, and he wanted to leave home
and get away from his stepfather. The headmaster gave him some career
advice, but they seemed to be living in different worlds. 'Oh yes, journalism,' said the Head, 'very good idea, you need to get a degree and go to
the *Manchester Guardian*.' 'Journalism is best tackled through University
and I can see him going to Balliol or to Trinity' was the note on his report.
That seemed completely out of reach, and not what he had in mind at all.
He told his parents that when filling in the question on the careers form
which asked, 'Do you want a job which needs a University education?'
he put 'doubtful'. He left school on 27 July 1954, just after his seventeenth
birthday on 3 July. As his elder brother, still at school, observed enviously,
he donned a trilby and went off into the world. The rest of his education
he did for himself.

4

The Newcomer

> I felt part of a privileged group, inside society and yet outside it, with a
> licence to scourge it and a duty to defend it, night and day, the street of
> adventure, the fourth estate.

'When the idea of journalism came up, I thought: "That's it!" It was instant
and final. It made everything else look boring.' The newcomer to the job
was articulate, ambitious and energetic. He had an ear for what was funny
and an appetite for what was interesting. And he was mad keen 'to do stuff
and start earning a living'. At seventeen he was good-looking, in a tall,
skinny, gangly way, with shaggy dark hair, huge dark eyes, fine bone structure, big teeth, a sensual smile, a charming way of looking aslant at people
from under his eyebrows, and an interesting accent. This good-natured,
hopeful, nice-mannered teenager had no idea how appealing he was. 'I
wish I'd known!' he would say, looking back.

As often, he was lucky. He narrowly avoided National Service. (Peter
didn't do it either, because it was deferred while he completed his four
years of training to be a chartered accountant.) It was abolished in 1960,
but, by the 1950s, there were many deferrals and exemptions for men of
Stoppard's age, born in 1937. His call-up papers arrived at his parents'
address in Long Ashton, Bristol, but there was no follow-up, presumably
because he wasn't yet a naturalised British citizen. He was grateful that fate
had intervened, and that he had avoided the prospect of what, in his imagination, was an endless vista of getting up very early, having cold showers
and going on marches.

As soon as he shed being a schoolboy and moved to his parents' house
on the edge of Bristol, he sold all his school books to a second-hand bookshop, and landed a job. This required some chutzpah: he just showed
up and got an interview with Eric Buston, the news editor of the Bristol
morning paper, the *Western Daily Press*, in Baldwin Street. The paper,
an old-fashioned provincial morning broadsheet, one of the few still in

existence, with a low circulation, didn't have many jobs going. But Buston saw something promising in this keen teenager, and hired him as a junior reporter for a starting salary of £2 10s 8d a week. (A more senior reporter would get about £13 a week; the Fleet Street minimum was £21, which would have seemed a gigantic sum then. His NUJ dues, which he started paying in November 1955, were five shillings a year.) He took it like a shot – it was just what he wanted. 'This was the life!'

Bristol, then, had no fewer than three newspapers, the *Western Daily Press* and two afternoon papers, the *Bristol Evening World* and the *Bristol Evening Post*. That suggests the city's importance, and its sense of its own importance. Historically wealthy, confident and grand, on the back of its eighteenth-century slave trade and its maritime splendour, the post-war city was reconstructing itself after the Blitz. Bomb sites were everywhere. The big ships no longer sailed up the Avon into the centre of the city. The giant Bristol industries – aircraft, tobacco, cars – were still thriving, but there would be closures and mergers ahead.

The hilly city, with its steep grey-stone streets and grand municipal buildings and dramatic river gorge, was a scenic place to live. The beautiful Georgian terraces and crescents of Kingsdown and of Clifton, up by Brunel's famous and spectacular suspension bridge, were mostly seedy and run down, but regeneration was beginning. The city centre would see some haphazard and ugly developments in the 1960s, old housing making way for new roads, but it maintained its confident, solid air. It wasn't a good place for everyone to live, though. Immigration had led to racism – as well as a new multiculturalism – in the city: the Bus Company employed no black drivers, and plenty of landlords turned 'coloureds' away. The dock workers at Avonmouth were still hired like slave labour, picked out for a day's work by a row of managers pointing from a platform.

In many ways it felt like a pre-war environment. The council, dominated by Labour and by the anti-socialist, parochial 'Citizen's Party', tended to be stuffy in its views. Old ways prevailed in many aspects of city life: no music of any kind, for example, was allowed to be played in the bars and pubs. The Lord Mayor, with his chains and his coach and horses, was a familiar figure. The council was notoriously stingy and unadventurous where the arts

BBC's Bristol-based documentary unit. Regional television was thriving. Television – and radio – drama had as much status, and provided as many opportunities, for up-and-coming writers, as the theatre. All of Bristol's young writers would write for TV and radio when they started out, with as much appetite as for the stage. This was the headquarters for the BBC Natural History Unit with David Attenborough at the helm, for BBC West (launched in 1957), and the independent channel TWW (Television Wales and the West). The cinemas showed New Wave films as well as Hollywood musicals and Westerns.

Not all the arts were so secure. The dance company, Western Theatre Ballet, was running at a loss, and (Stoppard noted) 'watches its overdraft like other companies watch their waistlines'. Although there was a long tradition of Bristol painters, inspiring for young artists such as Derek Balmer, plans to build a new art gallery, on land where a bomb site had been turned into a car park, hung fire for year after year. Stoppard covered this battle more than once in his columns, sometimes with precise attention to the architects' aspirations, sometimes with mock despair, as though in support of those obstructing the plans. The many little magazines, more often than not, were struggling or badly managed. The *Bristol Forum*, Stoppard noted in February 1961, 'is run in a way which would embarrass and discredit a troupe of itinerant horse dealers'.

This city, its everyday life, its people, its journalism and its arts world, was Tom Stoppard's university. It gave him just what he wanted. 'From a sheltered middle-class boarding-school half-life, I was admitted to a camaraderie of journalists with a ticket to worlds I knew nothing about – law courts, local government, theatre backstage, boxing matches, crime scenes, in fact "all of human life" as the *News of the World* used to say.' His time as a reporter there lasted from 1954 to 1962. It took him from the age of seventeen to twenty-five. Those eight years marked the shift in his life from immaturity to adulthood, and from journalism to play-writing. They also marked the shift in the city – and in England – from the leftovers of early-twentieth-century habits of life and ways of thinking to more experimental and colourful times. He witnessed that change, and was part of it.

Bristol in the late 1950s and early 1960s could not have been a more fruitful place for him. The combination of a compelling arts scene, particularly in the theatre, and a conservative provincial community ripe for satirising, was an ideal stalking ground for a young journalist. Perhaps more easily than he would have done in London, he could start to make his mark and be noticed. The everyday reporting he did gave him a huge range of materials to draw on; the drama and film that he saw and wrote about gave him his professional grounding. Almost without his noticing, the politics and responsibilities of journalism forged his attitudes to society. And he learned to write to a deadline – just.

He plunged in at speed, going straight off to do a night course on shorthand and typing. (Pitman shorthand came in useful in later years for note-taking in rehearsals.) On his first day at the office, he was sent out to learn the ropes with a senior reporter. It was to cover the West of England Lawn Tennis Championships, where he was much more excited to glimpse his favourite sports writer, Peter Wilson, than to see famous tennis players like Ken Rosewall wandering about. A more harrowing induction was his coverage of a car crash in which, misunderstanding what the hospital had told him, he 'killed a woman who was still alive'. It was on the Monday front page, and there had to be an apology. (She died later in hospital.) The mistake made a great impression on him. 'It was like the worst thing that ever happened to me in my whole life.' He used it in a story written under the influence of Hemingway and published ten years later: 'I remember I went into the lavatory and tried to make it not have happened but when I came out it was still there . . . I felt scared sick all day and in bed I felt so bad I started praying . . . I thought I'd had it for sure. I was still on probation.' It was the first lesson in the 'sacred trust' of journalism: to get it right.

At first his pieces were anonymous, but gradually he began to have his name or his initials on them. When he got his first signed piece – on a caving accident in the Mendips – he felt so happy he 'wouldn't have minded dying'. Other early signed pieces were carefully factual: on young couples wanting to buy more unusual homes as part of the era's 'hunger for fresh ideas', on the redesign of the Central Library, on the threat of demolition to the dilapidated Georgian terraces of Kingsdown, or on the contrast between the city's traditional coffee rooms and the new coffee bars full of students wearing 'flannels, pullovers and long hair'. But he rapidly developed a jokey way of putting himself into his reportage as 'we' – a faintly ludicrous, naive character – as in a piece on having to climb down a deep cave with experts from the Spelaeological Society ('We're frightened of the dark, and we want to see our Mum'), or buying a slave girl as a stunt for the Bristol University Rag Week (complete with picture): 'We keep ten yards in front of her and pretend that she belongs to someone else.' A report on the annual Goram Fair and its amusement park listed the possible treats: 'If you want a second-hand ungrateful goldfish, call at this address, and bring a bucket.' Dressing up as a very hot Santa Claus, wearing his costume over grey flannels, was not a soft job: it 'needed the stamina of a Grand National winner combined with the diplomacy of a White House barman telling Kruschev [*sic*] he'd had enough . . . In outright defiance of Mr Macmillan's call for restraint, I would support any pay claim by the NUSC (Earth Division).'

After a while the paper used him as its stop-gap motoring correspondent. Vintage car rallies, caravanning guides and traffic problems were covered with a light hand. The Great Britain guide for motorists depicted 'fair damsel . . . ye olde village green, ye olde village church and ye olde village cricket-team, all of which is ye olde baloney.' He can't share his neighbour's romantic passion for old cars like an 1897 Delaunay-Belleville: 'He calls them "she", I call them "it".' A list of rules for considerate drivers is parodied. 'It would be inconsiderate to pelt live-stock with orange peel.' 'Please remember to leave the countryside as you find it; ie. the tidy driver removes the body.' He spent most of his time on these assignments concealing the fact that he couldn't drive.

He liked being a reporter, and the feeling it gave him of being in the know: 'At a bus-stop, say – you felt this, you knew things, you'd talked to the detective in the case or the councillor at the committee meeting, you were the only person at the bus-stop who was inside something, and everybody else was outside; they were the people who bought the paper.' He learned to sub, editing copy on the 6 p.m. to 2 a.m. shift. In those days, newspapers were still being printed by letterpress, using metal type which could be changed by hand in the composing room up to the last minute before going to press, on the big flat surface traditionally known as 'the stone'. He loved the business of going down to the stone to lay out the page, in that era of hot metal 'which hadn't changed much since Charles Dickens was a reporter'.

Subbing was less exciting to him than reporting, but it taught him 'speed, accuracy and concision', and he was quick to pick up advice from the older journalists there, like Bill Bomford, who remembered him as fast and willing to accept correction. He wasn't an especially good reporter, but he had a turn of phrase. The editor, Sam Shapcott, a good-humoured, unflappable character, spotted him early, too: 'That new chap Stoppard is going to be good.' The newcomer might be teased for his accent and his inexperience, but that was all part of the robust atmosphere of the paper, where the walrus-moustached, Methodist Eric Buston presided disapprovingly over his team. This included John Tidmarsh and Brian Barron, who aimed to get out of Bristol and make their names in Fleet Street. The feeling was catching: 'When I was nineteen I used to walk up Fleet Street excited just to stare at the *Express* building and the *Telegraph* building.'

But that was fantasy. In the real world, there would be three or four jobs handed out per day – court cases in the morning, flower shows or committee meetings or some such in the afternoon, parish councils or dinners in the evening. The old-fashioned subs' room had big windows, long tables and ancient wall phones, scarce and much-fought-over old Remington typewriters – somehow Stoppard always managed to get hold of one – and suction tubes for shouting down to the editors or sending copy to the printers. It was the base for practical jokes like pouring cold tea down the tubes into the editor's ear, farting displays, late-night games of cricket with a ball made of paper, glue and string, which sometimes broke the windows, endless mugs of coffee and sandwich lunches, frequent trips to the pub opposite, the Windsor Castle, and competitions for who could write the most lurid American-style headline, like Bomford's 'Murder, Torture, Bloodshed in Reign of Terror'. Stoppard's best attempt was 'DOPE MODEL NUDE SLAIN FIEND LOVES PROBE MYSTERY

QUIZ'. When he went to New York for the first time, a few years later, in 1962, the first headline he saw was 'SLAIN EXEC LOVES PROBE'. 'I felt good all day.'

There was one female colleague in this joshing, competitive male newsroom. She was Isabel Dunjohn, beautiful, blonde and sunny-tempered, four years older than Stoppard. She had been on the paper for two years already when he arrived in 1954. Isabel, like her new young colleague, had had a complicated childhood. Her father, a difficult character, fiercely British, had disowned his Pomeranian Jewish ancestry and changed the family name. Born in the 1890s to immigrant Jewish tailors in East London, sent to South America at nineteen with £5 in his pocket, returning to fight in the war, and then working on the British Argentine Railways, he had met his English wife, an ex-suffragette and nurse, in Buenos Aires. They moved to England against his will, and Isabel, born in 1933, was the late daughter of an unhappy marriage. Conventionally brought up – boarding school, secretarial course, au pairing – she turned out to be remarkably good at the journalism class at her secretarial college, and was hired by Buston when she was twenty.

Isabel was amused by the two new boys, Stoppard and Peter Bond, who started out in jackets and ties, but were soon wearing long raincoats and long scarves and trilby hats, always with a cigarette hanging from their lips, modelling themselves on tough American reporters in the movies. In Stoppard's case the dashing exterior and witty turn of phrase was a light cover, as she soon realised, for an anxious, eager, ambitious, shy and unworldly character. They quickly became close friends. There was no shortage of girlfriends meanwhile: the effect which he had on young women left vivid memories behind. The actor Gwen Watford recalled (in 1992) his taking her out to a restaurant and then writing an article 'eulogising my eyes'. A Beauty Queen called Dolores never forgot her date with him at the Bristol Zoo when he was 'an up-and-coming handsome young journalist'. And there were some slightly more lasting relationships too. But to Isabel he was like a younger brother who needed looking after, always pale and hungry and stick-thin, getting endless colds, smoking non-stop, awake all night and oversleeping or falling asleep at the wrong times of day, always broke and needing the loan of a fiver, always turning up at her flat at meal times and eating like a horse, always funny, sweet and grateful. They would walk through the city together, and sit on the stone steps by the river Avon, endlessly talking. He told her all his plans and hopes. She was his confidante, and he adored her.

One of the all-absorbing things they talked about was the theatre, with which he was also falling in love, entirely because of the Bristol Old Vic. Isabel was more in the know than he was, to start with, and reported back from a visit to London in May 1956 that she had seen an extraordinary new play called *Look Back in Anger*, which he had never heard of. Theatre hadn't meant much to him at school, apart from one boy's performance at Pocklington, as Hotspur in *Henry IV*, when he realised that Shakespeare could be entertainment, as a comic show might be. But once he started going to the productions at the Old Vic, and particularly everything with Peter O'Toole in it, he became a fan. He was transfixed by O'Toole's performances in *Man and Superman*, and in the 1957 *Godot* ('I was immobilised for weeks after I saw it'). That first encounter with Beckett was an amazing experience for him. He responded to his poetry, his language, his jokes, to the extraordinary fact that the play 'kept you amused, absorbed, occasionally puzzled, and seemed to do so without really having any cards to play'. He didn't find Beckett depressing or nihilistic. From the first, he felt there was 'an extraordinary courage and stoicism in these characters who are legless, headless, in dustbins, lost, deserted'.

As powerful as the effect of O'Toole in *Godot* was his Hamlet, in the 1958 season. He saw it over and over again, rushing back from his assignments to try and catch 'O what a rogue and peasant slave am I' from the back of the theatre, though never quite remembering whereabouts in the play that soliloquy came. The performance enthralled him because it seemed to be inseparable from the text: the actor seemed to be confiding in the audience as if he was saying it for the first time. It was O'Toole's Hamlet which showed Stoppard what Shakespeare could be: that it was exciting, and that it made sense. His first theatre review, for the *Western Daily Press* in 1958, was a comparison of O'Toole's 'fire-breathing' Hamlet with Michael Redgrave's sensitive, wan performance at Stratford.

Dying to see you pet, completely dying, port in the storm that's
you . . . love if you get flu now i swear my heart will break up like a
jigsaw puzzle spreading tear-shaped drops of blood all over the room.
i'm thrilled & bucked up at the thought of you coming & i'm already
looking at my watch & shaking it.

By the time of that letter, for all his self-criticism, his career had taken a
jump. His pieces were being noticed. In the summer of 1958, he was lured
away from the *Western Daily Press* by Reg Eason, the fiery-tempered editor of one of the evening papers, the *Bristol Evening World*. He was easy to
poach – 'my demands were absolutely pathetic' – at a new salary of £11 9s.
He went on paying his union dues, but in 1959, a year in on the *Evening
World*, he didn't back a union strike, was censured and had his membership suspended for two months. It was an episode he would store up.

His colleagues – Charlie Wilson, Hilton Timms, John Smith – were a
tough professional bunch, who regarded him as something of an exotic
aesthete, with his dark looks, his shaggy hair, his Cossack-style coats
and his theatre connections. 'It was rumoured that he drank wine.' They
weren't convinced by him as a reporter – he seemed to them to lack the
killer instinct needed for putting his foot in the door to get a story, and
his prose was too stylish for matter-of-factual pieces. John Smith would
recall an incident when a gas main blew up in central Bristol and a double-
decker bus fell into the huge crater left in the road. Stoppard was sent off
to cover this major disaster, came back to the office and wrote a lengthy,
flourishing, metaphorical piece. Reg Eason, tearing his hair out, said he
couldn't understand a word of it, and told someone else to write the basic
two hundred words of factual commentary that were needed.

He did some gossip column work, filling in, for instance, for 'Barbara's'
regular column 'Chatterday', while complaining it wasn't really up his
street, as 'I'm literary. I know which side Hemingway was on in the Spanish
Civil War, and how many Brothers Karamazov there were, and things like
that. Intellectual you might call me.' He did the odd piece of social coverage, notably a cool satire on a roomful of Bristol beatniks. He may have
been a bohemian (at least in his stepfather's eyes), but he certainly didn't

think much of these bearded anti-establishment poseurs, sitting in deep thought, all dressed in black, in a roomful of smoke with a white rat wandering about, intermittently berating the evils of capitalism while living off parental allowances:

> There is something stagey about a room full of people all acting as if they are alone. This one needs a script by Ionesco . . . We go out, back into the materialistic world of little machines walking about in hats, thinking of the wrong things, pursuing the wrong values, corrupt, unjust, hypocritical, selfish and decadent. It's a hell of a life, isn't it?

What he took to with real enthusiasm, and did solidly for two years, was film-reviewing. Hilton Timms, the *BEW*'s resident film critic, found himself out-written by the new stand-in. He could see that Stoppard, whom he liked, 'coveted' his role, and was not best pleased to be told in the office, repeatedly: 'Tom did a great job on the films while you were away.' Timms used to 'gnash' his 'teeth in secret admiration and envy' over his stand-in's witticisms. The rivalry would be put to good use in one of Stoppard's first plays, which he started in 1962 and which ended up as *The Real Inspector Hound*. The critic Moon, the perpetual number two covering for the perpetually absent Higgs, fantasises the uprising of all stand-ins, second-in-commands, understudies and twelfth men: 'Stand-ins of the world stand up!'

Like his immersion in the Bristol Old Vic, the two years of film-reviewing he did from 1958 to 1960 were a vital education for him. He covered everything that came out, from new European cinema to Hollywood romances, from Westerns to film noir, from musicals to disaster movies. His reports were funny, no-nonsense, anti-sentimental, serious about how much films mattered, and as keen on popular blockbusters, if they were well made and well acted, as on experimental or small-budget films. So he waxed eloquent about Andrzej Wajda's *Ashes and Diamonds* as a masterpiece, an example of Polish cinema's search for expression by 'young intellectuals mastering a new medium', and was moved by a new Swedish film called *The Rainbow Game* which spoke to 'the younger generations'. But he was as enthusiastic about an 'enterprising and entertaining' thriller with 'no pretensions', like Joseph Losey's *Blind Date*, or a robbery movie with Rod Steiger, Eli Wallach and Edward G. Robinson, *Seven Thieves*, where it was 'enthralling' to watch the pieces of the jigsaw being fitted together, or a big Hollywood film with a message, like *On the Beach*, 'the best thing that ever happened to the Nuclear Disarmament campaigners'.

He was attracted by the new wave of English films where the 'little man' stood up for himself against the powers-that-be, like Richard Attenborough in Bryan Forbes's *The Angry Silence* resisting the power of the Trades Unions: 'If a man can't think for himself, well, there's no point in anything.' The film combined an attempt to entertain and to educate – a mix, he noted (with a tiny foretaste of *Jumpers*), which was like 'a row of chorus girls explaining Einstein's theory of light – and just about as rare'. That sort of breeziness about women on screen, very much of its time, was common in his reviews. There were plenty of blithe references to curvaceous starlets and pert little French misses, to 'a sex-pot who looks as if she is constantly coming up to the boil' or to being bored by Bardot 'in all her mammalian glory'. To set against that, there were heartfelt tributes to Kay Kendall and Jeanne Moreau, and a fixed dislike for the *Carry On* films in all their 'witless inanity'. (They 'will no doubt break box-office records so hey nonny no and sucks to Stoppard'.) On the other hand, he was unconvinced by the vogue for Bergman: 'The sacred cow is not my favourite beast.'

What interested him were films which brought serious material into the popular domain with truthfulness and excitement. He had no time for the Hollywood clean-ups of a rough classic such as *Huckleberry Finn*: 'Huck is Huck and MGM is MGM and never the Twain do meet (apologies).' But he enjoyed comparing two well-made versions of the story of Oscar Wilde – a story which would continue to fascinate him – one with Robert Morley and one with Peter Finch. He liked Jack Cardiff's adaptation of *Sons and Lovers*, with Trevor Howard and Wendy Hiller as the Morel parents, because it treated Lawrence's 'genius with the mixture of respect and individuality of a fellow creative spirit'. Watching Olivier's *Richard III*, a brilliant portrayal of a 'barbarous and sardonic evil genius', he lamented the 'crying shame' that 'the word Shakespeare keeps more people out of the cinema than a hot day'. (He would put that right, in time.) And he recommended Eisenstein's astounding *The Boyar's Plot*, the second of the *Ivan the Terrible* films, as an important event: 'Anyone who thinks that the cinema is nothing more than a comfy place in which to eat popcorn . . . should see what all the fuss is about.'

When he started work as a journalist, Stoppard lived in his parents' house, in a small guest bedroom which he shared with Peter when he was there. But when he started subbing, which could keep him at work till one in the morning, his hours didn't fit well with the family's domestic routine. The house was crowded. By 1955 there were two small children, Richard, now six, and a new baby, Fiona, Bobby's first daughter and her last, and late, child. (It was a mark of the family's lack of communicativeness and intimacy that when Bobby was pregnant with Fiona, when Stoppard was seventeen and just leaving school, she didn't mention this to him: he learnt about it from his brother. He found this very odd at the time, and always thought it odd.) He was relieved to move out and to get away from his stepfather. But from then on, even when he was regularly calling and visiting them, he would write his long letters home, telling his mother about all his doings. First he went to live at the YMCA, and then in a succession of flats and bedsits, one of them on Sion Hill. The landlord there was John Wilders, an academic teaching Shakespeare at the university, whose family used to call their sweet-natured, disorganised lodger 'Big Tom'. He painted his room a deep shade of red. Much of his time was spent at Isabel's Clifton flat, which she shared with her friend Madeleine Morley (who was rather keen on Stoppard) and, for a while, with O'Toole.

He took Isabel to meet his parents; she thought his mother was lovely, and very attractive, and his stepfather good-looking in a military way, but bossy and disapproving. The whole family sat on the floor and played Monopoly; but Ken sat in his chair and wouldn't join in. She could see he did not like his bohemian younger stepson, wasn't amused by him and was not on his wavelength. In 1960, Ken and Bobby, and their two small children – five-year-old Fiona by then devoted to her enchanting big brother – moved to the small town of Milngavie, outside Glasgow. (This would be grist for some comic articles about Hogmanay, Scottish fishing and terrible train journeys from Bristol to Glasgow.) They would stay there for seven years, and then moved on to Hale, near Manchester, then to Tettenhall in Wolverhampton, and, in the mid-seventies, to Hunsonby, near Penrith, in Cumbria. He was on his own now, with no more maternal comforts within reach. But there was a providential substitute, in the form of a much-loved theatrical landlady, Val Lorraine.

A lot of the Old Vic actors had lodgings at Grosvenor Lodge in Clifton, the large, comfortable Regency house of Val and her husband Bob, a civil engineer, and their musical children. Val was a generous matriarch who oversaw a bohemian houseful of actors and writers, cooking them proper meals, listening to their problems and looking after them. She had her own creative side too: she'd been a radio actor, and wrote occasional book reviews for the *Western Daily Press*, which revealed a strong, emotional character. She had no time for the 'condonement of self-pity'; she thought 'the most perverting vice of all is despair'; she was irritated by pretentiousness and by cynicism about infidelity; and (reviewing Martin Esslin's book *The Theatre of the Absurd*), she aired her belief that 'We are part of the chaos and the chaos is part of us. To recognise it, in spite of ourselves, acts as a therapy.'

This full-hearted character took Stoppard under her wing and was very quick to see his talent. Val Lorraine was one of the first to tell him that he was a much better writer than the other journalists around him. Her encouragement came at the right moment, and mattered to him. He became part of her household, moving into Grosvenor Lodge in 1960, paying £2 a week for his upkeep. Val told him he could have a free room as long as he got going with his writing. He told her his ambitions and worried about her when she was ill. She knew he could be lazy and chaotic and put things off; but she had faith in him from the start, and wanted him to succeed.

So did he. He wanted to be known, he wanted fame. A visit to O'Toole at Stratford, when he was playing Shylock, Petruchio in *The Taming of the Shrew* and Thersites in *Troilus and Cressida* for the RSC, gave Stoppard 'a taste of honey'. There was Peter, after the first night of *The Merchant of Venice*, sprawling over brunch, answering phone calls from congratulatory celebrities and reading the ecstatic reviews. Stoppard, enchanted by all this, told his mother: 'I'd like to be famous!' He wanted to be John Osborne or Arnold Wesker, not an anonymous reporter. It was much easier and more exciting to start out as a playwright than as a novelist. A playwright could write a hundred pages in a few weeks, most of which were white space, and it would last two hours on stage, and on Sunday Kenneth Tynan would devote a quarter of a page of the *Observer* to it, even if you were a completely unknown person and the play had no scenery. There you would be, with one bound, in the posh Sunday papers and literary weeklies. You would have credentials. You would be known. You would never have to explain yourself again. But when was he going to get down to any of this?

In the summer of 1960 he and Isabel went on a long Mediterranean summer holiday together. She was by then learning Italian in Perugia, to teach English in Sardinia. When he joined her, they went to Capri and Elba, travelling cheaply, living in the sunshine, staying in hostels, spending their days by the sea. On a deserted beach in Elba, Isabel lost a signet ring in the sand. It was decorated with a little bird, and she was fond of it. The next day they went back to roughly the same spot, and he was trickling his fingers through the sand, hoping without hope that he might find it: and he did. It came into his hand. Isabel didn't seem quite as astonished and grateful as he had hoped, but, in fact, she was amazed. And this little miracle made a profound impression on him. He wrote home about it: 'I'm not superstitious or particularly religious or anything like that but this disturbed me greatly . . . it really was fantastic, and I'll never forget it as long as I live . . .' Though that letter, as usual, was addressed to both parents, his next letter, to Isabel, makes clear that it was his mother, as ever, that he was really writing to. And he wrote to Isabel with equal emotion about the event. It was a secret only to be shared with his three female guardians, Bobby, Val and Isabel.

i told val about finding the ring at elba. i have only told two people, for val and my mother are the only two i want to know about it, it means so much to me and it disturbed me so much. it was so eerily uncanny that i feel it is not meant to be talked about just casually, i can't explain but seeing that ring in my hand was the nearest thing i've had to a religious experience . . . when we started looking for it i thought Please god help me find it because it means so much to her and i do love her so, and when the thing was suddenly in my hand i nearly vomited with shock.

In the aftermath of their summer together, he also sent her a wistful, romantic love poem, one of many he wrote for her. Such poems embarrassed him, looking back. But they are touchingly vulnerable expressions of a very young man's feelings, written in language utterly the opposite of his jokey, stylish public persona. This one was called 'My Dream':

> In sleep we walked through poplar guarded streets
> Threw stones beyond sea walls and they are falling still,
> We danced like wanton clowns, tumbled,
> And drank each other, mouth to mouth.
>
> Where are you now, who smelt the summer grass,
> Heard flowers hold their breath for our last shaking clutch?
> Awakening robs my mind, scatters
> Graveyard ashes on your sleeping face.

The 'miracle' of the ring had such a strong effect on him perhaps because it coincided with a vital moment of resolution. On his birthday, 3 July 1960, he was sitting on a beach in Capri with Isabel, feeling extremely depressed. He was twenty-three, and he had done nothing at all! There and then he made up his mind that he would go home, give in his notice to the paper, and seriously start to write a play. The decision fell into his hand, like the ring.

Talking it through with Isabel, he felt sure that Richard Hawkins, the proprietor of his old paper, the *Western Daily Press*, would give him some freelance work. He knew that the director at the Bristol Old Vic, John

Hale, was to be heard saying that Tom Stoppard was 'the only journalist who can write. (Ha!)' He knew he would have to reassure his parents: Bobby would worry and Ken would think it was irresponsible: 'I have an idea that you will not be half so pleased about this idea as I am . . . but . . . I lose money and gain time . . . it is the best thing for me . . . I'm feeling a bit scared but also confident and happy.' He thought he could get by on £5 a week at a pinch ('The main snag is I *cannot* write without cigarettes'). He couldn't live off the Lorraines without achieving anything – he had to earn back the faith which Val had in him, 'much more faith than I have in myself'. 'Because of her and because of you,' he told Isabel, 'no one else on earth – I want to write something good.'

5

Brennus

All in all, a pretty disgusting record of juvenile cynicism.

Going freelance so as to write plays still meant meeting deadlines, and it certainly meant counting up his income every month. Letters home were full of tottings-up: 'I want to earn as much as possible in March. I did enough work for £28 in February, and this month it should be well over £40.' Richard Hawkins, at his old paper, the *Western Daily Press*, hired him to write a weekly column at four guineas a piece. He took the name 'Brennus', after a mythical ancient king of Bristol, and a cartoon figure with a crown, sceptre, robe and beard decorated every column. The first, on 30 August 1960, was titled 'In Good King Brennus's Golden Days'. The idea was to report on local issues and events, but to keep it light and amusing.

The *Western Daily Press* had run into financial problems, and was taken over by the *Bristol Evening Post* in 1960, though it kept its own name and identity. (Brennus would make fun of these permutations, imagining a bewildered outsider trying to identify which paper he worked for: '*Western Morning News*? *Bristol Daily Press*? *Western Daily World*? *Western Daily Press*? *Bristol*—' 'Stop!') Hawkins put in a new editor on the *Western Daily Press*, Eric Price, a tough, philistine character, who bullied his staff and despised the arts. But at the same time Hawkins, overriding Price, decided to have an Arts page on the *Western Daily Press*, and he appointed as editor a writer and journalist called Anthony Smith, who had come to Bristol that year to work for the *Evening Post*.

Anthony Smith was a couple of years older than Stoppard. Unlike him, he was English through and through, and university-educated. He'd had a rather solitary childhood (an only child, his mother died when he was three, and he was brought up by an uncle and aunt and by his widowed father, an ex-RAF brewery clerk). He got a state scholarship to Cambridge to read French, but spent most of his time editing an arts magazine and listening to F. R. Leavis laying down the law on Eng Lit. He did his National Service in the RAF. He was a would-be novelist and poet, a lover of France, Irish literature, chess and cricket, and an opinionated critic with a passionate interest in new writing, which he would discuss at epic length with his friends Zulfikar Ghose and B. S. Johnson.

The first time he and Stoppard met, they were both reviewing the same film and didn't take to each other. Stoppard thought he was a university amateur and Smith thought he was some oik with inky fingers – or, as Smith put it, 'a loose-lipped lout in a brown suit'. But when Hawkins put Smith on the new Arts page, he told him to make use of Stoppard. The first commission, in December 1960, a piece on the new French cinema, in particular Truffaut's *Les Quatre Cents Coups*, arrived immediately. It was informed, thoughtful and elegantly written, arguing that it was the 'moral vacuum' of the characters (rather than the sex) which made French New Wave cinema so disturbing, and that these new young directors had, as Orson Welles had had with *Citizen Kane*, 'the gift of ignorance': 'they approach their material free of precedent'.

Smith and Stoppard joined forces on the Arts page, and became inseparable colleagues and companions for the next two years. They co-edited the page, talked endlessly about writing and life and their literary ambitions, larked about, and went in for lots of rapid, jokey to-and-fro gags – not unlike future conversations between Rosencrantz and Guildenstern. Most of their time together was spent at Grosvenor Lodge, where Smith, too, became one of the family, or in his attic flat in Clifton, the Paragon, with a breathtaking view of the bridge. After a while the Paragon also became the home of Smith's girlfriend Alison Kennedy, a French and drama student at the university, and for a time they formed a cosy threesome, another home-from-home for Stoppard. They worked, travelled and partied together, sometimes, with Isabel, as a quartet, though Isabel and Anthony were never soulmates. Possibly they felt like rivals.

The Brennus column and the Arts page sometimes overlapped in their content, and Stoppard also wrote an occasional gossip column, 'West's Week'. For Brennus, he cultivated a deliberate persona, modelling a breezy style on the comic writing he admired: Waugh, Thurber,

Perelman, Alexander Woollcott, William Saroyan, A. J. Liebling and the *New Yorker*, and his schoolboy hero A. G. Macdonell. (Looking back on Brennus with mixed feelings, decades later, Stoppard described him as 'indefatigably facetious'.) Brennus had his quirks and his habits, not unlike Tom Stoppard's. He slept late and wore suede boots, he always looked unhealthy ('Influenza has left us pale and wasted, precisely, in fact, as it found us'), he read three Sunday newspapers, he didn't own a television, he was gauche and accident-prone, and he smoked non-stop, especially with the first mug of coffee of the day: 'The first indispensable, golden, resuscitating inhalation . . . glory be, we're alive.'

Brennus had literary allusions at his fingertips: Gertrude Stein's 'a rose is a rose is a rose' for instance, came in handy for an autumn rose show, to prove she was 'characteristically wrong in triplicate'. He was snobbish about some popular cultural phenomena – John Betjeman, for instance, always being wheeled out whenever a Victorian paddle-steamer was in need of defending, or the fashion for rows of plaster ducks flying along living-room walls, the most 'ghastly cliché now available to the home owner'. But he could be cynical about more sophisticated art forms, too. The fame of *Beyond the Fringe* (in 1962) had turned 'iconoclasts into icons'. A poetry competition at the Cheltenham Festival in February 1962 had three judges, one of them Miss Sylvia Plath.

> These are three of Britain's fourteen poets. It is not easy to break into the Club . . . they take it in turns to publish books, which are reviewed by the other 13 in the 13 magazines which it is worth being reviewed in . . . The Cheltenham competition . . . will be a fight between the 11 poets who are not judges, or possibly only 10 if Mr Ted Hughes abstains on the grounds that he is the husband of Miss Plath.

Brennus took a perversely disillusioned stance on well-meaning journalists trying to launch a 'Bristol Forum' in 1960 to raise awareness of the arts in the city and to influence city planning: 'Their ridiculous optimism in embarking on a venture which is so obviously journalism with a conscience . . . has not a hope of succeeding.'

Brennus had it in for the city's pomposities and prejudices – patriotic ship-launches, stuffy municipal cocktail parties or grandiose displays of new trains. He enjoyed putting his head round the door of specialist societies, where the members took their hobbies with the utmost seriousness: tattooists, stamp-collectors, wine-tasters, show-dog owners, tiddly-winks competitors who are 'pushing back the frontiers of knowledge'. He didn't spare his audience. 'The average Brennus reader is a 43-year-old second-hand eggwhisk salesman who thinks Thomas Chatterton was a game-keeper and Santa Claus is a director of Coca-Cola.' (Chatterton was a son of Bristol and, in more serious vein, Stoppard lamented the city's poorly kept little Chatterton museum.)

Brennus loved an excuse for a silly anecdote or a comic riff. His first piece described a visit on board a minesweeper:

A six-year-old acquaintance of ours who experimentally intoned 'Hallo' into a speaking-tube was answered from below decks with a two-word Saxon expression, the second of which was 'off' and the first of which for technical reasons must be omitted from the *Western Daily Press.*

A whole piece was devoted to musing over a pocket diary published by one D. Harper for Rover Coaches, packed with 'a disproportionate mass of information' in seventy-five of its 127 pages, 'for the most part staggeringly and hilariously useless'.

. . . How often does one get bitten by a mad dog? How often – look me in the eye, Harper – how often is one asked to name the points of the compass in Portuguese? Speaking for myself, not once in the last 2 years . . . Should I be asked the way by a Portuguese sailor who has lost his compass, or get bitten by a mad dog, I would whip out my Rover Coaches Diary and in a matter of moments reply: 'Tack Sul-Oueste', or, alternatively, apply a caustic (carbolic or nitric acid) with a match or piece of pointed wood.

But, frankly, what are the chances?

That surrealist farcical tone, often in the form of dramatic monologue or dialogue, was Brennus's forte. A report on a tennis match was an excuse for a fantasia on the sound-word 'bonk': 'the sound of medicine balls dropping off the wardrobe onto a silk eiderdown, of goldfish falling on to a microphone, of a man hitting a soft football with a long cucumber, of a bubble car hitting a cow'. On a damp grouse-shooting expedition in Scotland, any attempt to phone 'the person known locally as The Telephone Whether Girl' to ask her 'whether it's still raining, whether the depression is lifting or whether she listens to the BBC or the BBC listens to her' ends in failure: 'She never replies. Desiccated of all emotion she is a zombie winding round and round a recording spool . . .' The joke would be remembered for the girl who is TIM, the 'Speaking Clock', in the radio play *If You're Glad I'll Be Frank*.

Already there were overlaps between Brennus and his alter ego Tom Stoppard, also given to surrealist inventions. Stoppard spun an oddball fantasy, for instance, out of the news of a bomb squad's having been called to the UN on the receipt of a package from a Mrs McCleary, containing a pie and a rocket and a copy of the ten commandments for Khrushchev. This took off into reminiscences of an Irish landlady in one of his Bristol digs, who was in the habit of sending mysterious brown paper parcels through the post. 'I ventured, "Are you really sending a Bakewell Tart to Mr Nehru?" – which, when you think about it, is not an easy thing to come right out with – and she replied "Yes, and the left half of a pair of galoshes."'

A sea lion called Fritzy escaped from Butlin's in October 1960, and the Performing Animal Defence League offered a reward to anyone who found him and returned him to freedom in the North Sea. Animal rights was an unproblematic target for satire in those days, and, without labouring his views, Stoppard invented an embarrassing train and boat journey with the reluctantly rescued Fritzy. In spite of his rescuer's attempts to shut him up, Fritzy laments:

'I want to go back to the circus. The food's all right and I left my girlfriend there, Mitzy . . . The sea is so *big* . . . Anyway, I've never learned how to catch fish for myself. At the circus they come in buckets . . . You wouldn't do this to me,' he said, beginning to cry. 'Oh, don't be a baby,' I said, picking him up to throw him in the sea.

Surreality reached its peak when Brennus started to make fun of his creator. Stoppard had argued that British political figures – such as Selwyn Lloyd – were in need of mocking by the equivalent of an American satirist such as Mort Sahl. The following week, Brennus took up the challenge, and offered himself in the role, in response to Stoppard, whom he called 'a maladjusted vegetarian . . . who watches television every night and then drinks till dawn', a 'dilettante who writes in his own blood on handmade papyrus'.

As time went on he got more critical of Brennus's 'whimsy' and decided, he told his parents, that it was better to make it a *factual* article, written interestingly and lightly. What he really wanted was a column like Peter Simple in the *Daily Telegraph* or *Punch*'s Charivari, of short ironic pieces. Meanwhile, the Smith/Stoppard Arts pages took up Brennus's topics – usually the council's philistinism – with a more serious slant. And Stoppard was still doing some reporting on city life, with some scathing pieces on racism in Bristol or on the by-laws forbidding music in pubs. Occasionally, if a single issue of the paper ran not only a Brennus column but also more than one Stoppard piece, he would use the byline 'Tomik Straussler': a private wave to the past. So Anthony Smith often called him Tomik. But mostly he wrote on the arts as himself. The page let him air his thoughts as to what mattered, what was changing, and what he liked. He was in interesting company. Smith got talented writers onto the page, including his friends Ghose and Johnson. Philip Hobsbaum reviewed new writers such as Peter Porter or Alan Sillitoe, Eric Walter White did the music, Derek Balmer the art, George MacBeth wrote about Hemingway, Richard Hoggart about culture, and a Bristol university student called Angela Carter started out with a piece on the raunchiness of English folk songs. Battles had constantly to be fought with the editor, Eric Price: one which they lost was an attempt to print an absurdist headline in caps for a piece on the Theatre of the Absurd, with the 'B' out of place, but Price, grimly, had the compositor put it straight.

being didactic, was Arthur Miller. Stoppard wrote eloquently about Willy Loman in 1961. Miller wasn't really interested in salesmen, he thought, but in a human being's frustrated desire for recognition, in 'the conflict between the individual aware of his own "specialness", and the society intent on reducing him to an integer . . . a dot without dimension in the great pattern of highly industrialised civilisation'. He noted that Miller was 'not grinding a political axe': *Death of a Salesman* was 'labelled Left by the far Right, and decadent by the *Daily Worker*'.

His admiration for Miller was part of his fascination with all things American – plays, films, novels, comedians, magazines, rock music. Eliot, e. e. cummings and Fitzgerald were part of his mental landscape. Edward Albee's *The Zoo Story*, he would say, was one of the plays that turned him into a writer. His passion for American work was something he shared with a lot of young, male, post-war English writers; in his case it had its roots in those glamorous gum-chewing American soldiers in Darjeeling.

Quite apart from Brennus's cool, Liebling-style quips, his fiction reviews showed how immersed in American writing he was – though not uncritically. Reviewing a collection of *New Yorker* stories in February 1961, he complained that the 'enfant terrible' was developing 'middle-age spread'. The latest crop seemed duller, apart from a 'superb' story by Philip Roth, 'Defender of the Faith', and Updike's childhood reminiscence, 'The Happiest I've Been'. Dos Passos's *Mid-Century* was 'a giant mish-mash'. Raymond Chandler, though addictive, 'passes through the system like a purge'. But Thurber he admired unconditionally. He felt a sense of affinity for his surreal stories and cartoons of 'the plight of the sane lunatic ever so slightly at odds with the lunatic sane'.

In the early 1960s he wrote two long pieces on American novelists. One was an interview he managed to get with John Steinbeck while he was living reclusively in England for a few months. Stoppard's colleague Peter Bond had tracked him down to a hideout in Somerset. Stoppard went and knocked on the door, and Steinbeck told him to go away. Lacking the doorstepping instinct, he at once backed off: 'I'm so sorry to have bothered you.' Steinbeck called him back. Since the young man had been so nice, he agreed to meet him in London. At the Dorchester Hotel, Steinbeck appeared out of place, a big, heavy, peasant-like figure. He told his young interviewer that early rejection could be good for a writer and early success harmful; that he wrote two thousand 'usable' words on a good day; that although he admired Hemingway he hated being compared to him all the time; and that he didn't talk about his work while he was doing it. He didn't think much of the Beats, and was amused by Truman Capote's comment on them, which in Steinbeck's version was: 'Well, it's just sort of ... *typing*, isn't it.' He believed that the only crime was 'dispassion, staticness, disinterest, *ennui*'. 'A good mind is never bored.' Steinbeck seemed more authentic to him than loud-mouthed Norman Mailer. He wrote, a little primly, but with feeling, in 1963: 'Mailer may one day be admired despite his opinions, which is the test of a writer, instead of because of them, which is the test of a propagandist.'

In April 1962, with Anthony Smith, he took his first, low-budget, plunge into New York. He was extremely excited to be going. They went on a charter flight from Bristol full of architects. Trying to assuage his mother's anxieties by teasing her, he said, yes, I have to fly, because the other 119 people are flying and have kept a seat for me. They slept on the couch or the floor of an apartment borrowed from someone they didn't know – an obliging absentee landlord who dropped by only occasionally, thereby confirming their high expectations of American hospitality. By the time they left his apartment, they were taking turns to sleep in his bed, and complaining that he hadn't replenished the peanut butter or the cinnamon toast. They saw off-off-Broadway shows, coffee-house comedians, Mike Nichols and Elaine May, and Lenny Bruce at the Village Vanguard. He met Mel Brooks, whose comic routine (with Carl Reiner as his straight man) as 'The 2,000 Year Old Man' had just taken off on the *Ed Sullivan Show*. Brooks took a shine to him, and sent him his record, a brilliant to-and-fro of ludicrous Yiddish jokes. Stoppard sent him a fan letter after he got home, reminding him of the 'funny-looking English boy writer . . . of middle-European extraction' he'd met, enthusing wildly about the 'inspirational humour' of the record, which he thought ought to catch on in England, and pouring out his latest plans and problems: writer's block, no money, in a state about deadlines, wanting to leave his 'lovely town' and move to London. Meeting

Brooks, he said, had been one of the best things that happened to him in New York.

He also made his way to the door of the *Village Voice*, via a contact with the theatre critic Jerry Tallmer, one of the paper's key people since it started up in 1955, in a seedy one-room office on Greenwich Avenue. The *Voice* was at the heart of New York bohemian counterculture. It was the first to publish Jules Feiffer's 'sick' cartoons, the first to report on the Living Theatre, or the Café La MaMa, or the American production of *Krapp's Last Tape*. Stoppard described it (for Bristol readers) as 'politically liberal and artistically obsessed', extremely 'in-group' (Ginsberg reviewed Kerouac, Mailer stopped part-funding it in a huff because of a typo in his weekly column), and 'the most relished reactor to any embryonic kicks in the American theatre'. There was nothing like it in Britain. It was exciting for him to have a few short pieces published there.

That early romantic feeling for America left strong traces. He would choose Bernstein's 'America', from *West Side Story*, as one of his Desert Island Discs, in 1985. The heroine of *Shakespeare in Love* (1998), ship-wrecked at sea, arrived, in an early draft, on the American shore at the end of the film, and greeted her brave new world with delight. Long before that, in 1976, he would caricature his fascination in a wild extended monologue, inspired by Lucky's unstoppable flow in *Waiting for Godot*, in *New-Found-Land* (written for an experimental American director), an exaggerated compendium of all the myths and clichés about the wonders of America. Looking back in 1995 on his first visit to New York, he said that he went as a pilgrim, and felt like Columbus the whole time he was there.

6

Walking on Water

> When people ask me what I do, I say I'm a writer.

American writing took its most magnetic form for him, as he began to do his own work, in the figure of Hemingway. One of his *Village Voice* pieces was a comparison of two equally inadequate biographies of his hero, by Lillian Ross (sycophantic) and by Dwight MacDonald (a hatchet job). 'Hemingway . . . can be spied between the two as a complete natural, engaging, bearish, bullish, joyous, witty, adolescent, pontifical, generous, and knee-high in pygmies.' He admired the man, and he was inspired by the prose style. Hemingway had died only a year before he went to America for the first time, on his birthday, and, when he heard the news, he wrote to his mother (unusually addressing the letter to her alone) with strong emotion. It wasn't just the tragedy of his death, or his incomparable influence on so many other writers, it was also that he had longed to meet him, and now it was too late. 'I don't get emotional about any other writer.'

Hemingway's plain speech and taut narrative, at once banking down and letting out pent-up emotion, his quick-fire dialogue, his disenchanted comedy, his immersion in landscapes, his toughness muddled up with bewilderment, had a powerful effect on him. When he first saw *The Birthday Party* in 1962, he thought of Hemingway. In years to come, he collected his first editions, wrote about him, attended Hemingway conferences and continued to admire him. Explaining in the 1980s why he got 'bitten' at twenty by Hemingway, in spite of the egotistical, ridiculous, self-parodying side of him, he talked about his 'tensile quality', his astonishing expression of 'the physical, sensual experience of life' (fishing, for example), his bold technical skills – how he would 'leap forward in time beyond the point we have reached in the story' – and how he got his effects 'by making the reader do the work'. In 2018, he was still a fan, rereading *A Moveable Feast* with excitement and admiration.

Brennus liked doing pastiche. One of his imitations – when undertaking a mildly uncomfortable assignment – was of a tough, macho foreign correspondent plunged into a war zone with the 'the whine of bullets' making 'a symphony of death' all around him. But he liked parodying Hemingway best of all. Enough of bullfighting novels, said Brennus in 1961. He was going to write a Hemingway cricketing novel, and here was an extract, called 'For Whom the Bails Fall: Death After Lunch'.

He looked at me and then the coin went high.

My mouth was dry the way it is when you haven't brushed your teeth. I brushed my teeth all right but this is how my mouth was. You can't explain these things but you try because maybe it means something and maybe it doesn't and in the end it doesn't matter, and you know that, too.

I need this luck, I thought. I need it bad because that's all there is. The coin spun high . . . and the earth moved away and under me.

He let me see it there. He didn't say anything, and then I stopped looking . . . It was a long way back. I walked into the room. They sat quiet, waiting.

'How did it go?'

'Fine,' I said. I didn't know how to tell them, but they knew how it was in my face.

'We're fielding,' I said. 'It's okay.'

'Sure it's okay.'

'That's what I said,' I said.

'We could have had such a damn good time batting together.'

'Yes,' I said. 'Isn't it pretty to think so?'

In a spoof CV sent to Smith early in 1963, he described himself as an up-and-coming young playwright who 'has travelled widely to New York (where he quickly established a reputation as a Hemingway parodist in the *Village Voice*)'. Hemingway seeped into his private writing, too. The summers of 1961 and 1962 were spent partly abroad, staying with the Smiths in a dilapidated castle in Blauvac, near Avignon, where Smith was friends with the eccentric chatelaine, hitch-hiking, and meeting up with Isabel in Spain and Italy. A love letter to her, written in an all-night cafe in Narbonne while trying to hitch to Spain, takes on a melancholy Hemingwayish tone: 'i want to sleep, and i want a lift in a Citroën Goddess all the way, and i want you, here now oh i do want you and i can't write . . .' A card to her the next summer from Pamplona, enjoying the bullfights, invokes *The Sun Also Rises*. Brennus takes this up in his report: 'It was a very fine fiesta and all the bulls were almost very fine too.'

A long letter to Isabel, probably from 1962, included a half-page of a story, of a man coming into a one-square town in Spain between sea and hills and seeing a crowd: 'So he got down off the truck wet and heavy-feeling in the heat and he went over with his shadow bunched round his feet and his pack sitting heavy on the white stones behind him and the truck grinding hotly across the square . . .' I don't know what this is, he says to her. Perhaps the beginning of a novel. He is missing her.

> you seem so far away. fuck it, you are far away. come close, write to me close. yaayyaa darling; i have to make up my own language for ending letters to you. the things you want to say have stopped meaning anything because words of love and farewell are used meaninglessly all the time, by people who don't mean anything of the sort, they just mean good-bye for now . . .

The cafe in Narbonne and the scene in the square got into one of three stories that were published in 1964, the first published products of his transition between journalism and play-writing. The stories use plain speech, punctuation-light paragraphs of action and description, broken slices of time, strange moments of intense consciousness, and dark grotesque comedy. The Hemingwayish manner gives a lot away: far more than Brennus's well-armoured comic riffs.

In the highly stylised 'Reunion', a self-pitying voice, talking to the woman he can never have, warns her against the man she's in love with (faintly invoking O'Toole): 'Those dashing artistic types always develop into wife-beaters.' 'What I miss', he tells her, 'is you approaching down

busy streets, and eating together and saving things to tell you and having things saved for me, that and driving on long journeys, and watching
you being pleased and watching you sitting in a chair.' The woman 'gave
off summer colours all year round'. (Isabel, he often said to her, was his
'sun-and-wine woman'.) The story, full of personal feeling, ends with their
unhappy parting.

'Life, Time: Fragments', made up of modernist, disconnected paragraphs, tells the increasingly surrealist life story of a failed writer – as
if Stoppard were running through all his worst moments and his worst
fears. He remembers the awful feeling of killing off a woman in a car-
crash report, in his first week as a journalist. He tries for a job on the
London *Evening Standard* because there was 'something slightly shameful
about being twenty-five in the provinces'. The editor asks him if he is interested in politics. Oh yes, he replies. 'Who, for instance, was the Foreign
Secretary?' Musing on the interview afterwards, he decides this wasn't a
fair question. 'He had only admitted an interest in politics, he had not said
he was obsessed with the subject.' (In later Stoppard-lore, this true story of
his interview with Charles Wintour would get changed: his silent joke to
himself becomes his witty repartee to the editor.)

Then he is abroad with the sunshine woman, reprising the cafe in
Narbonne, the scene in the square, the hitch-hiking, the moment on the
beach when he realises that 'whatever it was I'd been waiting for slipped
by then, between waves, as quickly as that'. Then, like a couple out of
'Prufrock' or *The Waste Land*, he and his lady make brittle night-time talk
about the need to kill off his literary heroes – 'Hemingway's an adolescent
philistine' – in order to clear the ground for himself. 'The models are no
good any more, we've had all that, we're on our own now.' Then we see
him, Beckett-style, lying on his bed, an ageing journalist contemplating
his passing life: 'I am drowning with the panache of someone walking on
the water.' In a paragraph he had already tried out in letters to Anthony
and Isabel, the failed writer, surrounded by rejection slips, but getting ever
closer to God, falls on his knees to an angel, who says: 'The Lord thanks
you for your contribution but regrets that it is not quite suitable for the
Kingdom of Heaven.' He kills himself. The body of the writer, and the

'body of his work' are discovered by a critic – the first of several predatory critic-biographers in Stoppard's work. 'So he made the writer quite
famous and he made himself a little more famous too.'

The best of the three, 'The Story', a dark farewell to his days as a reporter,
is a harsh moral tale about the careless destructiveness of journalism at its
worst. The narrator, a reporter on the *Sun*, is sent out – it's routine – to a
provincial courtroom. As usual, there's not much of interest. 'It took most
of the morning to get a line on a scrap-metal theft and a careless driver.'
Then a case comes up of a man, a Mr Blake, a teacher on holiday from a 'top'
school, who has 'fingered' a seven-year-old girl on the beach. He is a grotesque figure, 'red and tweedy' and grinning horribly, 'too fat and altogether
sick with where he had got himself'. He pleads guilty and gets fined. The
reporter decides to let it go, and shakes his head at the boy from the provincial weekly (a glimpse of the younger Stoppard?) who is going at it in his
notebook 'like a double murder'. He tells the man he isn't going to report it.
But the Press Services man, aptly named Diver, whose job is to pick up the
juicy tidbits and sell them to newspapers round the country, sharing his fee
with the journalists who feed him stories, asks as a favour for a paragraph
on the case. So the story of the indecent offence gets into all the papers –
and a week later, Mr Blake throws himself under a tube train. The reporter
gets his fee. 'I don't know what I spent it on,' the story ends. 'It got mixed
up with my other money and at the end of the month I was broke as usual.'

In all the mixed, prolific output of his ten-year apprenticeship as a
writer, from 1954 to 1964, 'The Story' is the first piece that puts its mark
down with complete assurance. Unlike any of his other early prose pieces,
it had an afterlife. Much extended, it turned into a television play, called
first 'The Explorers' and then *A Paragraph for Mr Blake*, aired in 1965. And
the commentary on journalistic morality, in the extended version, found
its way, many years later, into *Night and Day*.

These revealing stories, all connected to his Bristol life, were the first writings he published in hard covers. He thought perhaps he might write a
novel. But he knew, really, in the early 1960s, that theatre, not fiction, was
his business – and theatre was where he might find rapid success. He was

making all kinds of starts while he was at Grosvenor Lodge. In his mind's eye, he was consciously writing for Kenneth Tynan: what would he think well of? He tried a version of *Look Back in Anger*: that lasted for about five pages. Then he wrote three plays, all heavily indebted to what he had been seeing and reviewing, all garrulous and absurdist, all in some way about bewilderment and failure. None of them lasted in their first form. One of them vanished rapidly. All three of them were vital starting points.

The first to be written and the first to be sent out, *A Walk on the Water*, was a two-act comedy about a weekend in the life of George Riley, fantasist, unemployed inventor, sentimental patriot, chauvinist, self-promoter and self-deceiver. As in 'Life, Time: Fragments', Riley is a man 'drowning with panache while walking on water'. He is also the little man against society, the angry outsider familiar from many new plays of the time, holding forth in an English suburban pub and living room. Stoppard wrote it at Grosvenor Lodge to the beat of a Leadbelly song, 'Ol' Riley', one of Val Lorraine's favourites. He sent it to the artistic manager of the Bristol Old Vic, John Hale, who sat on it for nine months – he was 'too timid' to ask why – and then sent it back, but with a moderately encouraging reader's report: 'The central character, with his bombast and self deception, is well drawn, though without good acting he might become extremely boring. The whole thing rather depends on a mood . . . The construction of the play is professional.' He told his parents that *A Walk on the Water* was a naturalistic comedy, but that he liked his other play better, which took place 'nowhere' at 'notime'. This second play was a one-act dialogue, *The Gamblers*, for a prisoner and a jailer, set in a jail 'which has the feeling of a time when the fastest form of transport is the horse', on the night before the prisoner's execution. In the style of Vladimir and Estragon (and of the badinage that Stoppard and Smith went in for), they exchange one-liners on life, death, revolution, failure, hope, consciousness and fate, and, in the process, gradually exchange roles. The prisoner is self-assured and quick-witted, the jailer is 'older, fatter, duller'. He is the fall guy, the clown whose trousers fall down, the hangman who's never hung anyone before. He would really prefer to be a martyr, whereas the prisoner would prefer to lead a revolution. Each has been given their part to play, but the parts turn out to be interchangeable, just as, in their exchanges about revolution, the rebels and the tyrants are also seen to be, through history, endlessly interchangeable. The dialogue would sound familiar to any reader of *Godot* – or of *Rosencrantz*:

J: The neck is the weak point. Your spirits are down?
P: Right down.
J: In your left shoe?
P: The right shoe.
J: Strange.
P: Well, it was a fifty–fifty chance.
J: A gamble.
P: It could have gone either way.
J: There's no way of telling.

The main gamble, as far as they are both concerned, is whether there is anything to believe in, anything to hope for. In jokey fashion they are airing the same problems of consciousness which are going to preoccupy George in *Jumpers*, or Max and Lenka in *Rock 'n' Roll*, or Hilary and Spike in *The Hard Problem*:

P: How are you supposed to know you believe? How do you know
    you're not just hoping?
J: Because it works.
P: For you?
J: Of course.

As the prisoner says, it's all a gamble: 'It's gambling in the dark, of course. They don't let you look until it's all over and too late. And if you're right, and there is nothing at the end of it, you don't even know you've won. It doesn't bear thinking on.'

The third play he was working on was a surreal comedy and country-house murder-mystery spoof about two theatre critics, to be called either

am rather overwhelmed with my set-up.' Anthony was heartbroken, and wrote him a desolated letter. His best friend was going away and leaving him behind. If 1960s Bristol had been Renaissance Florence, then they were losing their Petrarch.

But there was a coda to his Bristol life. Early in 1964, a young film-maker, John Boorman, then head of the BBC's Bristol-based documentary unit, and encouraged by Huw Weldon at the BBC to experiment with real-life programmes, made a fly-on-the-wall, six-part television series about an 'ordinary' young couple, against the background of the changing city. He picked Anthony and Alison Smith as his 'Newcomers' in Bristol, as much for Alison's striking looks as for Anthony's literary ambitions. The film was made in the early months of 1964, culminating with a portrait of the city on the day that Alison gave birth to twins in May, and aired that month as the first series for the BBC's new channel, BBC2.

The Smiths' marriage is given a *cinéma-vérité* treatment in the context of a number of staged settings – the *Western Daily Press* newspaper office, a mixed-race nightclub, a black church service, an estate agent's office, a football match, the night-time streets among Bristol's down-and-outs, a party given by the Smiths, the hospital. It gives an eloquent social picture, an anthropological slice, of Bristol and its counterculture in the early 1960s, moving from staid county councillors to an anti-capital punishment protest, from dock workers at the Labour Exchange to young bohemians sporting beards and black polo necks, dancing the twist and listening to the Rolling Stones. The jerky, rough, improvisatory style was a bit like the Beatles' film of that year, *A Hard Day's Night*, or the film Boorman went on to make next with Charles Wood about the Dave Clark Five, *Catch Us If You Can*.

When Boorman went to the Paragon to start filming, the crew toiling up five flights of stairs to the flat with their camera equipment and setting up the first shot of the series, a pile of coats on the floor began to animate, from which Tom Stoppard emerged, with (as Boorman remembered) 'that innate elegance he possesses'. From then on, he was the visiting star of the show. Boorman thought he was brilliant, and that he would make a very good actor. The cameras follow him round addictively. He's seen in rapid motion throughout, dark, glamorous, funny, gawky and transfixing. He plays puppyish games, smokes non-stop, makes silly jokes, dances with all the beautiful girls at the party, and is cosily at home at the heart of the Smiths' lives.

He says to camera, tellingly: 'Although I almost try to have as few friends and as many acquaintances as possible, of those friends, I think the Smiths are as close as I need to have – or have.' The film was an artificial contrivance, of course: he had already gone, and *The Newcomers* was a kind of farewell to his life in Bristol. At one point he is heard saying: 'I think all of the things which count for me, which I look back on, began here.'

7

On the Scene

Preston: Funny man.
Angie: It's his job.
Preston: Funny peculiar.
Angie: He's funny ha-ha, too.

If he had planned to jump into the heart of what was soon going to be called 'Swinging London', he couldn't have come to a better place. *Scene* had just been started up by Peter Cook, satirist and comic genius, and Nicholas Luard, writer, cultural entrepreneur, gentleman adventurer and *bon vivant* alcoholic. They had met at Cambridge through the student revue Footlights. Cook – with Alan Bennett, Dudley Moore and Jonathan Miller – had just had a resounding hit in *Beyond the Fringe*, which took off at the Edinburgh Festival in 1960, transferred to the West End and was made into a hugely popular LP. Satire, from that moment on, was all the rage. *That Was the Week That Was*, presented by David Frost, another Cambridge Footlights graduate, began on television in the autumn of 1962. To keep up the momentum of *Beyond the Fringe*, Cook, with Luard, who had a legacy he wanted to spend, founded the Establishment, a Soho club in seedy Greek Street, on the site of a strip club, for satire, jazz, art and revue. It opened in October 1961, featuring the youthful John Bird, John Fortune, Eleanor Bron, John Wells and Dudley Moore, with Gerald Scarfe cartoons, and one-off turns by Frankie Howerd and Barry Humphries, making his first London appearance as Edna Everage. At the same time as the Establishment, *Private Eye* was launched. In 1962 it was sold to 'Cook & Luard Productions', and Nick Luard became *Private Eye*'s 'Lord Gnome'.

In July 1962, it was reported that a new magazine, *Scene*, was to be launched 'by the young men who have had a considerable success with *Private Eye*'. It started small and dingy-looking, and then morphed into an expensive glossy magazine, lamentably understaffed, produced first from a tiny Fleet Street office and then from a room above the Establishment.

The editor was Francis Hitching, later known for his interest in the para-normal. Kenneth Tynan called *Scene* 'virulently trendy in tone and sig-nally lacking in funds'.

It was exactly the kind of platform Stoppard wanted, though there were problems from the start. He complained bitterly to Isabel, and to his mother, about weekly cock-ups produced by a 'bloody amateur clutch of shoddy, careless disgusting stupid lay-out idiots who can't be trusted with anything'. 'Instead of blunders being rare and shameful they are more or less inevitable. One breathes a sigh of relief if something comes out okay.' But from September 1962 to April 1963 he reviewed over 130 plays, often writing two or three pieces for a single issue. As in Bristol, he wrote as himself and also under a pseudonym. When he was reviewing he wrote as Tom Stoppard and when he was interviewing he usually wrote as William Boot. He needed two bylines partly because he was writing so many pieces, and partly because he thought he ought to split his objective and his personal side. His critical judgements should be disinterested and authoritative. He 'clung to the idea that a play . . . had an innate score (out of 10, say)' and that his task 'was to deduce it and assign it'. Looking back in 1972, ten years later, he thought that had made him 'an awful critic', and that he'd been quite wrong to think there was 'an absolute scale of values', rather than trusting 'his own subjective responses' or understanding that 'the only thing that counted was the effect the experience had on me in my seat in the stalls'. By contrast, the real theatre critic was Tynan, who 'lived and ate and drank and sat around among actors and writers'. Neither Boot nor Stoppard, however, would ever be as personal or as ruthless as Tynan. As Stoppard said in 1972: 'I never had the moral character to pan a friend. I'll rephrase that. I had the moral character never to pan a friend.'

William Boot, in *Scoop*, Waugh's 1920s satire on journalism, long one of his favourite books, is the country-mouse nature correspondent who, by accident, finds himself bemusedly reporting on an obscure African insur-rection. Through a mixture of innocent beginner's luck, the cynical incom-petence and infighting of his rivals, and wildly farcical circumstances, he gets the scoop, and much against his will becomes a reporting hero. When he borrowed the name for *Scene*, Stoppard didn't make a character out of

'William Boot', as he had with Brennus. But Boot as the little man who makes his mark through a mixture of naivety and bloody-mindedness, in circumstances beyond his control, was an attractive figure to him. He held on to the surname for other uses.

The plan that Boot would get personal while Stoppard stayed Olympian was muddled from the start. He did two pieces about O'Toole, one in October and one in December 1962 (needless to say *Scene* messed up the illustrations), when O'Toole was poised between success as a stage actor and superstardom in *Lawrence of Arabia*. Boot wrote the first and Stoppard the second, but there wasn't much difference. The earlier feature was nostalgic for the 'underfed', shaggy-haired actor he remembered in Bristol, 'a hard-drinking bohemian causing havoc backstage' and 'blithely . . . dedicated to the ideal of being himself, at all times, without concessions to people or to circumstances'. But it also described a dedicated professional who always did his research. In the later interview, O'Toole talked about returning to the theatre in Brecht's *Baal*, because 'it imposes on me a discipline I don't normally possess'. He was also planning a film of *Godot*, to be shot in Ireland, with Jack MacGowran as Lucky and Frankie Howerd as Pozzo, because playing Vladimir at Bristol was the most intense experience of his life. The interviewer didn't reveal that he was helping O'Toole write this screenplay – which was really more of a transcription than an adaptation. The project came to nothing, as Beckett withdrew his permission. But working on *Godot*, line by line, was not a waste of Stoppard's time.

O'Toole swam out of Stoppard's world around now, but the following year, his huge success as Hamlet at the Old Vic had a strong effect on him. O'Toole's Bristol Hamlet had been a seductive beacon into the theatre; his London Hamlet led, by indirection, to *Rosencrantz and Guildenstern*.

O'Toole's involvement with Brecht and Beckett also overlapped with Stoppard's theatre experiences as a young reviewer. Given that he was twenty-five, new to the London scene, and still feeling a bit like a William Bootish country mouse, he was extremely definite in his views. He admired Brecht, but not for Brechtian reasons. His first review for *Scene*, of an anthology of Brecht pieces which had come to the Royal Court from

New York, with Lotte Lenya in the cast, noted that audiences responded to him not out of 'alienation', but – ironically – because they identified with the characters. They continued 'to pity Mother Courage whom Brecht damned as a war profiteer and Galileo whom he condemns for recanting'. It was his richness 'as a human being' which shone through these plays and made them great.

As well as marking his interest in Galileo, this was one of several pieces critical of ideology in the theatre, which he didn't warm to, and often found professionally inept. He thought Joan Littlewood was a genius and *Oh! What a Lovely War* a sensational piece of political music-theatre. He saw it on its first night, and next to him was a very old man with no teeth, who turned to him in the interval in tears and said: 'I was there.' That was what he thought wonderful and important about it, that it moved you and drew you in. But other agitprop productions from her E15 stable, done without her, could be dire. One standard flat package of 'workshop raw material' with social content seemed 'pretty . . . pointless'. 'It looks as if when it came to casting the show, the producer went into the street and blew a whistle.'

One of the most exciting things he saw was Jack MacGowran's one-man Beckett show, *End of Day*, at the New Arts Theatre Club. This was a venue for new work set up by Peter Hall and Michael Codron, whom Stoppard described, before their paths had started to converge, as 'the reddest of London management's new blood'. Beckett gave human beings 'a look of pity and ironic amusement, the exact opposite of laughing till one cries – crying till one laughs'. His characters were (as in Eliot's *The Waste Land*) 'caught between memory and desire'. And MacGowran embodied the comic essence of 'the Beckett refugee'. Stoppard noted, as of Brecht, that the audience response was not what the playwright would have wanted: 'It's so awful you have to laugh. When I saw it, hardly anyone did – they had come for punishment, as a misguided tribute to Beckett. He would not thank them for it.'

That production ran during the exceptionally cold winter of 1962, a winter which Stoppard would come to associate with the only time he met Beckett. It was at a party at the flat of Jack MacGowran's wife, Aileen

Gloria Nugent, and he would vaguely remember the BBC producer Reggie Smith being there, and possibly Louis MacNeice. Stoppard, the 'country bumpkin', was 'tagging on'. Gloria Nugent said: 'Do you want to meet Sam Beckett?' Overwhelmed, he asked, stumblingly, 'Why, where?' She said, 'He's in the kitchen.' And there was Beckett, with a small group of people, drinking and chatting. Stoppard would remember nothing of what they said; he just remembered being completely in awe. That feeling of being a fan in the presence of a great star, always very strong in him, had to do, he thought, with being an outsider – who finds himself accepted as being inside.

But he was not so venerating as a reviewer. Another new Beckett production, *Happy Days* at the Royal Court, with Brenda Bruce as Winnie, buried in sand, didn't work for him. In *Godot* and *Endgame*, 'something *did* happen, somebody *did* come, somebody *did* go'. There was no good reason why the play should be acted rather than read: 'dramatically it is not enough'.

What was the right line to steer in the theatre between laughter and pain? What was the effective balancing act between comedy, or ideology, on the one hand, and human feeling on the other? He liked quirkiness and oddity – William Saroyan's 'incurably curious', eccentric characters, for instance. He was interested in Muriel Spark's first (and, as it turned out, only) play, *Doctors of Philosophy*, which he reviewed alongside Saroyan and described as 'a thoroughly entertaining failure'. A farcical, surreal satire on academic aspirations, it has a well-read cleaning lady, three male characters all called Charlie (including a lorry driver and a nuclear physicist), and what Stoppard described as 'literate, spiky, concise' dialogue. William Boot interviewed Spark in the same issue as Stoppard's review. The interview quoted her saying: 'It is a question of reality – whether reality is only something you can touch, or whether there is an unreal reality – as I think there is.' The review described the play as 'a world of everyday reality made brittle by the admission of the unreal'. Spark 'chooses to make two characters step outside the play, as a crude example of unreality, and expose the scenery as plain scenery'. He went back to see it again and noted that 'the characters stepping in and out of the play' had been done away with, and that as a result it went better. Some of its ideas lingered in his mind.

But the absurd for its own sake didn't enchant him. Interviewing Spike Milligan's *Goon Show* writing partner John Antrobus, an unamused William Boot observed him falling about laughing at his own surrealist jokes (for *The Bed Sitting-Room*). Pure farce – like Brian Rix and *Pyjama Tops* – only interested him from the point of view of the box-office phenomenon: why did audiences come in their droves? He wanted to work out what audiences warmed to, as in a review of Ibsen's *Peer Gynt* at the Old Vic: 'Gynt, who compromises on every principle and evades responsibility, remains likeable, and that is how it should be.'

Individual performances, like Leo McKern's as Peer Gynt, or Michael Hordern's as a powerful Ulysses in Peter Hall's *Troilus and Cressida*, fascinated him, and he paid attention to actors' personalities and styles. Olivier's bizarre turn as a snobbish suburban Birmingham father in David Turner's *Semi-Detached* was 'a collector's item', his accent 'an indescribable and inconsistent sound achieved by hardly moving the lips'. Paul Scofield's Lear, in Peter Brook's memorable RSC production, was 'a high-moralled, over-principled autocrat', but not as moving as Alec McCowen's Fool. (The Cordelia of Diana Rigg, ten years later starring in *Jumpers*, could have done with a touch more innocence, he thought.) In interviews with William Boot, Susannah York came across as completely 'kooky'; the formidable young Sheila Hancock 'can put on a cool blue look that would freeze a humming-bird to an oven door'.

But he wasn't a theatre critic who just talked about performances. He had a more comprehensive interest in the way the whole thing worked. How could an old-fashioned, anachronistic play like Christopher Fry's *Curtmantle* (about Becket and Henry) still get across? Because of its 'visual and verbal beauty', its 'genuine theatricality'. Why didn't a well-written experiment like Edna O'Brien's first play, *A Cheap Bunch of Nice Flowers*, quite work? Because of structural flaws: 'Two of the six characters are utterly superfluous.' Where was the place in London theatre for the in-between plays, made with 'machined expertness', plays which 'obviously deserve a production and equally obviously are not good enough to occupy a theatre for the months needed to make a commercial profit'? (Answer: the Royal Court and the Arts Theatre, but even there they could feel 'uneasy'.) Why was satire, the most fashionable of genres, not finding its voice in the theatre in the way 'angry' plays had in the 1950s? What was the difference between off-Broadway, concentrated in a few blocks of Manhattan, and the scattered 'off-Shaftesbury' scene of London's alternative theatres, like the Court, or the Questors in Ealing? What could new playwrights hope for from the BBC, 'Aunty', with its Friday-night slots for 'thoughtful' drama, its Sunday-night 'family entertainment', its current reaction against kitchen sinks, and its 9.15 watershed for sex and violence ('with the exception of *Z Cars*')?

He was fascinated by what made for success, amused, for instance, that a play which ran on Broadway for 170 nights would be 'what the accountants call a failure and what the artists call a succès d'estime'. He paid attention to a round table discussion between William Gaskill of the Court, Michael Codron and James Saunders, comparing the commercial success of *Baal*, *The Caretaker* and Saunders's *Next Time I'll Sing to You*. Saunders's play didn't have Beckett's rigorous concentration, where 'everything counts, nothing is arbitrary'. But he admired the play very much. Saunders's characters, Dust and Muff, actors trying to work out the meaning of the play they are in, who 'kill time' waiting for a climax, Rudge the rhetorical writer-producer who starts up word games like cricket matches, all three trying to solve the mystery of the hidden life of Jimmy Mason the hermit, played by an actor who wants to know what kind of person he's supposed to be, made a lasting impression. So did the way Saunders 'left no stone unturned, expecting to find the truth not beneath any one of them but in what the stones look like the wrong way up'.

He was writing about theatre, as he said himself, with a 'realistic' combination of 'the aesthetic and the practical', thinking hard about the conditions and the venues for play-writing. But there was some Brennus-style joking, too. An imitation of a *Which?* consumer survey of value for money in the theatre drew up a comparative grid of the price of coffees, drinks, programmes and seats, and concluded that 'The Old Vic is the Best Evening Out (19 minutes per shilling, with reasonable facilities)'. A spoof attack on the glut of West End thrillers took the form of a dialogue between Slurp the Suave Critic and Rafferty the deceptively sleepy Inspector, who lays the sudden death of Mr Saunders, a thriller-writer, struck down in his library by 'a hide-bound edition of Agatha Christie's works', at the door of the critic: 'Slurp (with an insane, though suave, laugh): "You'll never get me alive!" (He eats his words and falls dead).' The idea for a play about theatre critics and a murder mystery was still in his mind.

Scene was struck down as suddenly and terminally as Mr Saunders in his library. Cook and Luard got Lenny Bruce to the Establishment in 1962, a difficult visit by the self-destructive American comic, who gave a dour performance which, when intelligible, was extremely filthy. They wanted to have him back in 1963, but the Lord Chamberlain intervened. Censorship, timidity and traditions of decorum were still doing battle with the new freedoms of the early 1960s, following on from the *Lady Chatterley* trial of 1960. (Stoppard took this theme up gleefully in *Dirty Linen* in 1976.) The legal costs destroyed the Establishment and *Scene*. Luard's trust fund ran out, his company was declared bankrupt and *Scene* folded overnight. Stoppard sent in a statement on 7 May 1963, calculating that he'd earned £877 5d over twenty-three issues and had been paid £632. He was owed £245, excluding expenses. But it was money he would never see, and he needed every penny he could get. He was nearly twenty-six, in London, with no job, no fame and no certain prospects.

His helpers and advisers were Isabel and Anthony, to whom streams of despairing letters were written at this time, and his agent Kenneth Ewing. When Stoppard climbed the stairs of 91 Regent Street, early in 1962, to Kenneth Ewing's tiny attic office in the Fraser and Dunlop agency, his luck was in. Ewing, ten years his senior, had been theatre-mad – especially Shakespeare-mad – since he was a student at Oxford. When he was, briefly, in the RAF (he loved flying as much as he loved dogs), he went rabbit-shooting with a young flight sergeant called Peter Hall, who became a lifelong friend. He then worked for the BBC's Eastern Europe service, and for a few years in the 1950s managed the Connaught, a well-respected provincial theatre in Woking. He was hired by the agents, and partners,

Jimmy Fraser and Peter Dunlop, in 1959, to initiate a literary list. Fraser and Dunlop (which in 1989 would merge with the distinguished literary agency founded by A. D. Peters and become Peters Fraser and Dunlop) specialised in theatre, TV and film writers. Ewing nurtured major comic writers for TV sitcoms like *George and Mildred*, *Bless This House* and *Man About the House*, but as well as the likes of Johnnie Mortimer and Brian Cooke, Barry Took and Marty Feldman, his literary stable would include Tony Harrison, Charles Wood, Adrian Mitchell, Michael Frayn, John Osborne, Anthony Shaffer and David Storey. (He got on best with men.) He was trusted by his writers, who stayed with him, for his intelligence and his loyalty – and his brilliance at reading and making a contract. Ewing was self-effacing, modest, and funny in a wry, low-key way. In a gossip-laden show-business world, he didn't speak ill of people or pry into their personal lives. He was honourable and generous; and could also be tough. His later colleague and partner Gordon Dickerson thought that he became one of the most stable elements in Stoppard's life. From 1962 until Ewing's death in 2008, he was a fixture, a member of the extended Stoppard family. When Dickerson and Ewing had their civil ceremony, years later, Stoppard was there; when Ewing died, it was Stoppard who spoke at the funeral, at the 'Actors' Church' in Covent Garden.

If Ewing had a fleeting hope that the gorgeous-looking young writer who had turned up at his door might be gay, that immediately vanished, and he rapidly adopted a tone of kind, steady reassurance with his new client, cheering him on ('How little reason you have to be depressed about *A Walk on the Water*') and making sure he was well looked after: 'Don't despair in my absence – Jill [Foster] will be here to hold your hand and Peter [Dunlop] to sign your cheques.'

They would speak on the phone most days, from the start and for as long as they worked together. Ewing was his good angel. Stoppard would ask him for a loan of £20 or so, on the basis of some nebulous and hypothetical contract, and Ewing would always lend him the money. In the summer of 1963, when he was stuck abroad on holiday with no money to get home, he telegrammed Ewing for £30, feeling abjectly embarrassed, and Ewing sent £50 by return. He noted that although Stoppard was broke and anxious in those years, he also had a kind of impressive bravado and stylishness. 'It was as if he knew his time would come.'

On one not-to-be-forgotten occasion, coming out of the office, Stoppard asked Ewing, as often, for a loan, and Ewing gave him what he had to hand. (In some versions of this story it's £40, in others, including Stoppard's, it's a fiver.) The next thing he knew, Stoppard had hailed a taxi to take him where he was going, and Ewing went home on the bus.

Ewing's immediate commitment to Stoppard was a gamble based on a hunch. And the plays they were trying to place were all about gambling: how roles might suddenly be reversed, how fortunes could change on the toss of a coin or the throw of a dice, how a high-wire act could topple or be sustained. At first the gamble didn't seem to be paying off. Stoppard tried *The Gamblers* on the producers of BBC Radio Drama in 1961, but it was rejected, after a long wait. Ewing sold *A Walk on the Water* early in 1962 for £100 (£50 on delivery and £50 on production), to H. M. Tennent, the operation of the powerful, conservative theatre manager Binkie Beaumont, known as the 'Fortnum & Mason of London theatre'. Tennent's sent the play out to a succession of distinguished thespian knights. Alec Guinness kept it for a while, but there was no way of rushing him. Ralph Richardson had expressed an interest, but he didn't think there was enough 'variation' in the main part – and he was 'dead against the musical lavatory' – one of George Riley's more spectacularly impractical inventions. As his play went the rounds, he began to see (he told his mother) that the 'ideal' in theatre was an abstract, and that 'compromise' was 'a necessity'.

He had more luck with his stories, thanks to Anthony Smith, who often came to his rescue in this uncertain time with loans and advice. Smith had been at Cambridge with Frank Pike, since 1959 a junior editor at Faber & Faber. Pike was hired by Charles Monteith, Eliot's successor at the firm, a mighty talent-spotter whose acquisitions for Faber in the 1950s and '60s included Beckett, Osborne, Golding, Hughes and Heaney. Like Ewing, Frank Pike was starting out in his job at the same time as Stoppard – and was looking for work by new writers, for a second anthology of stories called *Introduction*. Anthony Smith recommended Stoppard, who sent in four, and Frank Pike took three of them, the 'fragments' from the Bristol years. This too was the beginning of a long working relationship, and of a faithful bond with one publisher. To be accepted by T. S. Eliot's legendary Queen Square firm, even if only in an anthology, felt astonishing. He revered Eliot as a poet, and there are traces of Eliot all over his early work. He liked to stand outside the Faber building and point out Eliot's window. To belong to Eliot's publishing firm meant the world to him.

Frank Pike, a genial, shrewd editor, sent a few minor criticisms, which were anxiously received: 'I know the one you don't like. No one likes it, except me . . . However, thank you for your encouragement.' When the stories were accepted (Pike had checked with Monteith, who liked them, and became a devoted Stoppard fan), Stoppard replied with relief: 'Your [last] letter worked psychologically against me! . . . I was still struggling, getting more neurotic, when your next letter arrived.' Soon the tone would become more relaxed: 'Typewriter's bust. Have to keep winding carriage by hand. ("Cruel fate struck Stoppard at what turned out to be the zenith of his career, and thenceforth his output dwindled to occasional hand-wound notes".)' Stoppard outgrew the need to mind about Frank Pike's views; Pike would have to mind his. And, in matters of covers, print runs, blurbs and reissues, those views were often forceful. But their working relationship remained cordial and steady. It was a piece of benign teasing, years later, to name the pedantic editor in *Indian Ink* 'Pike'.

If there was no immediate take-up in the theatre, radio and television were just as desirable, and more lucrative, outlets. New writers could find plenty of opportunities there, either in BBC slots or in commercial TV. Two of his stories would be turned into TV and radio plays. Ewing's first success was to sell *Walk* to Associated Rediffusion TV. Michael Hordern, whose craggy, shambling, brow-furrowed eloquence made him a perfect Stoppard actor, was cast as George Riley, a part which he would reprise for the stage in 1968. A much-cut, unsatisfactory version of *Walk* was recorded on 15 November 1963 (Stoppard took an unnamed, transient blonde girlfriend, and Peter O'Toole, to the recording). But it was overtaken by world events. On 22 November 1963, John F. Kennedy was assassinated. Stoppard made no comment, other than to tell Anthony Smith that AR-TV had decided not to air their scheduled play, John Whiting's

Marching Song, on 25 November, because of its military content, but to put *A Walk on the Water* on instead, ahead of schedule, with no advance publicity. This rushed, botched job was the first professional production of a Stoppard play. Coincidentally, that was also the day on which Denys Lasdun was accepted by Laurence Olivier and Peter Brook as the architect for the new National Theatre. Two markers were set down that day for the next era of British theatre.

Stoppard came to be embarrassed by *A Walk on the Water*, as by most of his early work. He would call it his 'Flowering Death of a Salesman', a 'phoney' play 'squeezed out of' other people's plays. Robert Bolt's *Flowering Cherry*, a conventional drama of a suburban insurance salesman retreating into a fantasy life, Miller's *Death of a Salesman*, the farcical inventions of N. F. Simpson's *One Way Pendulum*, even the bar-room fantasies of the no-hopers in O'Neill's *The Iceman Cometh*, were all in the mix.

George Riley's professional inadequacy as a failed inventor who can only dream up surreally impractical concepts (like a pipe that will stay lit if it's smoked upside down), and his domestic bad faith, always threatening to strike out from home but in fact entirely dependent on his long-suffering wife and resentful daughter, are wildly at odds with the euphoric, boastful rhetoric ('Enter a free man!') with which he bolsters himself up. Half the time he's a ridiculous joke, a grotesque pastiche of a chauvinistic Englishman:

> Riley (*with scorn*): Dreams! The illusion of something for nothing.
>   No wonder the country is going to the dogs. Personal enterprise
>   sacrificed to bureaucracy. No pride, no patriotism. The erosion of
>   standards, the spread of mediocrity, the decline of craftsmanship
>   and the betrayal of the small inventor.
> Harry: It's terrible really. I blame youth.

But Riley's longing for excitement and for the unexpected, his belief in 'personal enterprise', his 'tattered dignity', have a kind of pathos too, especially in his long speech describing the lowering effects of ordinary life, when domestic chores are going on all around him, he is sitting at

while he wrote letters to Isabel and read Turgenev's *Sportsman's Sketches*. Ewing provided his fare home.

Bobby Stoppard became very anxious when she didn't hear from him on his long summer trips abroad in the early 1960s. She was always convinced that 'some dreadful fate had befallen him'. This irritated Ken, who found his arty stepson increasingly unsympathetic. Stoppard wrote, equally irritably, to Isabel, saying that he'd heard – perhaps from Peter, now working as a chartered accountant in Bristol – that 'my father was being very rude about me behind my back, & scornful of my life as "a writer". So as far as I'm concerned papa is dead till he's dead.' He struck a rare note of crossness in his letters home (in the summer of 1962), saying he was depressed and annoyed by her worrying: 'After all, I did have my 25th birthday abroad, not my 15th.' And then, relenting at once: 'I hope you're not still angry with me.'

He had one unconditional admirer in the household, and that was Fiona, who would anticipate her half-brother's visits with adoring excitement. As a small girl she would sit outside his bedroom door, waiting for him to wake up, while Bobby told her that Tommy should have his sleep-in. All the presents he brought her were cherished. Tender-hearted though she was – going fishing was always for her, as he put it, a 'conflict of loyalties between man and fish' – she still loved to go out on the river with him. Fiona was emotional and impulsive, as a teenager often at loggerheads with her father and upsetting her mother, and she left home very young. But she listened to her brother's advice. He was her hero.

Devotion and admiration were in short supply elsewhere. His letters and poems to Isabel became increasingly yearning. He invented pet names for them, Owl and Cat, Mush and Shmo, with little drawings. Before their holiday he sent her a poem, 'Night Thoughts', an effusion of unreciprocated courtly love, a cross between cummings and Provençal troubadour style:

> . . . When you walk the wind-stirred trees
> bear no other scent, no vines dare dance
> for me, and the sun's stare cannot warm nor please

as you warm and please me with a glance,

and when your lips
part I'm deaf to nightingales.
Invisible clouds eclipse
the stars for you, the moon pales.

O Lady, that summer has begun
to dim before your beauty.

The letters are just as touching and unguarded. After she's gone home, he writes from Dubrovnik that he feels 'very incomplete after being with you for 2 months'. Back home he is 'low' because 'I shan't see you for so long, when I should be seeing you every day for ever, or something.' It is she who encourages him, and it is their future together he is working for: 'my Isabel, who makes me want to write when I am too tired, dulled, lazy or weak to write anything for anyone else. Not that this will make us rich.' He regrets these outpourings, as he tells her in a revealing sentence about his dislike of self-revelation: 'All my inclinations – artistic, personal, ethic and moral – prefer reticence to over-explicitness. Over-explicitness embarrasses me, when I see it in a play, or in every single "serious" conversation someone traps me into.' But he continues to 'come clean with her', because he loves her, though he would write to her like this less often 'if I remembered more often that you don't love me'. Increasingly, he does remember it, and begins to accept that they won't, ever, have a future together. 'I don't know what I think about anything now, I just miss you badly & half think it's all hopeless.'

Meanwhile, Alison was pregnant and she and Anthony were getting married. He was going to be best man, which involved an overnight train to Bristol after the recording of *Walk*: 'My most respectable suit is that brown one, which necessitates brown boots. (If a worry), I'll appear in my second-best-man's grey suiting with Manfield winklepickers, black. (Please strike out all reference to footwear and file under *The Artist as Anarchist – The Stoppard Letters (1959–73)*).' He envied them their nesting, and often wanted to be back with them. 'What I want is an evening with you and alison in the womb, lots of fags, ingroup jokes, plans and optimism.' 'I do need a touch of the Smiths at regular intervals,' he told his mother. Part of him wanted to settle too, to make his own nest. And there was Jose, living in the same house. He did not fall in love with her. But he was attracted by her, and he liked the idea of being with someone who was in love with him: it made a change.

By the end of 1963 they were together, and he took her to Scotland to meet his family. Eight-year-old Fiona liked her at once; Bobby perhaps was anxious. Unusually, no letters to her survive from these months. And immediately there was a problem, though a problem in the shape of a great stroke of good luck. Charles Marowitz, the American theatre critic and director, a force in the alternative London drama world, whom Stoppard had praised in *Scene*, and who would go on to found Open Space and to work with Peter Brook, was asked by the Ford Foundation to recommend promising young writers for an international colloquium they funded in Berlin, with a mixture of young German writers and 'Anglo-Saxon' visitors. Their patronage was part of a post-war effort to reinstate West Berlin as a European cultural centre, working with the German writers' 'Gruppe 47', a literary network set up after the war. An invitation arrived in March 1964 asking him to come from May to September. There would be about eighteen people, including, in the Anglo-Saxon contingent, himself, Derek Marlowe, Piers Paul Read, and James Saunders – whose plays he greatly admired – and who was meant to mentor their work. All expenses were paid, they would have a scholarship of eight hundred Deutschmarks a month, plus travel, and there might be the opportunity to stage a play. Do not 'go off the deep end worrying about how I get there, what I live on, and also being kidnapped by the Russian police (MO-THER!)', he teased Bobby. He was not a worrier about things that might not happen. During the Cuban crisis, while people he knew were clasping their foreheads or weeping or sitting in Grosvenor Square, he could not rouse himself to participation or involvement, but felt completely fatalistic, assuming it would all get straightened out. He lived in a world of his own, he told his mother.

Berlin was an irresistible offer, but it upset Jose. She was distressed, frequently unwell, and 'irreconcilable to the German question'. They had to pack up Blenheim Terrace, and Jose was left behind in limbo, only a few months after they had got together, while he took his lucky chance. He had plenty of ideas. *Walk* needed to be rewritten as a two-act stage play. Kenneth Ewing knew the publisher Anthony Blond, who said that he would publish a novel if Stoppard would write one. He would get started on it at once: surely it must be possible to write a novel as quickly as a play? Perhaps it would be called *Jose*.

And Kenneth had had another idea, which came up in the car on the way back from an unsuccessful attempt to pitch a TV play to the BBC. They were talking about O'Toole's *Hamlet*, and Ewing said that he had often imagined a play about Rosencrantz and Guildenstern arriving in England. What if the mad King Lear had been on the throne at the time, and came to meet them! It was certainly a thought. When he took Jose to Scotland to meet the family, Stoppard also took some books about *Hamlet*, including the Shakespeare scholar J. Dover Wilson's *What Happens in Hamlet?* He thought 'Rosencrantz and Guildenstern at the Court of King Lear' might work as a title.

Berlin in the summer of 1964 was his first trip abroad as a writer, and it was a dream of luxury. This beat sleeping on the floor of an apartment in New York and hanging round the *Village Voice*. They were housed in a comfortable villa on the shore of Lake Wannsee, a quick train ride from the city centre. He wrote home excitedly: 'I have fallen on my aristocratic feet . . . you may worry about me a little but you'll soon realise I'm better off here with someone to clean up after me, feed me 4 times a day . . . and let me sit in the sun in the garden reading.' He was told he could rearrange his room as he chose, because the organisers knew that writers needed a sympathetic atmosphere. He didn't like to tell them he was 'a middle-class boy' who was quite happy with the atmosphere; he thought perhaps he should hang his carpet on the wall in case they thought he was a fake. They were left to do what they liked, the hope being that they would write something.

The German writers from Gruppe 47 were very avant-garde, and didn't have much contact with the 'Anglo-Saxons'. The Americans were the novelist and playwright Thomas Cullinan, and Peter Bergman, a counterculture radio host from LA, writing surreal radio comedies. George Moorse was making a short experimental movie, *In Side Out*, in which Stoppard played a cowboy in full kit, striding towards the Brandenburg Gate, his only known appearance in the movies, and one which confirmed his distrust of avant-gardism for its own sake. For the more serious business of writing plays, James Saunders was an intense and affable mentor, 'but with a tendency to treat each play as if he himself were writing it'. Saunders's work had a lasting influence on him.

His friend Derek Marlowe was writing a play about a scarecrow. The third of the British contingent, Piers Paul Read, a fastidious, observant young novelist, was the son of the poet and art critic Herbert Read. He had already been in Berlin for a year on another grant, and was writing his first novel, *Game in Heaven with Tussy Marx*. Stoppard was impressed by Read's adeptness at getting writers' handouts; he stuck a whiskey ad on Read's door which read: 'As Long As You're Up, Get Me a Grant'. Read thought Marlowe a bit of a poseur, a Beau Brummell type with flowery manners. Both Read and Stoppard were shocked to hear (via a letter from Jose to Tom) that while they were in Berlin, Marlowe's abandoned girlfriend had a baby. Read thought Stoppard charming and funny, and noted he spent a great deal of time playing Beatles records in his room while trying to write, and that his preferred drink was Cinzano and lemon. He noted, also, that Stoppard turned down the chance of a trip from Berlin to Prague for fear that he might be conscripted into the Czech army. Stoppard had taken advice from the British Council, who warned him there might be a faint risk of having to do three years' national service.

They got on very well. All three were alert to the atmosphere of Berlin. The Wall had only recently been built; people trying to get across from East Berlin were frequently shot at or killed. They saw Russian soldiers, young kids, in West Berlin, and went through all the red tape of going through Checkpoint Charlie when they visited East Berlin. They were aware of the military police, of 'people being spied on'. They had to carry proof of identity. Le Carré's *The Spy Who Came In from the Cold* had come out the year before.

As usual Stoppard was doing several things at once, in between bursts of writer's block. He finished with *Samuel Boot*, started, without results, to think about his novel, and turned *Walk on the Water* into a two-act play. The German theatre publishing and production company, Rowohlt Theater-Verlag, was on the lookout for any promising new talent, and set up a month's run for Stoppard's play – to be called, in German, *Old Riley Walked the Water* – starting in July at the Thalia Theatre in Hamburg. It was a very large space to fill with an untried play in translation. Stoppard went to rehearsals and was embarrassed, he told Anthony Smith, 'by their enthusiasm, by the size of the theatre, by the earnest discussion of psychological motivation'. He hid behind 'a frozen smile' the thought: 'You fools, the emperor is starkers.'

His fears were not groundless. The Hamburg audience, used to exciting British imports like the Beatles, was expecting a combination of Beckett, Pinter, a long-haired Beatle-lookalike and an Angry Young Man. In the event, they watched a play about an ageing self-deceiving dreamer in a domestic, suburban setting. Half the audience, relieved to have seen something they understood, cheered and clapped. The other, younger half booed loudly, 'in a storm of gleeful abuse'. Stoppard was dragged on stage to receive this mixed accolade, and stood there in a daze, for all the world like Henry James on the first night of his play *The American*. 'The thought flashed across my mind that they thought I was Jewish . . .' At the time, 'bowing inanely into a thousand seats of boos and bravos', it just seemed weird and hilarious, but then he felt depressed, and 'furious that I'd let WOTW represent me as a writer first time out'. He knew this was a false start, not an inglorious ending. *Walk* was done again in Vienna in 1966 as *The Spleen of George Riley*. It got a new title and much reworking before it played in London in 1968 as *Enter a Free Man*. By that time he felt very distant from it.

But he had the other idea to work on. *Rosencrantz and Guildenstern at the Court of King Lear* took shape as a one-act play in which, he told Anthony Smith, the characters were 'Fortinbras, Captain, Rosencrantz,

Guildenstern, Player, King Lear and Horatio, not forgetting Hamlet,' and most of the action took place on the ship going to England. Stoppard came to refer to this as a 'one-act verse burlesque'. But the verse in it is all Shakespeare's, interleaved with two kinds of prose. There were large dollops of Shakespearean pastiche, mainly spoken by Hamlet and Lear ('I see lunatics about me, every one as mad as the other'). And there were cryptic, witty, philosophical one-liners or rapid dialogue ('Who are you? where have you come from?', etc.), spoken by 'Ros' and 'Guil' and the Player, who, fleeing from Elsinore after his performance in the court play, wears a mask to look like Hamlet: 'I am a ham player, friend.' Ros and Guil banter with the Player, asking him to make the time pass with something more exciting than just 'incidents'. The Player swaps places with Hamlet, Ros and Guil land in England, meet the mad King Lear, who is not at all funny, and are put to death. The Player goes back to Elsinore to take part in the final act of *Hamlet*, and the real Hamlet gets back in time to see 'the final tableau of carnage', but too late to do anything. 'He is a man stuck in space,' Stoppard commented, adding: 'It is a bit screwy, but fun.' Hamlet leaves the play asking: 'What of me now? There is no end for a man caught out of the action.' Now he must perpetually 'walk the earth', a ghostly wanderer like his father. The play ends with his final speech, much in debt to T. S. Eliot:

I have time.
The sun is going down.
It will be night soon.
Do you think so?
I was just making conversation.
I have a lot of time.

In the later version of the play, 'I was just making conversation' is Rosencrantz's line. This early travesty of *Hamlet*, like the *Rosencrantz and Guildenstern* which grew out of it, is about swapped and uncertain identities, role-playing, wordplay, questions of choice and fate, and – as in *Waiting for Godot* – how to pass one's mortal time. But in this version,

Hamlet is at the centre, wearily estranged from his own play, a superfluous man left with no purpose on this earth. The emphasis is more on him and less on Ros and Guil, though they do get some of the badinage of the later version.

Ewing read it and wrote, shrewdly, that he 'very much liked the characters of R and G and their cross-talk, but [was] not so happy about the fact that in the end this becomes a play about Hamlet'. He noted a 'danger that the play drops to a parody of Shakespearian style'. Stoppard knew there was more work to be done, but he was 'fond of the play'. Now called *Guildenstern and Rosencrantz*, it had an outing in a small studio theatre in Berlin on the Kurfürstendamm, for a couple of nights in September. This was the work of the amateur Questors Theatre, a community enterprise in Ealing run by Alfred Emmet, who had an eye for new writers. James Saunders's *Next Time I'll Sing to You* was first staged there. They had recommended Saunders to the Colloquium, and he in turn invited some of their actors to come to Berlin and stage five short plays by members of the Colloquium. They then took the plays to their theatre in Ealing. Stoppard directed his own play, as unusual an enterprise for him as appearing in a film. Unfortunately the Rosencrantz was 'a total amnesiac when it comes to lines, and all is panic'. He asserted his authority: 'You should see me doing my Guthrie, striding about chain-smoking . . .' As soon as he got back to England, he started to rewrite it as a full-length play.

8

Rosencrantz and Guildenstern Are Dead

G: Who are you? where have you come from? where are you going? what
   are you going to do, how are you going to do it? and when?
Player: Why?
G: And why?

His return to England at the end of 1964 was a fraught moment. He needed to 'write like a madman', he told Anthony Smith, and he wanted to live 'by himself'. Perhaps he should go back to Bristol. He didn't see how he could afford to live in London, far less 'support a fellow human'. But Jose was offering to find them a flat in London. He thought the situation 'somehow has developed much more in her head than in mine'. All the same, they found a place in Pimlico, at 11 Vincent Square Mansions in Walcott Street, in the quiet streets of red-brick mansion flats between Vincent Square and the thundering traffic of the Vauxhall Bridge Road, near the river. It was a first-floor flat with the rooms opening out from a long corridor. Piers Paul Read had two tiny rooms, Derek Marlowe had another, and Stoppard and Jose were sharing a big room. Letters home, however, with details about his rent for the flat (£2 9s 0d a week including rates), his quest for second-hand furniture and Derek's cooking ('liver, potatoes and sprouts'), didn't mention her. But one of the letters describing life at Vincent Square Mansions said suddenly: 'I can't work unless I'm on my own' – something he would often say again. Read had the strong impression that he had wanted to drop Jose, and would have preferred to be on his own: 'and she said no'.

Derek Marlowe, when he wasn't out and about with beautiful women and rock bands, including the future members of The Who, was writing a theatrical adaptation of Gorky's *The Lower Depths*, and finishing his spy novel, *A Dandy in Aspic*. Spies were everywhere in the mid-sixties. *Dandy* was about a double agent who ended up having to assassinate himself, which Stoppard thought a dazzling idea, and Marlowe wrote it to the soundtrack of the year, the Righteous Brothers' 'You've Lost That Lovin' Feelin''.

These three good-looking, ambitious, highly talented young men, trying to make their way by their writing in the mid-sixties with very little to live on, all spent a lot of time thinking about money, success and fame. Marlowe remembered the three of them in the flat, in 1965, watching *Top of the Pops* (which had started up the year before). Mick Jagger, Stoppard's rock hero, was singing 'Satisfaction'. The three of them sat around talking about how the Stones were going to be millionaires. Which of *them* would make their first million dollars? 'They all thought Tom would be it, the first person, not a question of top dog, but big money, ie more than half-a-crown.'

Marlowe, as it turned out, got there first, but burned out later. He and Read would look on at Stoppard's career, increasingly from a distance but always with attention and admiration. They never lost that sense of having started out together, or that combative young-man rivalry. Stoppard sent Read careful, critical letters about some of his novels. Marlowe exchanged occasionally rueful remarks with Read about Stoppard's successes, as when reading *Jumpers*: 'I just wanted to see if it read as pretentiously as it played. It does.' When Kenneth Tynan wrote about Stoppard in 1977 for the *New Yorker*, he interviewed Marlowe, and cited him on the lack of emotion in Stoppard's plays and his inability to understand women. Marlowe told Read, mortified, that he had been badly misquoted. Tom, however, had been forgiving: 'Tom in his wisdom was Tom.' Marlowe died too young, in 1996, after a wildly volatile career and personal life. His son wrote to Piers Paul Read: 'Sadly he will never fulfil his ambitions . . . He was immensely proud of how much all three of you had achieved since the days, back in 1964, of flat sharing in Pimlico.'

Jose was the odd one out. Read was preoccupied with a tumultuous love affair and his Berlin novel, but was aware of considerable turmoil going on at Vincent Square. Jose made scenes, and more than once threatened to kill herself. In one diary entry of the time, Read coolly noted: 'Friction in the flat. Derek and Jose attack me, saying I am "cold". Jose angry that I have no time for her private life, threats of suicide, etc.'

Isabel, meanwhile, sat down to write a letter, probably at the end of 1964, and probably never sent. She said that she had become aware that she did care for him much more than she had ever realised. They had so much in common, they *talked* and got on so well, that it would be pointless – as he'd often said to her – not to go on and on. She had always loved him in her fashion, but it had taken her ages to commit. Yes, she knew there was Jose: but he didn't really love her, did he? Though she could be wrong.

These thoughts had come too late. He let himself go along with Jose's anxious need for reassurance and commitment. Towards the end of 1964, she proposed, and he agreed. (Isabel also got married, to her Yugoslavian boyfriend, late in 1967, and he went to her wedding.) They were going to get married in Scotland, where his parents were then living, and where Jose's sister was organising everything 'like Montgomery'. The wedding between 'T. Stoppard, Writer, Bachelor; Parents: Kenneth Frederick Stoppard, Sales Manager, Martha Eugenia Stoppard, previously M. S. Beck', and 'Jose Ingle, Information Officer, Spinster', took place in St Ninian's Episcopal Church, Troon, in Ayrshire, on 26 March 1965. He was twenty-eight and she was three years younger. His brother Peter was the witness. Settled as a chartered accountant in Long Ashton, in Bristol, in the house their parents used to live in, he had beaten his brother to it by a few years, and married Lesley Wilkes in 1961, with Tom as their best man. That happy marriage would last long years, until her death in 2016.

An undated page of typescript sent to Isabel imagined a wedding day from the bride's point of view, like a drowning man's life 'spinning' before his eyes.

Only I wasn't drowning. I was walking down an aisle to be married and, faint heart, was weary of it all . . . I knew I was panicking . . . This great step into the vast black unknown was more than a gamble. It was a mystery. Whatever happened after we spoke those solemn vows, meant to be taken seriously, spoken at the time with quiet determination by the parties concerned and forgotten generally within the year like a second rate film, I knew nothing about . . . Any other girl, I told myself severely . . . would be thrilled. The happiest day of her life, she's nailed him to the tree. Now he's here, all here, for at least the next year or two. Then, sex weary of her, he'll gladly cast an eye askance . . .

The female narrator imagines the prospect of divorce, supposes that the bridegroom will be too hung over from the last night's party to remember anything about the wedding, and expects that this day will be looked back on as an excuse 'to nag. And blame. Condemn and shame.'

'What with the marriage business and all', he wrote ruefully to his parents, writing had been interrupted. He needed to get on. The Stoppards went on living in Vincent Square for another year or so. But he also had a room in Soho which he was using as a writing space, by courtesy of an intriguing Scotsman, Gordon Williams, a colleague at *Scene,* who, in between ghost-writing footballers' memoirs, wanted to write an anarchic *Goon Show*-style radio serial. A fragment of their collaboration survives as *Doctor Masopust, I Presume,* in which a crazed surgeon orders an imaginary orchestra about, in a first glimpse of *Every Good Boy Deserves Favour* ('How can my enemies hope to destroy a man who has his own orchestra?') and spouts patriotic speeches, a bit like George Riley – and Ken Stoppard: 'Men of England . . . the bulldog breed, yeomen sons of this green and pleasant land, this other Eden set in a silver sea . . . I have come here to warn England against the menace of the new Europe – and if necessary to assume total power to protect the Great British from the clutching hands across the Channel.' (Britain had been trying to join the European Economic Community since 1961.) The partnership, in emulation of Dick Clement and Ian La Frenais, authors of the hit TV series *The Likely Lads,* came to nothing, but Williams went on to write a novel which was adapted by Sam Peckinpah as *Straw Dogs.* He also wrote what Stoppard considered to be the most telling book about journalism apart from *Scoop, The Upper Pleasure Garden.*

Another false start, also to do with patriotic rhetoric and the end of empire – against the background of the 1960s rush to independence of former British colonies – was a radio play meant for a series on the seven deadly sins. Stoppard chose Gluttony, and drew heavily on Waugh's *Black Mischief*. His play was set on the imaginary island of Baku, in the Arabian Sea. It has a missionary, William Moon, 'a sweet old man with the best intentions, without a clue about what is going on', a supporter of the passing empire, Sir Evelyn Travers, a gluttonous British Governor, Sir Dudley, and a beaming African postmaster-general who turns out to be masterminding the revolution. The Brits have their heads in the sand ('your average Baku islander is loyal and grateful, perfectly content with his lot, spends his time sitting around, harvesting the coconuts and so forth, singing hymns, dancing the bossa nova, playing baseball') and end up, mostly, being cooked and eaten. The episode was not aired.

A more rewarding piece of colonial writing was 'A Student's Diary'. This was an (unlikely) commission from the BBC World Service to contribute episodes in a drama series for its Arabic Service, to be written in English and translated into Arabic. It was a godsend: twenty-seven guineas for each fifteen-minute script, with 135 guineas on signature. The drama ran from April 1966 until February 1969; Stoppard wrote nearly seventy episodes during 1966 and 1967, alternating with another writer. The series told the story of Amin Osman, a Muslim from Jordan who comes to England to study at a large medical school in London. Stoppard referred to it as 'Ali in Wonderland', a joke which, like the series' treatment of immigration and cross-cultural misunderstandings, was very much of its time.

Amin, the naive traveller from another world learning the customs of the country, encounters false and true mentors. The first Englishman he meets on the ferry, an affable Brummie who warns him not to call it the French Channel, turns out to be a cocaine smuggler. Such cautionary tales abound. A girl Amin likes goes off with his best friend; a fellow student (called 'Farlowe') is killed in a car crash after having one drink too many. Everyone he meets teaches him something about England: that the English would 'form an orderly queue to get into *heaven*', that there is a north–south divide, what Guy Fawkes Night is about.

There were a lot of episodes to fill, and Stoppard mined his old Brennus columns ruthlessly – a hospital student rag, for instance, is lifted straight from Bristol. He didn't think anyone he knew would ever hear it. Amin's Jordanian background was left pretty vague – as far as Kenneth Ewing knew, 'he had never met an Arab in his life'. Bits of himself got into the story. He mugged up on medical textbooks (one episode is all about blood vessels), perhaps thinking of Dr Sträussler. In an exchange about wasting time, Amin says: 'I tend to put off my work until the last moment, but at the same time I don't seem to *do* very much with the time I leave empty. It stays empty.' A conservative countryman inveighs against 'the forces of radical protest', grimly foreseeing 'a liberal utopia in which traditions have given way to a uniformity that gives no offence but little joy'. Amin's irrepressible optimism has an autobiographical tinge: 'Who knows where fate will lead me now? The prospects are unlimited!'

His own prospects seemed unlimited but uncertain. A student production of *The Gamblers* was put on in Bristol by Anthony Smith in May 1965, which Stoppard went to with Jose, but he would have preferred that play to be forgotten about. The screenwriter Ted Willis rewrote *A Paragraph for Mr Blake* without telling him, so that when he took Jose to the recording for Associated Television at Elstree, he found it was full of 'corny scenes' he hadn't written.

Still, he was doing other things for radio and TV, though thinking of them only as 'stepping stones towards getting a play on the boards': 'I wanted to be in the theatre.' The radio proposals came from the BBC script editor Richard Imison, a generous supporter of new writers, who had liked the 'Just Before Midnight' plays. He pounced on Stoppard, 'Tigger-like', in the corridor of the BBC one day, with an idea for some plays about people in imaginary jobs or peculiar occupations. Stoppard immediately thought of the Speaking Clock. Since the 1930s the British public could dial up 'TIM', and hear a polite, clipped woman's voice, sounding rather like the young Queen, telling them what the exact time would be 'at the third stroke'. He came up with the brilliant 'wheeze' that this woman could be slowly cracking up, her interior monologue, 'something half-way between prose and verse', counterpointing her public time-telling voice. He thickened the plot by having her devoted husband, a bus driver, thinking she is being held hostage by the Post Office

('I want my Gladys!') and by scenes in which the desperate bus driver is put off the scent by the bureaucratic figures who control the 'dial-up' services, an essential part of the fabric of British life: 'We must keep a continuous check on all of them, because if you don't keep an eye on them they slide back.'

The joy of *If You're Glad I'll Be Frank*, which he always called *Glad/Frank*, is the internal voice of Gladys the Speaking Clock (who once wanted to be a nun) brooding on the silence of infinity and how it can't be confined by ticks and tocks, by 'routine-checking, schedule-setting time-keeping clockwork'. The voice of the clock is on the right of the page:

And they count for nothing
measured against
the moment in which a glacier
forms and melts . . .

At the third stroke it will be   At the third stroke it will be
too late to catch up, far
far too late, gentlemen . . .

Silence is the sound of time passing.
Don't ask when the pendulum
began to swing.
Because there is no pendulum.

Gladys starts by sounding like Prufrock, and ends up like Molly Bloom: 'and at the third stroke I will/yes I will yes at the third stroke I will . . .' Asked a few years later if the play represented a tragic sense of mortality, Stoppard replied warningly: 'The play is not the result of an apparent obsession with time. The obsession is the result of the play.'

Mortality haunts another radio play of this time, originally based on the idea of 'odd jobs', but which broke free from the series and grew into a longer life of its own, first on the radio, then on the stage. He started to write *Albert's Bridge*, alongside *Glad/Frank*, in the summer of 1965 (for a

£50 advance), but got stuck with it, rewrote it endlessly, with much encouragement and cajoling from Imison, and delivered it to the BBC a year later than promised. It was first aired, post-*Rosencrantz*, at 9.30 p.m. on 13 July 1967, directed by Charles Lefeaux (a change for him from *Dick Barton, Special Agent*) on the highbrow channel Network Three, a branch of the Third Programme. The *Radio Times* coverage said that 'Stoppard can be claimed as a radio discovery'. The play won two international awards in 1968, a Czech International Radio Plays prize and the Prix Italia, in the same year as Ken Loach's *Cathy Come Home*.

Like Gladys's modernist interior speech set against the pips of real time, *Albert's Bridge* counterpoints Albert's self-absorbed stream of consciousness with the real world below, as he paints his way along the 'Clufton Bridge', first as part of a team, then on his own – a wonderfully satisfying, solitary, unfinishable job: 'I'm the bridge man/web-spinning silvering spiderman . . .' The busy, worried town councillors of Clufton (straight out of Brennus's Bristol), Albert's demanding mother and domineering father, Kate the working-class girl he gets pregnant, marries and then ignores, all dwindle and grow tiny in his imagination when he's up on the bridge. He doesn't want to be 'content in his obscurity', any more than George Riley does: he wants to be 'sublime'.

Albert's moony, dreamy, artistic monomania is not the only aberrant point of view in the play. There's a member of the council driven mad by his own ever-elaborating statistics, and there's a would-be 'jumper' intent on suicide who can never make up his mind to jump: somehow the crazy world looks more orderly and manageable when he's up on the bridge. 'Come come, don't procrastinate!' says Albert, who just wants the bridge to himself. Compared with these other lunatics, Albert seems quite sane and endearing.

As often, Stoppard makes raids on the real world to bolster a strange, topsy-turvy invention. He does this with the moon landings in *Jumpers*, or the state funeral of Winston Churchill in his novel, or the death of Monroe in *'M' is for Moon*. The Forth Road Suspension Bridge had been opened in 1964, and it was being said that by the time they finished painting it, they'd have to start painting it again. Albert wants to see it on his holiday. (Second choice, the Eiffel Tower.) Clifton Bridge, of course, was also an inspiration. He used bits from favourite films – Harry Lime's deadly, scornful view of the world from the top of the Ferris wheel in *The Third Man*, or the men in *The Bridge on the River Kwai*, whistling 'Colonel Bogey' as they march. That's like the army sent to paint the bridge, catastrophically, at the end of the play, which involves a terrific final sound effect. There may be a glimpse of his own life, too, in Kate's lamenting at her neglect and Albert's bafflement: 'I did want her to be happy, too.'

Albert is a lapsed philosophy student, and has an already recognisably Stoppardian riff about what it would be like to be a philosopher's clerk: 'It'll be a matter of filing the generalisations, tidying up paradoxes, laying out the premises before the boss gets in . . .' His philosophy of life takes the long perspective. Only from afar can he have a sense of completion, but that entails complete narcissism and a chilling distance from other individuals: 'Is it a fact that all the dots have names?' The popular songs he croons to himself up on the bridge are love songs to himself: 'I've got me under my skin . . . I get a kick out of me . . .' Ah, says the jumper, 'the egotist school of song writing'. But there is another way to live one's life, involved with others, buried in detail and reality. Kate, in a telling line, says to him: 'Well, life is all close up, isn't it?'

Albert's lyric soliloquies dominate the radio performance, with a magnetic performance by John Hurt. But the play also makes an aural pattern out of the ordinary words of everyday work, so that cliché and banality get turned into a memorable comic tune.

Dad: Watch your feet, Albert. Mind your head, Charlie.
Charlie: You mind my head. Take care my feet, Bob—
Bob: Watch your feet, Charlie—
Charlie: Mind your feet, Dad—
Dad: That's my head, Albert—
Albert: Coming down . . .

It suited him to be given the germ of an idea – the seven deadly sins, eccentric occupations, minor characters in *Hamlet* – and then jump off with it and turn it into something surprising and original. He often said that he loved to be given something ready-made to start with, and that eighty per cent of his time as a writer was spent looking for something to write *about*. Two ideas proposed to him around this time were the germs for television plays. Like *Albert*, they both played with the idea of a man who tries to keep himself separate from the world. *A Separate Peace* was meant to be a matching half for a documentary about chess players, and part of a series on 'the pursuit of happiness'. But it ended up – as a 1966 BBC Thirty Minute play – not having anything to do with chess, and everything to do with a desire for a quiet life. A wealthy Mr Brown, who is perfectly well, checks into a nursing home because he wants to live there always. Like Albert, he spends his time happily painting, in this case a mural for his room. But the staff can't cope with a mystery patient who isn't ill, and a sympathetic nurse is set up to wheedle his secrets out of him – which are that he'd been at the nursing home as a child, and later been a prisoner of war, and wants to return, as a lot of Stoppard's characters do, to that childish sensation of helplessness, safety and passivity.

There's another two-faced informer in *Neutral Ground*. This was commissioned by Granada TV late in 1965 for a series reworking classical myths, but the series collapsed and the one-hour television play was not broadcast until 1968. *Neutral Ground*, a reworking of Sophocles's *Philoctetes*, was a Cold War spy story with Marlowe's *Dandy in Aspic*, John Le Carré and Greek tragedy in mind. He'd also been reading Edmund Wilson's book on the relation of art and psychic pain, *The Wound and the Bow* (the play's working title), and Norman Mailer's *Barbary Shore*. He wanted to do 'Shavian dialogue', pitting differing moral and ideological positions against each other.

In the original, Philoctetes, voyaging to Troy with the other Greeks, and owner of an invincible bow, is abandoned on a remote island, because of his disgusting suppurating wound, which no one can bear to live with. But the Greeks can't win the war, they need the bow, and they come back to get him, with a trick of wily Ulysses's, who uses an idealistic young warrior to pretend that he too has turned against the Greeks and to persuade Philoctetes to go with him. The young man succeeds, but at a cost to his own integrity. A version by Euripides thickens the plot by having the Trojans also in pursuit of the bow. Euripides, though, was deeply buried by the time Granada got to work on the play, rather to his regret.

Neutral Ground was Stoppard's first spy story, pointing ahead to *The Dog It Was That Died* and *Hapgood*. It was also his first foray into classical sources, and into writing about Eastern Europe. It's set in a no-man's-land village in Yugoslavia, where 'Philo' is rotting away. He is a double agent from a Soviet-dominated Eastern European country, whom the British have cast aside. His wound is his alcoholism. Bitter and hopeless, all he wants is to go home to die. The Odysseus figure, Otis the cunning American Cold War pragmatist, sends a young English agent, Acherson, to trick Philo into returning. The Russians are also after Philo, in the shape of two assassins called 'Laurel and Hardy', who are 'killers but fairly relaxed about it'.

But this isn't a comedy. Acherson's conflict between the individual good and the good of the country, between a useful end and foul means, is painful. He has to acknowledge Otis's ruthless belief that there are 'no neutral corners in this world', but he hates what he has to do. There's also a touching small boy, like the boy in *Godot*, who tries to look out for Philo, the first of many vulnerable small boys in Stoppard's work. At the dark heart of the play is Philo's bitterness about what the Russians did to his unnamed country – 'they have saved us out of existence' – and his memory of the small town he grew up in, before 'all the things that changed when the Russians came'.

In between writing radio and television plays and working on the new version of *Rosencrantz*, Stoppard rushed at his novel. The sparking-point was the state funeral of Winston Churchill on 30 January 1965, a huge national event. The novel – whose working title was 'The Funeral of the Year' – was delivered in August 1965, leaving him feeling very 'post-natal'. His publisher, Ewing's friend Anthony Blond – flamboyant, maverick, Jewish, independent-minded – was baffled by *Lord Malquist & Mr Moon*, and didn't think 'there was going to be a reading audience which will understand it'. But he told Stoppard that he always 'backed passion', and Ewing sent a telegram in September saying that 'Blond will publish and no doubt be damned.' He got an advance of £150. *Lord Malquist & Mr Moon* mixes up, as he loved to do, high and low culture, and steals from everything he'd been reading and seeing. He would describe it, looking back, as 'magpie pickings from (mostly) other people'. It's very theatrical, with chapters called 'Dramatis Personae', lots of farcical accidents and dramatic encounters, and characters leaving on the lines 'Exit Butler' or 'Exit Messenger'. Broken up with sudden cuts and shifts of view, it's also like a movie, in the mood of cold-eyed, stylised mid-1960s films like *Blow Up* or *Darling*. Comic strips, Westerns, *Carry On* films, thrillers, tabloid headlines and newsreel solemnities are stirred in with tributes to modernists like Joyce, Conrad and Faulkner, nods to Waugh, Wodehouse and Wilde, Pepys, *Tristram Shandy* and Cervantes, de Montherlant, Genet and Burroughs, traces of Sartre's *La Nausée* (in which the narrator, Roquentin, is trying to write the life of a marquis), comical allusions to *Hamlet*, and echoes everywhere of his hero Eliot.

Mr Moon carries a bomb around with him, like the anarchist Professor in Conrad's *The Secret Agent*. Like Joyce's Leopold Bloom in Dublin, he criss crosses the labyrinths of London while his wife is entertaining her lovers at home. And like Eliot's Prufrock, he is perpetually embarrassed, uncertain, and unable to make himself understood. He earns his living by offering his services as a 'Boswell' to people who want to have their lives memorialised: he's 'in the posterity business'. (This won't be the last of Stoppard's ironical jokes about biography.) At present he is working for Lord Malquist, an eighteenth-century-style dandy who rides about London in a coach and horses, dictating his *pensées*, when he isn't making love to Moon's wife Jane, a crude early version of Dotty in *Jumpers*, who is also being attended to by two rival cowboys, dressed in full gear, who refer to her as Fertility Jane. There's a lot of lipstick-and-undies bedroom comedy, with a nod to Joyce's pastiche of Gerty MacDowell in *Ulysses*. To thicken the 'plot', there's an escaped lion in St James's Park, a pathetic figure on a donkey who claims to be the Risen Christ, Birdboot the butler (to be saved up, with Moon, for *The Real Inspector Hound*), a murdered maid, the seductive, alcoholic Lady Malquist, and a coachman called O'Hara who changes race like a chameleon. That allows for Moon to ventriloquise the standard racist abuse of the time, which makes uncomfortable reading. The action culminates on the day that London has shut down for a great state funeral.

A philosophical debate is going on between the idea of style and the idea of order. Lord Malquist is a Wildean aesthete who believes in nothing *but* style. Like Albert on his bridge, he takes the distant view of human beings. People as individuals – other than himself – don't engage him. He's interested in the broad sweep of history. The state funeral, for him, marks the end of the age of heroism and great men. After that comes the age of style, in which the only role to play is that of the spectator, standing aloof. It would be easy to read the whole novel according to Malquist, as a youthful credo for aestheticism. Kenneth Tynan did so a few years on in his critical piece on Stoppard as a reactionary dandy, using Malquist's line, 'withdrawing with style from the chaos', as his title, and arguing that the phrase reflects the author's world view, one of 'extreme pessimism and therefore of conservatism'.

But there's a counter-view in the novel, equally dark but much less absolute. Moon argues with his patron that 'it's all *people*, isn't it? That's what the world *is*.' He can't hold all these people at bay or be indifferent to them. Like the would-be 'jumper' in *Albert's Bridge*, he is horrified by the feeling that the world is running out of control. That's why he wants to blow it, and himself, up. He views everything around him with bewilderment. His streams of consciousness are full of premonitions of disaster, for instance about the 'big power station' over the road:

The whole thing was at the mercy of a million variables which might fail in some way – strikes, silicosis, storms at sea . . . a derailment at Slough . . . a toothache in the wrong man at the wrong time – and at any time . . . people might stop deciding to be dentists (why after all should anyone want to be a *dentist*?) and there would be no one to kill the agonising pain in the back teeth of the black shiny-skinned miners who dig the coal which is put on the train which is derailed at Slough (yes and who will promise to go on milking the cows for the children of those who make the rails for the underground trains packed with clerks who take dentists for granted?).

Moon squeezed tight his eyelids against the returning accumulated fear which he could not separate into manageable threads.

But this wildly garrulous writer is also a perfectionist with writer's block:

He could not put down a word without suspecting that it might be the wrong one and that if he held back for another day the intermediate experience would provide the right one . . . Moon fearfully glimpsed himself as a pure writer who after a lifetime of absolutely no output whatever, would prepare on his deathbed the single sentence that was the distillation of everything he had saved up, and die before he was able to utter it.

That's one of many contradictions. He's a cuckolded husband who is still a virgin. He's a Boswell with no life of his own. He has no religion, though 'he sometimes wanted to be a Jew but had only the most superficial understanding of how to go about it'. What Moon really wants is to go back to childhood, when things felt safe:

'I think I'd like to go back to live in the country where I lived when I was small.'
　'Catch beetles.'
　'Press wild flowers.'
　'Climb trees.'
　'Make dens.'
　'But it wasn't always summer.'
　'No.'

Unable to decide whether life is random or inevitable, absurd or commonplace, he passes the time by interviewing himself, telling himself jokes and contradicting himself. 'I cannot commit myself to either side of a question'. He tells his wife: '"I was trying to face one way or the other and I got confused and fell over." *Let that be my epitaph.*' He can't act: 'He could only watch. He was a spectator.' There is a lot of overlap between Moon and his author – and between *Malquist* and *Rosencrantz and Guildenstern*. 'Spectator as Hero', he would note in 2005, would have done equally well as a title for the novel or the play.

Between 1964 and 1969, he kept a little black notebook of quotations, plot ideas, one-liners, poetry, reading lists, specimen titles and try-out pages of dialogue. It's a seed-bed both for the play and the novel (with a few foretastes of *Jumpers* and *Travesties*), which sometimes overlap on the same page. Eliot is everywhere in the Black Notebook. Stoppard marks his death (giving it as 5, not 4, January 1965). He drafts a passage about Malquist not caring about anything, which ends with: 'Till human voices wake us and we drown.' He tries out a line for Moon: 'My aim in life is to read, much of the night, and go south in the winter.' He puts in a whole poem, heavily indebted to 'Prufrock', written during or just after his time in Berlin:

> Isn't it time we went?
> When did the suggestion
> become a refrain
> and repeat itself into a question?
> (the nagging child who won't relent
> – isn't it time? isn't it time?)
> Time to turn and turn again
> Now turn and now repent
> the clocks that didn't chime
> the time you never spent
> and mourn
> irresolution, foetuses unborn
> the fuse you never lit
> (the languages you didn't learn
> the time you didn't give a damn
> and the time you did,
> the nights you didn't burn

down the cinemas in the Kurfurstendamm,
fight wars with dustbin lids,
scratch your names on a funeral urn
and mail it to Uncle Sam)

And all the things you never did
when you might at least have done the opposite.

Like this poet, Moon in *Malquist*, and Rosencrantz and Guildenstern (not to mention Hamlet), are full of 'irresolution'. *Malquist* is spattered with Eliot quotations from 'Portrait of a Lady', 'Prufrock' and *The Waste Land*: 'That is not it at all/That is not what I meant at all . . . And how should you presume? . . . Oh do not ask what is it/Let us go and make our visit . . . Hurry up please it's time . . .' At exactly the same time, he is scribbling lines from Eliot on the margins of a draft page of *Rosencrantz and Guildenstern*, where Rosencrantz, sounding very like Moon, is saying: 'I remember when there were no questions . . . when there were answers to everything . . . there were answers everywhere you *looked* . . . there was no question about it. People knew who I was. And if they didn't, they asked and I told them.'

At the bottom of this page are lines from Eliot's 'Portrait of a Lady': 'Attenuated tones of violins/mingled with remote cornets . . . I smile, of course/And go on drinking tea.' Under these quotes he wrote, rather ambiguously, the initials 'T.S.' As the play is rewritten and Hamlet's musings on time and mortality are given to Rosencrantz and Guildenstern, they often sound like Prufrock, anxious, indecisive, and haunted by mortality. And the whole concept of the play comes out of Eliot's poem:

No! I am not Prince Hamlet, nor was meant to be;
Am an attendant lord, one that will do
To swell a progress, start a scene or two . . .

But the Black Notebook isn't just an Eliot anthology. It's full of aphorisms – some quoted, some invented. A lot of these are about double identities, disguises and self-alienation: 'The drunken actor who said, "I come on in a minute" has the secret of identity, mortality.' (The Player in *Rosencrantz* will also say: 'I come on in a minute.') 'A play about a man defending himself – on charge of impersonating a solicitor.' 'I'm leading a double life – I feel like a spy in my normal surface life.' 'You'll know me because I'll be the only one in disguise.'

Many of the aphorisms have to do with style. He plunders lines he fancies from Beau Brummell and Frank Harris, from A. J. Liebling ('he zigged when he should have zagged') and Kenneth Tynan. He makes up one-liners for dandies: 'My aim is to go down in history in comfort.' He invents or steals quips about life-writing: 'He relies on his memory for his jokes and on his imagination for his facts.' Based on George Eliot's 'Among all forms of mistake, prophecy is the most gratuitous': 'Of all forms of fiction, autobiography is the most gratuitous.' 'To the Editor of the New Statesman: I have been commissioned to write a biography of myself.'

The notebook also contains entries about his feelings, which will go straight into the novel or the play, showing how personal – how autobiographical, in fact – Moon and Rosencrantz are under their disguises. One of these, marked 'Christmas Day, 1964', lies behind Moon's writer's block: 'And not a word written! I had put it off – and off and off – wanting to write "Ulysses" and afraid of ending up with "Portrait of the Artist". Now I'll be lucky to manage "Stephen Hero". Loud sing Goddam!' The date is annotated in red ink: 'Feb 24, 1965, etc.'

Another entry gets turned, almost word for word, into Rosencrantz's speech on being born 'with an intuition of mortality':

> What became of the 'moment' when one learned about death? There must have been a moment like that: the realisation of it. Yet I can't remember mine. A relatively minor revolution, like the first fuck, or even, in the case of a girl, the first period, must stay with one. One must be born with the knowledge of death . . .
>
> (I write this at 6 a.m., in bed after a sleepless night, and *still* I barely accept the fact of my own mortality.)

*

Stoppard told Isabel, in a long letter of February 1966, that he and Jose were 'comfortably broke' but that in his 'secret mind' he 'had fantasies of my book solving every problem but Jose discourages this *folie de grandeur*'. *Folie de grandeur* could be a definition of Lord Malquist's state of mind too, and when the novel came out, Stoppard described it, jokingly, to Isabel, as 'My fantasy life revealed.' He also noted ruefully: 'Most people seem to find it confusing, which I suppose it is, a bit.'

Blond published *Malquist* in August 1966, in the same week as the first production of *Rosencrantz and Guildenstern Are Dead*. Stoppard would frequently say that he had high hopes for the novel and low expectations for the play. By December, there had been a handful of reviews, some encouraging but mostly puzzled, and Blond had shifted 688 copies – though he did manage to sell it to Knopf for $1,000. He told Stoppard he should quickly write a second novel about astronauts and moon landings, since everyone else would be on to that subject soon enough. He took the point, but he never did write another novel. By 1973 Blond would be referring to 'poor Lord Malquist' and Stoppard had developed some good running jokes about how it had done very well in Venezuela and not so well in London:

I remember going into Foyles' bookshop in 1966 and being gratified to see a stack of Malquist-and-Moons on the New Fiction table. I counted them; there were twelve. A week or two later I went in again; there they were. I counted them again; there were thirteen! I saw at once what was happening. *People were leaving my book at bookshops.*

By the time he finished writing the novel, in the summer of 1965, Ewing had sent two acts of the new *Rosencrantz and Guildenstern* to the Royal Shakespeare Company. (It was also sent to the Royal Court, for one of their Sunday night performances, but got no response.) Stoppard had bumped into the RSC's dramaturge, Jeremy Brooks, in May, at the wedding of Michael Kustow (on his rapid entrepreneurial path through Bristol, Centre 42, the RSC and then the ICA). Brooks asked to see the two-act draft, and showed it to the men in charge. In 1965, Peter Hall was the artistic director. He'd been running the RSC since 1958, and had hugely expanded its remit, establishing the permanent company at Stratford and leasing the Aldwych for London productions. He was working with Clifford Williams, John Barton, Trevor Nunn, who would take over from Hall in 1968, and Peter Brook. ('Peter Brook . . . may be described as God in the world of which Peter Hall is Mammon,' Stoppard told Anthony Smith.) The rivalry with Olivier at the National was intense, and the setting up of the RSC's London base had been fiercely opposed by the National. Those tensions between the country's two new major subsidised theatre companies would run on into Peter Hall's takeover of the National from Olivier in 1973.

But it was a good moment for a promising young playwright hoping for a production at one of the subsidised theatres, especially with a play based on *Hamlet*. The RSC wanted to be experimental as well as classical. Trevor Nunn had been asked by Hall to run a short series of new plays in a London studio, while David Warner's *Hamlet* was playing in Stratford. Both Nunn and Hall saw the potential in *Rosencrantz* for that series. Nunn thought Warner might play Hamlet in that, as well. The RSC took out a year's option on it, for £150, in May 1965, enough for Stoppard to pay back his debts to Anthony Smith. He wrote the third act at speed.

By now *Rosencrantz and Guildenstern* had taken its recognisable shape. Hamlet had been pushed into the background, speaking only Shakespeare's lines; the double act of the two 'attendant lords' was now at the centre of the play. The collision of the three language-worlds – Shakespeare's tragedy, the Player's disillusioned theatrical oratory, and the two men's colloquial hesitations, deviations and repetitions – had clicked into place. It had become the play we know, the play which, over time, has come to feel as familiar to theatre-goers as *Hamlet* itself, or as *Waiting for Godot*.

Two men are sent for. They set out on their journey. They don't know what is happening or why, or what will be asked of them. They have travelled together before. But they don't know their own back-story. They only know what they have been told. They keep mixing themselves up with each other, and so will everybody else. We meet them as they stop on the road, tossing coins, with results that break all the laws of probability:

heads, seventy-six times running! Ninety-two times running! They seem to be stuck in time, or outside time. The Player and his rag-bag troupe of actors turn up, changing the pace with their willingness to please all customers (times are hard), their dreadful proficiency at sex and death, their world-weary knowledge, their quick-change cart of props and masks and swords. Rosencrantz and Guildenstern leave them high and dry in mid-act. Suddenly they are at the court, where the plot and characters of *Hamlet* roar in and out and around them, catching them up and letting them drop. They are given commands and instructions but they don't know how to act: they are spectators. The actors arrive, humiliated at having been left without an audience. The Player knows his way around the court. And he seems to know – from experience – what's going to happen to Rosencrantz and Guildenstern. He specialises in ominous, knowing aphorisms: 'Generally speaking, things have gone about as far as they can possibly go when things have got about as bad as they reasonably get.' 'Life is a gamble, at terrible odds – if it was a bet you wouldn't take it.' 'In our experience, most things end in death.' There is something sinister about him and what he makes his actors do, and he makes the two men uncomfortable and angry.

Nervous, lonely, bored and tense, they try to work out what's wrong with Hamlet and what they should be doing. They witness baffling bits of the key scenes of Shakespeare's play, which are no help to them at all. They watch the rehearsal of the play within the play, with their own deaths acted out. They see Hamlet with Polonius's body. They are sent to England. They are on a boat with Hamlet. They have no solid ground, and nothing to go on. 'England' doesn't seem plausible to them: what will they do when they get there? The players turn up again, 'impossibly' bursting out of the ship's barrels. While they sleep, Hamlet swaps the letter they are carrying, thus condemning them to death. They watch the Player acting death, a tour de force; and again see their own deaths acted out by the players. And then they disappear, never understanding why they were there, what was truth and what was lies, what the answers to any of their questions were, or, even, who they were.

They are characters in a play which is based on a pre-existing play, in which players play a play: the idea of infinite regression fascinated him.

Who are the 'real' characters and who are the actors? The Player gives his own answer (which can be as despairing or as comical as his interpreter chooses): 'We're *actors*, we're the opposite of people!' We already know that Rosencrantz and Guildenstern are characters in a play. Their ends are written. So what kind of choices do they have? Can they control or shape their destinies? Do they have any freedom at all? The fall of their coins, endlessly, improbably, turning up heads (until the one-hundred-and-first, very last throw), applies the laws of physics to a story about chance and fate. It's his first, gleeful meshing of science and drama.

All they have is words: 'Words, words. They're all we have to go on,' says Guildenstern, very like Hamlet. To pass the time and to keep themselves going, they play word games as if they were tennis matches: question games, thought experiments, logical arguments using syllogisms and hypotheses. They bat phrases back and forth at speed, trying not to drop a point: 'Dark, isn't it?' 'Not for night.' 'No, not for *night*. Dark for *day*.' 'Oh yes, it's dark for *day*.' The faster and funnier these are, the more they betray their panic and despair: Who do you think you are? . . . When's it going to end? . . . Why should it matter? . . . What are the rules? In between, Rosencrantz meditates dreamily out loud on the mysteriousness of toenails, or the terror of being in one's coffin ('stuffed in a box like that, I mean you'd be in there for ever. Even taking into account the fact that you're dead, it isn't a pleasant thought'). Guildenstern tries to analyse the laws of probability or work out their alternatives. Staring out front, they're longing for 'somebody interesting to come on in a minute', and terrified whenever they do. They keep trying to best Hamlet and he always gets the better of them: 'Half of what he said meant something else, and the other half didn't mean anything at all.' The words they rely on keep failing them. They can't even depend on clichés, which keep coming undone and turning into nonsense: 'It's all stopping to a death, it's boding to a depth, stepping to a head, it's all heading to a dead stop—'; 'home and dry – dry and home—'; 'No point in looking at a gift horse till you see the whites of its eyes.'

It wasn't just Shakespeare or Beckett – or Pirandello, or James Saunders, or Brecht, or Kafka, or Wilde – who lay behind this, though Vladimir and Estragon do pave the way for Rosencrantz and Guildenstern, just as Lucky and Pozzo do for the Player and his troupe. It was also the popular comedy he loved: Buster Keaton, Mel Brooks, Morecambe and Wise, *One Minute Please* (which turned into *Just a Minute* in 1967), *The Goon Show*. Behind it too lay his fond memory of Peter O'Toole's Bristol Old Vic Hamlet, and his joking, word-conscious friendship with Anthony Smith from those days. He often wrote his plays with a musical track playing repeatedly in the background. For this play it was Bob Dylan's 'Like a Rolling Stone' and 'Subterranean Homesick Blues'. Rosencrantz and Guildenstern suffer from homesickness; they'll never be home and dry. The word rings all through.

He splits himself between the two: Guildenstern seeking information, examining scientific solutions, wanting logical answers, and in the end grimly facing reality: 'We move idly towards eternity, without possibility of reprieve or hope of explanation'; Rosencrantz dreamy, vulnerable, childish, frightened. They quarrel, they compete, they are interdependent, they can't exist without the other: 'Don't leave me!' They exit, finally, almost at the same moment. Rosencrantz, like any victim of a cruel fate, is still lost in his innocence and bemusement ('We've done nothing wrong! We didn't harm anyone. Did we?'), Guildenstern is still searching for a cause and a plan: 'There must have been a moment, at the beginning, when we could have said – no. But somehow we missed it.' In the Black Notebook, he told himself what the play was about: '*Rosencrantz* is about the principle that every man is the centre of the world – and there are as many worlds as there are men. "That so much should converge on our own little deaths."' Under the play's linguistic brio and theatrical exhibitionism there's a deeply melancholy note, which sounds in their attempts to remember their past, or in Guildenstern's language of passing time:

We cross our bridges when we come to them and burn them behind us, with nothing to show for our progress except a memory of the smell of smoke, and a presumption that once our eyes watered.

Autumnal – nothing to do with leaves. It is to do with a certain brownness at the edges of the day . . . Brown is creeping up on us, take my word for it . . .

They seem almost to be their own ghosts, haunting themselves, already dead, as we know from the play's title – the line from *Hamlet* that gave him his story. Perhaps that's why the one major piece of *Hamlet* he omitted was the Ghost. He had the ghosts he needed.

Everyone in the play talks about death. Under all the playfulness and play-acting, it's the one reality. And death – real death, unlike stage deaths – is just nothing. 'It's the absence of presence, nothing more.' What Shakespeare's Hamlet is preoccupied by, and what the players spend their professional life doing best, is also what Rosencrantz and Guildenstern are brooding on. So they aren't in counterpoint or contrast to Shakespeare's play, although the joke of Stoppard's play is that they often sound that way. They share – and have their own modern version of – its profound human emotions. This fabulously light, playful, witty comedy was also a dark play about mortality.

Fifty years on, he remarked that if the RSC had sent it back, telling him, this is incomprehensible and not very funny, he would not have said to himself: 'Fools, they've missed a masterpiece.' There was still a lot more work to be done on it. Jeremy Brooks told him that a lot of 'the double-talk, amusing and stimulating as it is, needs cutting'. The resolution needed to be 'more positive', and they still weren't sure if it should be a three-act or a two-act play. Stoppard knew that the characters needed to be more 'humanised' and that 'Guil must be prised loose from my own character'.

He took it away with him on holiday in the autumn of 1965. They went to stay in a house on the borders of the Dordogne and the Lot with Anthony and Alison and the twins. But the family at close quarters was too much for them – or too much for Jose – and they moved across the valley, to a small village in the Lot, St Michel-par-Bretenoux, calling in on the others every day. On that long seven-week holiday, their first child was conceived, *Rosencrantz* continued to be revised, and they met some new friends of the Smiths. They were Miriam and Peter Moore-Robinson, a lively young couple living near Bristol. Peter, a bluff, gregarious Yorkshire Quaker, was a vet. Miriam was a high-flying young medic from a Jewish

family, a graduate from Durham University, just about to begin working as an assistant research director of a pharmaceuticals firm. They had
seen the Smiths in *The Newcomers*, and then spotted them at a cinema in
Bristol and got into conversation with them. (In Anthony Smith's version,
Miriam boldly introduced herself; in Miriam's version, her husband Peter,
to her embarrassment, made the first move.) The Moore-Robinsons began
to socialise with the Smiths in Bristol. They went to the student staging of
Stoppard's *The Gamblers*, though Miriam was too shy to say anything to
the playwright. The three couples, all in their twenties, converged on the
holiday house. Miriam observed how pretty and how thin Jose was, and
that witticisms simply poured out of Tom. She said to Anthony: 'Does he
talk like that all the time?' Tom was swatting at the flies, and she asked him
why he bothered. 'Every time a fly sits, it shits,' he said. That was their first
and only exchange. After the holiday, Alison and Miriam, and Miriam and
Jose, became friends. But Miriam was daunted by Jose's husband, by his
glamour and dazzle and wit.

Once Jose knew she was pregnant she decided to have her baby by 'natural childbirth', a popular 1960s choice which preferred relaxation methods and breathing exercises to drugs and epidurals. The father, instead of
being in the waiting room, was expected to participate. This father had
his doubts: a consultant anaesthetist he talked to called natural childbirth
'codswallop', and he was extremely apprehensive about being present,
'not having given birth before', as he said to Isabel. 'My ideas on childbirth', he would write a few years later, 'had been shaped by Middle Period
Hollywood. I was the one who paced about a bit at a safe distance, she
was the one who, without any intervening footage, sat up in bed looking
fabulous with a swaddled extra in the crook of her elbow.'

In the event, the baby was two months premature. Jose was walking
across Trafalgar Square one evening when labour started; she was rushed
into Westminster Hospital and gave birth on 4 May, after an extremely
painful two days. 'Mercifully I was expelled when the forceps were summoned,' the father wrote. 'Even in my most alarmist moods I had never
anticipated anything so frightful.' The baby was kept in hospital when Jose
went home; she went in to feed him, with a bottle, every day. They called

him Oliver (Lionel Bart's hugely successful musical was running in the West End, and Stoppard sometimes referred to his baby son as 'Oliver!'). Stoppard told Anthony: 'My mother is convinced that Oliver is an esoteric name and is upset about it – "Other boys will tease him unmercifully – why can't you give him a *nice* name like JASON." That's the provinces – way ahead of us.' By June, Oliver was home. He told his mother he had to get up and look at him every five minutes to make sure he was still breathing and hadn't been stolen by gypsies. He also noted that their social life was now over, and, in the same breath, that both his housemates, Read and Marlowe, had new books out: 'I seem to have been overtaken.' They were both sleepless, and he had 'yet to change a nappy'. To get some peace and quiet, they spent a few weeks in Bristol in Val Lorraine's house. Isabel sent a large cheque, and Jose spent most of it on a set of Beatrix Potter. In their joint thank-you, Jose told Isabel that 'Oliver is doing his usual trick of demanding attention as soon as I start doing anything'. She was an unconfident young mother with a tiny baby, a preoccupied husband working freelance, not much money, and no house to themselves.

At the same time as Ollie was born, the RSC option on *Rosencrantz and Guildenstern* expired. (By then Stoppard had tried sending it to the BBC, too, but it was rejected as 'long, wordy and rambling'.) Nunn was still keen on it for his studio series, but this plan fell victim to the expenses of the Aldwych season. He had to break this news to the disappointed author, who was living, as Nunn put it, in 'very frugal circumstances' and for whom this was clearly shattering news. When Peter Hall asked Nunn, soon after that, to do a production of a dark Polish comedy, *Tango*, by Sławomir Mrożek, Nunn immediately thought of Stoppard, and was able, as a kind of consolation prize, to offer him the job of rewriting Nicholas Bethell's literal translation. It was Stoppard's first European work, a foretaste of his later free translations of Lorca, Nestroy, Schnitzler and Havel. *Tango*, first staged in Warsaw in 1964, was a bitter, absurdist anti-Stalinist parable, about a young man whose parents are so liberal and decadent there is nothing left for him to revolt against, and who comes to believe in freedom through total power. This Eastern European satire opened at the Aldwych in May 1966, in a season which included Gogol's *The Government*

Inspector and Duras's *Days in the Trees*. Directed by Nunn, with Patience Collier, Robert Eddison and Michael Williams in the cast, and with Nunn taking over the main part from an actor in meltdown, it was the first writing by Stoppard to be spoken on a London stage.

Nunn also sent *Rosencrantz* to the Oxford Playhouse director Frank Hauser, and Hauser, with Ewing's reluctant agreement, passed it on to the student Oxford Theatre Group. Set up in the early 1950s, OTG took a revue and a new play every year to the Edinburgh Festival Fringe. (The revue nurtured talents like Alan Bennett, Maggie Smith, Terry Jones and Michael Palin, and, in 1966, Diana Quick.) The contract between OTG and Stoppard included travel expenses for him to Edinburgh, and ten per cent for OTG of all receipts from productions and adaptations of the play for the next five years. That turned out well for them.

Rosencrantz was supposed to be directed by an excellent undergraduate director, Andrew Snell, who recruited a good student cast. But, for personal reasons, Snell dropped out. The cast started rehearsals in the basement of the grotty Masonic Hall on Johnston Terrace where they all slept, ate and worked, directed by a stage manager from the Oxford University Dramatic Society, Brian Daubney, dropped in at the last moment and completely out of his depth. They were working from a script which had been badly mistyped. Some bits didn't make sense, some passages were repeated. The Ophelia, Janet Watts, a future journalist, said: 'We just thought it was modern drama!' There were two weeks of awful rehearsals, while they all told each other what a terrible play it was. The Rosencrantz, David Marks, a law student and the outstanding student actor of his day, very well up on modern drama, didn't agree. He thought the play was odd and special and moving: 'these two guys spinning in the void'. But he had a sinking feeling about the production, not helped by the fact that Guildenstern (Clive Cable) couldn't remember his lines, or that Daubney kept running away from rehearsals to walk up Arthur's Seat with his girlfriend.

Into this shambles came Stoppard, arriving at Waverley Station off the train from Bristol (while he and Jose and Oliver were temporarily at Grosvenor Lodge). He immediately set to work to salvage his play. To the Oxford students, all about eight years his junior, he seemed hugely cool. He wore a dark grey tweed suit with flared trousers and a stand-up 'Mao' collar, smoked Strand cigarettes, and was sparkling with alertness, attention and magnetism. (Word got back to their student friends in Oxford that the amazing Tom Stoppard had arrived, that he was incredibly charismatic and foreign-seeming, and that *he had never been to university*.) He sat up till two in the morning with the three leading actors, reading the script aloud and making corrections. Marks picked up his intonations, the rolling 'r's, the slight lisp and hesitations, the inflections, the funny public school phrases ('Tough beans, fellow!'), and based his Rosencrantz on Stoppard's manner. Stoppard worked through the play with the whole cast in the same way: 'Right, page one.' And off they went, with Stoppard directing, reading aloud, taking notes on their performances ('Very good scream,' he told Ophelia), professional, relentless, charming, serious and passionate. Queried on one phrase in the play, he replied: 'That's poetry, man!'

As they went along Stoppard made some rapid alterations, and wrote them straight into the actors' scripts, like a new bit about the mysteries of fingernail growth, a small addition which shows how the characters' to-and-fro works like a musical score, every note counting. The rehearsal script read:

R (*cutting his fingernails*): Another curious scientific phenomenon is
    the fact that the fingernails grow after death, as does the beard.
G: What?
R (*shouts*): Beard! What's the matter with you? (*Reflectively.*) The
    toenails, on the other hand, never grow at all.

Stoppard altered this on the spot to:

R (*cutting his fingernails*): Another curious scientific phenomenon is
    the fact that the fingernails grow after death, as does the beard.
G: What?
R: Beard. (*Pause.*)

G: You're not dead.

R: I didn't say they *started* to grow after death. (*Pause, reflectively.*) The
  fingernails also grow before birth, though not the beard.

G: What?

R (*shouts*): Beard! What's the matter with you?

The ending of the play, too, kept changing, and would go on changing.
The Edinburgh version ended with the two characters disappearing on
Rosencrantz's line: 'We've come this far. And besides, anything could happen yet.' Then the denouement of *Hamlet* is played out, up to Fortinbras's
last line, 'Go, bid the soldiers shoot.' In later versions, the two men would
have more to say in their last exchange, fading out on Guildenstern's line,
'Now you see me, now you—'. After their disappearance, the last scene
from *Hamlet* then ended with Horatio's final speech, followed by a brief
exchange between two new characters, two Ambassadors, cut short by
their being summoned, like Rosencrantz and Guildenstern all over again.
(That version lasted into the first edition of the play, but not the first performance.) Over time, there were something like eight different versions
of the play's conclusion. As Stoppard would frequently say, 'There is no
definitive text.' The shifting playscript, which would keep altering in its
many editions, reflects the uncertainties of the play itself.

The script had to be vetted by the Lord Chamberlain's Office, without
whose licence no play could be performed in Britain. The censor passed it
as a 'dotty but amusing' take on *Hamlet* by an 'undergraduate playwright'.
The 'World Premiere' of a play which was written for a big stage, with
trapdoors and 'other refinements', opened on 24 August 1966, in a small,
crumbling Fringe venue, the Cranston Street Hall, with a stage 'the size
of a ping-pong table'. Stoppard came up with Jose, having parked Oliver
with her sister. To the student cast, Jose seemed unexceptional, subdued
and out of place. It was two days after the publication of *Lord Malquist &*
Mr Moon and the airing of *A Separate Peace* on BBC2. The highbrow programme note described Rosencrantz and Guildenstern as 'a curious and
rather appealing couple':

. . . they are told little, they obey orders, and are somewhat bewildered, having been thrust into a situation which is nothing to do with them and which they hardly understand. Because of this they have the air of occupying a level above the action, a different level of reality. It must have been this which makes Wilde (in *De Profundis*) refer to them as immortal characters whose reported death is merely part of the play's mechanics; they march on.

In the interval, Stoppard was approached by two baffled local reviewers asking him questions like 'Are they supposed to be imaginary people?' The first reviews, which mostly came out the next day, were terrible. The *Scotsman* called it 'no more than a clever revue sketch which got out of hand', describing Rosencrantz and Guildenstern as 'a pair of knockabout comedians who bandy words instead of custard pies'. The *Daily Mail* said it was 'inexplicable throughout', the *Express* headed its piece 'Puzzle Play: What's It All About, Tom?' and the *Glasgow Herald* called it 'sub-Beckett' and 'sub-Pinter', 'as off-putting a piece of non-theatre as has been presented at the Festival for many a year'. The West End theatre manager Michael Codron went with his friend Jim Haines, and 'couldn't see beyond the wrinkled tights. We didn't think this was the genius of the twentieth century'. Audience laughs were few. The company, Janet Watts said, were 'aghast'.

But some people did like it. A young student named Ian McEwan who had hitchhiked from Brighton to Edinburgh, and went to it by accident, was enchanted. Stoppard took him to the pub and talked to him about literature; McEwan felt star-struck. On the first Sunday of the run, Ronald Bryden, the *Observer*'s theatre critic, covered the shows he'd seen at the Festival that week, with a smiling photograph of Stoppard at the top of the page over the caption 'The most brilliant début since John Arden's'. Setting the tone for a great many future reviews of the play, Bryden called it 'an existential fable unabashedly indebted to *Waiting for Godot*', with 'allegoric purposes' moving under the 'fantastic comedy', 'as witty and vaulting as Beckett's original is despairing . . . While the tragedy unfurls in this comic looking glass, you're too busy with its stream of ironic invention, metaphysical jokes and linguistic acrobatics to pursue them. Like

Love's Labour's Lost, this is erudite comedy, punning, far-fetched, leaping from depth to dizziness.' And then came the key sentence, quoted in the caption: 'It's the most brilliant debut by a young playwright since John Arden's.' The comparison might not have much force now. Arden's most famous play, *Serjeant Musgrave's Dance*, which opened at the Royal Court in 1958 to bad reviews, in fact took time to catch on, and his Marxist politics were utterly different from Stoppard's. But it was high praise. And the allusion to *Love's Labour's Lost* would have pleased him. One of his favourite endings was that play's: 'You that way; we this way.'

He read the piece early on the Sunday morning, in bed with Jose in their mediocre Edinburgh hotel room. He described the scene in a letter home. She was going through the papers; he opened half an eye, and, judging by her expression, thought he might as well go back to sleep for a couple of days. And then she showed him the Bryden review. That morning, Kenneth Tynan, since 1963 the literary manager at the National, was also reading the review. 'Minutes after reading Bryden's piece', Tynan recalled, 'I cabled Stoppard requesting a script.' Ken Ewing's office was deluged with similar requests: Bryden's review 'singlehandedly triggered off a huge reaction', Stoppard told his parents. He went to see Tynan in the 'wooden hut on waste ground' (a draughty prefabricated building in Aquinas Street) which was then the National Theatre office, in a state of awe and excitement. 'I began to stutter. Ken stuttered . . . So we sat stuttering at each other, mainly about his shirt which was pale lemon and came from Turnbull and Asser in Jermyn Street.' The National, at its Old Vic home since 1962, needed an exciting new success. Laurence Olivier was ill, the theatre was running at a deficit, the great plans for Lasdun's new building on the South Bank were grinding on with ever-mounting costs and endless squabbling. There were frequent and savage fallings-out between Olivier, John Dexter, the rebarbative Tynan and Lord Chandos, head of the management board. Retrospectively, Stoppard described the turbulent relationship between Tynan and Olivier as 'being joined in a continuous drama which intermittently broke surface in grievances and embraces'. Against this background, *Rosencrantz* was put on almost by accident. The season for 1967 was up in the air. There was a sudden gap in the schedule because John Dexter (who liked the play and would have directed it) had a row over the cancellation of an all-male *As You Like It*, and left the National that winter. There were several possibilities for a stop-gap, and *Rosencrantz* was one of them. Tynan told Stoppard effusively that he thought 'it was the best play they'd ever received' – but they all knew it was a risk. Stoppard would be the youngest, and the least-known, writer to have had a play put on at the National. Olivier was lukewarm, but was persuaded by being told they could save money by using the costumes from the old O'Toole *Hamlet*.

A contract was finalised on 1 October 1966 for a nine-month option on the play; Stoppard was paid £250 for the option. Three weeks later, after some competition between Penguin and Faber, Faber contracted to publish it in 1967, with an advance of £150 and a print run of fifteen hundred. The play was scheduled for the spring, alongside Strindberg's *The Dance of Death* and Chekhov's *Three Sisters*. Stoppard told Anthony Smith he was anxious about timing. 'I have a theory that plays go off, like fruit . . . Somehow, in a year's time the play won't be as good a play. It's not as good now as it was a year ago when I wrote it.'

The production was given to Dexter's twenty-five-year-old assistant, Derek Goldby, who had worked at the Royal Court and whose idols were Wesker, Littlewood and Brecht. There was a suggestion that Olivier might do the Player, but, according to Goldby, he pooh-poohed the idea of appearing in an unknown play directed by an assistant – and later regretted it. Stoppard told Olivier he thought of the Player as 'sneaky' and 'snake-like'. Olivier gave him a 'dubious' look, and instead the huge, flamboyant, old-school actor Graham Crowden was cast, who 'roared like a lion'. Otherwise, it was a young cast. John Stride as Rosencrantz was known at the Old Vic as Zeffirelli's Romeo, but Edward Petherbridge had only done small roles, and the Hamlet, John McEnery, had just joined the National.

Rehearsals did not go smoothly. Discussions about cuts and changes continued, with Tynan busily suggesting alternative endings; one script meeting with Olivier and Tynan went on until five in the morning. Tynan and Stoppard managed to resist Olivier's suggestion that the play should be given a happy ending, with Rosencrantz and Guildenstern coming back to life. He was impressed, though, by Olivier's suggesting that he put back a scene he'd cut after Hamlet kills Polonius. And he thought the fact he smoked 'Olivier' cigarettes 'sublime'. Stride gave a polished, dazzling performance at the first read-through; Petherbridge found it hard to learn Guildenstern's lines, and took much longer to find his way into the part. Crowden was so theatrical that he found it near-impossible to act the Player's 'death' as if it were real. Olivier came into one rehearsal, made a suggestion or two, and, turning as he left, twinkling at the cast, said: 'Just the odd pearl.' As the first night approached the cast got the jitters. Goldby had mostly kept the author out of rehearsals, but Stoppard asked to have one session with the actors. Goldby felt this undermined him; Stoppard feared that Goldby might be going to ruin his big chance. The production felt over-elaborate to him, too. The play is written for a bare, unfurnished, minimalist stage. Goldby, with the designer Desmond Heeley, the lighting designer Richard Pilbrow and the composer Mark Wilkinson, created a Gothic edifice of a sepulchral cobwebbed palace, a ghost ship coming up from below, a phantasmagoria of eerie lights and haunting music. 'One boggles at the whole thing.'

At the last full run-through, Olivier came to watch. He made one comment: 'Well, it will either work, or it won't.' The next night was the one and only dress rehearsal – and then the first night, to a full house, on Tuesday 11 April 1967. The lights went up on two men in Elizabethan costume, betting on the toss of a coin.

PART TWO

9

Success

Moon: . . . it is hard, it is hard indeed, and therefore I will not attempt,
to refrain from invoking the names of Kafka, Sartre, Shakespeare,
St Paul, Beckett, Birkett, Pinero, Pirandello, Dante and Dorothy L.
Sayers.
Birdboot: A rattling good evening out. I was held.

He hated first nights. To encourage himself, he bought a new blue suit for the event. Early on in the first act, a man in a dinner jacket sitting in front of him turned to his companion and said, 'I do wish they'd get *on*.' As a result, in the first interval he and Jose went to the pub next door, and – partly because Jose couldn't face it – didn't come back until the end of the play, to hear, not booing as at Hamburg three years before, but applause and bravos. Everyone in the theatre knew, at that moment, that this was a big hit.

The cast piled into cars and cabs and went from Waterloo to Kenneth Ewing's big, shabby-grand house, in a crescent off Clapham High Street, for the first-night party. Then Tom and Jose went back to Vincent Square. Fiona was there with Bobby. Derek Goldby, with a journalist friend, went to Fleet Street very early to get the papers as soon as they were printed. A legend grew up that Stoppard 'ran up and down' Fleet Street in the early hours 'from one machine room to the next'. He certainly appeared at the theatre for his first interviews the next morning, hungover and drinking glucose water, telling reporters some such story. But, looking back, he thought it was unlikely he'd have raced from Clapham to Fleet Street. More probably he went home, and picked the papers up early, round the corner at Victoria Station.

The reviews were ecstatic – even if one or two curmudgeons grumbled that it was 'all very clever, I dare say'. Praise came pouring out from Irving Wardle ('an amazing piece of work'), Ronald Bryden, again ('the most brilliant dramatic debut of the sixties') and Alan Brien ('real imaginative audacity'). Comparisons to Beckett, Kafka and Pirandello were frequent. Bryden made the point that the play drew on the 'Continental genre of modernised myth', citing Giraudoux, Sartre and Cocteau. The reviewer from *Le Monde* added Oscar Wilde and W. S. Gilbert to the mix. Harold Hobson, the first theatre critic to have seen the point of Beckett and Pinter, and as influential at the *Sunday Times* as Tynan had been in the *Observer*, said it was 'the most important event in the British professional theatre of the last nine years' – referring back to *The Birthday Party*. 'Its ingenuity is stupendous; and the delicacy and complexity of its plot are handled with a theatrical mastery astonishing in a writer as young as Mr Stoppard.' Hobson particularly responded to its darkness, as well as to its dazzle: 'Both [men] are equally baffled and helpless before the blank, terrifying, and unanswerable wall of life. It is a situation many people know well.'

It wasn't only the reviews that made Stoppard all at once successful and famous. There was a buzz around the play, an avid word-of-mouth, a feeling of excitement. Other playwrights had successes that year – Alan Ayckbourn's *Relatively Speaking*, Simon Gray's *Wise Child*, Peter Nichols's *A Day in the Death of Joe Egg* – but none had the same glamour. Nichols began a lifetime of comical, self-lacerating envy of the younger writer, whom he'd seen starting out in Bristol, and who now overtook him. 'Lucky Tom', he and Charles Wood called him.

For all its slow, awkward gestation, the play had a feeling of freedom, bravado and stylishness, and that's what audiences responded to. Once he had settled on the idea of turning the world's most famous play inside out, he had given himself, in his phrase, a free pass. He didn't quite realise, before his success, how bold he had been. He had wanted to do something new and unconventional, but if someone had said to him, how dare you take Shakespeare and muck about with him, he might have given up there and then.

His audiences found it entrancingly cool, modern and desirable. Young theatre-goers, in particular, felt it was *their* play. Partly it was the pleasure in seeing *Hamlet* upended, and of keeping up with the witty repartee. Partly it was the satisfyingly ironic theatrical self-consciousness of the experience. And partly it was that sense of bewilderment and exclusion, of not being in control, which Hobson had responded to. It felt very much of its time.

As with Beckett and Pinter, the play offered infinite room for theorising. He always insisted on its concreteness, simplicity and entertainment value: it was a comedy about two men thrown into a particular situation. His favourite take on it was from a journalist who said, Oh, I get it, it's two reporters on a story that doesn't stand up. But interpretations ran riot: it was absurdist; it was existential. He kept shrugging them off: 'I didn't know what the word "existential" meant until it was applied to *Rosencrantz*.' 'It had nothing to do with the condition of modern man or the decline of metaphysics.' This began a resistance to being over-read, for which he devised a jokey and much-repeated allegory:

> When I'm talking about my own work to somebody, my relationship with them is rather like that of a duped smuggler confronted with a customs officer. I truthfully declare that I am indeed responsible for this piece about two specific individuals in a particular situation. Then he starts ransacking my luggage and comes up with all manner of exotic contraband like truth and illusion, the nature of identity, what I feel about life and death – and I have to admit the stuff is there but I can't for the life of me remember packing it.

The play and its author resisted autobiographical interpretation, too. He acknowledged that Rosencrantz and Guildenstern were 'two sides of one temperament', that the two characters were 'carrying out a dialogue which I carry out with myself'. But this was the play of a writer who did not want to be confessional and who was, by nature, reserved and self-protecting; the more so for all the verbal dazzle. Asked about this, he would reply: 'I simply don't like very much revealing myself. I am a very private sort of person.' The most autobiographical thing about the play, he would say, was the close relationship between the predicament of the two characters and the predicament of the writer. How are they – and he – going to occupy the time before the next bit of *Hamlet* happens?

After the gamble paid off, Laurence Olivier would say that it was the production he was proudest of in his time at the National Theatre. (In ill health, he was ousted, and replaced by Peter Hall, in 1973.) He became fond of Stoppard, and, of course, very keen to keep him as a writer for the National. The play ran there for over three years, closing in May 1970. Every night of the performance, the theatre sold the Faber text (for eighteen shillings) in the foyer, an unusual strategy then. Copies sold at '50 per performance minimum'. Faber's original hardback print run, on 4 May 1967, of 1,500, would quickly come to seem ridiculous: but how could they have guessed what was going to happen? For the first paperback, in 1967, they printed four thousand; then they did a second edition, with many textual changes. Reprints followed almost annually, selling between twenty and fifty thousand copies at each reprint. By 1999 the play would have been reprinted twenty-three times. The print run between 2001 and 2008, for instance, was 510,587. The American publication of the play, by Grove Press, also went into many editions after its first appearance in 1967. Stoppard would always remember the arrival of the first Faber blue-and-pink jacket. He was at home with his parents in Milngavie, in Scotland, and he went round the house trying to find a book that would fit the jacket. He found one of Ken's fishing books, and propped it up inside the new cover, on his mother's dressing table, with two wing mirrors, to admire it back and front. He was twenty-nine, and looked back on this as the behaviour of a fifteen-year-old.

Everybody wanted to put on the new hit play. The 1968 programme note for *Enter a Free Man* noted that productions of *Rosencrantz and Guildenstern* 'are current or projected all over Europe, in New York, and in places as far apart as Tokyo and Buenos Aires'. Within a few years, it had been translated into twenty languages, including Czech, Danish, Dutch, French, German, Hebrew, Hungarian, Italian, Japanese, Russian, Slovak and Spanish. The German translator, who knew Beckett, told Stoppard that Beckett, after reading the play, said he was pleased that 'someone prefers understanding to imitating him'.

Within a year of the London opening, there were productions being put on in Paris, Vienna, Berlin, Munich, Stockholm and The Hague. In 1968 it was staged in twenty-three countries. In the next ten years, it had more than 250 productions worldwide. It won lots of prizes: the John Whiting Award, shared with Wole Soyinka; the *Plays and Players* London Theatre Critics Best Play award; the *Evening Standard* Most Promising Playwright award, with David Storey (for which Antonia Fraser was a judge). The Broadway producer David Merrick wanted him in New York immediately. An advance payment of $7,500 from Merrick went into his account in August 1967, and casting began at once for the New York production.

Success in the theatre was what he had wanted for years, and it changed his life. But the 'whirlwind' after *Rosencrantz* didn't go to his head. There was even an odd feeling of disappointment. Beforehand, all this would have seemed incredible, a spectacular leap. But once he had a hugely successful play on at the Old Vic, it didn't seem such an enormous jump after all. He was still the same person. Fame was very satisfying, and he took to it with ease. But admiration embarrassed him too. He was more temperamentally inclined to being a fan than a star. He hero-worshipped figures such as Tynan, or Olivier, or Hemingway, or Jagger. (And perhaps the flamboyance and the highly charged sexuality of these heroes of his suggested some wish fulfilment, in an essentially shy and decorous man.) He wasn't used to being treated like that himself.

He had work to do, some of it left over from before his triumph. There was no guarantee that this good fortune would last, and he needed, even more urgently now, so as not to disappoint his new admirers, to keep going as a playwright. After his birthday, he told his parents that he was distressed to be thirty: but 'at least I got a few things done just in time'.

Tynan wrote to Ingmar Bergman in June 1967, asking him to come to the National Theatre and direct Ibsen's *The Pretenders*, with Olivier and Gielgud, telling him they had asked Stoppard, 'the young English author whose *Rosencrantz & Guildenstern* has been a tremendous success', to do the translation. This came to nothing. Meanwhile, *Albert's Bridge* was broadcast in July, and won some prizes. An option had been bought on *A Walk on the Water* by a canny London-based American producer, Doris Abrahams, for £500 – a fortune for Stoppard in the pre-*Rosencrantz* days – and it was being cast, renamed first *Home and Dry* and then *Enter a Free*

Man. Michael Redgrave turned down the part because he thought he was too tall for George Riley, Richard Attenborough because he was filming.

Before *Rosencrantz and Guildenstern* went into rehearsal, the actor playing Rosencrantz had appeared in a Stoppard TV comedy, *Teeth*, which aired in the same 'Thirty Minute Theatre' slot in which *A Separate Peace* had appeared. In this cruel little farce for two male rivals and an interchangeable 'wife', which echoes *Malquist* in its harsh joking about cuckoldry, John Stride played the teeth-flashing, smug lover of the dentist's wife. Acting for the first time in a Stoppard play, John Wood played the vengeful dentist, who sends his wife's lover back out into the waiting room with green teeth and a terrible gap in his smile. The increasingly ominous duet between dentist and patient tosses clichés about debonairly, while the women in the waiting room talk like the women in the pub in Eliot's *Waste Land* ('got all her own teeth, has she?') about love and parting: 'I knew it was the end. And it was the real thing for me.'

John Wood had been a noticeable student actor at Oxford and a bit-part player at the Old Vic, in the 1950s, before he turned to television in the early 1960s. Dark, lanky, cutting and dry and witty, he was a brilliantly sardonic comedian, whose style was a perfect fit for Stoppard's cerebral game-playing and voluble male leads. After the dentistry, they became friends and theatrical soulmates. In the late 1960s, Stoppard would describe him as 'as close a friend as I'd got'. For many years he was Stoppard's actor of choice. As he said in a jokey double interview with Wood in 1975: 'I can't act, and I had to find someone who was tall, thin, neurotic and voluble to act for me . . . I write plays for somebody who can speak long speeches quickly.' 'Without appearing to do so,' added Wood. He played the harassed intellectual husband in the TV play *Another Moon Called Earth* in the summer of 1967, and told Stoppard that he badly wanted to play Guildenstern in the New York production of *Rosencrantz*. At that time Wood was so little known that he was considered a 'risk' for the part, but Stoppard thought 'his energy was the current that kept the play alive'. After that, and after a dazzling performance in Pinter's production of Joyce's play *Exiles*, he was snapped up by the RSC. Stoppard would write great, challenging parts for him: Henry Carr in *Travesties*, Ivanov in *Every Good*

Boy Deserves Favour, Housman in *The Invention of Love*. He would star in Stoppard's version of Schnitzler's *Undiscovered Country*, and returned to *Rosencrantz* as the Player for the 1987 New York revival. Stoppard knew he was a difficult man. Other actors, and directors, often found him arrogant and selfish, and he was a careless husband. But to Stoppard he was an actor of genius and an exhilarating friend.

Another Moon Called Earth pointed back to *Malquist* and ahead to *Jumpers*. Like *Malquist*, it is set on the day of a major national ceremony, the return of the 'lunanauts' from their journey to the moon. As in *Malquist*, a bedroom-bound adulterous wife, an unfaithful Penelope, provokes her weak intellectual husband, Bone, immersed in his writing of a logical history of the world, by receiving titillatingly close examinations from a visiting doctor. There is a learned hall porter (Crouch), a murder mystery, and an internal debate, as for Moon in *Malquist*, as to whether God's design for the world is random or determined. 'If it's all random, then what's the point?' For the anxious Penelope, the new fact of the moon landing increases the likelihood of randomness. If we are just 'another moon called Earth', then 'suddenly everything we live by – our rules – our good, our evil – our ideas of love, duty – all the things we've counted on as being absolute truths . . . they're all suddenly exposed as nothing more than local customs – nothing more . . .'

Stoppard would call it 'ProtoJumpers'. 'There's a thing I have about landing on the moon,' he told interviewers during *Jumpers*. 'It's much more than a location, it's a whole heritage of associations, poetic and religious. There are probably quite a few people around who'll go mad when the first man starts clumping around this symbol in size-ten boots.' 'The destruction of moon mythology and moon association in poetry and romance, superstition and everything, would be a sort of minute lobotomy performed on the human race.' The dottiness of Dotty, the moon landings and the philosophical argument over belief in God were wrapped together in his mind from the start.

Bone and Penelope blunder about in their comically hopeless marriage, with little bursts of pain and exasperation, in a practice run for Dotty and George in *Jumpers*.

Bone: You mean you're ill?

Penelope: . . . You don't care! All you can do is accuse me –

Bone: Really, Penelope, I never—

Penelope: How could you – ?

Bone: I make no accusations – I merely—

Penelope: You don't care that I'm not well—

The awful circularity and banality of this was close to the bone. Jose, already vulnerable, found her husband's sudden fame very difficult to manage. She felt isolated, and he was hoping that their growing friendship with John Wood and his wife, who also had a new baby, might provide 'mutual aid'. A few months after Oliver was born, in the summer of 1966, they had hired a nanny to help her look after the tiny, prematurely born baby. Alex Pyz, a young Polish girl from a hard-up Warsaw family, had come to London to learn English. She came for a few hours to Vincent Square every day after language school. She quickly became devoted to Ollie. She saw that Jose was in difficulties, but thought her clever and talented: she read a lot, she was a very good cook. And Tom was Alex's hero, then and for evermore. She couldn't travel with them to America because of her English classes, and she had to return to Poland at one point for family reasons. But Stoppard offered to house her and pay for her schooling if she came back. Alex would stay with them until the end of 1969. When she was away he kept in touch by letter, which included a teasing poem about her English – signed 'T Stoppard, fondest love, Jose & Ollie'.

> A yier ago tiday
> Myz Pyz juss
> arrifed on olliday
> for Chryzmuss
> (She spock like ziz all za time).
> But 345 days go avay
> till it vos Chrysmuss 1969
> so she az her olliday.

For vun yier she go to scoolz
and lerns er alphabat
and ridds Wirginia Voolv
and now she spicks like zat.

But life vizout er vood be so emty
vee invite Myz Alexandra Pyz
for Chryzmuss nincteen-senty.
(But she still spicks like ziz.)

Alex Pyz would say, sadly: 'I think Tom's fame was too big for Jose. She didn't know how to behave.' When the interviewers descended on the newly famous Stoppard, Jose would be seen in the photographs, lurking behind him and wearing an apron labelled 'Mrs Stoppard'. The high-achieving Miriam Moore-Robinson, by now a friend of Jose, saw this in the paper and shook her head: she thought it was not a good sign. And Jose was not happy. She found it hard to look after Ollie. She was beginning to drink a lot, at first a few beers, eventually as much as a bottle of Pernod a day. She began to anticipate being left behind, to test for the moment when he would abandon her, to be insecure about losing him (as he would put it) before he had any thought of being lost. If he had to go somewhere, she would at once ring up to find out if he was there. She became suspicious and possessive. All this mounted up gradually. There would be days of her staying in bed, of weeping or of sickness. In July 1967 he told Anthony Smith: 'Jose is unwell at the moment and I have promised a beckettian fortnight, nobody comes, nothing happens, nobody goes – after much tension of coming, happening and going.' Though he did not want to worry his parents, occasionally the problems slipped out: 'Jose not too well last week,' he would note.

They moved out of Vincent Square at last and into a much larger, more glamorous flat in South Kensington, in Queen's Gate Place, off the Gloucester Road. But, for rest and writing, they also rented Rosedene, an unpicturesque bungalow near Aylesbury, under the lee of Coombe Hill, in the Chilterns. It was in a nice setting, but very isolated, with limited public transport: at least one of them needed to learn to drive. Here, in the summer of 1967, Jose took to her bed, ill, tearful and depressed, and Stoppard, while looking after Ollie, wrote his next play. This was the play about the critics and the murder which he had long ago told Isabel he couldn't solve, and which was soon going to be called *The Real Inspector Hound*. As Bone keeps on saying to Penelope in *Another Moon*: 'I've got to get on with my work.'

It was a far cry from the Aylesbury bungalow to Broadway. Nor was it an easy run-up to Merrick's New York production of *Rosencrantz*. There were casting challenges – since of course the English cast had to stay put. The Player was to be the mellifluous-voiced actor Robert Eddison (Stoppard told Smith he would now write in 'numerous obscure and indeed impenetrable references to the invention of electricity'). John Wood and Brian Murray were cast as Guildenstern and Rosencrantz. The out-of-town run was to be in Washington. On 16 August, the Stoppards, with a young male nanny called Warren (who walked out on them in New York and had to be hastily replaced), embarked on the *Queen Mary*, for a nine-week stay in America. By coincidence, John Boorman, already a friend from *The Newcomers*, was also on board. He was going out for the opening of *Point Blank*. They spent five days crossing the Atlantic, playing chess, talking about their hopes and fears, both very apprehensive of how their first big hits were going to be received in the States. They were equally nervous but, as Boorman recollected, very pleased with themselves. They were 'a couple of swells'.

In Washington, Robert Eddison's beautifully spoken, Gielgudian performance, which Stoppard liked, bored the audience, and they kept walking out. David Merrick and Derek Goldby argued that for the even less tolerant New York audience, Eddison should be replaced by the understudy, Paul Hecht. This made Goldby very unpopular with the cast. For New York, the play had to be cut by forty-five minutes.

But when *Rosencrantz and Guildenstern Are Dead* opened at the Alvin Theater on Broadway on 16 October 1967, fronted up with a poster of the two of them as Hamlet's glove puppets, it was, as in London, an immediate hit. He couldn't bear to watch the first night. He and Jose went to a bar next door, 'smoking furiously and fretting'. Then the cast, in Broadway tradition, went to Sardi's, the theatre people's restaurant, to eat and wait for the reviews. When Stoppard walked in, the guests in the restaurant all clapped. The all-important Clive Barnes called him 'one of the finest English speaking writers of our stage'. Walter Kerr in the *New York Times* lavished him with praise. Jack Kroll in *Newsweek* called him 'the master comedian of ideas in the English language'. Only one critic, Robert Brustein, wrote a lacerating attack in the *New Republic*, deriding him as a 'theatrical parasite' and the play as entirely derivative, Beckett's *Godot* 'trivialised by a university wit'.

He was taken up, spoiled and pampered. To his great excitement, Marlene Dietrich came to see the play. Asked who he would most like to meet in New York, he opted for the legendary journalist Walter Winchell, and spent a strange night with the old man, being driven around in his car, which still had a siren on it, to crime hotspots in the city, and being met with some bewilderment by the young policemen, who had no idea who Winchell was. It crossed his mind, later, that he might write a play about him, but it didn't take shape. Admiring interviewers made their way to the luxurious apartment on Riverside Drive where the Stoppards were staying. Jerry Tallmer of the *Village Voice* remembered him sleeping on floors on his first visit to New York six years before. He was asked about his past, his family, his marriage, his writing plans, his modish clothes: a beautiful grey suit from the King's Road, a six-foot-long mustard-coloured scarf. Everyone thought him witty, lovable and charming. He told his parents that on television he 'did his Modest Young Englishman act'. Because this was New York, he was asked if he was Jewish. 'I don't know,' he replied. 'There must be some Jewish, somewhere.' He began to give his standard joking reply, lifted from a Jonathan Miller sketch in *Beyond the Fringe*: 'Well, I'm Jew-*ish*.'

Rosencrantz and Guildenstern ran on Broadway for 420 performances, transferring to the Eugene O'Neill Theatre in mid-run, and closing in October 1968. It had eight nominations for the Tony awards, the New York theatre industry's equivalents of the Oscars, and in April 1968 won four of them, including, most importantly, Best Play. The other nominees were Miller's *The Price*, Neil Simon's *Plaza Suite* and Peter Nichols's *A Day in the Death of Joe Egg* – which Stoppard admired greatly, though that was not much consolation to Nichols. The New York Drama Critics Circle gave it Best Play too. At the same time as the Tony awards, a production was put on by the American Conservatory Theatre company, newly established at the theatre in San Francisco by the combative, pioneering director William Ball. The production ran for three years, and it was the start of a long relationship between Stoppard and A.C.T. There was a production in Los Angeles, too, put on by another inventive West Coast theatre director, Gordon Davidson, for the Center Theatre group, at the Ahmanson Theatre, in the spring of 1969. When the play opened at the three-thousand-seater O'Keefe Center, in Toronto, in January 1969, it took $57,000 in its first week. The play and its author took America by storm, from coast to coast.

Rumours ran wild about how much he was earning, and how quickly, from this astonishing success. One gossip column reported that the New York production made him £100,000 within a few weeks, another that the play 'sent Stoppard's income soaring into five figures'. A 1969 interview reported that it had earned him £500,000. Kenneth Ewing told Tynan in 1977 that the published play had sold more than six hundred thousand copies in the English language alone, and that he would guess Stoppard had 'grossed well over three hundred thousand pounds'. During the early days of the New York production, a woman came reeling out onto the pavement outside the theatre, complaining that the play was incomprehensible. Bumping into the playwright, she said: 'What's it about?' And fed up at being asked this for the two hundredth time, he replied – or so legend has it: 'It's about to make me very rich.' In long retrospect, he would question whether he had said 'very'. Whatever the exact wording, the remark would be quoted back at him so often that he would come to regret it.

But it was true. On 11 July 1967, a few months into the run at the Old Vic, his bank balance was precisely £36 19s 6d. He was getting about £500 a month from the Old Vic. But he still had debts to friends and to his agent, and was paying for a press cutting service, a royalty to the Oxford Theatre Group, his commission to Fraser and Dunlop, and his taxes, as well as family and living expenses. From October onwards, once the New York earnings began to come in, his weekly earnings from the play began to hover around £2,500. His bank balance on 28 May 1968 was £2,857 10s 10d.

His brother Peter, at the Bristol firm of Touche Ross & Co., had been acting for him as his accountant since about 1965, and kept an overview of all his outgoings and income. In 1965 the biggest sums in any one month would be £250 from the BBC; and these were the outgoings:

> My rent is £3 per week.
> Electricity, gas, phone, £1 per week.
> Travel (professional) would be 10/- per week.
> Entertainment (drinks for agent, directors, etc) – £15 for the year.
> Stationery – £5 for the year.
> My trip abroad to France, Italy, Greece cost £150.

In January 1969, by contrast, he was writing to Peter:

> I see that on a net income of £40,754 we have put aside £35,652,
> leaving a *net*-net of about £5,000; £100 per week. My basic expenses,
> including housekeeping, Alex, standing orders, comes to about £60
> – but that's without clothes, petrol, hired cars, etc! So I'm obviously
> spending to my limits at least. No comment.

Peter made sure that there would be 'discipline' in this spending, and put an estimated tax liability aside in a separate account, so that his brother would never forget about the tax he was going to have to pay. Peter recognised that he wanted to spend money on 'things of the moment', 'nice interesting things' like a picture or a painted screen or a first edition.

He had never had real money before, but he knew what he wanted to do with it. He paid off his debts with, as he put it to Anthony Smith, an 'embarras de nouveau riche'. Now *he* could afford to lend money to friends in need, giving a £300 loan to John Wood in November 1967. He started up a regular fund of £50 a month under the name of 'Jose Boot and Oliver Moon'. He gave gifts to all the family in early 1968 when the Tony awards hugely boosted box-office sales: £75 each to Bobby and Ken, £20 to his half-brother Richard, £10 to Fiona, £100 to Peter and his family. Not wanting to seem patronising, he wrote delicately to Peter: 'It is conceivable that there is something offensive in my dropping you a hundred quid in this soulless manner – like an outsize tip – but I don't intend to make a habit of it – the Tony is a once-only thing, so it's a symbolically good prize to give away to family.' His regular expenses began to include car hire, tickets for shows (*HAIR!*), wine and cigarette orders from Victoria Wine, and an account at Hatchards bookshop – which he described to Peter as 'fantasy fulfilled'. For his journey to America he bought new luggage (cabin trunk, set of six suitcases), a dinner jacket, and evening clothes for Jose. Short, luxurious holidays in destinations he would not have dreamed of before – Madeira, the Bahamas, Bermuda, Florida – began at the time of the New York and LA trips. When he went to the West Coast he bought, among other things, a 1910 Tiffany-style table lamp ('unbelievably beautiful to my eyes'). Once he had learned to drive, he bought a BMW car, and they began to look for a house in the country. Most pleasurably, he bought paintings, books and clothes. He started bidding at Sotheby's sales for twentieth-century items like the manuscript of Waugh's *Scoop*, a Wilde letter, Hemingway first editions, a first edition of *The Waste Land*, a run of the magazine *Transition* and a complete set of *Horizon* magazine. He tried for a first edition of *Ulysses* in December 1969, which he hoped to get for about £150, but it went to America for £700. This was the start of a long passion for book-collecting.

He could indulge a taste for dandyism, at exactly the time when the boutiques and designers of Carnaby Street and the King's Road were catering for exhibitionist, androgynous modes. Men's fashions, like women's, were all about colour, velvets, flares, frills, cords, scarves, tassels, waistcoats, stripes. Mick Jagger's ruffles, the Beatles on the *Sergeant Pepper* cover, Nureyev's flowing, unbuttoned shirts, Pink Floyd's floral jackets and chiffon cravats, David Warner's long scarf as Hamlet, all set the fashions for modish men, a cross between Regency bucks and Ronald Firbank-style aesthetes. These styles suited him perfectly. Interviewers described him as wearing 'mod gear of his own design'.

Before his trip to New York, he went to Mr Fish, whose extremely desirable label read 'PECULIAR TO MR FISH', and was measured for two tobacco-coloured suits with orange-blue linings (it turned out they didn't fit). He bought seersucker shirts from the trendy shirt-makers Deborah & Clare in Beauchamp Place, with vertical stripes or little flower patterns. He bought silk scarves and a long Napoleonic coat from Biba. Miriam Moore-Robinson was struck by one particular outfit of his in the late sixties, which she thought a vision of joyful effervescence, and which consisted of 'tomato-coloured elephant-cord trousers, a granddad T-shirt with sleeves to the elbows in the same colour, a tomato and white silk scarf threaded through the trousers, and red leather slip-on shoes from Chelsea Cobbler'. A couple of years later, en route to New York again, he wore a pair of very beautiful Cuban-heeled canvas shoes made by Mr Sid, which were light tan, spattered irregularly with dark tan stars like the stars on the American flag. In New York he bought two more pairs from a Puerto Rican shop on 45th Street and Broadway. One pair was in lime green and darker green, the other pair was in bright Barbie pink. He went to the famous bootmaker in St James's, John Lobb, and had a pair of brown-and-black shoes made for him, which turned out to be as uncomfortable as they were expensive, even after they had been specially stretched. Looking back, he would attribute his passion for fancy shoes to one of his childhood books, Budd Schulberg's 1941 rags-to-riches story of an East Side Jewish kid turned Hollywood mogul, *What Makes Sammy Run*, who splashes out on shoes when he becomes a success.

It was a big change from the belted raincoats, black polo necks and trilby hats of his Bristol years. And in retrospect all this peacockery seemed silly, as though the wrong things had become important. Why wasn't he living a life of austerity and dedication, like a writer in a George Gissing novel? All the same, it was fun to have money to spend, and fun to dazzle and be eye-catching. As he said of himself, ruefully, decades later: 'I clearly had an exhibitionist streak in me in spite of being basically shy.'

In the run-up to the birth, they rented a flat in St James's Gardens, and he practised the drive to the hospital (he had only just passed his driving test, on a second attempt, in June). Jose gave birth on 20 September 1969, to a son, Barnaby, always called Barnie (later, Barny), at Queen Mary's Hospital in Roehampton. It was a much easier birth than her first, because she had an epidural to ease the pain. He wrote a piece for *Vogue* about the birth, jokily describing himself sitting by the bedside holding his wife's hand while immersed in a book about Einstein's theory of relativity – part of his homework for *Jumpers*. But by the time that piece was published, the marriage was over, and he was living with Miriam.

Her own marriage had not been going well, either. Miri and Piri, as their friends called them, had met in Newcastle, when she was in her twenties (she was born on 12 May 1937), and married in September 1962. Miriam Stern's family were working-class Orthodox Jews, her mother a convert. Her father, Sidney Stern, was a male nurse, her mother Jenny was a dinner lady. They were strong-willed, principled parents. She was brought up with a powerful work ethic and a resolve to be as successful as any man could be. As a medical student at Durham, she had been told that girls would get nowhere in the medical profession. To prove her point, she took the postgraduate MRCP (Membership of the Royal College of Physicians diploma) at Newcastle, specialising in dermatology, and got the top marks in the UK. Peter Moore-Robinson, a conscientious objector who had gone to jail for not doing his National Service, was training to be a vet. Her orthodox father was aghast that she was marrying a Quaker.

They moved to Bristol for Peter to study at the veterinary school, while she practised at the Bristol Royal Infirmary and worked in a clinical chemistry lab, getting to know the Smiths and through them the Stoppards. She decided to move out of medical research and into industry. She had an outstanding CV, 'at twenty-seven, the youngest doctor to have an MD and an MRCP'. When she got her job with the pharmaceuticals company Syntex in Maidenhead, they moved to Marlow. She had known for a long time that her marriage was a mistake. But she had her mother's caution always in her head, that 'as you make your bed you must lie there'. And she was intent on her career, working her way up to be managing director at Syntex, travelling all over the world giving presentations. (Peter's work, too, involved a great deal of travel.) She soon moved into the world of popular medicine, giving interviews, appearing on radio and TV, writing 'how-to' books about motherhood and health, and becoming one of the best-known medical gurus in the country. But that was to come. When she began to know Stoppard well, she was a busy, professional, ambitious doctor and businesswoman. She came across, in her early thirties, as a small, dark, expressive, vivid bundle of energy, intensely dynamic and extremely competent.

Literature and the theatre, though, were not her world, and her shyness of Stoppard continued, while they were seeing each other occasionally as a foursome. That shyness began to diminish as Miriam became closer to Jose, and more aware of their troubles. On one night, Jose rang her and asked her to come round at once. She had been drinking, and was threatening to take an overdose of pills. The live-in nanny was asleep; Stoppard was in London. Miriam got in her car and drove the short distance from Marlow to Bourne End. Miriam got Jose to bed and stayed in the house until he got back, very late. She asked him angrily how he could leave his wife in such a state. They sat in the sitting room, he very subdued. 'What kind of household are you running,' she asked him, 'if you don't know your wife is making these cries for help?' He was quiet, and apologetic, and said he was indebted to her. They began to talk about her work. Not looking at her, he said: 'You're the most high-powered woman I know.'

After that there was a shift; he began to be attracted, as much by her independence and professionalism as by her energy and sexuality. He made signals towards her. She smoked menthol cigarettes (later, she would become a spirited polemicist against smoking) and, after one visit to River Thatch, she saw as she was saying goodbye that he'd left a pack of two hundred on her car seat. She looked at him. 'Smoke more cigarettes, but put out longer stubs,' he said. (That was his own lifelong smoking method.) She began to feel that 'the air was crackling' between them. They were talking, on one occasion, about Ken Tynan. Stoppard was praising Kathleen Tynan, saying, with feeling: she lets Ken get on with his work, she is independent, she has a life of her own. Miriam thought: 'Ah, that's

what you have to be, to be looked upon with favour by Tom Stoppard.'
Rehearsals were going on for the *Rosencrantz* cast changes, and, in a group
of friends, he said he was going to see the opening performance by the
new cast. Do you sit in the audience? someone asked. 'I usually stand at
the back,' he said, and looked at Miriam. She read it as a summons, and
went to find him there.

After Barny's birth, Jose went on a 'crash diet' in advance of a holiday,
and he bought her an expensive slimming machine, which she hardly used.
They went to the Bahamas, in January 1970, joined by Kenneth Ewing
and by Peter and Lesley, and then to New York for a few days of business
meetings. The trip was unhappy and chaotic. Jose found travelling with
Ollie and the baby intolerable. There was a succession of nannies, and
many health problems. Dentists and doctors were summoned, hotels were
changed. Peter and Lesley observed the turbulence with dismay. It seemed
to them that Jose was incapable of looking after the children, and in a state
of desperate tension.

Back from New York, in the spring of 1970, Stoppard was in rehearsal
for a new play, *After Magritte*. In early April, he and Jose went to look at
a large, expensive house in Oxfordshire, with a view to moving; but the
prospect of taking it on felt like the last straw. 'I mean with a house like
that,' he wrote to Peter, 'you've got to *stay* married.' He was in love with
Miriam, and they were meeting secretly and writing love letters to each
other, in a state of 'fearful ecstatic excitement'. Looking back on these letters, he felt he had patronised her and undervalued her ambitions, and
that she had 'put him on a marble pedestal'.

She remembered one assignation, in a car park in Maidenhead, when
he said: 'I can't go on doing this.' Sometimes it was she who would say it
couldn't go on, and he would say to her – it was his 'tag-line' – 'It's all right,
really.' There may have been some opportunities for meeting provided by
friends from Bristol years, now neighbours in Chorleywood, Tim Corrie
(then working for Paramount) and his wife Hélène, who had known Miriam
well in Bristol, and the theatre director Geoffrey Reeves and his wife Rose.

By early summer, he had made his mind up, whatever the cost, 'to leave
River Thatch for good'. He planned to go while Miriam was away on a

work trip, so that it would be 'less messy'. But on Friday 17 July, in a cliché
of adultery that would suit a conventional, old-fashioned play, Jose – as he
remembered it – went through everything in his study and found Miriam's
love letters. It was the middle of the day; he was in town, at the Café Royal,
having lunch with Ned Sherrin. Jose summoned Miriam by phone from
work. Miriam was panic-stricken. She rang the Café Royal before she set
out and asked the waiter to page him with a message, which read: 'Jose has
found the letters.' He told Sherrin he had to leave, and what had happened;
Sherrin, a good friend, did not breathe a word.

Miriam found Jose cutting up the letters with scissors, weeping and
accusing her of betrayal. She told Miriam that he would never leave her
and the children, that Miriam had done a dreadful thing and would find
herself alone. Miriam believed her: why should he leave his family for her?
The scene went on for an hour and a half, the time it took him to drive
there from London. He came in, went over to Miriam, touched her knee
and said: 'It's all right.' And he dropped into her lap a little Woolworth's
key ring. She thought, 'It's not all right, what does he mean!' But as the
scene continued, he made it clear to them both that he had already been
planning to leave. 'And that', as he would say, looking back, 'was that.'

He asked Miriam not to go home – Peter was away, working in Cuba,
but he didn't want her to go back to their house – and sent her to the big
luxurious pub by the Thames in Marlow, the Compleat Angler. She waited
for him there. The Corries, in Chorleywood, remembered them arriving
in separate cars on a Sunday night, two days later. According to them, his
entrance line was: 'Isn't it wonderful, I'm with Miriam'; and hers was: 'Isn't
it wonderful, darlings, we're together.' They stayed there for a week, most
of that time in bed, and the Corries brought them cups of tea. Perhaps this
is a true story, perhaps an exaggerated memory, but, as other onlookers
and friends would say of their relationship, there was no missing its erotic
excitement and joy.

Peter flew back from Cuba, and Miriam met him at the airport and
drove him home. On the M4, she pulled up and told him she was leaving
him. 'Who for?' he responded. When she told him, he said: 'That's *great!*'
Because she viewed her husband as a socially ambitious lioniser, she took

it that he was pleased she was running away with someone so famous. But he also had his own relationships, and might have been glad to be freed. They went straight to see Stoppard, and the two men embraced each other. Peter Moore-Robinson divorced Miriam for adultery on 2 October, citing Stoppard as co-respondent, and the divorce was granted 'notwithstanding his own adultery committed during the said marriage'. He married twice more, became extremely wealthy through working in pharmaceuticals, and lived mainly in France.

Stoppard felt huge relief, and huge anxiety. Plans had rapidly to be made. The boys – Ollie now four, and Barny about ten months old – were to be visited every day. Jose's doctors' bills and support needed to be dealt with at once: careful systems for her maintenance were put in place from the start. River Thatch had to be put on the market – and was sold by the end of the year. Jose, with no one to depend on except her sister and her aunt and uncle, Gladys and Jim, went first to Somerset, then to a furnished flat in West Kensington, and eventually to a one-bedroom flat in Hemel Hempstead, near St Albans. The lovers too needed a place to live. Over the next two years they took a series of short rentals in the country, within easy reach of Miriam's job in Maidenhead. They started their lives together, in August 1970, in Telford Cottage, in Cookham Dean, which he had found through friends. She would always remember a thatched cottage, a green lawn, the sun shining on the lawn, the sound of the Beatles singing 'Here Comes the Sun', and feeling: 'This is the start of a new life.'

He wrote to Bobby (but among the hundreds of letters of his that she kept, this one has not survived), and then to Peter, the day after the break-up: 'A painful letter. I've left Jose.' He told his brother, who was probably not surprised, that 'only Ollie has kept me there for the past three years'. He said that he hadn't 'gone off with the au-pair' but with 'a 33-year-old doctor (married) whom I have known on and off for about five years'. His plans for leaving, he said, had been short-circuited by Jose's finding the letters: 'So here we are.' He would be seeing the children every day. He warned Peter he would probably be getting 'a bad phone call from Mum'. And he ended with a statement about himself: 'Look – however horrible things get, it's better than just carrying on in a resigned way married to someone I don't love, and not working, etc. *I had to change my life* – it's the only one I've got as far as I know and I don't believe in self-sacrifice.'

The greatest difficulty was over the boys. He was worried about their being brought up by Jose. Ollie learned in later years that Jose had threatened to drown them in the bath – though she would always tell the boys she never meant it. But that was an expression of her state of mind at the time. Not surprisingly, he wanted them to be with him and Miriam. But he did not feel he could impose this on Miriam – and he was acutely aware of Jose's maternal rights, and her feelings. He asked Miriam: how did she see their future? What would she most like it to be? She replied: I should like us to have Oliver and Barnaby with us. Others, including Jose's psychiatrist, advised that it would be better for the boys. On 22 August, he wrote to tell his parents that the boys were with them. (Jose may have been in hospital again at this point.) He told them: 'I simply know that they will be safer and happier with me and Miriam – it's a sort of ultimate cruelty (to Jose) for an ultimate good (the children's) and having come to that decision, that it's necessary, I intend to stand by it.' Bobby met Miriam a couple of weeks later, and he told Peter that he thought the meeting went very well. She was quickly reconciled to the change in her son's life: she would have seen what the problems were, and very soon he was writing home openly and happily about Miriam's career, her successes and their life together.

Miriam's life completely changed. 'One day I was a working woman with a demanding job as head of research in the pharmaceutical industry. And the next day I was the same woman but I had two babies.' She dedicated herself at once to being the best possible stepmother, in the same spirit of determination and perfectionism that made her want to be the best at her job. For Jose, Miriam taking her children was another act of betrayal, and she resisted it.

They were going to need a bigger house. In September Miriam found the Gatehouse, Gully Farm, part of the Hedsor Park estate, just outside Taplow. As he was driving there with her for the first time, down the long drive through Hedsor Park, he said: 'Miri, I said a house that would accommodate us, not *Versailles*.' This next temporary stay did indeed have much larger rooms, and a summerhouse in the garden for daytime work. His indoor study was in the big bedroom; he wrote into the small hours while she slept. Everything is *really* lovely here, he told his mother. 'We are as happy as it's possible to be . . . everything is well organised and I seem to have twice as many hours in the day as before.' The boys went twice a week, with their nanny, to Jose. Miriam wanted Alex Pyz to come back from Poland, but she declined.

A formal application for custody needed to be made. He would have to fight his case. He set about asking family, friends and colleagues who knew him well and had observed the marriage over many years to write depositions. Some, like Kenneth Ewing, were not willing to do so. Some, like Alex Pyz and the Corries, did so with reluctance, but feeling it was the right course; Alex said, sadly, 'I thought Tom would be the better father.' Friends – Anthony Smith, Val Lorraine, John Wood – were called on. There were clinical testimonies from the doctors and psychiatrist who had been looking after Jose. Family members gave their accounts. Bobby wrote some cautious notes about Jose, but he told Peter they were not very help-ful, 'except that they bear out the wealth of others' evidence.' He warned his mother, to avoid her painful disappointment, that he was not optimis-tic about getting custody. Peter, in a long, detailed, troubled account to the lawyers, Harbottle and Lewis, described Jose's inability to take care of the children over a long period of time. Tellingly, Jose's aunt Gladys wrote, so there were testimonies from her family too. The custody hearing took place on 28 October, three weeks after Miriam's divorce. Soon after, River Thatch was sold, and Jose moved out. They had to wait till 18 March to receive the result of the application, which went in his favour. Jose, 'the Petitioner', was granted 'reasonable access to the said children'.

Jose's version of events, told and retold to her sons as they were growing up, like a war story, was that Miriam had come as a friend and treacher-ously snatched away her husband because he was 'a rich successful man'. She used to say that Miriam had her committed to a lunatic asylum so that she could take her children. She often said that she should have asked for more money, that she had done badly out of the divorce. But, as Barny put it bluntly long afterwards, 'my mother was off the rails'. Both sons described their mother as irrational, fragile and disturbed. She became intensely religious – 'properly batty religious' as Ollie put it – and there were hallucinatory episodes. In later years, after much struggle, she gave up drinking, and would come to acknowledge, in a generous letter of gratitude to Miriam, that it had been the right thing for the boys to be brought up by her, and that she had not been fit to do so at the time. But in Ollie's view, she never got over it.

The new life, with two large-scale careers, two small children, nannies, house-hunting, a great deal of travelling, socialising, friendships, treats and adventures, at once filled up to the brim – and cost money. Maintenance payments came to about £300 a month. They had their portraits painted (in November 1970), by an artist called Ottilie Tolansky, at a cost of £340: 'We are very thrilled . . . both by the idea of having portraits in oils for posterity and by the paintings themselves.' For 'sentimental' reasons, he bought Miriam a 'big lump of amethyst' to hang on her symbolic key ring. He thought he might have to sell his first edition of *The Waste Land* to pay for it.

He was enjoying the big scale of Miriam's life and ambitions, as much as their personal life together. He told Peter in September that they had just spent a day in Durham, with 'Miriam lecturing impressively', followed by lunch with her parents in Newcastle. 'She had a 15-minute interview on the radio. I think I'm going to end up being slightly known as her husband.'

By June 1971, Miriam was pregnant, and *Jumpers* was nearly done. He wrote an awkward letter to Jose which moved quickly on from Miriam's news ('I meant to tell you but forgot that Miriam was having a baby') to talking about the play: 'Everybody who read it found it mystifying, Ken Tynan wanted me to cut my favourite speech.' When Miriam was three months pregnant they took an exciting trip in September to Tehran, to see Peter Brook's production of *Orghast*. It was a version of the Prometheus myth, with a new language invented by Ted Hughes, which fascinated him, staged at Persepolis from the end of August. Stoppard wrote up an interview with Hughes in October, for the *Times Literary Supplement*, describing *Orghast* as the most experimental use of language one could imagine. (A slight friendship developed, centred mainly on fishing.) As they walked across the desert, Miriam was wearing a kaftan – dramatic and colourful maternity wear, just right for this trip – which billowed out around her. He said: 'It's like following Gertrude Stein!'

Over the autumn and winter, while *Jumpers* was in rehearsal, they moved again, to High Barns, a house in a suburban village, Touchen End, near Maidenhead. Miriam's child was due in March, and she was looking for a permanent home for them to nest in. Early in 1972, Tom and Jose Stoppard divorced each other. On 31 January, Sir George Baker, presiding over the High Court Family Division, issued a decree nisi to Tom Stoppard, aged thirty-four, and to Jose Stoppard, aged thirty-one. He said that the decrees could be made absolute in a week, instead of the usual two months, so that (as Stoppard's old paper, the Bristol *Western Daily Press* reported) 'Stoppard can marry a doctor before their child is born in March.'

On 2 February, *Jumpers* had its first night at the National Theatre. On 8 February, the decrees became absolute. Jose's was granted because of her husband's adultery. His was granted because of the breakdown of the marriage in 1970: 'His wife behaved in such a way that Mr Stoppard could not reasonably be expected to continue to live with her.' Alimony was agreed at £3,000 a year, until Jose married again, or for life. Neither petition was contested. The *Daily Mirror* reported: 'Playwright Tom gets quickie divorce.'

Three days later, on 11 February 1972, at the Registry Office in Maidenhead, Thomas Stoppard (writer, previous marriage dissolved, father's name Eugen Sträussler, deceased) married Miriam Moore-Robinson (doctor, previous marriage dissolved, father's name Sidney Stern, nurse). Miriam was enormously pregnant. Ollie, who was nearly six, came in his school uniform. He was wearing his wellington boots, as his shoes couldn't be found that day; he sat on a chair, swinging his feet in his wellies, and eating an apple, while his father got married again. There was no honeymoon: they both went straight back to work, and Miriam went on working to the last possible moment. On 7 March, she was at her office in the morning, and went into hospital in the afternoon for the birth of their first child, William, in Westminster Hospital. He was a tiny baby, and one of Miriam's new friends, Marigold Johnson, vividly remembered her exclaiming dramatically over him a few months later: 'Look at him, he's *tiny*, I was working so hard, I starved him in the womb, and he's eaten all his fingernails!'

At first, relations with Jose, and arrangements for the boys, were difficult. Gradually, they became more routine and accepted. Stoppard was scrupulous over the maintenance, and responded to her needs. He paid for her rent, her car and her medical expenses. There would be many letters from Jose over the next twenty-five years, before long friendly and mild in tone, asking for help with holidays, or redecoration, or travel expenses, or doctors' bills, in addition to the regular payments he made her. He always responded.

But in the first two years after the break-up, the need for extra income, and the overriding desire to clear space for his work, made him extremely anxious in the middle of the new happiness, as his letters to his brother showed in the autumn of 1970: 'I want to keep at the work, having now had a quarter of the time I've given myself to finish the play [*Jumpers*]; I have not done a quarter of the work, of course . . . but it gets easier as it goes on, or less difficult.' He needed to take on a lucrative project quickly, but nothing seemed right for him at the moment except a screenplay of *Galileo* he was working on. He did bits of journalism for the money, like some *Observer* TV reviews, which gave him the chance to say what he loathed (Engelbert Humperdinck, wrestling, Simon Dee, *The Golden Shot*, *This Is Your Life*, *Hawaii Five-O*) and what he enjoyed. *Dad's Army*, *Z Cars*, *Pot Black*, *The Family of Man*, *Tom and Jerry*, *Late Night Line-up*, *Top of the Pops*, Somerset Maugham.

Meanwhile, he was 'nibbling' at his play. He told Peter:

I really itch to do it and exclude all else till it's done. I am getting a
bit depressed by not having a new play imminent, and every time
I open a paper I read about new plays by playwrights coming up
behind me and I'm feeling competitive (and losing). This is bad
for my morale. Since there is such a time-gap between a play being
finished and being produced, I feel that every week counts . . . This

lack of exposure is bad in every way. In fact I really ought to write an interim play, short, TV or radio perhaps, simultaneously with whatever longer project I take on, just to have something seen and heard within six months. [For *Jumpers*] I need to read for a month and write solidly for three or four . . .

Miriam wanted to make everything as easy as possible for him. There was one more short-term rental after Will was born, in a cottage near Binfield, twenty minutes from Maidenhead. But she had had enough of moving around – they were like a family of gypsies. A few months after Will's birth, she was pregnant again, and determined to have her second baby in their own house. Stoppard told her he had a fantasy of an elegant Georgian mansion. But the home she found for them was a large, rather ugly white pebble-dash Victorian house, with mock-Tudor beams going up to pointed roofs and a pillared porch. It was next to a roundabout with a pub on it, in Iver Heath. When she first took him to see it, he didn't even want to get out of the car. But inside looked better. Delightedly, he told an interviewer: 'It's the first house I ever lived in where the best room is going to be the room where I work.' Everything was set up around his writing: as he said, affectionately and ironically: 'Miriam has this exaggerated respect for what I do.' They moved into Fernleigh, on Wood Lane, in September 1972, and would live there for seven years.

Iver Heath, near Slough, the A40, the M4 and Pinewood Studios, was an ideal location. Miriam could get to Maidenhead in half an hour; it was a quick drive to London. Fernleigh was a solid, spacious house with lots of room for a family, and huge gardens. Downstairs there was a grand front room which nobody ever used, a tiny study or den for Miriam, a sitting room where they watched TV together, a breakfast room and a big kitchen with a round table, the main gathering place. There was a playroom for the boys, a billiard room, and an enormous study with diamond lead-pane windows overlooking the garden, two desks, one with cubby-holes, two walls of books and a Charles Eames chair and footstool. The study door was always open and the boys could always go in and out; usually it was in a state of 'organised chaos'.

Upstairs, a wide landing gave onto the main bedroom, with a balcony, a bathroom each and a dressing room, and the rooms for the children and an ever-changing series of nannies. The gardens, where the boys would spend a great deal of their time, had a towering leylandii tree, a tennis court, an orchard, a wilderness with an old pond, and gigantic rhododendron bushes. The gradual doing-up of Fernleigh was described in detail to his parents, as in: 'Today a man has knocked a door through the way from the back hall into the "playroom" . . . We spent much of the weekend trying to strip old wax off the wood block floors . . . the sitting room is now blue, bedroom yellow and white, bathroom blue and brown!'

The new life with Miriam was not all smooth going. As always, he needed to be alone for his work, and to get on with it when he needed to, ruthlessly. Miriam respected that single-mindedness. She made it clear to him and to his friends that she understood what it meant to be a playwright's wife. On her first meeting with Trevor Nunn, at the bar at the Aldwych Theatre, he took her aside and said to her: 'You will look after him, won't you?' She replied: 'Well, yeah, if he wants to write *Swinging from the Rafters*, I'll get rafters and a swing.'

But his capacity for withdrawing and reserve, for holding the other person at bay, and for not always showing sympathy when sympathy was needed, however generous and affectionate his feelings might be, remained. And he underestimated how startling and new the world of theatre was for her. So relieved was he to be with someone independent, charismatic and competent – and someone who was not drinking anything more than the odd glass of Cinzano, though even that would make him nervous – that he failed to realise, in the early days, how out of place she sometimes felt with his friends.

He wanted her to go out with him, and to show her off. He bought her a height-of-fashion Thea Porter outfit for party-going. Early on in their life together, he summoned her back from a conference in Berlin, so that she would go with him to one of Ken Tynan's parties. She remembered the talk there between Tynan and Roman Polanski and Ryan O'Neal. 'Where have I come to?' she asked herself, the doctor and businesswoman from Maidenhead. 'Which planet am I on?' Invitations would come for 'Tom

Stoppard and guest'. When they got to the party, he would plunge into the crowd and leave her on her own, to hold her own. People would ask her who she was, and she would say: 'And guest.' 'What do you do?' they would ask. When she said she was a doctor, their eyes glazed over. She had no reference points for their conversation about actors and new productions. On the way home, she would reproach him: 'You left me to sink or swim!' Instead of replying, 'Oh Christ, yes, I'm so sorry, next time I'll keep you under my wing,' he would say, 'What is your problem? You're more brilliant than any of them – of course you can talk to them.'

She began to understand how Jose had suffered from his fame and success; she too was feeling non-existent, worthless, in this new world. She even thought, at times, of leaving. But after two years of going home weeping from the parties, she decided to assert herself. When they asked her what she did, she asked them about their ailments. Immediately they all wanted to confide in her about their problems, physical and psychological. She remembered a very stylish party at the Oliviers', in the Barbican, with everyone dressed to the nines. Jonathan Miller was holding court on the floor. 'Well, he's a doctor,' she thought. 'And I'm another doctor.'

In this time of dramatic change, it might have been expected that less work would get done: and certainly there was a long five-year gap between *Rosencrantz* and the next production of a full-length play. But good work was compulsory and essential for his life, and the reasons for working well were multiplying. In the early 1970s, he embarked on an unconventional new theatrical collaboration which resulted, among other productions, in *After Magritte*. All through 1970, he worked on his historical screenplay of the story of Galileo. At the same time he was reading philosophy and physics for *Jumpers*. He wrote it over two years and was then involved in rehearsals; it opened in February 1972. When it was published, four months later, in June, it was dedicated to Miriam.

A few months after his divorce, the opening of *Jumpers* and the birth of William, he was in New York for a week, in the hot August summer, looking in on rehearsals of Theatre Four's double bill of *After Magritte* and *The Real Inspector Hound*, and discussing a New York production of

Jumpers with the producer David Merrick. He was doing some research for his next play, an idea about Lenin and Tristan Tzara and Joyce all being in Zurich at the same time during the First World War. He described the last two years of his life, freely and good-humouredly, in an interview for the *New York Post* with Jerry Tallmer, whom he had known since his first visit to the States and the *Village Voice*, twelve years before. He described what had been going on since he started *Jumpers*: 'I left Jose and I bought and sold houses and was divorced and was in and out of courts on the custody case and all this money going to lawyers.' Then there was a pause while he 'collected himself'. 'Two Years Passed', he said, as if reading a stage direction. He went back to work on *Jumpers* in November 1970 and finished it in August 1971. He talked about Miriam. 'She loves being a mother . . . And does all her work at the same time, five full days a week at the office. I don't know how the hell she does it, really. I suppose me working at home helps.' He described the move to Fernleigh, and his ideas for his next play. Ending the interview, on his way back to rehearsal, he said: 'I feel much better about myself. I have an enormous urge to do a lot of work now.'

'Tom Stoppard Doesn't Know'

> They never quite *understand* what it is they've seen. They probably
> wouldn't even agree on what it was.

Two men are driving along in a car. Suddenly, from the corner of their
eye, they see a man in pyjamas, with his chin covered in shaving foam,
and no shoes on, carrying what could be a football under his arm. No,
it's a tortoise. No, it's a peacock! The sight flashes by in about five-eighths
of a second. 'What the hell's *that*?' says one of the men in the car. 'I don't
know!' says the other. They never see it again. They never quite *understand*
what it is they've seen. They probably wouldn't even agree on what it was.
The writer doesn't want to write about the man, or the peacock. He wants
to write about the uncertainty of the witnesses. He is in the position of the
man who says: 'I don't know!'

This story, with variants, got into Stoppard's mind in about 1970, and
then became a favourite. In a lecture given at Notre Dame University in
1971, he referred to it as something he'd been told a couple of years before.
He would tell it many times after that, always slightly differently, but
always with the main story intact. The man, who is sometimes described
as living nearby in Little Marlow, collects peacocks – which tend to wander off, when they are newly acquired. He is shaving in his pyjamas, looks
out of the window, and sees one going out of his garden gate (or jumping
over the garden hedge). He rushes out of the house, just as he is, follows
and scoops up the peacock, and in that moment the car goes by. As he tells
the story, Stoppard acts it out, scooping up the imaginary peacock, and
then doing the 'Whoosh!' of the car zooming past, and then whipping his
head round in amazement to become the bewildered, fleeting witnesses.
It always gets a huge laugh.

Jokingly, it says what he wants to say about the uncertainty of the writer,
the impossibility of knowing anything definitely, the unpredictability of
the world, and the thin line between unreal absurdity and everyday life. It

also describes the situation of some of his characters: 'So when I'm asked what I write about, [I say] there are these two people in Elsinore, and they don't know why they are there . . .' 'What was *that*?' one asks the other. 'I don't know . . .' says the other, in perpetuity. *Rosencrantz*, he would sometimes say, was *Hamlet* as viewed by 'two people driving past Elsinore'.

His first use of the story was in *After Magritte*, written at the end of 1969 and put on in 1970, in unlikely circumstances. The strangeness of the play matched the oddity of its first staging. *After Magritte* was time off from the big exposure of the next National Theatre play, a small-scale *jeu d'esprit* which could be as reckless and playful as he liked.

It was Stoppard's first introduction to Ed Berman, a forceful, maverick character in London's anti-establishment theatre scene of the late 1960s and early 1970s. Variously described as a 'cigar-chomping American', a 'wild card', a 'zany visionary and astute self-publicist' and (by Stoppard) as the lookalike of a Boyar in *Ivan the Terrible*, Berman was a few years younger than Stoppard. He had jumped out of a conventional American upbringing (Harvard, Rhodes scholarship to Oxford), via anti-Vietnam War and Civil Rights activities, into community work in deprived areas of inner London. In the radical theatre of the time – Charles Marowitz's Shakespearean rewrites at the Open Space, Heathcote Williams's *AC/DC* (his attack on received attitudes to mental illness), the Royal Court's Theatre Upstairs, Wesker's Centre 42, The Roundhouse – Berman was focused on audience involvement and game-playing as an educational tool. He was a great breaker of rules. Centre 42's idea that 'the masses' should be lured into traditional theatres was not his way. Berman drove a 'Fun Art Bus' onto a council estate, rented tiny off-off-West End venues for short experimental plays, took over wastelands near railway lines and turned them into 'City Farms' and community gardens, and brought his 'Inter-Active Creative Game' methods to racially diverse urban kids – as with a show called 'Beowulf and the Dragon', staged on a canal boat in Paddington. Stoppard described him (in 1976) as dividing his time 'between the production company and work in schools, youth clubs, mental hospitals, community centres, playgrounds, remand homes and the streets'.

From 1968 and all through the 1970s, 'Inter-Action' was the umbrella name for these ventures. Ed Berman, as the guiding spirit of Inter-Action, called himself Professor R. L. Dogg. His group of actors – including some notable talents like Patrick Barlow, later one half of the National Theatre of Brent, Geoff Hoyle, a remarkable mime, the academic theatre-workshop creator Clive Barker, and the actors Stephen Moore and Prunella Scales – were known as Dogg's Troupe. When Stoppard got to know Berman, he asked him about his pseudonym. Berman explained it was so that when his collected poems were eventually catalogued, they would appear under the entry: 'Dogg, R. L.' Stoppard liked the patience of anyone who could wait that long for a pun as 'carefully-laid fuse' to go off, and not even be there when it did.

The first joint venue for Stoppard and Inter-Action was a Soho restaurant-club called the Green Banana, in Frith Street, run by a Guyanan actor friend of Berman's, Norman Beaton. The theatre director Geoffrey Reeves, a Falstaffian character who had known Stoppard at Bristol and now lived not far away at Chorleywood, knew Berman through Clive Barker. He brought *After Magritte* to Berman, with Stoppard's and Kenneth Ewing's permission. It was put on as part of Inter-Action's 'Ambiance Lunch-Hour Theatre Club'. (It was called Ambiance because Inter-Action had just moved from another, failed, West Indian restaurant venue of that name.) The lunchtime 'Not Quite Cricket Season of Almost British Plays' had short pieces by Howard Brenton, Beckett (*Three Dialogues with Georges Duthuit*) and N. F. Simpson, alongside *Magritte*, which ran from 8 to 18 April 1970. Stoppard was tickled by the way this was billed on the *Guardian*'s Arts page, which in those days had the venues in bolder type than the play titles: '**Coliseum, Drury Lane, Festival Hall, Green Banana**'.

The venue was a tiny low-ceilinged cellar underneath the club, with a spiral staircase going down to it. The sets had to be heaved in, ready boxed, from a van parked outside in the early morning (before the traffic wardens arrived) and then lugged upstairs again every afternoon. Stoppard asked Berman, when he came to see the show, why on earth they worked like this. The answer was, they couldn't afford their own theatre. When they did move on to a small one-room space in Rupert Street, which was called the Almost Free Theatre, as everyone paid what they could, if only a penny, he thought they ought to have a play written for them. So, for their 'opening ceremony', he gave them *Dogg's Our Pet* (an anagram of Dogg's Troupe, with Professor Dogg as a central character). On and off through the next decade, Stoppard wrote comic plays specially for Inter-Action – *The (Fifteen-minute) Dogg's Troupe Hamlet, Dirty Linen* and *New-Found-Land, Dogg's Hamlet, Cahoot's Macbeth* – as time off from the big works of the 1970s, *Jumpers* and *Travesties* and *Night and Day*.

The work for Inter-Action was what he always wanted theatre to be: 'a recreation'. Berman's enterprises were part of the spirit of the time, which Stoppard retrospectively described as 'simultaneously playful and desperately serious'. He loved being as wild and experimental as he liked in that context, in a way which would come to seem self-indulgent to him. Berman's philosophy of 'inter-action' also connected to Stoppard's lifelong belief that a playtext was the description of an 'event' which then happened in the theatre: 'you wrote a play and theatre was what happened to it'. The printed texts for Inter-Action were 'as much a description of an event collectively arrived at as an author's script', he wrote in 1979, after a decade of involvement with Berman.

Berman's collective theatre gave him an opportunity to wrong-foot those who by now had labelled him an establishment or conservative figure: 'it was nice to hitch my wagon to their star'. Which was not to say that he developed a preference for workshopped, collective rehearsal and performance methods. Scribbling a few notes to himself on a cold November morning's rehearsal of *Dogg's Our Pet*, with Geoffrey Reeves directing, he noted that his 'suspicion of participation theatre' was being remarked on, and observed wryly to himself: 'My idea of theatre: audience sits, listens and goes home.'

And for *After Magritte* to be funny, the opposite of improvisation or interaction with the audience was required. It had to be exact and formulaic, and every detail had to work precisely, like a piece of machinery, or the joke would fail. The idea was to expose surrealism's illusions as consisting of matter-of-fact, banal little events, all of which had a logical explanation. Surrealism was the very opposite of the play's strictly logical, rational intentions. He didn't want to break the natural laws and go into the world of dream and irrationality and the unconscious: that felt like playing tennis without the net. These thoughts spread through *Jumpers*, *Travesties* and *Artist Descending a Staircase*, but they started with *After Magritte*.

'When I encountered [Magritte's] paintings,' he said in 1980, 'I responded to their humour immediately and I enjoyed his jokes . . . but I also like the way he did things very carefully and perfectly.' That was how he wanted the play to be. He started with some try-out titles ('The Man in the Street, A Leg to Stand On, A Fiasco in One Act, The First Mrs Harris, Inspector Magritte's Last Case, The Flaming Tuba') and a 'first idea', a version of the anecdote from which the play grew: 'A blind man, one-legged, in pyjamas, carrying a peacock, standing at a bus stop, white-bearded, with a white stick under his arm and a pair of high-heeled shoes?' He put down two notes: 'Surreal without being arbitrary. Subjectivism is not enough.'

Magritte's bowler hats, window frames and watching eyeballs, float-ing fruit, light-bulbs and tubas – especially in his painting *The Menaced Assassin* – are all put to literal use in a bizarre scenario which in the end has to be made entirely logical and believable. Stoppard called it 'a nuts-and-bolts comedy' that works 'in purely mechanistic terms'. The resulting comic machine is, as he points out, more like Terence Rattigan or Agatha Christie than Beckett or Ionesco. Added to the mix are traces of *The Goon Show*, Thurber cartoons, *Real Inspector Hound*-style detective clichés, a touch of N. F. Simpson, the short surreal 1920s nonsense plays of Ring Lardner (much admired by Ken Tynan and Stoppard, with lines like 'the curtain is lowered for seven days to denote the lapse of a week'), and top-ical references whose comic value is now lost in time, for instance to *The Black and White Minstrel Show*.

The policeman looking in through the window at the incongruous opening scene (and at us) can make no sense of the following: a ceiling lamp in counterpoise with a fruit basket, a woman lying on an ironing board covered in a white bath towel with a black bowler hat on her stom-ach ('She could be dead, but is not'), a younger woman crawling slowly on all fours in a full-length ballgown, sniffing, a man with a bare torso, wearing the bottom half of a dress suit and green fishing waders, reaching up to the lampshade, and furniture stacked up against the street door. All that can be explained, and, at the play's end, so can another equally strange scene, which, like the equipoise of the lampshade and the fruit bowl, balances out the first tableau. In between, the Harris family (husband and wife and mother, or mother-in-law, it's never quite clear which) argue over another, offstage, scene which they have just witnessed in passing, after going to a surrealist art show at the Tate Gallery, which they were visiting because Mr Harris's mother (or mother-in-law), an accomplished tuba player, is 'a devotee of Maigret' – alias Magritte. Did they just see a blind man with a white beard and a white stick, hopping along in his pyjamas carrying a tortoise, or possibly a mandolin, or was it a one-legged football supporter wearing a West Bromwich Albion shirt with a football under his arm, with his chin covered with shaving foam, and brandishing an ivory cane? The argument nags on – and a good part of the comedy comes from the Harrises' low-level domestic squabbling. As in *The Real Inspector Hound* and, shortly, *Jumpers*, what's needed is a good sleuth. Only the appearance of Inspector Foot – 'Foot of the Yard!' – in hot pursuit of an escaped member of the Victoria Palace Happy Minstrel Troupe, can solve the mystery. Throughout the proceedings, the audience is reminded that 'there is obviously a perfectly logical reason for everything'.

Logical thinking in the service of theatrical entertainment runs from *After Magritte* straight on into *Jumpers* and the next Berman production, *Dogg's Our Pet*, a twenty-five-minute language game. Like the radio play *Where Are They Now?*, written at the same time as *After Magritte*, it makes fun of the rules and regulations of his vividly remembered public school life, as absurd to an outsider as any nonsense language.

When he offered *Dogg's Our Pet* to Inter-Action, *Jumpers* was just going into rehearsal at the Old Vic. To write that play, he had been giving himself a crash course in philosophy, especially Wittgenstein. He got to grips with the *Tractatus Logico-Philosophicus* and the *Philosophical Investigations*. 'I'd never read Wittgenstein before, and I read him several times without understanding lots of it – it's like reading poetry.' Wittgenstein made his presence felt in *Jumpers*, and, again, in the conference of philosophers in *Professional Foul*. Just as Magritte's paintings gave him the prompt for *After Magritte*, one of Wittgenstein's metaphors kick-started *Dogg's Our Pet*, which he thought of as 'a serious joke, a joke stood on something serious written elsewhere [by someone else]'. This was a small squib which anticipated bigger fireworks. In what became a lifelong habit, he grafted onto a dramatic event a hard problem in philosophy, history or science: language games, particle physics, chaos theory, consciousness, unlikely subjects for theatrical entertainment. It became one of his hallmarks.

Wittgenstein's *Tractatus* aimed to solve the problems of philosophy by showing how language works. His much later *Philosophical Investigations* (which contradicted a lot of the *Tractatus*) asked 'how we attach meaning to language'. This appealed to Stoppard, forever delighted 'by the way language and logic can be used or misused'. In the *Tractatus*, Wittgenstein said that language has 'a single underlying logic'. But in *Philosophical Investigations*, he argued that 'language has no single essence, but a vast collection of different practices each with its own logic'. He called the different ways we use language 'language games'. And the rules of these games, he said, are a 'social practice' set up by agreement within a 'tribe' or community.

Wittgenstein had been a house-builder at one time, and the illustration he uses for language games at the beginning of *Philosophical Investigations* is of a man building a structure and asking for the items he needs ('plank', 'block', etc.). But does he get what he asks for because his helper has a mental picture of a plank or a block? Do the meanings of words involve visualisation? Can the same words mean different things? *Dogg's Our Pet* steals this example to create a 'thought-experiment' about the arbitrariness of language, in the form of an absurd linguistic farce. He told Ed Berman that he liked the idea he'd found in Wittgenstein of a man on stage being thrown bricks which he builds into some steps, which he then climbs up on to harangue the audience. Berman was baffled, and asked him to explain. 'I don't know,' Stoppard said, 'I just like the idea of a man saying "brick" fifty times and then launching off into this tirade.'

Charlie, a school caretaker (like Albert on his bridge, a careful workman), is building a platform for a speech day. Charlie speaks English, but the schoolboys and the headmaster, Mr Dogg, and the lady who comes to give the speech, all speak the language of the tribe (or school), which of course is 'Dogg', and which like a lot of schoolboy lingo consists mainly of rude words. Charlie calls out in English for the objects he needs ('plank', 'cube', etc.), but the same words mean something else in Dogg. Much high-speed throwing from the wings and catching of objects, and hurling and receiving of unintentional insults, ensues, culminating in the visiting lady's speech ('Sod the pudding club' for 'I declare this building open', and so on). We also hear a voice on the radio speaking in Dogg, but in familiar 'inflections', whereby 'check mumble hardly out' clearly means 'Here are the football results', and 'Haddock Clock quite, Haddock Foglamp trog' is 'delivered with the inflections appropriate to, say, "Manchester City nil, Manchester United 3"'. 'The appeal', Stoppard noted, 'consisted in the possibility of writing a play which had to teach the audience the language the play was written in.' At the end, the frustrated and bewildered Charlie mounts the platform he has built and complains: 'I can take a joke as well as any man, but I've noticed a lot of language about the place and if there's one thing I can't stand it's language.'

A few months after *Dogg's Our Pet*, in January 1972, Berman asked Stoppard to write something for the double-decker Fun Art Bus. They toyed with the idea of a five-minute *War and Peace*, but that came to nothing. He was in the last weeks of rehearsals for *Jumpers*, which opened at the Old Vic on 2 February, but he broke off to give Berman *The (Fifteen minute) Dogg's Troupe Hamlet*, copyright T. Stoppard and W. Shakespeare – as much a parody of *Rosencrantz* as of *Hamlet*. The typescript went missing, but it surfaced a few years later, and was staged on 24 April 1976, to a small standing audience, on the concrete forecourt of the still unfinished National Theatre, with jokes about how long the building was taking.

This spoof mini-*Hamlet* had good comic timing. The National Theatre building had been in prolonged gestation since the late 1960s, accompanied by endless delays, quarrels, cost increases and resignations. Olivier stepped down as director in 1973, from ill health and exhaustion, the year after *Jumpers* opened at the Old Vic. Peter Hall took over, and decided in 1975 to move into the unfinished building on the South Bank. The Lyttelton

Archie: Lord Greystoke, it has been suggested that you are out of a
   book.
Greystoke: That is correct.
Crouch: And the author of this book was a novelist, wasn't he?
Greystoke: I have always understood him to be one's biographer.
Archie: Well, you can't say fairer than that, can you?

From the first runs of *Jumpers* in 1972–3 at the Old Vic, followed by the
Broadway production in 1974, the return of the play with a mainly new
cast for the 1976 National Theatre season, and then the West End revival a
decade later, in a production by Michael Codron at the Aldwych, it wasn't
only Tarzan who swung in and out. Some of the changes were technical
adjustments to do with the blacking out of the bedroom, the TV screen,
and Archie's 'dermatological' slides of Dotty's skin. (Not all theatres could
make use of a giant revolve like the Lyttelton stage at the National.) Others
involved subtle changes in George's character. In the 1972 version, as well
as failing the about-to-be-assassinated Archbishop, he is harsher to Dotty
(accusing her, for instance, of an 'aristocratic pretence' that she doesn't
know where her own kitchen is), vainer (giving his speech to an imaginary mirror) and more absent-minded (drinking out of the mug he keeps
his pencils in, and leaving a pencil in his mouth). One major early change
was due to Miriam's intervention. In draft, the play was called 'And Now
the Incredible Archibald Jumper'. There was only one copy of the script,
and it had to go in the post to Kenneth Ewing. Miriam offered to make
three copies at work, and couldn't be bothered to write out the whole title.
She just put *Jumpers* on the cover: and so it remained.

   Frank Pike at Faber, his admiring and patient editor, was warned what
to expect: 'I keep changing the script to make it work better, so I hope
you are prepared for some very messy galley proofs.' Successive editions
came out with authorial warnings. In 1972: 'In preparing previous plays
for publication I have tried with some difficulty to arrive at something
called a "definitive text", but I now believe that in the case of plays there is
no such animal.' In 1973: 'After some months' absence *Jumpers* returned to
the National Theatre in a slightly altered form. This edition incorporates

the changes because they seem to me an improvement on the original.' In 1986, in an edition which Faber rashly called 'definitive': 'This new edition incorporates some changes, mostly small but too numerous to specify, made for the 1984 [in fact 1985] production at the Aldwych Theatre.' He comments ruefully on his 'inconvenient habit of treating rehearsals as an opportunity to revise the text', a challenge to his publishers. It is a clear example (*Travesties* would be next) of his resistance to the idea of a definitive text.

This 'inconvenient habit' of revision was encouraged by his director, Peter Wood, who did the 1970s and 1980s productions of *Jumpers*. Wood went on to direct the first productions of *Travesties, Night and Day, The Real Thing* (in the UK but not in the US), *Hapgood* and *Indian Ink*, Stoppard's European plays, *Undiscovered Country, On the Razzle, Rough Crossing* and *Dalliance*, and the TV adaptation of *The Dog It Was That Died*. For years, Wood was his director of choice and theatrical soulmate.

Wood was about ten years older than Stoppard, and by the time of *Jumpers* he was one of Britain's most sought-after directors. He had come from a working-class rural background; his father was a Devon basketmaker and his mother a dressmaker. Besotted by theatre from childhood, he flourished at Cambridge as a Leavisite English student and a director. From there he went to the Oxford Playhouse and the London Arts Theatre, and made his name with successes as varied as O'Neill's *The Iceman Cometh*, Peter Shaffer's *The Private Ear* and *The Public Eye*, with Maggie Smith and Kenneth Williams, *The Prime of Miss Jean Brodie* with Vanessa Redgrave, and, at the Old Vic, with Olivier in *The Master Builder* and (as Tattle) in Congreve's *Love for Love*. He worked for the National, the RSC, the West End, European theatres, film and television. He was equally good at Restoration comedy, European drama, American classics, opera and new experimental work (he was the first director, in 1958, of Pinter's *The Birthday Party* and of Joe Orton's *Loot*, both of which had shaky starts). He developed strong relationships with playwrights, John Whiting as well as Stoppard.

Wood was a highly intelligent, authoritarian, even autocratic director (some called him 'The Commander'), a teacher who educated his actors and was a stickler for discipline and clear speaking. His rehearsals were uproarious, demanding experiences. Though in private he was a shy man with a fondness for animals, music, art and the countryside, and though he did not believe in '*Regietheater*', in which the director dominated over the proceedings, in rehearsal he had an exhibitionist, extravagant style. He had a brilliant flair for comic pace and structure, for finding spectacular, ingenious staging solutions, and for the coherent reading of a play. Younger actors loved the masterclasses they got from him, and some of his regular stars – Michael Hordern, John Wood, Felicity Kendal – adored him. But he had favourites, and some actors resented his forcefulness.

He and Stoppard developed an almost telepathic relationship. They understood each other very well, enjoyed each other's company, and had fun. They made a charismatic double act. Wood was an acute interpreter of his plays to the actors (he told the actor playing Archie in the American production of *Jumpers*, for instance, not to 'make value judgements about Stoppardian characters'). He always wanted him in rehearsal and welcomed his participation. Stoppard said that working with him was 'essentially collaborative and consensual'. He hugely admired his craft, his intelligence and his ingenuity. He loved the way Wood was on his wavelength, solved complex problems, and created particular atmospheres for each play through the music he chose, whether Keith Jarrett, ragtime or Bach. Stoppard responded to his suggestions, though he didn't always bow to his demands for clarification. Wood used, disapprovingly, the phrase 'retroactive exposition' to describe Stoppard's habit of mystifying the audience at the start of the play. He would say: 'Look, I am Rupert Bear, I'm sitting in the eighth row, listening to what you're saying, and I don't understand. Isn't it your job to make me understand?'

This long-standing professional love affair did not get off to a smooth start. Peter Wood was asked by Olivier to direct *Jumpers* because he had done an admired Beckettian production of *Rosencrantz* at the Nottingham Playhouse. But he was wary. *Jumpers* looked to him an alarming proposition – and, for a firm Catholic, a troubling one, too. He had heard that Stoppard really wanted Jonathan Miller to direct it. They had an uneasy first lunch, in a bad Italian restaurant on Southampton Row, and Wood

A family album: the Beck children in 1914. Marta is the smallest child.

Marta Becková in the 1930s.

Marta and Eugen Sträussler on their wedding day, 23 June 1934.

Dr Sträussler with colleagues and patients, Bata hospital, Zlín, 1938.

Baby Tomik, Zlín, 1937.

In flight from Europe, 1939: by ship to Singapore.

Tomik (*l*) and Petr Sträussler (*r*), 1940.

The Bata mothers and children in Naini Tal, 1942. Marta and Tomik far right.

Peter and Tom Stoppard, English schoolboys, early 1950s.

L OLD VIC ACTOR Peter O'Toole's contortions as he attempts to hit the
il Service ground, Filton Avenue, are watched by close-fielding pressmen
cricket match yesterday between the Bristol Old Vic and press critics.

The English game: cricket in Bristol, mid-1950s. Tom
Stoppard wicket-keeper, Peter O'Toole batting.

Isabel Dunjohn, Stoppard's first love, in the 1950s.

The aspiring writer in his mid-twenties.

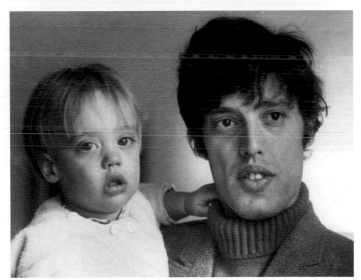

Wedding day, 26 March 1965, with his mother and stepfather.

Married life: Tom and Jose Stoppard.

Fatherhood: Stoppard with his first son Oliver, 17 December 1967.

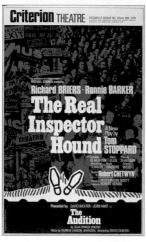

Rosencrantz & Guildenstern Are Dead, Old Vic, 1967: John Stride and Edward Petherbridge.

The Real Inspector Hound, first production poster, 1968.

After Magritte, 1970, at the Green Banana, Soho.

ROSEN-
CRANTZ
and
GUILDEN-
STERN
are DEAD

by Tom
Stoppard

Jumpers, 1972: Diana Rigg and Michael Hordern.

Lecturing at the University of Notre Dame, 1971.

Faber covers of *Rosencrantz & Guildenstern* and
Travesties.

Babysitting, 1972.

The Stoppard family at Fernleigh, 1975: Ollie, Barny, Miriam, Will, Ed, Tom.

left unconvinced. Then he talked to his friend Peter Shaffer and showed him the script, and Shaffer told him he was mad, that it was a wonderful play, and that he should immediately tell the National he wanted to do it.

Olivier warned Wood: 'You've got a very tricky bill of goods here with that boy.' Director and playwright began by circling around each other, Wood 'kid-glovey', Stoppard 'defensive'. But as they began rehearsals, they warmed up to each other. It was Wood who insisted on casting Michael Hordern, and who, during rehearsals, masterminded some vital structural changes. 'One day when I was out for ten minutes,' Stoppard said in 1974, 'Peter Wood cut a scene in two and played it backwards, and it was better. So we kept it.' But there were problems. 'A certain amount of boggling went on,' according to Stoppard, when Wood and Hordern first saw the enormous length of George's monologues. Hordern would say that he had a difficult time at first understanding the play, and a good many 'I *see*, yes *of course*' moments during rehearsals. Stoppard wrote a comic account of running between the rehearsals for *Dogg's Our Pet* and the first readings of *Jumpers* – with Diana Rigg, star of *The Avengers*, turning up in a fur coat and a vintage Rolls-Royce – while everyone was arguing about the character of Dotty and finding her too opaque. Some of the stage directions proved mightily challenging, 'like little time bombs that go off in the director's hands when he picks them up'. One of these was a recommendation that 'this ought not to take as long to happen as it does to describe it'. Another was a scene change which said, 'The bedroom forms around her.' Those five words, Stoppard would say, 'occupied fine brains for five weeks until the bedroom formed around her'. When Wood was rehearsing the 1985 production of *Jumpers*, he was still joking about that particular stage direction with Felicity Kendal.

Sitting in the audience at the Old Vic for the first preview, Wood 'looked along the row and there were nine people asleep'. More work had to be done. But when it opened, they had a triumph. Hordern's magnetically chaotic George and Rigg's 'luscious, lost' Dotty were acclaimed, and the praise poured out: exuberant, heady, witty, stimulating. Some critics found it static, wordy and difficult. It won the 'Most Overrated Play' of the year award as well as the *Evening Standard* Best Play of 1972. As the run went on, Stoppard began to feel that Hordern's performance relied too much on charm. But the production would take its place in theatre history as a huge hit, a theatrical landmark, and one of Olivier's greatest successes at the National Theatre.

Later productions of *Jumpers* had very different atmospheres. Paul Eddington, Tom Courtenay and, much later, Simon Russell Beale brought their own emotions and styles to George, Eddington with distraught anguish, Russell Beale with embarrassment and dismay. Julie Covington played Dotty more neurotically, Felicity Kendal more vulnerably and appealingly, than the glamorous Diana Rigg. Wood's 1974 American production, with the English actor Brian Bedford and the excellent Jill Clayburgh, did not go well. Wood had decided it needed Broadway-style glamour; there was an over-lavish set, swathed in pink carpet, a full-scale illusory dream sequence at the end, and a large team of professional acrobats who were much more expert than Stoppard had intended. The combination of these pyrotechnics and a rather stiff, British performance by Brian Bedford killed the laughter – as the influential New York critic Frank Rich scathingly observed – and *Jumpers* at the Rose Theatre closed after two months. This unfortunate Broadway experience would have a later effect on Stoppard's professional relationship with Peter Wood. But, New York apart, they could not have had a better start together. The first *Jumpers* gained a mythical status, and later productions were always compared with it.

After this triumph, when the National Theatre finally moved to the South Bank, what Olivier and Peter Hall wanted was Stoppard's next new play. But he had another allegiance too. Trevor Nunn had wanted to do *Rosencrantz* for the RSC and had been the first director to offer him work in the West End. Nunn looked on in an 'agony' of jealousy at the National's triumph with *Jumpers*, and he passionately wanted the next Stoppard play: 'You must know that if you told me that it was a conversation piece between two mushrooms, I would be agog with an expectation which is almost painful.' And the play was written for John Wood, who was at the RSC. So the RSC got *Travesties*, and, for the 1976 National Theatre season on the South Bank, Peter Hall got a revival of *Jumpers*. Stoppard felt he had 'a debt of honour' to the RSC. But ambition also played its part. Half-jokingly, but sounding more like the ruthless Archibald Jumper than the vulnerable George, he told the *New York Times* theatre critic, Mel Gussow, in April 1974: 'Beneath this carefully cultivated modest exterior I'm ravenous for vain publicity. I want to have *Travesties* on at the Royal Shakespeare when they revive *Jumpers* at the National Theatre, and I hope to have a play in the West End and a radio play at the same time. One night I'm going to wipe everybody out.'

13

The Home Team

One tried to behave better than oneself when in his circle – or his aura.

There was no painful five-year gap this time between two big plays. It took him about nine months to write *Travesties*. He started thinking about it in the spring of 1972, very soon after *Jumpers* opened. That autumn, Trevor Nunn (and Ronald Bryden) asked him for his new play for the RSC. He began it in March 1973 and finished it the following January. Rehearsals started in the spring of 1974, at the same time that *Jumpers* was opening in America. *Travesties* had its first night on 10 June 1974, at the Aldwych. The timetable was demanding and the concentration was intense. Meanwhile, family life swirled round him. He was completely part of it, but also preoccupied.

In 1973, Ollie was seven, Barny was four, and Will was a year old. (He was such a good-natured baby, his father said, that he was a *pleasure* to see at 5 a.m.) Miriam wanted to have a second child quickly. She was thirty-seven when Edmund ('my fourth and our last baby' by 'my second and last wife Miriam', as he put it) was born on 16 September 1974. He was named after two literary heroes, Edmund Gosse and Edmund Wilson. Stoppard wrote to Faber in August 1974, to say that he wanted *Travesties*, which would be published in February 1975, to be dedicated to his children, 'the last of whom will not be born till September'. The dedication is 'For Oliver, Barnaby, William and Edmund'. *Travesties*, though it has no children in it, is the play of his most intense period of fatherhood.

As well as being married to a famous, busy writer, Miriam was now the mother of a toddler and a baby and had Jose's two boys to look after. She had her managerial job at Syntex, which involved a lot of travelling, and, starting while she was pregnant with Ed, a media career. From 1974, she was one of the medical experts on Yorkshire Television's *Don't Ask Me*, a light mixture of scientific demonstrations and jokey audience-baiting, fronted by some outgoing personalities, among them Austin Mitchell, David Bellamy, Magnus Pyke and Rob Buckman (who became a friend). Later, in 1979, she had her own YTV show, *Don't Just Sit There*, and then started publishing a stream of medical advice books on pregnancy, baby care and parenting. Interviewed admiringly in 1975 as a 'brainy beauty' who worked a seven-day week, she declared, 'The more you take on, the more you are capable of doing.' She described her filming schedule, while pregnant: 'I do a full day's work at the office, then take a plane to Leeds, working during the flight. I meet the producer that night, get to the studio at nine next morning and we record the show the same evening. Then I climb on to a sleeper at 11 and I'm back in my office by 8.30 the next morning.' How did her husband feel about her work schedule? she was asked. 'He greatly approves of it. I think he's rather proud that I have such a responsible job, that I can hold down a senior position in my chosen profession. It also lets him get on with his own work at home. He is one of those writers who values his privacy.' He told her to 'have a go' at television, though she had no experience. 'He never advised me against doing anything.' His letters to his parents were full of proud details of her career, her travels and her high profile. He admired her energy and competence, as, jokingly, in November 1971: 'Miriam carries on earning her own keep while keeping us.' He clipped profiles to send them, of Miriam as super-wife, mother and medical director ('Busy? To the Children I'm Always as Fresh as a Daisy'). If she ever showed signs of wanting to stay at home with the boys, and give up being a scientist and a pundit, he argued against it: too much waste of intelligence.

As with everything else in her life, home was a major project. She turned herself into an ambitious gardener, though even she couldn't do all that herself without some help. She made Fernleigh comfortable and inviting in a traditional English way. There were antiques, prints, good pieces of furniture and indulgences like a Victorian glass case of stuffed birds or a big blue patterned Chinese carpet in the under-used front room. They had a double portrait done by Glynn Boyd Harte, an eccentric, old-fashioned young artist whom he'd met when giving a talk at the Royal College of Art. Boyd Harte painted them sitting on a spindly wooden bergère, with Miriam in a Thea Porter dress and he in stripy trousers and a black-and-white chessboard pullover, and they hung it over the sofa. Stoppard developed a passion for English watercolours, and bought what he could afford – over time, thirty or so paintings of the English seaside, the Thames, Derbyshire or Wales, by painters like John Varley and David Cox. He bought a tiny Thomas Girtin, too. And he went on buying books: Jane Austen, whom he started reading in expensive first editions, his favourite modernists, Hemingway, Joyce, Eliot, and runs of early-twentieth-century magazines like the *Egoist* and the *Dial*. They had a Fernleigh bookplate designed by Boyd Harte, with a picture of the house and their initials intertwined.

One of Miriam's domestic ambitions was to make sure that they would all have breakfast together when they were at home. It avoided the whole business, as he put it, of 'scrabbling around with a piece of toast in your hand looking for your shoes'. Ollie and Miriam would get up early and make it: porridge and boiled eggs, toast and thick-cut Oxford marmalade. This routine began at Fernleigh, but it went on all through the boys' childhoods. A few years on, when Will was a small boy, Miriam took him with her to a Harrods sale to buy a complete set of china, down to tureens and sauce-boats and teapots, patterned with yellow flowers, and they got it home together – with some difficulty, as she had parked boldly outside Harrods and the car had been towed away. Should we phone Daddy? Will asked. No, said Miriam, we're capable of sorting this out ourselves. Visitors to the house were impressed to see a full breakfast set permanently laid out in the breakfast room.

To the outside world, and in the media, Tom and Miriam Stoppard were seen as a hip and glamorous couple. One of her YTV producers told her they were even more famous than Paul and Linda McCartney. Looking at a photo of them together with Will, Stoppard said: 'I look just like an Italian film producer with his rock 'n' roll girlfriend.' But this wasn't a bohemian household, it was well ordered and domestic.

The ritual of family breakfast could be a challenge for a writer who stayed up all night working, had his mind full of his play, needed to read several newspapers every morning and was not very conversational before noon. The boys remembered a shattered figure appearing at the head of the table in pyjamas and an ivory silk dressing gown. He and Miriam would then share the school run. And he might then go back to bed, and start work later in the day, writing till two or three in the morning. When Miriam was travelling, the boys would see more of him, and had what they called 'Nursery Lunch' with him in the kitchen.

The school run distributed the boys, first to a little local PNEU kindergarten in a Victorian house, Eton End, and then to the Licensed Victuallers independent school in Slough, for Ollie, and Caldicott prep school for the other boys, twenty minutes away. Later, Ollie and Barny went to the Merchant Taylors' independent boys' school in Northolt (on the train), and Ed and Will went as boarders to Stowe. All this cost money.

Miriam was keen to make the boys' lives as active and independent as possible. She was a great believer in competitive sports. She maintained that you could condition children from an early age to play sport, and she would roll Will a big fluffy ball to kick at almost before he could walk. One of Will's early memories was of biting the pimples on the tips of his father's red wicket-keeper's gloves. Barny, though not especially keen on games, was a good rugby player; Will became an outstanding one. A regular sight at Fernleigh was of the boys 'bashing tennis balls' served up by Miriam, to her cries of 'Move your feet!' Later, both parents would make sure that they turned up, from wherever they were in the world, for school sports days and parent–teacher meetings. 'Mother' in *Hapgood*, shouting encouragement to her son from the touchline of the school rugby game, is a sighting of Miriam.

The boys were all treated the same, and in time formed their group allegiances. As a little boy, Ed was devoted to Ollie (who was otherwise rather solitary and separate) and followed him around like a puppy. Ed grew up to be the most like his father, and was closest to him. Will – everyone knew – was Miriam's pet. Barny and Will often fought. Their father noted grimly to himself, in the spring of 1977: 'Today Barnaby threatened suicide if William did not stop tormenting him. I think we must have a family conference.'

That note was made in a journal which Stoppard started to keep a year after Ed's birth, on 16 September 1975, in a handsome leather-bound book in which he wrote, intermittently, until he filled it at the end of 1979. He resumed it a few years later (in a grander but rather cumbersome book with wooden covers, a gift from Miriam) in the early 1980s. It was written for Ed, and so, although full of detailed accounts of his thoughts, work, travels, reading, social and family life, it also had a certain reserve. This was to be expected in a journal intended for a baby son to read as an adult, but it was also characteristic. On a trip to Greece in May 1977, he notes that the oracle at Delphi is known for two pronouncements, 'Know thyself', and 'Nothing too much'. 'This suggested an oracular compromise to me: "Know thyself but not too well."'

The pleasure he took in family life pours onto every page of the journal. There is plenty of chaos – one little boy throwing up all night, another one unable to sleep, rows and tantrums, breakages and tears, over-excited birthdays. But the tone is constant: tender, humorous and interested. In November 1975, Ollie, aged nine, has heard adults talking about the 'Atom Bomb' and starts to cry, saying 'I don't want to be blown up.' Stoppard writes, as if to Ed: 'Mummy [Miriam] says I have been over-protective, which is perhaps true, but it wrenched my heart. My idea of bringing you boys up is to contrive your happiness even to the exclusion of the world round the corner.' When he is away from them, he is painfully homesick. One typical entry is written on his Greek holiday: 'I'm missing you boys now much more than enjoying the voyage.' Another is written in a Washington hotel room during rehearsals for *Dirty Linen* in September 1976:

> I loathe being abroad on my own, in hotel rooms like this one . . . I
> miss you particularly. Your conversation is precocious for your age,
> and you are learning wickedness and incorrigibility from William.
> Barnaby, who taught it to William, is now en route from the
> whipping-boy status of William to the privileged and responsible
> heights of ten year old Oliver's calm existence.

Again from Washington (for *Night and Day*), in October 1979: 'I miss you and William so much . . . I think of you two in your school uniforms, after breakfast, sitting on the stairs, cuddling the cats.'

As they grew up, he was intrigued by their shifting relationships and their developing personalities – though he did once write, trying to describe one of them, 'I wish I was "good at character".' He took pleasure in noting their sayings and doings, in his journal and in his letters to his mother. On the way back from taking Barnaby and Will to a pantomime, Barny, aged seven, asked: 'Was Dick Whittington the cat or the man?' After a barbecue in the garden, he said: 'This is the best day of my life, including tomorrow.' Ollie, at six, taken to see *Dogg's Our Pet*, announced after five minutes: 'It's a very good play!' But he had never been quite sure 'what Daddy really did', and now, his father thought, he must be completely baffled. Ed, aged two, asked his father, sitting at his desk: 'Dad, what are you doing, doing your pretending?' A year later, 'flashes of lightning appear in [Ed's] sunny disposition. You are discovering that you cannot always have all that you want, and you are baffled and infuriated by this turn of events.' Two years on, 'your language at four years of age is eclectic to the point of public scandal. You and William are obsessed with all excretory functions, genitals, breasts, bottoms . . . all matters of prurient hilarity.' At four, Ed is praised: 'Your nature is to be well-disposed, if the world allows. Your enquiries are meticulous. Your pleasure in understanding things is a pleasure itself.' All through their childhood, he and Miriam tried to turn their home into a safe cocoon for the boys. He would often wonder if '*this* family is not entirely a preparation for the real world out there'.

Inevitably, Ollie and Barny had rather different lives from Miriam's sons. Every fortnight they made their regular weekend visits to Jose, going on the train to wherever she was living – a house in Southampton, a squat in Brixton, lastly a flat in Hemel Hempstead – and coming back in a taxi if there were no trains. Time spent with Jose was clouded by her unhappiness and unpredictability. By the evening she would be in her cups, making her complaints to the boys about the injustices done to her. As children do, they adapted; the difficult moment was always the transition, from the relative luxury of Fernleigh to Jose's place, and then back again. But their childhood double life did have a lasting effect. As Barny put it, looking back: 'Every two weeks you're going to a council flat in Hemel Hempstead with a schizophrenic alcoholic mother . . . and I think it threw me off.'

They didn't tell their father about what it was like with Jose, and he was unaware until years later that she was endlessly making her case to them.

He was simply relieved that they were all together, and happy in his family life. He was a benign and easy-going father – the opposite of Ken Stoppard – though sometimes absent-minded. In his classic 'father' pose, he would be reading a book with a baby slung over one arm. He didn't cook any of their meals – he couldn't really cook at all – but when Ollie was a baby he had changed plenty of nappies, and at Fernleigh he was on hand for bath-time and bedtime. They would both read the boys a story each, and then Miriam would sing to them. He read them Dahl's *Fantastic Mr Fox*, all in one sitting, or Sendak's *Where the Wild Things Are*, or Adams's *Watership Down*. There would be word games (especially on long car journeys), running jokes, treasure hunts for which he wrote the clues, and much family TV watching, like *The Two Ronnies*. Outside, he would kick a ball around with the boys and the two dogs.

He taught them cricket and took them fishing. Ollie, especially, took to this. They found a reservoir near Iver, well stocked with brown and rainbow trout. Stoppard took Ollie there and described the fishing in detail to Ken: 'we used big black fuzzy lures about half an inch long with a green flash for the tail . . . I caught a nice ¾lb rainbow.' It was their one area of communication.

Ollie remembered being sent off, at the age of about nine, to stay with his grandparents at Lazenby, near Penrith, so as to fish with Ken, whom he found daunting. Will thought he looked like a British colonel with a tweed blazer and tie, a grey-haired version of Stephen Fry in *Blackadder Goes Forth*. Ollie noticed that it was always Ken who cut the bread at meals – no one else was allowed to. He was still the family disciplinarian. But, as Ollie said, looking back, if you have a facade like that all your life, how can you drop it? His fishing expedition was nearly a disaster. It was August, not a good season for fly-fishing, and after a whole day, Ollie had caught nothing. Ken went off grimly to the car. But Ollie's granny – whom all the boys found loving and kind – stayed with him, and just when it was getting dark, he caught a twelve-ounce trout. Bobby eagerly pulled its gills out to kill it, cutting her finger as she did so, so that it could be shown to Ken, who was impressed and (unusually) gave Ollie a pound. It's a snapshot of Ken and Bobby in their sixties: Ken domineering and stern, Bobby as loving, fussy and anxious a grandmother as she had been a mother. Will would also remember as a teenager going fishing with his dad and his grandfather, and Ken making Stoppard, then in his fifties, climb into a hawthorn tree to rescue one of Ken's special silk fishing lines. Will noted that Ken was still treating the famous middle-aged playwright like a ten-year-old boy.

His writing life did not impinge much on the children, since it mostly went on at night. During the day, the study door was always open. Will inherited his father's sweet tooth, and became very familiar with his desk, as he knew he would find a regular supply of sweets there. The boys could wander in and out: there was no 'writer at work' warning. They were not even especially aware, until their teenage years, that they were the children of a famous playwright. He did not talk much about his work, either to them or to Miriam. Very occasionally he would read her something to test it out – a speech from *Jumpers*, the ending of *Travesties* – and she would feel anxious about her response. He would say: 'If *you* don't get it, then half the audience won't.' But, as he's observed, when writers ask their companion for an opinion they don't really want one, they just want confirmation. If he showed her something and she was not bowled over by it, he would rather wish he hadn't.

Ollie said of him, as a father: 'I'm not afraid of him – I've never had reason to be.' Ed did remember him being severe if he thought they were behaving badly. Very occasionally, when the boys were all thundering noisily around the house, he would shut them up. At times he got exasperated, as he said in a candid interview in the summer of 1976:

Yesterday I started work at half past nine in the morning and ended up at five o'clock in the afternoon in a foul mood because I'd been interrupted every twelve minutes by one of my four children or one of their three or four friends or telephone calls . . . It's domestic life. I wouldn't have it any other way. I can't bear that sort of monk writer. I knew one once who worked in a garage and they had to slip notes under the door. I think one should stop for the children and not make the children stop for the writing.

When things got too rowdy, it was usually Miriam who would read the riot act. Having been brought up by a fussy Jewish mother, she 'took a policy decision' not to be like that. But she could be bossy, and she could get wound up. She always felt that the children loved him more, and that she was the one they criticised.

Miriam Stoppard's Book of Babycare, her first book, was published by George Weidenfeld in 1977. At one of the publisher's dinner parties, Miriam had sat next to him and told him she wanted to write. Weidenfeld called across to his editor: this is Miriam Stoppard, she's going to write a book for us, see her tomorrow! Stoppard was always grateful to him for that. The book recommended a mild amount of discipline. Children should be encouraged to help with chores. But love, security and a sense of fairness came first: 'In our house truthfulness is rewarded, even though it involves confession to a wrong-doing. The two acts are treated separately.' The book also argued the case for working mothers ('My four sons don't turn a hair when their mother has to dash off to foreign parts to attend a conference – don't all Mums do that?'), though a supportive husband was essential. In this case, the supportive husband wrote the introduction to the *Babycare* book, a little-known publication of Stoppard's, 'the working mother being too busy at the office'. He didn't think 'the change of pen was detectable'. It summed up the book not as 'a book of rules' or 'a set of solutions', but 'an attempt to guide you into making *your* rules'.

Loving and affable though he was with his boys, he was not intimate or confiding. He didn't go down on his hands and knees to play with them, or pretend to join in their children's games. Sometimes, when they were trying to attract his attention, they felt he was in the room, but away in his mind. When he was writing, it was understood that he would be abstracted. Miriam always felt that when a play was underway there was a 'creeping feeling of excitement in the house'. She knew that at that point he needed to be left alone.

Ollie had the sense, at Fernleigh, that they were not solidly well off, perhaps only just afloat. They were living well in their big house, but they were living up to their limit. As the boys started to go to their expensive schools, Ollie, for one, did not take anything for granted. Perhaps the upsets in his early childhood made for insecurity. But he was right to detect some anxiousness. His father was never quite sure when the next tranche of income would arrive. Some of the mid-1970s letters to Peter, as his accountant, are nervy about cashflow. Fernleigh was expensive to maintain, the boys cost money, Jose had to be paid for, cars had to be serviced. They liked acquiring possessions and spending on treats and presents, wine and travel. Part of Miriam's regime was to take three family holidays a year, built into their complicated timetables. They went to the Algarve, to Italy or Corfu, on skiing holidays when the boys were a bit older. They had regular holidays in England and Scotland, often to the grand, old-fashioned Swiss Lodore Hotel near Keswick (now the Lodore Falls Hotel), overlooking Derwentwater. This involved some 'minor tramping', according to Ollie, some drives or a row on the lake: 'we weren't a walking family'. One summer's family stay at the Swiss Lodore in 1978 cost between £1,200 and £1,400.

Letters to Peter often used phrases like 'I don't feel particularly secure financially', or 'this might lead to short-term money problems'. He worried about his overheads and wryly lamented (as when confessing to the purchase of a £2,000 diamond ring for Miriam, or a Lalique vase for £800) his 'congenital extravagance'. 'I mustn't indulge myself unduly,' he would warn himself, or would promise Peter, after a December spree on first editions, in 1975: 'I will live as a monk in January.' The house sucked up money: 'The garden . . . needs a gang of workmen . . . the house needs painting. The wood is rotting. The roof leaks . . . Things fall apart. It's time to write a play, I think.'

Around the time of *Travesties,* he was always on the lookout for other work. A friend from Bristol, the young director and actor Robin Phillips, who had worked for the RSC (and later ran the Stratford Festival in Ontario), was having an interesting season at the Greenwich Theatre. He was making it into a lively out-of-town venue. He asked Stoppard to do a version for him (from a literal translation) of Lorca's *The House of Bernarda Alba*, his intense Andalucian drama of a house of women ruled by their autocratic widowed mother. Stoppard found it very austere: it was hard to 'make it bounce'. To his parents he described it as 'a quick adaptation job'. Frank Pike at Faber was not keen on publishing his version: he wished it had 'more Stoppard' in it. 'To adapt Lorca', Stoppard commented in an interview, 'you need to be a poet, a playwright, and fluent in Spanish – and I'm only one of those things.' But through Phillips's production of his version, in March 1973, he met Mia Farrow (who was playing Adela, and also Irina in Chekhov's *Three Sisters*) and became friends with her and her husband, André Previn. Stoppard and Previn first met in the lobby of the Greenwich Theatre, and got on extremely well from that moment onwards.

Phillips then asked him to direct the American comedy *Born Yesterday*, a stage play made into a 1950 film with Judy Holliday and William Holden. Advised by his friend Ned Sherrin, Phillips cast the popular comedian Dave King as the boorish businessman Harry Brock, and Lynn Redgrave as his girlfriend Billie Dawn, who starts off as a naive showgirl but wises up to his corrupt tricks. So Stoppard was directing some very funny and talented actors. He was nervous about it, and did it as a kind of dare, since he really wasn't a director – and was too timid with the actors to suggest that they should 'turn up the speed'. But he enjoyed it.

In 1973 he considered doing a treatment of a film on Virginia Woolf for George Cukor, but thought he should persevere instead with his play – and anyway, he thought Woolf was 'a bit of a precious bore'. He worked on a screenplay of David Hare's 1974 play *Knuckle*, for John Boorman, *Naked Without a Gun*. *Knuckle* is a thriller and morality play set in 1970s Guildford, in which the expat gun-runner Curly Delafield, investigating his naive, idealistic sister's mysterious disappearance (or murder, or suicide), finds himself entangled in the capitalist system he identifies with his 'civilised' father. To him, England is 'a shabby little island, delighted with itself . . . a jampot for swindlers and cons and racketeers'. Stoppard's adaptation, which had more action and less polemic than the original, came to nothing, and Hare didn't think much of it. But he spoke of Hare as 'the kind of writer-craftsman who appeals to me most'.

He responded to a suggestion from a TV company for a play in a series about 'crisis and re-birth', in January 1974, with a storyline called 'Hendrick's America', centring on a Citizen Kane-style mogul who is reinventing an idealised, imaginary American past through the means of late-twentieth-century technology. The idea was that 'the notion of freedom is a slippery one'. Another plot on 'crazed mogul' lines was called 'The Grapefruit Millionaire'. His new friend Previn, then resident conductor of the London Symphony Orchestra, as well as a composer, said to him: 'If you ever would like to write something which needs an orchestra, I've got one.' In response, Stoppard dreamt up a millionaire, orchestra-owning triangle player with a grudge against all musicians, a drug dependency and an obsession with fruit, a man 'who played the markets, mortgaged the whole caboodle and bought the orchestra, and . . . never regretted it'. This oddity, which looked back to an earlier, unfinished comic collaboration with Gordon Williams, *Doctor Masopust*, took another three years to be transformed into *Every Good Boy Deserves Favour*. At first he kept thinking too literally of how to use an orchestra, with silly jokes like a kettledrum that turned out to be full of porridge, or having the first notes of Beethoven's Fifth as part of the score. To which Previn responded by saying, more or less, 'I feel about that the way you'd feel if I said to you, Tom, I've had a great idea, why don't you write a play in which somebody says, *The son of a bitch stole my watch*.' The reference (to the last line of *The Front Page*) didn't have to be explained: that was why they got on so well.

Even while looking for well-paid work, he couldn't resist quirky or personal requests. A performance artist from Bristol, Neil Hornick, who produced a series of 'Captain Phantom' books for children, asked him to contribute to *Forwards!*, a collection of forewords which had to be written without knowing what was in the book or who it was by. Other contributors included Quentin Crisp, Adrian Henri, Terry Jones, James Saunders and Heathcote Williams. Stoppard enjoyed himself: 'I am delighted to introduce this book which I am greatly looking forward to reading, in so far as it is legible, in so far as it is a book . . . Well, I mustn't ramble on and keep you from all that follows, in so far as anything does.' Another introduction was a jaunty piece about the painter Glynn Boyd Harte, who had become a friend, for a 1976 exhibition.

His best-paying sideline at this time was for Joseph Losey, who had started work on a film called *The Romantic Englishwoman* but wasn't satisfied with the screenplay Thomas Wiseman had made from his own novel. The film, which came out in 1975 and starred Glenda Jackson, Michael Caine and an unfortunately cast Helmut Berger, was a story of adultery and double lives. The wife of an English novelist goes to Baden-Baden and has an erotic encounter with a 'poet' (in fact a crook, drug dealer and gigolo) called Thomas, who follows her home, menacingly. The novelist is writing about a wife who runs away to the Continent. The lovers flee to France, pursued by the husband, and by sinister gangsters who catch up with the con-man, while husband and wife return to their home and their previous lives. The film came across as opulent, hollow and chill. But its shifts in reality interested him (and would stay in his mind for *The Real Thing*). He tried to devise different tones for the writer's imagination and the wife's memory. He put in a film within a film, the writer-character's creation. (One of its working titles was 'The Malquist Affair'.) And he had some sharp touches – most of them not liked by Wiseman. The crook has 'poet' written in his passport. The wife measures her happiness in terms of what she has in her deep-freeze, and says: 'I've got an account at Harrods and a standing order to Oxfam.' Her feminist friend has a good line in cynicism: 'People make too much of sex. It shouldn't be anything you'd leave home for.' There is a touching small boy, one of many in his work. And the husband speaks with feeling about betrayal: 'The realm of possibility is a terrible country . . . What if the person you love is a liar?' It was his first major screenplay. One French reviewer said that the brilliant dialogue could equally well have been by Pinter or Stoppard.

A better-received and very different commission was a version of Jerome K. Jerome's *Three Men in a Boat*, aired as a BBC TV play in December 1975, directed by Stephen Frears, with Michael Palin and Tim Curry in the cast, and shot by the cinematographer Brian Tufano. He was fond of the book, with its innocent, knockabout pastoral, and it gave him the excuse, in Jerome's 'voiceover', for some affectionate descriptions of the Thames landscape he now knew well. In the 1990s, he re-adapted it for radio. 'Not all plays', he told an interviewer in 1981, 'are written because of a gut need to write about factor X':

The BBC asks you if you'd like to adapt *Three Men in a Boat* and
you don't think, 'These are not the times.' You say, 'Yeah, it's one
of my favourite books, I'd love to have a crack at that.' And you do
it. When it's a thing like that you're more a craftsman than artist. I
think it's right to take pride in one's craftsmanship as much as one's
originality.

Stephen Frears noted with amusement that Stoppard said to him, when
the film came out, 'We got away with it!'

But for all these commissions, the need to cover his living costs still
made him nervous. He thought about remortgaging the house, which in
1973 was worth between £65,000 and £70,000. He kept Peter up to date with
all his bills. The opening of every production had its expenses: first-night
flowers and presents for the cast like bottles of vodka; in New York, his
credit account with a limousine company, or extra bills at the Algonquin.
He was always watching the 'take', writing to tell Peter, for instance, in the
spring of 1974 about the Washington production of *Jumpers*:

> If my arithmetic is okay, I'll come into royalty when the play has
> grossed $284,000. After previews and two weeks it had grossed
> $137,000 . . . I'm told that we are pretty well full now, so in fact you'll
> start getting money from this current week's performance, a small
> amount. In a full week, my royalty should be pushing 4,000 . . .

There were many such letters. His calculations were always fluctuating;
he was always nervous about the future; he did not settle into feeling rich
and secure.

The complicated machinery of the Stoppard household and careers needed
a lot of back-up, from nannies and gardeners to secretaries, accountants
and agents. From 1975 onwards the whole edifice began to depend on the
presence of Jacky Chamberlain, who became Stoppard's PA, minder, typist, friend, diary-keeper and right-hand woman. Jacky, daughter of a catering manager for Victoria Wine, who had grown up in Middlesex and got

married at eighteen, started working for Miriam as a secretary at Syntex when she was twenty-one, in 1970. Miriam hired her partly because Jacky and her husband, David Chamberlain, were involved with the Questors Theatre in Ealing (which had put on the first short version of *Rosencrantz* in 1964), where Jacky stage-managed some of the productions. From the start, working for Miriam involved a few hours doing some secretarial work for Stoppard. In 1973, Jacky's son Daniel was born, her husband's work moved them to Scotland and she left Syntex, but kept in touch. When they moved back south two years later, Miriam passed her on, as a present (as she put it) to Stoppard.

From then on, Jacky would come in to Fernleigh every day, from ten until three, to sit at the typewriter in the billiards room and to do whatever was needed, sometimes bringing Daniel with her. She typed and retyped all the scripts, beginning with *Dirty Linen* and *New-Found-Land*. He wrote the plays in longhand, always on unlined A4 white sheets, in blue-black ink, with his current favourite fountain pen: 'There's usually one that has the nicest nib.' Then he spoke the pages, cues, punctuation and all, into a dictaphone, from which Jacky would type the script. Ed remembered hearing, as a small boy, the regular sound of his father 'talking and then playing back. Like a code. I couldn't figure out why he was vocalising the punctuation. [Ed puts on a deep, actorly voice:] *"Comma"*. *"Full stop"*. As textual changes accumulated, new versions would be typed up, or, if a whole new typescript wasn't needed, they would both be on the office floor cutting and pasting bits of script together. Eventually, Jacky got used to his handwriting and would type up the handwritten scripts. When he was travelling, pages that needed correction would go backwards and forwards by fax. For correspondence, Stoppard would scribble the replies he wanted to make on the bottom of the letter (frequently just 'No!' but as often as not taking care and time over the smallest request), and Jacky would type the letter. Later, when computers and email replaced typing with carbon paper on an IBM golfball, it was the same process: the email would go to Jacky and be printed out for him to annotate his answer. And she continued to get revised pages of script by fax, long after most people had phased out fax machines.

Jacky dealt with agents, editors, producers and publishers, handled all requests to him for speaking and writing, kept and organised his diary, paid his bills (in consultation with Peter), fixed their holidays and organised the complicated international rotas of rehearsals and play openings. She ran the big industry that was Tom Stoppard's working life, and she became essential to him and the whole family. Working in the house, she grew close to all the children. In the early days, she fielded difficult calls from Jose, and, when Miriam was away and he was looking after the boys, would make the 'Nursery Lunch'. She would keep the sweet jar and the cigarette box filled up on his desk (but, looking back, thought ruefully that she should probably have discouraged both). She dealt with moments of panic about deadlines and over-commitments, and helped him find the things that frequently went missing – his keys, his address book, his cheque book, his passport. 'Just calm down and look,' Jacky would say, while he was stomping about and tearing his hair.

Generally, though, he was not given to outbursts. She could see he didn't want to expend his energy on getting angry. If he was cross, it was usually with himself. She got used to his habits of procrastination. He would put off interruptions like interviews or photo shoots, or endlessly reschedule them, and eventually she would have to pin him down. But she also knew that he did not like to let people down.

Their work together moved from house to house and became a lifelong collaboration and close friendship. Steady, loyal and discreet, she made his life workable over forty years and more. She collaborated with his other teams at Faber and Grove and the agency. And she liked the buzz of working with actors and film people, the excitement of first nights and film openings, the sense that this was no ordinary job.

When her daughter Naomi was born in 1977 she was back at work two weeks later, taking the baby in with her. When the Stoppards went on holiday, Jacky and her family would stay in the house so that it was not left unoccupied. When her marriage broke up in 1978 and she started a new life with her boyfriend, Dave Matthews, whose two children moved in with them, Stoppard became a friend to the family. Jacky and Dave eventually got married in March 1999; the only reason Stoppard was not at their wedding was because *Shakespeare in Love* was up for its Oscar on the same night.

There was always a familial feel to Stoppard's close working relationships. He cultivated an affectionate, protective network. Funny thank-you notes would be scribbled to Jacky (or 'Jackie'): 'Thank you for being a wonderful Girl Monday to Friday'. 'To Jackie, a good type. From the grateful author. Tom. Actually – bless you, T.' He got in the habit of putting her name into the plays as a private joke – to keep her awake while she was typing, he would say. 'Chamberlain' is an MP in *Dirty Linen*, a clerk in *The Invention of Love*, an offstage character in the Associated Press office in *Night and Day*, one of the sports reporters in *Professional Foul*, an unseen cab driver in *Hapgood* and the English governess in *Voyage*. He often joked that 'Chamberlain' started to become more demanding about her characters and to ask for better roles in the plays. In his late play *Leopoldstadt*, her surname is given to two important parts.

Everyone who came to Fernleigh met and knew Jacky, and people did come. Stoppard hospitality was informal, work-related, family-friendly and not at all grand (though Peter Nichols did remember Stoppard pointing out how close Fernleigh was to Cliveden, and saying: 'Not bad for a boy from the *Western Daily Press*!'). Fernleigh was near enough to London for people to drive out for a Sunday lunch; a jovial letter of 1976 (to Jon Bradshaw, an American journalist friend) describes one such: 'We have had ten people to lunch. I have drunk two glasses of Madeira, three glasses of Macon Villages, two glasses of some German stuff, a glass of dessert wine and a glass of port. I have also eaten too much.' The Fernleigh guest list included André Previn and Mia Farrow, John and Christel Boorman, Trevor Nunn, Diana Rigg, Eileen Atkins, John Stride, Timothy West, Bryan Forbes, Roald Dahl, Clive James, Ned Sherrin and John Wells. These starry names were people he'd got to know through work; some of them were close friends.

John Wells was a congenial fellow spirit; Stoppard told his parents that he was the nicest man in London. They were much the same age, they found the same things funny and they liked each other's style. Wells was writing 'Mrs Wilson's Diary' in *Private Eye*, and, by 1978, the Denis

Thatcher 'Dear Bill' spoof letters, which he later turned into a one-man show, *Anyone for Denis?* Stoppard loved his company, and enjoyed the fact that when you were with him you might meet Isaiah Berlin or Princess Margaret. When he spoke at Wells's funeral, in 1998, he listed his achievements as 'teacher, actor, director, revue artist, essayist, playwright, editor, novelist, lyricist, librettist, journalist, translator, social historian . . . you felt that John was up for anything at any time'. Yet this highly gifted man was always, according to his wife, in awe of Stoppard's brilliance.

When they first became friends, Wells was with, but not yet married to, Teresa Gatacre. Teresa, a blonde beauty from an upper-crust family, daughter and sister of journalists (Christopher and Alexander Chancellor), had left school and married early, and had five children by her first marriage. In 1971 she and Wells had a daughter (who became the actor Dolly Wells), for many years officially known as the child of Teresa's first husband. Stoppard thought of their affair as a great romance, and when they finally married in 1982, the Stoppards became friends to the whole family; he was always especially nice to the children. Teresa Wells had a sharp eye, describing Fernleigh as 'a rather grim house on a roundabout near Slough', though always full of glamorous people. She noted that reviews of Miriam's TV programmes and health books were pasted up on one wall of the house, opposite reviews of Stoppard's plays, which she thought showed signs of competitiveness. John Wells, too, could be affectionately satirical about Miriam. Antonia Fraser, who knew him well, remembered him, among friends, doing a spoof of Miriam as a health guru. Miriam always knew the answer to everything, and her advice was always the exact opposite of what you might expect. John 'did' Miriam giving advice about how to treat a man found in the desert: '*On no account* give him a drink of water!'

Teresa Wells respected Miriam and thought her an admirable stepmother and mother. But it was Stoppard she adored. When John Wells became ill in the 1990s, he asked Stoppard to take care of Teresa after his death. This he did, out of affection for both of them. He summed up Wells as a 'decent chap' who raised everyone's standards of behaviour. In 1968, Wells wrote a potted autobiography in telegraphese, which began 'son merry clergyman saintly philanthropic mother'. Stoppard described him, in his eulogy in 1998, as 'merry saintly John'.

Two other couples played important parts in Stoppard's life from Fernleigh days onwards. Paul and Marigold Johnson were their neighbours in Iver. They had lived in Copthall, a grand eighteenth-century house on Iver's High Street, since 1958, and they got to know the Stoppards soon after they moved to Fernleigh. They were an exuberant, idiosyncratic pair, with pronounced views, strong personalities and a big network of connections. Marigold, née Hunt, whose father had been Churchill's doctor and her mother an actor, had been a Labour candidate, an anti-pornography campaigner, a psychotherapist and a worker for the peace process in Northern Ireland. Robust and forthright, in the 1970s she was bringing up four children (two of whom went on to have conspicuous careers in business and journalism) and sustaining a household which had its turbulent challenges.

Paul Johnson was a Jesuit-schooled and Oxford-educated historian and journalist who, in the 1950s and '60s, had been a fiery socialist, as red as his hair, editor from 1965 to 1970 of the left-wing *New Statesman*. When Stoppard got to know him, he was undergoing a dramatic Pauline conversion. In the mid-1970s he was working on his book *Enemies of Society*, a critique of the forces hostile to Western middle-class capitalism (summed up as Freudianism, Marxism and contemporary 'pseudo-sciences'). From that time, Johnson became a belligerent reactionary commentator, anti-Communist and anti-Trades Unions, a devotee and close adviser of Margaret Thatcher when she came to power in 1979, and a noisy polemicist lamenting the decline of the country's morality. He was also a prolific popular historian. It was less known that he was a talented landscape painter, mainly in watercolours.

Stoppard and Johnson became close friends. He described him, privately, as 'exceptionally kind, intelligent, erudite, good company and stimulating, as well as rude, though not rude to us often . . . also a very troubled man . . . Paul long ago defined the terms of right and wrong to his own Christian satisfaction and is fearless in applying them . . . He is stiff-necked, and right most of the time.'

He liked having this informed, argumentative character living down the road. He thought of Copthall 'as my gymnasium, where I go to exercise my mind with Paul'. Their mutual friend Antonia Fraser put the friendship down to propinquity: 'Tom loved having someone to go and talk to . . . whatever you can say about Paul, he's a very interesting man. I don't think they were drawn together by politics.' Over many years, they talked and corresponded freely and warmly. Johnson would write Stoppard long, gossipy letters from wherever he was, full of his opinions on the state of the world, often illustrated with miniature watercolours of the view from his window. He would hold forth on press freedom, religion, Stalin, Ibsen, Thatcher, Conrad Black, Salman Rushdie, writers and history, beautiful women (Johnson had a roving eye) and literary gossip: who was in or out at the *Spectator* or the *Daily Telegraph*, why 'Perry' Worsthorne had quarrelled with Kingsley Amis. They exchanged news on their purchases of paintings, their reading, their children's doings, their writing. So Johnson, while planning his book on *Intellectuals* (1988), picks up Stoppard's description of how his plays evolve: not logically from beginning to end, but through the visualisation of a key scene or moment, and that's where 'the really difficult acts of creation' occur. He often congratulated Stoppard on his work, as in 1990 on *Indian Ink*: 'You once said to me that you were not good at creating characters, but in fact in this play you have produced two sisters who are immensely full and rounded creatures . . . Dear Tom, you have such a wonderful mind as this play shows, so quick and sinewy and inventive.'

They would go to the theatre together, and Stoppard always got the Johnsons seats for his plays. He was very attentive to their children. When the Johnsons moved to London in 1984 (with a country retreat in Somerset), and Stoppard was living on his own, he would ring to say he was just round the corner, and could he drop in? Johnson would often write to say that he was 'yearning' for his company, or, in later years, wishing that they saw him more often. 'We miss you,' he wrote in 1990. 'Remember Dr Johnson's dictum, "Friendships should be kept in constant repair."'

Marigold also wrote to him, often thanking him for being 'a friend in need'. Johnson was for years a chronic alcoholic, and spent times in hospital while they were in Iver. Stoppard sometimes helped in difficult situations. Once, when their son Luke was about seven, Johnson was lying drunk in the bath and couldn't get out. Marigold and Luke tried to drag him out, to no avail. The doorbell rang, and it was Tom, calling round for a chat. Realising she was in difficulties, he called: 'Shall I come up?' Marigold said yes: 'if you don't mind, you could be a great help.' 'He came up to the bathroom, he saw at once what to do, he pulled Paul out of the bath, and said, I'd better dry you a bit and I'm going to drag you into bed.' It was not the only time he came to the rescue, without fuss and without passing judgement.

Stoppard's friendship with Paul Johnson and their mutual admiration for Margaret Thatcher in the 1980s contribute to the version of him as an establishment figure. He supported Johnson in his dramatic switch from the left to the right. 'To a great extent the change of Party-affiliation is an acknowledgement of changes in the Party policies rather than in Paul, who has held consistent moral views from which his politics derive,' he noted in July 1977. That was when he wrote an admiring review of *Enemies of Society*, calling Johnson 'an intellectual affronted by unreason, and a moralist affronted by relativism'. He dedicated *Night and Day*, his 1978 play about the Fourth Estate, to Johnson. ('That caused quite a shit-storm', observed the critic Mark Lawson, especially as the play was 'against the Unions'.) It was Johnson who introduced him to Thatcher, and he became her playwright of choice – 'inasmuch as she went to any plays', Johnson noted.

In 1983 Stoppard was a co-signatory of an open letter to the *New York Times* defending the US invasion of Grenada 'to restore democracy', alongside Johnson, Kingsley Amis, Hugh Fraser, James Goldsmith, Neil Hamilton, Roger Scruton, Nikolai Tolstoy, George Weidenfeld, Peregrine Worsthorne, Woodrow Wyatt and other conservative thinkers. He was on the board of directors, in the late 1980s, of the Committee for the Free World, headed by Midge Decter (wife to Norman Podhoretz, both leading extreme right American commentators), a 1980s neoconservative US think tank which had been behind that letter. Decades later, he joined the advisory board of Johnson's son Daniel's magazine, the highbrow conservative

Standpoint. These affiliations of the 1970s and 1980s need to be set in the context of his committed anti-Soviet activities. But his long friendship with Paul Johnson continues to surprise some of Stoppard's admirers and friends. Another leading journalist and historian, Max Hastings, whose thoughts on Johnson could be summed up by the phrase 'a raving lunatic', finds it extraordinary that Stoppard would have any time for Johnson. When Hastings asked him why he was fond of Johnson, Stoppard replied: 'Paul wants to be good.'

In old age, Johnson dismissed the attacks on Stoppard as a fellow right-winger. He called him, admiringly, 'a libertarian': 'someone who adds to the sum total of human freedoms instead of abstracting from them'. 'He's not a right-wing playwright at all. Tom is very willing to listen to anybody saying anything, he's a remarkably tolerant person, but on what he writes about, he's totally inflexible, and he wouldn't really bend his ear to anyone on the subject.' In Marigold's opinion, 'Tom doesn't like formal politics . . . It's about people.'

Her devotion to Stoppard did not quite extend to his wife, though she recognised that Miriam was stylish and impressive. She was a little miffed when they all went on a Swan Hellenic Mediterranean cruise together in 1977 (Stoppard read *Enemies of Society* on board), along with the *bon vivant* novelist Simon Raven and the cinematographer Freddie Young, and the Stoppards declined to go sightseeing with everyone else, preferring (as Marigold remembered it) to take a hotel room on shore 'so they could go and snuggle together'. 'Miriam hardly left his side,' Marigold complained; 'she was adoring.' She noted waspishly that on the blackboard in the Stoppard kitchen on which were written the day's instructions for the boys' lunch, the message almost always read: 'Fish fingers. Peas.'

Marigold's best friend was Antonia Fraser. They had been at Oxford together. The Johnsons often went to stay in Scotland with Antonia and her husband Hugh Fraser, and their brood of clever children. When her love affair with Harold Pinter began, Marigold was one of the first people Antonia told. So the friendship between the Pinters and the Stoppards overlapped with the Johnsons. No two writer-friends could have been more different in their politics and their personalities than Paul Johnson and Harold Pinter. It's a mark of Stoppard's interest in widely varying human beings that he liked and was liked by them both.

Stoppard got to know Pinter in the early 1970s, about ten years on from when he had mortifyingly tried to introduce himself at the Bristol Student Drama production of *The Birthday Party*. Pinter was seven years his senior and had been a mighty figure in the landscape of British theatre all through his youth. Pinter's plays of the sixties and early seventies – *The Caretaker*, *The Homecoming*, *The Basement*, *Landscape* and *Silence*, *Old Times* – were intensely interesting and important to him. Pinter was part of his panoply of modern writers in the same way as Beckett, or Joyce, or Hemingway were (all writers equally admired by Pinter). By the mid-1970s, they had drawn level in the theatre world. In 1973, Pinter was made an associate director of the National Theatre (by Peter Hall, with whom he would later fall out), while *Jumpers* was still in the repertory. *No Man's Land* was being written at the same time as *Travesties*, and was put on at the Old Vic, in April 1975, nine months after *Travesties* opened at the Aldwych. It wasn't long before they would be rated as equal names: a trivial example of this was a request (to which Stoppard agreed) to run an American Express ad in London theatre programmes, in early 1978: 'Pinter and Pasta? Stoppard and Stroganoff? Dine Out After the Show with Our American Express Card.'

But Stoppard would never speak of Pinter, as a writer, in the same breath as himself. Pinter was, to him, the complete man-of-all-parts. He was not only an astonishing playwright. In addition he was a writer for radio and TV and the author of powerful screenplays. And he was also an actor and director of note. In the early seventies, for instance, he directed *Butley*, a harsh comedy of an alcoholic literary academic in meltdown, by Simon Gray, who became a mutual friend, and, in 1970 at the Mermaid, Joyce's play of adultery, sexual confession and distrust, *Exiles*, with John Wood in the lead. *Exiles* is mentioned in *Travesties*, and had its effect on Pinter's *Betrayal* (1978) as well as on Stoppard's *The Real Thing* (1982). *Betrayal* made a great impression on Stoppard, four years before his own play on the subject. He noted to himself, after the first night in November 1978, that it was 'a very good play . . . deft, witty, clever, sad, and beautifully judged'. He was particularly struck by 'a wonderful speech – a declaration of love – in the last scene'.

Pinter's versatility, energy and hard work were extremely impressive to Stoppard, but that was the least of it. He thought of him as a writer who changed the rules of the game, who made people think about what the language of theatre could do in an utterly new way. Like Beckett or Joyce, he was transformative. Such game-changers, according to Stoppard, are extremely rare – and he didn't think he was one of them. 'The rest of us do things well, or very well, or indifferently.' 'Almost everybody refines', he said of playwrights in general, but 'almost nobody redefines'. When he saw a Pinter play for the first time he couldn't understand the choices the writer was making. He just had to go with it. Something 'completely counter-intuitive' was happening: Pinter was pretending that he hadn't written the play. It was as if he were saying: I know no more about this play than you do. What's there, I know, and you know, but we don't know anything else. He did not provide the 'back-story' for the characters; he asked the question: 'If the past can be obscure, why can't the present?' Instead of the author knowing the story before we do, the author, in Stoppard's phrase, 'seems to have got there late'.

When Stoppard first watched *Old Times*, in 1971 (in which the triangle of Kate, Anna and Deeley refer to various scenarios of their past, to do with sex and friendship, which may, or may not, be 'real'), he was frustrated. Why didn't the author explain, provide more information, tell us 'what really happened'? But he came to see that, like their mutual hero Hemingway, Pinter deepened his work by withholding things. The audience had to concentrate on the precise placing of words. 'The angel was in the detail.'

Professional admiration is one thing, personal fondness another. In this case, there was both. And it was mutual: Pinter liked and respected Stoppard as a writer and as a person. Stoppard's archive is full of notes and cards from him, affable and friendly though not intimate, and signed off with 'love'. There was also some wariness. Stoppard, generally a courteous and peace-loving person, knew all about Pinter's capacity for bristling rages. He was relieved never to have been in the crosshairs. He thought it was worth sitting down to dinner with a person who wrote what Pinter wrote, never mind his opinions, or how badly he might behave. The interest of it overrode the possible discomforts.

And they had one binding passion other than the theatre, which was cricket. Stoppard's bright red Slazenger wicket-keeper's gloves were much in evidence for Pinter's team, the Gaieties. From the 1970s onwards the games still arranged by Anthony Smith were interspersed with regular Pinter cricket fixtures against the *Guardian* team, followed by an evening in the local West London pub. Other playwrights on the team included Simon Gray and Ronald Harwood. As Antonia Fraser noted, nobody was chosen who wasn't a good cricketer. 'It wasn't about friendship, it was about beating the *Guardian*.' Tim Rice, the lyricist (riding high in the late sixties and early seventies with *Joseph and the Amazing Technicolor Dreamcoat* and *Jesus Christ Superstar*) had a team which played against Pinter's, and usually lost. He observed how seriously Pinter took the game. He was 'desperate to win, used to tell people to shut up talking and get on with it; he ruled it like a 1930s master from a prep school'. Pinter used to field in the slips and, according to Rice, was 'a dour opening batsman who would spend a long time in, not scoring too many runs'. The theatre critic (and biographer of Pinter) Michael Billington observed him 'patrolling the boundary, chivvying and encouraging the players, and urging them on to greater achievements'. Kenneth Tynan, himself a cricket fanatic, saw Stoppard playing dashingly and gracefully for 'Skipper Pinter' and 'his disciples' in a West London park in the summer of 1976. Antonia Fraser described a typical match in her diary for 29 July 1978:

The *Guardian* match at Gunnersbury . . . Ronnie Harwood ebullient and rather good; Simon [Gray] a great bat after having grumbled about his low position in the batting order last year; Tom as ever highly professional as wicket keeper in huge bright red gloves. Harold scored a duck, was mistakenly clapped heartily by us (Natasha Harwood [Ronald's wife] and me) as he walked back to the pavilion because we were chatting and hadn't noticed, thus he got into a wax. Furious with *Guardian* for having put on a fast bowler in a bad light, having taken off his own; etc. etc. All good fun. Many cheerful drinks afterwards at a pub in Strand-on-the-Green.

Pinter's private life, when Stoppard first came to know him, was not cheerful. His long marriage to Vivien Merchant was in the doldrums. Like Jose Stoppard, she was jealous of her husband's success, and an alcoholic; though the resemblance ends there, as Merchant was a fine actor who had inspired many of Pinter's plays and had her own public reputation. At the start of 1975 he and Antonia Fraser fell suddenly in love. They were both in their early forties, both famous, married and with children. They kept the affair secret for a time, though Antonia's close women friends rallied round. (Like Marigold Johnson, Antonia's other close confidante, Diana Phipps Sternberg – dashing beauty, interior decorator, inheritor and renovator of her family's Czech castle, Castolovice – was also a friend of Stoppard.) Then, leaked to the press by a wounded and vengeful Vivien Merchant, the affair became a tabloid headline, one of the most talked-about relationships between two people in the arts world since Arthur Miller and Marilyn Monroe. Quite apart from the exciting conjunction of the difficult, brilliant playwright and the charming, beautiful, much-loved historian, there was the frisson of the East End Jewish working-class left-wing writer going off with a member of the Catholic Longford/Pakenham tribe, the titled wife of an upper-class Tory MP. Antonia Fraser, though, always insisted that she and Pinter belonged to the same class, 'the Bohemian class'. Whatever their dramatic differences, it was an intense passion, and a life-lasting relationship. They were together from 1975 till his death in 2008. Stoppard became a fixture in their lives, and remained (as with Teresa Wells) a close and comforting friend to Antonia after she was widowed.

Antonia Fraser had met Stoppard before her life with Pinter began. She thought him very glamorous and exotic-looking, though it never occurred to her that he might be Jewish, and she liked him from the start. She saw him first when *Rosencrantz* got the *Evening Standard* award for Most Promising Playwright (she was a judge) and heard him tell the much-repeated joke – a joke Pinter also enjoyed – about his interview for a job at the *Standard*: 'He asked me who the Foreign Secretary was. I said I was interested in politics, not obsessed by it!' She met him after that at an evening with Derek Marlowe and Piers Paul Read, and was struck by the fact that he left early because 'he had a driver and didn't want to keep the driver out of bed'. She thought to herself: 'What a nice man! – when the whole point of having a driver is that he waits for you.'

The three writers together had fun. Amazed to find that Pinter didn't know what a clerihew was, Antonia started to write one and Stoppard finished it off. Antonia supplied:

> Said Harold Pinter,
> This is a typically Pinter winter.

To which Stoppard added:

> It's the pause
> Before it thaws.

She was fascinated by the differences between Stoppard and Pinter as writers, and thought of it as an unlikely friendship between two very different characters. Stoppard, she thought, was a true intellectual, Pinter was not an intellectual at all. His writing did not come out of intelligence; it was instinctive and passionate. One conversation between them in May 1976 summed up this difference to her. Antonia reported it thus:

> Dinner with Tom and Miriam Stoppard. The latter tackles Harold
> about the swearing in *No Man's Land*. 'This must be something in you,
> Harold, waiting to get out.' Harold: 'But I don't plan my characters' lives.'
> Then to Tom: 'Don't you find they take over sometimes?' Tom: 'No.'

They usually got on well as a foursome. Antonia was adept at defusing Pinter in explosive mode. She discovered after his death that he had kept among his possessions a place-card from a formal dinner, with her name on it, which she had clearly passed across the table to him during a row he was having: 'Darling – You are right. So SHUT UP.' But it was not all plain sailing. Once, in the early 1970s when the four of them were dining out together at Odin's restaurant, Miriam, still rather nervous of Pinter, asked him an unfortunate question: 'Do you think that a writer uses his personal experiences in his work, or is it mainly his imagination?' Pinter, outraged, at once lost his temper and berated her. Miriam cried. She thought that her companions might intervene, but neither of them did. The dinner had to be abandoned, and Pinter stormed out. In the car going back to Iver, she asked what she had said wrong. 'Oh Miri, come on, just think of his plays,' was the response: surely she couldn't really believe they were drawn from Pinter's own life. But why had he not come to her aid? 'I thought you could deal with it perfectly well on your own,' he replied.

Stoppard's version of the event was that she had raised 'the tired question as to whether a playwright is necessarily revealing hidden depths of himself in his characters, and Harold got steamed up'. Miriam, in his memory, 'held her own marvellously while Antonia and I refereed'. If they had leaped in to defend her, he thought, it would have been humiliating for her. 'Harold's position was somewhat mystical, investing his characters with free will. What he meant was that they habitually surprised him (so they should, in any decent work of art) but he showed a surprising fury against the jargon of psychology. A few days later he sent flowers – an unprecedented act according to Antonia.'

He relished the story of a similar dinner-table outburst, when Pinter was lambasting a hapless American woman ('You're an American, are you *aware*, are you *aware* of what America is doing') and Antonia intervened across the table: 'Harold, or *darling*, as I sometimes call you . . .' He denies the apocryphal and much-repeated story that when plans to rename the Comedy Theatre as the Harold Pinter Theatre were running into difficulties, he asked Pinter: 'Why don't you just call yourself Harold Comedy?' (In Stoppard's version, he made the joke to Michael Codron, who repeated it.) He was asked in 2014 by the 92nd Street Y, the New York arts and performance venue, to write a commentary on Pinter's interviews there. He listened to two of these, from 1964 and 1989, and described Pinter's interview manner in cricketing terms: 'When the ball is bowled at him he quickly plays a straight bat.' He wrote down the two utterances which seemed to him to have 'special resonance' with Pinter's life and work. They were: (1) 'There will now be a short pause to let any latecomers in.' (2) 'I would be very glad if you could shut that door at the back.'

Stoppard's and Pinter's political differences were marked. But from the late 1970s onwards, they shared a committed interest in what was going on in Eastern Europe, particularly Czechoslovakia, and a closeness to Václav Havel. When the Pinters visited Czechoslovakia for the first time in June 1989, and stayed with the Havels, they sent joint postcards to Stoppard. Havel said to them: 'I always sign in green, the colour of hope.' Six months later, he was president.

For all Pinter's loathing of Thatcher during the 1980s, he voted for her in 1979 (which he later bitterly regretted), mainly because of the disruption caused by wildcat strikes at the National Theatre to a Simon Gray play which he was directing. But, though Stoppard and Pinter differed on Anglo-American government, free speech in Britain, Thatcher, political theatre, Communism and the press, this was not what they talked about. Stoppard did not join the Pinters' much-mocked 'June 20' political discussion group in 1988 at their house in Campden Hill Square. He did not march in demonstrations alongside them and he did not sign the kind of petitions they signed. But he unswervingly admired Pinter's 'blazing honesty', and they did not quarrel. The most that Antonia Fraser would say about their differences was that they found Stoppard 'more right-wing than most playwrights we know, surprisingly right-wing by our standards . . . we vaguely expect writers to be on the left'.

Some time after Pinter's death, Stoppard would sum up, in one incident, the differences between them, by way of describing his own political shifts between the 1970s and the 2000s. This was in a speech he made when accepting the PEN Pinter Prize in 2013, which he shared with a Belarusian journalist. He said, as often, that he had always celebrated the freedoms he enjoyed as a citizen of England. 'I had never been censored or told what to write. As a citizen I never had to fear the knock on the door.' But he was beginning to feel, he said in 2013, that the freedoms he so valued were being mislaid.

Stoppard told a story to illustrate his point – a story in which Pinter has the last laugh. In 2005, Stoppard had visited Belarus, to give support to the Belarus Free Theatre, and talked to a dissident documentary film-maker, Yuri Khashchavatski. Stoppard told him (as often in such meetings) that he felt the discomfort of coming from a free country, talking to a journalist who had been subjected to violent censorship, and then going home to his freedoms. Khashchavatski replied: 'The fact that you can call your prime minister a liar and a criminal is not his virtue, it is your virtue, the virtue of your people.' Shortly after Stoppard got back from this trip, an elderly man, Walter Wolfgang, was forcibly ejected (to national outrage) by stewards from a Labour Party conference, for heckling Jack Straw over the Iraq war. Four days later, Stoppard's article about Belarus was published in the *Guardian*. Stoppard said in his 2013 speech that he then received a postcard from Pinter, which read, 'Ho, ho.' That postcard, in fact, took the form of (or else was followed up by) a much less gleeful missive, a polite two-page letter from Pinter which read:

Fascinated by your piece about Belarus. You are a goer. To open the door to that world & walk in. Thank you for it. I was of course also struck by your statement that you were going home to a country where you could call the P.M. a liar & a criminal in public. 'Up to a point, Lord Copper' . . . You no doubt read or witnessed the Wolfgang incident at the Labour Party conference? What did you make of that? . . . Love Harold.

The difference between them was most marked in their behaviour over their own plays. Theatre people often compared their experience of working with them. Stoppard's patient presence in rehearsal, engaged and responsive (though not always yielding), would be set against Pinter's legendary intransigence. Pinter's position was clear, and Stoppard understood it well. There was nothing for him to explain: he knew no more than we did. As for taking suggestion or bowing to others' wills, Petey's last words to Stanley in *The Birthday Party* – 'Don't let them tell you what to do' – was Pinter's mantra: 'I've lived that line all my damn life.'

There are many stories of Pinter refusing to answer questions when asked about motivation by the actors, or exploding with fury when changes were suggested. (There are as many about what a brilliant director he was and how many actors loved working with him.) Alan Ayckbourn, who was playing Stanley in *The Birthday Party* at Scarborough in 1958, often recalled 'asking Pinter about my character. "Where does he come from? Where is he going to? What can you tell me about him that will give me more understanding?" And Harold just said, "Mind your own fucking business. Concentrate on what's there."' It is unimaginable to think of Stoppard saying those words to an actor. His son Ed jokingly contrasted Pinter's begrudging agreement to change a tiny detail, like the number of a motorway, with his father's willingness to try out other people's good ideas. Trish Montemuro, stage manager at the National, remembered that during Pinter's (excellent) directing of Giraudoux's *The Trojan War Will Not Take Place* at the Lyttelton in 1983, there was nervousness among the crew: 'The actors called the director Sir – if we were at lunch and the lunch-tray wasn't clean enough – Sir will not be pleased.' Stoppard would never have inspired fear in that way.

One playwright who has been every bit as vigilant and fierce as Pinter in defence of his plays, David Hare, would have a revealing retrospective exchange with Stoppard in 2010. Hare had been embarrassed by the press coverage of the correspondence of his late agent, Peggy Ramsay, which included Hare being rude about Stoppard's 1970s screenplay of *Knuckle*. He wrote apologetically to Stoppard, saying he regretted his 'youthful combativeness' and had, also, come to find Pinter's 'touchiness' 'increasingly ridiculous'. He envied Stoppard his 'equanimity'. Stoppard replied that Hare should not reproach himself for not being 'accommodating'. 'If you were different the plays would be different.' Pinter's 'uncomfortable anger' was Pinter saying 'This is what matters, it's fucking serious!' Comparing himself both to Hare and to Pinter, Stoppard wrote: 'I accommodate too much.'

The theatre director who acutely experienced the difference between Pinter and Stoppard was Peter Wood, who had received a powerful riposte from Pinter, in 1958, to his request that the characters should explain themselves more in *The Birthday Party*:

The play is itself. It is no other. It has its own life . . . I take it you would like me to insert a clarification or moral judgement or author's angle on it, straight from the horse's mouth. I appreciate your desire for this but I can't do it . . . Everything to do with the play is in the play.

The two did not get on – Michael Codron observed 'a kind of *froideur*' between them – and the production, at the Lyric Hammersmith, was a disaster. Wood never worked with Pinter again. By contrast, he forged a sympathetic and fruitful theatrical collaboration with Stoppard – and a lasting relationship.

Of the friendships that began at Fernleigh in the 1970s, one of the closest was with Peter Wood. Miriam had a great affection for him. She enjoyed his flamboyance, his gregariousness and his style – and his kindness. She vividly remembered her first sighting of him, 'shirt open to the waist, [with] a big gold chain with a big gold medallion, smoking a Gitane' in his mannered way. She thought he was gorgeous. 'Don't get worked up, Miri, he's queer,' Stoppard had to explain (circa 1972). Her response was to tick Peter off and tell him he was 'wasted'. Wood became almost a member of the family, often going on holiday with them. He was one of many colleagues who turned into friends. Few people, in fact, got very close to Stoppard. Ronald Harwood, a fellow-playwright friend from the Fernleigh days onwards, said of him in 2014: 'I've known him since 1969 and I don't know him at all.' But everyone basked in the friendship that he did provide and loved being in his orbit. As he would say of his friend John Wells, he made one want to behave 'better than oneself'.

14

Travesties

If there is any meaning in any of it, it is in what survives as art.

The trio of Tom Stoppard, John Wood and Peter Wood was one of English theatre's most high-voltage combinations, and their outstanding collaboration was *Travesties*. They would work together again on Stoppard's version of a Schnitzler play, *Undiscovered Country*, at the end of the decade, and John Wood starred in two more Stoppard plays, *Every Good Boy Deserves Favour* and *The Invention of Love*, with other directors. But *Travesties* was the high point for these three theatrical stars in their thirties and forties. And there's a huge bounce of youthful high spirits in this play. Though it's shadowed by the war and the Russian Revolution, though it's full of insults and arguments, and though its focus is an ageing, forgetful narrator, it has a sunny, blithe feeling to it. It's a play of youth and freedom, with no failing marriages, no children, no parents, no responsibilities. Its absurd, love-struck, talkative characters show off and dance and sing and quarrel and make ridiculous jokes. Written in his mid-thirties, at a time when his life was solidly bedded down in family, children and wage-earning, it is full of uninhibited zaniness and exhibitionism, a young man's play and a farewell to being a young man.

Stoppard has often said that he is a playwright in search of a plot and that when the idea for a play springs at him it's 'as though at the far end of this gilded hall, the double doors have opened and a butler bearing a silver tray turns up and slowly approaches with the idea . . . which he just puts in front of me while the trumpets sound'. For this play – where there actually is a butler bearing a tea tray – the very first idea had come from Anthony Smith, who in the 1960s was writing a novel called *Zero Summer* (published in 1971) in which someone remarks that in 1916 Lenin, Tzara, Jung and Joyce were all in Zurich together: what if they had met? Stoppard asked him if he could use the idea, long before *Travesties* took shape. His first thought, around 1972, was that the play would set Lenin against Tzara

– perhaps a two-acter with 'one act a Dadaist play on Communist ideology and the other an ideological functional drama about Dadaists'. So from the start it was going to be concerned with 'whether the words "revolutionary" and "artist" are capable of being synonymous, or whether they are mutually exclusive, or something in between'. That seminal idea lingers on into the play's final speech: 'You're either a revolutionary or you're not, and if you're not you might as well be an artist as anything else . . . If you can't be an artist, you might as well be a revolutionary'.

It wasn't the first time, nor the last, he thought of writing about the Russian Revolution and its after-effects. In 1968 he'd said he wanted to 'commemorate, probably sceptically, the fiftieth anniversary of the Russian Revolution', perhaps basing it on 'that lovely group of octogenarians, who I believe inhabit a house in Bayswater, who had to flee in 1917 and who are hanging about waiting for the whole thing to blow over so that they can go back'. Now he read himself into the First World War, Tzara and Dadaism, Joyce and *Ulysses*, Marx and Lenin. That half the play takes place in the Zurich library, with Lenin writing his book on imperialism in one corner, Joyce dictating *Ulysses* in another, the 'librarianness' Cecily self-educating herself from A onwards (she has got as far as G) and Tzara cutting up Shakespeare sonnets, is a comic form of intellectual autobiography. A real library – in his case the London Library – was always essential to him; an imagined library, like the one in this play, is a perfect metaphor for how his mind works.

He immersed himself in the atmosphere of Zurich in wartime, with its mix of international exiles, artists, spies and revolutionaries, and wrote it up in a comic swirl of faux-tourist-guide clichés: 'the banking bouncing metropolis of trampolines and chronometry of all kinds', 'the riddled maze of alleyways' and the blessed, 'miraculous neutrality of it, the non-combatant impartiality of it . . . Switzerland, the still centre of the wheel of war'.

He read, for the first time, a great many of Lenin's writings and speeches. And he came to some strong conclusions, which stayed with him. Interviewed about politics and art in 1974, just after he had finished *Travesties*, he spoke firmly and passionately about Marxism–Leninism.

Leninism and Fascism are restatements of totalitarianism . . . The
repression which for better or worse turned out to be Leninism in
action after 1917 was very much worse than anything which had gone
on in Tsarist Russia . . . in the ten years after 1917 fifty times more
people were done to death than in the *fifty* years before 1917 . . . People
tend to think of Stalinism as being something else, a perversion of
Leninism. That is an absurd and foolish untruth, and it is one on
which much of the Left bases itself. Lenin perverted Marxism, and
Stalin carried on from there. When one reads pre-revolutionary
Lenin . . . one can see with awful clarity that ideological differences are
often temperamental differences in ideological disguise – and also that
the terror to come was implicit in the Lenin of 1900 . . .

He went on to argue, firmly, that 'Marx got it wrong'. In *Travesties*, as in
all his plays, contrary views are aired. But that commentary on Marx and
Lenin is not by someone who 'doesn't know' what he thinks. His reading
of Lenin – on revolution and class, on the duty of the artist to be at the
service of society – at a time when he was being constantly attacked from
the left for his lack of political seriousness, solidified his political vantage
point – which was bedded deep in his history and his childhood.

He packed Lenin's beliefs and pre-revolutionary history into *Travesties*.
In the first version of the play, an enormous speech delivered by Cecily at
the start of the second act explains Marxism, the origins of the revolution,
Lenin's path towards leadership (his brother's execution, his imprisonment in Siberia, his exile with his wife Nadezhda), and tracks his journey
from Zurich to the Finland Station in St Petersburg. He made a decision
to derive everything said by and about Lenin from documentary sources.
So while everyone else in *Travesties* is the subject of parodic caricature,
clowning and buffoonery, Lenin and Nadya are treated seriously as figures
from real history.

Of course Lenin had no time for Tzara – that, Stoppard would say, was
'one of the few things Lenin and I agree on'. He had already had a go at
Dada in *Artist Descending a Staircase*, a first sketch for *Travesties*. Now
he brought centre-stage the antics of Tzara and his co-conspirators, Hans

Arp and Hugo Ball, and their creation of a movement which blazed briefly and spectacularly in the cafes of Zurich, then moved to Paris, fizzled out and was overtaken by surrealism. (Later manifestations of Dada are glimpsed in William Burroughs and 1970s punk.) In reaction to the war's senselessness and horror, this nihilist phenomenon substituted childishness, anarchism and self-promotion for artistic talent and discipline and all the bourgeois values. It expressed itself through manifestos, nightclub performances ('noise concert for siren, rattle and fire-extinguisher'), 'simultanist verse', cut-up poems and acts of aggression against its audiences. In *Travesties* its spokesman is Tzara, whom Cocteau's biographer called, vividly, 'a destructive gnome, bellowing his non-poems in different languages', 'inhuman, sarcastic and contradictory', with his 'iron monocle and his plastic heart'. Stoppard presents him as an affected lightweight and show-off, a depthless caricature. But Tzara also gives the play a lot of its excitement. Though he loses all his arguments about art, his speeches are alive with effrontery and outrageousness. Stoppard 'found it persuasive to write Tzara's speeches . . . I found things to say for Tzara.' He is a caricature of the kind of dazzling showman Stoppard was sometimes accused of being – or accused himself of being.

In the end Tzara was set not so much against Lenin (though they do have some riotous clashes) as against James Joyce. One of Stoppard's main sources was Richard Ellmann's life of Joyce, first published in 1959. 'Ellmann's superb biography, whose companionship was not the least pleasure in the writing of *Travesties*', as he put it nicely, provided his real starting point. Joyce had come with his family, Nora Barnacle and their two small children (who notably do not feature in *Travesties*), from Trieste to Zurich in 1915. They were always on the move and had very little money. Joyce was teaching English, trying long-distance to get his play *Exiles* put on and *A Portrait of the Artist as a Young Man* published, going to the opera, having treatment for his eye trouble, and hobnobbing with all the other emigrants, writers, artists and 'café conspirators'. In public he would be found, at all hours, drinking, laughing loudly, talking about art, music and literature in French, Italian and English, making up limericks and singing bawdy songs. In private he was 'indefatigably' writing

Ulysses, whose hero, as Stoppard's Joyce says, is 'the most complete of all heroes – husband, father, son, lover, soldier, pacifist, politician, inventor and adventurer'.

Joyce was approached by a group called the English Players, with a plan to put on plays in English in this international and theatrical city. Ellmann noted: 'Joyce . . . was always ready to be diverted, knowing that no diversions could seriously affect his secret discipline. So he agreeably said, "Why not?"' The Players were hoping for support from the British consulate. But Joyce was already known to the British Consul-General in Zurich, Percy Bennett, for his anti-war doggerel satire, 'Mr Dooley' ('Who is the man, when all the gallant nations run to war/Goes home to have his dinner by the very first cablecar . . . It's Mr Dooley/Mr Dooley/The wisest wight our country ever knew . . . /Mr Dooley-ooley-ooley-oo'), his contributions to a 'neutralist' newspaper and – later – his refusal to enlist for military duty. Ellmann's account of Joyce's anti-British, neutral position ('he stayed out of politics and said little about the war') had a powerful effect on Stoppard's play, where Joyce is given the line: 'As an artist, naturally I attach no importance to the swings and roundabouts of political history.' Stoppard created a version of Joyce as the archetype of the genius who commits only to his art and remains neutral and uninvolved.

Because of Bennett's suspicion of the Irish émigré, the English Players did not receive as much support as they had hoped for when they put on their first production, Wilde's *The Importance of Being Earnest*, in April 1918. Relations were not helped by the casting of a minor consulate official, Henry Carr, in the part of Algernon. The absurd little story of what then happened between Carr and Joyce was Ellmann's greatest gift to Stoppard. Ellmann sums up the incident in a kind review of Stoppard's play, which took pleasure in his 'travesty' of history.

> Carr is not quite invented, although almost nothing is known about him . . . He and Joyce did not hit it off, Joyce finding Carr English and Carr finding Joyce Irish. Their relations were strained after the first performance, when Joyce slipped Carr the fee for amateurs rather than the slightly larger one for professional actors. To make matters worse,

he went to the Consulate next day to demand money for tickets that Carr was supposed to have sold. Carr contended that he had not yet received the money, and that in any case he had had to buy a new suit for the part. He called Joyce a cad and a swindler and threatened to throw him down the stairs. Joyce objected primly to this language as unsuitable for a government office, and went to a lawyer. He sued Carr for money and alleged defamation. Carr, backed by the Consul-General Bennett, countersued for the price of his suit. The litigation dragged on for months: in the end each won one case and lost the other.

In his introduction to *Travesties*, Stoppard describes how he leaped on that story when he read the biography. Details like Carr's purchase of a 'new suit' in which to play Algernon (specifically, 'some trousers, a hat and a pair of gloves') were catnip to the playwright, and at once suggested a vain man with a dandyish passion for clothes. Carr's insults, Joyce's 'prim' reaction and the drawn-out double legal cases were all wonderful material. And he loved the details of Joyce's literary revenge on Carr and Consul Bennett. Stoppard notes: 'Joyce won on the money and lost on the slander, but he reserved his full retribution for *Ulysses*,' where, in Ellmann's phrase, 'he allotted punishments as scrupulously and inexorably as Dante', and fictionalised them as two abusive, drunken soldiers.

In friendly exchanges between the playwright and the biographer (by then, coincidentally, starting work on a book on Wilde), Stoppard said: 'The play is anything but historical.' 'It's *not* an attempt at reconstruction and verisimilitude.' Hence his title – though he did also think of calling it 'gallimaufry', or ragbag. The play is a travesty of history, and all the historical characters are travesties, or caricatures, of their real, historical selves. Its plot is a travesty of Wilde's *The Importance of Being Earnest*. Henry Carr, in the play, says venomously that his legal battle with Joyce was 'a travesty of justice'. And each character thinks the other's view of art is a travesty of the truth.

Once he had found his story, he made Carr the pivot of the play. Just as the play swings between two time zones and two areas, the Zurich public library in 1917 and old Carr's room, so Carr has two roles (as Housman will, in *The Invention of Love*), as the young man about town in Zurich and the old man remembering his past. In *Travesties*, though, unlike *The Invention of Love*, the double part is played by the same person, a juicy challenge for the actor. Carr freed Stoppard to have fun with the historical coincidence of Joyce, Lenin and Tzara together in Zurich during the war. Jung, interestingly, had no part to play. There was enough going on without him, and – unlike *Jumpers* – this was not the kind of play where psychoanalysis could play a useful role. There is no analysis of character and no one going mad in *Travesties*, though madness is loose in the world.

And Carr, although comical, brings the madness of war into the play. In his argument with Tzara over the futility of war, Carr starts by voicing a string of clichés about patriotism and duty, rather in the tone of George Riley in *Enter a Free Man*. But gradually, as if an insistent tune is being played through his strange, unstable free association, the reality of war, and the terror-struck relief of getting out of it, comes hauntingly onto the stage:

> Great days! The dawn breaking over no-man's-land – Dewdrops glistening on the poppies in the early morning sun! The trenches stirring to life! . . . 'Good morning, corporal! All quiet on the Western Front?' . . . 'Tickety-boo, sir!' – 'Carry on!' – Wonderful spirit in the trenches – never in the whole history of human conflict was there anything to match the courage, the comradeship, the warmth, the cold, the mud, the stench – fear – folly – Christ Jesu! But for this blessed leg! – I never thought to be picked out, plucked out, blessed by the blood of a blighty wound – oh *heaven*! – released into folds of snow-white feather beds, pacific civilian heaven! the mystical swissicality of it, the entente cordiality of it! the Jesus Christ I'm out of it! – into the valley of the invalided – Carr of the Consulate!

Carr's presence turns *Travesties* into a memory play. (Over time, that focus would deepen.) 'I conjured up an elderly gentleman still living in Zurich, married to a girl he met in the Library during the Lenin years, and recollecting, perhaps not with entire accuracy, his encounters with Joyce and the Dadaist Tzara.' Since the historical dates don't quite fit the play's

1917 setting, the solution was 'to filter the story through the recollections of a fantasising amnesiac'. And because the play was 'under the erratic control of Old Carr's memory', 'the story (like a toy train perhaps) occasionally jumps the rails and has to be restarted at the point where it goes wild'. The script of *Travesties*, setting up its two locations, makes more of the idea of a memory room than the published play: 'The events take place in the memory of Henry Carr, and our view of the Room and of the Library omits detail in the way that memory might omit it.'

Carr concocts, in long, meandering monologues, his own version of history, with himself always at the centre of events. His self-deluded ramblings parody all the clichés of memoir-writing: 'My memoirs, is it, then? Life and times, friend of the famous. Memories of James Joyce. James Joyce As I Knew Him. The James Joyce I Knew. Through the Courts with James Joyce . . . What was he like, James Joyce, I am often asked . . .'

There are clear links to Stoppard's other plays (and to Peter Shaffer's *Amadeus*, which opened at the National in 1979, propelled by the aged Salieri's vicious and distorted memories of Mozart). Like Rosencrantz and Guildenstern, Carr is the minor character on the sidelines who sees events bafflingly unfurl before him, and when he could have intervened, does nothing. As with George in *Jumpers*, Carr's gargantuan monologues set the tone of the play. As in *The Invention of Love* or *The Coast of Utopia*, real lives underpin the plot. And as in *Indian Ink*, *Arcadia* and *Invention*, a quizzical light is cast on the business of memoir and biography. Stoppard would call *Invention* 'a memory play in which the protagonist has an unreliable memory': that could also be a description of *Travesties*. At the very end of the play, Carr's aged wife Cecily corrects all his facts, like Pike, the editor, in *Indian Ink*. 'I wish I'd known that you'd turn out to be a pedant!' Carr exclaims in exasperation, as Cecily reminds him that he never met Lenin, that he wasn't the Consul and – in a nice final twist to the whole comedy of misremembering – that it was Bennett, whom Carr has cast as his butler, who actually was the Consul. Joyce had his revenge on Bennett and Carr by turning them into grotesques in *Ulysses*; Carr reinvents the real people he dimly remembers; and Stoppard turns Carr and all the rest into imaginary characters in a play. Carr and Joyce have this exchange:

Joyce: Dublin, don't tell me you know it?

Carr: Only from the guidebook, and I gather you are in the process of revising that.

Joyce: Yes.

That is what writers do with history.

Reinventing history runs some risks, as he had already found when using the names George and Dotty Moore. After *Travesties* opened, he was 'somewhat alarmed' to get a letter from the real Henry Carr's second wife, who gave him some facts about her late husband's life and career. He thanked Mrs Carr 'for her benevolence towards me and towards what must seem to her a peculiarly well-named play'. Ellmann also received a letter from Mrs Carr, with the information (which he put into his 1983 revised biography) that 'in later life Carr, who loathed the sight of Joyce, told his wife unconcernedly that Joyce had presented him as a bullying villain in *Ulysses*'.

Stoppard's Henry Carr owes a debt not only to Joyce but also to Nabokov's *Pale Fire* (1962), in which the crazy, obsessive Charles Kinbote edits the late poet John Francis Shade's last work, 'Pale Fire'. Peter Wood noted the resemblance of *Pale Fire* to *Travesties*, 'in that it's narrated by an extraordinary, erratic old gentleman who has (a) a poor memory, (b) powerful reactionary prejudices, and (c) a high sense of fantasy'. Nabokov's influence stayed with Stoppard. He worked on a screenplay of Nabokov's *Despair* two years after *Travesties*. The figure of the pedantic editor would be remembered for Pike in *Indian Ink*. And, in a programme note for *Arcadia*, in 1993, he invented a quotation about Romanticism and attributed it to 'J. F. Shade'. Many years later, at a literary festival, he confessed that he had made up the quotation and 'attributed it to a professor whom I also made up'. The fact that this confession made headlines in 2015 shows the level of attention that Stoppard attracts. But only a few Kinbote/Pike types of pedantic sleuths noticed that the 'made up' professor's name in fact came from *Pale Fire*.

Joyce and Nabokov were linked in his play with a third great stylist, and another of his favourite writers, Oscar Wilde. *Travesties* borrows its comic structure, its characters, its jokes about class and society, and a lot of its dialogue from *The Importance of Being Earnest*. Tzara becomes Jack Worthing, Carr is 'the other one' (he can never remember Algy's name). Cecily and Gwendolen, Joyce's amanuensis and Lenin's devotee, are courted under false names by Tzara and Carr. Bennett is the revolutionary butler who provides a solemn running commentary on the Russian Revolution in the style of Wilde's butler Lane. Joyce's questioning of and disapproval of Tzara have the tone of Lady Bracknell ('Rise, sir, from this semi-recumbent position!'). Miss Prism's absent-minded swapping of the baby and the manuscript becomes Lenin's and Joyce's swapped folders of work. The rivalrous tea party between the two young women is done entirely in rhyming verse, to the tune of an old music-hall routine. He even planned to turn Lenin and Nadya into Canon Chasuble and Miss Prism, but lost courage.

In places Stoppard's jokes are almost indistinguishable from Oscar Wilde's. The sleight of hand is very skilful:

Algernon [in *Earnest*]: Lane's views on marriage seem somewhat lax. Really, if the lower orders don't set us a good example, what on earth is the use of them? They seem, as a class, to have absolutely no sense of moral responsibility.

Carr [in *Travesties*]: Bennett seems to be showing alarming signs of irony. I have always found that irony among the lower orders is the first sign of an awakening social consciousness. It remains to be seen whether it will grow into an armed seizure of the means of production, distribution and exchange, or spend itself in liberal journalism.

Lady Bracknell [in *Earnest*]: What are your politics?
Jack: Well, I am afraid I really have none. I am a Liberal Unionist.
Lady Bracknell: Oh, they count as Tories. They dine with us.

Cecily [in *Travesties*]: The gentleman who has his arm round your waist is a luminary of the Zimmerwald Left.

Gwen: Are they Bolsheviks?
Cecily: Well, they dine with us.

Without its being quoted, old Carr's entire narrative feeds off a line from Wilde's Cecily:

Miss Prism [in *Earnest*]: Memory, my dear Cecily, is the diary that we
   all carry about with us.
Cecily: Yes, but it usually chronicles the things that have never
   happened, and couldn't possibly have happened.

Stoppard said of Wilde: 'I think Wilde was *motivated* by style . . . with Wilde, style was not merely the means, it *was* the end.' His travesty of Wilde's mannered surface led to a play of styles. He often thought of a single gambit for a play: to start with a first scene which turns out to have been written by one of the characters, or to begin with a man being blown out of a pyramid of acrobats, or to have a body on stage which no one can account for. Here the gambit was to write a play in different styles. 'The pleasure of writing it', he said at the time of its 2016 revival, 'was to do with having different kinds of play going on in the same play.' The first scene is the most bewildering medley of all (he loved to baffle his audience at the beginning of a play), with Joyce dictating an impenetrable bit of *Ulysses*, Tzara spouting Dada nonsense poetry, and the Lenins speaking in Russian. Then there are whole scenes lifted from Wilde, a scene made up of limericks, a scene based on the section of *Ulysses* that's written in the style of the Roman Catholic Catechism, scenes drawn from the speeches of Lenin, a scene all in rhyme, and a scene, arising from Tzara's deconstruction of a Shakespeare sonnet, entirely consisting of Shakespearean quotations. Tzara appears as a 'Romanian nonsense' with a heavy accent and absurd manners; Joyce comes on making Irish jokes and singing Irish songs. To add to the gaiety, there are conjuring tricks and music-hall echoes, a strip show in the library, ludicrous puns and plays on words. The style of *Monty Python* (then at its height of popularity) mixes with Wilde. He would say, ruefully and revealingly: 'The passing show, the showing off . . . the pastiche and the jokes and the theatricality of it, was what the play was flourishing and boasting about.' 'I was writing the play to make the kind of exhibition of myself I was too shy to make in real life.'

For Wilde, style was art, art was style. For Joyce, the great artist is dedicated to the perfection of the craft, and his work outlasts history. For Tzara, all that is conventionally called art is rubbish, and anyone can be an artist. For Lenin, the artist must be the servant of the people, decadent art must be suppressed and the revolutionary must close his heart against sentimental aesthetic emotions – as, famously, Lenin resisted the tears that came when he listened to Beethoven's 'Appassionata'. In the heated, abusive battles over art which run through the play, we are nudged into agreeing that art is a matter of craft and talent, that art matters and that it will outlast us – as in the Shakespeare sonnet that Tzara cuts up: 'So long as men can breathe or eyes can see,/So long lives this and this gives life to thee.' When Stoppard imagined the historical characters justifying themselves to each other in the play's debate about art, it is Joyce who 'has the last word'. As he often says, he 'loaded the play for him', he was on his side – as in this speech about Homer's *Odyssey*:

An artist is the magician put among men to gratify – capriciously – their urge for immortality. The temples are built and brought down around him, continuously and contiguously, from Troy to the fields of Flanders. If there is any meaning in any of it, it is in what survives as art, yes even in the celebration of tyrants, yes even in the celebration of nonentities . . . What now of the Trojan War if it had been passed over by the artist's touch? Dust . . .

But Henry Carr also voices Stoppard's own down-to-earth reservations against allowing artists special treatment or pandering to their narcissism. In *Artist Descending a Staircase*, the three young men blunder into the front line and out again, a demonstration of their ridiculous self-absorption. The artists in *Travesties* are 'out of it', too.

Tzara: You could have spent the time in Switzerland as an artist.

Carr (*coldly*): My dear Tristan, to be an artist *at all* is like living in
    Switzerland during a world war. To be an artist *in Zurich, in 1917*,
    implies a degree of self-absorption that would have glazed over the
    eyes of Narcissus.

The most personal moment in *Travesties* is Carr's speech, slightly
reworked from *Artist Descending a Staircase*, about the unearned luck and
privilege of the artist, drawing on that childhood anecdote which Stoppard
often uses. 'I've always felt that the artist is the lucky man,' he said, as he
often said, in an interview while he was writing *Travesties*.

When I was at school, on certain afternoons we all had to do what was
called Labour – weeding, sweeping, sawing logs for the boiler-room,
that kind of thing; but if you had a chit from Matron you were let off
to spend the afternoon messing about in the Art Room. Labour or
Art. And you've got a chit for *life*? (*passionately*) *Where did you get
it?* What is an artist? For every thousand people there's nine hundred
doing the work, ninety doing well, nine doing good, and one lucky
bastard who's the artist.

For all the play's comic disguises, his own views are given there in
plain sight. And though you can't call *Travesties* autobiographical, his
own experiences are deep inside it. Everyone in *Travesties* is an exile, and
Joyce's play *Exiles* gets a deliberate mention. Characters speak in translation and take on double identities. It's a running joke that Carr always
calls Algy 'the other one': but everyone in the play has a double, an 'other
one'. Trevor Nunn remembered saying to Stoppard, while enticing him
to the RSC (though this is not a conversation Stoppard recalls): 'Why
don't you write a play about exile? . . . Because you are one really, aren't
you?' Months later Stoppard offered him *Travesties*, and Nunn thought
that was partly 'because we had once discussed the subject of exile', as
well as because Stoppard felt he owed the RSC a play.

Stoppard took the play to Nunn, one evening in his office above the

Aldwych, and read the whole thing to him. The director was riveted, and at once started imagining it on stage, while the reading was going on – even though Stoppard is not, as Nunn puts it, 'fundamentally an actor'. Nunn was very much hoping that when Stoppard had finished reading, he would ask him to direct it. But Stoppard firmly said that he wanted Peter Wood. 'It felt like a pie pushed in my face,' Nunn said – though he concealed his disappointment. He knew that Wood was a brilliant and funny director, and that it was the right decision. The other vital ingredient was John Wood. Nunn and Ronald Bryden, while luring Stoppard to the RSC, had suggested that his new play should have 'big parts for John Wood and Patrick Stewart'. Nunn's admiration for John Wood at the RSC, for instance his Hamlet-like Brutus in *Julius Caesar* in 1972, was boundless. Stoppard needed no persuading: he had John Wood in mind all the time he was writing *Travesties*. But he changed his mind about which part he should play. In a joint interview with the actor, Stoppard jokingly said it was all about height:

> I knew what Lenin looked like, so John had to be Tzara. Then I discovered that Tzara was a small dapper man so I had to find another way. Then I discovered that James Joyce was also in Zurich. John was Joyce for a while . . . then I came across this Carr figure . . . He's tall! So I wrote a play about Carr . . . if he was tall, John could play him.

Meanwhile, John Wood had been cast as Sherlock Holmes at the RSC, so *Travesties* had to wait until that had settled in. Carr was not easy to play: the challenges were the age changes and the monologues. John Wood described them as 'like huge interlocking curves . . . of varying radius'. But the part was made for him. 'Henry Carr's a lovely character; he's such an idiot.' 'With a play like *Travesties*, you get out onstage and you start and the play just picks you up. It's like being carried on a wind; it's very hard to put a foot wrong.' For all the excellence of John Hurt as Tzara and Tom Bell as Joyce, it was Wood's performance that left everyone gasping. Michael Billington remembered it as one of the greatest performances he had ever seen, with its 'vocal control' and 'lightning contrasts', and the outrageous

way it 'turned sartorial obsession into a sexual fetish'. 'As the aged, rem-
iniscent Carr, Wood was a querulous figure in a battered Panama and
dressing gown. As the sprightly younger Carr, speeding through Zurich
in blazer and boater, he resembled a Max Beerbohm cartoon in perpetual
motion.' Stoppard described Wood beginning, as old Carr, 'as an elderly
streak of mischievous self-regard' and then becoming 'young instantly by
the set of his body, the tension of his muscles . . . hopping as comically as a
cartoon cat stalking a canary'. He was in awe of his 'instinct for making his
body symbolise the changing levels of comedy, of reality, of mood'.

Travesties was a big success. It ran for a year at the Aldwych, then transferred to the Albery Theatre in the autumn of 1975, then went on tour. In the
States, it opened at the Ethel Barrymore Theatre on Broadway in October
1975, and had productions at the Mark Taper Forum in Los Angeles and
the Geary Theater in San Francisco early in 1977. It was staged all over
the world in the 1970s and 1980s, from Sydney to Bristol, from Paris to
Munich and Vienna. (Here, it felt to him very different and more serious:
'The middle-European sensibilities took over.') It won prizes and awards:
the *Evening Standard* Best Comedy, the New York Drama Critics' Circle
award, and three Tonys, including one for John Wood. And it sold well,
both for Faber in the UK and for Stoppard's American publishers, Grove
Press. Stoppard joked to his mother that they were going on holiday to
Jamaica on the proceeds of *Travesties*; the following year, on the proceeds
of *Dirty Linen*, they would probably have their holiday at the Holiday Inn
in Slough. Most critics, including the dominant New York reviewer Clive
Barnes, enthused: 'A tinderbox of a play, blazing with wit, exhilaratingly,
diabolically clever'; 'a miraculous display of verbal fireworks', full of 'sheer
intellectual shimmer'. Charles Marowitz (who had helped Stoppard on his
way to Berlin in 1963) wrote a piece in praise of it which was headed: 'The
theater's intellectual P. T. Barnum'.

But some found it heartless, overloaded and difficult. Robert
Cushman lamented in the *Observer* that he couldn't figure out what the
characters were talking about, and John Barber in the *Telegraph* complained about the undigested 'slabs of theory about politics and art'. In
the States, there were particular difficulties with the play's allusiveness.

Audiences dwindled. Carey Perloff, who from the 1990s was Stoppard's long-term director and friend at the American Conservatory Theatre in San Francisco, would find *Travesties* the hardest of all his plays to direct. 'Audiences do think, what are they talking about? If you don't know every word of *Earnest*, it's hard.'

The biggest difficulties were the Lenins, and Cecily's long history of Marxism and the revolution. Pinter was among a number of admirers in the London audiences who weren't convinced; he told Stoppard how good he thought the play was, but that he felt the only flaw was 'the slab of Lenin at the beginning of Act Two. I didn't understand its placing, measure and weight.' Ronald Hayman confirmed what many others thought when he said that 'the treatment of Lenin comes uneasily and unnecessarily close to historical accuracy'. On Broadway, the producer David Merrick was extremely anxious about those scenes. The Lenins were a bit bolshie, Stoppard told his parents. John Wood witnessed a lot of people walking out during the second half.

But there was at least one occasion when Cecily's long speech about Communism came off beautifully. When *Travesties* was to be staged in Paris, in 1978, he spoke to the director and told him he didn't have to do the whole of that speech. '*Mais pourquoi pas? C'est magnifique*,' the director said. (In telling this story, which Stoppard loves to do, he adopts a terrible cod French accent.) 'OK,' he told him, '*sur votre tête* be it.' After the play opened, they spoke again. How did Cecily's speech go? Stoppard asked him. '*Formidable, superbe*,' the director replied. 'I was thinking, God, this is the sort of audience I deserve. So I go to Paris to see it . . . and he was right. She did every word and you could have heard a pin drop. But she was stark naked!'

But 'the sodding Lenins' (as Stoppard came exasperatedly to call them) were not so easily solved. The problems are clear from the start, in the script, where at one point he commands a switch into bright white light ('no bumping around in the blackout'), the actors come out of character, pick up scripts, go downstage and read to the audience the passages on Lenin's attitude to art, with the actor playing Lenin referring to himself in the third person. That stage direction was soon abandoned.

Looking back, he felt his treatment of the Lenins showed 'timidity', a weakness he often accuses himself of. But in 1974 it was not easy to make fun of Lenin. 'One was dealing with a twentieth-century God, as one might be if one were writing about Freud.' He would come to think that he could have been much more playful with him. But for him to write a satire on Lenin, then, would have confirmed expectations he didn't want to gratify.

I was already being typecast as some kind of right-wing playwright, which I didn't think I was, and it seemed to me that's what I'd be expected to do. So the documentary thing was a way of treating them with a certain respect. I wouldn't do it now and I think it would have been a better play if I hadn't done it then.

Travesties went through more rewritings than any of his other plays. During the first rehearsals at the RSC (when Peter Wood made him write a bigger speech for Joyce), and the Broadway run, and again when the play was revived at the Barbican in London in 1993, directed by Adrian Noble, with Antony Sher as a boisterously energetic Henry Carr, changes continued to be made. A long, stylish riff by Joyce on monocle-wearing was cut, and later published separately. The main changes for the 1993 revival were cutting Cecily's speech right down and treating the Lenins more light-heartedly. He brought back, in one stage direction, the idea he had toyed with and discarded, of turning Lenin and Nadya into Wilde's Canon Chasuble and Miss Prism. He allowed Lenin, occasionally, to join in the Wildean pastiche. ('To lose one revolution is unfortunate. To lose two would look like carelessness!') He broke up the long sections of Lenin's pronouncements on art by having Carr listening, commenting – and often agreeing: 'There was nothing wrong with Lenin except his politics.' Twenty-three years on, and forty-two years since the first production, he went on tweaking and changing this now classic text for the production by Patrick Marber, at the Menier Chocolate Factory Theatre, in 2016.

A number of critics, notably – and hurtfully – his friend and erstwhile mentor Kenneth Tynan, criticised *Travesties*' frivolity and its portrayal of Joyce as 'the artist for art's sake . . . far above the squalid temptations of politics'. Of Joyce's statement in *Travesties* that *Ulysses* 'will leave the world precisely as it finds it', Tynan comments: 'So much for any pretensions that art might have to change, challenge, or criticize the world, or to modify, however marginally, our view of it. For that road can lead only to revolution.' The play confirmed Tynan's view that Stoppard had 'withdrawn with style from the chaos'. He called *Travesties* 'a triple-decker bus that isn't going anywhere'. But within two years of the play's first production, while *Travesties* was winning Tonys in America, Stoppard would be doing the opposite of 'withdrawing'.

The arguments in *Travesties* certainly expressed his view that the value of art is not dependent on its political position. 'I'm not impressed by art *because* it's political. I believe in art being good art or bad art, not relevant or irrelevant art.' The play asks 'whether an artist has to justify himself in political terms *at all.*' Interviewed in 1972, while writing it, he said that art wasn't 'important' politically, and quoted Auden saying that his poetry 'didn't save one Jew from the gas chambers'. But he was upset when the *Guardian* used that quote as its headline for the interview, and felt the need to explain that he'd been making a point about 'art in the short term, not the long term'. Art's importance was that it 'provides the moral matrix, the moral sensibility, from which we make our judgements about the world'.

And *Travesties* was not an apolitical play, in that Stoppard takes a moral view of politics, as well as of art. As he said in 1974: 'One can see with awful clarity that ideological differences are often temperamental differences in ideological disguise.' Forty years on, he was still saying that 'for as long as I can remember all political questions have resolved themselves into moral questions'. *Travesties* can be read as a forerunner of more serious political plays, where individual morality is always the test of any position. And the play sets up one of his main themes: that the independence of the artist is the hallmark of freedom in any society. It foreshadows plays soon to come about repression and censorship under Stalin and the Soviet regime. 'I think I enlist comedy to serious purpose,' he said of it. Yet it is also pure entertainment and joy: voices, styles, jokes, caricatures, music and dancing fill the stage, time switches back and forward at high velocity, and a rabbit is magicked out of a hat.

PART THREE

15

Terra Firma

> Right and wrong are not complicated – when a child cries, 'That's not
> fair!' the child can be believed.

History comes at Stoppard's people. Events swirl round and at them, and
with baffled anxiety and indecision they are caught up in things beyond
their control – whether it's bloody happenings at the court of Denmark,
state funerals, moon landings, the front line of the Great War or the
Russian Revolution. History challenges individuals to decide what is morally right and wrong, what matters and what is true. Stoppard's own 'luck',
in having evaded the catastrophic historical events of his lifetime, and in
living in a free country, was always in his mind. But what of those – especially the writers and artists, the teachers and philosophers, the journalists
and scientists, the actors and thinkers – who find themselves, by ill luck, in
the direct path of catastrophe?

In the mid-1970s, history came at him, and he found his cause, a cause
deeply connected to his own life. Glaring examples presented themselves
of what it would have been like *not* to have his historical luck. He rose
to the challenge of writing about them, but in his own way. He was certainly responding to a decade of being typecast as a wit, a dandy and an
apolitical entertainer. He had not been thought of as taking on political
issues. Yet his preoccupations with integrity, choice, freedom and coercion were continuous. What happened to his writing, and to his public
life, in the mid-1970s, was a development, not a sudden deviation, from
his earlier work. 'The Politicizing of Tom Stoppard', or 'A Playwright in
Undiscovered Country', some headlines had it: but this wasn't quite right.
More to the point was the long, acute appraisal of Stoppard by Clive
James (which he thought 'got it right'), observing that the poetics of his
'enchanted playground' didn't disqualify him 'from treating tough subjects'. In the 'verse-letter' James wrote for him (performed to a large audience which included the Stoppards, at the Institute of Contemporary Arts,

in the summer of 1975), he wrote: 'Your works are so much more/Than clever stunts.'

His inventions flew in all kinds of directions: a comic sketch with an invented language, a political satire with onstage orchestra, a naturalistic television play, a *Carry On*-style farce, a full-scale realist drama about journalism. But the essential link between all this work was language: its use, its censorship, its distortion, its relation to truth. 'The important truths are simple and monolithic. The essentials of a given situation speak for themselves, and language is as capable of obscuring the truth as of revealing it.'

When he started thinking about writing a political play he told himself: 'The truth is too serious for tricks.' But playfulness and irony were still his tools and ploys for expressing moral outrage. And squibs and sketches and light entertainments came bouncing out of him alongside darkening, even anguished, work. Wordplay delighted him all the while he was thinking about the responsibilities of language.

Wordplay was the essence of a light collaboration with Clive Exton, a regular writer for ITV's Armchair Theatre (whose plays included a 1969 spoof on parliamentary procedure, *Have You Any Washing, Mother Dear?*). This was *The Boundary*, a thirty-minute one-act comic thriller for TV, which was written, cast, rehearsed and recorded in a week. Two lexicographers, Johnson and Bunyans, are confronted with the mysterious vanishing act of Johnson's wife – and Bunyans' mistress – in a room swirling with disordered paper slips of dictionary entries. The wife, who assists on the dictionary, speaks in ludicrous malapropisms ('as I drifted back from the barn from which no traveller returns, back from the valley of the château of death, I heard every syllabub of your farinaceous attack on my parson'), the lexicographers entirely in dictionary definitions, puns and double entendres. An offstage cricket game provides the clue to the play's mystery. Exton thought it was 'all too Stoppardian'.

Ed Berman, still looming large in his life, asked him to write a play with an American 'connection', to celebrate the 1976 bicentennial and – ironically – Berman's forthcoming British naturalisation. Stoppard mulled over some ideas: perhaps he might write a play about Walter Winchell, the legendary crime reporter he once met in New York, or a play about his hero of plain, deep language, Hemingway. Meanwhile, he dug out his fifteen-minute speeded-up *Hamlet* for its appearance on the ramparts of the new National Theatre, in the summer of 1976. He wanted to have a go at every possible genre: 'Before being carried out feet first,' he said, 'I would like to have done a bit of absolutely everything . . . I find it very hard to turn down offers to write an underwater ballet for dolphins or a play for a motorcyclist on the wall of death.'

Cliché, double entendre, puns and pastiche were the motors of the double act he eventually contrived for Ed Berman. *Dirty Linen* and *New-Found-Land* started life at the Almost Free Theatre in Rupert Street in April 1976, directed by Berman, with some excellent character actors like Edward de Souza, Peter Bowles and the aged Richard Goolden, and went on to be his long-running hit in the West End and a big success in the States. A one-act play sandwiched inside a farce used the strategy he loved, especially for Inter-Action, of 'yoking things together with violence'. (He took the phrase from Dr Johnson on the metaphysical poets.) *Dirty Linen* was a wild deviation from Berman's original commission, and *New-Found-Land* was written to make the 'American connection'. But the two plays really don't have much to do with each other, except that both are set in the House of Commons, and both have to do with free speech.

The first idea for *Dirty Linen* was a sketch about upper-class British gents speaking entirely in foreign phrases, with a suggestion of murder: 'crime passionelle – rigor mortis – coup de grace – cherchez la femme – femme fatale – j'accuse – dulce et decorum est . . . In other words – a semantic exercise with corpse; my usual thing.' That's roughly how the play begins ('*Toujours la politesse – noblesse oblige – Mea culpa – Après vous*'), but the corpse has been replaced by a scandal. Writing it rapidly in January and February of 1976, he described the project ruefully to himself: 'I think the play is a slightly sexy farce, slightly about journalism. I hope to have a pretty girl in various stages of undress, so even if all else fails . . .' Three weeks later: 'What I have done is not so much a play as an elongated skit with a skittish title – "Maddie Sees It Through" – and a skittish hero-ine who has apparently compromised 109 Members of Parliament and the

Editor of the Times. So that's my pathetic triumph.' Then he dashed off the 'American' play, *New-Found-Land*, and showed the double bill to Miriam. Her reaction was disappointing. She said 'some of the jokes were cheap, that she didn't find it funny and it wasn't, even on its own terms, first rate'. Ed Berman agreed with her, and told him *Dirty Linen* was 'close to sexism' and that there would be hell to pay with the women's movement. Taking note of these objections, he improved it rapidly 'to the point of inconsequential adequacy'.

Dirty Linen is of its time, a send-up of what was then a wildly popular English theatrical genre. When he first went to London, Stoppard had interviewed Brian Rix for *Scene*, under the apt title 'Twelve Years Without Trousers'. Rix was the star of the long-running farces – *Dry Rot*, *A Bit Between the Teeth*, *Fringe Benefits* – which had been playing since the 1950s at what Stoppard called 'the goldmine known as the Whitehall Theatre'. Box-office takings could be 'a million pounds' for these 'Whitehall farces', all boisterous saucy high jinks, slamming doors, embarrassingly exposed bottoms, lacy bloomers, outrageous innuendo and madcap bedroom confusions. They all had two-dimensional stereotyped characters and eye-rollingly bigoted jokes, as on old seaside postcards, about mothers-in-law, homosexuals and curvaceous brainless 'dolly-birds'. And they worked through perfectly timed and crafted structural plotting. They moved theatres, had different authors and reappeared as movies or TV series, but the essential ingredients – as for the equally indestructible *Carry On* films and stage plays – were always the same. After the end of the Lord Chamberlain's theatre censorship in 1968, they got much saucier. They were avoided or condescended to by serious theatre-goers and critics, but they filled the houses.

Stoppard noted their lucrative popularity. When *Dirty Linen* opened, *No Sex Please, We're British* (by Anthony Marriott and Alistair Foot) was five years into its sixteen-year run – a farce in which the arrival of a load of unsolicited pornography in a suburban bank clerk's household cues a wild rampage of falling trousers, scandalous confrontations and laboriously risqué jokes ('I can't wait for you to take a look at my portfolio'). Michael Pertwee's *Don't Just Lie There, Say Something!*, with Brian Rix, had been made into a film in 1973 and then an ITV sitcom called *Men of Affairs*. Its basic gag, about a minister involved in a Bill to maintain the nation's moral standards, who turns out to be a serial shagger, and who is being exposed, in all senses, by a radical group of free-living beatniks, with a prurient press playing its part, lends the idea of hypocrisy in ministerial high places to *Dirty Linen*.

Stoppard was not a snob. He liked popular culture – *Monty Python*, *The Goon Show*, *The Two Ronnies*, rock 'n' roll, spy stories, American movies, going on *Call My Bluff* with Miriam. ('Samuel Beckett would never have gone on *Call My Bluff*!') He liked things that were very English. He relished terrible jokes and vulgar innuendo – as in the bedroom scenes with Dotty and her 'psychiatrist' in *Jumpers*, or the striptease in the library ('Get 'em off!') in *Travesties*, or the excruciating puns in *The Boundary* ('And her drawers – never found anything in them'). And he liked taking off from classic theatrical models. Remaking Shakespeare, Agatha Christie or Oscar Wilde was a pleasure to him, though he sometimes worried that that was all he could do. 'All my ideas for a play for Berman', he noted privately, 'are attached in some way to the bedrock of existing données – I can't float free. It is a temperamental weakness.'

Like other playwrights who took bedroom farce and made it their own – Joe Orton's *What the Butler Saw* (1969), a gleeful riot, just post-Lord Chamberlain, of sexual depravity and violence, or Alan Ayckbourn's 1975 *Bedroom Farce*, or Michael Frayn's later *Noises Off* (1982), in which a terrible repertory production of a farce called *Nothing On* drives the backstage comedy – he enjoyed the idea of applying his wits to parodying and subverting a much-loved English genre. And it certainly paid off.

The basic joke of *Dirty Linen* was to have a 'Whitehall farce' set in Whitehall. It picked up on some hot current affairs. The Profumo affair of 1963 was being echoed by the *News of the World*'s exposure of Lord Lambton's 'debauchery' with prostitutes (the Labour peer resigned in 1975), and the homosexual scandal surrounding Jeremy Thorpe was in all the tabloids, leading to his stepping down as Liberal leader in May 1976, a month after *Dirty Linen* opened. 'It looks rather more topical now than it did when I was writing it,' he told BBC's *Tonight*. The timing was

elegant, intelligent, magnificent – and one reviewer called it his best play. Both plays were translated into Czech in 1979. Havel wrote to Stoppard that he was 'very surprised by your ability to imagine the circumstance of ours'.

One more short theatrical curiosity sprang from the intense events of 1977, a play also about language and surveillance, inspired by Pavel Kohout's 'Living Room Theatre' productions. It was Stoppard's last collaboration with Ed Berman (after that, in the 1980s, the collaboration ceased, and Berman and his Inter-Action projects fell on hard times). *Dogg's Hamlet* rewrote and expanded his skits for Inter-Action of five years back, *Dogg's Our Pet* and *The (Fifteen-minute) Dogg's Troupe Hamlet*, with their speeded-up versions of *Hamlet* and the joke of teaching the audience how to understand the school-language of 'Dogg' as they watch the play. *Cahoot's Macbeth* was grafted onto *Dogg's Hamlet* in the manner of *Dirty Linen* and *New-Found-Land*. But it was a darker thing altogether.

A secret production of *Macbeth* is interrupted by an Inspector who speaks, Pinterishly – or Havel-like – in threatening clichés: 'It's as if the system had a mind of its own . . . I've arrested more committees than you've had dog's dinners.' Though he uses banal English, his references (columns of tanks, normalisation, one-party system) are all Czech. He and his superiors object to the free expression that can be smuggled in through Shakespeare:

> The chief says he'd rather you stood up and said, 'There is no freedom in this country', then . . . we all know where we stand. You get your lads together and we get our lads together and it's all over, one of us is in power and you're in gaol. That's freedom in action. But what we don't like is a lot of people being cheeky and saying they are only Julius Caesar or Coriolanus or Macbeth.

And the blood, tyranny and madness of *Macbeth* all too obviously relate to what is going on in Czechoslovakia – as in Macduff's cry: 'Bleed, bleed, poor country!'

Things get more confusing for the Inspector when Easy, the long-distance lorry driver out of *Dogg's Hamlet*, appears as Banquo's ghost, speaking

Dogg. The actors start to pick up Dogg from him and turn Shakespeare into Dogg: so 'Tomorrow, and tomorrow, and tomorrow' becomes 'Dominoes, and dominoes, and dominoes'. Dogg-speech allows the play to say out loud Stoppard's private words to himself about the tyrants: 'They're pigs.' 'Cretinous fascist pig,' says Easy, in Dogg, and gets away with it. As the Inspector notes, 'Words can be your friend or your enemy.'

Stoppard was not entirely happy with his double bill, given in a patchy performance by Berman's BARC company of American and English actors. But it had a robust life, opening at the Arts Centre at Warwick University in May 1979, then going to the Collegiate Theatre in London and to New York and Boston in the autumn of 1979 – and has often been revived. Critics preferred *Dogg's Hamlet* to *Cahoot's Macbeth*, which was felt to have too much Shakespeare and not enough Stoppard.

Cahoot's Macbeth (and other plays too, from *After Magritte* to *Dirty Linen*) had affinities with Havel's Kafka-like satires and black comedies, so much concerned with distortions of language, invasion of privacy, upended logic and bureaucracy run amok. Though their lives and fates were so different, the parallels between them were strong. Kenneth Tynan, who had introduced him to Havel's work, pointed out these parallels in his long piece on Stoppard for the *New Yorker*, published at the end of 1977. Tynan played up Stoppard's Czech-ness ('Essential to remember that Stoppard is an émigré'), comparing him also to Nabokov. But it was unfair – and unfriendly – of Tynan to use Havel as a stick with which to beat Stoppard. He contrasted them as the Czech playwright of 'burning conviction', courageously enduring silencing and persecution, and the 'bounced Czech' turned English conservative dandy, 'withdrawing with style from the chaos'. He praised his dazzling early work, which he rightly took credit for helping along, told the wicked story of Stoppard's trying to read *Jumpers* to a baffled Olivier, and inaccurately claimed to have single-handedly made the cuts that play needed. But he lambasted *Travesties* for preferring art for art's sake.

The character of Stoppard which he drew – whether as a writer, or playing cricket with Pinter's team, or charming a hall of students in Santa

Barbara, or dining at New College – was cool, clever, glamorous, witty and self-preserving. At the lecture hall, he noted: 'Tom's modesty is a form of egoism. It's as if he were saying, "See how self-deprecating I can be and still be self-assertive."' He made much of his looks, particularly the often-drawn comparison to Jagger: 'You might mistake him for an older brother of Mick Jagger, more intellectually inclined than his frenetic sibling.' He rustled up some old cronies and rivals (Geoffrey Reeves, Derek Marlowe, James Saunders, Charles Wood, Peter Nichols) to say how emotionally guarded he was, how he 'likes to be liked', how he always played safe: 'In matters of emotion, Stoppard is one of nature's Horatios; you could never call him passion's slave, or imagine him blown off course by a romantic obsession.' He noted that Stoppard had 'once said' that his favourite line in modern drama was from Christopher Hampton's *The Philanthropist*: 'I'm a man of no convictions – at least, I *think* I am.'

The subject of the profile took it steadily ('a distorting mirror, inevitably . . . For all that . . . he does a good job'), but did not enjoy it. It wasn't pleasant to be satirised by one of the theatrical figures he most admired, and to whom he was indebted. And this was a high-profile feature which attracted a lot of attention and would stay in the clippings forever. Most acutely, Tynan's treatment of his childhood – which shrewdly pointed up some gaps and mysteries – upset his mother, and therefore him. In the profile, Tynan reported a conversation with Stoppard about his family's past. Why, Tynan had asked him, could the circumstances of his father's death in Singapore, and his family's Jewish background, not be 'cleared up by his mother?' He quoted Stoppard in reply: 'Rightly or wrongly, we've always felt that she might want to keep the past under a protective covering so we've never delved into it.' Stoppard showed the draft of the piece to Bobby, who responded emotionally with a long, defensive letter, which Stoppard quoted back to Tynan. From those quotes, it seems that, as always, she played down their Jewishness. She said that they left Czechoslovakia because the Germans, 'going hysterically into everyone's ancestry . . . would have found that your grandparents had some Jewish relations in Austria, but up to then . . . nobody gave it a thought – we didn't know or care . . . your father and I were not religious in any way . . . it

really is getting out of hand when people call you an "émigré". Stoppard
told Tynan that

> much of her letter is taken up with explaining that for reasons which
> seemed good to her (and understandable to one who knows her) she
> felt that British chauvinism would put us children at a disadvantage
> among our new peers if much was made of her foreignness. She is
> now in a state – half guilty for seemingly shutting us off from our past,
> and half explaining that she never really did so.

A few years later, in 1981, when she was seventy, he asked her to write
down the story of her past. He sent her a handsome leather-bound notebook as an incentive, which she characteristically sent back ('it seems a
waste'). She wrote some pages in a cheap exercise book. But she left a great
deal out. It would not be for many years that he would discover what his
mother had been concealing.

He asked Tynan to make some cuts; but Tynan went ahead and printed
most of the article. A shorter version then came out in the *Sunday Times*,
with a cartoon of Stoppard by Mark Boxer, who also edited the piece.
Stoppard wrote to him with some irritation. Tynan had taken a long time
to write the feature; its critique of him for being over-detached was by
now, since *Every Good Boy* and *Professional Foul*, out-of-date and unjust.
'It looks, I would have thought, somewhat ill-informed,' Stoppard told
Boxer, calling it 'a car with a bent chassis'. 'It really brings on the shud-
ders . . . I think I'll stay in bed on Sunday.' In his journal, he noted that it
made him feel depressed and over-exposed, and was 'altogether unfortunate'. And it was no longer true: 'I have changed, and am changing, further
than the article can take account.' 'Don't take any notice of it,' he advised
his mother.

Tynan had misrepresented him. But Stoppard was tolerant, when he
admired people's work. Three years later, when Tynan died at fifty-three,
he spoke at his memorial, and said: 'For those of us who were working
in the English-speaking theatre during those years, for those of us who
shared his time, your father was part of the luck we had.'

Far from withdrawing from the fray, from the late 1970s Stoppard was fully engaged. And his relationship with Havel would continue for the rest of Havel's remarkable life. Ten years on, they would join forces as playwrights with Stoppard's free translation of *Largo Desolato*. In 2006, their alternative destinies would get into *Rock 'n' Roll*.

In 1984, Havel was out of jail but under surveillance. He had no passport and could not leave the country. Stoppard, at his request, went to the University of Toulouse to accept an honorary doctorate on his behalf. He read Havel's speech for him, which was published as 'Politics and Conscience'. It set impersonal systems of totalitarian power against the natural world and the humanity of individuals, and recommended 'antipolitical politics', 'politics as practical morality, as service to the truth, as essentially humanly measured care for our fellow humans'. Stoppard read the speech and made some comments, which he jotted down in note form. The last note was: 'All political questions are moral questions.' Back home in England, a few weeks after this trip, he wrote to him.

I'm feeling rather conscious of you today for a very peculiar reason. I dreamt last night that I had been sent to jail (I don't know why) for three years. My dream was about my first day in jail. I was in a terrible despair about being there and, in my dream, hoped it was only a dream but knew it wasn't. Then one of my children woke me up when he was going to school and after the first moment of relief that I wasn't in jail but merely in bed I immediately thought of you and how frightful it must have been when there was no possibility of waking up and finding yourself at home.

17

The Fourth Estate

There is nothing I feel more strongly about than a free press.

His political morality was inextricable from the value he put on true words, whether in the language of government or journalism or play-writing. He was a scrupulous and inventive user of language, who believed (as he said in a jokey 1972 review for *Punch* of the 'Supplement to the *Oxford English Dictionary*, A–G') in dictionaries as 'prescriptive' rather than 'descriptive', and who was a traditionalist about usage. When he watched his plays in rehearsal, making changes if it helped with pace and clarity and structure, the essential thing for him was that the language should be alive. In 1980 he said he had rewritten six pages of *Night and Day* three months after the play opened because 'they were inert. Now they are definitely ert.' That's the kind of wordplay which by now was being called 'Stoppardian' – an adjective which got into the *Oxford English Dictionary* in 1978. Reading an account in the *Sunday Times* of the death of a journalist – a death that sparked off the plot of *Night and Day* – he winced, even through the horror of the story, at the 'bad journalism' of the piece: 'putting together words for extra emotion but no extra information – "death commando", "terror-blast" (as a verb), just the sort of journalism it's not worth dying for'.

His love for the most exact and most exciting use of language cut across many kinds of writing. The plays came first, of course. Once he was on to the next one, he never stopped thinking about it, at whatever stage: the turning of an idea into a plot, structural challenges, a speech needing rewriting or a joke re-timing, and all the million issues of production – directors, auditions, set design, rehearsals, actors, previews, openings, box-office takings, transfers, translations, new productions, cast changes. The play of the moment was always in his mind.

At the same time, there was everything else: journalism, interviews, lectures, political speeches and protests, radio, television and films – quite apart from domestic life, social life, letter-writing, newspaper-reading, travel and, at the end of the decade, house-moving. He had enormous energy and stamina – and he felt time at his back. Writing to Piers Paul Read, in September 1979, he said that a lifetime 'felt so short now'. 'I am naively discovering the telescopic effect of personal, as opposed to historical, time. I have now been working for as many years as elapsed between the outbreak of the First World War and the outbreak of the Second. Is it possible?' He was counting from 1954, the year he left school. A year later, in his birthday month, after an intensive social week and faced with a deskful of unmet deadlines, he joked to his mother that he felt more like a nap: 'Over the hill at 43.'

But in fact he kept up a formidable pace of work. In the mid to late 1970s, alongside the political and theatre work, he wrote two screenplays, and worked on others that were never made into films. This (after *The Romantic Englishwoman*) was the start of a lifelong involvement with the movies. They provided a main source of income, but they were always a gamble. Sometimes they paid off. Sometimes they involved huge amounts of work for no results. Often they were frustrating experiences involving large numbers of executives who had money and power but very little idea of what he had in mind. Because he was being paid well, because other people depended on what he was doing, and because he had a scrupulous work ethic, he always took the film work completely seriously, even when he had no intention of having his name on the finished item. In the early years he also felt some excitement at working with famous film stars and directors and at the buzz of the film world. An unpublished section in a late-1980s interview shows up this side of him, the side that was a fan among stars. He was in Los Angeles to talk to Sean Connery (presumably about Connery's ill-fated involvement with the film of *Rosencrantz*), and somewhat in awe of him. 'The telephone rang and it was Paul Newman, another giant. So I laughed, and when he asked why I was laughing, I told him. A few minutes later the phone rang again, and a voice said: "This is Robert Redford." But it was Paul Newman, joking. So the groupie in me enjoys the social advantages of success.'

But he also treated movie-making with wariness, amazement, cynicism and, at times, dismay. These mixed feelings come out in his letters to his mother. He relished bad jokes about the industry, as in, 'The only poly-syllable word tolerated in Hollywood is delicatessen.' On a flight to Los Angeles in 1968 to talk to John Boorman about his first venture into the film world, the possible movie of *Rosencrantz*, he watched 'a film so bad that people were walking out at 35,000 feet'. But the long-drawn-out nego-tiations with MGM in the late 1960s for the *Rosencrantz* film (not the one which was eventually made, under different circumstances, in 1990) went beyond a joke. And he could never quite believe what he was being asked to write by film-makers and producers, as in 1979: 'Lew Grade (in theory) wants me to write a film based on Pushkin's *Onegin*, so Kenneth tells me, unless he's got it wrong and it's really the movie of the Onegin Line.' Ten years on, he was being asked to work on some very unlikely stories. 'Film people . . . ask me to do the oddest things, like a film about Peruvians, as if I would have the faintest idea how to write such a thing. I have also been asked to do a full length cartoon based on the Beatrix Potter charac-ters . . . I even considered it for 24 hours.' (One of the great lost Stoppard scripts?) Certainly he thought of this work primarily as paying the bills, as when in 1980 he was being asked by 'a film mogul' to do a screenplay of *Night and Day*, which he didn't know how to do but 'was making an effort', with domestic expenses in mind. When that was over he might be able to do some 'proper' work. In his journal, while working on a doomed screenplay called *The Frog Prince*, he wrote: 'Films are frogs insisting that they are princes . . . take the money and run.' And he quoted his old friend John Boorman: 'Making films is turning money into light and then back into money again.'

But he was pleased to be asked to work on the two books he turned into films in the 1970s, both by writers he admired: Nabokov's *Despair* and Graham Greene's *The Human Factor*. Utterly different in their style and in their characters, they were both about doubles – double lives, double agents. They were both novels written in the shadows of wars and conflict. Nabokov's was written, first in Russian, in the 1930s Berlin of growing Nazism. Greene's, published in 1978, drew on Communist involvement with South Africa's apartheid regime during the Cold War. *Despair* had a sensitive, disdainful, deluded Russian émigré at its centre, a chocolate-factory owner in Berlin who becomes obsessed with a vagrant he thinks is his double, and who plans to commit the 'perfect crime' by murdering him and taking on his identity. It was mannered and grotesque, like a comic pastiche of Dostoevsky. Greene's novel, darkly realist, written in a tone of weary disillusion, was about a conflicted Englishman with a hidden past, caught up in the plotting and treachery of others. Stoppard tried to be faithful to both styles.

He read *Despair* in the summer of 1976, and gave himself four weeks to write the script (while involved with the revival of *Jumpers* at the Lyttelton, the US production of *Dirty Linen* and his activities for Soviet dissidents). In October he took the script to Munich for a meeting with the director, Rainer Werner Fassbinder, and they agreed that Hermann should be played by Dirk Bogarde, who had done psychic torment so brilliantly in *Death in Venice* and *The Night Porter*. Bogarde got a call in his house in France from 'a rather high, anxious voice, which sounded . . . as if it were coming from the middle of a bus-station'. He turned his memory of the call into a polished anecdote:

> 'My name is Tom Stoppard,' cried the voice. 'We haven't met.'
> 'No.'
> 'I'm at London airport . . . I've just got in from Munich . . . I gather you aren't making any more films; am I right?'
> 'No. Wrong. I'm not making any more crap.'
> There was a short pause.
> 'I don't write crap,' he said crossly.
> 'I'm sorry. I wasn't talking of *your* work.'

In February 1977, they dined together at the Connaught: Stoppard found Bogarde funny, dapper, frail, and very sharp about money. There was a script conference at Bogarde's house in March, which did not go smoothly. Stoppard was 'reluctant to lay a heavier hand on the narrative in order to make [a] psychological point'; he was 'more afraid of being over-explicit than under-explicit'. He also assumed that Bogarde would play both Hermann and his 'twin'. Fassbinder had other ideas, Bogarde noted:

We sat round the table, pencils poised, scripts before us, while Mr
Stoppard feverishly re-wrote passages and then read them, eagerly,
aloud, while Fassbinder shrugged from time to time, showing a
marked indifference to what was going on, and frequently yawned.
It was perfectly clear to me . . . that he would make *his* version of
Despair, when the time came, and do exactly what he wanted.'

So it proved. When Stoppard saw the first version of the film, he
thought it 'very slow and pretentious. Fassbinder embraced the very sin
which I had implored him not to commit – he has brought all Hermann's
agony to the surface, to the death of comedy . . . for me it is a debacle.' He
wrote a candid letter to Bogarde, whose performance he greatly admired,
about the film's shortcomings, and, unusually, sent a copy of the letter to
his parents so that his views could be on record. When the film showed
at the Cannes Film Festival in May 1978 it won no prizes; when it was
released in 1979 it was 'a critical success' – some found it haunting and
impressive – and a box-office failure. The whole experience was frustrating. But the film's hall of mirrors and doubled identity stayed with him
for *Night and Day*. And he thought it was funny when Boorman told
him what Billy Wilder had said: 'It's very hard to imagine a farmer in
Nebraska saying to his wife, I feel like a movie, honey, let's go and see
Fassbinder's *Despair*.'

If Fassbinder was unbiddable, his next director, Otto Preminger, was
notoriously overbearing. When asked to write the screenplay of *The
Human Factor* for a Preminger film, he noted apprehensively in his journal that the director was famous for his 'violent temper'. And Preminger
at once started to hassle him, calling him up from New York: 'Are you
verking?' Stoppard, not a person to be bullied, sent Preminger a message
in the course of an interview in the *New York Times*: 'Tell him that Tom
Stoppard sends his love, that I am, and please not to do that again.' For tax
reasons (if he did the work abroad he would have less tax taken off his fee)
and 'just to get the work done', he went to a luxurious hotel in Brittany, in
July of 1978, and wrote the script in nine days, working from 10.30 a.m. to
12.30 at night, with breaks for swimming and eating.

He was faithful to Greene's story of the quiet, orderly Maurice Castle, working for MI6 and living in Metroland with his South African wife and her black child, his adopted son. Like Greene's old boss at MI6, Kim Philby, Castle is a double agent – because a Communist friend (now dead) helped Sarah and Sam escape from South Africa. Castle's weakness has always been, as his mother tells him, 'an exaggerated sense of gratitude for the least kindness. It was a sort of insecurity. You once gave away a good fountain-pen to someone at school who offered you a bun with a piece of chocolate inside.' (Greene's dialogue is word-for-word in Stoppard's script.) But he is exposed, finds himself the tool of corrupt international interests, is separated from his family and sent to Moscow, where he has never wanted to live: 'I'm afraid I'm not a Communist, just a casualty of the Cold War.' 'They'll cure you,' is the response. 'In a psychiatric ward?' he asks.

This job went better than *Despair*, though Graham Greene, with whom he had a polite exchange of letters, told Preminger that Stoppard didn't know enough about South Africa for the flashback scenes, and wanted his Afrikaner friend Etienne Leroux brought in as an adviser. Greene was also despairing when Robert Morley was cast to play a villainous MI6 character: 'Well, there is nothing to do except hope that Preminger has a stroke before the film is made,' he wrote to Stoppard. The film, released in the UK early in 1980, was workmanlike and unexciting (Stoppard let slip later that he thought it was 'awful'), but with a moving performance by Nicol Williamson. And Preminger, delighted by Stoppard's bringing Miriam and Ed, aged five, onto the set, turned out to be charm and kindness itself. Obviously this ogre had been misunderstood, Stoppard thought. Except the next minute, as he recalled it, 'a second assistant or someone said to him something like "Should we break for lunch, sir?" and Otto instantly blew his top. "Who are you? Who asked you?" – and sacked the man on the spot (though I doubt he stayed sacked.)'

The Human Factor, published a few years after Le Carré's novel *Tinker, Tailor, Soldier, Spy*, had its effect on Stoppard's double-agent plots, *The Dog It Was That Died* in 1983 and *Hapgood* in 1988. And the tough male world of international conspiracies, hard-bitten operators and *realpolitik* in both films, as well as the African background of *The Human Factor*, affected the tone of *Night and Day*. Greene's story also has at its heart the figure of a vulnerable small boy. That figure, so important to Stoppard at that time – 'there seems to be a ten-year-old-boy in all my plays' – returned in *Night and Day*, and is used as a litmus test for what is fair and just.

Night and Day is an argumentative action drama set in a male world, unusually bullish and hard-edged for Stoppard (there's nothing like it until *Hapgood* ten years later). The fantasy dictatorship of *Jumpers* has turned into a 'real' political plot. No other Stoppard plays have an African power struggle, mines, helicopters and jeeps, tanks, machine guns, flares and telex machines. But it also has a strong personal agenda. And in the middle of its macho jostling is a complex woman character, whose secret fantasy life cuts athwart the action. He wanted to write 'emotionally truthful scenes about a woman' in response to those who said that he didn't write good parts for women – or, as he caricatured it: 'There was always this bloke with the long clever speeches and these women fluttering about giving him feeds.' It was going to be about love at first sight – 'love and journalism', he told himself. It was a while before he realised that the play he wanted to write about journalism (and love) and the play he wanted to write about freedom were 'the same play'. The link came out of his feelings about Eastern Europe, but was roused up too by events close to home. The wars between left and right in Britain in the 1970s centred to a huge extent on the power of the unions: *Night and Day* was written on the back of the three-day week, Heath's struggle with the unions, and industrial unrest across the industries, from miners to garbage collectors to journalists. Stoppard dedicated the play to Paul Johnson because of their like-minded horror at the threat of state control, either in the Soviet Union or at home. Arguments over the closed shop – the employment clause that obliged you to be a member of the union if you worked – were hot issues in theatre and journalism, the two professions Stoppard minded about. He was a member of the Dramatists' Sub-Committee for the Society of Authors. This opposed calls for a closed-shop clause for playwrights writing for the subsidised theatres, the National and the RSC. He was one of several playwrights – like Pinter and Peter Nichols – who weren't members of a union. He was opposed to the National Union of Journalists' insistence on the closed shop. He thought the journalists' strikes of the late 1970s at the tycoon-owned papers – the *Daily Express*, the *Evening Standard*, *The Times* – were unjustified. He spelt it out in a letter to *The Times* in August 1977. 'A closed shop is a state of affairs where if, for example, I want to work for a newspaper, all I need is to avoid offending some person or group in a position to withdraw my right to do so, on that paper or any other. This is called absence of freedom of expression.'

A few years later, when the print unions, a year after the crushing of the miners' strike, attempted to resist modernising technology at the Murdoch papers, because it would led to mass lay-offs, and were outmanoeuvred and defeated by Murdoch's moving the *Sunday Times* to Wapping, he was 'gung ho for Wapping, for Murdoch, for Thatcher'. He thought they were freeing Fleet Street 'from the protection racket'. In later years, caught up in the debate about the Leveson Inquiry, he would look back critically on his 'zeal for an untrammelled press' and on his refusal to accept that media ownership by tycoons might involve quite as much censorship as the stranglehold of the unions. 'Now', he said in 2005, 'I'd be capable of writing a letter in reply to myself . . . Look at Berlusconi and Putin – it's complete manipulation and control.'

In the late 1970s he said repeatedly, in private and in public, that a free press was at the heart of 'English social virtues', and that the most important thing for a nation's health and civilisation was to have a press that could put all views objectively (for instance on Cambodia). When he compared Communist countries and the West, he would say: 'Again and again, it all comes down to a free press.' And, at forty as at seventeen, he was a journalism groupie. As a schoolboy, his fantasy was to be a tough, grizzled war journalist, sending back true facts under fire, from some-where in Africa. He loved meeting the big men of journalism, like Walter Winchell, or Ben Bradlee of the *Washington Post*. He asked Harold Evans, editor of the *Sunday Times*, to help him with his new play. He was well aware of how ruthlessly competitive journalists could be, and he knew about cheap, tacky tabloid journalism: he'd put all that into *Dirty Linen*. The sleaze was the price you paid for the independence. But like Maddie in *Dirty Linen*, he also wanted to tell people who despised the press: 'You don't know the first thing about journalism.'

As usual, once the idea for the play came into focus, he wrote it fast, through 1978. He wanted a situation where journalists' lives could be at risk in a dangerous country. The deaths of the journalists Nick Tomalin, in Israel in 1973, and David Holden, the *Sunday Times* Middle East correspondent, in Cairo, at the end of 1977, made a strong impact on him. He was a great admirer of the photojournalist Don McCullin. As a schoolboy in 1954, just about to become a journalist, he had read Steinbeck on the death of his friend, the great combat photojournalist Robert Capa, with emotion. He didn't want to set the play in Vietnam or Cambodia, because he wanted a locale where British journalists would be at the centre of the action. So he settled for an imaginary African country on the brink of a post-colonial civil war – just when the Ethiopia–Somalia war of 1977 had broken out. He told his brother Peter that he'd thought of going to Ethiopia or Somalia for a few days but it was 'too complicated'. The trouble with the African setting was that if he put a British-educated African politician into the play, he would end up sounding like a Stoppard character. As he said in interviews, he's 'the only African president who speaks like me'.

Waugh's *Scoop*, with its naive 'nature notes' columnist sent out by mistake to an African revolution, and inadvertently making fools of the hardened war hacks, was a major inspiration. Someone in *Night and Day* even says 'Up to a point, Lord Copper.' So was *The Front Page*, one of his favourite plays. He didn't want to start the play in 'the boardroom of a Fleet Street newspaper', it would be too much of a cliché, but when he came to write a film script (never made) of the play, he did start it in Fleet Street. All through the play, newspaper life is strongly present: in the angry telegrams from the editor written in telex-speech, as in *Scoop*; in the scorn of the London journalists for the provincial papers; in the battles between the union reps and the proprietors, the tyranny of the deadline for the weekly paper, the low tricks used by hacks in competition, the cheap tabloid headlines, the war-story clichés. All this material was close to his heart. He described the play, jokingly, to his mother, as 'an everyday tale of journalism folk'.

The play starts at full throttle: a helicopter roaring in, a jeep with head-lights full on, a machine-gun attack, a dramatic killing. As usual he was 'ambushing' his audience. It turns out to be the nightmare of the photo-journalist who is sleeping on stage. The play will act out that nightmare. It's like a scene from a movie, and *Night and Day* is full of echoes from the movies.

Three journalists converge on an English mine-owner's house in 'Kambawe', a Central African country caught up in a classic post-colonial conflict between a British-educated, repressive military ruler and a Communist-backed insurgency, with British business interests and international UN peacekeeping forces on the margins. The politics of post-colonialism are not the main subject, but we get what we need about the stand-off between the corrupt President Mageeba and the off-stage Colonel Shimbu, backed by Russians and Cubans, who wants to get control of the airstrip. There's some grim comedy about the relics of empire: the British outrage at Communist tactics, the journalists' hotel called the Sandringham, flowing with Scotch whisky, the condescension to the black house-servant (who turns out to be an ally of the revolution). The British mine-owner Carson (rather like Charles Gould in Conrad's *Nostromo*) tries to negotiate between the warring factions, in his own commercial interests: it's an intriguing bit of the plot, but not very involv-ing. The sinister figure of the dictator – who, as he points out himself, played Caliban, not Othello, when he was in England – dominates the second act more for his ominous contribution to the debate about a free press than for an insight into African politics. But the heart of the play is the relationship between the three journalists, and the feelings of Carson's wife, Ruth, the only woman in the play. She has her own views on jour-nalism, so there's a debate going on throughout about the advantages and disadvantages of a free press.

The rival journalists, most of whom are stuck, *Scoop*-style, in the near-est one-horse town with no good communications and no first-hand information, want the use of the mine-owner's telex machine. The tech-nology of the time – telex, the printers' stone, cassette tape, Nikon, Kodak and Leica cameras – is crucial to the action. The play is in love with the technical terms of the trade, the in-jokes, the war stories, the way the guys talk to each other when they are on a job.

Guthrie, the battered, tough, world-travelled photojournalist who will go into any danger zone to get the picture, ends up with the key speech about truth-telling. He's not a daredevil or a martyr – 'I don't intend to die for anyone' – but he stands for the function and value of the press.

> We're not here to be on somebody's side . . . We try to show what happened, and what it was like. That's all we do . . . I've been around a lot of places. People do awful things to each other. But it's worse in places where everybody is kept in the dark. It really is. Information is light. Information, in itself, about anything, is light. That's all you can say, really.

His colleague on the *Sunday Globe*, Wagner, is a cynical Australian who files stories from wherever there's trouble. 'I am not a foreign correspondent . . . I am a fireman. I go to fires. Brighton or Kambawe – they're both out-of-town stories and I cover them the same way. I don't file prose. I file facts.' He's furious because some anonymous freelance 'special correspondent' has scooped him with a front-page story in his own paper, an interview with the rebel Colonel Shimbu. Wagner imagines his rival as 'a boy-scout in an Austin Reed safari suit who somehow got lucky'. In comes Jake Milne, answering to that description, an optimistic idealist, fresh from resigning from the *Grimsby Evening Messenger* because he stood out against the local journalists' strike against the management. To Wagner, a union man, he's not just the boy who stole his story, he's 'the Grimsby scab'.

The argument is intensified by Ruth Carson's presence. She has (coincidentally) just had a one-night stand in London with Wagner, and she falls in love with Jake as soon as she sets eyes on him. She has her own reasons for disliking the press, having been raked over and hounded ('in that Lego-set language they have') as 'the other woman' in Carson's divorce from his first wife, and is eloquent on the 'grubby symbiosis' between 'the populace and the popular press'. She speaks the line that would always be quoted out of context as Stoppard's own view: 'I'm with you on the free

press. It's the newspapers I can't stand.' She prefers the unfettered competition between newspaper magnates to the union closed shop, and uses
the voice of her camera-mad little boy Alistair, a journalist in the making,
to spell out her point: '*His* theory – Alistair's theory – is that it's the very
free-for-all which guarantees the freedom of each.'

Ruth's secret erotic desires are a powerful focus. The long scene of her
seduction of Jake Milne at the start of Act Two, which (like Guthrie's
nightmare at the start of Act One) turns out to be a fantasy, existing in
a parallel world, night for day, is in sensual contrast to the macho talk in
the rest of the play. In the 'real' world of war and politics, urgent, complicated plotting and scheming and double dealing is going on, the outcome
of which is tragically fatal to Jake. Ruth and Wagner, two disillusioned,
compromised and bitter characters, are washed up alone at the end in
gathering darkness.

But the plot that matters is the debate about the fourth estate: the
unions versus the managers, tabloid rubbish as the price paid for press
freedom, the threat to that freedom under a brutal dictatorship. Mageeba's
most sinister line is: 'Do you know what I mean by a relatively free press,
Mr Wagner? . . . I mean a free press which is edited by one of my relatives.'
By contrast, Jake Milne makes an idealistic defence of banal, local British
reporting, in a speech that is untypically autobiographical, a tribute and a
valediction to Stoppard's Bristol days.

> People think that rubbish-journalism is produced by men of
> discrimination who are vaguely ashamed of truckling to the lowest
> taste. But it's not. It's produced by people doing their best work . . . I
> started off like that, admiring it, trying to be *that good*, looking up to
> Fleet Street stringers, London men sometimes, on big local stories.
> I thought it was great. Some of the best times in my life have been
> spent sitting in a clapped-out Ford Consul outside a suburban house
> with a packet of Polos and twenty Players, waiting to grab a bereaved
> husband or a footballer's runaway wife . . . I felt part of a privileged
> group, inside society and yet outside it, with a licence to scourge it
> and a duty to defend it, night and day, the street of adventure, the

fourth estate. And the thing is – I was dead right . . . Junk journalism is the evidence of a society that has got at least one thing right, that there should be nobody with the power to dictate where responsible journalism begins.

Jake's line to Ruth sums up the author's views: 'A free press, free expression – it's the last line of defence for all the other freedoms.' Guthrie and Milne, Stoppard told an interviewer, 'utterly speak for me'.

The play opened in November 1978 and was running well in May 1979 when Margaret Thatcher won her first victory for the Tories. She immediately set about her agenda of crushing the unions, privatising public industries, diminishing the power of the state and demonising the Marxist left. The Stoppards were all for it. Like Paul Johnson, they admired her greatly, and became social acquaintances in the 1980s. In October 1982, for instance, she was the guest of honour at the historian Hugh Thomas's house, with Stoppard, Isaiah Berlin, Stephen Spender, Anthony Powell, Philip Larkin, Jack Plumb and Nicholas Mosley – 'all men'. 'The PM is impressive, never stuck for a riposte, and utterly convinced of the superiority of Englishness over Frenchness Germanness and Spanishness.' On another occasion she invited him to dinner with Reagan at 10 Downing Street. Miriam did an assured, tender and respectful television interview with Thatcher in 1985. In retrospect, he noted her philistinism and her divisiveness; at the time, she seemed to him what the country needed. 'Mrs T was my heroine,' he would say, 'entirely on the issue of print unions . . . I hated what the printers were doing to my precious newspapers. Thatcher and Murdoch saved the day.'

The mood of *Night and Day* matched the start of Thatcherism. This did not endear him to his old enemies on the theatrical left (the phrase 'militant conservatism' has been used of the play), but that did not worry him, though he knew the 'faint aroma' of being a reactionary would hang around him for the rest of his life. The play also involved him in an argument with David Hare, whom he admired. This wasn't a quarrel over the play's treatment of the unions, but over what Hare saw as his idealisation of a revolting profession. Stoppard said of the argument, looking back: he thought I romanticised scumbags. Hare's own play about British journalism, *Pravda*, would take a very different line in 1985.

Hare read the play a few months before it opened, and told Stoppard, in a long, fierce letter, that it had 'provoked him beyond measure'. Didn't Stoppard realise that journalists *wanted* to be degraded, *wanted* to have their prose slashed by sub-editors and wanted 'cretinous capitalist proprietors', so that they could have a permanent excuse for 'the indifference of their own standards'? Didn't he know how many journalists 'believe one thing and write another'? All Fleet Street journalists know they're writing 'mind-numbing shit', but they can't help it, they say, because they aren't free. 'I am very shocked that you, who in *Professional Foul* and *Jumpers* is so clearly arguing for careful stewardship of the truth should now befriend one of its principal enemies.' His play was going to 'give comfort to all the bad consciences of the newspaper business'.

Stoppard read the letter and put it in the bag he always carried around with him. He had just come back from a quick trip to Pittsburgh, where *Every Good Boy* was performed in September, and had been given his travel expenses – about $1,500 – in cash. He was taking an afternoon nap in the bar of the Arts Theatre, where rehearsals for *Night and Day* were underway, when his bag was stolen, with all the money and David Hare's letter. Stoppard told Hare that as a result he was having to reconstruct his argument from memory. But he responded firmly. He was 'profoundly right', and Hare was only 'trivially right'.

> Do I really have to cull the five newspapers delivered to my house
> this morning to convince you that there is as much baby as bathwater
> and that you ought to think this thing through before you tip them
> both out in a fit of bad temper? You have made the utterly boring
> discovery that journalism contains at least as many incompetents,
> fools, sloths and cynics as any other trade, and you have embraced the
> superannuated half-truth that the entire press is the personal property
> of a few capitalist barons . . . Your letter is not simply unconvincing
> ideologically, it has got reporters wrong.

He referred him to Ruth and Guthrie's arguments in the play, who were *'both* right'. He wasn't romanticising journalists. Don McCullin, his main inspiration for Guthrie, *was* brave. 'I could list you a hundred instances of the British press *as it is* being a force for truth and justice.' But just because the press *was* at times 'inaccurate, slanted, malicious, deluded, etc', Hare seemed to be saying: 'Let's only have plays showing how contemptible all journalists are without exception or qualification.'

Hare replied that in losing his briefcase Stoppard had also lost sight of Hare's argument – he hadn't said all journalists were corrupted, but he did see a profession in which 'it is common to write what you do not actually believe'. This produced a 'profound cynicism'. He had never met a playwright who said: 'I had to say that but I don't believe it.' Stoppard wrote back to say that his bag had now been found, and that the thief, 'thinking only in the short term, had taken the money, but left your letter'. Rereading the letter, he didn't think he'd misrepresented Hare's argument. Sure, a journalist might often have a piece cut 'in such a way as to distort what he wished to say'. But usually the cutting was inept or hasty, not the result of 'malicious principle'. Hare said he 'often' met journalists who disowned what they had written. 'I have never met one. Not one. Ever.'

Hare had one more go, only a couple of weeks before the play opened. It amazed him that Stoppard, 'who has attacked interference with writers' work in the incomparably worse way it's attacked in Russia, should be so attracted to a profession in which, on however much smaller a scale, it is NORMAL for people not to write their best'. Why, he asked, was that cynical movie about journalists, *The Front Page*, so attractive to them both? 'Because we both think how nice it would be to be innocent of self-doubt, and not to care; there is something very attractive about that kind of cynicism. But you are fucked, Tom because you have moral seriousness written all over you, and don't tell me you don't.' Hare regretted the quarrel, and their friendship survived it. In 1985, doing publicity for *Pravda*, he wrote to Stoppard correcting a rumour that he had described *Night and Day* as 'appalling'.

In their debate, Stoppard stands firm, while making it nicely clear from the tone – as with the joke about the bag thief – that the argument was not going to become a quarrel. He tended not to quarrel. But the exchange made a strong impression on him, and, so soon before the play opened, it came as a challenge. While Hare generalises passionately, Stoppard refers him to the particular points of view represented in the play, which he felt he was defending.

Before the play opened, he was anxious about it, confiding to his parents: 'There are days when I lose confidence in the play & think – oh yes *this* is the one which stops the Stoppard carnival! We shall see.' And some critics were underwhelmed by its realism and its talkiness – for them it was too like Shaw and not enough like Stoppard. 'A descent into naturalism' was one judgement. Peter Hall thought it was 'about too many things, everything that is in Tom's head at the moment . . . He has tried to make it into one play. It's four at least.' But the English audience liked it. This was a play written for Michael Codron and for the non-subsidised, commercial theatre, Stoppard's second play for Codron after *The Real Inspector Hound*. And Codron's commitment paid off, though there were plenty of technical headaches – he had to search around for a theatre that would be able to cope with a jeep coming on stage at the start of the play. At one point he told Stoppard that this wasn't going to be possible. 'No jeep, no play,' the answer came back.

In November 1978, *Night and Day* was part of a Stoppard boom: there were no signs of the 'carnival' coming to a halt. *Every Good Boy* had had a triumph in New York, and *Night and Day* was one of four plays of his overlapping in London. *Dirty Linen* was having its thousandth performance (though it had become 'coarse and slow', he thought). *Dogg's Hamlet, Cahoot's Macbeth* was still on, and about to open in the States. His adaptation of Schnitzler's *Undiscovered Country* – worked on with rapidity and enjoyment straight after finishing *Night and Day* – opened at the National in 1979. To cap his triumphs, he won a big international prize that summer, the Shakespeare Prize, awarded in Hamburg, which came with acclaim, a cheque for £6,000 and 'a huge medal' of 'the Bard in relief'. It also allowed him to donate a sum to a young person in the arts or media, which he gave to Paul Johnson's son, the journalist Daniel Johnson. He divided the windfall up between a painting, 'deserving causes' and all the family, urging his parents to accept £500 without demur.

There were queues for tickets for *Night and Day* at the Phoenix Theatre and the play won the *Evening Standard* Best Play award in January 1979. Diana Rigg as a cool, pantherish Ruth and John Thaw as a rough, tough Wagner, in a rousing production by Peter Wood, were a great draw. As often, Wood persuaded Stoppard during both the UK and the American runs to do a lot of rewriting, including some extra speeches between Wagner and Ruth, to deepen and to clarify the characters. Diana Rigg had regular rewrites slipped under her dressing-room door. But she loved the part. Looking back decades later, she would say: 'I adored it. I knew this woman. She speaks her thoughts, it's very novel. It wasn't difficult to do – it was a gift. A wonderful part for a woman, so brilliantly concise and wry and witty.'

Things did not go so well with the play in Australia, early in 1979, where Stoppard spent a few weeks, when he could hardly afford the time, to monitor a mediocre production of *Night and Day* and one of *Dirty Linen*, and to give his theatre talks to adoring students, cheered up by a cricket match (between Queensland and Western Australia) at the Perth Literary Festival, and by dining with Warren Mitchell at a restaurant called An Elegant Sufficiency. ('One longs to set up a pie-shop in competition – The Vulgar Excess or The Crude Parsimony.') He was made much of – 'for the first time I felt a bit famous', he told his parents – though at one social event he sat next to a woman who told him she loved his plays, and went on to describe her favourite, 'which turned out to be *Bedroom Farce*'. On the way to Australia, the flight stopped to refuel at Bombay. He sent a postcard to Bobby from the transit lounge: 'I set foot again after 33 years . . . I wish I could leave the flight and go straight to Darjeeling.'

When *Night and Day* went to the States, there were problems. Diana Rigg left the first cast in London, because of a back injury she had got from lifting the body of the dead acrobat in *Jumpers*. (To her regret, she has never appeared again in a Stoppard play.) Maggie Smith took over as Ruth at the Phoenix, and then in the States, with Susan Hampshire replacing her after a few months. There was some trepidation before Maggie Smith began – she was a force to be reckoned with – but she was 'miraculous', according to Peter Wood and to Stoppard, and gave one of the great memorable performances in a Stoppard play, like Hordern in *Jumpers* or John Wood in *Travesties*. Smith gave Ruth's inner turmoil and desires an edgy expressiveness. Stoppard thought she did something impossible, like being in two places at once: inhabiting the character totally, while simultaneously seeming to stand outside it, making an ironic commentary on her own behaviour. When they opened at the Kennedy Center in Washington, he gave her – it was his little joke for his lead actresses – a Head Girl badge.

But between the Washington opening and the New York run it became apparent that the actor playing Wagner was all wrong for the production, and the excruciating business of replacing him had to be gone through. Stoppard hated such situations, though he would always put the needs of the play first. He wrote home: 'Life in the theatre – I'm glad I only write the damn things.' And even with Maggie Smith getting huge praise, the play had, as Codron put it, a 'rocky road' on Broadway, and lost money – though a line about America's cowardly record of dealing with Africa got a surprising burst of applause every night. New York, Stoppard noted wryly, was the only place where 'Shavian' was a term of abuse. On one night, he told his parents, '*100* people left during the play!!' He and Peter Wood were quarrelling over the production; he was doing endless interviews; he felt 'over-attended' and over-exposed, unhappy and irritable. Stuck in a hotel room for weeks while he worked on the show, he was homesick. He wanted to see his boys and he wanted to be with Miriam. He lamented in secret: 'Oh let it all be over so that I can come home . . . Dear me, this is not the life I had planned, either as a writer or as a father.'

Home, by then, was Iver Grove, which they bought in the summer of 1979 and moved into between 19 and 24 September. They had been very settled in Fernleigh. He had written *Travesties*, *Artist Descending a Staircase*, *Galileo*, *Dirty Linen* and *New-Found-Land*, *Every Good Boy*, *Professional Foul*, *Night and Day*, as well as screenplays and his adaptation of *Undiscovered Country*, in that comfortable, ugly house. He was happy there. He often wrote bursts of pleasure into his journal about everyday life there, the boys going about their business, the domestic bustle, the view from his study, as on a wintry day at the end of 1978: 'Outside my window: the lawn pearly with dew, bare trunks and branches of trees some shades darker than the fog which is and conceals sky; you [Ed] in blue and green anorak walking sturdily, your straight-haired roundhead tucked in against the damp.'

But they had often remarked on a perfect house near them which could be glimpsed, hidden away behind trees, at the other end of their road, Wood Lane. Miriam passed it all the time on her way to and from work in Maidenhead. Early in 1979, just as she was due to go on a trip to Mexico, she heard it was for sale, and boldly drove up its winding driveway, past the giant mulberry tree at the entrance. She sat there amazed at what she saw, before the owner shooed her away. Back home, she said (more or less): 'You've always said you wanted red rosy Georgian brick instead of white pebble-dash – take a look at this house!' As she remembered it, she then went on her business trip, to be met on her return at the airport with his announcement that he'd made an offer on the house – and in alarm she said to him, but I only told you to take a look! In his memory, it was *he* who told her that he'd heard the house was for sale, during one of her phone calls from Mexico, and she said to him (more or less): 'Go and buy it.' And then he went and looked at it. And when he saw it, he thought – as he put it – 'well, *shit*.'

Iver Grove was indeed a very impressive house. It is a beautiful, small-scale, early-eighteenth-century brick mansion described by Pevsner as 'one of the finest houses in Bucks in the Baroque style of that date'. It's our favourite period, Stoppard told his parents. Estate agents referred to it as an exquisite Grade II listed Georgian villa. A sale notice for the house and its grounds in 1865 described it as 'a commodious old-fashioned mansion' with 'pleasure grounds of rare magnificence', a 'nobly timbered park' of thirty acres, double coach house and stabling for seven horses, a small enclosed farmyard, a pretty undulating meadow and three excellent kitchen gardens. Country-house architecture writers enthused about its purple brick with red brick dressings, its amply spaced bays and its west frontage, a three-bay pediment on giant Doric pilasters with a matching cornice and frieze, and a front door with a porch on Tuscan columns. Inside was a high hall with black and white marble tiling and a sweeping central wooden staircase, the pride of the house, with – in Pevsnerese – 'slender-faceted balusters'. The wood for the staircase came from Nelson's HMS *Victory*, and the floorboards were from the Armoury in the Tower of London. It was not a huge mansion – more of a jewel, a 'Queen Anne doll's house' as Stoppard described it – but with lots of outbuildings and vast grounds.

It had a colourful history. They would have liked to call it a Vanbrugh house, but in fact it was the work of John James, a good church architect and contemporary of Hawksmoor (their neighbour Paul Johnson was quick to spot this), who designed it for Lady Mohun, widow of a notorious rake and gambler, who was killed in a duel in 1712. The adventurous Lady Mohun then married a much younger man and had the house built between 1722 and 1724, as a country retreat for occasional use. But she died in 1725, and after that it was owned by country-loving aristocrats, the Gambiers, who created a famous garden of rare pansies. Then it fell into disrepair, and in the Second World War the house and stables were requisitioned and used for storage for telegraphic equipment for the Polish army (our wartime allies). Heaps of electrical junk were still lying around in the stables. After the war the house was done up by the Ministry of Works, listed by English Heritage in 1954, and then privately owned.

They were strongly advised not to buy it – by the bank and, at first, by Peter, keeping a careful eye on his brother's accounts. Friends who knew Fernleigh thought they were mad – though friends who had seen Iver completely understood. At one point they nearly lost heart, but they both knew it was, as Miriam said, 'the house of our dreams'. It was just as convenient as Fernleigh for her work, for quick access to London and for the boys' schools. She thought it would be their ultimate house for the rest of their lives together.

There were plenty of other things going on in the summer and autumn of 1979. *The Human Factor* was being filmed, he was in New York working on *Night and Day* and seeing *Every Good Boy* at the Met, they had a family holiday in Corfu, he had four plays running at once in London. But the Iver plans were at the centre of their lives. They had to take the risk of buying the house before they could be sure of the outbuildings, which were owned separately, and which they knew they would want for their work, as although the house had lots of bedroom space, it had fewer reception rooms down-stairs than Fernleigh. Now-unused stables set round a cobbled courtyard, a red-brick coach house with Dutch gables, a huge walled kitchen garden, a little cottage (with a sitting tenant) and another small house for the gar-dener, a ten-acre field, a great number of trees, a tennis court – these were all part of the attraction, and had to be charmed out of a nice old gentleman who, fortunately, had seen and admired Miriam on the television.

It was a major purchase, made at a time when he was spending lavishly. Thinking aloud about how he had used his Shakespeare Prize money that year – on a Peter De Wint painting of Windsor Castle, on rare first edi-tions of Hemingway and Jane Austen – he said to himself, perhaps not very convincingly: 'I suppose it's awful to be so privileged/lucky/wealthy etc.' Fernleigh sold for £150,000. Iver Grove cost £190,000, the outbuild-ings and land another £40,000. He remembered buying his first house, River Thatch, in 1968, for £14,000. He couldn't quite believe that, just over ten years on, he had bought a property for £230,000. (When the house was sold, nearly twenty years later, it went for £1.35 million; in 2007 it changed hands for about £5 million.)

But his satisfaction was intense. He had always had a fantasy of a beau-tiful country mansion, a 'trophy' house, and he loved the eighteenth cen-tury, its grace and order. He wouldn't mind ending his days in a country house near Bath, reading Jane Austen and *The Times*. He could see the potential of Iver's grounds, and he had a passion for fruit trees. One day, he thought, they would have peaches growing against the south-facing wall of the kitchen gardens. As soon as the house was theirs, they picked six pounds of mulberries from the tree that guarded the entrance. He would not be doing the gardening, though, or the interior decorating. 'I write plays, that's my excuse.'

Iver Grove was his complete idea of a beautiful English house. But essentially it was Miriam's project. She grasped it with passion, energy and organisational prowess. As her son Will would say, 'like all the places Miriam has ever lived in, what they end up looking like is not what they looked like at the beginning.' It was a five-year plan: to redecorate the whole house first, then to refurbish the outbuildings as their workplace and to redesign and expand the gardens, eventually to put in a swimming pool. As a start, the tennis pavilion was moved from Fernleigh to Iver. Paul Johnson lent them his enormous Guido Reni painting of the Archangel Michael driving Satan out of Paradise, to go at the top of the stairs. An eighteenth-century portrait of a young girl in blue, in Gainsborough or Thornhill style, captured their hearts at an auction and was bagged for £700, giving him intense pleasure. There were already heaps of furniture at Fernleigh which wouldn't all fit into Iver – the move took 'umpteen pantechnicons', he told his parents. But Miriam kept rushing home in high excitement with spoils from the Thames Valley antique shops – a Georgian commode, a tallboy, a bookcase – most of which she had bargained hard for. He enjoyed all this, and loved this side of her. At one point she dragged them all off to a cattle market in Thame to buy agricultural equipment. He was impressed that she was making *coloured plans* for the walled gardens: 'It will be the Versailles of back gardens!' he exclaimed.

He felt sad to say goodbye to the Fernleigh 'era', and sad that Ed would probably not remember its rooms and gardens. But they closed their life in that house in style, giving a big lunch party in the garden on a Sunday in September two weeks before the move. Miriam lavishly cooked Indian food (with masses of curry left over for the freezer) for guests whose names the host listed in his journal: Otto Preminger, André Previn (now separated from Mia Farrow and with a new partner), Kingsley Amis and Elizabeth Jane Howard, Roald Dahl and Patricia Neal, Stephen Frears, the Johnsons and their son Luke, Harold Pinter and Antonia Fraser, John Stride and his wife, Bryan Forbes and Nanette Newman, the Wellses and Derek Marlowe – who would have vividly remembered the Stoppard of Vincent Square Mansions.

On the day of the move, 19 September, the family walked down Wood Lane in procession to the new house. Oliver was thirteen, Barny was celebrating his tenth birthday the next day, Will was seven (and would remember having his eighth birthday at Iver the following March) and Ed was five. They would be living out of packing cases for some months to come. In the chaos of the removal days they ate some of their meals at the nearby Holiday Inn, where he would occasionally retreat to write in solitude. He had a moment of paternal pride when Ed, observing a packet of Brie on the hotel table, said: 'An isosceles triangle!' Then he went off to the States to deal with *Night and Day*, and Miriam set about getting the painters in, the sofas and rugs ordered, the watercolours hung and an architect hired to design the plans for the outbuildings.

She began to get the feel of the rooms, pinning colour swatches and fabric samples onto the walls, changing her mind about greens, finding exactly the right lamps and curtains. It took her two years to get the sitting room just right. The dining room, and their bedroom, and his little sitting room next to their bedroom, their dressing room with two bathrooms, followed suit. She knew that there wasn't room in his brain for this kind of thing. And she knew that their marriage worked well because they had their separate areas of interest. In her later words: 'I never expected to get anything from him that I didn't.' His running joke about doing up the house was, 'you make the decision, I'll write the cheque'. (Though her own income from her Syntex and TV work and her books, would also go into Iver – she didn't like to be dependent.) If she asked for his view on a Turkish carpet, his interest was limited – but he liked having the carpet. He could see that this might have been frustrating for her. She was working and taking care of the children and travelling, and also pouring her energies into furnishing the house, and not always getting quite the reaction she hoped for. He caricatured his response: 'Oh that's fine, well done, and stop talking about that now, I'm trying to think about this play, and you keep banging on about furniture and carpets.' There were occasional explosions, shouting and tears and making up. But on the whole her energetic involvement with the *things*, and his concentration on his work, made a good balance.

The conversions to the outbuildings and the work on the gardens progressed in fits and starts, as and when they had the money. The coach house became an enormous two-floor work space, coloured bright red and orange. She worked downstairs with the Syntex secretaries and a desk for Jacky. Upstairs, at the top of a fire-engine-red metal spiral staircase and behind plate-glass windows, was his gigantic study, about forty feet long, where he kept his reference books and hung the framed autographs of writers he had started to collect, and had his huge partner's desk. The children said it looked like a shopping arcade; he said it was the kind of study Mussolini would have liked.

Over time they added a billiards room, a darkroom for Miriam's photography, and what they called a 'conversation pit', a little sunken agora or mini indoor theatre, with carpet-lined seating round the wall for lolling on. Outside, the tennis court was floodlit, and there was, eventually, a glass-covered pool (which he preferred looking at to swimming in) and a croquet lawn. Miriam designed a Japanese water garden with a waterfall and a series of descending ponds. Reclaiming the history of Iver Grove, she turned herself into an expert on pansies, and created an exceptional garden with hundreds of species, and decorative, eighteenth-century style murals on the brick walls. He would have a circular stone sundial made for the wall of the garden, with a design of pansies and the inscription: 'For Miriam who made this garden 1982'. (This hobby began expensively, when vast numbers of annuals were bought, under the impression they were perennials.) In the early 1980s, frequent entries in his journal noted that she was 'gardening non-stop'.

In 1981, her parents, Sid and Jenny Stern, moved down from Newcastle to live near them in what had been the gardener's cottage, partly to help with house- and child-sitting. They kept up the devout Jewish practices which had been the context of her childhood, with a mezuzah on the cottage door, celebrating shabbas on Friday nights, in the grounds of their daughter's very secular household. He liked and respected his parents-in-law. Bobby and Ken, who moved during the Iver years from Penrith down to Tipton St John, near Sidmouth, in Devon, visited occasionally; but it was hard to persuade them to make the journey, unless he could promise Ken some fishing and persuade Bobby that she wouldn't be a nuisance. Instead, his weekly or twice-weekly letters reported on their doings.

When they first moved into Iver, Miriam was on sabbatical from Syntex to write two more of her health and baby books and to do more television. It was nice to have her there in the kitchen, but now, he thought, she would understand what a writer's life at home was like: 'interruptions till evening'. Every so often, as the great five-year plan proceeded, he would complain, mildly, about the noise and the disruptions – it was a bit like the Forth Bridge round here, he said, while the waterfall was being constructed. Lady Croom's extensive landscaping project for Sidley Park, in *Arcadia*, ten years on, owes something to Miriam's early Iver Grove days.

The boys all remembered climbing up the spiral staircase to his huge study in the coach house and taking sweets from his desk drawers. They were never turned away or told they were interrupting. But they had slightly different reactions to the move. Oliver, already in his teens and always slightly separate from the others, thought of Fernleigh as his real childhood home, and never felt the same about Iver. He felt it was a show house, less usable than Fernleigh. Downstairs was all taken up with the hall and the big sitting room; the next floor up was his parents' rooms; the top floor was for the children's bedrooms and (for a time) the nanny, and the children's playroom. They spent most of their time in the high-ceilinged, rather awkwardly shaped kitchen. Barny also found Iver less warm and comfortable. An eighteenth-century aristocratic lady's country resort didn't suit a twentieth-century family of six so well. For him, the move to Iver accentuated the difference between the time he and Ollie spent with Jose in her flat in Hemel Hempstead and their life in the grand house.

But all the boys found the Iver acres a wonderful playground. For the younger boys, Will and Ed, Iver was like a secret secluded garden. They both went to Caldicott school (where they played a lot of sport, and had no troubles, though the school went through a bad history of abuse cases in that period) and then to Stowe as boarders, where both were bullied for a time, Will especially. For him, at that unhappy time, Iver was his refuge. At home Miriam's two boys fought, a lot, kicked rugby balls about and played tennis day and night through the school holidays. Barny didn't join in the sport, but Ollie and the two younger boys would fish, sometimes in the local gravel pit, sometimes on trips with their father to the river Kennet.

Within months of moving they were having barbecues and lunch parties for eighteen, and a regular marquee party every summer for about 130 people (mostly from his world, rather than the Syntex world), with caterers. When Miriam got fed up with cooking the Christmas dinner for all the relatives, they decided to have a Christmas family holiday abroad on alternate years. People turned up continually for production meetings and script conferences and interviews. Gardeners and nannies and workmen and secretaries came and went.

Their closest neighbours – the Johnsons and their children, Tim and Hélène Corrie (who had known him from the Jose days) and the music producer Deke Arlon and his wife Jill, a writer, who lived in a manor house near Beaconsfield – all thought the house imposing and beautiful, and enjoyed neighbourly visits. They saw Iver as Miriam's project: Trevor Nunn called life there 'exuberant' and 'Miriam-led'. Some old friends wondered whether the setting entirely suited him, and thought the house might be changing him slightly, that there was more emphasis on wealth and glamour. The old battered Wolseley was changed for a BMW, the pink shoes and frilled shirts morphed into Armani suits. But there was bound to be a bit of jealousy from those who had known him a long time. Antonia Fraser, who thought Miriam was terrific, said to her nicely, on her first visit to Iver: 'I'm going to be guilty of one of the seven deadly sins, envy.'

Everyone was awed by Miriam's style and management: the astonishing walk-in cupboard filled with hundreds of pairs of shoes; the racks of designer clothes, all ready for her to appear in public at a moment's notice; the rows of shelves full of home-made jam ('where did she find the time to do *that*?' Diana Rigg, a friend of Miriam's since *Jumpers*, asked herself). Ashtrays with lids were spotted all over the house. Miriam became an anti-smoking evangelist in her television years, and people would hastily stub out their cigarettes if she came into a room. She knew there was no point in trying to persuade him to give up, but asked him to smoke only in his study or outside the house. The lids on the ashtrays were an amicable compromise.

Visitors noticed that the boys were fed mainly on microwaved frozen food and left to their own devices. The neighbourhood boys and school friends who would come round regularly (Jamie and Tim Arlon, Ben Corrie) loved the fact that you got microwaved tagliatelle and went out to McDonald's if you were with the Stoppards – and that there were quad bikes at their house, a great craze for the boys at Iver in their teenage years. The father of the house was often around, kindly, benign, interested in the boys and their friends. Tim Arlon was starting a band and he and his mates sat around at Iver trying to think of a name for it; Stoppard joined in. Later, when Arlon was making music in LA, Stoppard would make a point of visiting their studio if he was in California. Ben Corrie, his godson, had a correspondence with him that went on for years, and mattered a great deal to him.

At Iver Grove, Stoppard was lord of his estate, loving husband, family man, generous host and party-giver, employer, friend, public figure. But this was also the person who moved out of his baronial study, where he never really got much written, and sat at the kitchen table, after everyone else was asleep, drawing the next play out of himself in silence and solitude, writing into the small hours. That was the real thing.

18

Undiscovered Countries

> Haven't you ever thought what a strange uncharted country is human
> behaviour?

Rooted in his family life, and often complaining of the endless travelling
that his work entailed, he also liked going to new places. He said to his
mother: 'I'd like to go everywhere *once*.' This referred to the prospect of
an unlikely trip to the Galapagos Islands, made in March 1981 for the
Observer.

He went with the head of development for the World Wildlife Fund,
Ivan Hattingh, and they flew to the Galapagos by way of a few days in the
rainforests of the Amazon. Stoppard read his Darwin (*The Voyage of the
Beagle* gave one 'a spooky view of the penny dropping' about evolutionary adaptation), did a great deal of homework and talked to everyone he
met. For describing the wildlife, he used his old Brennus-tricks of joking
imagery – baleful marine iguanas 'with jaws like mean old men', a cac-
tus 'hardly bigger than a shaving-brush', a swallow-tailed gull that looked
'as if it had come from Hamley's'. The innocence of the creatures, their
lack of fear, amazed him: 'the sea-lion lies down with the snorkler'. Of the
four species he encountered – wildlife, scientists, tourists and National
Park officers – it was the scientists who interested him the most. They all
seemed exceptionally happy people. The German director of the research
centre, Friedemann Köster, told him that the biologist was 'the ideally fulfilled man'. What about art and aesthetics? the playwright asked him. Oh
yes, Köster replied, the aesthetic stimulus had been of great use in his
study of the enormous king vulture. The big question for one happy young
ornithologist from Ohio, who was spending the best part of three years
on the islands, was 'Why do finch beak sizes vary within the species?' 'He
declined a peppermint because he didn't want to get used to luxuries.'

The Galapagos was his furthest expedition at this time. But he was often
on the move. Productions of his plays took him to Australia, America and

Europe. He travelled for pleasure on family holidays (skiing at Chamonix, sunshine in Jamaica, rainy views of Derwentwater at the Lodore Hotel), to give lectures and in support of his political causes. And his intellectual travels, through the 1980s, took him deep into the European worlds of Austrian and Austro-Hungarian writers from Vienna and Budapest. He inhabited those countries in his imagination with pleasure and sympathy.

One of the literary figures for whom he was willing to travel was his hero Hemingway. When he started collecting first editions and writers' autographs, he got to know Marguerite Cohn, who owned the House of Books on Madison Avenue, where Stoppard often made his way on trips to New York. Margie, whom he described as neat, busy, birdlike and enchanting, shared his passion for 'that physical object known as a book'. She would send him rare Hemingway-related materials – a monograph by Hemingway's sister's gardener, as he joked. She felt to him more like a friend than a book dealer – and he seemed to her 'one of the most thoughtful persons she had ever known'. At the end of 1977 he went to see an exhibition of Hemingway drafts and notebooks at the University of Virginia. In 1982 he spoke at Northeastern University, in Boston, at a Hemingway conference, where he mused on writers' afterlives, the 'ebb and flow between reputation and oblivion', and explained why he 'got bitten . . . and stayed bitten' by Hemingway. It wasn't just 'the way he got his effects by making the reader do the work', or how he creates 'different kinds of music' in prose, it was his 'personal morality', the celebration of 'the physical, sensual experience of life', 'the ordinary business of living and surviving'. When Margie Cohn died in 1984 he spoke at a celebration in her honour. As part of the network of American book dealers and collectors to which Margie Cohn belonged, he also forged a link with the Grolier Club, distinguished centre for American bibliophiles. One of these, Jack Hagstrom, transmitted Stoppard's admiration, at Margie Cohn's memorial, to the poet Richard Wilbur, and then sent Stoppard a copy of Wilbur's poem 'The Ride', which Hagstrom had printed. It hangs in Stoppard's house among many other framed autographs, first editions and broadsides. The adventure of collecting, and the delight in the book as a well-made object, never left him.

His Hemingway lecture was one of many appearances that took him all over America. Public lecturing, mainly to throngs of rapt, eager literature and theatre students, had begun at Notre Dame in 1971, when he burst on the scene, famous from *Rosencrantz* and in the middle of writing *Jumpers*, long-haired and hip, smoking and joking, clowning with a huge audience, and appearing to make it all up as he went along. From then on he became a part-time public performer, constantly inundated with invitations to speak in America, Europe and Australia, as well as at home.

Once set, the pattern of his lectures would remain roughly the same. Some trusted anecdotes would stay permanently in his repertoire. Like a jazz player, he would riff on similar themes and return to favourite stories, like the one about the man with the runaway peacock. He described his method, when he started out as a public speaker, as 'a series of non-sequiturs, loops, digressions – at the end you might see some sort of pattern'. Without exactly invoking *Jumpers*, he isn't unlike his absent-minded philosopher who begins his lecture: 'Secondly! . . .' Though he wasn't an actor, he knew all about timing, staging and pace, how to get a huge laugh, and how to get an audience eating out of his hand. He rarely used a script. He liked to joke about the contrast between himself as a creative writer and theatre person, and the academic venues where he often appeared.

He often spoke, particularly in the early days, about the need to free the play from the constraints of the classroom. So he would have ironical fun with numerological analysis, or the tracing of literary allusions ('it would be a very curious audience indeed who sits there murmuring, "Ah, Chekhov", or "Yes, Alfred Hitchcock"'), or far-fetched theories about the deep meanings underlying a play. It wasn't that he had it in for 'critics' theatre' or the study of a play 'in a classroom between hard covers', though he did get a big reaction from students – laughter and applause – when in his early lectures he said he had 'no academic interest in the theatre, none whatever'. It was that he spoke, above all, as an empiricist, a practical man of the theatre – or, as he sometimes called himself, 'a brazen pragmatist'. He would insist that a play is not set in stone. 'I think art is an empirical experience, and theatre, because it is different every night, and because it is different from seat to seat, simultaneously, is perhaps the most empirical of them all.' In a phrase he used repeatedly, 'theatre is an event not a text'. Or: 'The event defines the text as well as the other way round.' 'You wrote a play and the theatre was what happened to it.' He gave his lectures titles like 'The Event and the Text' or 'The Less than Sacred Text'. The idea connects to the refusal of ideology and didacticism which is at the heart of his nature.

He would take his examples from productions he had seen or heard about, and from whichever of his own plays was currently in production or was at the front of his mind. He would often refer to Shakespearean productions to show how a director's concept, or a piece of acting, or staging, or lighting, could change or add to the printed lines. 'When we refer to Shakespeare as our greatest writer we refer to him as the author of an event and not merely of a text.' He was hugely impressed by Trevor Nunn's powerful *Macbeth* (done at The Other Place with Judi Dench and Ian McKellen in 1976) because it was a sort of 'chamber-*Macbeth*', very simply dressed, on a bare stage, which got to the heart of the play. Peter Brook's legendary 1970 *Midsummer Night's Dream*, in its white-walled circular gymnasium, with Titania 'sitting on a large red feather boa hanging from the flics . . . while below her, walking about on twelve-foot stilts, Puck, twelve feet in the air against that white wall, staggered about on his stilts, while the earthlings searched high and low for the playful and whimsical spirit that was interfering with their little lives', stayed with him (and many others) not just because 'it was a beguiling and exciting spectacle', but because 'it gave literal expression of the central idea, which is metaphorically expressed as "different levels of reality"'. Brook's 1962 *Lear*, with Paul Scofield, made a profound impression on him. Brook put the scene of Gloucester's blinding just before the interval. Gloucester was 'staggering about' with blood pouring from his eyes – it was 'quite grisly' – and the servants were 'jostling him and . . . being extremely callous towards him' (not as in the text, where they offer him whites of eggs to salve his eyes, which Brook cut). As this was going on, 'Brook brought up the house lights' so that 'in a strange kind of way you were implicated'. He was less admiring of a *Hamlet* at the Royal Court theatre (by Richard Eyre, in 1980, with Jonathan Pryce) where the Ghost was wrenched up, with an 'awful retching noise', out of Hamlet's stomach. That meant sacrificing the first scene of the play ('Who's there?'), with its 'real theatrical excitement' – 'it goes off like a motor-bike'. What he found 'repeatedly thrilling and time-less' in Shakespeare and made him 'vibrant in the modern theatre' were those 'rapid, sharp exchanges which drive the action on', rather than the big set-piece speeches. Not all reinterpretations, though, were to his taste, particularly not the ponderous kind of production which gave Italian Fascist brown boots and shiny belts to *Coriolanus*. 'I don't think theatre works as parable; it works as metaphor.'

When he talked about working on his own plays, he would go into vivid, specific detail about a piece of stage mechanism that took the audi-ence by surprise, or the improving of a joke that wasn't getting the right reaction, or the tussle that often went on, particularly between him and Peter Wood, between '*my* reluctance to be over-explicit and *his* fear that the audience isn't being given enough information. I like to get the shock of [the audience] finding things out, and in some cases, Peter saves me from their *never* finding out.' Many actors and directors bear witness to Stoppard's willingness to make changes so that the text will become the best kind of event. They also make clear that it is *he* who wants to be in control of those changes. He doesn't want other people altering his texts, though he is interested when a director does something quite unexpected with one of his plays – like an Italian production of *Rosencrantz* in which Rosencrantz was a woman and the whole play was staged in a series of Perspex boxes, or that notorious French production of *Travesties* in which Cecily's speech on the history of Marxism was begun stark naked and continued as she put her clothes on.

Stoppard's favourite metaphor for the creating of a theatrical event was the making of a *noise* – as when working with Peter Wood on *Night and Day*:

My plays for me – in my head, before anyone gets hold of a text – make a certain quality of noise, which rises and falls at certain places, and slows and speeds up at certain places, and much of our rehearsal consists of my trying to explain what this noise is like, and trying to make the actors make this noise; and then Peter [Wood] and the actors working from the other end show me how the action can speed up in a different place, and not get loud there but get very quiet, and it's my turn to be shown an alternative orchestration for these voices.

When you write a play it makes a certain kind of noise in your head, and the rehearsal and staging is an attempt to persuade the actors to reproduce this noise . . . But theatre is a curious equation in which language is merely one of the components.

His lectures were, for a time, a major source of income, and a great help when, in the early 1980s, he was worrying about paying his taxes. In 1982, he hired a lecture agent, Selma Warner, and she created a programme of American appearances for him. He plane-hopped across North America, touching down at San Diego, Kenyon College in Ohio, the Library of Congress in Washington, Emory University in Atlanta, Florida, Harvard, Ontario. Meanwhile, there were plenty of public commitments at home – the prestigious Clark Lectures at Cambridge in 1980 ('I'm worrying about them,' he told his mother; 'I think I'm going to have to *write* them in the end'), a talk for the Shaw Society in 1983, a lecture at Darwin College in Cambridge in 1985, and so on incessantly. Wherever he went, there would be parties and dinners for him, everyone would want to talk to him, ecstatic thank you letters would follow in his wake. The Professor of English at Rice University in Houston wrote to tell him that the waves of 'barely controlled hysteria [which Stoppard had clearly joked about] emanating from the audience on Thursday night testify to the enthusiasm which your appearances generated. You were extremely generous with your time and energy, answering questions all afternoon, shaking hands (in Texas we call it "pressing the flesh") and then delivering a stunning informal address in the evening.' Impeccably polite and obliging, always seeking out the least important person in the room to talk to, he nevertheless found the 'social obligations' of these lectures the most taxing part. He was irritated when journalists infiltrated the proceedings; Selma Warner responded to his complaint in November 1982, agreeing that 'a reporter has no business in the classroom, and yes the social aspects can also be controlled'.

In 1984 he gave up these lecture tours: it was too hard to combine them with rehearsals, productions, writing and family life. The extra money they brought in (about $2,500 per appearance in the early 1980s, plus first-class fare and the best hotels) would be replaced by the income he got from doing screenplays. But he continued to speak often and widely, and not only because he needed the money or was promoting a new play.

He was being awarded a stream of honorary degrees, from Brunel, Bristol, Sussex, Leeds, York, London University – so many that he sometimes forgot which ones he'd got – and he would speak when required on these occasions. He became vice-president of PEN in 1983 and did his duty – meetings, speeches, introductions. For one of these, he noted that 'during a previous PEN effort to raise funds for the cause, an enthusiastic donor whipped out his cheque-book with the cry, "Writers in prison? Capital idea! Best place for them!"'

What he joked about was also what he took seriously. His high-profile commitment to the cause of 'writers in prison' and political detainees in Eastern Europe was now built into his life. While *Night and Day* was playing in New York, in the autumn of 1979, he chaired the Sakharov Hearings, 'an examination by testimony of Soviet repression', in the very room where the House Un-American Activities Committee had held court in the 1950s. He 'presided' in the chair in which Senator McCarthy must have sat. He took to the role, he confided to his journal, like 'a fish to water', and felt proud of his chairmanship, though he knew that the really important business was the 'appalling and moving catalogue of Soviet gangsterism recalled and recounted by a procession of exceptional men and women'. He was profoundly impressed by the statements of 'ordinary' Russians, Lithuanians and Ukrainians.

His connection to Havel remained close, and he went on speaking out about what was going on in Prague. In 1981, he was refused a visa to go back to Czechoslovakia, no doubt because of his writing and activities on behalf of Charter 77, and wrote an open letter to President Husák, published in *Index on Censorship*, ironically describing his thwarted attempts to get back into the country of his birth, and his friendship with Havel. 'Frankly, Havel's prison sentence has been a great nuisance to me. Every week or so I have to ask myself what I can to do to help him instead of being able to get on with my life and work.' One of his reasons for returning was to 'shake the hands of a few people who have fallen from grace and to reaffirm, use-lessly, that they have not been entirely forgotten and ignored'.

Asking himself 'what I can do to help' took different forms. His pub-lic gestures ranged from representing Havel for his honorary degree at Toulouse University in 1984 and making radio appeals for *Index*, to co-signing a letter of protest (alongside Kingsley Amis and Norman St John Stevas) about the arrest in Prague of some leading Czech jazz musi-cians. In 1986 he asked Beckett for the use of a photograph for *Index*. (Beckett wrote a play about theatrical censorship, *Catastrophe*, for Havel, in 1982, and his own plays were banned in Czechoslovakia.) Stoppard was put out when *Index* published the image, to be used on a T-shirt, with a gag in Beckett's mouth and the caption: 'If Samuel Beckett had been born in Czechoslovakia we'd still be waiting for Godot'. But in response to his apology, Beckett wrote: 'Dear Tom, nothing against it, all best, Sam.'

Between 1979 and 1986, years when he was also writing and staging *The Real Thing* and working on a revival of *Jumpers*, he wrote free translations of Austrian and Hungarian plays which, though separate from his polit-ical activities, were connected to them intellectually and emotionally. As with his 'translation' of Havel in 1986 and, much later, of Chekhov plays, this work had a great deal to do with his own history and temperament. Even though they were all jobs which came at him, rather than him seek-ing them out, they are part of his ongoing concerns. There is hardly a time in his life, in fact, when he is not writing in some way about Europe and Eastern Europe, exile, journeying and homelands, from *Travesties* through to *Coast*, *Rock 'n' Roll* and *Leopoldstadt*. Even the most English of his plays – *Jumpers*, *The Real Thing*, *Arcadia*, *The Invention of Love* – have the sense of an outsider at the edge of the English establishment, or an argument about what makes England or Englishness worth having, or a foray into an undiscovered country.

His European translations were like 'gifts', time off from writing his own plays, while ensuring he had something running in the theatre. They drew on his dexterity and comic skills, his appetite for pure entertainment and broad comedy. The mixture of tightly worked control, linguistic freedom and playfulness that had gone into farces like *After Magritte* or *Dogg's Hamlet* or *Dirty Linen* was on full display in these adaptations.

He always worked from literal translations and couldn't read the original German or Hungarian in which the plays were written – any more than he could read or speak Russian or Czech. But his enjoyment of European culture and history was plain to see in these translations. He responded to these plays because of something they had in common: sophistication, irony, cosmopolitanism, civilised intelligence, worldliness. These authors – Arthur Schnitzler, Ferenc Molnár, Johann Nestroy – came out of a Viennese or Austro-Hungarian tradition which Stoppard found profoundly appealing. He often thought that if not for the Second World War he would have been a writer in direct descent from Joseph Roth or Stefan Zweig, writers who greatly attracted him. He is fascinated by that literary intersection, somewhere between the Czech–Austrian satirist Karl Kraus and the Austrian philosopher and novelist Robert Musil. Behind them stand Rilke and Kafka. What is the attraction to him of that culture, which he would draw on deeply, much later, in *Leopoldstadt*? It is, in great part, its Jewishness. It is a culture, he says, which elevates and values the best in music, painting and writing. And that is a vein, too, he notes, which runs all through modern Russian history, through Soviet times. In his words: 'Everything altered around it, but the thing itself was accommodated and perpetuated, so that under Stalin, if you were a great poet or dancer, it meant something.' The serious public work he did in the 1980s on behalf of Soviet Jews living in the post-Stalinist USSR was connected to his light-hearted involvement with these European plays.

He often tells the story of how he came to adapt Arthur Schnitzler's *Das weite Land*. In rehearsal one day with Peter Wood for *Night and Day*, he noticed a 'literal' of the Schnitzler on the director's table. Wood said he was planning to put it on in a new translation. Feeling rather put out, like a neglected lover or a betrayed wife, Stoppard asked why *he* wasn't doing it. I would never have thought you would want to, Wood replied. Would you? He immediately said yes. The same sort of thing would happen, years later, when Michael Grandage asked him if he would do a new version of Chekhov's *Ivanov* for his Donmar season in the West End in 2008. It was a single phone call. Don't you want to reread it first? the director asked him. No, I'll do it, said Stoppard straight away. He knew when something felt right for him.

He had had some contact with the Vienna Burgtheater, where Peter Wood often worked; *Das weite Land* was in their repertoire. His German translator, Hilde Spiel (distinguished but touchy), was Viennese. Now he immersed himself in the work of one of Vienna's most notorious play-wrights, and in the period around 1911, just before the deluge, which he had already inhabited with *Travesties*. Arthur Schnitzler, born in 1862, was part of an avant-garde group of artists in Vienna before the war, notorious for his sexual frankness and his erratic personal life (wild affairs, a failed marriage, a daughter who killed herself, a disgrace to the army). Worldly, cynical and erotic, he was the chronicler of a decadent, hypocritical, bour-geois Austrian society in which he was both an insider and a misfit. He was interested in psychoanalysis, dreams, madness and suicide, and had links to Freud, Hofmannsthal and Richard Strauss. After his death in 1931 his books were banned and burnt by the Nazis as Jewish, decadent filth. But his dark satires had a lasting influence. The scandalous *Reigen* – *La Ronde* – of 1897, pursuing the sexual merry-go-round of ten couples, was made into a film by Max Ophüls in 1950, and given a new version by David Hare in *The Blue Room*. *Liebelei*, a bitter 1895 tragedy of wronged love and self-sacrifice, with a shooting and a suicide, which Stoppard turned into *Dalliance* in 1986, was also filmed by Ophüls. It has often been restaged, with more banal titles – *Flirtation*, *Reckoning*, *Playing with Love*. Schnitzler also inspired Kubrick's *Dream Story*. And more than one film was made of his 1911 play *Das weite Land*.

The usual translation of the title was *The Vast Domain*, but Stoppard caught the play's ironic melancholy by turning it into a phrase from *Hamlet*. *Undiscovered Country* evokes Ibsen, Wilde and Chekhov, too. A frivolous bourgeoisie is dancing on the edge of an abyss, falling in and out

of love, ignoring the politics of the outside world. There's an Ibsenesque
idealistic young woman who wants to climb to the top of a mountain, a
woman caught inside a troubled marriage, a worldly-wise doctor. Painful
emotion is covered over with brittle, suave repartee. Their 'bogus civility'
is a thin veneer. Stoppard told his mother that he thought Schnitzler was
better than Ibsen, 'at least as comedy mixed with tragedy'.

His version makes the most of the comedy. He leaps at the ridiculous characters in this group of leisured Viennese, with their mansions,
their good cigars, their love of entertainment and their holidays in the
Dolomites. He has fun with the overdressed young man on the make,
the dim society matron, the nouveau riche banker's wife and the spoilt
playwright who despises the people he writes for: 'End of Act Three, the
audience rushes deeply moved into the bar'. He drops in Viennese jokes
about light opera and psychoanalysis, and makes the most of an ongoing
tennis match as a metaphor for the 'foolish games' of all the lying lovers.
Epigrams about trust and faithlessness, youth and age, love and sex, honour and dishonour, ricochet to and fro.

He cuts the dialogue with as sharp an edge as can be. When he started
work, he felt anxious about getting an exact equivalence for the original.
But when *Undiscovered Country* went into rehearsal, with his star team,
Peter Wood and John Wood, he began to loosen up. At the first read-
through, some of the things the actors liked best were the things he had
made up, and it was hard to know when to stop doing that. Of one satisfying aphorism he had invented, which wasn't at all true to the original
but felt right, he said: 'It was like being given a box of Lego which is put
together, and there's this one piece which is the wrong size. And I never
knew what to do until I decided to put in my own bit of Lego.'

He put his distinctive mark on the dialogue. 'I sometimes think women
who are good mothers possess the gift of being so for their husbands too'
(in a literal translation) becomes (in Stoppard's version): 'The mark of a
good wife, mothering her husband.' 'One doesn't like to be a stooge' is
toughened into 'I won't be made to look a fool.' A married woman saying goodbye to her young lover tells him, in his version: 'You'll live. It
was lovely. Let's call it a day.' Epigrams are pointed: '"He had too many

affectations." "What he had was style. They're often confused." 'In my opinion, yearning is a necessary part of the soul's economy. Relationships are all the better for it. In an ideal world more and more people would see less and less of each other.'

That's the view of the play's central character, Friedrich Hofreiter, a wealthy light-bulb manufacturer. He is a manipulative egotist, perpetually unfaithful to his wife in an attempt to rediscover lost youth, witty, fatalistic, vain and restless. Though extremely attractive, he has a sinister, morbid quality. Around him circle his troubled wife, his faithful doctor friend, his ex-mistress, a young girl who passionately adores him, and his older alter ego, an ageing, philandering hotelier who has a key exchange with Friedrich about the possibility of loving the person you betray and the impossibility of knowing the heart of another person:

> Haven't you ever thought what a strange uncharted country is
> human behaviour? So many contradictions find room in us – love
> and deceit . . . loyalty and betrayal . . . worshipping one woman, yet
> longing for another, or several others. We try to bring order into our
> lives as best we can; but that very order has something unnatural
> about it. The natural condition is chaos. Yes, Hofreiter, the soul . . . is
> an undiscovered country as the poet once said . . . though it could
> equally well have been the manager of a hotel.

Stoppard referred to his version of *Undiscovered Country* as 'a craftsman's job, not "my soul speaks through Schnitzler"'. But there were suggestive prompts here for his own next play.

For all its dark truths about love and the soul, what most struck audiences was the amazing theatrical showmanship of Peter Wood's Olivier Theatre production, designed by William Dudley. It was a complicated production to mount, not helped by a stagehands' strike in the run-up to the opening on 20 June 1979. In the big cast, there were moving, polished performances, from John Wood as Friedrich (perhaps a bit *too* busy in the part demonstrating his versatility and intelligence, Stoppard thought), Dorothy Tutin as his tormented wife, Michael Bryant and Joyce Redman.

But what people remembered above all was one particular piece of stage-craft. When Stoppard talked about plays as texts that turn into events, this was one of his favourite examples: the fabulously exciting transformation of a country mansion near Vienna into the entrance hall of a mountain-eering hotel with an elevator. Better than any dialogue, he thought.

> As we got to the end of Act One and time to do the scene change, a lot of dry ice began to be pumped from all around. After a very short time the stage was up to about shoulder height in this white fog . . . The next thing that happened was that in the middle of the stage – out of this fog – a fist holding an ice-axe went straight up and was followed by a shoulder with a coil of rope, and then a little woolly hat, and then a mountaineer was standing there; he started pulling on his rope, and pulled another mountaineer up out of this fog . . . Then . . . a third person with woolly hat and ice-axe and whatever came through. It was very interesting. They all stood there and clapped each other on the back and congratulated each other . . . and by this time the fog was beginning to disperse because the dry ice just – whatever dry ice does . . . These three mountaineering guys were then just standing in this hotel lobby with the lift going up and down. For years afterwards . . . somebody says, 'Undiscovered Country, you . . . you did . . . you wrote that? That was wonderful, when that fog came in and the mountaineers . . .' I say, 'Yeah, I wrote that.'

That theatrical bravura was at its most spectacular in the next Wood-and-Stoppard fling with European comedy. On the Razzle, worked on rapidly and staged in 1981, first at the Edinburgh Festival and then at the National, was a different kind of Viennese spectacle from Undiscovered Country. Johann Nestroy belonged to an earlier generation – he died the year Schnitzler was born – and to a world of farce, pantomime and musical comedy. Nestroy was a singer, an actor, a playwright, a composer, an enter-tainer and a hugely popular Viennese theatrical phenomenon. No cyni-cal melancholy, world-weariness or introspection here: the social satire was much broader and the pace was quicker. Nestroy loved wordplay and regional dialects. He had music and songs in all his plays. His comedy of 1842, *Einen Jux will er sich machen* ('He's out for a fling'), was a free translation of a little-known English one-act comedy. It told the story of two country mice who abandon the shop for a spree in the big city, while their master goes to court his wealthy fiancée and the master's niece tries to run off with her boyfriend. There is an explosion of coincidences, disguises, chases, crises and comic reunions. It was a huge success. It was adapted, twice, in the 1930s and 1950s, by the American playwright Thornton Wilder, who grafted on the character of Dolly the Yonkers matchmaker (played by Ruth Gordon in a famous production), leading eventually to Barbra Streisand and Louis Armstrong in *Hello, Dolly!*

In Stoppard's version there was no matchmaker, no dialect, no music and not much respect for the original text. He felt he could be joyously free with this funny old farce. Most of the dialogue was his own invention. His version was laden, possibly over-laden, with puns, double entendres, malapropisms, misfiring clichés and gleefully filthy sexual innuendo. Much of the plot depends on a very slow pantomime horse called Lightning (a joke he would use again for the tortoise in *Arcadia*), and the play did go like lightning. The audience didn't have time to stop laughing before the next joke came along.

Everyone has a verbal tic. Zangler the ludicrous grocer puts his foot in his mouth every time he opens it. His glib, opportunist, bungling servant Melchior does the word 'classic' to death. The ingenue niece says 'it's not proper' to every suggestion. The country-mouse heroes, Weinberl and Christopher, swap lofty, sentimental hopes and dreams and pronouncements on the class system, while wriggling in and out of endless scrapes. There's a whole raft of jokes about the Scottish mania which has hit Vienna after Verdi's *Macbeth*, involving kilts, sporrans and Mac-iavelli: 'Even the chocolate cake – Sachertartan!' There are quick nods to other comedies, from the Marx Brothers to *My Fair Lady*. There are excruciating puns: 'the wurst is yet to come'. There are lots of jokes about language, perfect for a play in translation set in Vienna, including a saucy French maid, a messenger from Belgium speaking cod 'foreign' ('Ich comen looken finden

Herr Sonders'), a spoof on Italian waiters, and some Anglo-German misunderstandings:

> Melchior: What weather we're having, eh! Turning out a bit dank. Is it
>   cold outside?
> German man: *Bitte?*
> Melchior: Is it? Last night was definitely dank. Would you say tonight
>   was as dank or not as dank?
> German woman: *Danke.*
> Melchior: (*amazed*) Danker?
> German man: *Bitte.*
> Melchior. Please yourselves.

Silliest of all are Zangler's mishaps with language – 'God in Himalayas!' 'Quick, fetch me a half-witted cab you hansom fool!' – where cliché takes on a surreal life of its own:

> Zangler: I feel like the cake of the week.
> Weinberl: That's very well put, Chief.
> Zangler: I don't mean the cake of the week—
> Weinberl: Not the cake of the week – the Sheikh of Kuwait—
> Zangler: No—
> Christopher: The clerk of the works—
> Zangler: No!
> Weinberl: The cock of the walk?
> Zangler: That's the boy. I feel like the cock of the walk.

Zanglerism is catching, so Melchior starts talking like his master, as if he's involuntarily learnt to speak Dogg: 'Don't have dinner with him, miss! – he'll alter you before the dessert – no – he'll desert you before the altar.' 'What is all this nonsense?' comes the reply, and that's the delight of it. No one knows what's going to come out of their mouth next, what they will have to invent to get out of a scrape, or who they are going to have to pretend to be. Shakespeareanly, 'Christopher' is a woman who is playing a boy pretending to be a woman disguised as another woman: 'I'm not the woman you think I am. I'm not even the woman you *think* is the woman you think I am.' Mistaken for someone else, Melchior indignantly erupts: 'I am about the only person here who isn't pretending to be someone else!'

Everything depended on how it was done, and as soon as they went into rehearsal Stoppard and Wood became, as always, their own comedy duo, working together to squeeze every inch of laughter, every turn of surprise, out of the script. Felicity Kendal, a star of stage and screen, famous in her mid-thirties for the television sitcom *The Good Life*, and playing big parts in that National Theatre season of 1980–1 (Desdemona to Paul Scofield's Othello, Constanze in Peter Shaffer's *Amadeus*), was cast as Christopher. Though Shaffer and Stoppard were very different kinds of writers, she thought that what they had in common was the writing of 'great arias' for actors.

It was her first job with Stoppard and Wood. She watched this 'exceptional team' with delight as they worked their magic tricks and joked at each other's expense to put the actors at their ease. She saw that Wood had a superb comic talent and understood exactly what to do with a Stoppard script. It was a long, tough rehearsal period, a big cast, a very complicated play to put on, and physically demanding – but it was fun.

Her Christopher was a magnetic comic turn: husky, jaunty, crop-haired, wide-eyed, quick-thinking. At first she had no idea how to 'get' a young boy. She felt she was being too 'feminine' or – 'ghastly!' – too like Oliver Twist. She used her own nine-year-old son as a model. She could see that Stoppard, with his four sons, knew all about boys' behaviour too. (For the boys, especially Barny, *On the Razzle* with all its rude jokes was a favourite among their father's plays.) The turning point came when she realised that her feet looked too small. She asked for her boots to be two sizes bigger. Then the whole thing 'came together'. After that she had no anxieties at all. She knew she was good in this play.

This was her first phase of working with and getting to know Stoppard, and she was one of three actors in the production who then became part of his team. The others were Dinsdale Landen and Michael Kitchen. For Kitchen, stylish and suave, the whole production was a dream of pleasure, though it was also extremely hard work. He 'had never had a better time in a rehearsal'. Wood and Stoppard's first idea had been to cast him as Weinberl (played eloquently by Ray Brooks) but he was even more pleased with Melchior. For a time he would become close to the Stoppard family, and forever after he would think of Stoppard with unbounded admiration. 'He is to theatre and screen and intellect what Federer is to tennis. Elegant, durable, brilliant, beautiful.'

Dinsdale Landen, one of Stoppard's favourite actors – a comic genius, he thought – played Zangler, and he too became a good friend. Stoppard loved his pompous, grandiose, absurd performance, with his handlebar moustache, jingling spurs, too-tight uniform and booming, plummy voice. He loved the way Landen kept making up extra jokes on the spur of the moment. In the restaurant scene, full of near-miss encounters, colliding waiters, screens, revolving doors and rapid exits, Zangler at one point hears the voice of Melchior emanating from somewhere, and can't work out where it's coming from. To Stoppard's delight, in an impromptu stroke, Landen looked into the hanging flower-basket, suspended over the table, as though in some strange way Michael Kitchen might be inside it. In the next scene, Zangler is chasing his niece and her lover through a garden. The Lyttelton stage has a revolve, which was put to maximum use in Carl Toms' design. There was a ladder leaning in the corner of the garden and Landen shouted 'A ladder!' and then ran through the central passage of the summerhouse, which was revolving. Then he emerged from the direction in which he'd entered, and cried out: 'Another ladder!' Stoppard was enchanted by this invention. It still made him laugh years later, thinking about it.

Everyone in the show was having a ball; so were the audiences. But there were criticisms. The early ones were from Miriam, who thought some of the puns were worked to death, and from his mother, who read an early draft and complained that it was too rude. This produced a heated reaction. Where were these four-letter words she was complaining about? There weren't any! Yes, there was a huge amount of sexual innuendo, but the original was riddled with it. And was it any worse than Morecambe and Wise? He explained that one particularly crude passage was needed because he was working towards the line, 'This place is beginning to lose its chic for me': 'which is a funny line *only* if the speaker has just said something very coarse'. Ruefully, he added that perhaps there was so much sex in the play because Miriam had been away for three weeks.

> I'm afraid I've made the Coachman in Act II *sex-obsessed* – *I* think it's funny but perhaps I'm losing my objectivity as middle-age overtakes me . . . or Miriam's lengthy absence, of course – the sort of thing that probably won't occur to anybody when *Razzle* is set for O Levels: 'Explain Stoppard's motivation for making the Coachman obsessed with sex'. Only Oliver will answer: 'His wife was in America for 3 weeks – next question'.

More seriously, he said that he didn't want to be too faithful to the original. He needed to 'find a tone which updates the romp'. And with some irritation, the forty-four-year-old playwright told his mother: 'I do *know* what I'm doing'.

There was considerably more irritation at being ticked off, in a lengthy *Sunday Times* review by the poet and theatre critic James Fenton, for his 'complete misunderstanding' of the dynamics of Nestroy's plot. Fenton criticised Stoppard for apparently not realising that Weinberl had been played in the original production by Nestroy himself, and had had a more important role to play than Stoppard allowed him. It annoyed Stoppard that Fenton would assume that he would not have done his homework. Other critics, like Irving Wardle in *The Times*, enjoyed the comedy's 'atmosphere of inspired lunacy', singling out for praise Kitchen and Landen, Kendal's 'marvellous, quick-witted performance' and Harold Innocent's 'sex-crazed coachman'. Peter Wood got the Laurence Olivier award for best director, and the play had a long afterlife, in the States and in regional theatres.

His returns, a few years later, into European drama and 'undiscovered countries' were not in quite such a joyous spirit. A rare foray into Russian opera in 1983, a version of Prokofiev's satirical comedy *Love for Three Oranges* done for Glyndebourne, was an entertaining commission. But his 1984 version of Ferenc Molnár's *Rough Crossing* wasn't such a happy experience as *On the Razzle*. His second Schnitzler, *Dalliance*, at the National in 1986, was a melancholy romance, more bitter than sweet. That year he also did his version of Havel's *Largo Desolato*, a desolating work.

But soon after *On the Razzle*, in 1982, he made another witty foray into foreign territory. He was asked to write a play to celebrate the sixtieth anniversary of the BBC, with his favourite radio director, John Tydeman. The result was a one-hour comedy called *The Dog It Was That Died*. It harked back to the wild radio inventiveness of *Artist Descending a Staircase* or *Glad/Frank*, to the unpredictability of *After Magritte* or *Jumpers*, and to the espionage world of *Neutral Ground* and his film of *The Human Factor* (whose plot also involved a dog that dies). It even has a character who's interested in 'consonantal transposition' and starts to teach his listener this new language, as with *Dogg's Our Pet*, or Zangler infecting Melchior with his spoonerisms.

As that suggests, *The Dog It Was That Died* plays mainly as zany high jinks. Tydeman thought it wonderfully silly and over-plotted, but also a stunning vehicle for radio effects. Stoppard thought it 'very lightweight'. It's full of wildly eccentric English characters who take their own particular obsession completely seriously. The smooth upper-crust spymaster is building a Gothic folly in his garden, which doubles as a donkey sanctuary run by his bossy wife, who is having an affair with his opium-smoking boss. There's a cheese-obsessed vicar, and a rest home for broken-down spies, built on the edge of a cliff, where the lunatic inmates (in a steal from Edgar Allan Poe) are indistinguishable from the staff, and the doctor in charge has 'bats in his belfry'. It's full of funny radio moments, like the sound of someone clutching a pair of red-hot forceps while being kicked by a donkey as a vacuum cleaner starts up and a roomful of clocks strike the hour.

Inside the farce is a dark story of a desperate person. Purvis, the depressed double agent, has been manipulated by both sides in the Cold War to such a degree that he can hardly remember which side he is on. He tries to get both sides to remind him of what the arguments were, but his English manager, Blair, is not much use to him: 'I never really got

beyond us being British and them being atheists and Communists. There's
no arguing with that, is there?' He has become a hollow man, 'like one of
those Russian dolls . . . which fit into one another as they get smaller'. He
no longer knows whether there is the last doll in the middle, 'the only one
which isn't hollow'. 'Perhaps I'm not even a set of dolls any more, perhaps
I'm an onion. My idealism and my patriotism, folded on each other, have
been peeled away leaving nothing in the middle except the lingering smell
of onion.' He's given up to uncertainty: 'I hope I'm right, though I would
settle for *knowing* that I'm wrong.' Even his suicide, the first time round, is
a muddled, farcical botch.

The Dog It Was That Died is Le Carré-like in its disillusioned treatment of the Cold War. (Apparently David Cornwell, who didn't yet know
Stoppard, wasn't best pleased by seeing this play referred to in *Punch* as 'Le
Carré-cature'.) It looks ahead to *Hapgood*, which reuses Blair's name and
role. *Hapgood* too will have a strong feeling for England at its heart. Purvis
finds that in the end his only 'remaining affinity' is 'with the English character', seen at its most bizarre at the rest home. Unpredictable English
eccentricity is preferred to an ideology which explains all mutations and
tragedies as part of 'historical inevitability'.

Aired in December 1982, and compellingly played by Dinsdale Landen
(with Charles Gray, Penelope Keith, John Le Mesurier as the doctor with
a worrying nervous laugh, and Kenneth Cranham as a dogged, anxious
investigative agent), *The Dog It Was That Died* was more of a success than
he expected. It won the Giles Cooper award for radio drama, and was
turned into a play for Granada TV by Peter Wood in 1989 (less effectively,
in spite of the performances by Alan Howard as Purvis and Alan Bates as
Blair).

The vulnerable side of a tough profession was also the subject of a film
script he worked on in the early 1980s called *A.O.P.* The title stood for
'Attack on the Principal', and 'the Principal' was the secret service code
for the president. He had always been fascinated by the bodyguards in
the American newsreels, and after the attempted assassination of Reagan
in March 1981, that fascination turned into an idea for a film. He went to
interview a secret service agent in Washington, and even visited a training

school (where he noted that security was as tight as for 'the real thing'). He wasn't thinking of a screenplay 'mainly concerned with fast cars, flying bullets and snipers at windows', but about the conflict in America between 'security and democratic rights'. He was remembering, nostalgically, the time in his childhood in India when America seemed romantic. His character was a young man who's left his home town and goes back there to protect the president, with an aura of glamour about him. But he's sacked from that job and becomes the bodyguard for a famous rock star, a Jagger or a Dylan. (This was a decade before Clint Eastwood in *In the Line of Fire* or Kevin Costner in *The Bodyguard*.) He is despised by his former colleagues, but becomes part of a world where, whatever the underground lives of the artists are like, the music itself – rock music which, like Stoppard, the young man has grown up with – commands respect.

The bodyguard film didn't get made, and nor did a screenplay based on P. D. James's novel *Innocent Blood*. A more serious and challenging project was a request from a producer, Fred Brogger, to write a play for TV about the Polish workers' movement, Solidarity. He began work on *Squaring the Circle* early in 1982, while he was in the middle of writing *The Real Thing*, and for the next two years he struggled with the frustrations of trying to mount a joint British and American film project. Between 1982 and 1984 he often complained about this tiresome saga. What began as an interesting challenge became 'a long irritation', a distraction from his stage play. But having committed to the project, he stuck with it, along a very bumpy road.

In March 1982 he described himself as 'stuffed with information': 'I know more about Polish politics than anyone else in Iver.' He took reams of careful notes on the history of Solidarity and Poland under Communism. But he was already worrying about the genre. As he started to write, he felt it was boring: 'it seems to be neither a play nor a documentary'. By April 1982 he had a script, but it would take another two years, and £1.25 million spent, before a much-altered version was aired. And even that was not the end of the story.

He was writing about living history, about a situation that was still unfolding dramatically. Out of the conflicts between the Gdańsk shipworkers and Poland's Soviet-dependent government came the Gdańsk agreement for independent Trades Unions, signed in August 1980, and the founding of Solidarity the following month. A year later, the shipworkers' hero Lech Wałęsa was elected president of Solidarity. Two months after that, in December 1981, the Polish government, under General Jaruzelski, imposed martial law (arguing that this would avert a Soviet invasion), which meant political repression, arrests, assaults, sackings, curfews, censorship and price rises. There were huge demonstrations in August 1982. But it would take years before Poland, moving with the great shifts all across Eastern Europe, had a general amnesty for political prisoners in 1986 and elections in 1989. Wałęsa became president in December 1990.

Stoppard was writing the film between 1982 and the end of 1983, in the middle of the martial law period. No one knew what would happen next. But at the time of writing, it all looked bleak. The first scene of the play was the meeting between Polish First Secretary Gierek and Brezhnev, in the Crimea, in July 1980, during the outbreak of activism in Gdańsk; the last scene was the imposition of martial law in December 1981 and the arrest of the Solidarity leadership. So he began it only two years after the events it described.

Given this context, he was convinced that a straight factual documentary was not the right approach. And it wasn't in his nature to write an unambiguous play. He wanted to give, 'Rashomon-style', multiple, contradictory accounts of events, and for the audience to be made aware of the dangers of the documentary form. So he created a narrator of 'acknowledged fallibility' who gives us alternative versions of historical scenes, and asks: 'What is the reality supposed to sound like?' 'Everything is true,' the narrator tells us, 'except the words and the pictures.' On the first page of the script he finished in April 1982, there was an asterisk next to 'Narrator', and the footnote read: '*: The Author.'

There followed Brogger's long search for a director, for the money, for locations and for a cast. (Stoppard had an unfulfilled hope that John Hurt might play Wałęsa.) They entered the territory of compromise. The British director Mike Hodges (famous for *Get Carter* and *Flash Gordon*) liked Stoppard's ambiguous author-narrator, and was willing to add an

even quirkier figure, a witness who could quiz the narrator on his version of events; that witness turned into five different Polish characters.
But the American company, Metromedia, who agreed to put $800,000
into the film, wanted the narrator to be a famous American film star,
and didn't like the 'witnesses'. It turned out they hadn't seen the page
with the asterisk, on the 1982 script, which identified the narrator as the
author. Stoppard thought he could persuade them (over several trips to
Los Angeles all through 1983) that 'the script required the narrator and
the author to be the same person'. But he was wrong. Metromedia, in the
person of Steve, or Bruce, or Dale, or Chuck, or Bob, 'and way beyond
Bob, somewhere at the top of the mountain, the mysterious figure of
Mr Kluge, remote as Buddha', continued to insist on drastic simplifica-
tions in the interests of 'advertiser support'. 'It became rapidly clear that
Metromedia had bought not merely the right to show the film but the
right to alter it in any way they liked.' As often, he was forced to ask questions about the rights of the author. If it came to a fight, did 'authority'
rest with authorship? Evidently not.

Mike Hodges took his name off the project. Stoppard felt he had to
continue trying to get the best result he could, so he went on patiently
'horse-trading' – and clawing back some of his original script. But Hodges
never quite forgave him. 'I love Tom Stoppard,' he said in 2002, 'but he
really was naive in this instance . . . The Americans . . . were insulting their
audience by dumbing it down . . . Tom should never have compromised.'
The US version took its own shape. Channel 4's UK version, aired on 31
May 1984, was titled 'a film by Mike Hodges and Tom Stoppard'. In the end
it was not quite as bad as he feared. It won an Emmy, which Stoppard went
to LA to collect (without Mike Hodges), and the Critics' Prize at the Banff
TV festival in Toronto. By the end of 1985, the very different US version
had still not been aired.

At the time, Stoppard adopted a resigned, ironical tone: 'That's showbiz,'
as he said to his parents. It wasn't lost on him that the historical betrayals
and compromises he was writing about were being echoed in the relatively
trivial production problems he was having. Still, he found it 'as upsetting
as any situation I've been in as a writer', and he reproached himself, too,

for naivety. He wrote some dismayed pieces about the business, one of them as the introduction to the first Faber edition of *Squaring the Circle*. 'Strewth, what a story,' commented Frank Pike.

Even without the drastic changes imposed by Metromedia, there were big differences between Stoppard's first, unpublished 1982 script and the published text of 1984, which was (more or less) what was seen on Channel 4. The 1984 version did much more spelling out and explaining ('You won't understand Poland's attitude to Russia until you understand some Polish history'). He put in more jokes, like a Russian banker called Finansky. But he did maintain his unreliable approach, for instance giving three different versions of a scene between Wałęsa, Jaruzelski and Archbishop Glemp, or showing us a solid-looking, book-lined room which proves to be a temporary studio set. The character you might want to sympathise with, Kuron, the intellectual radical writer, who foreshadows the romantic revolutionary exiles of *The Coast of Utopia*, is as fallible as anyone else.

For all its ambiguities, a definite view underlies the film. Stoppard's own anti-Marxist belief that 'theories don't guarantee social justice, social justice tells you if a theory is any good' is strongly voiced by the narrator, who calls, as Stoppard so often does, on a child's view to prove his point: 'Right and wrong are not complicated – when a child cries, "That's not fair!" the child can be believed.' And the narrator spells out the play's essential premise:

Between August 1980 and December 1981 an attempt was made in Poland to put together two ideas which wouldn't fit, the idea of freedom as it is understood in the West, and the idea of socialism as it is understood in the Soviet empire. The attempt failed because it was impossible, in the same sense as it is impossible in geometry to turn a circle into a square with the same area – not because no one has found out how to do it, but because there is no way in which it can be done.

The struggles of Solidarity, Havel's incarceration and the continuing injustices and repressions in Czechoslovakia kept his mind close to Eastern Europe all through the 1980s. He became deeply involved with the cause of the 'refuseniks', the Soviet Jews who wanted to emigrate from the Soviet Union to Israel and elsewhere, who were treated as 'outcasts from Soviet society' if they applied for visas. They were sacked, demoted and attacked, and mostly denied permission or left in limbo. An international campaign was being mounted on their behalf, especially in the States. The cause seemed to him a morally crucial one, bound up as it was with human rights and freedom of choice. His own childhood history underlay his involvement – though, in the 1980s, in spite of the memoir he asked his mother to write in 1981, her history was still obscure to him.

His strongest motive for involvement was his horror of Soviet Communism and a deep sense of injustice. In 1983 he opened a Soviet Jewry exhibition at the House of Commons. A few years later, in 1986, he wrote a piece for the *Daily Mail* – not his favourite outlet, but he wanted to reach a big audience – about the KGB's cynical release of the mathematician Anatoly Shcharansky to the West, after years of imprisonment and harassment. Though Shcharansky's release was a cause for celebration, behind him stood 'an immense column of refuseniks who are trying to follow him out'. On 17 February 1986, he organised a dawn-to-dusk vigil on the South Bank, a roll call for Soviet Jews who had applied for and been refused visas of emigration from Russia. (The event led to an award for services to Soviet Jewry in July that year.) Nine thousand refusenik names were read out – a fraction of those who had applied for visas – and as each name was uttered, a red carnation was thrown onto the courtyard outside the National Theatre. He wrote to all the well-known people he could think of to get their participation. Piers Paul Read was one of many who received a formal invitation to come and stand outside the National Theatre. Stoppard told him that more than a hundred 'public figures' would read out the names, and that there would be big coverage of the event. The celebrity readers included David Owen, David Steel, Ken Livingstone, Neil Kinnock, Ronnie Corbett, Melvyn Bragg and Twiggy. The Broadway producer Emanuel Azenberg, who had begun his friendship and working relationship with Stoppard on *The Real Thing* and was a supporter of Israel, flew over from New York with Senator Bill Bradley, famous American basketball player turned politician. Why was he making the trip? Manny Azenberg asked Bradley. Bradley replied: 'One, it's good politics; Two, I believe in the cause; Three, I'll be having dinner with Tom Stoppard.'

Stoppard's involvement in Cold War anti-Communist activities strengthened his links to Margaret Thatcher (a great heroine to most Czech and Russian dissidents at the time), whom he invited to take part in the roll call. She declined, as she felt it would 'weaken her ability to assist Soviet Jewry', but told him she sympathised 'very much' with the cause. Another who declined was Isaiah Berlin. He told Stoppard that his sympathy with the cause was total, but that with painful regret he had to refuse to be publicly critical of the Soviet Union because he had living relatives there, and could cause them harm.

His pro-Jewish and anti-Soviet activities did not go down well with his parents. Ken Stoppard had become increasingly xenophobic as he got older, and very much disliked his famous adopted son campaigning for Russian Jews. Bobby, as always, wanted a quiet safe life, for herself and for him. She had put her life in Eastern Europe behind her long ago, and she was anxious that his high profile might put him at risk. And she disagreed with his position. 'Tomáš,' her complaint would run – in his paraphrase of it – 'don't you realise most people are happy in Czechoslovakia? They don't know they're living in this prison society you're talking about. We've got to England. Don't make waves.'

Out of kindness and tact, he muted these activities in his letters to her. In February 1980, for instance, when he took part in a recreation of a Czech dissenter's trial in Munich, he only mentioned it in passing, 'because you don't like my getting too "involved"'. But their disagreement came to a head with the 1986 roll call event, and, for once, he spelt out his arguments, in one of the most challenging letters he ever wrote to her.

About the Soviet thing – I really hate upsetting you, but I suppose not quite enough to override my own arguments for doing it. I could have told you two months ago but what's the point? – it would only worry you for 2 extra months. I agree with most of what you say – I would even put in extra arguments, eg a Russian Jew is infinitely better

off than half the population of half the countries one reads about –
Africa, Latin America, Haiti, S.E. Asia, etc, etc. AND there certainly
are plenty of things in the 'West' which are far from wonderful . . . *and*
millions of Russians, including Jews, live perfectly reasonable lives
without the slightest desire to change them – none of this is news to
me. On the other hand, Russia, unlike Haiti, etc, is one of the great
and powerful nations which, like America and Europe, considers
that it represents a norm and a standard and a type of society which
aspires to be a model for the world in general . . . so it merits scrutiny
just as Britain or France or America do, but in the latter case the
scrutiny can come from within – abuses are frequent and widespread
but at least they are a) acknowledged *as* abuses, ie the system going
wrong and b) subject to examination by press and TV and c) subject
to correction by the law of the land. But in Russia the abuses are a) the
system working as designed b) not subject to examination or criticism
and c) not subject to law because the legislature is not separated from
the government as it is in the West . . . so I think it's right to 'interfere'.

Now – your main point is: let someone else do it, not Tom. Why?
(apart from the fact that I hardly ever do anything anyway). You don't
really think the Russians are going to shoot me?! And if I thought
there was the remotest chance of your cousin's children or anybody
else in Cz. getting into disfavour I *really* would keep my head down
(Isaiah Berlin and Nureyev both have mothers in Russia and quite
rightly *never* do anything political) but even the Communists don't
blame anyone for the actions of a second cousin who left the country
at the age of 18 months! Havel . . . is much more likely to get a
backlash as someone connected with me.

. . . You seem to say that I don't 'need the recognition' but I can't
believe you think I'm doing it for that – I dislike having my name in
the papers and try not to except when I owe it to a producer of my
plays. The fact is that . . . *you* have no idea how bad things can be and
if they were happening to Fiona you would be on the South Bank
yourself! I've been lucky all my life, it almost makes me believe in the
stars, and the way I can live, including O, B, W & E, really begins with

that fate making me an 'English writer' instead of a Czech one, and I don't think one should necessarily take it for granted and get on with one's own life and say hard luck to everyone else.

I'm a bit confused as to your other argument. Are you saying that there's an anti-foreign streak in English society and I shouldn't keep reminding people that I wasn't born at the age of eight in Retford?? I've *never* found the English like that, the opposite if anything.

I keep telling journalists that my being born in Cz. is irrelevant to all this, which is true in the sense that I feel English and love England and have not an iota of feeling transplanted (although I have an enormous nostalgia for India) – it's odd really. I have no emotional feeling for Europe at all, and it's almost arbitrary that I involve myself a bit in Czechs and Russia etc – except that I do think Communism is anti-human. I know it intellectually not emotionally.

. . . You know I love you and it upsets me to upset you – I'll keep my head down now for a couple of years. It's not a way I *like* to spend my time, it's a sort of occasional necessary nuisance which I think I owe to my good luck.

19

The Real Thing

To speak of being familiar with a loved one is a contradiction in
terms . . . Lovers should be referred to as constant unfamiliars . . .

Max, an architect, is sitting alone, building a house of cards. His wife
Charlotte, an art dealer, comes home. The door slams, the house of cards
collapses. 'It's me,' she announces. She has been on a trip to Switzerland,
and brings him back a present. Max needles and quizzes her. She sees
there is something wrong. He tells her he has been through her things and
found her passport. He assumes she has been unfaithful. His questioning
of her is witty and sardonic, congratulating her on the inventiveness of her
fake airport presents, guessing at the number of lovers she has. She tells
him there is a right thing to say if only he could think of it. She is sorry he's
had a bad time, but he has done everything wrong.

> Max: Is it anyone I know?
> Charlotte: You aren't anyone I know.

And she leaves, shutting the door behind her. He gets out her present.
It's an Alpine snow globe. He shakes it and the snowstorm fills the stage.

In the next scene, Henry, a playwright, is preparing his appearance on
Desert Island Discs, rather despairingly, since he's supposed to be a brilliant intellectual, but the only music he really likes is 1960s pop songs.
('I'm going to look a total prick, aren't I, announcing that while I was telling Jean-Paul Sartre and the post-war French existentialists where they
had got it wrong, I was spending the whole time listening to the Crystals
singing "Da Doo Ron Ron".') His wife Charlotte, an actor, treats him
sharply. Max and his wife Annie, also both actors, come to call. In the
foursome that follows, we get two revelations. First, quite quickly, that
Max and Charlotte are the actors playing 'Max' and 'Charlotte' in Henry's
play, *House of Cards*, which is what we were watching in Scene One. And

that Charlotte is not enjoying the run of the play, since in her view Henry can't write parts for women. ("'Fancy a drink?" "Let me get you a drink." "Care for a drink?" That's Henry's idea of women's parts.') Second, once the others are out of the room, making 'dips' for drinks, that Henry and Annie are having an affair, and are poised on the verge of giving their secret away. Annie wants to – she is rash and passionate – and Henry doesn't, in case it turns out not to be the real thing. Two offstage characters are talked about. One is Henry and Charlotte's daughter Debbie, a punk-ish, horse-loving teenager. The other is Annie's good cause, a Scottish soldier called Brodie, whom she met on a train and who's been sent to prison for burning a wreath on the Cenotaph as an anti-cruise-missiles gesture. A protest movement is growing around him. Max and Annie are moved by his story, Henry and Charlotte are not.

The Real Thing turns and turns these relationships and configurations around, as in a hall of mirrors. To put it simply: the playwright leaves the actress he is married to, who is acting in his play as the wife suspected of infidelity, and goes to live with another actress, who is married to the actor who is playing the man in the playwright's play who suspects his wife of infidelity.

Stoppard's version of *La Ronde* spins round as follows. Max finds out that Annie is betraying him with Henry – while Henry's *Desert Island Discs* programme is playing on the radio – and she leaves him. The play is as ruthless with Max as Annie is: we don't see him on stage again. Henry and Annie set up together, at first in bliss. He is trying to write a play for her to star in, as Charlotte starred in his last play. She is acting in Strindberg's *Miss Julie*. He speaks with delight of being in love, but seems not quite in love enough for her, or not enough to be jealous, or to stop fancying other women.

Two years later they are still together. Henry hasn't written his play for her; he is writing a blockbuster sci-fi film script to pay off his alimony bills. Annie is acting in a Jacobean tragedy of incest and passion, Ford's *'Tis Pity She's a Whore*, with a young actor called Billy, who has fallen for her, and for whom she develops a *tendresse*. She also wants Henry to draw attention back to Brodie's cause by doctoring his agitprop play and getting it put on. In response, Henry performs a big speech, with cricket bat, on the difference between good and bad writing.

There is a scene between Henry and Charlotte, cynically tolerant friends now, in which Charlotte tells him she had nine lovers during their marriage, as she thought he wouldn't care. ('It used to bother me that you were never bothered . . . By the time I realised you were the last romantic it was too late.') There is a scene with Debbie, about to leave home at seventeen with a fairground musician, who is scornfully unromantic about sex and, though fond of her father, impatient with his rhetoric and his views. (These two scenes started as separate entities, and then got merged into one.)

In a mirror image of the two earlier scenes of betrayal between 'Max' and 'Charlotte' and Max and Annie, Henry waits for Annie to come home from Glasgow, where she's been playing Ford's incestuous lover with Billy. (We have seen Annie and Billy meeting on the train to Glasgow, in an echo of the first scene of Brodie's play, and we see them rehearsing their love scene in 'Tis Pity.) Henry has gone through her things, because he thinks she may be unfaithful to him. He is feeling the betrayal which 'Max' was so witty about in *House of Cards*, and which Annie put Max through when she left him for Henry.

Annie and Billy act in the TV film of Brodie's play, rewritten, as Annie requested, by Henry. She carries on a relationship of a kind with Billy, but stays with Henry: she assures him that she loves him and that he is not replaceable. He is jealous, in love and in pain. In the last scene, Brodie finally turns up, awkward and ungrateful, to watch his TV play in their house. He doesn't think much of the rewrite. ('I lived and put my guts into it, and you came along and wrote it clever.') Annie reveals that his political act had never been a real protest, just an attempt to attract her attention. Insulting and insulted, he leaves, a misfit in this play to the end. As Annie and Henry are about to go to bed, Max phones, to tell Henry he has found a new love. The pop music that marks every scene plays us out on 'I'm a Believer'. We're left supposing – and hoping? – that Henry and Annie's love will survive and they will stay together. Stoppard would say: 'I think that the right two people found each other, and will sort of survive.'

But he would also say that perhaps it was appropriate 'to end on a note of suspension'.

'For better or worse, that's it – the love play!' That was his summing-up of *The Real Thing* in 1983, and from then on he referred to it as 'fairly straight-forward'. Twenty-five years on, he would say dismissively that there was nothing intellectually challenging about the play. The trickery was all in the structure. The first scene typically 'ambushed' his audience. 'To write a play in which the *first* scene turns out to have been written by one of the characters in the *second* scene,' he said to his mother, while writing it: would that be criticised, as he always was, as 'too clever by half again?' He added that, given this premise, 'willy-nilly the character had to be a play-wright (whose wife is acting in scene one – clever by three-quarters??)'. He would frequently say he would have preferred the main character to be a novelist. 'I thought it might indicate that one had run out of everything, if one started to write plays about people who write plays.' But once he had decided on the trick of the first scene, that was how it had to be. And it followed that the other characters had to be actors, and that the play was in part, as he put it, about 'reality/as distinct from theatre'.

The play makes the audience think about theatricality throughout, even though it's a realistic drama of love and marriage. It is patterned with repeated motifs and balancing acts. The returning wife, carrying a plaus-ible gift from her travels; the jealous husband going through the wife's things; the pop love songs as musical clues to emotion; the middle-class social ritual of making dips to go with drinks; the pick-up on a train; the play within a play: all these ingredients come around, as if we are on a perpetual revolve. He loved these layerings and mirrorings. His play about a playwright is as tightly crafted as an Austrian farce, as finely balanced as a house of cards.

Writing a play about a playwright, and a play about love, led to the obvi-ous conclusion that he was writing autobiographically. That was another reason he hadn't wanted to have a playwright as his main character. It's going to look as if it's all about me, he thought. Joking to Bobby, while writing it, he said: 'The wife turns out to have had 9 affairs so I thought

I wouldn't make her a doctor.' The real Charlotte, in the second scene, is scathing about this problem of overlap. It was no fun playing the wife when she was married to the author. 'All those people out front thinking, that's why she got the job . . . and also thinking that I'm her . . . "It's me!" – ooh, it's her! – so that's what they're like at home.' Nor did Stoppard want people to think, 'Ooh, it's him!'

But this was slippery ground. He said of Henry: 'He does have my prejudices.' And he frequently acknowledged that 'there's a lot of me in it', or at least that Henry 'expresses some of the notions I have about writing'. 'I don't know if it's autobiographical, but a lot of it is auto something,' he said in 1983. When the play was revived in 1999 he dropped his defences. 'Of course, he is me because it's intellectually autobiographical. In most of my plays, there's someone who's nearer to being my spokesperson than anyone else.' But there was always a caveat. 'Because *The Real Thing* had an English playwright editorialising about writing and love and marriage and all that, it was perfectly obvious that when he was waving his prejudices around, he was pretty much speaking for me. But then so are the other people (in the play) who contradict him. That's what playmaking is; you have to take everybody's side.'

Henry may be speaking for Stoppard, but that doesn't mean we like him. He is also self-absorbed, sarcastic, pernickety about language, over-bearingly loquacious and emotionally inadequate. How much we feel for him depends a great deal on the performance. The same is true of the other characters. During the first days of rehearsals for the London run, Stoppard told Bobby that the cast was very good, but that so far Polly Adams was too *nice* for Charlotte and Roger Rees was too *quiet* for Henry. 'But there's time to make them nasty and loud.'

Henry has his author's 'conservative temperament' (as Stoppard said of himself) – and his musical tastes. The lyricist Tim Rice, whom Stoppard had got to know playing cricket in Pinter's team, remembered Stoppard calling with a question for him while he was writing the play. Rice prepared himself for something challenging. The question was: 'Is it the Crystals or the Ronettes who recorded "Da Doo Ron Ron"?' Rice told him it was the Crystals – and he said, 'Oh no, I wanted it to be the Ronettes.'

The exchange gets into the play. And there's a funny riff on Henry's preference for the Righteous Brothers' 'You've Lost That Lovin' Feelin'' as 'possibly the most deeply moving noise ever produced by the human spirit', over
Maria Callas singing in 'a sort of foreign musical with no dancing which
people were donating kidneys to get tickets for'.

Henry also resembles Stoppard in his passionate pedantry about the
English language. His prissy use of 'an hotel', not 'a hotel', his physical recoil
at the cant phrase 'the caring society', his pain at Max's mixed metaphor,
'He got hammered by an emotional backlash' ('I'm sorry, but it actually
hurts') are the comic symptoms of a deep emotion.

The Real Thing is one of the Stoppard plays that doesn't feed off another
text. He said of it proudly: 'Here we are all on our own. No coat-tails!'
No *Hamlet*, no Wilde, no Wittgenstein. But there are plenty of echoes.
There's more than a touch of Coward's *Private Lives* in the badinage
between the two couples. The cruel erotic talk of Strindberg's *Miss Julie*
casts a troubling shadow across this 'liberated' play. Ibsen's *A Doll's House*
is faintly heard in the wife's closing of the door as she exits her marriage. A handkerchief provides a clue to infidelity, as it does in *Othello*.
And a fierce language of lust and desire comes roaring onstage with two
extracts from *'Tis Pity She's a Whore*, Giovanni's wooing of his sister and
their post-coital love scene. Ford's rich sensual rhetoric ('Such lips would
tempt a saint, such hands as those/Would make an anchorite lascivious')
is not available to Stoppard's twentieth-century characters – when Henry
talks about 'dignified cuckoldry' he is being deliberately fusty. No more
can these post-Freudian, liberal, agnostic middle-class lovers go in for
the sadistic misogyny, eye-gougings, poisonings, stabbings, tearing out of
hearts, suffocating with pillows and suicides involved in the jealous love
stories of Ford and Shakespeare. But under the civilised modern surface
of *The Real Thing*, those savage emotions boil up through the stage language of the past.

The play offers us some modern contrasts of language too: the sophisticated style of a West End comedy of manners, the polemics of left-wing
theatre, the clunky clichés of popular film or the poignant banality of
1960s pop songs: 'Then I saw her face, now I'm a believer . . .' ('Strange

how potent cheap music is,' as Coward has it in *Private Lives*). It is in this mongrel literary context that Henry holds forth about his respect for words. 'Words,' he says, are 'innocent, neutral, precise, standing for this, describing that, meaning the other, so if you look after them you can build bridges across incomprehension and chaos . . . I don't think writers are sacred, but words are.' This is often quoted in isolation, but it belongs to its dramatic context.

Henry thinks Brodie's political play is a rubbishy, 'jerry-built' abuse of language. He makes it sound like a caricature of all protest writing: 'war is profits, politicians are puppets, Parliament is a farce, justice is a fraud, property is theft'. This satire, like the argument about newspapers in *Night and Day*, comes out of a particular moment: the Thatcher ascendancy (Stoppard was lunching with Thatcher and Reagan in July 1982), the left-wing theatre of the 1980s, the start of the big anti-missiles protests. While he was writing the play in autumn 1981 there was a huge London march against nuclear weapons, a resurgence of CND. Jimmy Boyle, the Glasgow gangster turned novelist, a *cause célèbre* in the early 1980s, lurks behind the character of Brodie.

Brodie is an easier target for Henry's boot than Tristan Tzara was for the other Henry in *Travesties*. (A third Henry takes a bow in the title. *The Real Thing* is also a short story by Henry James, in which the artist-narrator says that 'the ruling passion of my life was the detestation of the amateur'.) Unlike Tzara, Brodie barely gets to answer back. Annie speaks for him indignantly: 'You're jealous of the idea of the writer. You want to keep it sacred, special, not something anybody can do . . . Then somebody who isn't in on the game comes along, like Brodie, who really has something to write about, something real, and you can't get through it.' But it is Henry's cricket-bat speech, and not Annie's repudiation of it, which becomes the most famous moment in *The Real Thing*:

Shut up and listen. This thing here, which looks like a wooden club, is actually several pieces of particular wood cunningly put together in a certain way so that the whole thing is sprung, like a dance floor. It's for hitting cricket balls with. If you get it right, the cricket ball will travel two hundred yards in four seconds, and all you've done is give it a knock like knocking the top off a bottle of stout, and it makes a noise like a trout taking a fly . . . (*He clucks his tongue to make the noise.*) What we're trying to do is to write cricket bats, so that when we throw up an idea and give it a little knock, it might . . . *travel* . . . (*He clucks his tongue again and picks up [Brodie's] script.*) Now, what we've got here is a lump of wood of roughly the same shape trying to be a cricket bat, and if you hit a ball with it, the ball will travel about ten feet and you will drop the bat and dance about shouting 'Ouch!' with your hands stuck into your armpits. (*Indicating the cricket bat.*) This isn't better because someone says it's better, or because there's a conspiracy by the MCC to keep cudgels out of Lords. It's better because it's better.

The witty metaphor shows off just the kind of stylish elan it's talking about. And it comes out of the English traditions that Stoppard loves. Every word increases our sense of the cultural security of Henry and the alien inadequacy of Brodie, the working-class Scottish prisoner of conscience.

The cricket-bat speech had been gestating for a long time. It came out of his 1970s journal entries, where he had noted down: 'Good prose is sprung like a cricket bat.' Nearby in the journal was the sentence he had copied down from Auden: 'Poetry is the displacement of private instability into the public arena,' with his own twist on it: 'Politics is the displacement of private instability into the public arena.' That got into *Travesties*: 'Ideological differences are often temperamental differences in ideological disguises.' Now it was given to Henry: 'Public postures have the configuration of private derangement.' He told interviewers that the Auden quotation was one of the crucial spurs for the play.

When Annie reveals, at the end, that Brodie's political gesture was just a means of attracting her attention (and then slams a bowl of dip into Brodie's face, like a custard pie thrown into a clown's face), Henry's point is proved. The playwright has it both ways. Polemical art like Brodie's isn't the real thing; and Brodie's politics were not genuine in the first place, they were just driven by personal 'instability'. He was aware, at the time and later, that he was using the Brodie character unfairly as a target, like a coconut shy – though in performance he can have more dignity than on the page.

In general, Stoppard maintains that however good his plays are, they usually have at least one thing wrong with them. He judges *The Real Thing* to have been 'pretty good' when it was about love and marriage and friendship, but not so convincing when it was about a young uneducated soldier going to jail for desecrating a war memorial. He knew that the argument with Brodie was heavily weighted in Henry's favour. Perhaps, while writing it, he hadn't worked out how much Henry's political animus against Brodie came out of a sense of rivalry. But then he had always believed that the writer was the beneficiary of his subconscious.

The cricket-bat speech is about authenticity: what does the job, what rings true? It applies to language: how good can it be, what are the tests for its authenticity? And it also applies to love. How do you know the real thing? How do you keep it? And how do you write it? Henry is on shakier ground here. 'I don't know how to write love,' he tells his lover. 'I try to write it properly, and it just comes out embarrassing.' Stoppard likes this self-referential moment: in a play about love, his playwright complains that *that* is what he can't write about.

Everyone in *The Real Thing* has a different register for love. Annie wants it to be impetuous and risky. She knows there is a cost: 'Better to tell them,' she urges Henry. 'It's easy. Like Butch Cassidy and the Sundance Kid jumping off the cliff. It's only a couple of marriages and a child.' She leaves Max boldly: 'it's better than all that lying.' (Max, abject in love, has no words to argue with except 'I love you' and 'please don't.') She picks up Brodie and then turns on him. She encourages Billy and then discourages him. She wants Henry to be jealous: 'You don't care enough to *care*.' She knows that he is irreplaceable to her, but that also involves hurting him: 'I have to choose who I hurt and I choose you because I'm yours.' Charlotte, an older and more cynical character, thought her infidelities would not affect Henry, because he never took the trouble to tell her his feelings. His view of the marriage was that once the commitment was made, it could look after itself. Charlotte puts him right, afterwards:

There are no commitments, only bargains. And they have to be made again every day. You think making a commitment is *it*. Finish. You think it sets like a concrete platform and it'll take any strain you want to put on it. You're committed. You don't have to prove anything. In fact you can afford a little neglect, indulge in a little bit of sarcasm here and there, isolate yourself when you want to. Underneath it's concrete for life.

He was an idiot to think so, she tells him. And he goes on being an idiot with Annie, even though he loves her so. One of *The Real Thing*'s suggestive questions, not spelt out, is whether a person's character makes all their relationships turn out the same way. Billy gets 'under her radar' partly because Henry has not renewed their commitment. He realises this, late on: 'It's as though I've been careless, left a door open somewhere while preoccupied.' Yet self-absorbed, sarcastic Henry is the play's one true romantic. His daughter Debbie knows this. She is the next generation: treating sex just as biological attraction, rejoicing in free love as free of 'propaganda', impatient with her father's posturings, as in his play:

Henry: It was about self-knowledge through pain.
Debbie: No, it was about did she have it off or didn't she. As if having it off is infidelity.

Just get on and do it, and don't invest it with mystery and sacredness and guilt, thinks Debbie, going off with her rucksack on her life's adventures. She gives a forceful, if brief, kick to Henry's moral language of love, which runs through the play like music:

I love love. I love having a lover and being one. The insularity of passion. I love it. I love the way it blurs the distinction between everyone who isn't one's lover. Only two kinds of presences in the world. There's you and there's them.

It's to do with knowing and being known . . . Knowledge of each other, not of the flesh but through the flesh, knowledge of self, the real him, the real her, *in extremis*, the mask slipped from the face . . . A sort of knowledge. Personal, final, uncompromised. Knowing, being known. I revere that.

Charlotte is right to call him 'the last romantic'. But there's a gap between his eloquence about love and how he acts as a lover. And when love is betrayed, he is reduced to as few words as the next man: 'Oh, please, please, please, please, *don't*.' He loses his balance.

For love to bring happiness – and that is our best hope in this world, if we are 'believers' in love rather than in any other form of worship – there has to be balance. 'Happiness is . . . equilibrium,' says Henry to his daughter. 'Shift your weight.' The three dots in the middle of the line – a kind of pause or breath – keep the thought steady. What does it mean? That happiness requires a sense that things are stable, in order, as they should be. But also that there must be equilibrium between lovers, a balanced give and take. You may have to shift your weight to get to that place. Quoting the line in an interview, Stoppard stands up and demonstrates, moving from foot to foot, and saying: 'Equilibrium is pragmatic. You have to get everything into proportion. You compensate, rebalance yourself so that you maintain your angle to your world. When the world shifts, you shift.'

The line is the fulcrum of all the play's images of balance: the fragile structure of the house of cards, the concrete platform that can take any strain, the words that can 'build bridges across incomprehension and chaos', the tilt you may be able to give to people's perceptions 'at that axis where we locate politics or justice', the construction of a cricket bat. To make the best use of the bat, you have to stand steady, shift your weight, hold your balance. Like a pyramid of acrobats, or a suspension bridge, or the 'leverage' Archimedes needs to move the world, or the impossibility of squaring the circle, the application of geometry to engineering is his favourite tactic for asking: what will *work*? It's the most resonant, and possibly the most autobiographical, line in this eloquent play about emotion.

*

The Real Thing was dedicated to Miriam. The dedication was a tribute to their life together; and perhaps also a thank-you to her for encouraging him to write 'the love play'. She had been urging him to write about emotions. He kept being accused of being a cold fish, and she knew this was preposterous. 'Tom,' she commanded, 'you'll have to write a play about love!' If he thought that *Night and Day* was a good enough account of a woman's emotions, he needed to think again. But he was very reluctant, she said, to write about love and sex. She remembered Tynan asking him to write a sketch for *Oh! Calcutta!*, but, like Henry, he couldn't do it: 'it just comes out embarrassing'. When he wrote about sex, he was decorous and shy. Miriam thought he was too private a person to go into 'that vulnerable area'.

But everyone else, he noted, seemed to have a play in them about adultery among the liberal literati. Pinter had written *Betrayal*, Peter Nichols had written *Passion Play*. Perhaps he should have a go, and then move on. *The Romantic Englishwoman*, with its writer writing a film about adultery inside a film about adultery, had left a trace. And *Undiscovered Country* had a powerful after-effect. He often quoted the phrase from Schnitzler about 'yearning', or 'longing', being good for the soul ('In an ideal world more and more people would see less and less of each other'). Henry was not unlike the witty, selfish Friedrich. And Schnitzler's merry-go-round of adulterous passions, his dark sense of the heart of the loved one as an undiscovered country, haunted *The Real Thing*: 'To speak of being familiar with a loved one is a contradiction in terms . . . Lovers should be referred to as constant unfamiliars . . .'

There were more private sources for the play. He wrote it 'with some emotion', he said, looking back, because it was about a love affair and a married couple. The painfully intense time of his double life, towards the end of the marriage to Jose, was far enough away now to be mined for a play – even though it was certainly not confessional. Traces of his own past show up – Jose going through his things, the sudden revelation of the affair, the writer who does not pay enough emotional attention to the person he is living with. There may have been a family trace, too, of Fiona's difficult runaway teenage years, in Debbie's independence – he told Bobby that the woman playing Debbie had a similar face to Fiona. Closer to home, the wife in *The House of Cards*, always leaving on business trips and coming back from the airport, has a working life like Miriam's. In the time leading up to *The Real Thing*, and during it, both of them were working at full stretch, travelling a huge amount, and often apart. Somewhere in that time, he would say, he 'got upset about something'. But that 'something' was not anything he would tell his biographer. What he did say about himself as a husband was that arguments could arise from his innate – and dreadful – consistency in being aloof and detached. He gave Henry his own tendency not to speak out enough about his feelings, to take commitment for granted. Some years after *The Real Thing* was written, when he and Miriam were separating, he said to her: 'I left a door open. I wasn't careful enough. I didn't say enough.' And added: 'But Miriam, I loved you so much.' To which she replied: 'Really? You never told me.' This poignant exchange was recalled by her many years later; and the words she remembered his saying were almost the same as Henry's: 'It's as though I've been careless, left a door open somewhere while preoccupied.'

According to most Stoppard-watchers, this play marked a sea-change. It became the thing to say about him, that up to *The Real Thing* he was witty, brilliant and unfeeling, and with that play he became warmer and more self-revealing. 'Stoppard as We Never Knew He Could Be', 'The Tin Man Had a Heart After All', 'Stoppard Gets Emotional', read the review headlines. All concurred that *The Real Thing* 'fits almost no preconceived notion of the kind of playwright he is thought to be'.

Many theatrical colleagues and close friends would say that it was more self-exposing than anything that had come before. The play's producer, Michael Codron, was still saying in 2010: 'This was Tom Stoppard showing his heart at last.' The play's first Annie, Felicity Kendal, by the time of *The Real Thing* one of his favourite actors, looking back in 2004 after many years of love and friendship, called it 'a very raw play, for him; he's usually pretty guarded, emotionally'. David Hare, who watched his work with attention and had a great admiration and affection for him, recalled with amusement their exchanges on this topic. Whereas Hare (Stoppard told him) didn't mind writing lines like 'I love you', or 'you mean so much to me', Stoppard found that difficult to do. Confessional plays like Eugene

O'Neill's, where people talk about their emotions all the time, Stoppard found embarrassing. Hare thought that it was hard for him to be 'sincere'. That reserve extended from the plays to the person: 'He's unreachable'. (Hare was not alone in feeling this.) *The Real Thing* appealed to audiences because it felt more direct and accessible. Still, Hare thought it was quite wrong to say that suddenly, with *The Real Thing*, 'the man has a heart'.

Stoppard acknowledged that in his mid-forties he was 'shedding his protective skin'. It had taken a long time to shake off the 'bottled-up' legacy of the family and school he had come from. And he continued to be quite in favour of bottling up. But *The Real Thing*, he agreed, did let more of himself out. He could see why it felt like a different sort of thing. But it's misleading to say that *The Real Thing* marks a sudden change of heart. It is a mistake to think there was no emotion in the early plays, no longing and tenderness, no sense of loss and grief, and no autobiographical content. Sadness, mortality and melancholy, confusion and vulnerability, thread through the playfulness of *Rosencrantz* and *Travesties* and *Artist Descending a Staircase*. There is deep sadness in *Another Moon Called Earth*, in *Where Are They Now?*, in *Every Good Boy*. Infidelity was the subject, years before, of *Funny Man*, and more recently of *Night and Day*. The anguish of a marriage that isn't working, of breakdown and spoilt love, is at the heart of *Jumpers*. Ten years before, he had ended his TV film, 'Tom Stoppard Doesn't Know', with that quotation he loved from James Saunders's *Next Time I'll Sing to You*: 'there lies behind everything . . . a certain quality which we may call grief'.

But because he had to a degree unbottled himself in *The Real Thing*, because his characters were, at last, saying 'I love you' and 'please don't', because the main character was a playwright, because the play was full of poignant pop music and conversations about marriage and love – and because of the title – audiences and critics felt it as more direct and emotional. And so the accepted view took hold, that suddenly the cold fish had grown a warm heart.

Like *Night and Day*, *The Real Thing* was a commercial play for the West End, done by Peter Wood and the designer Carl Toms, and produced by

Michael Codron and his partner David Sutton. It ran at the Strand Theatre from 16 November 1982 for over two years – an unusually long run in the 1980s. It was an expensive proposition for Codron. Kenneth Ewing asked for an advance of £10,000 on Stoppard's behalf, which Codron would recall, sharply, as 'a huge amount of money then'. He had the impression there might be a shortfall in the Stoppard accounts. Another £5,000 was to be paid within twelve months, with a royalty of 7.5 per cent 'till recoupment' (the point when the producer has repaid his investors all the money that he raised to put on the show), and after that of ten per cent. The contract also specified £25 per day expenses during rehearsal, and the right of approval of director, designer, opening cast and American producer. Once the bargain had been struck and the contract signed, Stoppard wrote to Codron that he was as pleased as punch to be working with him again. 'You deserve better than an over-demanding author but like Queen Victoria I will try to be good.'

The play took about eight months to write, mostly at night in the kitchen at Iver Grove, and the first version was finished early in February 1982. (He gave Miriam a bound copy of the manuscript, including its numerous different versions, 'the first two or three pages done twenty-three different ways'.) The right opening cast was essential for the play's success, and a number of names were floated for the main parts, including Ian McKellen, John Wood and Cherie Lunghi. But there was no doubt about who should play Annie. Stoppard told his parents in February 1982 that he, Peter Wood and Michael Codron all wanted 'Felicity Kendall' – a misspelling he soon wouldn't be making. The part was not written with her in mind, but he couldn't think of anyone else as right for it. But she was busy at the National (in *On the Razzle* and *The Second Mrs Tanqueray*) until October, so they waited to schedule *The Real Thing* until she was free.

Kendal already felt part of the Stoppard team, and she enjoyed playing Annie, though she knew (as future Annies would also find) that it was hard to make the audience engage with her: 'In *The Real Thing*', she said in 1985, 'the woman is very blatant about what she needs and feels and it's difficult to gain the sympathy of the audience.' She saw her as the centre of the action. 'Everything that happens is going on round her, because of her.

The whole point is she's saying, this is me, take it or leave it. He does write these very strong women, not necessarily aggressive, but themselves.' She found that kind of woman 'comparatively easy' to play. She and Roger Rees were friends, and Stoppard thought they were very good together – as did the reviewers. Kendal's Annie was described as intriguing and 'kittenish', 'subtly combining impishness and passion'.

She was an ideal actor for Stoppard, who always put 'clarity of utterance' first, before any other quality. So did she, having had what she called a 'rather old-fashioned' training: 'Say the lines, and let the audience hear them, and the author will do the work for them; don't start mumbling away thinking it's all to do with your emotions.' She saw that the performer's job in a Stoppard play was not to try to interpret on his behalf; some things in his plays were meant to remain ambiguous. Her job was not to over-explain but to be 'real'. 'I'm trying to work out how the author wants me to do this character; and then to convey that as clearly as possible to the audience, so that I'm doing the author's speaking for him.' He would often say to her, in rehearsal: 'Don't try and make that funny; just say it, and I'll do the work for you.'

As always he and Peter Wood were having fun together in rehearsal. Kendal relished the warmth and closeness between them. He thought it was a very nice and gifted company. Of course all kinds of problems arose. One of these was the character of the daughter, who comes late into the play. Codron couldn't see the point of her. 'Do we have to have that scene?' But Stoppard 'was fighting for the daughter' – there were things he needed her to say – and in the end Codron admitted he was wrong.

As the play went from rehearsals into previews and performance, and then transferred to America, many changes were made. Some had to do with making sure the audience 'got' the shift from Scene One to Scene Two. A line he longed to cut, because it was so crudely over-explanatory, was Henry's to Annie in Scene Two: 'My wife plays with your husband six times a week and twice on Saturdays.' Some had to do with lessening Henry's resemblance to himself – so he got rid of him saying on *Desert Island Discs* that he was a journalist before he became a playwright. Some changes had to do with tone: 'carnal knowledge', in Henry's speech about knowing the loved one, became 'a sort of knowledge'. And he was always looking to speed things up. So, in Annie's big speech about her conflicted feelings for Billy and for Henry, an eloquent passage was cut on how she regrets the pain she is causing him.

Kendal knew by now that this constant revision was part of how he worked. 'It's rewritten and rewritten again and again . . . like sculpting something. By the time the play opens, it's already in a publication – but that doesn't mean that's how it's going to stay. The next edition will have the changes.' Just after *The Real Thing* opened, he said:

> One of the slightly alarming things about writing plays is that you spend a long time thinking about what ought to be said . . . and then in four weeks with actors in rehearsal and for empirical reasons, like the dragginess of a scene, you just chop these things out and never think about them again . . . You have these ruthless conclusions about whether the length of a scene is being justified by its dynamics, and when it's not, you have to change the equation. You either have to make it more dynamic or make it shorter – and I usually end up making it shorter.

'A text that leaves no room for discovery will, in the end, be mechanistic,' he said, while the play was in rehearsal in New York. 'It's like a bridge which is absolutely rigid; it has no play in it, no sway in it. It will break the moment the pressure goes wrong.'

This, as always, was a challenge for his publishers. He had redoubled his commitment to Faber by having their American division publish him in the States. He and Ken Ewing had come to feel that Grove Press, who had published him in America since *Rosencrantz*, were not taking good enough care of his books. (He went back to them in 1998 with *The Invention of Love*.) However, he was annoyed with Faber over *The Real Thing*. He felt they had 'missed a trick' by not having it published as an original hardback and by printing a smallish first run of six thousand copies. He wrote crossly to Frank Pike: 'I only write a full length stage play every four years or so and for want of a better phrase [they] are after all the "major work". After the big success of the play, Pike apologised: 'It is embarrassing that we were caught out by what a hit it has been.' But Stoppard too was embarrassed by the fact that, as usual, Faber's first edition differed in many details from the play that was running on stage by the time the book came out. The next edition had quickly to incorporate the changes. He referred to this as 'the Stoppard Second Edition fiasco'. After the play had been massively revised for the New York production, the American arm of Faber published a 'Broadway edition'. Many more editions followed of this hugely popular play.

He had not been sure of its success. Just before the opening night he wrote to Bobby: 'My name is HUGE in lights outside, like Coca-Cola in Piccadilly Circus. I feel a bit fatalistic about it all. I hope it works.' At the first night, John Boorman said to him, it's quite Shavian, isn't it? Very close Shavian, Stoppard replied.

The reviews were mixed. He totted them up for Bobby: 'We ended up being hated by *The Times* and the *Express* and liked by the *Mail*, *Telegraph*, *Guardian* and *Evening Standard*. So if all three Sundays like us we should be ok for a while.' *The Times*, he said, hated it so much he 'almost shrieked'. That was Irving Wardle, who summed it up as 'cleverness with its back to the wall'. Milton Shulman wrote cruelly of 'Pirandello role-playing, Shavian badinage and Barbara Cartland gush in a play whose adroit twists manage to disguise its obviousness and whose wit compensates for its glib solution'. Robert Cushman in the *Observer* called it 'distressingly like other people's plays' about middle-class adultery. There were attacks on its lapses into 'complacent caricature'. But, meanwhile, Stoppard's conservative friend Roger Scruton praised the play, in *Encounter*, for its 'masterly and devastating criticism of . . . the jargon-ridden language of revolution'. *The Real Thing* settled the view of him in some quarters as England's most right-wing playwright. Henry's prejudices were often identified with Stoppard's, and he was attacked for 'creating a straw-man in the figure of Brodie'.

There were mixed reactions to the witty, stylish direction and the cool, elegant set. Carl Toms created a set of translucent, Japanese-style grey gauze panels which rose and fell to frame the action. There were projected scenes of London, and a painting of Henry and Charlotte in their living room, to give an effect of infinite regression. The Strand Theatre was warned it would be a 'highly technical and complex production'. The original design had to be 'seriously compromised', he told Bobby, as it needed 'twenty stage-hands to shift things up and down and around, and Codron baulked. I don't mind – it makes no sense to have a production which can't afford to keep open if it isn't three-quarters full all the time. (This is what happened to *Jumpers* in New York – it closed taking more box-office than plays which ran on merrily for months.)' That was the voice of a hardened, practical man of the theatre.

The final effect was suave, mannered and sleek, rather than intense and passionate. Frank Rich came over to see it for the *New York Times*, and savaged what he called 'a preposterously gimmicky production'. But there were good reviews too, audiences loved it and came pouring in, and it won the *Evening Standard* Best Play award.

He had been having some qualms about his favourite director. Their rehearsals together were always a riot of joking and showing-off and brilliant wheezes. Perhaps working with Peter Wood was *too* much fun, too much like having a party. He remembered rehearsing *Night and Day* in the same building as a friend who was rehearsing a thriller on another floor. He looked in on them, and there was a very serious atmosphere, as if they were doing *Murder in the Cathedral*. Then he went back to the hilarious rehearsal of his own 'grown-up' play. The contrast stayed in his mind. As did the misfiring *Jumpers* in New York, when he felt he and Peter had been like 'babes in the wood' on Broadway.

But a big American opportunity was on its way. The veteran Broadway producer Manny Azenberg was in London, and his friend the director Mike Nichols suggested that he go and see *The Real Thing*. Nichols already knew of Stoppard, and had sent him P. D. James's novel *Innocent Blood*, with a view to his doing the screenplay. Nichols liked the sound of *The Real Thing*, but Azenberg told him they would not be able to get it – Peter Wood would be transferring his production to the States. Then came the killer review by Frank Rich, and any American interest in the production immediately died. Azenberg saw his chance, and told Codron he would take it, but not in that production. Mike Nichols would do a new one. Stoppard wanted this to happen. He hugely admired Nichols's films, notably *Who's Afraid of Virginia Woolf?* and *The Graduate*. Nichols had already had big Broadway hits with *Plaza Suite* and *Annie* and Neil Simon's *Barefoot in the Park* and *The Odd Couple*. And Stoppard wanted his play to be looked after for an American audience, by somebody inside the New York theatre scene. 'So that', Stoppard said fondly, looking back, 'was Mike in my life.'

It was a delicate moment in his relationship with Peter Wood, who had expected – and was contracted for – his production to be transferred to America. Stoppard felt rather guilty. True to his character, he wanted everybody to be happy, and – as he put it, ruefully – 'very often you can't make everybody happy'. But, equally characteristically, he put the play's interest before his affection for his old friend and colleague, with professional steeliness. Wood and Codron came to a financial agreement, whereby Wood was 'paid for not doing it' (in Azenberg's blunt phrase) and continued to get his royalties from the American show. It was enough money for Wood to renovate his country property. In Codron's office the play became known as 'The Roof of the Barn'. Author and director were too good friends for this to spoil their relationship, and they went on working together after that. And Stoppard knew it was the right decision.

Manny Azenberg now took charge. A child of the Yiddish immigrant Bronx, now fifty, he'd had his first Broadway show about twenty years before, and was famous for his partnerships with Neil Simon, for the musical *Ain't Misbehavin'* and for his work with Athol Fugard. Shrewd, forceful, humorous, benign, battle-scarred, a man of the New York commercial theatre to his bones, and a man also of strong feelings and principles, he found working with Stoppard an excitement and an education.

Their first challenge came with raising the money to put the show into the Phoenix Theatre on 45th Street. Azenberg managed to raise about two thirds of the $740,000 this would cost. Under the Broadway theatre royalties system, everyone – producer, actors, author, director, designer – was entitled to be paid a percentage of 'the gross' (the gross weekly box-office receipts). But this was becoming increasingly problematic in the 1980s, as production costs for Broadway shows rose, and producers

found it harder to recoup the cost of the show. The advance royalty payments might exceed the production costs, and the investors wouldn't get
their money back. To avert this, Azenberg wrote to everyone involved,
making plain what everyone had asked for and asking everyone to take
a cut so that the show would survive. 'And the guy that took the biggest
blow, and willingly,' Azenberg remembered admiringly, 'was Stoppard.' He
immediately said he would take less than his contract had stated. This was
good behaviour, but it also worked to embarrass those who might have
held out for a bigger royalty. As it turned out, the play became a huge and
very lucrative success. At the end of the run, Azenberg was able to send
Stoppard $12,000 to make up for what he had waived. He didn't have to
do that – but both of them now trusted each other completely, in a profession where trust was crucial, and often went missing. 'Tom Stoppard
writes well and behaves well,' Azenberg concluded. Using the language
he'd learned from his military service, he said of him: 'I would want him
in the foxhole. He won't run away. And when the bullets are flying, he's
there.' Citing Henry's line, he thought he had perfect 'equilibrium' in his
relationship to the world. And he admired his commitment to the work.
Stoppard moved to New York for two months, to be there every day while
the play was in rehearsal. Azenberg noted that he knew the name of the
backstage doorman and the doorman's wife, asked them how they were,
was never rude, and had no snobbery and no narcissism in him. 'The
word in Yiddish is, he's a mensch.'

Before he started working with Stoppard he was 'frightened to death
because he was so intelligent'. But Azenberg wasn't a man to mince his
words. He was watching the first out-of-town performance of *The Real
Thing* in Boston, sitting at the back of the theatre, when Stoppard tapped
him on the shoulder and asked him what he thought. Azenberg told him:
'Ten minutes into the second half I wasn't paying attention, I was looking
at the scenery.' Stoppard said, 'You're right.' He went away, and came back
five days later with some radical cuts and changes. 'Is it better?' From then
on Azenberg knew exactly how to work with him. There was no point
beating around the bush. 'He's so smart, he can discern when he's being
bullshitted.'

The cast for the American production was exciting, and excited to be doing the play. Jeremy Irons, newly the sexiest English actor in the world because of *Brideshead Revisited*, had called his agent to say that if he didn't get him Henry on Broadway he would kill him. Christine Baranski was playing Charlotte. Stoppard described her as like 'a thoroughbred race-horse, and with a great sense of humour'. The daughter was played, charmingly, by a teenaged Cynthia Nixon. Many years later, long after starring in *Sex and the City*, she would return to the play as Annie. The Annie of 1984 was Glenn Close (Meryl Streep had turned it down), then very well respected in New York theatre, but not yet the famous film star of *Fatal Attraction*. She found Annie underwritten – 'she doesn't get to talk back', she complained – but she played the part passionately and sensually. Azenberg witnessed a discussion in rehearsal about whether or not Annie had actually slept with Billy: it was ambiguous in the text, and Close wanted there to be a more specific moment of revelation. All looked to the author, including Nichols. 'And Tom came over and said, "Well, if you have to sleep with him, sleep with him!"'

This was the only time Stoppard worked with Mike Nichols, and it was a very satisfying experience. Nichols was six years older than Stoppard, and like him was a Jewish immigrant from Europe with a changed name, the son of a Russian doctor who had emigrated to Germany and then fled the Nazis. His father, too, had died when he was young, and members of his family had perished in the Holocaust. From his success as a satirical comedian in a legendary 1950s partnership with Elaine May, he became one of America's most admired – and awarded – film and theatre directors. He was funny, quick, supremely talented and sometimes scathing – you would not want to be his target. His personal life was complicated, and he was in his third marriage, to the writer Annabel Goff-Davis, when he came to know Stoppard. He had a gift for friendship. He was a wealthy, lavish host, with a taste for civilised living (which included a magnificent ranch above Santa Barbara for his Arabian horses and a farm in Connecticut). 'He's good at comfort and joy,' Stoppard said of him. He was a person of strong, impulsive enthusiasms. Stoppard said that 'he invested completely in somebody he decided was a good thing'.

In September 1983, the Stoppard family took a long trip to America, taking in Disneyland, Wyoming, Santa Fe and Las Vegas, and ending up on Nichols's ranch in San Ysidro, so that he and Stoppard could talk about the play. Then he settled into New York for the rehearsals, while a new cast took over the play in London. He was relieved that audiences didn't entirely disappear after Kendal and Rees left the show – but it never felt quite right to him without them. The New York *Real Thing* was a very different kind of production, much more naturalistic, and faster. 'The New York first act takes 53–55 minutes', Stoppard noted, preoccupied as always with timings, 'and in London it lasts an hour.' The set, with its furniture fixed to a revolve for speed of action, was more realistic, the relationships felt more impassioned, and there was more sexual heat between Irons and Close.

He found the rehearsal process engrossing. Nichols did not play games, though there were plenty of funny moments. In one rehearsal, Stoppard approached Peter Gallagher, the actor playing Billy, and asked him: 'Could it be more *plangent*?' Peter Gallagher looked for help to Mike Nichols: 'Plangent?' he asked Nichols, who replied: 'Fucked if I know!' He was congenial, but also serious and decisive. He allowed for 'deep discussion' of the play. In rehearsal he was dedicated, analytical and without ego. Actors trusted and liked him. As they would say: 'he loved you to a safe landing'. Glenn Close relished his advice to her and Irons: 'If you ever get lost, just drown in each other's eyes.' On the first day of rehearsals, Nichols asked him if he wanted to say anything to the actors. Stoppard said: 'I don't have much to say – but I think it shouldn't be in a rush – the characters should take it quite slowly.' And Nichols said, 'Yes, absolutely – either that or very very fast.' Remembering this and laughing, Stoppard said: 'That guy had *style*.' A stagehand came in, at one point, holding up two hardback chairs. One was indistinguishable from the other. He shouted into the stalls, 'Mike, which chair?' Mike pointed and said: 'THAT one.' Stoppard thought, Christ, I could never be a director. Afterwards, he asked him what was it about that chair? Nichols said, 'Nothing. You have to answer immediately, you can change your mind later.'

Everyone who watched them working together was struck by how well they got on. Jeremy Irons's wife Sinéad Cusack, watching rehearsals and seeing the show many times, thought the way they operated together was extraordinary. This was her first encounter with Stoppard, and she at once felt a strong sense of affinity with him. And although she did not yet know him well, the play seemed to her a profoundly autobiographical revelation of Stoppard's character.

The loving friendship between Stoppard and Nichols which began on *The Real Thing* was an unbreakable one. Stoppard found Nichols enchanting. They laughed at the same things and they didn't have to explain their references to each other. He felt that Nichols was 'a perfect fit' for him; and he was also a fan. The journalist and media star Diane Sawyer, who married Nichols a few years afterwards, in 1988, and was with him until he died in 2014, was a close witness of their long friendship. She thought of them as two great 'voyagers' who used very different navigational tools. As a person, and as a director, Nichols was attuned to tiny shifts in human behaviour, to which he applied a kind of X-ray. He admired Stoppard's metaphysical, intellectual intelligence. And he liked the fact that in spite of that intellect, Stoppard didn't judge people. Nichols was an extrovert, an unstoppable anecdotalist, but he loved the way Stoppard would puncture or conclude an anecdote with dry precision. They shared, too, a mixture of worldliness and solitariness. They were both curious, adventurous, gregarious, much-travelled people, but both of them 'lived for what they were able to think'.

They did not meet often, but would make a point of doing so whenever they were in each other's country. They would call each other and talk about family, work, professional life and personal problems (both would have their troubles over the next few years). Nichols said that if he had been a playwright he would have been overjoyed to be like Stoppard. 'He's the most expressive playwright of our time . . . He has no apparent animus toward anyone or anything. He's very funny at no one's expense. That's supposed not to be possible.' He thought of him as 'the only writer I know who is completely happy'. Perhaps they always showed each other their sunniest side. And they praised each other unstintingly in public. When Nichols took the Tony award for best director for *The Real Thing*, he said to the audience, in delight: 'I get to receive this, and I get to be Tom's friend.' He was one of the people Stoppard wanted to write well for: as if, when he was writing, Mike Nichols was in the space between the rooms.

The Real Thing opened on Broadway in January 1984 and was an enormous success. This was the moment when Stoppard 'took' New York. The reviews were ecstatic. Frank Rich was entirely won over by the new production. This is 'not only Mr. Stoppard's most moving play, but also the most bracing play that anyone has written about love and marriage in years', he wrote. Instead of being known as the author of *Rosencrantz*, he now became known as the author of *The Real Thing*. All box-office records at the Plymouth were broken: five days after it opened it had taken more than $700,000. It turned him into theatre's equivalent of a rock star in America, and made him large sums of money. For Ken Ewing and all at Fraser and Dunlop, this was their client's first huge commercial success, outstripping *Rosencrantz*. By the second month of its American run it was earning him £12,000 a week. He knew he had to pay taxes on that, but still, he was enjoying the wealth. From now on he would be in the limelight, his plays and his private life a topic of interest. He never thought of himself as 'famous' outside the small world of theatre. *Rosencrantz* had made him well-known and talked about. But this success jumped him to another level of recognition. One tiny example: when he was arrested for speeding, in England, and had to pay a fine, in March 1985, it got into the North American papers: 'STOPPARD SPEEDS!'

Will and Ed – now twelve and ten – had a taste of the excitement of *The Real Thing* in New York. During the rehearsals they came over for half-term with Miriam, and then again for the opening. They were taken up the World Trade Center by Mitch Erickson, Stoppard's long-time New York stage manager, went to a basketball game at Madison Square Gardens with Manny, were bought football helmets by Miriam and proudly rode the subway wearing their new puffa jackets. They saw part of the play. Will was impressed by hearing the Monkees' 'I'm a Believer', as his father had been playing it non-stop at home. Ed realised at this point that his father was 'a big deal'. Until then he had always thought of his mother as the famous one. Even Barny, by now a rather disaffected teenager, was pleased to be taken by his father to see the play a few months into its run: they stayed at the Carlyle, took in a Sondheim musical, saw Dustin Hoffman in *Death of a Salesman* and went shopping for clothes on Lower Broadway. Ollie, at eighteen on the point of leaving school and home, rapidly became aware that the income from this play made the Stoppard lifestyle, as never before, 'easily achievable'.

The opening was a glamorous event. There was what he described as a 'huge awful' first-night party at the Tavern on the Green for 650 people, crawling with journalists, and then he and Miriam flew home on Concorde. The *New York Times* noted: 'This city has fallen madly in love with *The Real Thing*.' It won the Drama Desk award for Outstanding New Play, and five Tony awards: Best Play (beating Michael Frayn's *Noises Off* and David Mamet's *Glengarry Glen Ross*, which Stoppard greatly admired), Best Director, and Best Actors for Irons, Close and Baranski. Other playwrights sent enthusiastic congratulations, and Leonard Bernstein said he was passionate about it. David Mamet told Stoppard that he had stopped going to the theatre in the US because no one seemed to be writing about anything: 'your deeply-felt play was deeply felt by us'. Peter Shaffer said he had savoured and crunched it up and swallowed it with relish.

Both in New York and in London, it was a fashionable night out. Jacky was inundated with special requests for tickets. Mick Jagger took his pregnant girlfriend Jerry Hall. Princess Margaret went twice ('Heavens, perhaps she thinks it's her story!' he said wickedly to his mother, who loved to hear about the royals). When it looked as if Jeremy Irons would be leaving the show, David Bowie offered to take over from him. 'You probably don't know who he is,' Stoppard wrote to his parents. 'He is a sort of Mick Jagger though more versatile and he's done a bit of acting.' At the time, at Jagger's request, he was trying to think of a subject for a musical comedy with Jagger and Bowie, but with no success. When Jagger and Bowie came to lunch at Iver to discuss the project, 'the children were for the first time impressed'.

The play had a personal effect on many people. It was one of those nights at the theatre which makes you think about the way you have led your own life. Manny Azenberg, after watching *The Real Thing* day after day, proposed to the woman he had been living with for seven years. He hadn't wanted to get married because he hadn't wanted to get divorced again. But the play seemed to make it possible. Clive James, who went to see it with his wife Prue, told Stoppard that they had recited the dialogue just ahead of the characters: 'We discussed how you managed to plant the microphones in our house.' The novelist Angela Huth wrote a story in which a couple quoted a speech from the play to each other. An American actor, writing a fan letter, thought that 'wives, husbands, ex-wives, ex-husbands, mistresses and lovers would say to each other: "There – that – that's what I mean. That's what I was trying to say."' Another fan said that she had watched the play with her husband, her lover and her lover's wife, and the only thing she and her lover wanted to do then was to go and see the play again together. He was very tickled by this. Lots of people thought it was autobiographical. Stoppard remembered a friend of Miriam's saying to her in shocked tones, after the first night, when they were on their way to the party, 'Miriam, what have you been *doing*!' In the States, he had to keep fighting off personal questions from interviewers: 'I very, very rarely run off with an actress.'

The Real Thing sat at an intersection in the middle of his life. The breakdown of marriage and infidelities it dealt with pointed backwards and forwards. The personal assumptions that were made about it didn't become true until long after he wrote it. Its dedication seemed to alter its meaning as time passed. The people it newly involved him with – Felicity Kendal, Mike Nichols, Sinéad Cusack – would give his life a different shape. And it marked a transition in his work.

There were full houses on Broadway while Irons and Close were in the play, and then it dropped off, closing after sixteen months – during which time he went over to rehearse every new cast – in May 1985. 'One can't complain,' Stoppard wrote home ruefully, 'even though at the beginning everybody was having delusions of grandeur with the play running two or three years. My plays don't seem to. They run out of genuine customers and after that the mass public sees right through them – nothing like as good as Neil Simon after all.' In London, it went through four changes of cast at the Strand and closed in March 1985, after three years. Meanwhile, it was much in demand in Europe, as *La cosa vera* in Milan; in Vienna, where the Peter Wood production was revived; and in France as *La Vérité vraie*. The relationship with the French translator, Guy Dumur, did not go well, and had to be broken off. He wrote politely to Dumur in January 1985, regretting the episode, and telling him, in passing, that 'for different reasons' 1984 had not been 'my favourite year'. For all the great success of his play – or *because* of all the exposure and travel and demands and high pressure – he seemed at odds with himself, and a note of trouble and anxiety kept creeping into his private journal.

As a curious coda to *The Real Thing*, Stoppard recorded his *Desert Island Discs* for the BBC on 22 November 1984. It was broadcast on 12 January 1985. Unlike Henry, he did not choose 'The Skaters' Waltz' or take *Finnegans Wake* as his book. He took Dante's *Inferno* in a dual Italian/ English version – he would need something to stretch him intellectually, like a book of chess problems or a history of mathematics, but this would enable him to learn a language. His luxury was a plastic football to kick around while thinking of something to write. His musical choices stayed true to what he loved. There was pop music (the Beatles' 'Love Me Do'), there was America (*West Side Story*), there was England (Vaughan Williams's 'Fantasia on a Theme by Thomas Tallis'). 'I have an intense empathy for England – I feel very English,' he told the courtly Roy Plomley. There was Previn's music for *Every Good Boy*. Stoppard revealed to Plomley that the boy playing the triangle in the play was a gesture to his having been 'the famous triangulist of the Darjeeling school band'. There were two haunting piano pieces which Peter Wood had used in their productions, William Bolcom's rag, 'Graceful Ghost', and a section from Keith Jarrett's mysterious 'Köln Concert'. And there were two Bristol-connected numbers. One was the jolly foot-tapping 'Jump for Joy', by the Avon Cities Jazz Band, a fixture in Bristol in his time there. The other was Bessie Smith's 'Careless Love', his choice out of the eight records. It spoke to him of 'first love, last love'.

His first love Isabel Cortan heard the programme in Bristol and wrote to him, care of *Desert Island Discs*. She had been moved to hear him choose the Bessie Smith, which had been one of 'their' songs, long ago. 'I wasn't remotely surprised to hear from you,' he replied. 'I think of you often and after 15 (?) years a letter was overdue.' A sporadic, affectionate, nostalgic correspondence ensued. Once, in an emotional mood, twenty-five years after *The Real Thing*, he began a letter to her: 'My first love, dearest Dizi.' They met occasionally, and have stayed in touch for the rest of their lives; she would be at his eightieth birthday party in 2017.

The Real Thing was a play about breaking faith – but also about keeping the faith. Its author was a faithful friend to those he loved, and faithful to his past.

20

Crossing

In the end we all have our secrets. That's how we live.

The meaning of life is not something which one can summarise or
verbalise one way or the other and then hand over like a piece of
information – it's not an object, it's more like an elusive spiritual state –
and the more one needs it the more elusive it becomes.

On 19 March 1984, a few months into the New York run of *The Real Thing*,
there was an awkward clash between work and family life. He had to make
a quick trip to New York to check on the play and to Chicago, with Mike
Nichols, to see an actor who might be the next Henry after Jeremy Irons.
Miriam was going with him. But Iver Grove was full, as often, of decorators
and workmen; Barny wasn't feeling well; and Ed was playing in a Caldicott
school rugby sevens tournament. They agreed that Miriam should stay
at home to deal with all that. But as he was leaving for the airport, she
decided she wanted to go with him after all. So he cancelled his solo ticket
and booked two seats on Concorde that evening. When they got to New
York, she was too tired to watch the play, while he had to dine the actors
till one in the morning and then, after four hours' sleep, fly to Chicago.
Miriam called home from there to learn that 'Captain E. Stoppard' and the
Junior Colts had won their tournament against eight other schools, and
that Ed had scored every point in the first two games. She was in 'floods
of tears and self-recrimination' at having missed his triumph. He too was
desolate. 'I love watching Ed playing rugby more than almost anything
in the world.' They flew back on the 22nd. This 'ill-timed and exhausting
expedition' cost him about £6,000.

The incident shows what a tricky balancing act it was, juggling their
work and their commitment to the boys, and how upsetting it was when
things went wrong. Not to mention how much he could now afford to
spend, and how crossing the Atlantic at a moment's notice was a regular

part of their lives. And it shows too their loving involvement with the growing boys, as they shifted from children to teenagers, and from being mainly at home to being at boarding school or away.

Ed, small, charming, determined and sociable, and Will, a less confident character, were both sports-mad. At home they played tennis all summer long, rode their quad bikes and used the new Iver pool. Stoppard called home 'The Iver Grove Leisure Centre'. At Caldicott they were dedicated rugby and cricket players, leaders of their teams. The boys' sporting triumphs and defeats were witnessed with emotion. 'A bad afternoon watching poor Eddie's tiny team getting slaughtered,' Stoppard wrote home in January 1983, 'and he was scrum-half and captain, so it was sad.' 'Will, wicket keeper, let through ten byes and was in tears over this. I remember feeling exactly the same way when I used to be a wicket keeper.' 'One forgets how nerve-racking the whole business is, watching one's children going in to bat.' He still played himself now and then. In July 1984, the Caldicott parents played Caldicott's First XI. Will was top scorer for the school (35) and his dad was top scorer for the fathers (54). That was the last cricket for him for that particular summer: a few days later, he went into hospital for a double hernia operation, which took a couple of weeks to recover from. He did not make a fuss about such things.

Ed had other gifts than sport. When he published his first story in the school magazine, both parents decided proudly, 'this boy is obviously Renaissance man'. He had a feeling for words (he was always making up funny words and accents as a child) and he loved the look and feel of his father's Sheaffer pens. He was the kind of boy who charmed everyone and looked as if he would fall on his feet. His father's love for him poured onto every page of his journal.

Will, Caldicott's star rugby player, played in the All England Rugby Competition in 1985, and his parents drove him all over England and Wales to his matches. When he moved to Stowe as a boarder, and went through some bullying which he didn't tell his parents about, rugby was his lifeline. He enjoyed his mother's high media profile, but his parents' fame was also a challenge to him when he was a boy. He once told Miriam that he didn't think he could live up to their reputation, and he was always aware, at school and later in his life, that there would be high expectations of him because of them. Miriam said to him: 'You have nothing to live up to, and we will always support and love you.'

In their parallel, other life, Barny and Ollie continued to visit Jose regularly and to take holidays with her. Barny was more interested in art and film and model-making than in sport, though he did play rugby at Caldicott and at Merchant Taylors', where he went from 1983 to 1984. That rather conservative, disciplinary school didn't suit him, and his father decided to take him out of there and send him to a 'crammer' in West London. In his teens Barny separated himself somewhat from the other boys, and spent a lot of time with the music producer Deke Arlon's family in their big house nearby.

Ollie, quiet and reserved, left school for Bristol University in 1984, where he lived in spartan student accommodation, and switched after a time from geology to physics. He and Ed were still close; Ed looked up to him as a wise elder brother, and learned from him. He and Will, in their early teens, once casually gave Ollie a fishing rod for his birthday without wrapping it up, and Ollie had been hurt. It was one of the few moments when their father gave them an explicit moral lesson. Look, he told them, Ollie would have preferred it if you'd got something less expensive and bothered to wrap it and put a label on it.

Fishing was always a passion for Ollie (Will got the bug too, in his teens) and he and his father had days out on a river or a lake, sometimes with Michael Hordern, an addicted fisherman. Ollie had also become a good cook. On one of the grander Iver Grove occasions, in September 1984, Prince and Princess Michael of Kent came to dinner. The fellow guests – as listed in a letter home – were 'Mrs Jeremy Irons', Michael Kitchen, a close family friend at that time, and John and Teresa Wells. Ollie and a friend cooked 'quails eggs, turbot, lamb and apricot', and it all went off very well.

That dinner party was an example of what Stoppard would call, to his parents, 'posh dos', or his 'court circular': a meeting with Charles and Diana, helicopter trips with the Kents to Glyndebourne (which he called 'The Royal Flying Visit'), dinner at Number 10 with the Thatchers and the American president, Princess Margaret and Zandra Rhodes. He took a

semi-comical tone about all this, as when they flew back for a day from
skiing in Chamonix, in March 1985, for dinner and an overnight stay at
Windsor Castle: 'There is a pub called the Windsor Castle down the road
and it is possible I have got the whole thing wrong and we are being put
up there.' The family skiing holidays were part of the 'lifestyle' they were
enjoying: not so much fun, though, when he broke his shoulder on the
slopes, on the last day of 1984. He was always a rather tentative skier, as
John Boorman, whose family went on some winter holidays with the
Stoppards, recalled. On one occasion he slid off the piste and ended up in
some trees. Miriam called down: 'Tom, what are you doing down there?'
He replied: 'I am doing my best to rejoin you.'

In 1986, the family discovered grouse-shooting. Ed's Caldicott rugby
team was playing against a prep school near Crieff, in Perthshire, and the
Stoppards found their way to the nearby Cultoquhey Hotel. Cultoquhey
was a big, cosy nineteenth-century manorial house with open fires and
old furniture. Anna and David Cooke, the owners, brought up their children there, and hosted shoots. For a while the Stoppards (Ollie, Ed, Will
and Miriam, though never Barny) went there regularly, sometimes for
Hogmanay, sometimes in the late summer during the season. This was not
the kind of large-scale grouse-shooting where the shooters stand waiting
in the butts, the grouse are driven in front of the beaters, and huge bags of
birds are collected up. David Cooke preferred the more active, small-scale
kind of shoot, where the beaters and the guns walk up together in a line,
and the dogs go in front and put up the birds. Stoppard wore a tweed jacket
with jeans and sported a gun, but he wasn't really in it for the shooting:
Anna Cooke thought he preferred going 'on the hill' for the sake of the walk
and the family being outdoors together. They also went on a few nearby
winter shoots on the estate of Diana Rigg's then husband, Archie Stirling.

For Stoppard, Cultoquhey became a favourite place. He would spend
part of his time upstairs writing: *Arcadia*'s grouse-shooting scenes would
have their origins here. He left his cigarette butts all over the house, ate
large quantities of Arbroath smokies and Scottish cheddar, and charmed
the entire household, from the smallest boy to Anna's mother. Anna
remembered a day on the moors when a little boy, a friend of her son, who

was desperate to go on the hill, trod on a needle, which worked its way up through his boot. He didn't want to give up the shoot, but was limping badly. When Anna took the lunch up to the shooting party, she saw Stoppard carrying this child down the hill, back to the car on the track below.

They fitted these diversions into their formidable timetables. Miriam was in China, the Philippines and Thailand for the whole of March 1983, filming her YTV Television show, *Where There's Life*; Stoppard and the younger boys went out to visit her in Bangkok and Manila. A few weeks later, she would be up at 5.30 a.m. to go on breakfast TV to plug her 'baby book', and then out to Los Angeles for more filming. In 1984 she was TV Woman of the Year at the Variety Club of Great Britain awards, and winner of the ITV Personality Award. He too was endlessly travelling – in the summer of 1984, for instance, when his triumph at the Tony awards in New York was followed by a prize at a festival in Taormina, in Sicily, where he was given the keys of the city and watched a four-hour open-air *Hamlet* in Italian. When he was away from home, as in Vienna for the first night of *The Real Thing* in March 1984, in a luxurious hotel, he felt 'alas' that he was on his own, but added: 'feel no alas at having turned away temptation, again'.

An apocryphal story (told with relish by Michael Codron) has it that, around this time, he was making a phone booking for a lunch in a restaurant across the road from where one of his plays was running. The restaurant manager asked him for his name, and then asked him to spell it. Stifling the urge to tell him to go outside and look at the theatre opposite, where his name was up in lights, he spelt it out slowly: S-T-O-P-P-A-R-D. And the manager said, 'Oh, you mean, as in Miriam!' Her level of fame attracted malice. Angela Carter, adding a 1980s 'Afterword' to her 1971 novel *Love*, dropped in a satire on a glamorous female psychiatrist on the board of directors for a detoxification centre who 'is also a director of three pharmaceutical companies, hosts a radio phone-in on neurosis and is author of a nonfiction bestseller, *How to Succeed Even Though You Are a Woman*. She is a passionate advocate of hormone-replacement therapy. She drives a Porsche, rather fast.' It was well known in theatrical circles that a group of playwrights' wives had founded a club called the WOW, the 'Wash Out Wives'. The idea came from John Osborne's wife Helen, and the other members were Thelma Nichols, Penny Mortimer and Christopher Hampton's wife Laura. This 'anti-feminist' group of non-working wives was said to have been created 'as an antidote to the frenetic fame of Tom Stoppard's wife Miriam'. Miriam herself called it a 'cabal' and said she felt uncomfortable with them, as they talked about nothing but their husbands' work.

Sometimes when Miriam was on her travels, he felt 'desolate and exhausted'. 'Everything is clouded.' She was away, for instance, on his forty-fifth birthday, in July 1982. 'I am in a bad patch,' he wrote in his journal. A new tone of melancholy comes into these entries during the years of *The Real Thing* – though that may be the result of their being written when he and Miriam were apart. 'I'm in terrible trouble,' he wrote in August 1982. Early in 1983, he had lost his 'terra firma' and felt 'depressed and insecure'. Later that year, before their trip to the States and his starting work on *The Real Thing* in America, he was suffering from insomnia, felt he was using his time badly, and was cross with himself and the world. And the next spring, just as *The Real Thing* was triumphing in the States, he felt dissatisfied with life and with himself, and 'fairly pissed off with everything'. These are scattered journal entries over several years, mixed up with much more cheerful notes. But they point to some disequilibrium in his life. One unhappy moment, in April 1983, gave rise to a poem called 'Lament'. He had always wanted to buy Miriam a string of pearls, but had never got round to it. And then she bought herself some while she was away in Tokyo, at the airport duty-free shop. However much he would try to recompense her in pursuit of those pearls, he would 'never catch them up'. 'And you're my only girl,' the poem ended sadly.

Anecdotal accounts provided by friends, many years later, pointed to signs of unease in the mid-1980s: of his having dropped round to the Corries' house one day and confided his difficulties with Miriam's intense involvement with her work, or of his getting exasperated with her in public, at a school parents' meeting, because she grilled Deke Arlon about her own career when they were supposed to be concentrating on the boys. Some would remember her competitiveness with him – though she herself said she had no such emotions. The big, Miriam-driven operation that was Iver Grove came to feel burdensome to him at times. He headed one letter to Peter, detailing their expenses on the house, with the ironic address: 'Xanadu'. To one interviewer who came to see him at Iver in May 1989 he burst out exasperatedly, setting his luxurious life in the context of Havel's imprisonment and the fatwa against Rushdie: 'I mean, look at this fucking house and everything.' By the late 1980s, his letters to his parents and his appointment diaries gave the impression that their paths were diverging. 'They led such different lives,' their friend Marigold Johnson would say. Ollie had the retrospective impression that for years 'they had separate lives in the same house'.

He wrote no original play between *The Real Thing*, in 1982, and *Hapgood*, begun at the end of 1986. But he was entangled all through that time, from his mid to late forties, in a mesh of activities, including screenplays, an opera libretto, a television play, two major adaptations for the National, a translation of Havel, revivals of his plays, directing and public political work. While all this was going on, his personal life was slowly changing.

Three very different projects cut across his work on *The Real Thing* between 1982 and 1984. One was *Squaring the Circle*, with all its obstructions. One was a contribution to the screenplay of his friend Terry Gilliam's film *Brazil*, which he worked on in the summer of 1983 and into early 1984. For Gilliam, it was a much longer and more arduous process, which involved a series of collaborators and a long and bloody battle with Universal Pictures. He had started work on it in 1979, and it was released in 1985.

The film was a futuristic satire of a nightmarish totalitarian society, set in a dystopian world of computerised bureaucracy in which a downtrodden, besuited worker, Sam Lowry, a cog in the wheel, tries to break through his dreary life with dreams of a fantasy woman and the sabotaging of state systems. With switches from black and white to lurid colour, wild scenes of explosions, satanic mills and machine-gunning security forces, and long, psychedelic dream sequences, many of which Gilliam had to cut, it's as if Orwell's *1984* were crossed with *Alice in Wonderland* and Chaplin's *Modern Times*. One film critic described it as 'neo-futuristic-retro chaos'. It had a remarkable cast, with Jonathan Pryce as the bewildered hero and Robert De Niro as a canny plumber-saboteur, and strong support from British actors like Ian Holm, Ian Richardson, Bob Hoskins and Jim Broadbent. Stoppard had some friendly, if critical, to-and-fro with Gilliam about the script (into which he introduced the idea of an idyllic English landscape that turns out to be 'a gigantic roof-garden'), but found the end product 'a bit bleak, a bit relentless for my taste'. Still, *Brazil* was nominated for two Oscars, including for its screenplay, won the Los Angeles Film Critics Association awards for best director and screenplay, and became a cult film. When asked, in 1999, which of 'his' films he liked the best, he demurred from calling them 'his', but listed *Brazil* with *Empire of the Sun* and *Shakespeare in Love*.

The third distraction from *The Real Thing* was, of all things, an opera. This was done to oblige their friend George Christie, manager and owner of Glyndebourne. He enjoyed the ritual of going to Glyndebourne with Miriam – black tie, picnic, long intervals in the beautiful grounds of the Sussex opera house – though opera, as *The Real Thing* had made clear, was not his chosen form of entertainment, and he had to take strong mints with him to stop himself falling asleep and snoring. But he was intrigued by Christie's suggestion that he should do a version of Prokofiev's *The Love for Three Oranges* for Glyndebourne's touring company. This was a truly international concoction, based on an eighteenth-century Italian *commedia dell'arte* play, with a French libretto, and performed in the 1920s first in America and then in the Soviet Union. It is a farcical fairy tale (set, as he translated it, 'once upon a time, in the world of make-believe') about a melancholy prince, who suffers in Stoppard's version from 'galloping malingeritis'. He cannot laugh, until he catches sight of the bloomers of the wicked witch, Fata Morgana. In revenge, she condemns him to search through the world with the court jester Truffaldino for the three oranges ('I'm dreaming of an Orange Christmas'), pursued by the demon Farfarello, until he falls in love with the princess Ninette, who gets turned into a giant rat and then back into a princess. (In the original, the prince says at this point: 'What an amazing thing to have happened! And how beautiful she is!' Stoppard's version goes: 'Well, fancy that. And I rather think I do.') The rude, anarchic quality of the piece appealed to him, and he had a good time putting in large numbers of silly jokes. He worked – from a literal translation – with the conductor Stephen Barlow and the Canadian opera director Robert Carsen.

He and Carsen met many times, often at Iver, in the summer and autumn of 1983, and they got on well. Carsen watched with fascination as Stoppard worked out, with lightning speed, how to adapt the jokes to the music. He could see that opera was not Stoppard's 'thing', but that he was amused by the challenge. And it took him, as Carsen noted, 'about five seconds' to realise that he had to fit the stresses to the music, so dialogue couldn't be switched about as it could in a play: 'He had to make all his jokes to fit the rhythm of the French text.' He wrote a funny, neatly crafted version, much enjoyed by the singers and the audiences, and reused (for instance at a Sydney Opera House production in 2005). Carsen noted that Stoppard turned up to rehearsals much more often than the average translator.

Out of that collaboration came a good friendship. After Carsen left Canada he had gone to the Bristol Old Vic Theatre School, so they had Bristol in common. By the time he met Stoppard he had been living for some years with the wealthy bisexual socialite, engineer, inventor and patron of the arts, Jeremy Fry (of the Quaker Fry's chocolate family). This charismatic personage had a grand house, Widcombe Manor, in Somerset, and had created an informal colony for writers in Provence, Le Grand Banc, in the Lubéron. Fry's philanthropic work included renovations of the Bath Theatre Royal and the Arnolfini Gallery in Bristol. His circle included not only Princess Margaret and Lord Snowdon (who had an affair, and a child, with Fry's wife), the artist Craigie Aitchison and the director Tony Richardson, but also some of the best new talents in the opera world, including Carsen, the designer John Pascoe and the dramaturge Ian Burton. Le Grand Banc became an occasional writing refuge for Stoppard, and sparked off his attraction for that beautiful part of the world. He liked Jeremy Fry, and was impressed by his worldly prowess. He would put these friends, as a little private tribute, into *The Invention of Love*, where there are two undergraduates called Carsen and Fry.

Stoppard worked with Robert Carsen again, in 1987, on a revival of *Rosencrantz* for the Roundabout Theatre in New York, with John Wood returning to the play, this time as the Player. When French productions of his plays were being put on, Carsen would advise him on the translations. He became a renowned opera and theatre director, working in America and Europe, and Stoppard saw many of his productions, in La Scala or Salzburg or Aix-en-Provence. Carsen found being with Stoppard exciting and inspiring. Talking to him felt like an exchange of crackling energy, where you have to be at your best and also find you are better than you thought you could be. Carson relished his generosity, his attentiveness and his patience. He appreciated his reserve, his mixture of the very private and the very public. He liked the fact that Stoppard was always the same with everyone, irrespective of status or fame. He admired his craftsmanship of his work and his attention to language. Carsen thought Stoppard had an almost musical ability to create 'an extra dimension' in his work, 'a dimension of expression or of thought beyond what is normal'. To him, Stoppard was 'a School of One, like Janáček is a School of One'. He described him as an alchemist.

The alchemist was at work, after *The Real Thing*, on three major theatre pieces, all adaptations from European and Eastern European texts. *Rough Crossing* was the next big Stoppard production after *The Real Thing*, opening at the Lyttelton on 30 October 1984. He wrote it that spring and summer, and delivered it on his forty-seventh birthday – remembering how on his thirty-fourth, he had read *Jumpers* to Olivier and Tynan. It was intended as a dazzling comedy to follow on from the panache of *On the Razzle* and the theatrical twists of *The Real Thing*. The original, *The Play at the Castle*, was by the Jewish-Hungarian playwright and novelist Ferenc Molnár, who had fled Budapest when the Nazis came. It was adapted in 1926 by P. G. Wodehouse, in his play-writing days, as *The Play's the Thing*. In the Molnár/Wodehouse versions, the farcical action is set in an Italian Riviera castle, where a playwright-producer, his collaborator and a young composer arrive to take by surprise their leading lady (with whom the composer is in love) and show her their new work-in-progress, a romantic operetta. Unfortunately, the three of them overhear her making love with her old flame and fellow actor. The distraught composer tears up his score and rushes out; the cunning playwright has to persuade him that what they have overheard was a rehearsal of a love scene for their operetta.

Stoppard was much less faithful to his sources than he had been with *Undiscovered Country*. He turned the Italian castle into a cruise ship – the SS *Italian Castle* – going from Cherbourg to New York. The 1920s have turned into the 1930s, the operetta into a (terrible) Broadway musical with chorus girls, *The Cruise of the Dodo* (the title the result of a typist's error). The pastiche is as much of Noël Coward, or generic Broadway musicals, as it is of Molnár or Wodehouse.

There is a plethora of running gags. The composer, Adam, has a (temporary) speech defect which holds up his reactions, so that he always replies to the last remark but one. The spoof play, which takes up most of the second act, is a fiendishly complicated farrago involving an international jewel thief, a gang of white slave traders, a kidnapped baby, a shipful of French tarts and a ping-pong tournament on the Venice Lido. The overheard 'love scene' is a concoction of excruciating clichés ('you've plucked out my heart like the olive out of a dry Martini and dashed me from your lips!'). The ship's captain and the ship's telephone operator have written their own plays and keep asking the writers to read them. There are some nice Stoppardianisms, like the lover's rebuff ('I was the love of your life!' 'That was another life'), or the jewel thief's explanation of his compulsion, which the actor assumes is another typo ('Perhaps I was starved of affectation as a child'), or the playwright's complaint at his actors' 'sine-qua-nonchalance'. Following on from the ingenious Melchior in *On the Razzle*, there is an inspired comic character, the steward Dvornichek, a landlubber who has to rapidly acquire his sea-legs and his nautical lingo, persistently drinks all the cognacs he's been asked to fetch, and turns out to be a brilliant dramaturge. All the characters are vaguely international, rather than Hungarian: 'My assumption about Dvornichek is that whatever his nationality his English is mysteriously perfect.'

The playwright-producer, Turai, is a manipulative man of the theatre who puts the show before everything. So there are plenty of self-reflexive jokes about the business: plays that start bafflingly with 'chaps talking about something they evidently know all about and we know nothing about' and which require a character to come on and explain the plot, a writer who 'tells the story but doesn't understand character', scenes with no good lines for women, and actors who have the effrontery to criticise the plays they are in, or, even worse, to offer to rewrite them:

> In all my born days I have never encountered such brass. I have had actors who won't take their trousers off, I have had actors who won't work with cats or in the provinces, in short I have had from actors every kind of interference with the artistic process but I have never had an actor with the effrontery to write.

For all his vanity and bad temper, Turai has that theatrical sixth sense which can always magic the rabbit out of the hat. He is like Henslowe, a decade on, in *Shakespeare in Love*: 'Strangely enough it all turns out well.' 'How?' 'I don't know. It's a mystery.' So says Turai: he has 'the strangest feeling . . . that everything is going to be all right'.

But, on this occasion, it wasn't. It ought to have worked well. The favourite team was assembled: Peter Wood and Carl Toms as director and designer, André Previn (who could never get over Stoppard's complete inability to hold or recognise a tune) to write what Stoppard called 'some deft and charming' music, Michael Kitchen following his Melchior with an equally funny Dvornichek. Stoppard especially liked Kitchen's wheeze of having boots with slots in the heels, which would fit onto two studs on the stage, so that as the ship pitched and rolled he could sway at incredible angles to the deck. Toms created an elaborate revolving art deco ship's set with a 'Pisa Salon' in which the Tower of Pisa stopped leaning when everything else was at an angle. There was a chorus of girls in yellow oil-skins, gold lamé and red feathers.

But there were difficulties casting the show. John Wood was not available, so John Standing was cast, and played Turai with camp languorousness. Neither Diana Rigg nor Felicity Kendal was able to play the diva, and Sheila Gish was cast. Standing and Gish got on badly with Peter Wood in rehearsal, and, after his experience with Mike Nichols, Stoppard was getting impatient with Wood, too: he thought he talked too much in rehearsals, was too slow and wasn't concentrating on the right things. He commuted endlessly from Iver to the National, feeling cross and uneasy. Rehearsals had an unhappy atmosphere, and the play still felt 'rough' on opening night. He knew what was wrong: 'The play is almost tosh anyway and needs fleetness and energy. Without it, it is tosh rampant, or rather couchant. I'm depressed . . .'

They didn't get away with it. Though everyone adored Michael Kitchen, in general *Rough Crossing* got a 'frightful press'. What should have been 'a delicate trifle', one critic complained, had become a 'leaden-footed' and 'interminable' parody. Another called it 'a decidedly over-cooked goulash'. It was noted that the production was fitted out like the *Titanic*, and suffered much the same fate. The play was taken out of the National's repertory by February 1985. Just before that, in the interval of seeing *Coriolanus* in the Olivier Theatre, he popped into the back of *Rough Crossing* (he told Anthony Smith) 'to find a small subdued house tittering in a rather depressed way and it was a relief to get back to Ian McKellen in his underpants'. Yet the early audiences liked the jokes and enjoyed themselves. After he took a ruthless red pencil to it (cutting out the chorus, for instance), it had a number of successful revivals, though not in London.

The best review *Rough Crossing* got was a wicked parody in a play by Stoppard's old Bristol acquaintance Peter Nichols, *A Piece of My Mind*, which opened early in 1987. Nichols, like his friend and fellow playwright Charles Wood, had watched Stoppard's career for twenty years with mixed feelings. In *A Piece of My Mind*, the washed-up playwright and would-be novelist Ted Forrest is consumed with uncontrollable envy of the dazzlingly successful, universally praised 'Miles Whittier'. Though Nichols said that the play was more about Wood (as in 'Forrest') than himself, and more about the whole issue of 'celebrity and publicity and fame' than about Stoppard in particular, there's no mistaking the Stoppardian flavour of Miles Whittier's latest, universally acclaimed comedy, whose ecstatic reviews make Ted Forrest throw up with a bad attack of the spleen:

Headline: 'Pink Champagne. Few playwrights of any epoch would dare bring together such disparate elements as Miles Whittier does

in his dazzling comedy *Starboard Home*. Mahatma Gandhi, Rudyard
Kipling, Anton Chekhov and Nellie Melba meet on a P&O liner,
bound from Bombay to London. Soon they are ordering magnums
and, in a classic drunk scene, concoct the peach and ice-cream dish
that finishes by slipping down the Australian prima donna's ample
bosom . . . His dialogue sparkles like vintage champagne . . . So
spellbound by his shimmering wordplay that we are hardly ready for
the sudden depth, the sound of a heartbeat as strong and tender as
Chekhov's own . . . Word-spinning brilliance. Wilder than Wilde – an
Oscar winner . . . He had us reeling from the theatre, our feet on the
pavement, our heads among the stars, glad to have been one of the
privileged few at this once-in-a-lifetime marvel . . .'

Aren't you happy for him, his wife asks Forrest. 'I wish him dead,'
Forrest replies. But the debonair Miles Whittier, darling of all audiences,
the lucky man who always escapes disasters and comes on stage in a rosy
glow and a shower of confetti, passes over and beyond him like a meteor.

While Stoppard was writing *Rough Crossing*, in May 1984, he went to
Toulouse University to represent Václav Havel for his honorary degree,
and to read out his acceptance speech, 'Politics and Conscience'. The contrast between their situations was sharp: Havel unable to leave his country,
and writing under duress, while Stoppard seemed to be riding high in his
charmed life. Early in 1985, Havel dedicated to Stoppard – as Stoppard
had dedicated *Professional Foul* to him – his play *Largo Desolato*. (The
phrase meant 'a mood of slow disintegration'; Havel told Stoppard it was
a musical marking in Alban Berg's 'Lyric Suite'.) Stoppard took on the task
of making a 'speakable' English version out of it from a literal translation.
He told Ewing that he wanted his royalties donated to the author. He kept
as faithfully as possible to Havel's melancholy play of the dissident philosopher Leopold Kopřiva, who feels he is losing his way, in private and
in public life. Havel noted that his own 'post-prison despair' infected the
character, and his biographer called it a musical meditation on 'the weight
of human existence', written out of 'existential anguish'. Stoppard's version
of Leopold's predicament was filled with heartfelt intensity:

Why can't I get my life clear! It was wonderful when nobody was
interested in me – when nobody expected anything from me, nobody
urging me to do anything . . . why can't I . . . forget everything and
start a completely new life? . . .

I lack a fixed point . . . I'm not really doing anything except listening
helplessly to the time going by.

Havel thanked him for his dedication to the task: 'Who else would have
more feeling for this sort of thing than you?' The play was put on in the
studio theatre of the Bristol Old Vic, opening, in a rather muted production, on 9 October 1986, and then, more vigorously, at the Orange Tree
in Richmond, in February of 1987. Stoppard went regularly to Bristol to
help it on its way in the late summer of 1986, once his other translation of
that year, *Dalliance*, was safely embedded at the National. He kept Havel
in touch with how it was going. In a short piece for the Bristol Old Vic, he
wrote of his pleasure in doing the job:

Anyone who cares for the theatre as a form, and cares for good work,
should take pride in Havel who has kept his head and his humour in
circumstances in which, as Bertram says to Leopold, 'any of us would
have cracked'. I am proud to know him and to have had a part in
bringing his new play to the English stage.

It was a far cry from *Largo Desolato* to *Dalliance*, which he worked
on early in 1986. It opened at the National on 27 May of that year, three
months after he organised the roll call on the South Bank on behalf of
Soviet Jewry, and a few months before *Largo Desolato* opened in Bristol.
The two plays, though utterly unlike, were both dark comedies. *Dalliance*
took him back to Schnitzler's *fin-de-siècle* Viennese world. *Liebelei* was
a simpler and sadder piece than *Das weite Land*, but again set love as a
light game of 'dalliance' up against love as an experience of life-changing
romantic intensity – the real thing. There is a quartet of young lovers,
predictably contrasted. Of the two young men, playboys and Hussars, one,

Theodore, is a boorish hedonist, the other, Fritz, has a romantic heart. Of their two girls, Theo's Mizi, a wardrobe mistress, is a light-hearted cynic. Her friend Christine, a poor music copyist, devoted to her widowed father, a violinist at the opera (the most poignant character in the play), is an innocent who has fallen deeply in love with Fritz, unaware that he has a married mistress. Theo tells Fritz he should take love lightly, Mizi tells Christine that 'men are all the same'. Christine longs to know all about Fritz, but he fends her off. No one can know everything about anyone: 'In the end we all have our secrets. That's how we live.'

A bohemian supper *à quatre* is broken in on by the jealous husband, who challenges Fritz to a duel. He pays a visit to Christine's attic home, and imagines another life, of simple, trusting fidelity, before he goes off to meet his fate. In the last act, Christine hears of Fritz's death, and discovers his infidelity to her. She is plunged into disillusioned, suicidal grief: 'He was God and salvation and I was his day off.'

Stoppard adapted this Schnitzler play as freely as he adapted *Rough Crossing*. He played up the theatricality of the Viennese setting and the contrast between romantic comedy and tragic melodrama, and put in his signature tune of a play within a play. So the last act is set not in Christine's home, as in the original, but backstage at the theatre, where a Viennese operetta, 'The False Hussar', is in rehearsal. The light opera cuts ironically across the tragedy. A few critics objected to his infidelity to Schnitzler. But *Dalliance* was a success: 'One of the most enjoyable plays in London' . . . 'A gripping critique of masculine loyalties' . . . 'offers a good cry and some insights into the Stoppard creative sensibility', they said of it. Peter Wood was back on form in what Stoppard described to Frank Pike as 'a typically grandiose Stoppard/Wood version', there was a strong performance by Brenda Blethyn as Christine, and support from the excellent actors in the 1980s National company, like Michael Bryant and Sara Kestelman. Audiences were lapping it up, he noted with satisfaction.

He had something in mind for a new play, at the end of 1984 and the start of 1985, something about a mathematician, but he couldn't quite get hold of it. He told Anthony Smith, at the start of 1985, that he was reading lots of mathematical books, 'little of which I understand'. In his journal he noted: 'I am reading books about mathematics and wondering: where is the play?' Meanwhile, there was a great deal to keep him in business. Revivals of his plays were constantly being staged and he always paid them attention, and there were new casts to be rehearsed for long-running productions. Early in 1984, *Dirty Linen* was being put on at the Redgrave Theatre in Farnham, *Enter a Free Man* was opening off Broadway, Peter Wood was doing *The Real Thing* in Vienna, and the third London cast of *The Real Thing* needed rehearsing. At the Manchester Royal Exchange in the spring of 1984, Tom Courtenay and Julie Walters were playing in a production of *Jumpers* which he admired, though the critics were not very enthusiastic. That didn't matter, since every seat was sold out before the opening night.

A year later, in May 1985, he agreed, exceptionally, to direct one of these revivals of his plays. Edward Petherbridge, his first Guildenstern, and Ian McKellen had been asked by Peter Hall to run an Actors' Company at the National. They asked Stoppard to direct *The Real Inspector Hound* in the Olivier Theatre, with Petherbridge as Moon and McKellen as Inspector Hound (alongside Eleanor Bron and Roy Kinnear), in a double bill with Sheridan's *The Critic*, directed by Sheila Hancock. It was a clever combination, since Sheridan's satire on eighteenth-century theatre, with its mocking critics, Dangle and Sneer, nicely matched Stoppard's send-up of clichéd theatre criticism and bad West End thrillers. He liked the idea, though it meant commuting in and out of London during the summer months for rehearsals, and it made him nervous. He wasn't sure whether the play was funny any more. He thought it would feel like a period piece. In the event he enjoyed this rare outing as a director, and was amused by the practical problems he had set himself, like how to get Mrs Drudge the charlady to throw a mock-bearskin rug over a stuffed corpse without appearing to notice it. The double bill went well, and travelled to Paris and Chicago. It turned out that the play *was* still very funny, but also now seemed more of an investigation of illusion and reality, and less of a parodic squib – perhaps because audiences had been trained up in Stoppard since 1968.

The most important revival of the mid-1980s, and the biggest Stoppard event – personally as well as professionally – in this complicated stretch of time between *The Real Thing* and his next new play, was that of *Jumpers* at the Aldwych in 1985, for a limited six-month season. He told his parents, with some excitement. that Felicity Kendal and Paul Eddington were going to do it, with 'P. Wood again of course'. There was a strong support cast too, with Simon Cadell as a suave Archie, and Bones played by Andrew Sachs (famous for Manuel in *Fawlty Towers*). He took the opportunity to do a lot of rewriting, and he and Wood reinstated the dramatic appearances of Captain Scott and Tarzan in the play's coda. The production, geared for a commercial West End audience, but without the lavish resources of the National, was a spectacular affair, designed ('again of course') by Carl Toms. Vivaldi's 'Gloria in Excelsis Deo' was set against the theme from *Star Wars*, Captain Scott and Tarzan made their flying entries in a space suit and swinging from a grapevine, and Kendal, in fabulous clinging sequined décolleté, sang from a glittering silver crescent moon suspended above the stage.

He had some anxiety that the Hordern/Rigg production had taken on such mythical status that no new production would live up to it. 1985 was a very different world for *Jumpers*, thirteen years on. The political rhetoric of the hard left, the moon landings, arguments over logical positivism, were distant historical phenomena. The political context now was the Falklands War and the miners' strike, rampant privatisation and the first inklings of the stock market's Black Friday in 1987, the year when Thatcher was re-elected and declared there was no such thing as society, only individuals.

In this mid-1980s *Jumpers* the emphasis was more on human predicaments and less on philosophical argument. The play felt more personal, and less difficult, than in 1972. Eddington gave an anguished performance as George, in which, as one critic observed, you could feel the pain of a marriage 'audibly splintering'. Kendal was a glamorous, brittle Dotty. Not everyone warmed to her performance, Stoppard alerted his mother, but 'I like her.'

Like all new productions, it had its rough moments. In the opening week, Eddington kept forgetting his lines, and was thrown by 'a religious maniac in the audience shouting "yes!" every time he asked the question "is God?'" Sonia Friedman, who would later become a major producer and Stoppard's friend, was then an eighteen-year-old drama-school student, doing evening work at the Aldwych. Her job was to operate the follow spot (the single pinspot, manually controlled, that follows a particular actor around the stage). Her most important cue, almost at the end of the play, was to pick out Felicity Kendal's head while she was singing on the top of the crescent moon. Friedman was sitting backstage absorbed in a book, with her head-cans off, and missed her cue. The next thing she heard was a whistle from the stage and someone screaming at her down her cans. Kendal was sitting on the moon, in a total blackout. The star was not pleased. Friedman was fired.

But, glitches apart, the production was a big success. There was excitement in the papers about Kendal and Eddington playing husband and wife, as they'd been the opposite halves of the two couples in the 1970s sitcom *The Good Life*. There were gossip features about Stoppard's popularity ('he doesn't like the label or the stereotype of intellectual'), Kendal's allure ('Felicity Kendal swops green wellies for all-out glamour') and the 'coach-loads of pundits' turning up to see the show. It had a strong run during its six months, from 1 April to 1 October 1985, and Michael Codron and Stoppard hosted lavish parties for the fiftieth performance and for the last night. Stoppard felt warmly about the whole production. He wrote to Paul Eddington: 'The spirit of happiness and affection which seemed to be present at all the rehearsals and which has continued in the performances has been a vital ingredient in the unbelievable success . . . and you . . . were the mainspring of that . . . [I am] inexpressibly grateful.'

That mood of 'happiness and affection' was intensely felt. By the end of the run, he and Felicity Kendal – both married, both parents, both famous names – had fallen in love. She had been part of his theatrical 'family' for a long time now. He had been resisting his growing emotions for her and trying to ignore them; but (in his phrase) in the end not. The next thing he worked on was *Dalliance*, a story of secrets, affairs and infidelity set in the world of the theatre. And the next new play he wrote – which he began work on at the end of 1986 – was *Hapgood*, with a big leading part for Kendal.

*

Before that play took over his life, he had another job of work to do. From May 1985, while *Jumpers* was running, and on and off for the next two years, he was working on his first collaboration with Steven Spielberg, *Empire of the Sun*. It was a screenwriting job he felt much more involved with than *Brazil*, and the beginning of a long working relationship with Spielberg and with his producer Kathleen Kennedy. They had recently founded Amblin Entertainment, with Kennedy's husband Frank Marshall, and they had had a huge global success with *E.T.* in 1982. It was David Lean who suggested to Spielberg that he make a film of J. G. Ballard's 1984 novel, which centred on a young boy. Lean didn't want to make it himself – he told Spielberg he was too old to direct children but that Spielberg 'was good with kids'. Stoppard had already started doing an adaptation of the novel with another director, Harold Becker, but Becker left the project. When Spielberg took over, he had not met Stoppard, though he knew that 'he was a great playwright'. He flew him out to Hollywood, and they began their conversation.

Ballard's novel told the story, based on his own childhood experience, of the brutal Japanese takeover of the Shanghai International Settlement after Pearl Harbor. When the Japanese invaded China, the American, English and European inhabitants of Shanghai had kept up a fragile neutrality within the Settlement. In 1942 the Settlement was broken up and they were mostly sent to the Lunghua internment camp, where conditions were harsh, and many of them died. Ballard, as a teenage boy, spent three years living in the camp with his parents, until the end of the war. Forty years on (and after writing some extraordinary novels whose surreal cruelty and strangeness indirectly reflected his childhood experience) he at last turned this part of his life into fiction. Shanghai and his childhood there had become to him 'a dream-like pageant'; the war and the camp had remained in his mind's eye in all its horror. He got rid of the parents, and had Jim, from ages eleven to fourteen, surviving on his own in the chaos of wartime Shanghai and the camp. Jim, hyperactive, garrulous and excitable, is in love with aeroplanes, with the Japanese pilots, with the American airmen and their culture, and with the war itself. His parents, and the bourgeois schoolboy English life he led in their suburban-style house, become a peculiar distant memory to him during the war. He becomes a scavenger, an opportunist, a watcher and a survivor. He sees everything, from the corpses and brutal beatings in the camp to the glaring light of the atom bomb going off in Nagasaki.

Stoppard greatly admired this story of what he called, in his screenplay, at first 'a lucky boy', and then 'an undernourished, undersized, over-experienced fourteen-year-old'. But as soon as he met Spielberg, there were battles to be fought – or, as Spielberg put it, 'we immediately butted heads'. Stoppard told his parents that 'naturally he is throwing his own ideas into the script so just as naturally the poor writer has to go home and try to accommodate them'. Spielberg would recall that he 'had a lot of crazy ideas' about the changes he wanted to make to the book, while Stoppard 'had a lot of rational ideas about how things should stay the same'. He was impressed that Stoppard 'was not rolling over', but 'was defending . . . the truth of Ballard's experiences growing up in World War II'. It was unusual for Spielberg to meet a writer who stood up to him; and it became the basis of a respectful friendship. He described Stoppard, admiringly, as 'intransigent'.

They never saw eye to eye about the film. Stoppard wanted to be faithful to the strangeness and harshness of Ballard. Spielberg wanted the film to be more emotional, and, in Stoppard's view, more sentimental. 'Jim too uncharming', came the production note on an early draft. Spielberg's version introduced more of a personal conflict over Jim's allegiance between his American mentor, Basie, and the Englishman who tries to keep up Jim's public school education with Latin verbs and English poetry. In the film, Jim forges a silent, poignant relationship with a Japanese boy who becomes a kamikaze pilot. His reunion with his parents is emotionally charged up, with a recitation by Jim of Rupert Brooke's 'there's some corner of a foreign field/That is for ever England'. Stoppard objected to the heavy-handed pathos of this sort of thing, firing off a series of cross memos. There should not be a 'warm' reunion scene between Jim and Basie. The rivalry over Jim between the British and the Americans in the camp should be more 'implicit'. The ending was horribly sentimental. 'Why don't we give Jim a little dog at the beginning', he wrote witheringly, 'and then the dog could show up too.' And did Jim have to quote Rupert Brooke? He'd much prefer it if it could be a quotation from Dryden:

> Happy the man, and happy he alone,
> He, who can call today his own:
> He who, secure within, can say,
> Tomorrow do thy worst for I have lived today.

And if Spielberg didn't like the Dryden, he would write the bloody thing himself and pretend it was 'something old'. Sometimes sheer exasperation took hold: 'Have you guys got something against apostrophes?' He knew that he couldn't stick too closely to Ballard's novel, 'but', he reminded the film people, 'he did write a grown-up book with these complicated, surprising and believable psychologies'. In the end he admired the film, which looked sensational and had an exciting cast (the young Christian Bale as Jim, John Malkovich as Basie, and strong British actors like Miranda Richardson and Robert Stephens). But in his view Spielberg had wanted to turn it into too much of a 'boy's adventure story'. Spielberg knew that Stoppard felt 'that he had put too much liquid refreshment into Ballard's experience'. For all their differences, good will prevailed. And when all the work was done, Spielberg, Kennedy and Frank Marshall sent Stoppard an extra cheque of $50,000, as 'something more than just thank you' for 'work above and beyond'.

When shooting began at Shepperton Studios in March 1987, the script was still being changed. Ballard, who lived near Shepperton, was invited to appear as an extra. He watched the transformation of his novel with interest, observing that the 'Hollywood film company came down from the sky' 'like a jumbo jet crash-landing in a suburban park'. Stoppard reported to his mother that it seemed to him entirely characteristic of the film business 'that after two years of writing a script one ends up re-writing it the day before shooting started'. The whole thing was 'a typical Hollywood operation – they needed a pre-war Packard and bought one at Sotheby's! Then they bought an identical Packard so they wouldn't have to ship the Packard to and from China!'

Between the shooting of the film and its opening in Los Angeles in December 1987 – where it wasn't a huge box-office success, as people confused it with Bertolucci's *The Last Emperor*, and it didn't win any Oscars – there was a 'typical Hollywood operation' over the credits. Spielberg often employed several writers on his films, sometimes without letting them know about each other. Stoppard discovered that he had also hired Menno Meyjes, who worked with Spielberg on *The Color Purple* (1985). He was annoyed that he had not been informed about this. Not wanting to be confrontational, he met Meyjes and talked to him politely about the situation. But when he found that Meyjes was to have equal billing as a screenwriter, he argued, on principle, that this should not be so. The case went to 'credit arbitration' with the Writers Guild, and Stoppard won. (Film producers submit their list of credits, but anyone who has worked on the film has the right to object to that list, and the Writers Guild has the job of carrying out a 'credit arbitration' on these claims, to determine what the 'substantial contribution' to a screenplay is and whose that is.) While this dispute was going on, Stoppard asked Kathy Kennedy what Meyjes had done for the film. Surely he had not provided much of the screenplay? She replied, yes, he contributed two very important things: one was the boy's crew cut and the second was the boy's leather jacket. This was a very illuminating moment for him. He recognised that those two visual details communicated Jim's allegiance to the American pilots, in a way that words could not.

Early on in the film, a knowing member of the English community says to Jim's father: 'I'd get Mary and the boys out altogether. Somewhere safe. Singapore.' Later, the news comes through of the Japanese occupation of Singapore. Working on *Empire of the Sun* took Stoppard back to his own childhood experiences. Spielberg thought that, although they never discussed it, Stoppard might have felt some identification with Ballard's story, since he too was a 'displaced person'. Stoppard told his mother that the novel was 'rather depressing and close to home . . . about a young boy whose family was caught by the war in Shanghai, and how he survived the war'. He told Spielberg that 'if the true subject of this film has to be put into one word the word would be "survival"'. He finished his work on the film just before his fiftieth birthday.

PART FOUR

21

Doubles

We're all doubles . . . We're not so one-or-the-other.

He celebrated his fiftieth birthday with a big party at the Garrick Club on 30 June 1987. Lots of his friends, family and supporters were there – including Ken Ewing, his agent for twenty-seven years, the Faber team, who had been publishing him since 1964, and Michael Codron, who was about to produce their fifth show together. The birthday marked the middle of a life in which friends and colleagues stayed on board for the duration.

This significant birthday came in the middle of a busy and complicated year. It was a source of great anxiety to him that Barny, seventeen in 1987 and about to go to art college in Bournemouth, had to have an operation, the start of difficult times for him. Stoppard took Barny with him to LA and Tokyo in July. There were other family travels that year: to Spain in April, on a Swedish boat trip from Gothenburg in June, fishing in Somerset in August, another fishing trip with Ted Hughes, a December holiday in Scotland for the shooting. The most exotic journey was to celebrate Miriam's fiftieth birthday in May. The two of them went to Egypt to see a production of *Aida*, with Placido Domingo, in the temple of Luxor. This 'once-only' trip for well-heeled cultural tourists included two nights in Cairo and some sightseeing. Given his feelings about opera, Miriam thought that his taking her there 'really was an act of love'. Asked in the interval if he was having a good time, he replied: 'Well, it's better than *Aida* without Luxor.' But he enjoyed the Nile. He sent a postcard to Jacky of a line of Bedouins praying with their kneeling camels by the Pyramids, with the note: 'Everyone here is very respectful to Miri, as you see.'

For work, he went to and from the States all year long, first to do some lectures at Harvard, then for the American launch of *Dalliance* in New Haven, then for Robert Carsen's production of *Rosencrantz* at the Roundabout Theatre, with John Wood given his head as a flamboyant, larger-than-life Player, then for meetings in LA about *Empire* with

Spielberg and for the start of negotiations about the film of *Rosencrantz*, which Stoppard was going to direct. In London, there was a revival of *Every Good Boy* in June at the Festival Hall, and of *Rosencrantz* in the West End, with a well-known pair of TV comedians ('The Oblivion Boys'), Stephen Frost and Mark Arden, directed by Peter Wilson. As always there were proposals to be turned down, some more easily than others, like the suggestion he might adapt Kingsley Amis's Booker Prize-winning novel *The Old Devils*. He wrote to his brother Peter: 'I don't think that a lot of old Welsh drunks is my cup of tea.'

He finished *Hapgood* early in 1987, in the hopes of a spring production, but it had to be delayed. Rehearsals started at the beginning of 1988. Fed up with the endless commute from Iver to rehearsals – and so as to have a place of his own – he rented a furnished flat in Cadogan Square in Knightsbridge for the duration of the show. Miriam, meanwhile, rented a flat in Albany, in Piccadilly, and then a small Mayfair flat in Clarges Mews. Iver was becoming a weekend house. When the lease of Cadogan Square ran out in May, he took a more permanent step, and bought an unfurnished flat in Chelsea, for £180,000. ('Can I afford it?' he asked his brother Peter. The answer was yes.) This was an airy, modern, white-walled space, in a smart block of flats called Chelsea Crescent, in the riverside enclave of Chelsea Harbour. It had a panorama of the river Thames, between Battersea and Wandsworth Bridge, with Chelsea Harbour Pier jutting out into the river and a sidelong view of St Mary's Church, Battersea, on the Surrey side, upriver. Everything was spick and span, with underground parking below, and round-the-clock porterage, and a regular cleaner. There was a hallway, a large L-shaped sitting-room with a kitchen off it, one big bedroom and one much smaller. The river, full of its traffic, was always in his eye. It wasn't a homely area, but there were cafes and restaurants nearby and the kind of shops where you could buy Belgian chocolates and Lalique glass but not a bottle of milk. (Milk was delivered.) At first it was mainly a work space. Gradually it became his home, as he filled it with his clothes, and his big desk from the study at Iver, and bought an enormous sofa, and put his prints and pictures and framed awards on the walls. Not much cooking went on. If any of the boys came to stay they would eat breakfast with him in the kitchen while he read his way through a pile of newspapers. They had a pact to ignore each other until lunchtime.

He told his parents that he needed a London base just for 'convenience', and that the Chelsea flat was mainly to be used as an office for making the film of *Rosencrantz*. But he loved his 'Chelsea bolt-hole'. He lived there for six years. In the autumn of 1994, he moved upstairs to a flat more than twice the size, in the same building, with much more space for his books. This was number 44 Chelsea Crescent, his London home for nearly twenty years. The estate agents, who sold it for £875,000, described it as 'a most spectacular bright and spacious sixth and seventh floor penthouse mai-sonette'. Downstairs was a living space ('magnificent studio-style recep-tion room'), a kitchen and a big dining room with sofas and a dining-room table, all with river views. Upstairs was a room as wide as the whole of the downstairs floor, with two big desks, one for his current work and one for business. There were three balcony-terraces. The bedrooms (two and a half, the half a child's room) and their bathrooms got the morning sun and looked out onto a goods line where the empty Eurostar trains went by on their way to be washed. Gradually, blocks of new flats sprang up all around. Chelsea Crescent was the opposite of Iver Grove, full of the complications of managing a big estate, where marriage and children and social life had come to determine the way of life. By the late 1980s the children were in their late teens and early twenties, and the marriage was coming to an end. The way he lived his personal life contracted. It suited him; he was glad to be absolved. He relished the freedom, the gregarious solitude, and not having to make domestic arrangements.

He would date his separation from Miriam from the time of the pur-chase of the first Chelsea flat in May 1988. But it was two years before their separation became official, and meanwhile they continued to be close, privately and publicly, and completely committed to the boys, as one by one they left home and went out into the world. Jacky, discreet as ever, managed their complex diaries and their increasingly separate arrangements. She came to Chelsea Crescent two or three times a week, and spent the rest of the time at Iver. In 1990 she and her partner Dave

Matthews moved to Winchester for his job, but her working arrangement with Stoppard continued.

Hapgood was delayed for six months because he, Codron and Peter Wood all wanted Felicity Kendal in the main part, but she was pregnant just when rehearsals would have started for a production in the spring of 1987. Very soon after her and Michael Rudman's son Jacob was born, she was back on stage. Her lead part was extremely challenging; the situation was complicated; the company was not an entirely happy one; and the play was not easy to do. Kendal took all this on board with typical determination.

They had been theatrical collaborators for seven years. This new play was written with her in mind. While they were rehearsing it, he started to write a radio play about India, for her, which became *In the Native State* and then the stage play *Indian Ink*. *Arcadia* was written in the early 1990s for her to star in. In 1998 he did a version of *The Seagull* – his first Chekhov – so that she could play Arkadina. For ten years or so, between 1988 and 1998, Kendal was his muse, his colleague and his lover. But they never set up home together. Through his years as 'Felicity's consort' (his phrase), he was living, essentially, on his own.

She was forty-two in 1988, and one of England's best-known actors. This was mainly because of *The Good Life*, which ran on BBC TV from 1975 to 1978. Her blonde, kooky, lovable character, Barbara Good, one half (with Richard Briers) of the suburban duo in contrast with their high-falutin neighbours, Penelope Keith and Paul Eddington, had made her a nationally popular star. She was brought up first in Birmingham, but was taken to India as a baby. She went back there when she was six, with her much older sister Jennifer. Their parents, Geoffrey and Laura Kendal, were actor-managers who ran a small touring company which put on classical English drama – from Shakespeare to *She Stoops to Conquer* – all over India. 'The Firm', as they called it, was mainly English, but was joined by the Indian actor Shashi Kapoor, who married Jennifer. Felicity Kendal started acting before she could walk. She went to convent schools (her mother was Catholic) and spent the rest of her time travelling and performing. The story of the Kendals' company was the inspiration for the 1965 film *Shakespeare Wallah*, directed by Ismail Merchant in his partnership with James Ivory and Ruth Prawer Jhabvala, with Felicity Kendal, at eighteen, as the young love interest. In her 1998 autobiography, *White Cargo*, she told the story of 'The Firm' and of her upbringing.

Her extraordinary childhood, driven by the domineering perfectionism and adventurous spirit of her father, himself a talented actor, made for an odd temperament: 'My nature', she said of herself at eighteen, 'was outwardly sweet and a bit fey, but this masked a will of iron and a selfish determination to succeed at all costs.' She was the baby of 'The Firm', and because she was small, round-faced, big-eyed and blonde, she attracted diminutives: 'Foo', 'Fu' or 'Phoo', later 'Flick'. She was very bound up with her long-suffering and talented mother, her sister and her sister's family, and caught between love for and rage at her father. At eighteen, she decided she had had enough of their life in India, and, to her parents' dismay, went to England to make a career.

After a difficult start, she began to get parts in television and on stage. She married, at twenty, an older, divorced actor, Drewe Henley, and they had a son, Charley, in 1973. But the marriage broke down painfully. She had an affair with the writer Robert Bolt, then married the Texan-born theatre director Michael Rudman in 1983. By this time she was a big name. Quite apart from *The Good Life*, she starred in Ayckbourn's *The Norman Conquests*, played opposite Gielgud, was a striking Viola in a BBC TV *Twelfth Night* (1980), and played Desdemona to Scofield's Othello around the same time as *On the Razzle*. Just after *Hapgood*, she was Beatrice in *Much Ado* with Alan Bates, starred in *Ivanov* and played Ariadne Utterword in Shaw's *Heartbreak House*, with Scofield and Vanessa Redgrave.

She and Stoppard had many affinities. Their childhood in India was a strong bond, and her account of hers, in *White Cargo* (written towards the end of their relationship), shows how much her experiences influenced his version of India in *Indian Ink*. Like him she was very committed to her sons and involved with her family. After she married Michael Rudman, she converted to Judaism, his faith: Stoppard wrote her a poem to mark the event.

Her approach to theatre tied in with his. She was not a Method School actor who went in for psychological immersion in the character. She believed in attention, hard work, observation and linguistic rigour. Gossip columns played up her glamour and allure: 'Saucy, sassy and so sexy' was the headline in the *Daily Express* when the columnist William Hickey listed her as a 'national treasure'. But under that public display she was disciplined, impatient of fools and extremely tough. She needed to be. The break-up of her first marriage was followed by tensions in her second. In 1984 she suffered the tragic early death of her sister Jennifer – a death which inspired the lost sister of *Indian Ink*. Both her parents died, too, in the years when she was with Stoppard, her father after several years of being paralysed by strokes.

She was brought up in a household of two actors who constantly see-sawed between talking about their work and family life. That kind of companionship was very familiar to her. All her affairs and marriages were with people 'in the business'. While she and Stoppard were partners, they were able to be completely professional with each other in rehearsals. Colleagues never felt he was treating her differently from the other actors. It was easy for her to move from a good working relationship to finding (in her phrase) 'comfort in the friendship'. He said, wryly, looking back: 'We were attracted to each other when we did *Jumpers* . . . and *unprecedentedly*, in the case of actors and writers and directors working together, we sort of fell in love.' Certainly there was a determined flirtation going on. According to a reliable source, she would send him Kendal mint cakes, asking if he fancied one. She was an enticing and seductive person, and it was nice to be falling in love again.

Getting to know him intimately in the middle of his life, she found him not only attractive, but also kind and loyal, with a very fast brain, and a 'tremendous sense of humour'. 'He likes himself. He's not a discontented person . . . He enjoys everything about being who he is.' She was aware, though, that niceness was not the whole story. She knew that he was aware of the effect he had on others. She saw that there was a very strong will under the charming, benign exterior, and that the impeccable manners were his form of armour. There was nothing in the world he wouldn't do for the people closest to him, especially his sons. But she also found him self-protective and reserved. In rehearsals he was charming and funny, but 'completely stubborn'. 'This is what is going to happen' was his attitude, 'and I'm not going to *please* you.' 'Of course you must tell me,' he said to one actor, 'I will listen to all your suggestions . . . and then I will do what I want.' He didn't want actors to be nervous of him – but she thought that he liked a little bit of awe.

He fell in love with her through their professional closeness. As an actor, he thought her deeply serious about the discipline of theatre, as well as being a brilliant comedienne. She knew how to perform 'his kind of stuff'. She had an inborn gift for timing. She understood wit and comedy. She cared about language. Now she was playing the most powerful woman's part he had written so far, created with her in mind. It was an irony of the situation, and an example of how imaginative writing works, that Miriam also recognised some of her own qualities in this character.

During the rehearsals for *Hapgood*, Stoppard did a long interview (in the rented flat) with Shusha Guppy for the *Paris Review*. These interviews are meant to give a definitive, vivid portrayal of a major writer caught at a particular point in their life. He talked a lot about *Hapgood*, because he was in the middle of it. Towards the end of the interview, Guppy tried to get through his polite defences:

Interviewer: It is often said that a writer's output is the product of psychosis, of self-examination. Is there any indication of this in your case?
Stoppard: You tell me!

It is a typical response. He did not think of his plays as confessional. All the same, *Hapgood* came out of a time of doubleness in his life, and secrets, double lives and conflicts of interests are at the heart of the play.

He had been thinking about it for several years. At the end of 1986, he described it in a letter to his mother. The new play was a sort of spy thriller, and had taken him a long time to work out. He would have done it sooner if he were any good at plots. 'I've ended up with a plot which is quite preposterous so I'm fairly nervous about the whole enterprise.' He had read three John Le Carré novels for the play – 'all extremely good'. He

had stolen all Le Carré's jargon, so 'I hope he didn't invent it'. He himself
was not particularly interested in spies, 'it was just a way of getting something off the ground, but as it turned out, the plot which I thought was
merely a necessary excuse for the play is turning out to be most of the
play'. The letter went on to describe the boys' rugby games at Caldicott and
the team that Ed had captained for the last time, before going to Stowe: 'I
must say I'm mad about all 15 of them, and feel very sad that it's all over
now.' This reads like a deviation from *Hapgood*, but it isn't. In other letters
home about the play, he tells them that it is named after the main character: he was 'off' clever titles. He mentions that it had to be delayed because
of Kendal's pregnancy; that he had hoped John Wood would play the spymaster, but the part has gone to Nigel Hawthorne; and that he hesitates
to send them a copy because it has one character (Hapgood's delinquent
'twin sister') who swears a lot. His mother didn't like swearing. These letters point to some of the challenges of *Hapgood*, which at every stage was
a difficult project. But he knew what he wanted it to do, and had a strong
idea for it.

He had been reading about mathematics over the last couple of years.
That led him on to a fascination with quantum physics, and he read in
and around the subject with the same kind of autodidactic excitement
that he might bring to reading about Wittgenstein, or eighteenth-century
landscape gardening, or Greek poetry. How could such complex specialist
subjects be harnessed to a dramatic, entertaining plot and also provide a
way of thinking about human behaviour?

He already had an interest in the physics of coin-flipping, Euclidean
geometry and astronomy. And he was fascinated by what followed from
the point when classical physics, with its certainties and fixed viewpoints,
gave way to the counter-intuitive doubleness and relativism of quantum
physics. 'For centuries mathematics was considered the queen of the
sciences because it claimed certainty . . . But then . . . the mathematics of
physics turned out to be grounded on *uncertainties*, on probability and
chance. And if you're me, you think – there's a play in that.'

He read the kind of accessible books on quantum mechanics 'which
any first-year physics student is familiar with'. He sat up all night at Iver

Grove with Ollie, who had been doing physics at Bristol, using him as a sounding board. Ollie, looking back, was affectionately accurate about the limits of his father's expertise: 'You can be interested in physics, but you don't actually know anything about it if you haven't got the maths, I'm afraid . . . He couldn't integrate an equation, if you see what I mean.' Ollie was as humorous about this as his father might have been: 'It's like telling a folk singer they're not Mozart. No, they're not, but that doesn't mean they shouldn't sing folk songs.' He was very touched that, in gratitude for his help, *Hapgood* was dedicated to him.

Talking to Ollie was just the start of it. He read the legendary American physicist Richard Feynman's 1964 Cornell lectures, *The Character of Physical Law*, especially the one called 'Probability and Uncertainty: the Quantum Mechanical View of Nature'. That gave him the basis for the speeches in *Hapgood* about physics – sometimes almost word for word. He read J. C. Polkinghorne's 1984 *The Quantum World*, and, as usual going to the horse's mouth for information, he asked Dr Polkinghorne to read an early version of the play. Bits of their correspondence were published in the first *Hapgood* programme. He read about Heisenberg's uncertainty principle, and he read John Gribbins's *In Search of Schrödinger's Cat*. (A hypothetical cat, enclosed in a steel box with a Geiger device that could trigger the release of a toxic acid, is, by the rules of quantum mechanics, both dead and alive until the box is opened to discover the result. The cat gets a mention in the play.) He was gripped by the counter-intuitive behaviour of subatomic particles, which Feynman describes in terms of impossibility and unpredictability:

> We know how electrons and light behave. But what can I call it? If I
> say they behave like particles I give the wrong impression; also if I
> say they behave like waves. They behave in their own inimitable way,
> which technically could be called the quantum mechanical way. They
> behave in a way that is like nothing that you have ever seen before.

Science can be mystifying, says Feynman: 'How can it be like that?' we ask of it. It teaches us that 'the future is unpredictable'. To put it another way: 'Quantum mechanics describes the interaction of particles at a sub-atomic level, where the "common sense" rules of classical mechanics no longer apply.'

Stoppard loved the fact that the language of quantum physics could involve mystery and wonder. He put a Feynman quotation about that in the *Hapgood* programme. It was a rather baffling clue for an audience with, quite possibly, no background in physics, reading the programme before the play began:

> We choose to examine a phenomenon which is impossible, *absolutely*
> impossible, to explain in any classical way, and which has in it
> the heart of quantum mechanics. In reality it contains the *only*
> mystery . . . Any other situation in quantum mechanics, it turns out,
> can always be explained by saying, 'You remember the case of the
> experiment with the two holes? It's the same thing.'

Stoppard said in his letter to Polkinghorne that it was the difficulty in 'reconciling the mathematical language with a commonsensical view of what is *possible*' which filled him with amazement.

At the heart of quantum theory is Heisenberg's uncertainty principle: 'When measuring the position and momentum of an electron, one can determine either the position or the momentum but not both. The act of measuring one quality affects the other quality, and thus one gets different results based on which quality is measured first.' 'The act of observing alters the results,' as in what Feynman calls 'the case of the experiment with the two holes'. In Feynman's words: 'You can't invent an apparatus which can determine which hole the electron passes through that won't at the same time disturb the electron enough to destroy the interference patterns.'

The experiment Feynman is referring to demonstrates 'the dual nature of light, which can behave either as waves or as particles, depending on how it is observed.' Stoppard, in his *Paris Review* interview, calls the 'wave/particle duality of light' the most familiar example of 'the mystery which lies in the foundation of the observable world'. Here is the experiment described in detail:

If sub-atomic material (ie., light) is shot through two holes and against a light-sensitive recording device, a wave pattern will form on that backdrop, revealing that the material is functioning holistically like a wave. However, if we closely 'watch' the material as it is being shot through the two holes, the material will generate particle patterns, revealing that this same material is now behaving like particles passing discretely through the two separate holes . . . [This is] the strange particle behaviour that is the cornerstone of quantum physics. The crucial point is that in the subatomic world, two sets of characteristics – wave and particle behaviour – can simultaneously inhere in the same entity.

The scientist who provides the explanations in the play puts it more simply:

Kerner: Every time we don't look, we get wave pattern. Every time we look to see how we get wave pattern we get particle pattern. The act of observing determines what's what.
Blair: How?
Kerner: Nobody knows. Somehow light is continuous and also discontinuous. The experimenter makes the choice. You get what you interrogate for.

This is a central image for the play. But quantum physics is not the *subject* of *Hapgood*, as philosophy was, to an extent, the subject of *Jumpers*, or language was the subject of *Dogg's Our Pet*. Here, the science works as a useful extended metaphor, or parallel, rather like football in *Professional Foul*. *Hapgood* is a complicated Cold War spy thriller: *Tinker, Tailor, Soldier, Spy* with added physics. 'The language of espionage', he thought, was a perfect fit for the duality of quantum mechanics.

He had been interested in double agents for a long time. As in *The Dog It Was That Died*, his 1982 radio play, he was drawn to the absurd or tragic predicament of the double or triple agent who had been 'turned' so often he can barely remember why or what for. Purvis, in *The Dog It*

Was That Died, says: 'I've forgotten who is my primary employer and who my secondary . . . the side I was actually working for . . . got lost.' Kerner, *Hapgood*'s physicist-spy, echoes him: 'Frankly, I can't remember which side I'm supposed to be working for, and it is not in fact necessary for me to know.' Purvis and Kerner are contrasted to a British spymaster, in both plays called Blair (a name then with no political associations!), for whom everything is either/or, us or them, cut and dried.

As in *The Dog It Was That Died*, however ruthless, opportunist and grotesque the activities of the Western intelligence operatives may be, they are working in the interests of a preferable system. Englishness – here in the shape of public school education, small boys playing rugby, rule-breaking, eccentricity and linguistic richness – is worth defending. The earlier version of the play is more explicit about this, when Hapgood says, of her son's public school education: 'I like all that manners maketh man stuff, and competition and talking properly and being magnanimous in victory and defeat.' *Hapgood* is not a political play in the same way as *Every Good Boy* or *Professional Foul*, but Kerner, the double agent, speaks for his author when he says (as Stoppard often said): 'The West is morally superior, in my opinion. It is unjust and corrupt like the East, of course, but here it means the system has failed; at home it means the system is working.'

Writing a Cold War spy thriller towards the end of the 1980s was timely, though it felt familiar, even then, rather than thrillingly new. One of *Hapgood*'s problems is that because of its context it has dated – unlike, say, *Travesties* or *Rosencrantz*. Reagan's controversial Strategic Defence Initiative, the anti-ballistic missile system intended as a defence against Soviet attacks – known, not affectionately, as Star Wars – had been launched in 1983. It involved research, funded by the US Air Force, into the physics of anti-matter. By the early 1990s it had become discredited and was abandoned – though its supporters argued that it had helped to bring about the end (then) of the Cold War.

This historical moment gave the play a Soviet double agent who is a quantum physicist researching particle-beam weapons for the Star Wars project, close links between MI5 and the CIA, and a definite trace of

Margaret Thatcher in the character of Hapgood. She is the single, powerful, managerial woman in an organisation surrounded by men. (In an early version, she has a female secretary, Madge, but this was changed to an unflappable young male assistant, Maggs, so that Hapgood would be the only woman on stage.) It was a bold reversal of thriller conventions to have his key operator not be a George Smiley or an Alec Leamas, but a young, attractive, single woman with a sex life and an illegitimate child.

Hapgood, a dauntingly effective intelligence operator, can act her way out of any predicament, play chess in her head while decrypting coded messages, fake a double identity, break the rules of the organisation, shoot a target, memorise any sequence of events on a mental grid, instantly grasp the most complicated of counterplots, and make a perfect cup of tea. She also has her vulnerabilities and desires. She is involved in different ways with all the men in the play. She has had an affair with the Russian scientist-agent, Joseph Kerner, while she was 'turning' him, and has had a son by him, now twelve. She has always kept her son's parentage secret, and has sacrificed their relationship to her job. She is an object of desire for Ridley, the rough, young, reckless, dubious gangster of the organisation. She is in love with Blair, the urbane, conservative spymaster. She arouses baffled admiration from the hard-nosed American CIA agent Wates. And she would give her life for her son Joe, an endearing, rugby-mad English public schoolboy who doesn't know he has a Russian spy for a father.

Joseph Kerner – 'Joseph K', caught in the Kafkaesque mirror-world of Cold War espionage – alien, homesick, a man of imagination and melancholy, is at the moral heart of the play, and the character closest to his author. As a foreign second-language speaker, he waxes enthusiastic on the British jargon of espionage – 'Safe house, sleeper, cover, joe . . . I love it' – which Stoppard so relished in Le Carré's novels. (He would soon be working with Le Carré on a film, *The Russia House*, and becoming a friend, but Le Carré remained politely silent on the subject of *Hapgood*.) One of Kerner's main roles in the play is to explain the parallels between quantum physics and spying. Whenever he talks about wave/particle theory or electrons, he's really talking about what's happening in the world of double agents.

Kerner: The particle world is the dream world of the intelligence officer. An electron can be here or there at the same moment. You can choose. It can go from here to there without going in between; it can pass through two doors at the same time, or from one door to another by a path which is there for all to see until someone looks, and then the act of looking has made it take a different path . . . It defeats surveillance because when you know what it's doing you can't be certain where it is, and when you know where it is you can't be certain what it's doing . . .

Different kinds of language clash in *Hapgood*: the language of science, the jargon of the espionage world, tough-talking American CIA lingo, public school slang, British euphemisms, chess talk, and a human language of love and desire. Stoppard enjoys mixing this kind of thing – 'Ma'am, this is a 500 millisecond-repeat transponder-transmitter locked on seventeen megahertz with a lithium battery and a gate interruptor' – with Hapgood's tender phone calls to her son about his guinea pig or his rugby boots. There is a constant to-and-fro between what is 'personal' and what is professional or technical. There's a startling contrast between the language of Hapgood the formidably controlled manager, and Hapgood's 'twin', sloppy, shouty and sweary. There are good jokes about linguistic misunderstandings – Kerner's misuse of English jargon, or the bafflement of the American at what in English counts as friendly usage:

Wates: She calls me Wates.
Blair: It's a sort of compliment.
Wates: It doesn't sound friendly.
Blair: Mister wouldn't be friendly.
Wates: You call me Ben.
Blair: That's another sort of compliment.
Wates: She doesn't call me Ben.
Blair: That would be friendly but not necessarily a compliment.
Wates: She calls you Paul.
Blair: Yes, but we're friends.

Wates: Can you explain this in some way I'd understand it?
(Blair *considers the question.*)
Blair: No, I don't think so.
Wates: You guys.

Kerner's scientific explanations have some of the most romantic language in the play:

> I could put an atom into your hand for every second since the world
> began and you would have to squint to see the dot of atoms in your
> palm. So now make a fist, and if your fist is as big as the nucleus of one
> atom then the atom is as big as St Paul's . . . Every atom is a cathedral.

That comparison is a loaded one. The mystery of quantum physics lets in the possibility of God: 'Who needed God', says Kerner, 'when everything worked like billiard balls?' *Hapgood* has a tightly controlled plot in which everyone seems gridded onto their operational path. But in fact it is random, messy, bewildering and open-ended, and includes in its grimly realistic universe the possibility of religious belief, changes of heart, and even of happy endings.

From the start we're in a world which seems highly organised but is also extremely confusing. Double and triple agents are passing secrets of scientific research about Star Wars to the KGB. An MI5-style British counter-intelligence unit has a mole in it. Almost everyone is under suspicion, and a sequence of scams and staged encounters is set up to reveal the traitor. The play begins in a London swimming pool with a rapid, balletic mime accompanied (in the first production) by Bach's Suite in G Minor. There are four cubicles, there is a CIA agent on watch, and Hapgood, as it turns out, is concealed inside a shower cubicle under an umbrella, from where she will emerge fully dressed, bone dry and poised for action. Russian and British agents, Kerner and Ridley, come rapidly and bewilderingly in and out, swapping towels and briefcases, going to the pool and returning. How many of them are there? Who is tracking whom? It is like a pastiche of a spy movie. It is also meant to represent the movement of electrons.

('An electron can be here or there at the same moment.') But the audience cannot possibly know this.

Nor can they know that the stage direction requires a location which is 'variously circumnavigable in a way which will later recall, if not replicate, the problem of the bridges of Königsberg'. (Kerner, originally a citizen of Königsberg, like Kant, will explain that there are seven bridges criss-crossing its river, and the inhabitants have a game of trying to cross them all without crossing any of them twice: an insoluble problem until you realise that you need two walkers.) If you happen to be a quantum physicist, you might realise straight away that 'the first scene is a witty representation of the two-slit experiment'. But for most of the audience, as Stoppard said, 'as in other plays I've written, the first scene is supposed to be virtually incomprehensible . . . for ten minutes, it's just sort of "Hellzapoppin"'. That's sort of a mannerism of mine. Then you clear it up and begin to explain it.' Before long, we grasp that the key to the scene – and to the whole play – is that there are twins involved. There are two Russians, and there are two Ridleys. Later, there will seem to be two Hapgoods. Twins are like double agents; and twins are like electrons. Each one can be its own alibi.

The challenge was to make the plot clear while keeping up the suspense. Understanding the plot turned out to be as much of a struggle for the actors as for the audience. He had to write a long 'Hapgood Crib' to explain it. It shows a logical mind intently at work – and also shows that he is quite happy not to know everything about his characters. Their back-stories are obscure to him.

> Twelve years ago the Russians put Kerner in as a sleeper, i.e. someone who pretends to defect and can be reactivated later, perhaps years later, as a spy . . . Hapgood, aged 26, has the job of debriefing Kerner. She breaks his story and turns him into someone who is prepared to work for the British. At least that is her perception . . . During these months of debriefing Hapgood falls for Kerner and conceives Joe . . . The identity of the child's father is suppressed . . . as the child's father Kerner would have lost his credibility as an 'authentic' Russian

sleeper, and therefore his usefulness as a British double. But . . . my own assumption about Hapgood is that by the time the child was born the love affair was well over . . . Hapgood has carried a torch for Blair for years – possibly the Kerner episode was merely an interruption of that . . .

The crib goes on to explain how a leak has been discovered coming from Kerner's lab – or Hapgood's office – and how the meet at the pool, designed to catch the spy, goes badly wrong. Who is giving real secrets to the Russians, who has opened the briefcase, who has taken the planted roll of film? Blair suspects Kerner (rightly, as it turns out), Wates suspects Ridley and Hapgood, and Hapgood and Kerner (also rightly) suspect Ridley. He has to be flushed out. Hapgood, Kerner and Blair act out a scene to make Ridley believe that Kerner is the traitor, that Joe has been kidnapped and that the only way of rescuing the boy is to restage the scene at the pool, so that the Russians will release Joe in exchange for real infor- mation. Then Hapgood, to deceive Ridley and to enable her to be in two places at once (and to give a juicy acting opportunity to Kendal), pretends to be her own twin sister, a delinquent, promiscuous character who seems to be the exact opposite of the Hapgood we know. Finally the scene at the pool is returned to, the two Hapgoods are revealed to be one person, and the twin Ridleys are fatally exposed. (*Hapgood*, as he noted, is the only one of his plays in which a character is shot on stage.) But still nothing is solved. In a melancholy coda, we learn that Kerner was a sleeper after all, and may go back to Moscow; and Hapgood, who has been personally betrayed by Blair, is going to leave the service. What is the good of the service any more, in any case? The Cold War is coming to an end, and any clear-cut idea of 'us and them' is blurring and fading. That is what these characters and their author thought in the late 1980s.

Kerner reads a lot of spy thrillers, but he wishes they could be more like scientific experiments, where the problem is revealed at the start. 'I don't understand this mania for surprises . . . In science . . . what is interesting is to know what is happening . . . First, here is what we will find; now here is how we find it.' As Stoppard says of the play: 'In a normal spy thriller you contrive to delude the reader until all is revealed in the dénouement. This is the exact opposite of a scientific paper . . . *Hapgood* . . . is not a whodunnit because we are told who has done it near the beginning of the first act, so the story becomes *how* he did it.' We learn early on that Ridley is the traitor and that he has a twin. Then we are shown why and how. It interested Stoppard to find that although the audience knows that they are watching a series of fake scenes intended to expose Ridley, they still get sucked in and find themselves in suspense. Like the characters in the play, the audience is in a double state of mind.

But it rapidly became an irritant to him that the plot was obscuring what really interested him in the play. His Hapgood Crib concluded: 'To be blunt, I don't think that the mechanics of the plot bear scrutiny at all and I don't think that they ever will. The trouble is they don't remotely interest me, they're just a necessary nuisance to provide the opportunity to write about this woman who in Blair's words is "a sort of double".' In another memo, he wrote: 'Spare me a critique of this plot. The play is about dualities and uncertainties and about two people pretending to be one person and one person pretending to be two people, and a cartload of such things, and was perforce written in the hope that we would keep our eye on the cart rather than on the tottering five-legged horse behind it.'

Central to the play, he said, was 'the proposition that in each of our characters . . . the person who gets up in the morning and puts on the clothes is the working majority of a dual personality, part of which is always there in a submerged state . . . Inside Hapgood One there is a Hapgood Two sharing the same body; and that goes for most of us.' In a radio interview with Kate Kellaway, he said: 'We all of us have . . . a Stoppard Two and a Kellaway Two who emerge under pressure.' 'It's not really a dual personality,' he told another interviewer. 'It's just that one chooses to "be" one part of oneself, and not another part of oneself. One has a public self and a submerged self.' Is one real, the other false? he was asked. 'No, they're both part of the whole person.'

The theme is spelt out by the Eastern European character Kerner, in a speech which echoes lines in Havel's *The Garden Party*: 'We all are a little bit what we were yesterday and a little bit what we are today; and also a little bit we're not these things . . . so that none of us entirely is and at the same time each one of us is not entirely . . .'

> Kerner: We're all doubles . . . We're not so one-or-the-other. The one who puts on the clothes in the morning is the working majority, but at night – perhaps in the moment before unconsciousness – we meet our sleeper – the priest is visited by the doubter, the Marxist sees the civilising force of the bourgeoisie, the captain of industry admits the justice of common ownership.
> Blair: And you – what do you admit?
> Kerner: My estrangement.

Hapgood is different to different people, and they all call her by different names ('Mother', Mrs Hapgood, Betty, Elizabeth, Lilichka, Yelizaveta, Mummy, Celia Newton or 'Auntie' when she is being her twin sister). She separates the personal and the professional, but they keep overlapping. Her formidably controlled professional self shows glimpses of a rule-breaking, anarchic streak. When she pretends to be her twin, her delinquent self takes charge, and she can lose her inhibitions and be Ridley's lover. Ridley is a tough, gung-ho killer, but he wants Hapgood and will put the safety of her son over the espionage game. 'Be yourself,' he tells her, at their last moment together: but it isn't so easy. Blair is careful and rule-bound, but will put her son at risk and set personal involvement aside in the interests of the organisation. Even Joe the schoolboy has a secret strain of melancholy – perhaps to do with fatherlessness, we don't know: 'Once when he was really little, he got unhappy about something, he was crying, he couldn't tell me what it was, he didn't *know* what it was, and he said, "The thing is, Mummy, I've been unhappy for *years*."' Kerner is so doubled he no longer knows which self he is: caught between countries, allegiances and languages, he is also a father who can't know his own son and a lover who lost his moral compass, because 'there is something terrible about love. It uses up all one's moral judgement.'

Doubleness had always preoccupied him. From the time when he was splitting himself between Brennus and Stoppard, or inventing the split selves of Rosencrantz and Guildenstern, or the prisoner and jailor in *The Gamblers*, or Birdboot and Moon in *The Real Inspector Hound*, to the double identities of Ruth and 'Ruth' in *Night and Day*, twin selves were built into his view of human nature. Later there would be the two Housmans in *The Invention of Love*, and his alternative life as Jan in *Rock 'n' Roll*.

He spoke of his own doubleness quite often. If he were writing a book about himself, he thought it would be the obvious thing to talk about. He played down the split between being Czech and being English, or the doubleness involved in being in love. That would have been too revealing. But he admitted to other kinds of doubleness. In a 1988 interview, he described himself as 'a very emotional person. People wish to perceive me as someone who works out ideas in a cool, dispassionate way but I don't think that's my personality at all.' And he called himself 'a modest person hiding a proud person, I suppose'. When he told his mother that he was going to call *Hapgood* after the main character simply because he was 'off' clever titles, he was not telling her the whole story. The name carried two selves inside it. 'Happy and Good, perhaps. Or Happenstance. Perhapsgood.'

'Getting *Hapgood* ready was exhausting and frustrating,' Stoppard told Shusha Guppy. 'It has as many scene changes, light cues, sounds cues, etc, as a musical.' There were other problems too. Kendal had come back to work too soon after giving birth, and was exhausted and finding it difficult to concentrate. She was worried about letting him and the others down. Rehearsals were not easy, and 'not as much fun' as usual. Peter Wood was frustrated. He kept asking Stoppard to explain the plot more clearly but – he said later, with some bitterness – 'the day had passed when he listened'. The out-of-town run, before the play opened in April 1988 at the Aldwych, in a too-large theatre in Wimbledon, went badly. There were technical glitches. Word began to get around that the play was 'difficult'. Stoppard kept on rewriting and changing things around. Three acts became two. The revisions and notes to the actors were endless. Roger Rees, as Kerner, and Kendal were both used to this, but she still found it challenging. And she could see that Nigel Hawthorne (who had been cast as Blair mainly because of his brilliantly urbane civil servant in *Yes, Minister*) was unhappy. He was not used to the playwright coming in night after night and saying, 'could you do this in a different way'. There was a disastrous company call at the Wimbledon Theatre during the previews. Kendal was lying down throughout, feeling wretched. She had wrenched her shoulder (from playing a scene where Ridley deliberately injures Hapgood), and she had flu. Hawthorne was having what she described as a 'tizzyfit'. Peter Wood issued a directive to the author. 'Tom: you cannot rewrite any more.' Kendal went to rest in her dressing room, between the matinee and the evening performance. And under her door came a piece of paper in Stoppard's familiar writing, which read: 'You don't have to do this if you don't want, but if you're up to it I wonder if you could try these lines.'

Changes went on all through the Aldwych run. A few months in, Stoppard wrote a note to Hawthorne and Rees, telling them that he thought their first scene together (which takes place in the zoo) had become 'too much about reactions' and not enough about the physics. 'The balance between exposition and exhibition of "character" has changed.' This was the last straw for Hawthorne. He sent him a long, angry, handwritten letter that night from his dressing room. 'You are now asking us to reduce the degree of humanity and by doing so, your contention is that the scene will be easier to follow. I would have thought the opposite to be the case . . . You seem to be advocating the sacrifice of relationship to theories . . . It makes the play an absolute bugger to perform night after night.' He understood that Felicity was 'frequently instructed to make Hapgood less approachable. Stricter and colder,' while he was being told to make Blair 'harder and more ruthless'. He did not like the way things were being handled. 'Any thought of the four of us [Stoppard, Hawthorne, Wood and Kendal] working as a "team" went out of the window yonks ago.' He had been confused when he first read the play, but he had thought it would all come clear in rehearsals. But they were the 'least creative rehearsals I've ever attended. They were dominated by you and Peter who were playing games with the cast to see how much of the play they understood.' He was angry at being patronised. He refused to be thought of as 'a mindless actor'. He concluded: 'I love you as a man and puzzle that the warmth you give out so constantly and effortlessly is excluded from your plays.'

Stoppard was understandably nervous about *Hapgood*'s fortunes. Wood's production had some thrilling moments, particularly its opening (a big back-projected map of London which opens out into closer and closer detail as a red dot moves around it in pursuit of the suspect), and its design for the scene at the zoo, with two giraffes which look as if their necks emerge from one body. Roger Rees was a delicate, magnetic Kerner. The expression of 'spellbound joy and agony' on his face as he listened silently on the phone to the voice of his son, who does not know him, was a particularly beautiful moment. And Kendal, for all her exhaustion, was exciting and dynamic in 'her' part. Stoppard was particularly pleased with the young actor who played Ridley, Iain Glen, almost straight out of drama school. When he read for the part, Stoppard at once recognised that he had the right 'body language'. Codron and Wood wanted to carry on auditioning, but he said no: 'It's over, there's no question.' That was always his favourite example of a moment when he intervened in the casting and felt he had got it exactly right.

There were high levels of expectation for his first new stage play for six years. One critic likened it to 'the theatrical equivalent of the launch of a new British car'. As Michael Billington left the Aldwych on the press night, a woman behind him said to him, 'How is your physics?' That set the tone for the play's reception. There were a few enthusiasts: Ronald Hayman, reviewing it for BBC Radio 4's *Kaleidoscope* programme, was sympathetic, enjoying it as part of Stoppard's 'Theatre of Audacity'. Billington said it was baffling and fascinating and made the audience 'work like blazes'. But most reviewers were exasperated: 'exposition at the expense of emotion', 'a surprising lack of theatricality'. Irving Wardle in *The Times* was particularly dismissive. 'It comes across as a bright idea which has laboriously to be harnessed into shape, and which generates precious little in the way of dramatic action.' It 'made the audience feel stupid', and ended with 'crashing sentimentality'. Friends wrote kind, even enthusiastic letters, but were often puzzled. He was depressed and defensive about the play's reception: 'It's been written about as though it were incomprehensibly baffling . . . My impression is that your ordinary punter has less trouble with it than some of our critics.' But plenty of people came out saying, 'I'm none the wiser.'

As Manny Azenberg said: 'The audience is ready to kill him.' A rumour circulated that he had been found in tears after the opening night, saying 'I can't remember how to write plays any more.' *Hapgood* ran for its allotted six months at the Aldwych, and Codron was quite pleased with the audience figures, but it won no awards. The view settled in that it was a hopeless flop, his first big failure since *Rosencrantz* had made him famous twenty-two years before.

The reception of *Hapgood* harshly exposed the issue of 'difficulty' which ran all through his writing life. With *Jumpers*, or *Travesties*, 'difficulty' was received as 'brilliance'. Audiences felt flattered and excited by being asked to keep pace with the wit and brio and verbosity of those plays, even if they didn't understand every word. But going along with the acclaim for brilliance went accusations of heartlessness and unintelligibility. That 'too clever by half' label, which *The Real Thing* had mostly done away with, came back with *Hapgood*.

'I'm not trying to make the plays difficult, God help me,' he would say. 'Nobody could think that one would just be mischievous or perverse and try to make life hard for the audience.' But it was his nature to be allusive, intellectual and demanding. He was a playwright of ideas who also wanted his audiences to love him. He liked carrying out 'thought-experiments' on stage, like a scientist or a philosopher, and seducing audiences into going along with those experiments through laughter, excitement and surprise. He *wanted* to put them under the pressure to work it out for themselves as it went along. That was part of their enjoyment. He often said that the sound of laughter is the sound of comprehension, and, also, 'the sound of people congratulating themselves. If the joke had been made that much easier, you wouldn't get the laugh – they'd have nothing to say "Well done!" about.'

Hapgood was thought of by many as a failure – though in his view it was a kind of success. But it led him on to using scientific theory in another kind of play, which endeared itself much more to the audience. The relative failure of *Hapgood* paved the way for the great triumph of *Arcadia*.

Before that, the immediate challenge was getting *Hapgood* to America. Peter Wood's production, with Roger Rees alone remaining from the original cast, went to the enormous Doolittle Theater in Los Angeles (with Judy Davis as Hapgood), and to the Geary Theater in San Francisco, in the spring of 1989. Then the play was put on by A.C.T. Theatre in Seattle, in a new production, in the autumn of 1990. But there was no transfer to Broadway, and it took another four years for *Hapgood* to go to New York.

Stoppard rewrote the play extensively for its first American transfer. Peter Wood persuaded him to put in a fifteen-minute speech, after the mime scene at the pool, giving the audience the back-story and explaining the action. It was delivered by Wates, in his tough, gun-slinging prose, as if debriefing an audience of FBI listeners, with slides of all the characters coming up on a screen behind him. 'Okay, I'm Wates,' it begins, 'and you want to know what the hell is going on and why and so forth.' Stoppard thought this was 'a frightful idea' and hated compromising his play in this way, and the 'interminable and unendurable' speech did not survive for long. It didn't do the play much good, in any case. The previews were not too bad, but the Los Angeles subscription audience – 'completely packed houses of sullenly silent southern Californians', as one critic put it – had paid for the entire season in order to get tickets for *Phantom of the Opera*, and were not expecting, or wanting, anything like this.

Hapgood eventually arrived in New York, at the Lincoln Center, in November 1994, by a lucky combination of circumstances. Since working with him on *The Real Thing*, Manny Azenberg had wanted to bring Stoppard together with the director Jack O'Brien. A remarkable and versatile director, O'Brien, then in his mid-fifties, had started his theatre work young, at Michigan (where his mentors were Tyrone Guthrie and the actor-director Ellis Rabb) and on Broadway in the 1960s. He could turn his hand to anything, whether it was big musicals (*Porgy and Bess*, *Into the Woods*, *Hairspray* in 2002), or Shakespeare, or modern drama: Thornton Wilder, William Saroyan, August Wilson. Since 1981 he had been the artistic director of the San Diego Old Globe Theatre, where he stayed until 2007, with many forays onto Broadway and into opera, radio and TV. He had had hopes, in 1989, of doing *Hapgood* at the Old Globe, and Azenberg had introduced him to Stoppard in New York at an awkward meeting where O'Brien, in awe, had pretended to know something about fishing in order to impress him. Then he had tried to get the rights for *Rough Crossing*, without success. After these non-starters, there was a stroke of luck. The American star Stockard Channing – whom Stoppard could easily imagine as Hapgood – was starring in John Guare's play *Six Degrees of Separation* at the Royal Court, in the summer of 1992. Boldly, he took a copy of *Hapgood* to the theatre and asked her if she would be interested in doing it in New York. He told her it was his 'loose tooth play', the one that had gone missing. She said yes, but on condition that the director should be Jack O'Brien, with whom she had worked before. It would be put on by André Bishop at the Lincoln Center, in the Mitzi Newhouse Theater. Stoppard knew that O'Brien had wanted to do *Hapgood* in San Diego and would have liked to do *Rough Crossing*, so he began their working relationship with a feeling of guilty compunction – a familiar emotion for him. At their first meeting at the Lincoln Center, he presented O'Brien with an enormous glossy art book. 'I know this is a bit naff,' he said, 'but I'm going to give it to you anyway.' O'Brien, who had never heard the word 'naff' before, was tickled pink. Awe and admiration were mixed up at once with delighted affection: they were going to be friends for life.

An effusive, open, emotional character, O'Brien says of Stoppard: 'When I look at him I see one of the most fascinating, compelling, sexy human beings in the world . . . one of the most attractive human beings alive.' He thought everything about him, including his brain and his love of language, was 'deeply erotic'. And eroticism was the key to what O'Brien brought to the plays. He often thought that the British productions of Stoppard's work were too cerebral and austere. He wanted to direct his plays for passion, sex, human interest, relationships, 'blood'. He wrote to Stoppard:

> It's not the machinations of the plot that attracts me; it's the characters . . . I love this play because I feel very strongly for them all: the poor bastards, they are not unlike us, striving in spite of an enormously involving work ethic, intense and completely dangerous, to have some semblance of a life . . . I'd trim out anything that doesn't build the tension, relate to the relationships . . . basically, Tom, I found the play 'sexy'.

The science was 'a bit of a blur' to him, but Stoppard reassured him: 'I know you don't know what it's about, but it's not that difficult.' O'Brien had time for a crash course from Stoppard in quantum physics before rehearsals began, as Channing was making a film. 'I could remember enough to do the play,' O'Brien said. 'I got it for about two or three months.' But it wasn't the physics that fired up this production, it was the human situation. Azenberg felt the same about this as O'Brien: 'waves, particles, who cares!' What mattered in the play, in Azenberg's view, was the story of a mother protecting her child.

Stoppard chopped and changed the play, cutting about twenty minutes off the running time, greatly simplifying the science and making the plot clearer. He took to calling it a 'new-fashioned melodrama', because 'it operates on a heightened, slightly implausible level of life'. He was closely involved, as always, with rehearsals. After the first run-through of Act One, O'Brien nervously asked him what he thought, and he said, caustically, 'Well, aside from the fact that the *four wrong people* are in the room, I think it's fine.' It was a lesson to O'Brien on how witheringly sharp he could be, and he set to work to get the actors to be more like the people Stoppard had in mind. He got his close friend the jazz artist Bob James to write an evocative, catchy score for the production, and teamed up with the designer Bob Crowley, who had just had a great success designing Nicholas Hytner's National Theatre production of *Carousel*. It was Crowley's first collaboration with O'Brien and with Stoppard, and this too became a firm alliance. On the revolving stage of the Mitzi Newhouse, Crowley gave *Hapgood* a realistically bureaucratic set, crowded with filing cabinets and office furniture.

Stoppard reassured André Bishop, who was worrying about whether the audience would get it: 'Don't worry, it will all become clear.' All the same, Stockard Channing would come off stage on some nights saying, 'It's like Stonehenge out there.' But the play was much more of a success at the Lincoln Center than it had been in London or on the West Coast. The run was extended three times, to the end of March 1995 – by which time, amazingly, he had two plays running concurrently there. Channing liked the part so much that she wanted to do it as a film, and said she would buy the rights. To keep control of his work, Stoppard offered to write the script. But he quickly cooled: 'I'm so bored by the idea of it!' he told his mother. He sat in California on Boxing Day 1996, trying to work out how to make all the characters follow each other around in the first scene, and realised he just didn't want to do it. There was a simple solution: to send the money back and not write the script. Channing was very disappointed, but it was 'a huge relief for me'.

By the time *Hapgood* came to New York, six years after its original production, his life, and the world, had greatly changed. He wrote in the Lincoln Center magazine that the play takes place 'on one week in 1989 just before the Berlin Wall was breached'. And in the script, he made one or two alterations to suggest that the play (originally written between 1986 and 1987) was taking place then, in November 1989. Kerner, telling Blair that the system in the West is morally superior to the system in the East, makes no prediction, in the 1988 text, of any possible revolution. In the 1994 edition, he says: 'But the system can change.' Blair is sceptical about this, allowing a nice ironical moment for the 1994 audience: 'Budapest in '56 – Prague in '68 – Poland in '81 – we've been there! – and it's not going to be different in East Berlin in '89.' Events had overtaken the play: in the six years between its first appearance and its New York production, it had ceased to be contemporaneous, and had become historical, in a way he could not have imagined when he started writing it.

22

Script Doctor

What country, friends, is this?

Trying to write a screenplay of *Hapgood* was nothing but trouble to him and he was glad to give it up. But he was much involved with film work, especially in the early 1990s, when, because of the changes in his personal life, he needed the money. This work ranged from adapting his own work, to writing whole screenplays from other writers' novels, to advising on an already written film, to contributing bits of uncredited dialogue. He had a contract for two years in the early 1990s with Universal Pictures to look over what they had in the pipeline and choose three pictures to work on. And, after *Empire of the Sun*, Spielberg used him regularly as a consultant and often asked him to improve, or invent, sections of dialogue in his films.

He was wary of adapting his own plays into films. He wrote for his medium, knowing exactly how to make his ideas work in the frame of a theatre, or through the sound of radio, or, occasionally, inside the box of television. The material didn't transfer with ease – even though he once said that 'inside any stage play there is cinema wildly signalling to be let out'. He had written a screenplay of *Night and Day*, and there would be approaches for films of *The Real Thing* and *Arcadia*. But the only time (until 2017) that he adapted one of his own plays into a feature film, which he directed, was *Rosencrantz and Guildenstern Are Dead*, which, after some obstacles and delays, was released in the UK in May 1991.

There had been an earlier screenplay, written in 1968 for John Boorman and MGM, but MGM – having paid an enormous sum for the rights – decided they couldn't afford the budget. (And they thought Rosencrantz and Guildenstern weren't 'sympathetic' or 'identifiable' enough characters.) Twenty years on, Stoppard had another approach. Like his working relationships with Mike Nichols and Jack O'Brien, this came via Manny Azenberg. Azenberg was friendly with the film producer Michael Brandman, who had been dazzled by *Rosencrantz* in New York in 1968 and had long wanted to make it into a film. Azenberg loved the idea and said he wanted to co-produce. He put Brandman in touch with Stoppard. They got on well, and work started: raising the money, casting, writing the screenplay, looking for locations, choosing a director. Stoppard suggested that John Boorman should direct, since he'd been going to do it originally, but he was busy. Going through other possibilities with Brandman, he began to realise that they were all too much in awe of the original. The only person who would be disrespectful enough would be him: 'I didn't care to defend any of the play. I wasn't interested in protecting [it].' He cut the text ruthlessly, curtailed the Player's philosophising and put in more bits of *Hamlet*.

The funding depended on getting a big name. In December 1987, Stoppard had a meeting with Sean Connery. He agreed to star as the Player, and the money came in as a result. As Stoppard made clear to interviewers, 'The money was for a Sean Connery film, not a Tom Stoppard film.' Rosencrantz and Guildenstern would be played by well-established actors, Roger Rees and Robert Lindsay. Because of Connery's tax requirements, they would have to film outside the UK or the USA. He and Brandman went to Budapest and to Yugoslavia, looking for Elsinore in Dubrovnik. They took Brandman's son Miles with them, and Brandman would always remember how kind Stoppard was to him. Plans changed, and they settled on Toronto, where there was a big enough studio for the designer John Napier's lighting grid – which in the end proved too expensive to build. They were going to use 'Canadian fake-ancient university buildings' for Elsinore, and Lake Ontario for the sea.

A few weeks before he was due to begin filming, at the start of 1989, Connery let Stoppard know that he had an as yet undiagnosed throat condition (it turned out to be non-malignant polyps) which meant that he would not be able to work. Stoppard flew to LA to try to persuade him not to pull out, but to wait. Because Connery's doctors had told him to stay silent for a month, in the hopes of healing the condition, Stoppard wasn't able to have a meeting with him, but spoke to his wife. He explained that they had already started to spend the budget which had been raised because Connery's name was on the film. Connery got annoyed, and felt that he was being 'harassed'. In his view, the *Rosencrantz* people hadn't understood his situation. In their view, it was a breach of contract, and the producers sent him lawyers' letters. Connery settled out of court for $300,000 – a great deal more than he would have made from being in the film, which had been agreed as six weeks' work for £75,000. His biographer surmises that it was 'perhaps' a measure 'of how distressed he was by his health problems that the habitually litigious Connery chose to buy himself out of Stoppard's movie'. He had an all-clear from his doctors in April, and at once started making *The Hunt for Red October*, a big blockbuster film based on a Tom Clancy novel, playing a Russian nuclear submarine commander. The out-of-court settlement involved a gagging agreement on both sides, but months later, in an interview in *The Times*, Connery gave his side of the story. 'I couldn't tell anybody about my throat,' he said, 'and I was on a month's silence. Then they came round with a lawyer and they wouldn't believe it, they thought I was on some dodge. I've since had four operations . . . Normally I would have sued Stoppard out of the country. He and my wife were privy to what the whole thing was about . . . No, Stoppard behaved very badly.'

Stoppard replied, in a letter to *The Times*, that both sides had agreed not to speak about the settlement. 'Connery has forgotten this and at the same time maligned me.' He went through the chain of events.

> The producers of *Rosencrantz* had an obligation to substantiate the reason for their being unable to deliver the Connery film as contracted, and it was their unsuccessful attempts to get Connery's co-operation on this which he now characterizes as 'they thought I was on some dodge'. Connery says that but for his throat 'I would have sued Stoppard out of the country'. He is confusing different parts of his anatomy. Connery paid up because he didn't have a leg to stand on.

The letter was, typically, both stern and funny. Looking back, he would regret it, and felt that he should have kept quiet; at the time, he needed to defend himself and the producers.

Connery's settlement would partially fund the remaking of the film, but it was still a difficult situation. They would have to recast and start all over again. Stoppard asked Harrison Ford if he'd be interested, but Ford was otherwise engaged – possibly, Stoppard thought admiringly, doing his carpentry in Wisconsin. They talked to Richard Dreyfuss, over lunch at Orso in Los Angeles. He said he would do it, but they would have to wait a year. Dreyfuss was a big star, but not as big a star as Connery – so there would be a financial risk. Stoppard, Brandman and Azenberg called an emergency meeting. Should they go ahead with the film? They decided to take the risk, on condition that each of them would contribute a third of any financial losses. It was a gentleman's agreement between friends, and they shook hands on it.

Because Dreyfuss was a younger actor than Connery, they needed to rethink the casting of the two main parts. Stoppard realised he had been thinking of the actors of his generation as still being the age they were when *Rosencrantz* was first put on, because 'I thought I was still twenty-eight.' They cast the next generation of rising stars: Gary Oldman as Rosencrantz, Tim Roth as Guildenstern, and Iain Glen, so brilliant in *Hapgood*, as Hamlet. Brandman's wife Joanna Miles played Gertrude and Ian Richardson was a wily Polonius.

Toronto was abandoned, and they went back to Yugoslavia, in autumn 1989, when Eastern Europe was in dramatic upheaval. They were still struggling with the money, and Stoppard made urgent fundraising phone calls from Croatia, doing a producer's job as well as a director's and a writer's. They were selling the film in advance not only to different countries but to different media, and money had to be raised (in part from Disney Studios) for the video as well as for the film. Everything had to come out of the overall – and modest – budget.

Elsinore became a combination of two castles outside Zagreb, and a series of interiors created by the production designer Vaughan Edwards, on the sound stages of the Zagreb film studio Jadran. The shoreline scenes were filmed in a vast cement quarry. The whole experience, from first to last, was, for Stoppard, 'a valuable lesson in pragmatism'. The external scenes are empty, rocky landscapes, with Rosencrantz and Guildenstern in hats and boots and cloaks on horseback, looking like characters out of a Western, spinning coins into the void. The internal scenes take place in vast castle rooms with elaborate murals and imposing furnishings, galleries and marble staircases. Pieces of paper swirl around in the wind, shutters bang, tapers burn. The court appears in a fast-moving gang, surging in and out alarmingly. The players, elaborately bedecked, do *Monty Python*-style comic turns and masquerades. Instead of waiting for the next thing to happen to them, Rosencrantz and Guildenstern stomp from room to room in the castle, their footsteps echoing hollowly. Everyone is dressed in full Elizabethan rig, but the pair talk and act like young modern guys caught in the wrong costume and the wrong era. Their question-and-answer game is played over a disused tennis net (a vestige of his 1960s screenplay). Dreyfuss is a knowing, hard-edged, fast-talking Player; Tim Roth is foxy, quick and impatient as Guildenstern. The heart of the film is in Gary Oldman's Rosencrantz, a performance, as Stoppard described it, with something 'ineffably sweet' about it. Moon-faced, long-haired, puzzled and hopeful, he is in a world of his own. His speech of fear about what it would be like to be shut in a box, delivered lying on a marble tombstone, is at once funny and troubling.

Looking back, Stoppard thought the whole film was over-rehearsed. But some things happened on the spur of the moment, in a joyously amateurish way. The film's running gag – which has nothing to do with the original play – is that Rosencrantz is a latent scientist ahead of his time, like Galileo. He keeps accidentally inventing things: a Big Mac, a paper plane, an aircraft propellor. He shows these proudly to Guildenstern, who carelessly chucks them away.

The film feels theatrical rather than cinematic. Stoppard always thought it was too long. His imagination worked through ideas and language, not visual images. Kathy Kennedy, Spielberg's producer, put it politely: she could see that in that film he was 'drawing from theatre' and had not imagined (in spite of his earlier experience in the medium) that writing for the movies needed to be so different.

He knew that a good screenwriter who is 'thinking cinematically' has 'a qualitatively different way of writing'. By contrast, his screenplays were 'epic, picaresque stage plays . . . Telling the story by moving the camera is something I don't think about.' Over twenty years later (talking about

Parade's End) he would say: 'To this day, I don't write in pure cinematic language the way a screenwriter probably aspires to. I write scenes – often quite long scenes – mainly because I still get seduced into writing six lines where one-and-a-half will do.' Nor was he a natural director. Brandman noted that once he had decided to do the job, he spent a few days on the set of Mike Nichols's film *Working Girl*, to find out how Nichols did it. He asked Terry Gilliam: 'Would you like it to look like *Lassie Come Home* or would you like it to look like Bergman?' After a few days of shooting, Brandman came up to him and said: 'The camera isn't moving very much.' 'It was at that point', he said in an interview, 'that I realised that it wasn't moving at all. I was doing seaside photography.' He depended heavily on his cinematographer, Peter Biziou, who was very quick and decisive.

Many years later, he was talking to Spielberg about Mike Nichols. Spielberg was relaying something Nichols did in *The Graduate*. He had Anne Bancroft in the background, out of focus, with Dustin Hoffman in focus, at the moment when Bancroft realises that he is seeing her daughter. At that moment Nichols used a 'rack focus', that is, he combined the narrative of her understanding something with her face coming into focus, so that the two things happen simultaneously. Stoppard knew that he would never have thought of doing something like that: a Stoppard film would all be 'dialogue-driven'.

He told an interviewer after *Rosencrantz* was made that the whole thing was very enjoyable. This came out, misleadingly, as: 'The whole thing was very easy.' But it wasn't easy, it was difficult. And, after the film was shot and edited, the problem was that, as he put it, 'everything stays the way you leave it'. Nothing could be further from live theatre. After making *Rosencrantz*, he understood why David Lean had once said that 'the hardest part' of making a film 'was knowing how fast or slow to have the actor speak'. Because 'the damned thing stays the way you left it'.

In 2015, there was a twenty-fifth anniversary Blu-Ray reissue of the film, for which Michael Brandman did a long interview with his old friend. He asked him why he had not done other screenplays of his plays. *'Because they're plays,'* Stoppard replied.

Some reviewers complained that the film was too wordy and that the play was never meant to be a film. But it had its admirers. Pinter sent him an enthusiastic note, interesting for what he liked about it: 'I really think you've done a wonderful job on *R&G*. The sense of alienation, of isolation, is extraordinary, and the shifting levels of reality (now you see it now you don't) are brilliantly done. The film is both very funny & deeply mysterious. *Many* congratulations. It's a great joy.'

Before any reviews appeared, it was entered for the forty-seventh Venice Biennale Film Festival in September 1990. The competition for the Golden Lion statue for Best Picture was stiff. Jane Campion's adaptation of Janet Frame's *An Angel at My Table*, which had a passionate following, and the Merchant Ivory film *Mr and Mrs Bridge*, with Paul Newman and Joanne Woodward, were in the running. The expected winner was Martin Scorsese's film of the Italian-American mob scene, *Goodfellas*. After *Rosencrantz* was shown on 5 September, Stoppard flew back to London and asked, breaking the rules of the Festival, that he might be told the result in advance; he couldn't face going back to Venice to see *Goodfellas* win. 'Please return to Venice,' came the message. That night, he phoned Brandman, who was in Toronto, saying that he would never forget the stunned looks on the faces of Scorsese, his family and the whole Warner Brothers gang when *Rosencrantz* was announced the winner. Gore Vidal, who was chairing the panel of judges (which included Omar Sharif), described Stoppard's film as 'a tribute to the force of the mind, of wit and of logic in human affairs'. Stoppard himself thought *Goodfellas* was in another league altogether, and told Scorsese he would have voted for him – 'don't blame me!'

Then, as Azenberg put it grimly, the bill came in. They had a shortfall of about a million dollars, and they all lost money on it. Now they had to honour their three-way agreement. Stoppard's cheque for $330,000 arrived immediately. That was what Azenberg meant by wanting to have him with you in the foxhole.

The difficulties with the making of *Rosencrantz* were minor in comparison to some of his other experiences in that world. It was a very different matter to be a 'script doctor' for a film written by someone else – or by a number of other people, who might not know that their work was being rewritten. Film is 'a different moral universe', he once said to Tim Corrie, for a time his film agent. This view helped him to be laconic rather than dismayed: 'Who knows what goes on in Hollywood?' He often spoke dismissively about his film work to Bobby: 'I don't get worked up about Hollywood any more.' 'Film writing is junk-food.' When he was feeling at his most cynical about Hollywood, he described it as 'advanced technique in the service of arrested development'.

He would often say that 'the film-writing world has its own rules'. 'The feeling the writer has in the theatre is *quite different* from the feeling the writer has in the movies.' The main difference is that 'the writer is there to serve the director who himself [*sic*] is serving the narrative. It's nothing like the theatre which is the other way round.' Another of the differences is that 'you can astonish the audience too easily in the movies'. But a more creative difference was that in film you could change the frame. As he said while making the film of *Rosencrantz*: 'In the theatre you've got this medium shot, fairly wide angle, for two and a half hours. And that's it folks.'

'I enjoy doing films,' he told an interviewer in 1989, 'but it isn't a continuation of one's life as a writer. It's a detour.' And, he added, it's one's livelihood. His film agents, Tim Corrie and then Anthony Jones, at Peters Fraser and Dunlop – created in 1989 out of the merger between A. D. Peters' literary agency and Fraser and Dunlop's film, TV and theatre agency – were making big deals for him. But he was selective, and would not accept work on 'any old screenplay' just for the money. The film agent Bob Bookman, who liaised for a time with Anthony Jones in representing him in the States, assumed that Stoppard thought of the Hollywood film work simply as something that paid the bills. For instance, in the spring of 1991 he did five weeks' work for Universal and was paid $100,000 a week. Bookman noted that it was an unusual writer who would be paid on a 'weekly' retainer, for thousands of dollars, to come in towards the end of a film to do 'character polish' or 'dialogue polish'.

He often found this kind of work frustrating, burdensome and time-wasting, especially if it cut across play-writing. Though, as he says, 'there's a difference between completely wasted time and time which would have been better spent'. His agents' view was that he was pragmatic about his film work and idealistic about his plays.

But as far as Steven Spielberg and his Amblin producer Kathleen Kennedy were concerned, he brought to this work the same commitment as he would to a play of his own. In the teams of writers he used for every film, Spielberg particularly respected Stoppard, who on the whole enjoyed working with him. (That was unless Spielberg called him for a script conference when he was taking a shower.) According to Kennedy, Spielberg would often send him scripts just to see what Stoppard thought of them, before beginning work on a project, and was influenced by his views. Stoppard had a nose for what would make a good film. He could do comedy, dialogue and structure like no other writer. Also, as Kennedy put it, 'he's quite wonderful in the cutting room', where everything can be moved around. Even when Stoppard wasn't there, she would imagine his voice in the room, looking at a line or a scene and saying, 'Why is this not landing?' Stoppard knew that he was 'very useful in the editing suite'.

He was rigorous and critical. Spielberg said that he improved his films by challenging him. *Empire of the Sun* was a case in point. He made Spielberg defend his ideas, 'be authentic' and 'truthful'. He would have made a powerful barrister, Spielberg thought. 'He's great at catching me when I'm trying to be quaint or cute. He doesn't like quaint, he doesn't like cute.' He sums up their relationship with this ambivalent phrase: 'He has been a consistent blessing-in-disguise in my career.'

Stoppard's work on the script of Spielberg's 1989 film *Always* shows up that stubbornness. This was the story of a daring fire-fighting pilot (Richard Dreyfuss) who is killed on one of his missions and sent back to earth by his guardian angel in white (Audrey Hepburn, in her last role) to look after his loved one (Holly Hunter) and lead her into the arms of another handsome young firefighter. After a long farewell speech, 'That's my girl,' says the Dreyfuss character at the end, smiling and with a glint of a tear in his eye, 'and that's my boy,' as he turns to walk away from them down the runway and the music swells up. Stoppard told Spielberg what he thought of the last long speech, having held fire because he had the impression Spielberg thought it was okay. He thought it was '(a) soapy . . .

(b) obscure ... (c) illogical ... (d) untrue ... (e) bad writing ... (f) pseudo-poetical meaninglessness'. And he sent him another version. Spielberg thanked him effusively for the changes, telling him that to work with him was like working with the seventh cavalry – he came to the rescue at the last possible moment.

Also in the late 1980s, he worked on a film of Laurens Van der Post's African novels, *A Far-off Place* and *A Story Like the Wind*, which he thought should be told from the point of view of the boy in the story – as in *Empire of the Sun*. That script foundered, and the film wasn't made until some years later, by Disney. In 1988, he threw himself into a very different job for Spielberg, writing chunks of dialogue for *Indiana Jones and the Last Crusade* ('Indy III'), in which Indy (Harrison Ford) and his father Henry (Sean Connery) search for the Holy Grail, pursued by evil Nazis. He started by rewriting the dialogue for Connery (this preceded *Rosencrantz* events) and then Harrison Ford asked for him too. Spielberg wanted Stoppard to turn the father–son relationship into a comedy, and gave him a free hand. He loved the 'loose and generous' way Stoppard rewrote the script and the risks he took. He bombarded Spielberg with suggestions, all in the interests of speed and structure: 'Steven, personally I don't go for the stuff in this scene at all ... I also think we've had enough stuff about what the Diary means to Henry ... the scene slows things up too much.' Connery plays Henry, Indy's father, as a tetchy, fusty academic in a three-piece tweed suit with briefcase, umbrella, bow tie and fob watch, who never gives his daredevil son any praise or encouragement until the very end. Stoppard gave him comic catch-lines at hair-raising moments – 'Our situation has not improved', 'This is intolerable' – and bursts of eloquence, as when rousing up a flock of seagulls with his umbrella to fend off the Nazi pursuit: 'I suddenly remembered my Charlemagne – let my army be the rocks and the trees and the birds in the sky.' Their father–son exchanges are heartfelt, as when Henry finally says 'Well done' to Indy. Passages of dialogue like this are all Stoppard's:

Indy: Do you remember the last time we had a quiet drink? I had a milkshake.

Henry: Hmmm . . . What did we talk about?

Indy: We didn't talk. We never talked.

Henry: And do I detect a rebuke?

Indy: A regret. It was just the two of us, Dad. It was a lonely way to grow up. For you, too. If you had been an ordinary, average father like the other guys' dads, you'd have understood that.

Henry: Actually, I was a wonderful father.

Indy: When?

[*Henry looks up from his Diary.*]

Henry: Did I ever tell you to eat up? Go to bed? Wash your ears? Do your homework? No. I respected your privacy and I taught you self-reliance.

Indy: What you taught me was that I was less important to you than people who had been dead for five hundred years in another country. And I learned it so well that we've hardly spoken for twenty years.

Henry: You left just when you were becoming interesting.

Stoppard wrote most of their scenes, did not want to be credited, and was paid a great deal of money. A letter from Kathy Kennedy to Ken Ewing in October 1989 makes clear how much: '[Steven] feels the deal that was presented was $500,000 at $100 million of gross receipts and an additional $100,000 at each additional $25 million of gross receipts. Tom can rest assured that when Steven said he would see close to a million dollars, he feels quite confident that figure will be reached.' The film took $474.2 million at the box office. To put this in context: *The Hunt for Red October* took $200.5 million; *Rosencrantz*, a low-budget independent film, took $739,104.

All through the 1990s, Stoppard wrote uncredited words for Spielberg's Amblin films, including the poorly received *Hook* (with Robin Williams as a grown-up Peter Pan and Dustin Hoffman as Captain Hook), and *Schindler's List*, for which he rewrote one scene. He told his parents in January 1994:

The enormous success (critical success) of *Schindler's List* is very
pleasing to me because I was a champion for the script which S.S.
sent me for comments a couple of years ago and I stopped him from
'improving' it and generally supported the writer. I also helped Steven
to arrive at a definitive version, a (very) few of the lines are mine,
faxed to Krakow during filming. I hope Steven gets his Oscar at last.

And he did.

He provided uncredited work, too, for a surprising range of Universal
films: *Mom*, in which a Los Angeles mother turns into a werewolf; *Medicine
Man*, about a cancer researcher in the Amazon rainforest tangling with
native medical beliefs (Sean Connery again); *Beethoven*, a family comedy starring a lovable St Bernard; *Charlie*, a biopic directed by Richard
Attenborough, which Universal pulled out of and which eventually came
out as *Chaplin*; and Stephen Gyllenhaal's romantic drama *A Dangerous
Woman*, with an unstable heroine played by Debra Winger. He had to scotch
the rumour that he had been involved in the script of Richard Donner's
1992 *Lethal Weapon 3*, though he wasn't sure if it was 'in his best interests
to deny it'. Later, he would work on *Restoration*, from Rose Tremain's novel,
and, uncredited, on Scott Rudin's fantasy horror film *Sleepy Hollow*, Ridley
Scott's *Nottingham*, which after many challenging years became *Robin Hood*,
and Disney's 102 *Dalmatians*, as a favour to Glenn Close. One of the lines of
his which survived in the movie, and which he and Close particularly liked,
was 'You may have won the battle, but I'm about to win the wardrobe.'

He advised on such film scripts with his usual meticulousness and
energy. He knew how annoying it could be to have to take someone else's
comments on board. 'This is the most irritating note for a writer to get,' he
told the Universal producer Casey Silver in 1991. 'I call it the Portia Note
– "let's lose this pound of flesh" – and it's left to the writer to point out that
some of the heart, kidneys, lungs and liver are connected to it.' But he was
ruthless in his notes: 'Inert, lumpy dialogue.' 'Fudgy.' 'Eh? I don't get it.' 'Is
this for real?' 'This stuff gets sillier and sillier.'

He would be similarly unsparing, years later, with *Robin Hood*, a vehicle
for Russell Crowe, which he took on because he admired Ridley Scott,

who thanked Stoppard for being so 'specific and diligent'. Some of his notes read: 'Boring line and implausible plotting'; 'anachronistic by a few hundred years'; 'an impossible phrase in 1199'; 'otiose and hi-faluting'; or, more exasperatedly: 'for the forest gods' sake will you save this fuck-up!' He referred to the film drily as 'Robin Hood invented Socialism', and kept his name off the credits when it was released in May 2010.

The advice he gave was very often about the tone of a film, as for *A Dangerous Woman*: 'What you've got here is a movie that could be as cheesy as *Peyton Place* or as truthful as *Mockingbird*.' His notes on *Mom* observed that

> there are at least three kinds of movies here which don't properly square with each other . . . I have no problem with humour based on stereotypes (eg smothering Jewish mom) . . . the bits I like are scuppered for me by the 'sincere' passages . . . I find [those bits] a terrible turn-off . . . At the same time I've got a suspicion that I'm culturally (Englishly) unqualified to tell this movie what it ought to try to be doing.

Often his work on a film would only be in the early, advisory stages. He had conversations with Spielberg's collaborator on the *Indiana Jones* movies, George Lucas, about *Star Wars* (the first trilogy was re-released in 1997), and made some suggestions. He often chose film work because he liked a particular director, such as Ridley Scott. *Blade Runner* was one of his favourite films, along with *Chinatown* (which made him weep), *Some Like It Hot*, *Sweet Smell of Success*, *Casablanca*, *The Third Man* and *The Godfather*.

When it came to writing whole scripts to which he put his name, he was drawn to complicated plots, preferably with historical substance: Cold War spy thrillers, Second World War code-breaking, gangster movies and detective stories. The nearest he came to this genre of writing in his plays was in *Night and Day* and *Hapgood*. But movies led him into different kinds of plot and language. Between 1989 and 1991, he did an adaptation of E. L. Doctorow's novel *Billy Bathgate* for a Disney film directed by Robert Benton, which involved working with Jeffrey Katzenberg, Disney's studio executive, who later joined forces with Spielberg at DreamWorks. Katzenberg was a tough business operator who drew up an agreement with Stoppard to hold back full payments on *Bathgate* until he saw whether Disney's input into *Rosencrantz* would be recouped. But Stoppard could be every bit as tough, in his own elegant way. He agreed with Katzenberg (early in 1990) that it had been appropriate for Disney, in the fundraising stages of *Rosencrantz*, to 'show prudence in the case of a first-time director facing up to a quite complex film on a difficult schedule'. But now that *Rosencrantz* was successfully completed, Katzenberg might feel 'that our arrangement is perhaps over-prudent or even superfluous'. Rather to his surprise, Katzenberg paid up at once. Stoppard was just as firm about his expenses for the work on *Billy Bathgate*. He told Ken Ewing that he was getting $1,000 a day for two four-day trips to New York, entirely on *Bathgate* business. But he needed the producers to reconsider that figure: he had taken a two-room hotel suite 'because I prefer not to sleep and work in the same room', and he had upgraded one of his return journeys from first class to Concorde, so that he wouldn't be 'travel-mugged' when he got back.

He met Doctorow and liked him, and was interested in the novel, in which a young Bronx boy gets taken up, and then thrown out, by the gangster Dutch Schultz, whose girl he falls in love with. The film's cast included Dustin Hoffman, Nicole Kidman and Bruce Willis. But he was disappointed in it, because they turned the young boy into a young man and did 'their usual thing of sanitising everything and making it simple'. It was generally felt to be a clichéd New York gangster movie, much less exciting than *Goodfellas*. Doctorow himself disliked it – but novelists often dislike adaptations of their books.

He was working with well-established conventions, too, in his screenplay of *Poodle Springs*, which he wrote around the same time as *Billy Bathgate*, in the early 1990s, but which did not get made until 1998. This was a late Philip Marlowe story which Raymond Chandler had left unfinished at his death in 1959, completed years later by the novelist Robert B. Parker. Marlowe has married a rich socialite in a Californian gambling town closely based on Palm Springs, where he finds himself investigating corruption, blackmail and killings among the very wealthy. (The marriage doesn't last.) In the film, updated by Stoppard to 1963, Marlowe, in his trilby and raincoat, seems 'well, *dated*', an old-fashioned kind of romantic investigator in a harsh, free-living new world. The billboards behind him are advertising *From Russia with Love*, the women's book of the day is *The Feminine Mystique*, the kids are listening to the Beach Boys and Dylan's 'The Times They Are a-Changin''. The script makes much of this poignant anomaly and does some slick Chandler/Hemingway parody dialogue: 'The Galahad of the mean streets,' someone tells Marlowe. 'It's a different Camelot now.' The film will end, off screen, with the assassination of Kennedy.

He was extremely pleased to be asked to do the screenplay of John Le Carré's *The Russia House*. The novel was set in 1987 and published in 1988. The film, directed by Fred Schepisi, came out in 1990. So this was up-to-the-minute work, dealing with Gorbachev's Russia and the last stages of the Cold War. It is a characteristically caustic, disillusioned novel about the vested interests involved in the arms race, the mutual suspicions between American and British intelligence (as in *Hapgood*), and the 'corrupt and anachronistic' world of an ever more futile intelligence system.

Scott 'Barley' Blair, an upper-class English publisher given to alcohol, jazz and girls, is caught up in a plot between MI6 (the branch dealing with Soviet affairs, known as the 'Russia house') and the KGB. It involves a manuscript which has been smuggled out of Russia by an idealistic Soviet physicist ('Goethe', changed to 'Dante' in the film, as being more pronounceable), revealing the chaotic state of Soviet military technology and nuclear capabilities. A young Russian woman publisher, Katya, with whom Barley falls in love, is a victim of the situation. Complex intrigues and betrayals ensue. In the end Barley puts his personal affections ahead of any loyalty to his government. In Katya's words: 'You swore to me that you would always prefer humanity to nations and that when the day came you would act like a decent human being.'

The film was, as Le Carré put it, a 'stellar affair', with Klaus Maria Brandauer, Sean Connery, Michele Pfeiffer, and some stylish English

The study, Fernleigh, 1977.

The Stoppards' Fernleigh bookplate, designed by Glynn Boyd Harte.

English family life: fishing with Will.

Every Good Boy Deserves Favour, with John Wood, André Previn and orchestra, Ian McKellen, Royal Festival Hall, 1 July 1977.

Mark Boxer cartoon to Kenneth Tynan's profile, 'Withdrawing with Style from the Chaos', 1977.

Tom Stoppard with Harold Pinter, 1980.

Undiscovered Country, 1979, with Emma Piper,
Dorothy Tutin, John Wood and Sara Kestelman.

Stoppard and director Peter Wood on the set of
Rough Crossing, 1984.

The Real Thing, New York, 1984: Jeremy Irons
and Glenn Close.

The Stoppards: a much-photographed couple, 1979.

Iver Grove: 'a very impressive house'.

Stoppard at fifty: Jane Bown portrait, 28 June 1987.

The film director: Stoppard on the set of *Rosencrantz & Guildenstern*, 1990, with Tim Roth and Gary Oldman.

The Czech friends: Tom Stoppard with Václav Havel.

Hapgood, 1988: difficult rehearsals, with Felicity Kendal and Peter Wood.

In the Native State, 1991: Stoppard with Felicity Kendal and Peggy Ashcroft.

Felicity Kendal as Hannah in *Arcadia*, 1993.

Rediscovering his mother's Bata shoe shop in Darjeeling, January 1991.
In his study at Chelsea Harbour, early 1990s.

In rehearsal for *The Invention of Love*, 1997.

actors like James Fox and Stoppard's friend Michael Kitchen playing the MI6 bureaucrats. The casting of Connery involved a comically awkward meeting between the star and the two writers. It was the first time David Cornwell had spent any time with Stoppard. On their way to show Connery the script at his hotel in Park Lane, Stoppard told Cornwell about the difficulties over *Rosencrantz*. Cornwell was amused to find Connery showing off the grandeur of his hotel suite ('£100 a night, and free mini bar'), addressing him as 'Young Mr David', flirting with him and sidelining Stoppard. They sat on the sofa while Connery turned the pages of the script, saying 'too long, too long'. According to Cornwell, Connery expostulated, of one speech in the script: 'If anybody said all of that to me, I'd kick him in the balls!' As they were leaving, Stoppard turned to Cornwell and said, 'I think I shall have to find a new typeface for irony.' Cornwell didn't know if Connery had heard him.

David Cornwell was drawn to Stoppard from the moment he met him. And he was pleased that the film got going so swiftly: he was in awe of Schepisi's efficiency. But he felt that Stoppard was not 'cut out for popular film-making. His home is on the stage.' He thought the script was slow and 'mysteriously uneventful'. When he put forward some 'friendly objections', he soon discovered, like Spielberg, that 'Tom was not biddable.' At one point in their discussions, Stoppard said somewhat waspishly to him: 'Are you telling me how to write a script?' 'Which', Cornwell noted drily, 'I was.' Stoppard resisted any suggestions from Schepisi that Le Carré might do some rewriting. When the film was three drafts in, he told Frank Pike (who wanted to publish the screenplay) that he had arrived at a 'streamlined version which I have done under the pleasant but remorseless direction of Fred Schepisi . . . My favourite bits aren't in it any more. That's the movies.' In the end, Cornwell acknowledged that the screenplay was a faithful narrative and 'an enormous homage to my words'.

The Russia House was the first Western film to be shot on location in the Soviet Union, in Moscow and Leningrad (as it then was), under Gorbachev's glasnost policy. It had three premieres: the first in New York on 4 December 1990, where Stoppard sat at Spielberg's table; the next in the UK in February 1991; and the third in Moscow, in November 1991, for which he sent a formal message of good will: 'It was a privilege to be associated with a film which we all hope is only the beginning of a tradition of East–West exchanges between film-makers, and an affirmation that art has no frontiers.'

This was the only time he worked with David Cornwell, but, as often, the professional collaboration led to a lifelong friendship. Cornwell observed him acutely. He saw him as hugely courteous, iron-hard when needed, universally sympathetic and generous, incapable of betraying a friend. He loved what he called his 'whizzy creativity'. Culturally, he found him very 'mittel-European', conservative with a small 'c', with an outsider's love of England, intellectually in the tradition of Bulgakov, or Joseph Roth. He felt they were kindred spirits. They had both loathed their public schools as teenagers, they had both had an absent parent. They shared, Cornwell sensed (though the two men never talked about this), a kind of inner darkness, a secret condition hidden under 'the performance-art of life'. In both of them, he thought, there was an enormous amount of concealment. It did not suit their art, for either of them, to look inside themselves too deeply.

The relationship meant a lot to them both, though they did not meet often. Cornwell divided his time between Cornwall and Hampstead, and had a horror of the big public, social occasions which Stoppard took on so easily. They dealt in their own way with celebrity: Stoppard, as Cornwell put it, with some awe, 'came out of the trenches and took it on'. He, by contrast, was ruthless about putting off visitors if he was in the middle of a book – a discipline which Stoppard envied. They wrote affectionate letters to each other (Cornwell signing off, 'we love you dearly'), they met with their families, or Stoppard would occasionally drop round to visit him in Hampstead. They would pick up their conversation easily. Stoppard would ring and say, 'Don't cook, I'll just come by, I just want soup.' It became a family mantra for David and Jane Cornwell that 'what Tom wants is soup'. When the Cornwells thought he might need it, they offered him sympathy and a refuge. Stoppard has had a few warm friendships with other writers: Anthony Smith in his youth, Paul Johnson, Harold Pinter, Antonia Fraser, Václav Havel, Michael Frayn, and, in later years, Patrick Marber,

Julian Barnes and Daniel Kehlmann. Of these, his loving bond with David Cornwell was of the first importance to him.

The Russia House was a fast job of work compared to the other screenplay he adapted from a novel about war and military espionage. This was *Enigma*, which he worked on intermittently between 1995 and 1999, but which did not come out until 2001. Robert Harris's bestselling 1995 novel fictionalises the secret Second World War work of the cryptographers at Bletchley Park, that legendary Victorian house in a small Buckinghamshire railway village, where Oxbridge mathematicians and intellectuals worked day and night to crack the German codes, supported by a team of female ciphering clerks, and greatly aided by the work of the Polish Cipher Bureau in Warsaw. No real-life figures from Bletchley such as Alan Turing or Dillwyn Knox appear in Harris's novel and Stoppard's screenplay. But the hero, Tom Jericho, has a faint trace of Turing, in that he's a brilliant young Cambridge mathematician who has had a breakdown and is the genius of the tweedy, eccentric group of code-breaking boffins.

The film begins with Jericho coming back to Bletchley in 1943. The Germans have switched their U-boats to a new code. Jericho has to crack it before a huge convoy of US merchant ships encounter a phalanx of German U-boats. His task is complicated by the presence at Bletchley of a suave intelligence officer, Wigram, who knows there is a traitor in their midst, and by his hopeless love for the gorgeous and faithless Claire. She turns out to have been embedded at Bletchley by Wigram as a honey-trap for any possible traitor. But she has fallen in love with, and given secrets to, a glamorous Polish code-breaker who is seeking revenge (by getting information to Russia's enemies, the Nazis) for Stalin's massacre of Polish officers before the war. Claire's dowdy, clever flatmate Hester (played well against the grain by Kate Winslet) helps, and loves, Jericho. So the film is as much the rite of passage of a nervy geek turned action man and finding romantic consolation, as it is a reimagining of Bletchley.

Stoppard's involvement came about through Mick Jagger. He was friendly with him and his then wife Jerry Hall, he went to his concerts when he could and he loved his music. He was a fan as well as a friend, and when he thought about fame – which he quite often did – Jagger's global fame put his own into perspective. As he said, being out and about with Mick Jagger brings it home to you that you're *not* famous. Jagger has been famous for fifty years in the foothills of the Himalayas or the Mexican desert; he would be stopped on the street in Outer Mongolia. There is nowhere he can go where people don't know who he is. Stoppard considers this with awe, interest and some envy.

They had already thought of working together. In 1983 Jagger suggested that he and David Bowie collaborate with Stoppard on a musical comedy film. Stoppard said he was 'stupid' about musicals, but perhaps they might do something about 'the shady side of the City'. (The idea surfaced many years later as part of the plot of *The Hard Problem*.) In the autumn of 1990 Jagger sent him a tape of his new album, *Wandering Spirit* (which came out in 1993). He was thinking of creating a theatrical show. Stoppard asked him, perhaps with 'Sympathy for the Devil' in mind, if he was at all interested in the Faust story. 'Quite a lot of the things you've written might have been written for the situation – eg "Satisfaction" sounds like Faust upping the ante. A device which appeals to me, theatrically, is to bring a false Jagger, a double – so that you also sing the Devil, who, as we know, has the best tunes.' Nothing came of that. But in the early 1990s, Jagger started a film company, Jagged Films, with co-producers Victoria Pearman and Steve Tisch. *Enigma* was to be their first feature film – Jagger owned an Enigma machine, which was used as a prop – and they asked Stoppard to write the screenplay. It was their only collaboration.

He thought the novel presented difficulties of plot and structure, but the story interested him. Robert Harris went to Chelsea Harbour for a first discussion. They had a coincidental personal link, as Harris's wife, Gill Hornby, was the daughter of Miriam's one-time Syntex secretary. As Stoppard said to his mother: 'Small world. Big cliché.' Stoppard sat Harris down on his blue sofa, poured him some white wine from Fortnum & Mason and cross-examined him for two hours in a tone of 'unrelenting if good-humoured antagonism'. Was this scene credible? Would someone really have thought that then? 'Oh, come on,' he said at one point, 'that's bollocks, isn't it?' It began to dawn on Harris that he had 'caught the bug' of the story of Bletchley Park. Later that day Stoppard called Harris and said he would do it.

He committed himself to a three-month writing period and immersed himself in twenty books on 'Bletchley, codes, convoys, etc.' He was also reading a 1940s wartime diary called *To War with Whitaker* by Hermione, Countess of Ranfurly, which made him feel nostalgic. 'The England the war was fought for has gone,' he wrote to his mother. That mood coloured the script. He also met two elderly ladies who had been 'debby girl' clerks in the Bletchley Huts. One of them told him that all the girls from the Bletchley days were relieved and delighted that he was going to do the film. He commented grimly: 'poor girls don't know that that makes no difference in the end the producers will change it any way they like if they like'.

He went to stay with the Harrises, and with the Jaggers in France, to work on the film. Harris got many late-night phone calls with detailed questions such as 'Could an Enigma machine have been hooked up to a car battery?' They visited Bletchley together, and Harris described the stunned silence in the local pub when he, Stoppard and the producer Michael White were joined by Mick Jagger and Jagger's bodyguard.

Stoppard struggled with the plot, and with the studio executives' desire to turn it into a romance between Jericho and Hester. 'Of course Paramount pay [us] and tell me what *they* think, and I'm left to solve the problems. The movies!' He finished in May 1996 – by which time he felt bored with it. But as usual that was only the beginning. The first draft was too complicated – 'like a fugue or a game of 3D chess', Harris thought. Five years then passed, as directors were sought, Paramount pulled out, Jagger toured Hollywood studios trying to sell it, Michael Apted came on board as producer, Stoppard wrote a third version, $13.5 million (a relatively small budget) was raised and stars were courted. Eventually the money came in and filming started in 2000, with Chicheley Hall standing in for Bletchley. The film that emerged from all this was a solid thriller in Hitchcockian, Buchanesque style, with a complicated time sequence, an unlikely James Bond-style finale and rather stereotypical characters. It was greeted with mixed, though largely respectful reviews.

There were some complaints that Turing did not figure and that the heroic work of the Polish allies had been unrepresented, and furthermore traduced by having a fictional Polish spy at Bletchley. Stoppard responded to this charge, in personal letters to Polish complainants, by donating £250 to a Polish memorial in Bletchley, and in a letter to the *Daily Telegraph*, surprised that anyone would 'take a fictitious Pole to be a slur on Poland's well-known heroism and sacrifices in the war'. Prince Charles, who attended the film's premiere, took an interest in these complaints, and was assured by Stoppard that future showings of the film would include an extra credit to 'the Polish Cipher Bureau' for 'its critical early work in cracking Enigma'. He hoped that Prince Charles shared their own pleasure in the film's 'old-fashioned virtues, moral and aesthetic'.

At one point in this long and arduous process, Jagger threw an opulent party in December 1996, at which Harris encountered a smooth Paramount executive who assured him that all would be well. He 'loved us – loved the script, loved the story, loved everything. He put his hand on my shoulder and looked me in the eyes. "Have faith," he said, in a read-my-lips voice. "We. Will. Make. This. Movie." "Now I know we're in trouble," said Tom afterwards.'

Enigma was not the only screenplay which took up his time in the 1990s, while he was in the middle of writing major plays. Some of this work came to nothing. Universal was considering making an animated film of Andrew Lloyd Webber's musical *Cats*. Spielberg showed some interest, and there was a meeting between Lloyd Webber, Stoppard and Spielberg in LA in 1994, at which Lloyd Webber, to Stoppard's interest and amusement, told Spielberg that *Phantom of the Opera* made more money than Spielberg's highest-grossing films – *E.T.*, for instance – because the price of the tickets for *Phantom* was so much higher. That meeting was inconclusive, and then Trevor Nunn – the director of the musical, who had started work on a film script but gave it up – encouraged him to write it. Stoppard was not especially keen on musicals: he had never been in a hurry to go to *Les Misérables*, even though he had been in Nunn's office many times, 'with *Les Misérables* outside the window where Trevor can look at the queue'.

He had turned down the chance to adapt Gaston Leroux's novel into the musical *Phantom* – much to his sons' regret – and felt no urgency about seeing it. 'You feel that *Phantom* is there, like the Eiffel Tower. There's no rush.' (Later, he did a bit of work on the sequel to *Phantom*.) Working with Lloyd Webber – as with Previn – made him aware of his complete lack of musical ear. 'I don't think he realises that all tunes sound the same to me.'

But he decided to do *Cats* because he liked the poems. He saw it as a 'puzzle problem': inventing a plot which the songs would fit into. His script had the cats going all over London – up into the gallery of St Paul's, into the Tower, down into the sewers. The play, he told his mother, takes place entirely on a rubbish dump – 'not enough variety for a film, so I'm changing it and doing my bit for tourism'. He introduced Eliotic jokes and allusions and dramatic action. 'Curiosity', he told Spielberg, was going to be the cats' fatal flaw. And there were other Stoppardian touches. There's a cat with nine lives who keeps counting his lives on his paws and finally runs out of luck. Mungojerrie and Rumpelteazer are always being confused with each other, like Rosencrantz and Guildenstern. There is an elaborate 'TRANS-MOG-GRIFICATION' of ordinary cats to Jellicle cats. The long-lived Deuteronomy introduces a witty montage of English historical events. There's a climactic fight between the wicked Macavity and the hero Mungojerrie on a footbridge above rushing water which Stoppard annotates: 'Think of Sherlock Holmes and Moriarty on the Reichenbach Falls.' Macavity has lines from *The Waste Land* ('My nerves are bad tonight' . . . 'There will be time, there will be time after the taking of toast and tea'). And when Macavity disguises himself as a blind cat guiding the other cats to the dangerous waters of the London sewers, he tells them, just as Charon will in *The Invention of Love*: 'I am the Ferryman down there. It's customary to give me a coin.' Universal's plan for an animation eventually stalled. (A film of the stage show came out in 1998, and a controversial film with computer-generated images mixed with live action, in 2019.) 'I couldn't feel less animated,' he said of it gloomily at one point. But his script shows how much he relished working with Eliot's words. And there was something of him in at least one of Eliot's cats:

The greatest magicians have something to learn
From Mister Mistoffelees' conjuring turn
And we all say,
Oh! Well I never! Was there ever
A cat so clever
As magical Mr Mistoffelees!

A proposal which interested him much more was a suggestion from Kathy Kennedy that he write a screenplay for Amblin of a long novel by Nicholas Mosley, *Hopeful Monsters*. An inventive and prolific novelist, who also wrote a critical biography of his father, the Fascist leader Oswald Mosley, he was writing an ambitious series under the title 'Catastrophe Practice'. *Hopeful Monsters*, which was published in 1990 and won the Whitbread Prize, was the culmination of this series. Over a long time span, from 1918 to 1939 and on into the 1970s, and a range of international settings, a group of friends and lovers struggle to discover a pattern in life and new forms of experience – political, social, sexual, intellectual. The two main characters, the English Max and the German-Jewish Eleanor, have parallel, connected lives. Nazi Germany, Stalinist Russia, the Spanish Civil War, East End anti-Fascist riots, the invention and dropping of the atom bomb, the creation of Israel are all described. Rosa Luxemburg, Einstein, Heidegger, Wittgenstein, Hitler and Franco have walk-on parts. The cinematic possibilities are rich.

But it is also a very intellectual novel – and 'not easy going', as Stoppard warned Bobby, sending her a copy. Nietzsche, Kleist, Dostoevsky, Freud, Jung, Lawrence, *Faust*, *The Magic Mountain* and *The Waste Land* are strong influences. Biology, philosophy, psychology, anthropology, myth and fairy tale are all brought to bear. Problems in physics – of interest to Stoppard – like wave/particle theory, are introduced in order to ask whether the observer affects or creates what is observed. What evolutionary conditions might produce a new kind of consciousness? Out of anarchy and revolution, might a new kind of humanity emerge? And what kind of 'chance' or 'miracle' could bring about such a mutation? The 'hopeful monsters' are the new growth from an old strain. Perhaps 'they would not want to destroy'. Stoppard took notes: 'The central idea is that the "environment" – modern world – becomes insupportable – We have to mutate to adjust . . . one could create an aesthetic/moral environment to encourage hopeful monsters. The texture of the environment is of violent death . . . images of death – fire – persecution – bigotry – must be the foundation.'

He held these ideas in his head for several years in the mid-1990s. He read up on the context, and wrote many pages of research notes. There were endless meetings and script conferences, and a long search for an A-list director. In August 1995, for instance, he was picked up in a car from Chelsea Crescent at 7 a.m. on Saturday 12th, took the 8.45 a.m. flight to New York, went in a limo from the airport to the St Regis hotel for a development meeting, did a working dinner, and took the Monday night flight home, getting back on Tuesday morning. This was a normal pattern for his film work.

He had some interesting exchanges with Nick Mosley. But, after a few years, and no film ever made, he came to think of 'the whole exercise [as] a sham, it's simply not a proper film for Hollywood but they seem to be happy to pay to prove it'. The first draft, in 1993, took him three months, in the middle of other things. After that, he had Jacky type so many versions that she started calling it *Hopeless Monsters*.

There was one screenplay which, after long delays and difficulties, did have a triumphant outcome, and became one of his best-loved pieces of work. For many people, *Shakespeare in Love* is the title they most associate with his name. It started life routinely, in the early 1990s, as a script he picked out of the Universal pile in fulfilment of his contract. Though the final product was richly Stoppardian, it was not his idea, or his title. The original script was by an American screenwriter, Marc Norman, who pitched it to a friend of his in Hollywood, Ed Zwick, a producer for Universal. Norman got the idea from his son, who was reading *Romeo and Juliet* in college, and asked his father what the guy was like who wrote the play. The pitch was for an American film with superstars. Julia Roberts was cast, but she would only do it with Daniel Day-Lewis, who wasn't interested.

I've ever seen.' But then came the all-important 'numbers', the National Research Group ratings for a sample audience's reaction. They were only middling. Harvey Weinstein had become possessive about the film and had started to think of it as a potential Oscar winner. He wanted a rom-com with a happy ending. It should end with Viola in the wings watching Shakespeare acting. She would be his bit on the side. Never mind about the wife in Stratford! Reshoot! Rebuild the set!

Madden and Stoppard fought their corner, on this and also on some phrases in the script which Weinstein thought too arcane. They had to stand up to him. (What else was going on at the time was not in view, and not known to Stoppard or Madden. Twenty years on, Paltrow was one of the film stars involved in the charges of sexual misconduct against Weinstein.) In these battles, Madden found Stoppard steady, 'dismayingly patient', generous, collaborative, pragmatic and resolute. And in the end he found the logical solution. Viola would give Will the plot of *Twelfth Night*, just as Marlowe had for *Romeo and Juliet*. They would have to part, but she would be his muse and his next heroine. It was a nice joke – Shakespeare always gets his plots from other people – and it solved the problem. Weinstein got what he wanted: *Shakespeare in Love* swept the board at the Oscars in March 1999, seven years after Stoppard had started work on it. And they got their revenge. Buried deep in the 'extra materials' on the DVD of the film, alongside some other deleted scenes, is a scene shot in the tavern. 'What is the ending?' says Henslowe. 'By God, I wish I knew,' Will replies, off camera. Henslowe retorts: 'Let us have pirates, clowns and a happy ending, and you'll make Harvey Weinstein a happy man.' John Madden jumps in front of the camera in a feigned panic, shouting, 'Cut! Cut! CUT!' And everybody laughs.

In the first ending they shot, Viola is washed up, from the sea and the shipwreck, on a vast beach. (It is Holkham Sands, in North Norfolk.) She starts walking up the beach and encounters two figures, a sailor and a Native American, covered in war paint. In the far distance, 'there rises the ghostly shimmering outline of the skyscrapers of modern Manhattan'. She speaks her first line, a question to them. The sailor replies: 'This is America, lady.' And with a big smile she says, 'Well – good!' and walks on 'to meet her Brave New World'. For the revised ending, they airbrushed out the two men and the exchange, and have her simply walking away from us up the beach towards the distant woods, while we see Shakespeare writing her first line, under the title *Twelfth Night*: 'What country, friends, is this?'

23

Changing States

> All portraits should be unfinished. Otherwise it's like looking at a
> stopped clock.

The years between his two best films, *Empire of the Sun* and *Shakespeare in Love*, when so much 'script doctoring' was going on, were, more importantly to him, the years of four major plays, and of revivals, adaptations and productions all over the world. He was in his prime; he was also at a time of upheaval and stresses. That, as he puts it, 'was – life'.

He often measured his own lucky and privileged life story against his friend Václav Havel's. Early in 1989, an American interviewer, sent to talk to him at Iver about *Hapgood* for *Vanity Fair*, found him upset and ill at ease, having just heard that Havel had been sentenced to another nine months in prison by the Czech government. But by the end of that year, everything would change in Communist Europe. Throughout this astonishing time, Stoppard would stay in touch with Havel as much as he could.

In the autumn of that year, there was a stage production of his 1972 radio play, *Artist Descending a Staircase*. A young director, Tim Luscombe, a graduate of the Bristol Old Vic Theatre School, was asked by Dan Crawford, who ran a small experimental theatre in Islington at the King's Head pub, to do it. Stoppard did not especially want *Artist* to be made into a stage play, but he was kind and courteous when he came to rehearsal. Luscombe remembered being tactfully handed small scribbled notes from him at the end of the day's work. The play transferred to the Duke of York's Theatre in the West End, and then to a huge New York theatre, the Helen Hayes, where it had a short run in December 1989.

Before *Artist* opened in New York, it was staged for a week in a theatre on the campus of Duke University. Stoppard flew out to be with the cast on 9 November 1989. It was the day of the fall of the Berlin Wall. While he was in North Carolina, in the week of the preview, 11 to 18 November, the Velvet Revolution was taking place in Czechoslovakia.

On 17 November, a large student demonstration was suppressed by the police in Prague. In the ensuing days, there was a growing series of mass demonstrations. On 24 November, Dubček, the reformist First Secretary who had resigned after the Soviet invasion, returned to Prague and, alongside Havel, addressed two hundred thousand people in Wenceslas Square. The Communist government resigned, and on 10 December the first non-Communist government of Czechoslovakia was formed. On 29 December, Václav Havel became president.

Tim Luscombe remembered that while the cast were living together in a hall of residence on the Duke University campus, Stoppard would go straight to his room, every evening, to make phone calls. He had assumed that Stoppard was phoning home. But it later transpired, Luscombe said, that he had been talking to Havel on a nightly basis. Whether he was giving advice, or encouragement, or discussing strategy, Luscombe did not know, and Stoppard does not remember. But his connection to Havel, as he metamorphosed from censored and imprisoned playwright to national leader, remained close.

Havel came to London with members of his new government in the spring of 1990, and Stoppard went to the dinner Thatcher gave for them at Number 10, on 21 March. (Miriam was amazed to meet bohemian writers and artists who were now members of the Czech government.) He was there again when Dubček came to the Czech Embassy on 30 November 1990. He would go back to Prague, from then on, numerous times. In May 1991 he made his first visit since 1977, for a production of *Travesties* at the Realistické Theatre (for which Havel asked him to waive his royalties). He sent a long account of the new Czechoslovakia to his mother. *Travesties* 'was a very pertinent play to the Czechs', he told her. 'In the Lenin bits they laughed their heads off, having all been force-fed with a good socialist education.' He noted how rapidly Thatcherite free-market privatisation was taking over, 'for better or worse'. The new government consisted entirely of people who had been 'banned intellectuals'. Havel's press secretary (and future biographer), Michael Žantovský, was the translator and director of *Travesties*. The Mayor of Prague had translated *Hapgood*. The Minister of Defence had been a literary critic. 'You couldn't invent Czechoslovakia at the moment.' He visited Havel at the enormous palace where Husák had installed innumerable horrible-coloured bathrooms, and at his country house, for lunch with Havel and Olga and their mutual friend Diana Phipps. 'Václav works incredibly hard on a frightful spread of problems – he showed up at the theatre for my party after *Travesties* having travelled straight from some distant town where he had been persuading the coal miners not to strike. I felt quite trivial.' In 1994, there would be another visit to Prague to share a platform with Havel at a PEN conference. Their friendship continued unbroken, if long-distance, until Havel's death in 2011.

Thatcher's dinner for Havel in March 1990 was the last public outing he and Miriam had together. Their separation was gradual, undramatic and good-mannered. They agreed on it in 1988, by which time he was with Felicity, and Miriam was in a relationship with the businessman and industrialist Christopher Hogg – whom Stoppard would later work with, congenially, on the board of the National Theatre. They agreed to wait for two years before telling Ed. Towards the end of 1990, they broke the news to the four sons. This was partly because the papers had begun to run stories about his new relationship with Felicity Kendal, whose marriage with Michael Rudman had broken down and who had moved out of their house, with her two boys, in September 1990, amid what the tabloids called 'mounting speculation'. She was being 'consoled' by Stoppard, the papers said. That month her birthday appeared in Stoppard's appointment diary for the first time.

Oliver, by then twenty-four, was away in Bristol, about to move to Nottingham with his new girlfriend Marie, who became his wife, and trying to write up his thesis. He was going through difficulties, and would later give up physics and become a postman in Norfolk. His father's second divorce hardly affected him. The first Barny heard of it was in a phone call from a journalist. He was twenty-one, and was trying to make a living in the music and video business. In the next few years he would spend some time at Iver and a lot of time in the States.

The younger boys were still at boarding school, and they were told at the same time. Ed, sixteen years old, wrapped up in his own world, was not much disturbed by the break-up. He had his own way to make: he would take his A Levels two years later, then go to Edinburgh University to read French, and then to LAMDA as a drama student. As Miriam remembered it, when they told him what was happening, his father asked him if he was okay. Yes, Ed said, blithely. 'What do you *mean*, yes? This is your mother and father who are going to separate!' But you are so obviously friends, was Ed's response.

Will was eighteen, in his final year at Stowe. He hadn't been aware there was anything wrong, as by now the family were leading such scattered lives, but he was not shocked or startled. He was only concerned that they should all go on having family dinners together as normal, and wrote a thoughtful letter to his father, telling him that he wasn't worried by it, as long as they were both happy and that 'it doesn't disturb the communal activities of the family'. Will left school in the summer of 1991 and then went to Bristol to read psychology – but only for a term. University wasn't for him, he decided, and he went into the music business, first as a road manager for a band, and then founding a management company – always with help and support from his father. He was the closest to Miriam, and was aware that she was deeply upset after the separation, and was trying to protect them from her feelings. She wanted to behave well, and to be remembered as the mother who behaved well.

While the 'media frenzy' was going on, she kept a guard on herself in public and in private, but not quite always. In November 1990 she appeared at the 'Women of Distinction' lunch to present an award, and made a shaky speech about the need for female solidarity: 'I hate it when women put other women down. I wish we could be more supportive of one another.' This was duly reported in the tabloids: 'Perhaps the tearful Dr Miriam Stoppard was thinking about her own situation when she hit out this week at the treachery of women.'

For them both, though, family solidarity and their continuing friendship was what mattered. He was at pains to explain things to the rest of the family: to Fiona (who had had a daughter, Ami, the year before, fourteen years after her son Leo, and so was very preoccupied), to his half-brother Richard and his wife Susan, who were sorry to hear the news but not closely in touch, and to his brother Peter and his wife Lesley, who had not seen it coming. Most importantly he needed to make the situation clear to Bobby and Ken, so that she would not worry. There were many letters and phone calls telling his mother that everyone was all right, and demonstrating how close and friendly he and Miriam still were.

In December 1990, the Stoppards had their last holiday together in Scotland, at Crieff, still a favourite place for them. Anna and David Cooke and their family were aware of the gossip columns in the *Daily Mail* and the *Express*: 'Although he will leave for Scotland next week for one last Christmas with his wife Miriam, playwright Tom Stoppard will soon be free to pursue his friendship with actress Felicity Kendal – friends say the Stoppards are to divorce.' Anna's mother, who was very fond of the family, was sad. You'll see, it will all come right, she said to Miriam. No, Miriam said, he's in love with someone else. Stoppard did not go back to Crieff after that: Anna Cooke thought he would have felt awkward returning there with another companion.

After the holiday, on 28 December 1990, Stoppard issued a formal statement through his lawyers, Harbottle and Lewis, the same lawyers he had used for his divorce from Jose: 'Tom and Miriam Stoppard, who have amicably maintained separate residences for some time past, have agreed on a legal separation.' There were headlines and photographs: 'It's over for Tom.' There was no mention of divorce, and Miriam had no idea or thought of it at that point. He then immediately went on a journey to India, his first since childhood.

Felicity Kendal and Michael Rudman were divorced in March 1991 (and three weeks later Rudman was sacked as director of the Chichester Festival Theatre). She and Stoppard were invited out as a couple now. She moved into a house in Chelsea which he helped her buy. Reporters would snap them when they were out shopping together or with her younger son Jacob. The intrusive press coverage continued, on and off, for the next couple of years. It was particularly spiteful about Miriam, who, as a 'superwoman' figure, was an easy target: 'The woman who told us how to give birth, bring up our children and run our sex lives was very publicly dumped in favour of her husband's regular leading lady.' An unpleasant piece, with a grotesque cartoon, in Murdoch's and Andrew Neil's *Sunday Times*, in May 1991, began: 'For Tom and Miriam and Michael and Felicity, adultery and its attendant angst has been their bread and butter.' The Stoppards had been a 'Golden Couple' who invited the cameras into their house 'when it suited them for publicity purposes'. 'Friends' were cited on Miriam's competitiveness with Stoppard. Miriam was quoted as saying: 'Tom said I had wings and showed me how to fly. I am eternally grateful.'

Old friends who had not been in close touch with him for years wrote letters of sympathy, some wildly at variance with the real situation. His old flatmate Derek Marlowe told him (from his own experience) that he knew what hell he must be going through, the months of guilt, the worry about the children. Isabel wrote wistfully from Bristol, hoping that he had found what he wanted and needed. The Cornwells offered him a country retreat with them. The Pinters, who knew about the scourge of publicity from their own early days together, wrote supportively and rang up to make sure he was all right. The only armour against such exposure, Antonia knew, was that you are happy with what you have done. We're your pals, she told him, and we're here. Also: one does survive.

He was very happy, he told his mother in February 1991, and would not have been able to be so if Miriam and the boys were unhappy. Apart from the embarrassment of its all feeling like 'Hollywood behaviour', and apart from the publicity, everyone involved – Miriam, the boys, Felicity and her sons, Miriam's parents – were fine. On Sunday 12 April, he and Felicity gave a lunch party for a hundred people at Chutney Mary, a newly opened, fashionable Indian restaurant in the King's Road, a statement to all their friends about their new life together. It was a big theatre and media gathering, drawing on both their lives, with guests including Peter Hall, Sheridan Morley, Richard Eyre, Peter Nichols, Ronald Harwood, Ian McKellen and the Braggs, as well as close friends like the Johnsons and the Pinters, Michael Codron and Ned Sherrin.

He told Miriam that year that he wanted to be divorced. She had not expected it. Somehow she had imagined that the marriage would continue in some form. She was shocked, but said to him, at once: 'I'm glad you love somebody enough to want a divorce.' She knew and had known for some time, as she put it later, that there was not enough love in their own relationship to sustain it. And she thought back sadly to what he had said to her when they were separating (sounding like Henry in *The Real Thing*): 'I left a door open. I wasn't careful enough. I didn't say enough.'

Miriam was not jealous, or angry, but she did grieve. She wrote pages about her emotions, and then threw them away. It was painful to read in the tabloids that she had been 'supplanted', but she tried to ignore that, and to behave with civility – since the level of civility in her marriage had always been very high. It was the *idea* of their life together which she bitterly regretted, and she criticised herself for not foreseeing its end. Stoppard thought, by then, that their lives were sufficiently separate for her not to be in pain: but, judging from her own retrospective account, he was wrong about this.

Stoppard's petition for divorce, on a form headed 'Two years' separation and consent', gave his grounds for separation as 'irreconcilable differences'. The date at which 'the petitioner came to the conclusion that the marriage was in fact at an end' was 'at the time of our separation in May 1988'. His address was given as 35 Chelsea Crescent, and hers as Iver Grove from 1988 to 1991 and then Clarges Mews. The divorce was heard at Somerset House on 11 February 1992, twenty years almost to the day since their marriage in the Registry Office at Maidenhead, granted on grounds of having lived apart for two years, and made absolute in June. It was a mid-life event. The Stoppards were fifty-four; Kendal was forty-five; Oliver was twenty-six (and appalled by being so old), Barny twenty-three, Will twenty and Ed eighteen. Bobby was eighty-one, and he took pains to put her mind at rest about the divorce.

By 1990 Iver Grove had become something of a white elephant, and there were always upkeep problems. The huge business of sorting out their possessions and putting the house on the market began in the early 1990s. He moved out, more or less, at the end of 1991, though he still spent some time there. In June 1992 he told his parents that Iver Grove was looking lovely and that he didn't like the thought of not having it, 'or rather of some stranger having it'. 'But I suppose it will have to go in the end.' The boys made intermittent use of Iver all through the 1990s. Barny would remember that the main house had been mothballed but that he and Will would stay in the gardener's cottage and their friends would come and visit. It all felt strange to him in those last years, like the mansion at the end of *Citizen Kane*. There were piles of stuff stored in the stables, and, as he recalled it, people who lived locally would break into the stables and make off with pieces of furniture. Eventually, long after the divorce, in May 1997, Iver Grove was sold for £1,355,000.

Traces of the Stoppards' life in that beautiful grand house lingered on for decades, through three more sets of owners. Some of Miriam's carefully chosen wallpapers and drapes remained, as did the bright red spiral staircase in the coach house up to his study. The mulberry tree at the entrance lived on, still yielding its annual crop. But the once stylish 1980s covered pool gradually turned into an outdated – and malfunctioning – problem area. The Victorian glass case of stuffed birds, one of the many decorative objects from Fernleigh, stayed on, a sad unwanted remnant, in an alcove of the back stairs. The round stone sundial on the wall of the flower garden, with its design of pansies, reading 'For Miriam who made this garden 1982', was never taken down. But the rare pansies vanished utterly, the murals on the garden walls faded and bleached, the water garden that took so much labour to make fell into disrepair. The big swirling energy of the Stoppard family life moved on, fragmented and reshaped itself elsewhere.

There were other changes and preoccupations. Jacky went on working with him after her move to Winchester. He told Bobby that he could not imagine managing without her. But he did change another long-standing arrangement. His brother Peter was retiring from his accountancy firm, Touche Ross, and Stoppard decided this was the moment to take his financial affairs elsewhere. From 1992, he was looked after by Diane Ruskell, a good friend of Jacky's, at a Marlow-based firm, Brewer, Clark and Partners. When she broke away and set up her own firm, Ruskells, in 1997, he went with her. She found him a pleasure to work with, straightforward, entirely uninterested in complicated financial deals, and – unlike some of her other 'showbiz' clients – not in the least temperamental. They worked in a relationship of complete trust.

Peter had spent years making sure that his brother kept enough in reserve from his 'substantial income' to pay his taxes. His judgement on Stoppard's attitude to money was that he wasn't recklessly extravagant, but liked treats and luxuries. Peter was slightly hurt by the move, but saw that it was the right moment for it. One extra expense incurred at this time was a bill for dental implants. Stoppard was having a lot of trouble with his teeth – and he knew why. 'Too many jelly babies,' he told his mother ruefully. As with all his medical interventions, he took this stoically.

As well as his passionate interest in what Havel was doing in Czechoslovakia, there were other public involvements at this time. He spoke up over the 1989 fatwa against Salman Rushdie, and, on its third anniversary, in February 1992, shared a platform with Günter Grass, Martin Amis and Rushdie himself, under the title 'What Is to Be Done?'. The discussion was televised live for the BBC and his speech was published in the *Observer*. He argued, as he did in other contexts, that there should be no special favours done to writers, and that if they were seen just as 'writers closing ranks for literature' or 'Western liberals come together to deplore attitudes uncongenial to Western liberalism', that would not be useful. Freedom of expression was 'not unimportant' to him but was not a fundamental right and was not the central issue. He believed that the death sentence handed out to Rushdie by the government of another country invoking religious law, an 'extreme sanction which is strange and repugnant to us', was 'deeply wrong on the level of humanness which binds us all', but not because Rushdie was a *writer*.

> If I were to open a pub and, through a combination of amazing ignorance and misplaced enthusiasm, were to call it 'The Mohammed', I dare say a fatwa would be coming my way pretty smartly. Would the publican merit your intercession more than, or less than, the writer? I hope you would reply: equally . . . I have never been comfortable with the idea that words have a preferential status over and above the discomfort they may give others simply because someone has chosen to write them.

This led to an exchange of views with the philosopher Ronald Dworkin, to whom Stoppard wrote: 'As a writer I find it embarrassing to insist on across-the-board rights for anything I choose to write, any place, any time.'

His public responsibilities expanded when he joined the board of the National Theatre (while Richard Eyre was managing director), where he would serve for thirteen years. He regarded it as an honour, and felt it was right to 'pay back' one of his main theatrical homes – though he was anxious there might be a conflict of interest. His first meeting, on 11 October 1989, began with Richard Eyre's tribute to Laurence Olivier, who had died that summer, 'the great buccaneer actor-manager who was also a Hollywood film star'. Eyre said he felt diffident about leading this tribute in the presence of Tom Stoppard, whose eulogy on the death of Ken Tynan ('he was part of the luck we had') had set a standard difficult to emulate. The board stood in silence. The next item on their agenda was to welcome Stoppard. Eyre sent him an appreciative note: 'I was enormously grateful for your presence at the Board Meeting the other day. It really helped to focus the discussion, not only by what you said, but the authority with which you said it.' He wrote in his diary: 'Board meeting. I describe the aim of the NT to present what couldn't or wouldn't be done in the commercial theatre both in content and style. Tom S says it's for [i.e. the NT stood for] the best of everything: our greatest asset is our integrity.'

The chair of the board was the highly effective Lady Mary Soames. Fellow members of the board, a mixture of legal, diplomatic, entrepreneurial and theatre interests, included Michael Palliser, Michael Codron, Lois Sieff, Sarah Hogg, Sonia Melchett, Victor Mishcon, Peter Parker and Judi Dench. Over the years other names came in: Dipak Nandy, Ian McKellen, Joan Bakewell, Sue McGregor, Ben Okri, Chris Smith, Lola Young. Not all these names attended meetings regularly, but Stoppard did. Christopher Hogg, Miriam's partner, was appointed chair in July 1995.

There were two big, difficult issues in those years. One was the development plans proposed in 1994 for the South Bank building, very publicly opposed by the original architect, Denys Lasdun, and only partially carried out. Stoppard never liked the brutalist look of the building, but he felt for Lasdun and thought his views should be respected. The other was the succession to Richard Eyre as director of the National Theatre. Stoppard was closely involved with this between 1995 and 1996, and it was he who first tentatively approached Trevor Nunn, found out that he was interested and urged the board to snap him up. His last year on the board also coincided with the appointment of Nicholas Hytner to replace Nunn. By coincidence, all three of these director-managers, Eyre, Nunn and Hytner, ended their regimes at the National by directing a Stoppard play: *The Invention of Love*, *The Coast of Utopia* and *The Hard Problem*.

In the everyday management of the theatre, there were constant discussions about the renovation of the building, programming, touring, the Arts Council grant, relations with the unions, the deficit, the National's public profile and audience figures. As one of the National's leading playwrights Stoppard would find himself receiving reports on the box-office take, or the scheduling plans, or cast changes, or West End transfers, of his own plays. On one unfortunate occasion, it was explained to the board that the first preview of the 1995 revival of *Rosencrantz* had to be cancelled 'for operational reasons'. He kept quiet.

In board discussions he listened more than he spoke. When he did contribute, he was clear-headed and pragmatic, sometimes sounding a cautionary note, and only occasionally allowing himself (rather to Eyre's surprise) to ramble. He kept a sharp eye on the press coverage of the theatre, and he wasn't above dealing with small details. The front-of-house carpet needed renovating. More seating was needed for people eating at the Olivier buffet. They should discount seat prices for the less popular shows. They needed to decide what touring was for: was it 'to show the flag or make money?' If they accepted commercial sponsorship for a musical they should ask themselves 'what recognition would the sponsors require?' Eyre found him a wise and supportive adviser, who would warn him when he felt Eyre was over-dramatising a problem. His voice can be heard coming through the dry board minutes, as when discussing, in 1990, whether productions could be made less elaborate to save money. He didn't think the National Theatre productions were 'ostentatious'; the public 'got its money's worth'. He believed that 'words, unfortunately, did not count as much with audiences as visual presentation'. When discussing the new building plans, he said that the scheme 'looked careful and not at all greedy'. And it was right to refurbish the building. It was part of making the National Theatre more welcoming to 'another generation' and ensuring its achievements were appreciated: 'What was happening on stage, at the core, was being re-invented all the time, and people took that for granted.'

At the time he joined the board, his work beyond the National Theatre was in full spate. In the early 1990s, there were new productions: of *Rough Crossing*, at the King's Head and in Brooklyn, with music by André Previn; of *Hapgood* at A.C.T. in San Francisco; and of *The Real Inspector Hound*, with *The (Fifteen-minute) Dogg's Troupe Hamlet*, by the Roundabout Theatre off Broadway from July to October 1992. There would be a major RSC production of a much revised *Travesties* in the autumn of 1993. That summer BBC Radio 3 broadcast all his radio plays, just before the film of *Rosencrantz* won the Golden Lion award at Venice. Faber published the radio plays in 1990 and again, with additions, in 1994, which gave him the chance to write a tribute to John Tydeman. Film work continued apace – including the first, unproduced version of *Shakespeare in Love*. And, in the early 1990s, he was working on two major plays.

So, in his mid-fifties, he was much in the news and had a high international profile. Around this time, understandably, he began to have a horror of publicity, and a dread of biography. He was going through all his papers while leaving Iver, and sold his first tranche of papers and manuscripts – keeping back anything personal – to the American archive where many British authors have deposited their papers, the Harry Ransom Center at the University of Austin at Texas. Oddly enough, Anthony Smith was selling his many letters from his old friend to the same archive, and wrote to ask him if this was all right. He also wanted Stoppard to publish his old Bristol arts pieces. Stoppard replied: 'What a coincidence. I too have just done a deal with Austin. How ridiculous to know that your letter to me and my reply will both end up there. *Cui bono?*' He added that he had a horror of things appearing 'in a book', such as the letter he had written to Dirk Bogarde in 1977 about Fassbinder's *Despair*, saying: 'It's rubbish, Dirk.' And he certainly did not want to reprint his journalism. When his archive arrived at Texas in the autumn of 1993 he gave a talk to the Austin students. It touched on the relationship between the private life, the publishing and editing of written materials, and biography.

> Without meaning to, without having any secret agenda, one is constantly obscuring the tracks of one's own life – on a very trivial, domestic level . . . Whenever I happen to read something which attempts to reconstruct the past from scraps of evidence, not hearsay, no – absolute black and white, written-down documentation, people's notes, whatever – the process of doing such, invariably it seems, leaves out the fallibility of the person producing this evidence, the innocent fallibility. And if you reconstructed the last two weeks of my life, it would be full of errors because I'm so sloppy about the evidence I leave. It's so misleading . . .

These feelings got into the plays of the early 1990s, at a time when his private life was being so much exposed. Predatory and inept researchers of the past are figures of fun in his next two plays. And he kept coming back to his belief that the work should stand on its own and that his own life was not directly reflected in his plays. The way 'I feed off myself', he would say in an interview in 1998 about *Indian Ink*, is 'more to do with the thoughts I have had than the days I have lived'. The exchange with Anthony was part of an increasing anxiety about what might happen to all the personal letters he had written. He was interviewed at the end of 1992 for Michael Hordern's memoir, and told Bobby that he hoped no one would ever write his biography or publish his letters. 'Burn everything,' he told her. (She didn't.) He was reading Larkin's letters, which had just come out. Larkin had sent him a copy of 'Aubade', and as a humorous return gift, Stoppard had sent Larkin a poem he had written for Miriam. Larkin had been kind in response, but imagine if he had said something vile about it! There it would be, forever in the letters. When the book about Hordern came out, he disliked the feeling of being 'raw material' in someone else's Life. If you wrote a fan letter to an actor, it was always exaggerated: and there it was, cold on the page. Mark Lawson, who interviewed him in the

spring of 1993, described him as having 'a sense of doom' about the prospect of a biography. Like Oscar Wilde, he thought it added a new terror
to death. When he went back to India at the end of 1990, for the first time
since leaving at the age of eight, and wrote a piece about it, he sent it to his
mother saying: 'I hope it's not too personal.'

Yet touches of autobiography crept in all over the place in his writing.
Introducing a fundraising volume for the Bristol Old Vic in 1993, he spoke
fondly of it as his alma mater, the place where he 'caught the bug' of life
in the theatre: 'I was a junior reporter when I entered the Theatre Royal
for the first time, and it still feels more as if it entered me.' A light piece
for a collection edited by Antonia Fraser in 1992, *The Pleasure of Reading*,
took him back to his purchases of the *Dandy* and *Beano* 'in the shop near
the Capitol Cinema in Darjeeling' and 'the library on the troopship which
brought us from India when I was eight'. And his India play was full of
personal traces.

He had already written most of *In the Native State* before he went back
to India. It was written for, and dedicated to, Felicity Kendal. Their childhood Indian memories – hers of theatrical touring, his of schooldays –
overlapped. Like him, but a decade later, she had been in Darjeeling. The
Kendal troupe had often performed for maharajahs in their native states
– paralleling his memory of being taken by his mother to a rajah's palace.
He knew her family stories, and of the tragic early death of her elder sister
Jennifer in 1984. *In the Native State* was in part inspired by that sisterly
relationship, a consolation to Felicity for Jennifer's death. He got to know
her mother, Laura, who died the year after he wrote *In the Native State*,
and when he rewrote it for the stage he dedicated it to her memory. The
redoubtable Geoffrey Kendal was felled by a succession of strokes during
the time that Stoppard and Kendal were together, and died in 1998. He
also became friends with the Kapoors, Jennifer's widower the actor Shashi
Kapoor, and their grown-up children. His return to India was closely
bound up with that family. He told Bobby that he had been around 'non-
stop' with Felicity's relatives in India, and he made his trip to Darjeeling
with Kendal's nephew, the photographer Karan Kapoor, who took the pictures which illustrated the essay he wrote about his return, 'Going Back'.

was a frequent visitor to the Jaipur Literature Festival. He returned, always, with the same sense of pleasure, excitement and nostalgia.

In the Native State was commissioned by his old radio producer John Tydeman, who was retiring. It was recorded for BBC Radio 3 in January 1991, and transmitted on 21 April 1991. So it overlapped closely with 'Going Back'. And the play was also about returning and remembering, and the perils of reconstructing the past.

There is a tenderness and eroticism to the India play not quite like anything else in his work. It is light and sweet about sexual attraction, in the mood of *Shakespeare in Love*, which overlapped with it in time – and which is also about a woman inspiring a male artist. But here the inspiration goes both ways. His first idea was to have a 'conversation between a poet and a painter. While the poet was having her portrait painted, she would be writing a poem about having her portrait painted.' What she is writing affects the mood of the painting. Her poems are moist and pulsating, in tune with the dripping hot weather and the 'exoticism' of the setting. (He wrote and rewrote these poems exhaustively: this was the only time he aired his private passion for writing poetry in a play.) As the play unfolds, her clothes will come off, and there will be a secret painting of her naked, an intimate portrait of an Englishwoman in the formal tradition of Indian paintings of sexual delight.

In Indian art, every work has its *rasa*, as the Indian painter explains to the English poet. '*Rasa* is juice. Its taste. Its essence. A painting must have its *rasa* . . . which is not *in* the painting exactly. *Rasa* is what you must feel when you see a painting, or hear music; it is the emotion which the artist must arouse in you.' There are nine *rasas*, and each has its own mood, or colour. 'The *rasa* of erotic love is called Shringara . . . and it is aroused by, for example, the moon, the scent of sandalwood, or being in an empty house.' The *rasa* of erotic love colours the play, full of heat and sexuality, and dominated by the character of the free-living, sensual – and mortally ill – Flora Crewe.

Rasa came late as an idea for the play. Browsing in a shop in Tottenham Court Road, while he was in the middle of writing it, he picked up a book on Indian art (quite possibly B. N. Goswamy's *Essence of Indian Art*, published in 1986), discovered the concept there and knew at once how useful it would be. (In ancient Sanskrit dramatic theory, *rasa* is applied above all to the art of theatre and dance; it also has a profound influence on modern Indian film, as in the work of Satyajit Ray.) You could call this good luck, or complete accident – or, as he put it, the God of Playwrights taking a hand. Before that, in 1988 or 1989, he had started the play, as usual, with several ideas at once. He wanted to draw on his memories of India, by way of 'using what I've got', as he said in interview: 'I've got India. It feels that one should be using it sometime sooner or later.' He wanted to write a part for Kendal which had to do with their shared Indian memories, and to write about the British Raj and colonialism, and to do something with the idea of the painter painting the poet. His first notes try out some of these ideas, like someone noting down the ingredients of a dream, in a list headed 'Radio':

A woman is writing a poem.
A painter is painting her.
A person is speaking to the painter.
All three are being filmed.

The poem develops.
The painting develops.
The film is edited –

Real poet? – Documentary on painter? On both?
The poem is about the painter painting
The film is about – ??

Someone is Indian – the poet?
Someone is talking of Empire – ??

Narrative development –
Woman is colonised –

Poet is English –
Painter is Husband –
Film maker – ? Indian . . .

Poet is English –
Painter . . .

As a radio play, *In the Native State* could be flexible with time and place. Like all his plays of this decade, it is a memory play, moving between two times, which asks how accurately the past can be re-found. Different forms of narrative inside the play – painting, poetry, letters, editing, biography, history – provide competing ways of telling a life story.

The radio play moves between India in 1930 and England in the present day – around 1990. In the stage version, there are also scenes set in present-day India. The Indian setting is the imaginary 'native state' of Jummapur, in the year of an exceptional heat wave, and of Gandhi's non-violent protest march against the British tax on Indian salt production, the start of his civil disobedience movement, which eventually led to independence. These states were ruled by local princes. But they were British protectorates, whose rulers were usually loyal to the British, and they were kept an eye on by the British Residency, representing the Governor-General of India. The typical protagonists of a 'native state' feature in the play, from local nationalists and literary types, a wealthy hedonistic rajah, a young British army officer at the Residency and the stuffy English expats, to a comically canny house servant and a little boy, the 'punkah-wallah', whose job it is to wave the fan to keep the English lady cool.

But 'native state' also applies to the play's heroine, the English poet, who comes to India for the first time at the age of thirty-five. Flora Crewe is the daughter of divorced parents whose mother died on the *Titanic* with her lover. She brought up her much younger and equally free-spirited sister, now the mistress of a Communist politician. (The politician's name is Chamberlain, in his usual offstage tribute to Jacky.) Flora has had numerous affairs, broken off an engagement to a millionaire crook, modelled for Modigliani and quarrelled with Gertrude Stein in Paris, hung out on the edges of Bloomsbury, and writes volumes of erotic, experimental poetry with 1920s-style literary titles: *Venus in Her Season, Nymph in Her Orisons*. She has come to India to give lectures to Theosophical Societies and Book Clubs on 'Literary Life in London': 'I was surprised you did not mention Virginia Woolf.' 'I seldom do.' She has also come to India for her health – though she soon becomes aware that most people *leave* India for their health. Flora is impetuous, worldly and gallantly stoic about the lung disease which is soon to kill her. We hear her voice through her poetry and her letters to her sister. She has a Wildean dryness: 'I seldom cry, but never in the electric light.' Above all she is independent and liberated. She intends to stay in her 'native state', and not be taken control of or colonised by anyone else. She uses men, as her sister will say of her, 'like batteries. When things went flat, she'd put in a new one.'

Flora causes a stir. Everyone who meets her wants to give her their own version of India. She is being painted by an Indian artist, Nirad Das, a mixture of Hindu nationalist, lover of Indian culture and Anglophile. His mixed education, split between a 'vernacular' school and an English-style Bombay boarding school, founded on the imperial principles of Macaulay (whom Stoppard enjoyed reading) that all Indians should be taught English, sums up his divided nature. At times he verges on a comic stage Indian, saying things like 'I am top hole,' or "This is a red-letter day without dispute.' The play has fun with language differences – which are also political markers. Nirad and Flora have a running joke about Anglo-Indian usages, in a wild parody of *Hobson-Jobson*, brimming over with his pleasure in the words he's known since his childhood:

> Flora: While having tiffin on the verandah of my bungalow I spilled kedgeree on my dungarees and had to go to the gymkhana in my pyjamas looking like a coolie.
> Das: I was buying chutney in the bazaar when a thug who had escaped from the choky ran amuck and killed a box-wallah for his loot, creating a hullabaloo and landing himself in the mulligatawny.

India to the Romans, he tells her that it was the Indians who were the Romans: 'We were up to date when you were a backward nation.' When he defends his father's mild nationalist protest (he threw a mango at the Resident's Daimler), for which he was imprisoned, she angrily makes the case for the empire: 'We made you a proper country! And when we left you fell straight to pieces like Humpty Dumpty!' As usual both sides of the political case are made. But whatever we think of her views, old Mrs Swan's nostalgia for the India she knew, in the Himalayan country near Nepal, which she still thinks of as home, is eloquent and touching. The play ends movingly with a last flashback, her visit as a girl of eighteen to Flora's grave a year after she died:

Orchards of apricot – almond – plum – [. . .] up in the North-West . . . I was quite unprepared for it when I first arrived. It was early summer. There was a wind blowing. (*Cross-fading, wind.*) And I have never seen such blossom, it blew everywhere, there were drifts of snow-white flowers piled up against the walls of the graveyard. I had to kneel on the ground and sweep the petals off her stone to read her name.

'He's really a soppy old thing,' said John Tydeman, lovingly, commenting on the play.

For Anish Das, trying to do his dead father justice, and for Eleanor, remembering her dead sister, and for Mr Pike, relentlessly sleuthing, time travel is only possible in their imagination. The clock cannot be put back, any more than what England did to India can be wiped out. That's the trouble with biography: however hard you try, you cannot go back in time, in the way that this play can. *In the Native State* – and *Indian Ink* – make a wicked satire on the editor-biographer, who is always getting things wrong. Stoppard liked the idea of a kind of Flann O'Brien narrative, as in *At Swim-Two-Birds* (a book he loved) where characters rebel against their narrator and editorial commentary gets mixed up with story-telling. The idea of 'the commentator making points about the material which he is part of' went back to *Rosencrantz and Guildenstern* and *The Real Inspector Hound*.

In the radio play the voice of Pike, with his southern American accent, irritatingly intrudes all through Flora's story, doggedly filling in the gaps and putting us right, 'telling you things you already know or don't need to know at that moment'. He is often barking up the wrong tree. At one point, in a nice fusion of the two time zones, Flora shouts down a barking dog as if she is telling Pike to shut up.

In *Indian Ink*, Pike is an onstage character, and more coarsely ruthless: 'This is why God made poets and novelists, so the rest of us can get published,' he says. There are new scenes in which he goes to modern-day Jummapur in pursuit of the last links to Flora's story. He teams up with an Indian literary critic (with satirical views on the persistence of Indian Anglophilia) and they track down the site of her dak bungalow, which was burned down during Partition. Only the tree which Flora mentioned in her letters, 'a big green tree with monkeys and parrots in the branches', remains. (It's an inverted echo of Stoppard's wistful discovery, in 'Going Back', that the tree he went back to Darjeeling to find had long ago been cut down.) They interview the Rajah's grandson, and they find a very obscure old man, the lavatory attendant in their hotel, who was the little boy who worked the punkah in Flora's dak bungalow, and saw Nirad Das painting her portrait. Pike is beside himself with excitement at the chance of meeting the old man after dinner. A typical biographer, he can't wait. '*After dinner?* He could *die* while I'm eating!'

In *Indian Ink*, Mrs Swan spars with Mr Pike, putting him off the scent, warning him not to write a book about Flora, and telling him: '*Biography* is the worst possible excuse for getting people wrong.' To our delight, some of Flora's secrets evade him. The key to her life is not in biography or editing but in the heart of those who loved her, and in art: her poetry, her letters and the paintings of her. The different portraits of Flora are like ghosts, haunting the play. As she says in *Indian Ink*: 'Perhaps my soul will stay behind as a smudge of paint on paper, as if I'd always been here . . .' Modigliani painted her in the nude, but the painting was burnt. Das did a sketch of her lecturing, but tore it up. The portrait he painted of her, in a blue dress, which ends up on the front of her *Letters*, is unfinished. All the better, says Flora: a finished picture is like looking at a stopped clock. The secret portrait, of a nude Flora set inside a bejewelled miniature in traditional Indian style, is only seen by Flora and Nirad, and eventually by Anish and Eleanor. 'How like Flora,' says Mrs Swan: she means, how like her to have chosen to be painted thus. It is an Anglo-Indian picture, in which the English woman and the Indian artist are set free and joined together through the work of art. Perhaps they were lovers, but we don't know that, and nor does Mr Pike. The interior life of Flora Crewe is as evasive as the objective truth about Indian history.

'I'm the only person in England', he said in 1995, 'who never saw *The Jewel in the Crown*.' Tydeman may have cast Peggy Ashcroft to play Eleanor Swan partly because of her part in that famous ITV series about the British Raj, but Paul Scott's novels and their adaptations were not a direct influence on Stoppard. He had been reading about India long before he started to work on the India play. Now he read Naipaul, and the BBC India expert Mark Tully, and *The Autobiography of an Unknown Indian* by Nirad Chaudhuri, and a great number of books on Indian history, politics and art, including Emily Eden's *Up the Country* and Charles Allen's *Scrapbooks of the Raj*. And *Hobson-Jobson*, the classic nineteenth-century glossary of Anglo-Indian vocabulary. Of course he had read Forster. *A Passage to India* shadows the play, and is mentioned in it: 'Otherwise, it's hanging over the play like an unacknowledged ghost.' The relationship between Flora and Nirad Das echoes that between Adela Quested and Dr Aziz; the members of the British Residency are satirised as Forster's colonialists are; the British officer, Durance, is a nicer version of Adela's fiancé Ronny Heaslop; Mrs Swan has a touch of wise, mysterious, cranky Mrs Moore.

The play attracted the same kinds of criticisms as Forster had, for caricaturing the Indian characters, or lacking understanding of the nationalist movement, or sitting on the fence about colonialism. In spite of the forceful arguments for Independence it contains, he was accused of having treated pre-Independence India as 'a kind of English Eden' and of identifying with Mrs Swan as his 'conservative mouthpiece'. There would be complaints that Indian women made no appearance in the play, that it depoliticised the end of empire by 'moving political questions into the bedroom' and that it was 'an exercise in feeding what was left of the Raj nostalgia machine in the 1990s'. He himself liked the play's refusal of ideology. 'It's much more an intimate play than a polemical play,' he said of it. 'It's a very cosy play in many ways . . . worryingly cosy sometimes. But I really enjoy its lack of radical fierceness.'

Felicity Kendal called the radio play 'a little jewel in his crown'. The stage version, in her view, 'lost a little bit of its delicacy'. It was very well cast. With her dryness and allure, she was exactly right, he thought, as Flora. Saeed Jaffrey had a nice cameo as the Rajah. At the tender heart of the radio play was a beautiful performance by the eighty-three-year-old Peggy Ashcroft. It was her last part; she died later that year. In the first read-through, the young woman playing Eleanor's younger self at eighteen could not be there, and Ashcroft said she wanted to read it, and had thought she was going to play both parts. And she did read it, eloquently, but both Tydeman and Stoppard knew she could not possibly play the eighteen-year-old. When they told her this, she was upset. Tydeman left it to Stoppard to persuade her, by asking her to listen back to the recording. After that she had to agree with them: 'Ah well,' she said sadly, 'there you are. You get older.' Stoppard consoled her. The girl was a different person from the old woman, he said to her. What you are at twenty is not what you are at eighty. Tydeman, listening, thought he was impeccably tactful.

The radio play was well received, and caused a buzz of publicity because of the links with Kendal's Indian childhood and their new relationship. He was pleased with it, and thought that by comparison *Indian Ink* was just a piece of craft-work, an enlargement of the original idea. It upset him if his radio work was overlooked. He had a sentence (which he later cut) in his introduction to the Faber reissue of his radio plays, saying how galling it was when people described *Arcadia* as his first play since *Hapgood*: 'poor *In the Native State!*'

Initially he intended to make a straightforward stage version of the radio play, for a production by Dan Crawford at the King's Head Theatre in Islington, scheduled for 1992. But he decided he needed to start again from scratch. He wrote apologetically to Crawford.

> It won't do to stage it in its radio-script form. I want to write it again as a stage play without trying to 'save' the radio play. I don't quite

know how to do it . . . I don't think it can be simply put on stage like
Artist Descending . . . I know this is disappointing but I hope not
incomprehensible.

Instead of going straight ahead with the adaptation of the India play in
1992, he was writing the first screenplay version of *Shakespeare in Love*,
alongside other film work, and engrossed in writing his next new play,
Arcadia, which he had started the year before and which would be staged in
1993. And he was celebrating his fifty-fifth birthday, in August that year, with
a holiday on Richard Branson's Caribbean island of Necker. They were a big
party: Felicity and her two boys, one of his nephews, Barny, Oliver and his
partner Marie, Ed and a friend. (Will, to his lasting annoyance, had to stay
home for a music tour he was managing.) They were 'all in one place and in
one house on one island for ten days', as he told Bobby. This was one of the
longest times he spent uninterruptedly with Felicity, and the only time, too,
that his sons got to know her. It was a luxurious, convivial interlude.

After the holiday, *Arcadia* took over, and it would be a couple of years
before he went back to the India play, with a new title, which he said was
a combination of 'holy inspiration and the work bench'. *Indian Ink* was
staged in 1995. There had been talk of its going to the small theatre at the
National, the Cottesloe, but by 1995 *Arcadia* had had a long run there,
and had transferred to the Haymarket. So Michael Codron took *Indian
Ink* for the Aldwych, and it ran there (after a short out-of-town preview at
the Yvonne Arnaud Theatre in Guildford) from 27 February 1995, for ten
months, overlapping with *Arcadia*. As it turned out, this production was to
be the final collaboration between Stoppard, Michael Codron, Peter Wood,
Carl Toms and Felicity Kendal. Peter Wood found it magical, because 'it
allowed [Stoppard] to be a poet'. It was the last time they worked together.

In *Indian Ink*, the 'present time' was moved back five years to the 'mid-
1980s', so, in 1995, it became a history play twice over. In a new beginning, it
started with Flora writing to her sister about her arrival in Jummapur, not
with her reading her poem while being painted. There were many changes
to the switches between the two time zones, which co-existed (like *Arcadia*)
in one, fluid set. Eldon Pike became an onstage character who visits India

in the 1980s. The characterisations became more emphatic. In the dialogue between Anish and Mrs Swan, a more melancholy note was struck. Mrs Swan was a Communist in 1930 and has become a conservative; Anish's father was a nationalist in 1930, but reverted to nostalgic Anglophilia. 'He must have – altered,' Anish says. Mrs Swan replies: 'Yes. One alters.'

As always he jibbed at having to give explanations, and he and Peter Wood had their usual arguments about this: 'I'm always disappointed by the degree of explicitness which is forced out of me . . . Peter is constantly at me to help [the audience].' There was much discussion about whether it should be made clear that Flora and Nirad sleep together (as there had been in *The Real Thing* about Annie and Billy). One tiny detail took up a lot of time. When Nirad explains *rasa* to Flora, he gives 'the scent of sandalwood' as an example of what can arouse it. Much later in the play, he lends her his handkerchief. In the radio play, she says: 'Your handkerchief smells faintly of something nice. Is it cinnamon?' But Wood wanted Flora to say: 'Is it sandalwood?' so as to remind the audience of *rasa*. Stoppard noted, during the run of the play: 'I refused to let the word sandalwood appear in the scene – to everybody's fury. Two or three nights ago, I relented.' The change – like many of the small production changes – did not get into the published text. Of course different audiences picked up different things. He was delighted that two people in the audience laughed when Flora, being shown the Rajah's fleet of cars – a Rolls, a Bentley, a Bugatti – recognises one of them as 'a Brancusi'. A fax sent to the stage door, three months after the play had opened, for the attention of Margaret Tyzack and Paul Bhattacharjee, showed how closely he was listening. It concerns two lines between their characters after Mrs Swan's outburst about how the British made India a 'proper country'.

Anish: Oh yes . . . I am a guest here and I have been . . .
Mrs Swan (*calming down*): No, only provocative.

Wood had asked Tyzack to speak the line as if it were a question. Stoppard wrote to the actors:

Forgive my ungilding this lily but the interrogative 'only provocative' is not what I meant and it bugs me, so I have asked Peter if I may withdraw his suggestion of the other week. Paul, if you slightly slow down the feed 'and I have been . . . ', ie use the three dots, his finding his way to the right word (which might have been 'careless') it gives Mrs S a moment in which to complete/correct the sense of his statement quite simply. I hope this isn't annoying. Love, T.

Michael Codron, who thought the play 'suffused with the spell that India clearly had for Stoppard', was anxious about it in its pre-London run, and he too gave Peter Wood a great number of notes. But Codron came to love the production, with its 'haunting Indian reed music . . . and Carl Tom's gauzy, gliding sets'. There were eloquent performances by Felicity Kendal (who was replaced later in the run by Niamh Cusack), Margaret Tyzack, and Art Malik as Nirad. Stoppard maintained that he didn't know Malik had starred in *The Jewel in the Crown* – though he did know 'he was the villain in Schwarzenegger's *True Lies*'. On the opening night, he was seen edging his way into a middle-row seat, apologising to his neighbours for disturbing them, and then saying amiably: 'After all, you wouldn't be here if it weren't for me.'

But it got mixed reviews. One critic complained that throwing a mango at the Resident's car was a pretty soft-edged critique of empire. And because of the huge response to *Arcadia*, still running at the Haymarket Theatre, he became somewhat the victim of his own success. *Indian Ink* was described as a weak follow-up, even though it was, originally, written earlier. 'You don't have to think *Arcadia* a masterpiece to be stupefied by *Indian Ink*,' one critic wrote, calling it 'a clunky and obvious reworking' of the radio play. Another lamented that it 'had neither the emotional impact nor the intellectual razzle-dazzle of *Arcadia*'. It did not transfer to Broadway, and it would not often be revived. All the same, the India play kept a place in his heart, and for those who worked on it with him, it was 'one of the happiest experiences of all the Stoppards'.

24

Arcadia

Thomasina: Yes, we must hurry if we are going to dance.

Valentine: And everything is mixing the same way, all the time,
irreversibly . . .

Septimus: Oh, we have time, I think.

Valentine: . . . till there's no time left. That's what time means.

Begun in 1991, worked on through 1992 and staged in 1993, *Arcadia* is a mid-life play. It is written at a time of looking back and looking forward, just as the play looks back and forward. The parallel lines spoken by Septimus and Valentine in the last act hold in one mental space the moment in which we still have time to act, and the prospect that time will in the end run out, for us individually as well as for the universe: 'we have time'/'there's no time left'. The play is full of anxiety and sadness about time. But it is also a comedy of time, and timings, and plays with time in enchantingly light and suspenseful ways.

Arcadia is a truly original play, and seduced its audiences and readers by being so new and ingenious. The thrill of discovering revolutionary ideas, for the scientists, poets, historians, landscape gardeners and geniuses who inhabit the play, mirrors the ebullient inventiveness of the thing itself.

Time had always been on his mind. It goes right back to his experiments of the 1960s, under the influence of Eliot, with the inexorable ticking taxi meter that measures out Dominic Boot's day, or Gladys the speaking clock made dizzy by the infinity of time ('Silence is the sound of time passing'), or the early version of *Rosencrantz and Guildenstern at the Court of King Lear*, ending with Hamlet's soliloquy: 'I have time . . . it will be night soon . . . I have a lot of time.' Out of that came their play, which they spend killing time, stuck in limbo, not knowing their fate, while scenes from *Hamlet*, in another time zone, keep rushing in on them at fast-forward speed. Time bumping backwards in curious jolts, in *Artist Descending a Staircase*; the sadness of lost time cutting across the present in *Where Are They Now?*; Henry Carr in *Travesties* talking us back into past time through his fallible rememberings; *Hapgood*'s particle-like twins operating in two times at once; the see-saw of *In the Native State* (and then *Indian Ink*) from the present to the past: all these plays make us think about time. Now, in *Arcadia*, time is the subject: what is happening to it; how we live in it, not knowing our fates; whether those things which have become 'lost to view will have their time again'. Though we must inevitably be lost in time, perhaps time can be conquered, and the past conjured up.

As usual, this was not his only idea. *Arcadia* is about knowledge, sex and love, death and pastoral, Englishness and poetry, biography and history. Not to mention chaos mathematics, iterated algorithms, Fermat's Last Theorem and the Second Law of Thermodynamics. It is a play with one set, set in two time zones. It is a comedy with a tragedy inside it. And it is a quest story, which he kept reminding himself, in his notes, to keep in focus: '*Simple narrative must be prime*. The poet – the critic – the duel – the Suitor – the Garden – the Waltz. The searcher – the quest – the discovery – (and being wrong) –.'

Set at the start of the nineteenth century and in the late twentieth century, it brings together two kinds of revolutions. One is the shift between Enlightenment and Romantic culture. The other is the recent shift between classical science and new ways of thinking in maths, physics and biology. Neither of these happened all at once. Nobody wakes up one morning to find they are suddenly a Romantic poet as opposed to an Enlightenment satirist (Byron was both), and Newton's laws weren't instantly replaced by quantum physics. But the play suggests turning points.

Its two time zones, which run in parallel, converge at the end of the play. So do the two strands of the arts and science, which are not opposites, as some people say, but have a great deal in common, and can be equally creative. The cunning beauty and delight of *Arcadia* is how its ingredients – human, romantic, intellectual, scientific – are meshed together to make a perfect whole.

In *Hapgood*, quantum physics and Cold War spying were effortfully brought together. In *Arcadia*, his eclectic reading led to a more rewarding outcome. He told Bobby in 1991 that he had been reading for a play 'about the Romantic/Classical temperament, I mean the change between'. He had been browsing in books on Byron and Romanticism in Paul Johnson's library, and reading about the history of landscape gardening. And he continually followed new developments in science. He said later: '*Arcadia* came out of the subjects that had been my enthusiasms over years and years.' He started with two thoughts, how to put 'chaos' in a play, and how to have a play with one set, moving through time.

His own self-education was itself an example of what fascinated him: how the mind works things out, how knowledge is acquired and put to use. He enjoys writing plays in which thinkers make sense of the world, or apply logic and reason to what seems impenetrable. He loves to set up complications that require acrobatic feats of ingenuity to solve. He likes to show characters wondering if there is any order inside apparent randomness, like Mr Moon in *Malquist,* or Rosencrantz and Guildenstern tossing coins. He is interested in people who are obsessed with proving the unprovable, like George in *Jumpers,* or who are gambling on a completely new way of thinking, like the ridiculous Tristan Tzara, or Joyce the modernist genius, or the stubborn Galileo. How do new systems of thought come into the world, and what kinds of people might think them?

Although he is famously a playwright of ideas, who often says that he starts from the idea rather than from the plot or the characters – or his own life – there are always people mixed up with the ideas. Part of what attracted him to quantum physics was the compelling personal voice of Richard Feynman. When he heard that Feynman had died, in 1988, just after *Hapgood* was launched, he said: 'I don't think I've ever read [an obituary] which caused me such a stab of grief as I felt on reading of the death of an American physicist whom I had never met and whose work was way out of the reach of my understanding.' He knew that it was, fundamentally, 'grief for myself': he had wanted to send him *Hapgood* as 'an object of tribute'. But, more than that, he had wanted Feynman to know that he had tried to cross the 'great divide in our culture' between science and art. Reading Feynman had confirmed his view that 'science and art are more like each other than unlike . . . [they] are not just *like* each other, they sometimes seem to *be* each other'. He called him 'an aristocrat in science and a democrat in almost everything else'.

He responded as strongly to James Gleick's popular 1987 book on chaos theory, which he read soon after *Hapgood* was done. He was gripped by its account of the new science challenging orthodoxies in maths and physics, and of the solitary, embattled, creative, sometimes unrecognised scientists who brought it to light. 'Genius' in science and in art seemed similar to him, and the idea of 'genius' is vital to *Arcadia*.

Quantum physics had appealed to him because it involved doubling and uncertainty, a drastic change from the fixed certainties of classical physics to the realm of unpredictability. Chaos theory, too, involves the relationship between order and randomness, something that had interested him for a long time. He liked the idea of putting something so unlikely and new into a play.

Chaos theory 'attempts to systemize that which appears to function outside of any system. It describes a world in which there is chaos in order, but also order in chaos'. Stoppard calls it 'a reconciliation between the idea of things not being random on the one hand and yet unpredictable on the other hand'. It appealed to him because it had to do 'with the unpredictability of determinism'. In fact, 'chaos theory' is a distorting term, because it makes it sound as if it is all about randomness. And for non-scientists, confusingly, it is the same word that we use in everyday speech when we are talking loosely about a state of hopeless disorder. Some scientists prefer to use the term 'deterministic chaos', so as to get in both sides of its meaning, order *and* unpredictability.

Nor is it just one science. Chaos theory is a hybrid. It mixes together maths, physics, biology, economics, astronomy. It can apply to fluctuating population growth or weather forecasting, turbulence or earthquakes, eclipses or heartbeat patterns, the formation of snowflakes: to any dynamical system where apparent randomness is found to contain order. Grandly put, it is 'a science of the global nature of systems'.

'Chaos' got going in the 1970s, so when Stoppard was reading about it, it was still an excitingly new, radical change of direction. In Gleick's words: 'Where chaos begins, classical science stops'. Newtonian, classical science argued for an entirely determined universe. It maintained that given enough information, we can predict future events. The nineteenth-century scientist Pierre Laplace proposed that one could infer from the deterministic laws of the universe a vast entity, or intellect, which could 'embrace in a single formula the movements of the greatest bodies of the universe and those of the tiniest atom'. Or as Thomasina Coverly puts it in *Arcadia* in 1809, several years before Laplace: 'If you could stop every atom in its position and direction, and if your mind could comprehend all the actions thus suspended, then if you were really, *really* good at algebra you could write the formula for all the future.' But classical science ignored, or dismissed as monstrosities, what Gleick calls 'the irregular side of nature, the discontinuous and erratic side'. Galileo (whose distant shadow haunts *Arcadia*), Newton and their scientific descendants searched for regularity. But that meant 'disregarding bits of messiness that interfere with a neat picture'. The new science wanted to ask big questions: 'How does life begin? What is turbulence? . . . In a universe ruled by entropy, drawing inexorably toward greater and greater disorder, how does order arise?'

Chaos theory took the messiness and disorder on board. Gleick tells the story: 'The modern study of chaos began with the creeping realization . . . that quite simple mathematical equations could model systems every bit as violent as a waterfall. Tiny differences in input could quickly become overwhelming differences in output.' Chaos theory paid attention to aperiodic systems – systems which 'almost repeated themselves but never quite succeeded', like weather, or animal populations. It dealt in non-linear equations, 'which express relationships that are not strictly proportional, and generally cannot be solved', unlike solvable linear equations. Before that, 'almost no one in the classical era suspected the chaos that could lurk in dynamical systems if non-linearity was given its due'.

Chaotic systems have three key properties. They are non-linear, they are deterministic, and they exhibit 'sensitive dependence to initial conditions'. The general reader knows about sensitive dependence through the image of the butterfly effect: 'A butterfly stirring the air today in Beijing can transform storm systems next month in New York.' As anyone knows who has missed their bus to work, or watched a theatrical farce, 'small perturbations in one's daily trajectory can have large consequences'. 'Chaos' is a description for the 'rapid amplification' of a small difference to 'kingdom-shattering proportions'. A well-known nursery rhyme (in Benjamin Franklin's version) sums it up:

> For the want of a nail the shoe was lost,
> For the want of a shoe the horse was lost,
> For the want of a horse the rider was lost,
> For the want of a rider the battle was lost,
> For the want of a battle the kingdom was lost,
> And all for the want of a horseshoe-nail.

Valentine, the twentieth-century computer scientist and biologist in *Arcadia*, puts it like this, with excitement and delight: 'The unpredictable and the predetermined unfold together to make everything the way it is . . . the smallest variation blows prediction apart.'

But chaos is not entirely chaotic. Apparently random effects, it transpires, follow universal mathematical laws. 'A complex system can give rise to turbulence and coherence at the same time.' Order in chaos can be modelled in phenomena as wide-ranging as the population growth of grouse (Valentine's research project) or the vagaries of the stock market. The mathematician Benoit Mandelbrot, one of the strange geniuses in Gleick's story of chaos, who influences *Arcadia*, created a picture of reality which showed that 'within the most disorderly reams of data lived an unexpected kind of order'.

How can these patterns and order be traced and made sense of? Chaos scientists looked at how the behaviour of dynamical systems bifurcated endlessly. As systems respond to variations in input, the graph of their behaviour bifurcates, and then bifurcates again, ad infinitum, into a condition of chaotic randomness. But 'within those random states, windows of order reappeared'. Mathematicians use feedback loops, or iterated algorithms, to establish patterns of bifurcation. These algorithms – as we learn in *Arcadia* – would be impossible to work out with pen and paper, even if a genius could imagine them in her head. They can only be done with electronic calculators and computers.

Thomasina was trying to do in the 1800s a mathematical process that was first used in the early 1970s. Stoppard resisted, rather firmly, the frequent suggestion that she was based on Byron's daughter Ada Lovelace, the mathematician who worked with Charles Babbage and anticipated computer programming, called her methods 'poetical science' and died in her thirties. He heard about Ada after *Arcadia* was written, from Robert May, the physicist turned biologist, one of his main scientific advisers for the play. May worked on population changes in species, and he used 'functional iteration' as a way of describing these changes each year through 'a feedback loop, each year's output serving as the next year's input'. 'The output of one calculation was fed back in as input for the next.'

Nearly two hundred years after Thomasina had intuited this process, her calculations come to light. Valentine describes her achievement to a character who knows nothing about physics or maths and so is a useful stand-in for the audience and the reader. 'She's feeding the solution back into the equation, and then solving it again,' he explains.

> . . . It's how you look at population changes in biology. Goldfish in a pond, say. This year there are x goldfish. Next year there'll be y goldfish. Some get born, some get eaten by herons. Nature manipulates the x and turns it into y. Then y goldfish is your starting population for the following year . . . Your value for y becomes your next value for x.

Any sixth-former doing maths knows about algorithms: the magic is in Thomasina's anticipating them. As Stoppard says: 'You do not have to be Einstein to have the idea of feedback, the idea of the algorithm which just operates on itself. The problem was that there were not enough pencils or paper or time to do it often enough. To do it so many times that the pattern emerges.'

Algorithms can be used to draw the irregular shapes of nature. Fractal or fractional geometry – terms coined by Mandelbrot from the Latin for 'broken' and from the English words 'fracture' and 'fraction' – was a way of measuring qualities that otherwise have no clear definition. Mandelbrot's example was the degree of roughness or irregularity in a twisting coastline. Fractal geometry enabled mathematics to describe, explore and mirror the unpredictable forms of nature. Gleick explains it eloquently. You used 'a shape to help visualise the whole range of behaviours in a system'. You looked at materials like 'the fragmented landscapes of an earthquake zone' so as to calculate 'the irregular patterns of nature'. You could study 'the way things meld together, the way they branch apart, or the way they shatter'.

Fractal also meant 'self-similar'. 'Self-similarity is symmetry across scale. It implies recursion, pattern inside of pattern.' Fractal geometry produces detail at finer and finer scales, as in the image of a person reflected in mirror after mirror after mirror, infinitely receding. Mandelbrot liked to quote Jonathan Swift:

> So, Nat'ralists observe, a Flea
> Hath smaller Fleas that on him prey,
> And these have smaller Fleas to bite 'em,
> And so proceed ad infinitum.

Self-similarity got into the content – and the structure – of *Arcadia*.

Thomasina writes in her mathematics primer that she has invented 'a method whereby all the forms of nature must give up their mathematical secrets and draw themselves through numbers alone'. Valentine explains how it works: 'If you knew the algorithm and fed it back say ten thousand times, each time there'd be a dot somewhere on the screen. You'd never know where to expect the next dot. But gradually you'd start to see this shape, because every dot will be inside the shape of this leaf. It wouldn't *be* a leaf, it would be a mathematical object.' Thomasina Coverly has worked out how a mathematical drawing could simulate an apple leaf, and Valentine reproduces the image on his computer two hundred years on. He calls it 'the Coverly set', in tribute to 'the Mandelbrot set', his beautiful, complex computer images of fractal shapes.

Some years after *Arcadia* came out Stoppard had a public conversation with Robert Osserman, deputy director of the Mathematical Sciences Research Institute in Berkeley. He said then that what fascinated him in the idea of fractal geometry was that 'there is a complementarity in the notion that math describes nature, and that nature is following mathematical rules . . . Numbers have a kind of social behaviour, they're not simply tools of description.' Thomasina 'understands . . . that it's not actually the equation in itself, it's the way you . . . manipulate the equation, the way you pull the solution back into the equation in a feedback loop, which generates shapes . . . That, in the end, is what is moving about the idea that nature is written in numbers. That it's generative.' It was the parallel behaviour of nature and mathematics that fascinated him, just as the parallel creative energy of the arts and the sciences was one of the play's subjects.

Algorithms were not Thomasina's only discovery. The past time zone of the play jumps, in a non-linear fashion, from 1809 to 1812. She is thirteen when it starts and nearly seventeen when it ends. When she is thirteen she notices, as a child might notice, that you can only stir the jam in your rice pudding one way: 'If you stir backwards, the jam will not come together again.' Yes, says her tutor Septimus, the Newtonian, classical scientist, who at this point knows more than his pupil, time will only go one way, and 'we must stir our way onward mixing as we go, disorder out of disorder into disorder until pink is complete, unchanging and unchangeable, and we are done with it for ever'. Thomasina agrees with Septimus: 'You cannot stir things apart.' Gleick calls this 'entropy explained in five words'.

Three years later, she has become wiser than her tutor. She has worked out that there is no such thing in the universe as an 'unchanging and unchangeable' state. Centuries ahead of her time, she has grasped the Second Law of Thermodynamics. She has worked out that 'the heat equation . . . goes only one way'. That is, she has foreseen the law of entropy, which tells us that the universe is evolving from order to disorder. Heat, according to the Second Law of Thermodynamics, can only flow in one direction, from hotter to colder. There is no way back in time, no backward swing of the pendulum. The idea that the world's energy, heat and light will eventually run out and the universe at last be nothing but dark void runs like a sombre drumbeat under the life and vitality of the play.

Gleick gives an example of 'the inexorable tendency of the universe, and any isolated system in it, to slide toward a state of increasing disorder'. He explains – like Thomasina telling Septimus about stirring the jam – that if you have a bath with two separate compartments, one containing water and one containing ink, and you remove the barrier between the compartments so that ink and water mix together, the mixture never reverses itself. This is the part of physics 'that makes time a one-way street'. 'Everything tends towards disorder. Any process that converts energy from one form to another must lose some as heat. Perfect efficiency is impossible.'

But Gleick does provide some consolation, which affects the mood of *Arcadia*. What chaos theory shows is that 'somehow, after all, as the universe ebbs towards its final equilibrium in the featureless heat bath of maximum entropy, it manages to create interesting structures . . . Nature forms patterns . . . The universe is randomness and dissipation, yes. But randomness with direction can produce surprising complexity . . . Dissipation is an agent of order'.

Stoppard leaped on these ideas with excitement and poured them into his play. As always he relished the technical language of specialist disciplines. 'Noise', for instance, is the scientist's word for 'error', or 'observational uncertainty'. It is 'what scientists blame for the inaccuracy of their measurements'. Too much noise, in *Arcadia*, is what drives Valentine off course in his research. In the play, 'noise' becomes a metaphor for extravagant and ridiculous behaviour, especially that of the fame-seeking literary don Bernard, a very noisy character. 'Trivial' means, for scientists, redundant information that doesn't lead anywhere or proofs with no value. In the play, it is a telling word for what matters and what doesn't. Personal relationships and the achievements of individuals, says Valentine, are 'trivial' compared with the search for knowledge itself.

He also borrowed the concept of 'bifurcation' for the play's structure. 'I have a secret agenda,' he told an interviewer, 'but I wouldn't lay it on the audience. The play mimics the way an algorithm goes through bifurcations into chaos . . . [It] bifurcates two or three times and then goes into the last section which is all mixed up. So, it's very chaos structured.' He liked making the play mirror the idea of 'self-similarity': the present reflecting the past, and the two time zones converging in a long final scene which is both disorderly and patterned.

That the shape of *Arcadia* mirrored the structure of fractal geometry was not something the average theatre-goer would notice. We do get an education: there are lots of science lessons in the play, in both time zones, so that we will understand. Audiences can congratulate themselves and feel flattered when they 'get' it. But probably no audience is going to pick up on everything.

For instance, early on in the play, Thomasina makes fun of Fermat's Last Theorem. She tells Septimus that when Fermat left a note in the margin saying that he didn't have room on the page to add the proof of the theorem, the note was 'a joke to make you all mad'. Towards the end of the play, we come to understand that she has left a similar teasing note behind her about what will come to be known as the Second Law of Thermodynamics, which will indeed drive Septimus mad. Half the audience won't know what Fermat's Last Theorem is, though some will know about his legendary marginal note and the fact that scientists have been trying to solve it ever since. (Uncannily, soon after the play opened, a Cambridge mathematician, Andrew Wiles, announced that he had found the proof of the theorem after years of secret work. Later, his proofs would be questioned, but during the run of the play a note about Wiles was slipped into the programme at Stoppard's request.) As usual, he is doing a delicate balancing act. He wants to please and satisfy the whole audience, but he also wants one person – or possibly ten people – to relish and understand everything, and he is writing for those people, while keeping everybody else happy.

Science is used in the play as metaphor, not as information for its own sake. After *Hapgood* and *Arcadia* he kept being invited to speak to scientific audiences; but he always did so by talking about science as metaphor. In one of these talks he noted that the reason the exchange between Thomasina and Septimus about heat loss works so well is that the word 'entropy' is never mentioned. It is 'pure metaphor'.

Ed Stoppard was nineteen when *Arcadia* came out, and not yet certain he would be an actor. He would one day play Valentine, in the 2009 revival of the play. He understood exactly what his father was doing with the science, as in the speech when Valentine is explaining chaos theory:

> If you went: 'So, this is a speech about chaos, fractals, maths, questions of scale,' you'd think, you're kidding me. But on the few occasions I got it right you could hear a pin drop . . . What the audience isn't doing is understanding chaos theory. What they *are* doing is feeling for a moment the emotions it arouses in a person who does understand it . . . Audiences leave feeling . . . they've connected emotionally. Theatre is not about understanding, it's about connecting – it's about emotions.

What we are made to care about in *Arcadia* is not the workings of chaos mathematics, but life itself. Though he has described it as 'a big *talkfest* in one room', the engine that powers the play is not abstract discussion. It is the excitement and the passion that go with the quest for knowledge. Finding things out is as exciting as sex in this play – and can be as misdirected and chaotic. The seekers after knowledge are constantly running into trouble and setting off on false trails. *Arcadia* is certainly a play to do with science, but it's also a comic farce, and a love story, and the history of an English house.

One of the clues he took from Gleick was a comparison between scientific and aesthetic changes. Mandelbrot and his followers, Gleick says, preferred Beaux Arts architecture, with its fantastical Gothic elaboration, to the clean orderly lines of the Bauhaus or the Seagram Building. 'The new mathematics of fractal geometry brought hard science in tune with the peculiarly modern feeling for untamed, uncivilised, undomesticated nature.' Gleick draws a parallel between Newtonian science and the eighteenth-century preference for orderly, tamed gardens over unregulated wilderness, before the turn to the picturesque.

Arcadia begins just as that turn is taking place. The play's large country house in Derbyshire, set in 'a typical English park', is undergoing

major landscape 'improvements'. The offstage owner of Sidley Park, Lord
Croom (Croom is the name of the earldom, Coverly is the family name),
has hired a 'landskip gardener' to transform his ancestral grounds. As in
many big country houses in the 1800s, where the landed gentry retreated
from London to hunt and shoot, plot politics and hold large house parties, 'improvement' was all the rage. The formal Italianate gardens of the
Elizabethan and Stuart periods, all straight lines and mathematical patterns, had given way, in the mid-eighteenth century, to gently ornamental
'arcadian worlds' of meandering walks, clumps of trees 'companionably
grouped at intervals', curving watery rills and lakes, and meadows, as Lady
Croom approvingly describes them, 'on which the right amount of sheep
are tastefully arranged'. 'Capability' Brown was everyone's favourite garden designer. These natural-looking private landscapes, made for walks
and circuits, were enlivened with carefully placed features. It's one of the
many good jokes in *Arcadia* that when we first hear about these features
they sound like convenient spots for adultery: '. . . the gazebo, the boat
house, the Chinese bridge, the shrubbery'. ('Oh no! Not the gazebo!')

But it's farewell to the gazebo and the shrubbery. All that was being
sacrificed to the fashion for the picturesque. Aesthetic arbiters, famous
in their day (Uvedale Price, Richard Payne Knight, Humphrey Repton),
drew on pictorial models to create wilder, emotional landscapes, meant
to play on the observer's sensibility and feeling for untrammelled nature.
Lord Croom's garden designer, Mr Noakes (a fictive version of Humphrey
Repton), is going to turn Sidley Park's 'Arcadia' into a rough, irregular
scene, in the manner of the landscape painter Salvator Rosa, with wild
waterfalls dashing against rocks, a fallen obelisk, a grotto and – an essential feature in any self-respecting gothic landscape – a hermit's cell. 'The
whole thing', Hannah the landscape historian observes, 'was brought home
in the luggage from the grand tour . . . It's the Gothic novel expressed in
landscape. Everything but vampires.'

Lady Croom is appalled by her husband's plans and the disruption
they are causing: 'Where there is the familiar pastoral refinement of an
Englishman's garden, here is an eruption of gloomy forest and towering
crag, of ruins where there was never a house . . .' Her brother, Captain

Brice, protests: 'Is Sidley Park to be an Englishman's garden or the haunt of Corsican brigands?' This is comical, but *Arcadia* also takes the turning point seriously. Hannah speaks passionately of how it marked 'the decline from thinking to feeling', a move from 'paradise in the age of reason' to a 'setting of cheap thrills and false emotion'. In a sentence that was cut from her speech, she is even more emotional: 'All destroyed by the vandals and Goths – that's my name for the landscapists, God rot them.'

After three years of improvements things are no better, and Lady Croom rounds on the hapless Mr Noakes. 'What you painted as a forest is a mean plantation, your greenery is mud, your waterfall is wet mud, and your mount is an opencast mine for the mud that was lacking in the dell.' As for his hermit's cell, how is he going to get anyone to live in it?

Noakes: I am sure a hermit can be found. One could advertise.
Lady Croom: Advertise?
Noakes: In the newspapers.
Lady Croom: But surely a hermit who takes a newspaper is not a
    hermit in whom one can have complete confidence.

Lady Croom is a bossy conservative who likes to keep order. And the life of Sidley Park seems to be ruled by custom. Guests come to Derbyshire during the season for the shooting of birds. In the winter they all go back to London. The daughter of the house, who in due course will be married off, is given lessons from the resident tutor. The son of the house goes to Eton and learns to shoot. However, we soon find out that this traditional English aristocratic house is a topsy-turvy domain of adultery, scandals and feuds. Lady Croom's idea of 'the decorum due to a civilised house' is that her teenage daughter's tutor (with whom Lady Croom is having an affair, among others) should shoot dead in a duel the cuckolded husband of Lady Croom's rival, Mrs Chater, a wonderfully reckless offstage character who has made love to everyone in the house and is Lady Croom's brother's mistress. So much for decorum: this enclave of English tradition turns out to be rather like Schnitzler's *La Ronde* – or *Undiscovered Country*. Chaos is running riot within the orderliness.

Sex is rampant, from the irresistible first line of the play, where the thirteen-year-old Thomasina asks her attractive, worldly, ironical tutor: 'Septimus, what is carnal embrace?' He certainly knows the answer. ('Is it the same as love?' 'Oh no, it is much nicer than that.') When he is not teaching Thomasina, he is pursuing Lady Croom, making love to Mrs Chater in the gazebo and placating her idiotically vain husband, a poet of no talent at all (before he becomes an unqualified botanist), with the promise of a good review for his new work, 'The Couch of Eros', so that he doesn't have to fight a duel with him. The scene in which he gets Mr Chater to persuade himself that his wife's adultery is a proof of her loyal support for his literary efforts is a small masterclass in absurdity.

One member of the shooting party, as befits a play set at the dawning of Romanticism, is the notoriously dangerous, dashing and seductive Lord Byron, Septimus's school and college friend, with whom all the women are in love. (That includes Thomasina by the time she is sixteen, true to the fashions of the time: every sensitive young woman had a copy of 'Childe Harold's Pilgrimage' and a picture of Byron above her dressing table.) It is one of the play's brilliant stratagems that Byron remains tantalisingly unseen throughout, but is key to the plot. He has been brought to Sidley Park by Septimus, he goes out on the shooting parties, and he upsets the son of the house, Augustus, by claiming his hare and telling Augustus that 'he missed by a hare's breadth'. 'His conversation was very facetious,' Augustus complains. He lets slip to Mr Chater, with unfortunate consequences, that Septimus has given Chater's first poem a terrible review in the *Piccadilly Recreation*, he flirts with Lady Croom and makes love to Mrs Chater, and he leaves the house with Septimus's copy of Chater's poem, containing some incriminating letters. He is at the centre of the climactic, offstage, night-time farrago in which a duel is narrowly avoided, nocturnal visits are exposed, and hasty departures made from Sidley Park by the Chaters, Captain Brice and the great poet himself, about to quit England for ever.

On stage, meanwhile, we are always in one room, elegant and bare, with high French windows looking on to 'light and air and sky', one large table and an architect's stand. The table is covered with objects and papers and books, including a theodolite and a tortoise called Plautus 'which is sleepy enough to serve as a paperweight'. For part of the time, this scene is a quiet haven for Septimus and Thomasina's lessons, where the pupil begins to intuit mathematical possibilities far beyond her tutor's capacity. Their exchanges are full of curiosity, wit and affectionate playfulness: 'Septimus, do you think God is a Newtonian?' 'An Etonian? Almost certainly, I'm afraid.' They seem like oases of civilisation next to the noisy, farcical turmoil of the adult world.

Thomasina observes all that with a kind of innocent, pre-sexual wisdom, rather like Henry James's Maisie. At age thirteen, she doesn't think much of carnal embrace. She hates Cleopatra, who 'turned everything to love' and 'made noodles of our sex' by falling for Caesar, who 'burned the great library of Alexandria'. She minds more about knowledge than sex. What arouses Thomasina's passion are the lost plays that were destroyed in that fire, or the possibility of drawing nature through geometrical forms, or the discovery that 'the heat equation . . . goes only one way' – as she tells Mr Noakes, proud of his new 'heat engine', 'the Improved Newcomen steam pump'. 'Improve it as you will,' she tells him, 'you can never get out of it what you put in.' Thomasina herself is full of heat and energy. Alert, eager, funny, spontaneous, childish, she catches our hearts: 'an uncomplicated girl' who also happens to be a genius. There is no other Stoppard character like her.

Septimus and Thomasina are surrounded by books, paper and ink. Paper is everywhere. Grouse-shooting records, gardening diaries, landscape-design drawings, sealed love letters, a challenge to a duel, a poetry book with an inscribed dedication, a review, a maths primer, a Latin lesson, a portfolio, the diagrams for a new heat engine, Thomasina's scribbled drawing of an imaginary hermit, her sketch of Septimus and the tortoise, are exchanged, slipped inside books, borrowed, left lying about or hidden away. In one deliciously breathtaking exception to this accumulating paper trail, Septimus burns an unread letter from Byron. The modern-day historians of the play, trying to read their way back in time, exclaim hopefully, or despairingly: 'Paper is what they had. And there'll be more. There is always more.' 'Somewhere there will be *something* . . . if only I can find it.'

In the present-day scenes, the set remains the same, and, as Stoppard advises, 'there is no absolute need to remove the evidence of one period to make way for another'. There's still a tortoise sitting on the table, but now his name is, humorously, Lightning. The books exist 'in both old and new versions', but, as the table collects 'an inventory of objects', anachronisms simply become 'invisible'. This has been nicely described by one critic as 'seeing double': 'Part of the playful fun of the drama is seeing the casually handled objects of 1809 become the intensely scrutinised, and generally misleading, archaeological clues of 1993.' The characters in the past are excited about the possibilities of the future. The characters in the present are trying to excavate the past. As Stoppard once explained it: 'The scenes set in the past show what happened, and the present-day scenes show people trying to work out what happened.'

The Coverly family is still in residence at Sidley Park. Both parents are offstage characters who make their presence felt. The present-day Lord Croom is a bad-tempered reactionary eccentric ('My father never replies to typewritten letters'). His wife (Hermione) is excavating the history of the gardens, and seems to be every bit as randy and as bossy as the earlier Lady Croom. The elder son, Valentine, is a nervy, emotional computer scientist using the family game books as data for his algorithms on population growth. The younger, Gus, shy to the point of torment, perhaps autistic, never speaks, but watches and listens. He seems to be the genius of the place, with an uncanny intuition of its past. The daughter, Chloe, is sexy, tactless, posh and sweet. All three Coverly children seem to be 'channelling' Thomasina in different ways: as scientist, as genius and as susceptible young woman.

The two historians who are visiting the house in quest of the past appear to be exact opposites. Hannah Jarvis, serious freelance landscape and literary historian, is researching the Sidley Park hermit as an image of the turn from classicism to Romanticism, and helping Lady Croom in the gardens. She has also written a revisionist feminist account of Byron's mistress Lady Caroline Lamb. The other visiting literary historian, a showy 'Media Don' from Sussex University, Bernard Nightingale – or 'Peacock', his perfect alias when he doesn't want Hannah to know his name – is a self-serving careerist. He is pretending to be in quest of the minor poet Ezra Chater (who he is quite sure is a different person from his contemporary, Ezra Chater the minor botanist) but is really hoping to find some scandalous new information about Byron, and will stop at nothing. By unlucky coincidence, and in one of many neat parallels between the early and the modern time zones, he has given Hannah's book a scathing review: they are bound to be opponents. They meet on the day the house is being tidied up in preparation for the annual costume ball.

The Romantic period scenes are written in an elegant, rich, witty and poetic language, never quite slipping into parody, though with echoes of Restoration comedy, Jane Austen and Wilde. Septimus and Thomasina spar like sharp-tongued partners out of Congreve: "'A fancy is not a discovery." "A gibe is not a rebuttal.'" Lady Croom can sound like a cross between Lady Catherine de Bourgh and Lady Bracknell: 'Do not dabble in paradox, Edward, it puts you in danger of fortuitous wit.' Peacock (author of *Headlong Hall*, the 1816 satire on the rage for 'improvements' and English upper-class idiocy) gets a nod. There's a slight trace of Shaw, perhaps because Felicity Kendal had just been starring in *Heartbreak House*, Shaw's dark, apocalyptic, English-country-house political satire. Fragments of Byron's voice are heard, both satirical and ravishingly lyrical.

By contrast the language of the present has lost heat, and has declined into cliché, swearing, windbaggery, cheap shots and banalities. (The two time zones and the biographical quests are a bit like A. S. Byatt's 1990 *Possession*. Byatt has said that Stoppard told her he 'pinched' his plot from her.) Gus, the shy genius, has decided never to speak, as though silence is preferable to this kind of language. But at moments these modern characters *can* speak with beautiful thoughtful intensity, when they are voicing their passions, in science and in the arts. No character is only classical (reserved, rational, sceptical) *or* romantic. Valentine the scientist is much more emotional and sensitive than Bernard the literary historian. Caustic, brusque, independent Hannah also has strong emotions. She has long ago given up on the idea of marriage: 'I don't know a worse bargain. Available sex against not being allowed to fart in bed.' (There's more of her failed love life in early manuscript versions of the play.) Yet she attracts the deep friendship of Valentine and the silent adoration of Gus.

Chloe has a theory that the reason disorder gets into the system is 'all because of sex': 'the only thing going wrong is people fancying people who aren't supposed to be in that part of the plan'. The play certainly proves it. There is almost as much shagging going on in present-day Sidley Park as there was in the Regency period. Bernard, a cheapskate, parasitical kind of Byron, has it off with the mother and the daughter, and can't even resist making a pass at Hannah. Everything for him is about phallic self-assertion, conquest and triumph: 'The Byron gang are going to get their dicks caught in their zip'. Hannah calls him 'arrogant, greedy and reckless'. Going through all the evidence he can find 'like a bloodhound' and rough-riding over all the bits that don't fit his theory, he leaps to the sensational conclusion that Byron, visiting Sidley Park in 1809, cuckolded and then killed Ezra Chater in a duel – and *that's* why Byron left England for ever.

We get tremendous satisfaction from seeing Bernard air his conclusions – the copy of 'The Couch of Eros' with the incriminating letters! The challenge to a duel! The scathing reviews of Chater's poems! – while all the time we have been seeing what actually happened. But no amount of sceptical questioning stops Bernard in his tracks, and he plunges headlong into his moment of headline fame: 'Bonking Byron Shot Poet', 'Byron Fought Fatal Duel, Says Don'. Unfortunately for him, Ezra Chater turns out not to have fought a duel or been killed by Byron, but to have lived to introduce the first dwarf dahlia to England. Bernard is humiliated ('Fucked by a dahlia!'), and Hannah gets her revenge.

But Hannah too gets things wrong. She had come to Sidley Park convinced that its hermit was a madman, a symbol of 'the whole Romantic sham', living alone with his tortoise, covering pages and pages with 'cabalistic proofs that the world was coming to an end'. With Valentine's help, Hannah begins to piece together the true story of Sidley Park. She realises that the hermit wasn't an 'idiot in the landscape'; no, the hermit was the tutor. 'The Age of Enlightenment banished into the Romantic wilderness! The genius of Sidley Park living on in a hermit's hut!' This comes as a shock to the audience, too. But why did Septimus Hodge spend the last twenty-two years of his life incarcerated and alone, writing indecipherable pages that would eventually be burnt? Hannah has to come to one more realisation (something we already know): who the genius of Sidley Park really was. Valentine shows her on his computer the beautiful mathematical shapes that Thomasina had been intuiting. And only then do we learn from their conversation that Thomasina died, on the night before her seventeenth birthday, in a fire from the candle in her room.

While we are still reeling from this, the two time zones converge, in the very last scene, in a perfect theatrical moment. Thomasina comes running on stage, where Hannah and Valentine are working. It is the day before her seventeenth birthday. The childish conspiracy between her and Septimus has turned into something different. He has promised to teach her the daring new dance from Germany, the waltz. She is trying to teach him about the one-way action of heat, but her theorem is beyond him: 'It will make me mad as you promised.' The modern-day cast dress for their costume ball, and become indistinguishable from their ancestors. Thomasina and Septimus waltz, and she asks him to come to her room. But, for once making the moral choice, he says no: and that – we know – will be the death of her. Gus presents Hannah with her missing piece of evidence for the identity of the Sidley Park hermit, Thomasina's drawing of Septimus and Plautus. He asks her, silently, to dance with him. The two couples dance, together and separately, across time, and the play ends as though in the timeless moment of Eliot's 'Burnt Norton':

> Time present and time past
> Are both perhaps present in time future
> And time future contained in time past . . .
> . . . at the still point, there the dance is . . .

Bernard has been banished from this final scene, like a fallen Lucifer. He has managed to offend everyone, just for the hell of it, including the harmless Valentine, whom he attacks as the representative of the sciences. Why should scientific research get all the headlines and all the money? 'Don't confuse progress with perfectibility . . . Quarks, quasars – big bangs,

black holes – who gives a shit?' He prefers Byron. It's an extreme statement of the 'two cultures' position, which Valentine knows is absurd:
'He's not against penicillin and he knows I'm not against poetry.' All the
same, Bernard's ruthless investment in literature has its admirable side.
For all his low motives and ridiculous exhibitionism, he has a 'visceral
belief' in himself, in those moments of 'certainty for which there is no
back-reference'. There is not such a huge gap between him and Valentine.
Jumping to conclusions ahead of the proofs is, as Valentine sees, 'just like
science'. Stoppard puts this comparison right at the heart of the play. He
says that when Bernard talks about 'the creative moment', the 'gut instinct'
coming from 'the part of you which doesn't reason', 'he describes something which I believe is the same experience known to scientists in *their*
most creative moments'. It's the point 'where art and science intersect'.

These were strong, personal feelings. *Arcadia* was not an autobiographical play. But it had to do with a great many things in his own life
– not least his experience of sexual attraction disrupting a well-ordered
life. It links to other works – *Galileo, Hapgood, Hopeful Monsters*, and
the youthful passion of *Shakespeare in Love,* which overlapped with it.
It borrows a hare and a tortoise from *Jumpers.* It draws on his love of
English traditions, embodied in the Derbyshire country house where he
first went to school, which he often described as his 'Arcadia'. It used his
experience of grouse-shooting in Scotland, his childhood memory of the
gardens of Chatsworth, his familiarity with Stowe, from Ed and Will's
school years there, and Miriam's ambitious garden improvements at Iver
Grove. Valentine has something of Oliver in him. And his own distaste
for unprincipled journalism, predatory biographers and intrusions into
private lives (as in *Indian Ink*) energises the character of Bernard.

But there is part of him in Bernard. The play sets a noisy comical performance artist, an academic Tristan Tzara, up against reclusive thinkers and silent watchers. The showman and the hermit are both sides of
Stoppard. The balancing act in *Arcadia* between rationality and emotion,
heat and cool, is also a personal one. In a much later interview, he said:
'You have to include a certain kind of objective cold-bloodedness in the
playwright . . . What I do is something colder perhaps as well as warmer.

The cold part is that I want to work on your emotions in a self-conscious way as well as exploit my own immured subconscious.'

And work on our emotions he does. Why is *Arcadia* such a moving play? Because it has to do with loss. Stoppard in interview recalled a nice moment in Evelyn Waugh's autobiography where Waugh noted that his first edition of H. G. Wells's *The Time Machine* had sixteen pages of advertisements for popular novelists of 1895, much praised, and 'all, today, quite forgotten'. Byron, lacerating his fellow writers in 1809 in *English Bards and Scotch Reviewers*, observes that most of them will be consigned to oblivion:

> E'en now, what once-loved minstrels scarce may claim
> The transient mention of a dubious name!
> When fame's loud trump hath blown its noblest blast,
> Though long the sound, the echo sleeps at last;
> And glory, like the phoenix midst her fires
> Exhales her odours, blazes, and expires.

It is perfectly true. Coleridge and Wordsworth and Southey are objects of Byron's ridicule, and their names did survive; but so are some writers called Clarke, Hewson and Kenney. And who are they? They might as well be Ezra Chater!

Some losses are trivial, some are tragic. Thomasina laments the plays that were burnt in the library at Alexandria. So the classical poet-scholar of *The Invention of Love* (already taking shape in his mind during *Arcadia*) will speak sadly of those lost plays and the near-loss of Catullus's work, and *Rock 'n' Roll* will be haunted by the disappearance of a great part of Sappho's poetry. The 'fragmentary survival of the great poets from antiquity has tremendous potency for me', he said. In the early 2000s, he gave a paper on the Roman love elegist Cornelius Gallus, for a group of classicists, which refers back to Thomasina's lament for the lost plays of Aeschylus, Sophocles and Euripides. Likewise, only a few lines of Gallus's work survived. He notes that Gallus makes a brief appearance in *Antony and Cleopatra*, disappearing with the stage direction: 'Exit Gallus'. Stoppard minds a great deal about these exits. As he said in interview while *Arcadia* was playing, 'Anybody who writes plays wants them to survive and be revived, to survive the writer's death.'

Arcadia is full of losses. A girl born in 1796 and dead in 1812 is imagined to have intuited chaos theory and the Second Law of Thermodynamics. But nothing comes of it, because she didn't have a computer, because she dies young, and because, had she survived and married, she would probably not have been able to be a scientist. (This is made more emphatic in his much later, unproduced screenplay of *Arcadia*, which adds the line: 'Perhaps she'd be famous if she wasn't a girl.') Septimus cannot prove or disprove the theories she has left behind because he has no way of working them out and no one to talk to. And his papers are all burnt. Thomasina foresaw that heat will consume the universe, the stars will burn out, energy will run down and darkness take over. Byron saw it coming, too, in his apocalyptic poem 'Darkness', of 1816, quoted by Hannah, which begins, terrifyingly:

> I had a dream, which was not all a dream.
> The bright sun was extinguish'd, and the stars
> Did wander darkling in the eternal space,
> Rayless, and pathless, and the icy earth
> Swung blind and blackening in the moonless air . . .

It ends:

> The waves were dead; the tides were in their grave,
> The moon, their mistress, had expired before;
> The winds were wither'd in the stagnant air,
> And the clouds perish'd; Darkness had no need
> Or aid from them – she was the Universe.

Can anything be salvaged from the losses? Septimus believes that we should not grieve for what is lost, because it is made up for by what will survive:

We shed as we pick up, like travellers who must carry everything in their arms, and what we let fall will be picked up by those behind. The procession is very long and life is very short. We die on the march. But there is nothing outside the march so nothing can be lost to it. The missing plays of Sophocles will turn up piece by piece, or be written again in another language. Ancient cures for diseases will reveal themselves once more. Mathematical discoveries glimpsed and lost to view will have their time again.

Stoppard has said that he is more inclined, like Thomasina, to grieve over what is lost: 'It matters; it seems to matter a lot.' On the other hand, Septimus is saying that 'one has to accept the world as it is and not the world as it could have been. You operate from what you have.' Hannah and Bernard, trying to find their way back into the past, are at the mercy of what they can find and what has survived, and their exasperated, ever hopeful cry (the cry of all biographers) is: 'There must be *something*, if only I can find it!' Their quest for the past is largely a comedy of mistakes, missing data and misinterpretations. All the same, as Bernard says, you have to turn every page, and then you might find something. Not everything vanishes. Some things can be proved. At the very last, when Gus hands Hannah Thomasina's drawing of Septimus and Plautus, she thanks him, saying: 'I was looking for that.'

If Septimus is right, then not everything will be lost, burnt and wasted. And Thomasina is right to exclaim: 'Oh, phooey to Death!' She does live on, strangely. Valentine may doubt – unlike Hannah – that it could have been the girl, not her tutor, who was the mathematical genius. But he can still work out on his computer and bring to life the algorithm which Thomasina understood could describe a form of nature: a leaf of an apple, fruit of the tree of knowledge.

We must all be consumed by time, and the world is heading for cold darkness. That is what gives this beautiful play its melancholy strain: '*Et in Arcadia ego*'. But melancholy is not the dominant mood of the play. It is full of froth and energy, light and spirit, sexual heat, busy plots, excitement, intellectual adventure, jokes, curiosity, inventions and dancing. The energy of life itself is summed up by the quest for knowledge. That is what defines us and makes us human. Hannah says: 'It's wanting to know that makes us matter. Otherwise we're going out the way we came in.'

Arcadia was the first stage play since *Hapgood* five years before (*In the Native State* had been broadcast, but *Indian Ink* was still to come) and he was understandably protective of it. 'It's the usual thing,' he told his mother in April 1992, wryly anticipating the reviews, 'bookish, too clever by half and he can't do emotions.' At the first night, turning to a young friend of Barny's, Jamie Arlon, he asked anxiously: 'You understood this, didn't you? It was easy, wasn't it?'

Peter Wood was not asked to direct this time, to his regret, though he did do it in Zurich, and then directed *Indian Ink* (and *Arcadia* again at Chichester in 2000). Stoppard gave *Arcadia* to the National, at its artistic director Richard Eyre's invitation. Eyre was sent the script in mid-June of 1992, and wrote in his diary that it was 'very Stoppardian – by which I mean original, witty, intelligent – but, less characteristically, is very passionate and moving.' The two men liked and respected each other. They had a lunch together at which Stoppard realised Eyre was assuming that he would direct it himself. This was awkward. Stoppard had written the play with Felicity Kendal in mind, as he told Bobby: 'I wrote Hannah as something Felicity might do, not had to do (note the title is not "Hannah").' She had been working with Trevor Nunn, whom she greatly admired. Nunn had badly wanted to do *Travesties* at the RSC, and he had done the first production of *Every Good Boy*. Kendal told Stoppard that he ought to take this chance of working with Nunn. Kendal and Stoppard talked on the phone the day after his lunch with Eyre, and she said, more or less: 'Look, I know it's difficult, but you've just got to be tough, and phone up Richard and say, there's a misunderstanding.' Stoppard grasped the nettle, and rang Eyre to tell him that he wanted Nunn to direct *Arcadia*. Nunn remembered, years later, having been sent a copy of the play containing a note from Stoppard, asking him if he would direct it. Nunn wrote back, on 22 June 1992, praising the play and saying that 'if there were any possibility of me being involved with *Arcadia*' he would 'hug it in carnal embrace'.

Richard Eyre vividly recalled the phone call. 'I was standing in the kitchen when he rang', Eyre remembered, 'and it was like a spear through the heart. I didn't have any choice. I said, Well, it's a wonderful play, I'm very sad, but you must have the director you want.' It was a bad moment for them both. 'Tom is such an utterly decent man. He was in agony. Stuttering and sweating at the end of the phone and praying that I wouldn't say, You absolute bastard. And of course by then I'd fallen in love with the play. So it was heartbreaking.' Eyre wrote in his diary: 'He says he should have said that he wanted Trevor to do it when he first spoke to me about it, instead of saying that it could be directed by either of us. He's promised Trevor a play for twenty years. Oh well, *tant pis*. I felt humiliated, but I'm not quite sure why. It's my fault for having jumped to the conclusion that since I was running the theatre I would have *droit de seigneur*.' Stoppard was well aware that another kind of person would have taken this badly. But he also knew that Eyre was, in his words, a complete gentleman. He told Michael Codron (who would manage the play's transfer from the National to the Haymarket), 'I got on a tramline and got off clumsily – I think the play will be directed by Trevor after all – I feel a bit flat and foolish.' Codron told Eyre that presumably the change of heart was the result of 'pillow talk'. No one involved in this difficult theatrical episode ever forgot it, though each of them had their own version of it.

Stoppard thought Nunn was a great director, the best analyst of a text there could ever be – a skill Nunn partly attributes to having been taught English literature by F. R. Leavis at Cambridge. They agreed, too, on casting. There were no big names, apart from Kendal, playing brilliantly against the grain as a frumpish, grumpy, awkward Hannah. Stoppard watched her performance developing with unbounded admiration. (Nunn says he had Germaine Greer in mind for her character.) Harriet Walter was an imperious, elegant, roguish Lady Croom, and Bill Nighy, not yet a superstar, but much admired for his work for David Hare, was magnetically flashy and posturing as Bernard. There were also some highly regarded, little-known young actors. Sam West, son of Timothy West and Prunella Scales, was a sensitive Valentine. Stoppard told his mother that when Jose was expecting Oliver, she went to antenatal classes with Prunella Scales, who was pregnant with Sam. 'So now the bump is in my play.' The other new stars of the show were the entrancing Emma Fielding as Thomasina and Rufus Sewell as Septimus. Sewell was 'the new hot young actor', with a fascinating physical presence. As Stoppard put it, he knew, magically, just where to put his feet, and his body language was in tune with the character. There was strong competition for his part, Nunn remembered: 'A guy came in and did very good work but we couldn't quite see the wit and the daring – so we didn't cast him – he was called Ralph Fiennes – then a bit later a guy who had the wit and was very naughty and wicked but we couldn't quite see the intellectual grasp – he was called Hugh Grant.' Nunn asked Stoppard to choose between Fiennes, already very well known, and the unknown Sewell. Stoppard said he thought they ought to cast Fiennes but he wanted Nunn to overrule him. Fiennes went on to make *Schindler's List*, and Hugh Grant to become a famous actor because of *Notting Hill*.

The actors found the play difficult. Nunn wanted it to be him, not Stoppard, who did the explaining – otherwise he would just be the person who told the actors where to stand. He had to keep his authority with the company. Stoppard was there most of the time in rehearsal, but he would wait to be asked for his views. He took detailed notes all day long, full of tiny points of emphasis, instructions for the actors ('Plot doesn't work if Bern. isn't bigger than life'), instructions about tone, as between Septimus and Lady Croom ('too much of a love scene?'), and points for information: 'When were matches invented?!' At one point Nunn suggested he should absent himself for a few days to give them all a breather and allow them to make mistakes.

Robert May was brought in to talk to the cast about chaos theory. The younger actors were very keen to master this, and he wrote detailed notes and drawings of algorithms for Emma Fielding. Kendal didn't really 'get' the science. But she loved her part and the play, and in her own way understood it completely: '*Arcadia* is an incredibly complicated, intricate piece of work but at the heart of it there's huge love and grief . . . But sentimentality he sees as an enemy.' As in *Hapgood*, they put their private life aside in rehearsal, and the company had no sense of that affecting their work.

South Africa, in Sweden and Slovenia. In Germany, the playwright Daniel Kehlmann noted, they treated it as frivolous light entertainment, 'boulevard theatre'. In Zurich, Peter Wood's production looked and felt quite different from Nunn's, with a 'shabby, beat-up' set and a big Poussin mural, so that, as Stoppard said, 'one of the main subject matters of the play was in your face the whole night, which was a terrifically good idea'. In Paris, it was done at the Comédie-Française, in 1998, a prestigious though rather heavy-handed event. Robert Carsen, his opera-director friend, helped to save some of the jokes in French, and Julian Barnes told him what had been lost in translation: '"Salvator Rosa" has become "Wuthering Heights" (eh?), "When Father Painted the Parlour" has become "God Save the Queen"'. Barnes noted that (as with his own novels in French) some 'gentrification, or gentilising', had taken place in the French, 'otherwise known as smut-avoidance'. This was one of many translations of the play, which also went into Catalan, Czech, German, Hebrew, Polish and Turkish.

In New York, in the autumn of 1994, *Hapgood* opened at the Mitzi Newhouse Theater at the Lincoln Center, where it ran for four months. *Arcadia* was heading for America at the same time. Manny Azenberg thought a Broadway theatre would be best, but Stoppard opted for the Vivien Beaumont Theater at the Lincoln Center. Meanwhile, *Indian Ink* opened at the Aldwych, in February 1995, with Kendal. That opening coincided almost exactly with the New York previews of *Arcadia*, which started on 2 March. *Hapgood* was still running next door. It closed on 26 March, and the press night of *Arcadia* was 30 March. Just as, the year before, he had had two plays concurrently at the RSC and at the National, he now had two plays overlapping in New York. He wrote to his mother: 'I must admit when I saw the side-by-side posters at Lincoln Center I thought – "My goodness!"'

However, *Arcadia* in New York was not an entirely happy experience. André Bishop, the manager of the Lincoln Center, had thought it would be perfect for the Beaumont Theater's thrust stage, but he felt that Nunn (who was also busy with *Sunset Boulevard*, and was hard to pin down) had not spent enough time with the designer working out how different it would be from the Lyttelton's proscenium stage. There were terrible acoustic problems, and the actors had to be miked, an unusual thing then, much disliked by the older members of the company. Richard Eyre, in New York directing David Hare's *Racing Demon* at the same time, dropped in for the end of *Arcadia*'s press night on 30 March 1995, and complained in his diary: 'Why don't architects *care* about acoustics? It's like designing a car without wheels.' He went on to tell a (rare) Stoppard blue joke. 'I was standing in the foyer with Tom and a woman came up and gushed, how wonderful his work was, how much pleasure she had from it, etc etc. Tom was very polite, then she went and he turned to me: "Why don't they ever offer you a blow job?"'

However much pleasure the audiences were getting, and however ecstatic the New York reviews, *Arcadia* did not transfer to Broadway, did not win any Tonys, and ran at the Lincoln Center for only four months. Meanwhile, though, it was starting its journey all over America, as a favourite at hundreds of regional theatres and student and amateur groups. At Penn State University, in 1995, a whole year was given over to a 'Penn Reading Project' on the play.

One of the American highlights was a fine production for A.C.T. at the Stage Door theatre in San Francisco in October 1995. His connection with A.C.T. was a long one, which had begun in 1968 with the then director William Ball's production of *Rosencrantz* at the Geary Theater. In 1989 the San Francisco earthquake almost destroyed the Geary, but A.C.T. survived, putting on its productions in different theatres all over the city. In 1991 William Ball died and Carey Perloff became the director. *Arcadia* was her first Stoppard; she would do almost all his plays after that, one of the few women directors to work with him regularly. She came to his attention first because she was so energetically persistent about getting the performing rights for *Arcadia* out of the Lincoln Center. Then they corresponded intensively during the production, and met for the first time in London in 1996. It was the beginning of an excellent working relationship and a close friendship.

Perloff's background made her a perfect match for Stoppard. Her mother, Marjorie Perloff, of whom Stoppard became extremely fond, was a distinguished English literature academic, married to a cardiologist, and

a Viennese Jewish émigré, who among many other books wrote an eloquent autobiography of her family and her childhood exile, *The Vienna
Paradox*, which had a great influence on him. Carey Perloff had a classical education as an undergraduate and studied Sappho and Catullus, had
done graduate work at Oxford and married an English lawyer. She was a
writer herself as well as a director, a very good reader of plays, decisive,
loquacious, determined and perceptive.

She understood him from the start. He reminded her of her own
European Jewish ancestry. She saw how much 'clarity of utterance' mattered to him, how he saw his texts as pieces of music and wanted the actors
to look after the words. She appreciated his appetite for knowledge, his
reticence, his moral nature, his complete absence (unlike many male playwrights) of condescension to women, his respect for actors and his interest in the *craft* of theatre. She was in awe of his mind, but they were at
ease with each other, and she was amused by his quirks, like (later on) his
inability to use a computer, and his idiosyncratic texting habits. His first
text to her read: 'Am off to Paris and thence to Japan'. No one else, Perloff
said, uses 'thence' in a text.

At the end of 1995, *Indian Ink* closed at the Aldwych and a revival of
Rosencrantz and Guildenstern opened at the Lyttelton Theatre, directed by
Matthew Francis, with Alan Howard as the Player, Adrian Scarborough as
Rosencrantz and Simon Russell Beale as Guildenstern. Russell Beale, who
had played Guildenstern when he was a schoolboy and was told by his
English teacher to think of the play as lightweight, found it extremely moving. He felt it as a play about disappointment, about being lost and irrelevant, not being thought to matter. He found two other things about the play,
returning to it: that it was extremely easy to get lost (he and Scarborough
once went round twice with the tennis-game 'question and answer' scene),
and that you could not rely on the audience already knowing the play, even
though, by then, it was a 'classic' of modern English drama.

During the early 1990s Stoppard was doing other jobs too. He worked
on a long, frivolous narrative for Lehar's *The Merry Widow*, full of
innuendo and punning, set in *fin-de-siècle* Paris, which Dirk Bogarde

performed with world-weary elegance at a Glyndebourne Festival Opera concert performance at the Festival Hall in July 1993. He adapted his 1977 TV version of *Three Men in a Boat* for radio; it aired on 29 December 1994. He was writing *The Invention of Love*, and still working on *Enigma* and *Hopeful Monsters*.

As *Arcadia* garnered prizes (the Olivier award, the *Evening Standard* theatre award, the New York Drama Critics' Circle award), was adapted for radio with the original cast, sold thousands of copies and was performed worldwide, he kept being asked, all the more so after *Shakespeare in Love*, if he would turn it into a film. He didn't want to do it: what would be the point, when it worked so well for the stage? Many years later, he gave in to pressure from the producer Scott Rudin, and wrote an (as yet unproduced) screenplay for him between 2015 and 2017. But he never felt the need for a film. The play was enough. He would say of it: '*Arcadia* just fell out, like a game of patience.' It will last as long as there are actors and theatres. The play was the answer to its own question: what will survive of us?

He was rueful and funny with Bobby about his fame, as when being reluctantly summoned back to Pocklington School as a famous old boy, or joking about the fact that the satirist Miles Kington was putting on a play at the Bristol Old Vic called *Waiting for Stoppard*: 'so I finally got a title!' (Kington wrote to him hoping that he would take out an injunction against the use of his name, which would help with publicity; be as rude about me as you like, Stoppard replied. But the squib was a harmless and admiring pastiche.) He was mildly amused when he went to a satirical performance by the comedian John Sessions at the Royal Academy about the Victorian painter Frederic Leighton, to find that the character of Disraeli was being done in the voice of Tom Stoppard. His fame always made him feel something of a fraud. He often had attacks of imposter syndrome. Flying back from the States on Concorde in November 1994, he told Bobby that the only valid reason for being thought 'an important writer' was the way they look after you; the rest was an embarrassment: 'I keep wondering when they'll find me out, in fact it's 27 years undetected.' He often mentioned his dread at the thought of having his letters published or his biography written.

But she heard a good deal about his public life as an 'important writer'. He was much involved on the board of the National Theatre with the process of replacing Richard Eyre with Trevor Nunn. He joined the committee of trustees of the London Library, his major research resource for many years, where he would become increasingly involved. He was summoned for jury service in January 1996, but managed to 'charm his way' out of it. He was elected to the Other Club, an all-male dining club founded by Churchill, which met at the Savoy eight times a year, while parliament was sitting. It was limited to fifty people, mainly politicians, 'but also the likes of John Mortimer, Bernard Levin, Robin Day, and, I suppose, me'. He didn't think he would fit in, as 'every time I see a politician on television, I think, what a game', but he enjoyed the conversation, and even found himself chairing a dinner, surrounded by cabinet ministers and 'Lord Tom Cobley and all': 'I kept thinking *this is ridiculous, how did it happen?*'

He often told her about such outings, like an evening in February 1996 spent at George Weidenfeld's, in company with Bernard Williams and

Isaiah Berlin, to meet Shimon Peres, whom he thought very impressive. He 'kept quiet and listened agog'. He told her about treats like Rolling Stones and Pink Floyd concerts, and about his glittery friends – almost all met through work – Spielberg, Jagger, David Bowie, Andrew Lloyd Webber. He told her whose funerals and memorials he had gone to: Miriam's father's, or Michael Hordern's, or Kathleen Tynan's in 1995, in the same church where he had spoken at Ken Tynan's memorial service fourteen years before.

Wherever he was in the world, he tried to ring every Sunday, 'even if just to say hallo and goodbye', as she put it. She would get postcards or airmail letters, or descriptions of his travels on his return. In the summer of 1994 it was Sydney (for a production of *Arcadia*) and Tahiti; for several summers in a row in the mid-1990s he was at Jeremy Fry's village in Provence, Le Grand Banc, trying to write his Housman play in his own little cottage. His greetings to her might come from Italy or the Hague, California or Philadelphia. She sent Sarka lists of his travels, as in October 1993: 'Paris, Zurich, Freiberg, Strasbourg in four days!' He told her he wasn't bothered about Christmas, or whether he was alone for it: the nicest Christmas he could remember was sitting in the flat in 1992, writing the first page of *Arcadia*.

He knew she enjoyed hearing about what they called his 'posh' events, and would tell her when Princess Margaret was coming to *Arcadia*, or Buckingham Palace had invited him to a reception, or lunch at the Queen Mother's home in Windsor. He described this kind of visit as 'one of those "if Mum could see me now!" occasions'. He became friends with Daniel Chatto and Princess Margaret's daughter, the painter Sarah Armstrong-Jones, because Kendal's agent, Ros Chatto, was Daniel Chatto's mother, and they went to the wedding, which he described in detail. In the year of the break-up of Charles and Diana, it was clear where his sympathies lay. He wrote to Bobby with horror about the massacre at Dunblane: 'It's impossible to get over it. I thought – what is the point of anything on my desk when such a thing can happen.' But then he added grimly: 'I hope to god Di doesn't take her royal compassion up there.'

One of the most satisfying 'posh' stories he had for her was his visit to Chatsworth in the summer of 1995, a nostalgic return to Derbyshire and the beginning of a good friendship with a remarkable character. He was invited by Andrew Cavendish, the Duke of Devonshire, whom he'd met through the London Library and the Other Club, to give out the first Heywood Hill literary prize on 23 June 1995. The award, for 'a lifelong contribution to the enjoyment of books', named after the smart London bookshop owned by the Duke, took place at Chatsworth in a jolly ceremony complete with brass band and provisions. In 1995 it went to Patrick O'Brian (and the following year to Penelope Fitzgerald). Stoppard was delighted to be asked, because it meant he could go back to his childhood places. He went fishing in Dovedale, looked at his school again, and found their old home, Rosegarth. It all 'looked so unchanged', he told his mother. Okeover Hall had been completely done up; it was odd 'to think of us boys looking out of those dormitory windows at the hillside where we sledged in the winter of '47'. He turned up late for dinner at Chatsworth after his day on the river, wearing his wellies and his Barbour, and was urged to join all the black-tied and bejewelled guests; his supper had been kept warm for him. The next day he was shown the treasures in the library.

Chatsworth, which he described as 'a nice mixture of grand style and unpretentiousness', had been run for forty-five years by the Duchess of Devonshire, the last of the Mitford sisters, known as Debo to all her friends, a person of great energy, competence and charm, who had turned Chatsworth into a highly successful commercial operation in which she closely involved herself. She was a spirited, aristocratic doer, not a reader. 'As a literary moll', Stoppard wrote, introducing a memoir she wrote in 2001, 'the Duchess was a hoot.' Her bedside books, he noted, were *Fowls and Geese and How to Keep Them*, the *Oxford Book of English Verse* on India paper, and, 'most precious', *The Last Train to Memphis: The Rise of Elvis Presley*. Evelyn Waugh once gave her a mocked-up copy of one of his books with all the pages blank. But she was a close friend to many writers and artists, among them Patrick Leigh Fermor, Alan Bennett and Lucian Freud. Stoppard would now become one of these, and she would write him short, funny, enthusiastic notes in her emphatic handwriting. He found her humorous, kind and welcoming. He loved going to the great house he had known from the outside as a child, and being invited to what he thought of as the sort of country house weekends you might read about in books. He was fascinated by the 'one degree of separation' there was between his world and her world. And he always felt like something of an impersonator, or imposter, when he was there, attempting to appear more relaxed than he was.

On his own rather different domestic front, he gave Bobby lots of detail about his move upstairs to and refurbishing of 44 Chelsea Harbour, the long-drawn-out process of getting rid of Iver, and the doings of the four boys: Ed reading French at Edinburgh, Oliver with Maric in Norfolk, giving up his physics dissertation and trying his luck at opening a food shop (which only lasted a short time), Will in the music business, Barny in the film business. He told her about the celebrations he and Miriam held for Will's twenty-third birthday, a dinner for seven, and for Ed's twenty-first, a fishing trip, and about the presents he'd had for his own fifty-eighth birthday, a set of library steps from Felicity, and a cake from Jane Asher's fashionable shop in the shape of him reading in the bath.

He amused her with funny stories, like his account of acquiring a personal trainer called Nigel and going to the gym, in the summer of 1996, as he was worried he never took any exercise. 'Nigel my trainer puts me through various pathetic trials of strength and stamina and embarrasses me by saying "Perfect!" "Superb!" while all around me there are people with muscles grimly getting on with it by themselves. I feel I want "Intellectual" on my T-shirt.' He took a deeply affectionate tone with her, as when he had missed sending a present on the day of her birthday: 'Dear best of all mums – all you have is me unwrapped – and all my love.' He often teased her about being a fusspot and treating him as if he were a child, as after a visit to Sandringham – 'yes, Mum, I remembered to write to Prince Charles' – or when telling her he was walking to the theatre for rehearsals through Central Park: '(no, Mum, I won't get mugged)'. As she and Ken got less mobile, he and Peter suggested they might move into a flat or a bungalow. But 'don't get into a fuss about it'. He chided her: 'You're getting into a tizz about things which *don't matter* – I wish you wouldn't!!' He tried to lend her some of his own phlegmatism, as when he sent news of his sons: 'At least they are all in one piece, no trouble, no illness, no one in jail, no one miserable, and one should just be thankful.' When she was fretting about Fiona or Richard, he told her that it was no good trying to change grown-up children's lives. One must just 'make the best of it'.

But worry she did, and if she hid her darkest feelings from him, she let them out in her letters to the distant but friendly Sarka. His personal life was a source of anxiety to her. She told Sarka that she had thought his marriage would last forever, she worried that he was taking care of all his boys financially, and she felt his relationship with Felicity was insecure. His play is a great success, she told Sarka in 1994, 'but I want him to be happy *in his private life*'. It was all part of her family worries, along with her son Richard's problems in his marriage and Fiona's challenging life with little money and two children. Ken had been ill with emphysema for over ten years, and he was also, as she put it, 'a great hypochondriac', who spent a lot of money on homeopathic remedies. He made constant demands on her and was often moody and difficult to live with. Her own health was not good, with her diabetes and increasingly poor eyesight. She fretted constantly about her Czech family and especially about Irma. She wrote many, often unanswered, letters to her distant relatives, and spent hours, sometimes in the middle of the night, thinking about her memories. One letter she wrote to her son in March 1994, wishing him luck with the *Travesties* transfer to the Savoy Theatre, and anxious about the news of the IRA mortar attacks at Heathrow, remembered his father's death in February 1942, at the age of thirty-four, and their arrival in Bombay on that same day. She told Emil Máčel, who was writing to her from Zlín with bits of family history, that she lived strictly in the present and could not afford the luxury of dwelling on the past. But her mind returned to it continually.

In the early summer of 1996, she became ill; she couldn't eat properly and she was very tired. She was booked to go into hospital for an endoscopy, and he urged her to go private – he would pay for everything. Waiting to go in, she told Sarka that 'Tomik's 59th birthday' was coming up, 'so I will think about that day in Zlin when he was born, and we were all together'. In July, while she was in hospital, he sent her the first pages of the new play. It was a comic scene in the underworld. 'It has *just* occurred to me', he wrote, in a humorous and tender compliment to her, that 'the subject matter might strike most people as unsuitable for hospital reading but you and I can rise above that.' All through the summer he tried to persuade her not to worry about anyone else and not to go to any trouble for any family visitors. By September there was a possible diagnosis of an umbilical hernia. At this point he pushed back against her resistance to anyone 'making a fuss'; he felt he had trapped himself into a condition of 'keeping mum – no pun intended'. It was very like the way she had made it impossible for him to ask questions about their past. On 7 October 1996 she wrote to Sarka to say that her news was 'not very good'. She had been in hospital twice and the doctor had come to the house the day before to tell her that she had cancer of the pancreas. 'I must get used to it, and I don't know how much time is left to me.'

The family came down to Devon – Tom and Fiona and Ami first, then Richard, then Peter and Lesley. The night before she was due to go back into hospital, he sat up all night, writing her a long letter, thanking her for very many things and telling her how well she had done for them all. He thought she would have time to read it in hospital and that it would help her. It would be a source of painful regret to him that she did not read this letter (which does not survive). Before they left the house, on the morning of 11 October, only four days after her letter to Sarka, Bobby was in the kitchen with a baking tin in her hand, and she said to the others, there's a chicken in the oven, make sure Peter and Lesley have some roast chicken. In the car on the way to the hospital, she said crossly to Fiona, 'And Tom hasn't got any sweets.' She knew that he ate them to keep him awake on the long drive back to London, and she was worried about him, as always. That was the last thing she said. As soon as they got to the hospital in Sidmouth, she was given an enormous dose of painkillers. She didn't speak again, and rapidly became comatose, but when Richard arrived, Fiona noticed that she made an annoyed gesture with her hand, as if to say, he shouldn't have come all this way. Within hours of getting to the hospital, she died. It was a profound shock to them all.

On the first day of rehearsals, in August 1997, David West came to talk to the actors about Latin pronunciation. Richard Eyre noted his warning to them: 'Don't copy me exactly, I'm from Aberdeen.' Eyre was very nervous that day, starting work on his first ever Stoppard production. But Stoppard said to him: 'This must be just another day for you, you do it all the time. I only have one of these every five years.' He was there almost every day in rehearsal, 'droll and self-mocking, generous and sanguine', as Eyre described him, though sometimes a little too 'interventionist'. They got on very well, and Eyre was happy to be working with him at last. Ironically, the situation was the reverse of *Arcadia*. The incoming head of the National, Trevor Nunn, had wanted to do *Invention*, and had indeed thought he was going to, since Stoppard talked to him a great deal about the play when they were both in New York, and they went on discussing it – at one point, Nunn remembered stopping him from switching Acts One and Two around. But, this time, Stoppard felt it belonged to Richard Eyre. And because he was a year later with it than expected, it turned out to be Eyre's last production at the National.

When Eyre first read the play he thought it was 'incredibly dense . . . I can't see the wood for the wood or the trees for the trees.' 'I admire it but can't yet love it,' he told himself in his diary. But he was amazed at how well Stoppard imagined unrequited homosexual love. Once in rehearsal he started to understand the 'symphonic' structure of the play, and became 'very fond' of it. The company worked well together; Trish Montemuro, stage-managing, thought the atmosphere was very good, and the old familiar kinship between John Wood and Stoppard was wonderful to see. The relationship between Wood and the compelling young actor Paul Rhys as Housman worked especially well. There was a difficult technical rehearsal, when Eyre was on edge and snapped at Stoppard, but they made it up the next day. Anthony Ward's set was complex, a cyclorama of back-projected images (of Oxford, river banks, clouds and sky) and a back wall of grey bookshelves, with Charon's boat coming round on the revolve. (The boat was a nightmare, Trish Montemuro remembered.) It looked better, Stoppard thought, when the play transferred from the Cottesloe to the bigger Lyttelton stage. By that time Eyre had gone: the first night of *The Invention of Love* was his last night at the National, a strange and melancholy experience for him.

In November 1998, Michael Codron took the play to the Haymarket, after a short run at the Yvonne Arnaud Theatre in Guildford. For a West End transfer, as usual, he had to find 'angels' – financial backers – to support the play. It wasn't an easy play to get backing for, and the run (which went to February 1999, at which point Codron needed to bring *Fascinating Aïda* into the Haymarket) did not do very well financially.

Invention started afresh in the States, with new productions, first at A.C.T. in January 2000, and then at the Wilma Theater in Philadelphia in February 2000. Both places were second homes to him. Blanka Zizka, the Czech director of the Wilma, who with her husband and fellow director Jiri Zizka had left Czechoslovakia in the 1970s because their work had been banned, regularly put on his plays (by 2016 she would have done twelve Stoppard productions) and brought to them what Stoppard, fondly, called her 'off-centre, visionary' and unwavering approach to the theatre. He liked going to Philadelphia very much and he liked the way his plays were done there. He and Carey Perloff, at A.C.T., were by now firm friends. As a classicist by training she was the perfect director for *Invention*, and its American premiere at A.C.T. went well. However, during rehearsals, her house nearly burned down, and she directed it in a state of disruption and stress. Stoppard's gratitude to her was profound – and the production found some nice touches, like the effect of dream-like, whirling lights which took Housman away at the end of the play. Some preview audiences found it too long, and when a few people left before the end, the sound of the seats closing went through him, he told Perloff, 'like a spear'.

Stoppard asked Richard Eyre if he wanted to do *Invention* in New York; Eyre wasn't sure it would work there. Instead, it was offered to André Bishop, to be put on by the Lincoln Company at the Lyceum Theatre. Jack O'Brien and Bob Crowley renewed their Stoppard collaboration from *Hapgood*. In O'Brien's view, they turned *Invention* into a more passionately gay, less intellectual play. Crowley created an atmospheric setting, with a black mirrored floor, little movable models of books and Hellenic statues, a set with a series of 'dream-rooms' that could switch from a theatre to a railway station to a river bank, realistic Victorian costumes and lots of bicycles and boys. He felt that he had got to the 'heart and soul' of the play. He loved its feeling of the past catching up with the present, of the past never going away.

But they had one bad moment with the author. At the end of Act One, as AEH is giving his long speech, as if to a group of students, on translating Horace's love poem to Ligurinus, the stage direction tells us that 'Jackson is seen as a runner running towards us from the dark, getting no closer.' O'Brien and Crowley decided to use the famous image of Leonardo's 'Vitruvian Man', morphing into the figure of Jackson. Stoppard hated it. It's a cliché, he told them crossly. But it's one of the great moments in Western art, O'Brien said. 'Exactly,' Stoppard replied, and left the room. But soon enough he came back. 'I see,' he said, 'it wasn't a cliché *then*.'

The reception of *Invention*, in both countries, divided those who liked its scholarly wit and were moved by its language and deep feeling, and those who found it over-informative and repetitious, the work of an auto-didact. It won awards (the New York Drama Critics' Circle award, the *Evening Standard* Best New Play award) and had many admiring reviews. One exception was a vicious attack by the reviewer David Sexton, who said it was so insufferable, tedious and vulgar that he thought there must be something wrong with the state of English theatre that so many people admired it and the audience seemed to be enjoying itself. No one criticised Stoppard for appropriating a gay love story, as perhaps they might now. He was plagued, though, by attentive fact-checkers. When the philosopher John Lucas wrote to him correcting a date in the play, he replied that the play was stuffed 'with chronological "errors"! . . . the play is a memory play in which the protagonist has an unreliable memory; not a biography'.

He was impatient, too, with those who thought he had made Wilde the hero of the play at Housman's expense. (Adam Phillips was one of the reviewers who saw it Stoppard's way: 'it is Housman's vulnerability rather than Wilde's that is made to seem the more inspired, the more resilient'.) His argument with Daniel Mendelsohn over this, in the pages of the *New York Review of Books*, became a burden to him. He wished that he'd done what he usually did, which was not to respond to criticism. He told David

Hare, later, that the exchange had 'bled me of creative energy for a month of back-and-forth, about something which would have disappeared down the plug-hole'. To set the record straight, he made a point of saying, in interviews, that he thought Housman was 'a heroic person', in his rectitude, his 'morally steadfast defence' of scholarly standards and his fervent and scrupulous love of language.

He kept telling people that the play was 'not biographical . . . The whole thing never happened – it's all going on in Housman's head.' In a lecture for the London Library in October 1997 called 'Reflections on "Biographical Fiction"' (which mostly consisted of funny comparisons between doggedly factual and creatively inaccurate biographies of Housman), he argued in favour of invention. How do you get to the truth about a person? He gives an example from an edition of Goethe's letters of how *not* to do it. 'In his later years, Goethe mentioned in passing: "And then at the age of seventeen I fell in love for the first time." The editor made a footnote here. It said: "Here Goethe was mistaken."'

Perhaps fictional biography could do better. 'A fictional treatment of A. E. Housman . . . choc-a-bloc with inaccuracies, might deliver the man as truthfully as a much fatter book of carefully deployed facts.' When in doubt, he encourages the biographer, speculate! The real test of biographers is 'how they deal with what isn't known, not with what is – most of all, the workings of the human mind, and that's a country which borders mine.' He concludes: 'I am in pursuit of an impudent claim that in biography, though not in classical scholarship, there is no special virtue in accuracy if it is not the right kind of accuracy, and no special vice in inaccuracy unless it is the wrong kind of inaccuracy.' He sounded like his own version of Oscar Wilde: 'It's only fact. Truth is quite another thing and is the work of the imagination.'

The biographical facts of his own life were concealed, as usual, inside his invention. But some of the truth about him was suggested by it, too. He often said in interviews that he had become a more self-expressive, less guarded writer, and that he had been shy of self-revelations in his early work. In this play he seems to have split himself between the theatrical, exhibitionist, stylish Wilde, who turned his life into a performance, and the shy, self-concealing Housman, who poured his hidden emotions into his art and into the pursuit of knowledge. Housman speaks fervently in the play (sounding as fervent as Hannah in *Arcadia*) in praise of 'useless knowledge for its own sake . . . It's what's left of God's purpose when you take away God.'

Asked which is his favourite of his plays, he has said that although he thinks *Arcadia* is his only 'perfect' play, he personally loves *The Invention of Love* because he so enjoyed writing it. The remark about *Arcadia* is one he later wished he hadn't made, as sounding vain and grandiose. A sphere could be a perfect sphere, but how could a play be a perfect play? But he stands by his affection for *The Invention of Love*. And there is personal feeling all through this 'historical' play. His youthful unrequited love for Isabel might explain why he is so good at imagining another kind of unrequited love. His wistfulness about not having been an undergraduate colours the Oxford scenes: 'I have a romantic idea about the University I never attended,' he said. 'Oh to be twenty-one, reading Greats at Oxford!' He turned sixty on 3 July 1997, as he was finishing the play, nearly a year after his mother's death. A sense of mortality gives the play its elegiac tone.

27

The Scar of Time

> I have nothing that came from my father, nothing he owned or touched,
> but here is his trace, a small scar.

On 14 June 1997, a few weeks before his sixtieth birthday, the announce-ment of the Queen's Birthday Honours included a knighthood for Tom Stoppard for 'services to literature'. Among other figures from the arts world honoured that year were Dame Cleo Laine, Sir Roger Norrington, Sir Donald Sinden, James Bowman, CBE, Gillian Lynne, CBE, and Victoria Wood, OBE. He was the first playwright to be knighted since Terence Rattigan. Congratulations tumbled in. Michael Codron wrote to 'a very parfitt gentil knight'. David Cornwell sent 'Hooray and much love' to 'Sir T'. Kenneth Ewing wrote with delighted affection. A leader in the *Guardian*, headed 'Arise, Sir Tom', said:

> Never was a chevalier more chivalrous; never was a dramaturgical
> personage more modest . . . From his first big hit . . . he brought
> an intellectual intensity, anarchic wit and heightened linguistic
> consciousness to the British stage which has no precedent . . . The
> playwright is there to render mortality immortal and immortality
> mortal. We have no greater practitioner of that art than Sir Tom.

He was deeply pleased to be Sir Tom, though he never made a song and dance about it. When Teresa Wells asked him if he was more embar-rassed or proud, he said, 'Proud, *of course!*' He knew there were writers who turned such honours down, but his response was, quite simply, 'How wonderful.' To Peter, he said: 'What a shame mum isn't here, isn't it?'

His sixtieth birthday on 3 July 1997 didn't involve lavish celebrations: the night before it, he went to see Alan Howard's Lear with Felicity, Will and some of his friends; the team at the agency arranged a river-boat trip to a restaurant in Putney; and a few days later he went up to Edinburgh to see Ed graduate. *The Seagull* was running, *Shakespeare in Love* was back on his desk, he made trips to Ireland and to France. There was some publicity, including a long profile by Kate Kellaway in the *Guardian*, subtitled 'Tom Stoppard, sexy at 60'. She described him as not sedate or stolid enough to be sixty, or a knight. He was a 'flying buttress' rather than a 'pillar of the theatrical establishment', elusive, divided between seriousness and frivolity, 'politically contradictory' and 'adept at making his character into a slipknot' for any potential biographer.

He may not have felt, himself, like a theatrical monument, but, in his sixtieth year, his worldwide reputation as one of the country's leading playwrights was unshakeable. Among the living, only Harold Pinter was as famous; Alan Bennett, Alan Ayckbourn, Caryl Churchill, Michael Frayn, David Hare and Peter Shaffer were none of them household names in the same way.

On 11 September 1997 – while *The Invention of Love* was in its last weeks of rehearsal – he went to the French Embassy to be made Officier de l'Ordre des Arts et des Lettres, the second grade of the distinguished honour given by the French Ministry of Culture to artists and writers, or, in the official words of the order: '*les personnes qui se sont distinguées par leurs créations dans le domaine artistique ou littéraire . . . en France et dans le monde*'. Ed and Will came, Peter and Lesley all the way from Bristol, Fiona and her partner David, Richard from King's Lynn, Jacky and Dave from Winchester. Peter Wood was there, and Teresa and John Wells, in very poor health. Frank Pike represented Faber. The agency came in force: Kenneth Ewing and Gordon Dickerson, Nicki Stoddart, Anthony Jones, Ewing's assistant Rose Cobbe, Tim Corrie and his wife. Not all were currently working with Stoppard: Gordon Dickerson had left PFD, Tim Corrie had been replaced by Anthony Jones as his film agent, and Stoppard was now working more with Rose Cobbe than with Nicki Stoddart. But it showed their loyalty and affection for him that they were all there.

Like Jacky, and his editors at Faber, these were his friends, companions and allies. It was more than a job for them. They protected his interests, looked after his welfare and made his working life as smooth-running as they could. They would come, when they could, to every first night, every public lecture and every major event and celebration in his life. At Christmas and on birthdays they would all get presents and cards. They were part of the permanent Stoppard family.

Kenneth Ewing's old-fashioned, stubborn, principled, affable ways still suited him very well. Ewing did everything in longhand, never used a dictaphone, mocked up all the contracts himself in advance and would then talk them through in detail. The PFD Stoppard team, which after Ewing retired would essentially be Anthony Jones, Rose Cobbe and St John Donald, knew that Stoppard sometimes had to be persuaded to put his mind to business matters. But once he was giving his full attention, he was forensic, concentrated, fast (super-quick at long division) and not to be messed with. He would phone them and come in often: the PFD Chelsea Harbour office was close to the flat. For the making of every new contract, there would be long meetings, which would conclude with much teasing of Ewing by Stoppard.

In making his contracts they knew he was concerned with the status of the writer, and that he kept a sharp eye on how that status was treated in the commercial theatre, for instance in terms of the division of the royalty pool. They knew he wanted to control the choice of director for his plays and liked to be involved in casting. In some contracts Stoppard would get 'right of approval' of director, designer, opening cast and American producer. He was sensitive about the timings of productions. He did not like an overlap between a new production and a revival; he wanted to be able to concentrate on rehearsals for one play and not be caught between two productions. He was uneasy if he thought that one Stoppard play might steal the thunder of another: there was some firm correspondence, for instance, with the director Bill Kenwright, who wanted to bring a new production of *Rough Crossing* to London at the same time that *Arcadia* was opening in 1993.

The timetabling of any given year, when there might be several productions going on at once in England, Europe and the States, had to be carefully planned between Jacky and the agency. He was very dependent on them all for getting things right. It was the same at Faber. There would be some to-and-fro between him and Frank Pike – later, Peggy Butcher, and then Dinah Wood – on revisions, prefaces, collected editions and suchlike. Because Faber knew that he would always revise his plays after the first edition came out, with his agreement they kept the first printing down to a low number and then printed the revised edition in greater numbers a few weeks later. They always consulted him on details such as discounting the plays for sale in the theatres, the layout of the cast page, cover images and publication dates. But, in general, he trusted them to look after his plays.

PFD dealt with contracts, royalties, transfers, licencing in foreign territories, production companies, fees, publishers, translations, film rights and credits, and many other aspects of the big machinery of his professional life. But, like Jacky, they also fielded mountains of miscellaneous requests, both serious and trivial. In 1997, for instance, Rose Cobbe sent on a request from *Reader's Digest* asking if they could put a Stoppard epigram – 'If an idea's worth having once, it's worth having twice' – into their 'Quotable Quotes' section. He said it was a misquotation of a not particularly quotable comment in conversation, and better forgotten. A public relations company pitching for the business of Pommery champagne had noticed a reference to 'a bottle of Pommery' in *Invention* and wanted to know if they could quote him as a fan of the brand. Cobbe told him she would say she couldn't get hold of him.

Jacky, in Winchester, continued to deal, similarly, with all manner of approaches, while still doing all his typing, personal business, finances and travel arrangements for him. Her mailbox just after the opening of *Invention* was typical. Among the fan letters, factual corrections, requests from translators, actors wanting to be cast in his next play, students of his work needing help with their essays, and convenors of arts groups wanting to put on readings, there were approaches from the Housman Society (had he thought about writing a play about John Maynard Keynes?), from a Vassar professor wanting to put on a shortened version of the play ('If you're talking about losing, say, ten minutes, I don't mind, but if you mean much more than that, on the whole it would be better to choose a different play'), an offer of a new translation of Propertius from someone who'd seen him being interviewed by Charlie Rose, correspondence about a production of *Invention* to be done in Gdańsk, and an invitation to travel to New Zealand with a lady who had put a personal ad in *The Times* describing herself as 'Aged, battered crone seeking pleasant footloose young man'. Most of these received answers. So did a polite letter from a professor at the University of British Columbia, Ira Nadel, informing him that Methuen would be publishing the biography he had written of him, and asking for a meeting. They did meet once, and Nadel talked to others, including Anthony Smith and Peter Stoppard. Stoppard said he hoped it would be 'as inaccurate as possible'. The biography, a thoroughly researched, detailed coverage of his public and professional life, with an emphasis on his Jewish history and on the double identities in his plays, came out in 2002. He did not read it.

Three months after the party at the French Embassy, on 12 December 1997, he went to Buckingham Palace to be knighted. Prince Charles wielded the sword, and photographers took his picture outside. He looked glamorous, youthful and delighted. Then there was a lunch at the Ritz with Will and Ed. It was a triumphant conclusion to his sixtieth year.

But for all his public honours, his high profile, his first biography and his array of professional commitments, his life was not steady or fixed. There were changes all around. Friends' lives, of course, were constantly shifting: he was much in demand at birthdays, weddings and (increasingly) funerals. Kenneth Ewing turned seventy, then Paul Johnson: Stoppard was on hand with speeches and tributes. Harold Pinter had his sixty-eighth at the Ivy, Andrew Lloyd Webber celebrated his fiftieth (black tie and dancing). Simon Gray got divorced, and married Victoria Rothschild; both were his friends. Derek Marlowe, that flaming early talent, died far away, at fifty-eight. His dear, funny friend John Wells died of cancer, at sixty-one, in January 1998. He spoke movingly at his funeral and at his memorial, and kept a kind eye on Teresa.

His own life, too, was going through another quiet upheaval. From around the time of his sixtieth birthday, gossip began to circulate about the break-up of his relationship with Kendal, though neither of them spoke about it in public. There was no dramatic moment of separation. But both of them relished their independence, both were extremely busy in their professional lives, and both began to feel that there was going to be no more to the relationship than there had been. They had always been 'on and off', and they had not chosen to live together or get married. The complications and consequences of that seemed impossible or alarming to them. Looking back, Stoppard found it hard to explain why it ended. In his version, they were fine as they were; but they had run out of steam. Into that loss of intensity and enchantment another strong attraction began to make its way.

The relationship ended during the course of 1997. Kendal's father, who had been incapacitated for some years, died in May 1998, a hard time for her. Later that year she published her autobiography of her acting childhood, a kind of tribute to him, full of the memories of India which had also influenced *Indian Ink*. Some time after the break-up, she was reunited with her ex-husband Michael Rudman, with whom she remained. She and Stoppard stayed on good terms: they went to each other's shows, they socialised occasionally, and often spoke on the phone. Though she keeps the private story of their life to herself, she speaks of him to this day with fondness, humour and respect. If there was pain and sadness, it was well managed, and outweighed by affection and loyalty. It is one of the striking features of his life that he has stayed friends with his ex-partners.

The tabloids which had harassed them when they first got together had a field day with these rearrangements. There were gleeful rumours of other relationships. In June 1997, a *Daily Mail* journalist spotted Mia Farrow on a visit to John Boorman at his home in Annamoe, in County Wicklow. She was filming in Ireland, and was staying in one of Boorman's cottages with two of her children. Stoppard was also visiting Boorman for a few days. Farrow, like Boorman, was an old friend of his: they had known each other since his first collaboration with Previn, and there are friendly notes from her, over years, sending love to Miriam. The three of them went out to the village shop, and were snapped together. Boorman was erased from the picture, and a romance was deduced from the resulting image of Stoppard with his arm over Farrow's shoulder. This 'news' item zoomed round the world: 'Mia Farrow and Tom Stoppard spotted strolling the Irish streets of County Wicklow'. The *New York Daily News* picked it up: '*Farrow and Stoppard in the Name of Love?* Has Mia Farrow found love again?' The *Sydney Morning Herald* reported that 'Mia Farrow is the main squeeze of British playwright Sir Tom Stoppard.' Even the *Observer* picked up the story, saying that 'the couple' had been reported 'buying groceries together'. Later clippings incorporated the rumour as historical fact, as in: 'Mia Farrow's former significant others, André Previn, Philip Roth and Tom Stoppard remain friends . . .' Boorman remembered that for the next few days there were photographers swarming over his land, and it cost him, as he had to install an electric gate. He also noted that Stoppard's relationship with Kendal was coming to an end at that time. Boorman told him he should explain to her what had really happened. No, Stoppard replied, he was not going to defend something that did not require defending.

At the end of September 1998, the *Daily Mail* ran a front-page piece about the break-up, with a huge photograph of Kendal under the headline 'Curtains for the Tom and Felicity Show' and a report that the relationship had ended 'acrimoniously'. 'The couple, who did not live together but could not bear to be long apart, are not even speaking any more . . . what went wrong between them seems destined to remain a mystery . . . everyone expected them to marry when their respective divorces came through. But it didn't happen.' Feature writers picked up on the story, but were met with polite silence by Stoppard and brush-offs by Kendal. To doorstepping reporters, she would respond briskly: 'Have a nice day.'

A few years later, Stoppard was in France when Kenneth Ewing phone to tell him that he was all over the front pages of the tabloids again. With a sinking heart he looked up the story. It said that Marie Helvin, model, ex-wife of David Bailey and close friend of the Jaggers, had moved into his flat with eleven pieces of luggage. But – according to Stoppard – he had only once been alone in a room with Helvin, and had certainly never had a romantic moment with her. The story was so out-of-the-blue that he even found himself wondering whether Helvin had planted it; but he knew it was hard not to become paranoid where the tabloids were concerned. And, even though he was a weathered public figure, it still amazed him that the press could just 'make things up'. These sorts of intrusions coloured his views on journalism and privacy. Meanwhile, his 'relationship' with Helvin settled into the clippings.

The real new thing in his life was more quietly managed. From the spring of 1998, the appointment diary Jacky kept for him began to include references to Sinéad Cusack. As with Miriam and Felicity, he had known her for a long time before they fell in love. When Jeremy Irons and Glenn Close were together on stage in New York in *The Real Thing*, she was often in the audience. He knew her work well as an actor with the RSC. The shift in their feelings for each other was slow, gradual and private: and it was a complicated situation, especially for her. Partly for these reasons, this change in his life involved a new place to live. The references to her in the appointment diaries were usually linked to his increasingly frequent trips to France, where they would travel on separate flights.

He had spent several summers with Robert Carsen and Jeremy Fry at Le Grand Banc, in Provence, and loved it. Now he found his own Provençal house, in the medieval village of Lacoste, in the Vaucluse, forty kilometres from Avignon. Lacoste, with steep cobbled stone streets, stone arches and grey stone houses with red tiled roofs, has a spectacular setting and some equally spectacular history, since the castle at the top of the hill had been the home of the Marquis de Sade. Stoppard's house was a seventeenth-century stone cottage high up, near the church with its belfry, with big views over the village roofs, across to the village of Bonnieux and the hills beyond. It had thick walls and an interesting shape, with a long room on both floors which was wider at one end: the 'fat' end of the room downstairs was the kitchen, upstairs it was his study. He had a small infinity pool built, and a sauna, and stone terraces in the garden, which was full of lavender and roses. Carsen designed his kitchen for him. Just down the road was a *boulangerie*, and there were cafes and a little hotel. He bought it in October 1998. This was to be a retreat and refuge for him and Cusack, and a place for him to work. He read for, and wrote, his next big play there, and for several years his diaries were full of trips to Lacoste. By 2001, though, he was complaining that it had become too trendy. Everything changed after Pierre Cardin bought de Sade's castle – and thirty other houses in the village. There was also a big American art college in the village, and the narrow streets filled up with students. Cardin opened galleries and shops, an opera festival started up, all the old houses were done up to the nines, and the village became, according to his old acquaintance the music producer Deke Arlon, who had a house nearby, 'one huge art exhibition'. There was a public footpath overlooking his garden, and at one point the house was burgled. Stoppard told Anthony Smith that there were too many 'Sadists' thronging past his door, and now that Cardin had bought the château, next there would be Sadists in smart blazers, and it would all be too much. A long-running feud developed between those who relished Cardin's commercialisation of Lacoste and those who hated it. Lovely though it was, the French retreat had its drawbacks. In 2007, he sold the house for £745,000. (Its sale price in 2010 was £1.24 million.)

His hidden life in Lacoste, where he was beginning to work on *The Coast of Utopia*, had to be fitted into the gaps between his public life. As usual, he had pieces to write and appearances to make, including, in 1998, giving a masterclass in Birmingham for David Edgar, and getting an honorary degree at Hull University. His involvement with the London Library increased: after his lecture on fictional biography he became vice-president in 2000, and then president in 2002: it would be a major commitment.

One of his many public talks was given in January 1999 at the New York Public Library, later published as 'Pragmatic Theater' (under the suave editorial hand of Bob Silvers) in the *New York Review of Books*. He had been asked to talk on 'Technique and Interpretation in the Performing Arts'. 'If there were ever a title dreamed up to strike me dumb,' he began, 'this one verges on inspiration.' It was like asking a rock climber to talk about the notion of technique: he would probably describe it as 'climbing up rocks in the way that seems to make the best sense if you don't want to fall off the rock'. A seemingly light 'improvisation' followed, on the essential pragmatism of theatre, and on his preference for 'common sense and a common understanding of storytelling'. Asked recently by a student what he expected from an actor, he had replied (as he always did), 'clarity of utterance', and been met with a nervous laugh of reproach. But, he said, it 'really is the first thing I ask for'. He proposed that a playwright's 'technique' is the control, and ordering, of the information that flows from the play to the audience – and gave an inimitable example:

> There's a man on the stage and a woman on the stage. The man says, 'Would you care for a drink?' The woman says, 'Yes, I think I might. I'll have a whiskey and soda.' This mildly uninteresting exchange becomes more interesting, more dramatic, depending on the information we have. It's more interesting if she's a member of Alcoholics Anonymous. It's more interesting if we know the man to be a successful poisoner; most interesting of all, perhaps, if we have already seen the man's roommate use the Cutty Sark bottle for a urine sample.

But, in fact, the ordering of information as the main example of a playwright's technique can only take us so far. He could think of many directors of Shakespeare who subvert the playwright's ordering of information. And, in any case, we don't like to think of 'genius' being only a matter of 'technique'. *The Importance of Being Earnest* was originally a four-act play; it was Wilde's manager who told him to cut out one of the acts. Wilde was the genius, the manager was the technician. As usual, Stoppard emphasised theatre as an event which takes over from the playwright's original words. In the process of staging a play, it's as if a complete object, like a sonnet, is 'thrown into a kind of spin-dryer'. When *The Real Thing* was first put on, he and the company agonised over exactly when the audience should 'get' the twist in the second scene. When it was revived seventeen years later it didn't seem to matter. 'A play which *depends* on keeping its secrets isn't worth seeing twice.'

On the other hand – the talk is a fine display of Stoppardian free association – there is a kind of 'grown-up art' which draws its value from withholding information. Take the sinister lodger in Max Frisch's *The Fire Raisers*, who turns out to be the town's visiting incendiarist and sets the house on fire. The meaning of the story is unexplained, and the play's power is the stronger for it. In his youth, three plays that meant a great deal to his generation were *Look Back in Anger*, *Waiting for Godot* and *The Birthday Party*. Osborne's play was shocking, but it 'withheld nothing'. With the other two, it was different. Beckett and Pinter 'broke' the usual contract between the play and the audience, that you would be given a certain amount of information. Unlike surrealism and Dada, which he thought 'intrinsically worthless', these plays were not 'irrational' or 'arbitrary'. They did what Shakespeare did: 'the simultaneous compression of language and expansion of meaning'. He ended with another of his favourite examples, of a playwright who can 'still turn our hearts over' with words, whatever happens to his work in the spin-dryer of production. This was his early mentor James Saunders. Beckett, Pinter and Osborne, he said, in their different ways, had inhibited him when he was young from feeling he could write a play; but Saunders made him feel 'he could do that'. And he quoted the speech he loved from *Next Time I'll Sing to You* about 'grief' being like a deep, unseen carp, swimming under the surface of the water.

As well as giving speeches and classes, and continuing his commitment to Index on Censorship and PEN, he also got involved in the 1990s, through Trish Montemuro, with a charity called War Child, co-founded by David Wilson, an agent, and the film-maker Bill Leeson. Appalled by the war in Bosnia–Herzegovina, they set up a charity to help Muslims and Christians – especially the children – in East Mostar, one of the most terrible places of the war. During the siege of Mostar, War Child sent a mobile bakery into the war zone. Rock stars like Bono and Brian Eno got involved. Stoppard was asked to be a patron. There was a big event at the Royal Festival Hall, at which he spoke, and he gave some financial support. (Later, the charity ran into major problems with accountability, but it survived that troubled phase.) Eno got other musicians together and produced a record called *Help*, which raised well over £1 million, and he persuaded Luciano Pavarotti, who was singing regularly at charity concerts in Modena, to do a concert in aid of War Child there in 1995. A music therapy centre was set up in Mostar in the tenor's name. In December 1997, very close to Christmas, Stoppard found himself in a helicopter flying to Mostar with Pavarotti, Bono and Bianca Jagger.

He wrote a piece for War Child which, not for the last time, claimed back Cecil Rhodes's notorious quotation: 'You are an Englishman. That means you have drawn first prize in the lottery of life.' To him, he said, this much mocked statement was no joke. He told the story of his childhood and his English adoption, his involvement with Charter 77, his strong sense of being 'a child of fortune', and his 'romantic attachment' to 'freedom of expression' as the basis of 'all civil freedom'.

In 1998 and 1999 there were several new productions of *Arcadia* in Paris, in Prague (where as usual he saw Havel), in Riga, by the bold Latvian director Alvis Hermanis, and in Dublin. *The Real Inspector Hound* had a sparky revival in the spring of 1998, directed by Greg Doran, in a double bill with another sixties hit, Peter Shaffer's *Black Comedy*, at the Comedy Theatre, with funny performances by David Tennant, Nicola McAuliffe and Anna Chancellor. *On the Razzle* was done at the Wilma Theater, and early in 1999, Carey Perloff put on a new production of *Indian Ink* for A.C.T. in San Francisco. She felt it was a very personal play, close to his heart.

Some of the biggest demands on his time, at the end of the 1990s, came, once again, from *Shakespeare in Love.* Having lain dormant since 1992, the project was revived in 1996, and for about two years he and John Madden worked on the script and fought their corner together. Shooting began in June 1998; the New York premiere was in December, and the London opening, in Leicester Square, on 19 January 1999. The reviews were excellent, though some critics objected to too much clever knowingness, or to its English Heritage costume drama atmosphere. But most were charmed by its sweet romanticism, its wit and its swagger, and so were audiences. It was a huge box-office draw, making over $100 million for the domestic 'take' and over $289 million worldwide.

On 24 January 1999, at the Golden Globe awards in Beverly Hills, it got awards for Best Comedy film, Best Actress and Best Screenplay, jointly awarded to Marc Norman and Stoppard. John Madden (who was nominated for Best Director but lost out to Steven Spielberg) remembered with delight that after Norman's long acceptance speech, Stoppard came up to the podium as the red light was already flashing, and just said: 'In my country, when you hear the words Wrap It Up, it means your flies are open.' The audience erupted. The Golden Globes were the precursor to a bevy of other accolades, the Actors Guild awards (where the whole cast won for an outstanding performance), the BAFTAs (Best Film, Best

Supporting Actress for Judi Dench), and numerous joint awards for Best Screenplay, at the Berlin International Film Festival, and from the Writers Guild of America and the New York Film Critics Circle. But the most important thing, of course, was the Oscars.

When the film of *Rosencrantz and Guildenstern* won the Golden Lion award at Venice nine years before, all the betting had been on Scorsese's *Goodfellas.* At the seventy-first Academy Awards, held at the Dorothy Chandler Pavilion in Los Angeles on 21 March 1999, the expectation was that Spielberg was going to win Best Picture and Best Director with *Saving Private Ryan.* His film had eleven nominations, *Shakespeare in Love* had thirteen.

Stoppard was as keyed up as anyone. He had brought Kenneth Ewing with him, who found it all quite overwhelming. The whole team were staying at the Four Seasons hotel, and John Madden described Stoppard as being in a state of 'puppyish' exhilaration. The night before the awards, there was a Miramax party for which Stoppard had written a skit called 'Two Gentlemen of Queens'. President Clinton's impeachment had ended the month before with his acquittal, and Monica Lewinsky was in the news. Tina Brown's much-talked-about magazine *Talk,* funded by Miramax, was about to be launched. The sketch, reported on by gossip journalists covering the Oscars, was full of louche topical jokes, for instance about Tina Brown wanting Lewinsky to have a child by Bob Weinstein in time for the Christmas cover of *Talk.*

The awards for the film upset all predictions – not least Madden's, who thought of it as a small quirky English comedy next to the huge Normandy landings blockbuster that was *Saving Private Ryan.* When Harrison Ford opened the envelope for Best Picture, there was a long pause before he made the announcement, as if he couldn't quite believe that *Shakespeare in Love* had beaten Spielberg. There was much rejoicing, lorded over by Weinstein. The film also won Best Screenplay (presented to Stoppard and Norman by Goldie Hawn and Steve Martin), Best Actress for Gwyneth Paltrow, presented by Jack Nicholson, Best Supporting Actress for Judi Dench, Best Art Direction, Costume Design and Score. Madden was thrilled, though he lost, again, to Spielberg, who consoled himself with

Best Director and a special named award. Paltrow made a tearful speech, thanking everyone from Weinstein to her angelic agent to every beloved member of her family. That was as nothing to the ecstasy of the Italian actor Roberto Benigni, who, when announced as the winner for his performance in *Life is Beautiful*, climbed and leaped his way onto the stage and exploded extravagantly: 'My body is in tumult! It is a colossal moment of joy! I would like to be Jupiter and make love to everybody!' When Stoppard, looking grand and pleased, got to the stage, after waiting with polite composure while Marc Norman spoke, he said: 'I'm behaving like Roberto Benigni *underneath*.' After a huge laugh, he told them not to clap, 'or they'll play the music'. Very rapidly, he made his points, thanking the Academy and Marc Norman, the producers Donna Gigliotti and David Parfitt 'who played good cop and very sweet cop to Commissioner Harvey', and John Madden – 'who's available'. 'And since Gwyneth mentioned her agent I thought I'd mention mine. He's older and nicer. Ken Ewing is my guest tonight. I sent him my first play thirty-eight years ago and we're still here. Thank you. And for the hell of it: Hi, Ollie, Barny, Will and Ed.'

Will joined them afterwards; he had some work on in LA with a music colleague and wouldn't have missed it for the world. He and his friend met up with his father and Ewing at the Beverly Hills Hotel, hired by Miramax as their headquarters for the evening, and Will said: 'We're going to show you how you do this properly. Once you've won an Oscar, you don't need a ticket, you just go where you want to go.' Their 'Avalon stretch' was waiting to take them from party to party. Stoppard kept saying: 'We're not going to get in!' And they teased him: 'What do you *mean*?' Ewing had the Oscar clutched between his legs in the back of the car. Will loved it all. He noticed afterwards, as others did, that the Oscar was never paraded or on show in the flat. He admired this modesty and lack of showiness in his father. Back in England, a veteran Fleet Street journalist, John Smith, watching the Oscars on the telly, remembered sharing a typewriter with the young Stoppard at the *Bristol Evening World* in 1958. That boy had gone far.

The combination of *The Invention of Love*, *Shakespeare in Love* and its Oscar, the break-up with Kendal and the knighthood prompted lots of coverage. In one interview of 1999, he spoke again about his writing methods. 'If you can steel yourself just to blunder off into the dark, and keep alert to the way it might go, then God will come to your aid.' He had learned 'not to try to figure out everything before you start'. The hardest part of writing plays, for him, was 'inventing the story . . . I always begin with something very abstract.' But feature writers were increasingly insisting on the personal rather than the abstract. There were several pieces – yet again – on how the beating heart of Stoppard was at last being revealed. With some exasperation, he told one journalist that 'of course' he was a romantic, whatever the clippings had said about his heartless brilliance. A 1999 profile, "The Heart in the Closet", said that his 'dizzying mix of acrobatic philosophy and philosophical gymnastics' and resistance to autobiographical writing was shifting into 'a new, emotionally naked Tom Stoppard'.

This line on him was confirmed by a new production of *The Real Thing*, put on in the summer of 1999 at the Donmar Warehouse Theatre, and directed by David Leveaux. Leveaux, a one-time English student at Manchester University who started directing very young, had worked with Beckett at the Riverside Studios and in East Berlin, with Pinter at the Almeida, and on plays by O'Neill. Funny, observant and clever, he had a fund of good stories about working with these giants. One of his favourites was a memory of sitting with Beckett in a pub in East Berlin. They were approached by a wild-eyed fan, who said to Beckett, 'I've been reading your work for forty years.' Beckett looked up from his Guinness after a pause, and said: 'You must be very tired.'

Sam Mendes, director of the Donmar Warehouse Theatre, made Leveaux associate director and asked him what he would like to do. Leveaux had seen *The Real Thing* in his twenties and didn't make anything of it; now he was in his forties and knew what it was about. Stoppard agreed to the revival, though warily (he always thought revivals came too soon), and approved the choice of director. He immediately warmed to Leveaux, whom he found congenial and easy to work with, and who understood his work very well. Leveaux persuaded Stoppard that this was a good time and place for *The Real Thing* to come back, seventeen years on. There would be a new generation of audience, and the Donmar, a boldly experimental venue, would give it a different treatment. The play still had a reputation as a dazzling exercise in verbal gymnastics; Leveaux wanted audiences to find how romantic, moving and 'real' it was. He wanted to make it new. He advised the actors not to think of Stoppard in the boulevardier, English-comedy tradition of Noël Coward, but more in the company of European writers, or writers using English as a second language: Conrad, Kundera, Nabokov. The Donmar was an uncluttered space, and the designer, Vicki Mortimer, created an elegantly fluid, low-key set of plain panels, much simpler and less high-tech than the Mike Nichols Broadway production. Stephen Dillane and Jennifer Ehle were quite different, too, from Felicity Kendal and Roger Rees, or Jeremy Irons and Glenn Close, more inward, poignant and vulnerable.

Leveaux quickly got used to having Stoppard in the rehearsal room. He found him a formidable presence, but never overbearing, and often playful. Sometimes he asked Leveaux, as if uncertainly: what do you think my role should be? And Leveaux would simply reply: 'But you're here!' He would jump in when he thought a line was overwritten or unclear. Leveaux felt that he was reinvestigating the play. He was rueful about its feeling like a period piece: it was 'such a genteel expression of sexual attraction' compared with a contemporary play like the young writer-director Patrick Marber's *Closer*. He'd always thought himself squeamish about sexual explicitness, and he thought it even more now.

Though he had the sound of the first productions in his head, he did not impose it on them: he knew this production would have a different rhythm. This one, he said wryly, was 'the deconstructivist version' of his play. But he could also be sharp. He minded very much about inaudibility – he always listened out for the word 'if', and noted when it was swallowed – and he had his intransigent moments. One actor complained of a speech: 'I don't know why he says this – it feels like a riff, rather than something he needs to say.' Stoppard replied: 'When I write plays, I write the name of the character in the margin, and I put what they say. Then I put the name in the margin and put what *they* say.' There was an electric silence in the rehearsal room. It was the equivalent, Leveaux knew, of Harold Pinter saying, mind your own bloody business. Don't over-interpret, don't invent motivation, Stoppard was saying. He didn't quarrel or bully, but he could be fierce.

The production was much liked, and transferred to the West End and to Broadway. Stoppard's first-night card to Leveaux read: 'Thank you for making me famous.' Praise came from friends and admirers, including a note from Tony Blair, one from Patrick Marber, who became a friend and colleague, and one, touchingly, from Glenn Close, saying how much the play and their friendship had always meant to her. All reviews agreed that Stoppard was a more emotional writer than he had been given credit for. It was, as ever, a simplification: there had always been deep emotion and expressions of his feelings in his plays. But the sense of a more self-revealing Stoppard was intensified, at this time, by an extraordinary piece of personal writing. It was called: 'On Turning Out to Be Jewish'.

Bobby's death, followed by Ken's, made it possible for him to reclaim his Czech story. Sarka's revelations to him about the family history, in 1993, had had a deep effect on him. And in part because of his friendship with Havel, his connections to the Czech Republic were alive in many different ways. Roger Scruton had invited him to be a trustee of the Jan Hus Education Foundation, which had begun in 1979 as a series of underground philosophy seminars and which continued to support education in the Czech Republic after the Velvet Revolution. In January 1994, a translation of *Arcadia* was put on at the Teatr Wybrzeże in Gdańsk. He donated his royalties from the translation to the Gdańsk Theatre Trust. That March, he was made an honorary member of Czech PEN, and went that autumn to the PEN conference in Pilsen, which was when he met Alexandr Rosa at the hotel in Prague. In February 1996, he was elected to the Honorary Board of the International Festival Theatre in Pilsen. In April 1997, another *Arcadia* was put on in Prague, where his plays were often produced. That summer, there were catastrophic floods in the Czech Republic, and he sent money to relief agencies. In 2004, he would stand on the stage of the Czech National Theatre in Prague and tell the audience that his connection to the country and its history was 'ineradicable'.

That history had been a tragic one for many members of his family, as for the country as a whole, and his knowledge of this had gathered pace since his mother's death. He had a letter from Emil Máčel in Zlín some months after Bobby died, and only then realised she had been in regular correspondence with him about their family history – and that Emil had sent his account of the Bata Czechs to her in the week she died, too late for her to read it. He was still in contact with Vera Somen, once Gellert, his childhood companion and the daughter of Nelly Gellert, Bobby's best friend in Zlín. Vera, who lived in Kenya, had occasionally visited Bobby and Ken over the years. After Nelly's death, in 1994, Vera and her brother Andrew Gellert had an affectionate exchange with him, recalling their mothers' close friendship, and they wrote to him again after Bobby's death. He told them about Máčel's researches, and that he was going back to Zlín. The Gellerts, in their turn, would revisit the childhood home with their families. Vera was amazed that, until his meeting with Sarka in 1993, Stoppard had had no idea about his mother's Jewishness, since it was something she had known all her life. She had often looked at the headlines about Stoppard which called him a 'Czech-born English playwright', and asked herself, 'Why don't they say Czech-born *Jewish* playwright?' She never knew that Bobby – or Marta, as Vera always called her – had hidden the story from her sons. So it never occurred to Vera to say anything to him about it.

Between 22 and 24 May 1998, he made a brief trip to Zlín from Vienna, where he had been doing some work, returning to his first home for the first time in nearly sixty years. He met Peter there, and they looked at their old house, and met Emil and his wife, elderly, helpful and benign. On return, he wrote to his classical friend David West that he had just spent two days revisiting his birthplace: '*lacrimae rerum*'.

The next year, he returned for a more thorough investigation of his past. This was partly for his own satisfaction, and partly for the essay he had undertaken to write. In London, in April 1999, he met with the widow of Dr Albert, who had been the head of the Bata hospital in Zlín in his father's time. The ninety-six-year-old Mrs Albertova vividly recalled the day, sixty years before, on 14 March 1939, when the Germans were coming and the Jewish doctors had to flee. One of her two grown-up daughters, Zaria, then six, now sixty-six, remembered Dr Sträussler particularly well.

The next month he went back to Prague, on 18 May 1999, and was met at the airport by Sarka. They were joined by her father, Jaroslav Rosa (son of Bobby's eldest sister Wilma), and by Alexandr Rosa and his mother, Vera (daughter-in-law of Bobby's sister Berta). Those sisters, he knew from Sarka, were among the members of his family who had perished. Now he was going to see the evidence. On 19 May the Rosas took him to the Pinkas Synagogue, next to the Old Jewish Cemetery. The synagogue had been closed under the Communist regime, and only reopened in 1995. In the 1990s, the names of the nearly eighty thousand Czech and Moravian victims of the Nazis had been hand-painted onto the walls, grouped by their home towns. There he saw the Beck family names (under Zlín) and the Sträussler family names (under Brno), with the dates of their deaths: his maternal grandparents, Rudolf Beck (died 28.7.1944) and Regina Becková (died 16.4.1944), and his aunt, Berta Kindová (died 26.1.1943). There also were his aunts Anny (died 9.1.1942) and Wilma, who died in 1943, and there were Eugen's parents, Julius and Hildegard Sträussler (died 9.1.1942). Sarka noted that while they were in the synagogue, Stoppard was very quiet, took notes and did not show his emotions.

She saw him off on the train to Zlín, via Otrokovice, four hours east of Prague, through that lush scenery of hills and fruit orchards, to the town of his birth, in its deep, wooded river valley, with the houses climbing up the picturesque hilly slopes. He met up with Peter, and they were guided round Zlín, as before, by Emil, who had been sending them family trees and historical details about the Sträusslers and the other Bata doctors and their fates. To Peter, also, these were new facts; he wrote to Emil Máčel before the visit: 'If I understand your note, our mother's parents both died in Terezin, which is new, and shocking, news to me.'

At the Máčels' 'communist-era' size flat, there was a comically awkward moment: the Máčels' parrot bit Stoppard, drawing blood, and Eva Máčel rushed to her medicine cabinet, much embarrassed. Once that was sorted out, they went again to the street with the almost identical neighbouring little red-brick houses, with their paved paths up to the front doors, where the Sträusslers and the Gellerts had lived, at what had been 2619 and 2617 Zálešnà III, since renumbered 18 and 22. The occupants of what had been the Sträussler house, at number 2619, were somewhat wary of them. But the Gellerts' house, 2617, was still lived in, amazingly, by the wife of a Bata doctor who had moved into the house in 1939, after the Gellerts left, and when the Gellerts visited in 2003 she excitedly welcomed them in.

They saw the Hotel Moskva, once the Bata Community House, still with its cinema, and they went to the hospital and the obstetrics unit where they had been born, where they met doctors and nurses. They were introduced to Zlín's Medical Officer for Health, a formidable lady, Olga Groschlova, whose son Filip Groschl acted as interpreter.

Among the letters he wrote on his return was one to Gore Vidal, congratulating him on *The Smithsonian Institute*, which Vidal had sent him. 'I have been visiting Zlín,' he told him, 'the place of my birth which I left in April 1939 aged 1½ and staring at the little brick Bata house where the Sträusslers lived until my father fled with his family to keep an appointment in Singapore . . . it was very moving and rather upsetting.'

He would make many more visits to the Czech Republic. In 2004, coinciding with a film festival, he took Fiona and Richard to Zlín, again with Peter, and in 2007 he went with Peter to Brno, the home of their father and paternal grandparents, where he was awarded an honorary degree. He stayed in touch, as was his way, with Emil and Eva Máčel, until Emil's death in 2015. But this visit in 1999 was the one which at last unlocked the whole story for him. He wrote it up in a long piece, for which he provided photographs of his mother and his family. It was published in the first issue of *Talk*, which gave it the title 'On Turning Out to Be Jewish'. Tina Brown, the editor, had asked him first for a piece on the state of British theatre; but, having nothing to say about that, he gave her this instead.

Talk's first front cover, in September 1999, showed Gwyneth Paltrow crouched on all fours in leather gear ('Gwyneth Goes Bad'). Its contents included a big profile of Hillary Clinton, which, a year after the Monica Lewinsky affair and a few months after his impeachment, sensationally attributed her husband's philandering to his abuse as a child. There were revealing pieces on the presidential candidate George W. Bush and on the grieving Mohamed Al Fayed's theories about his son's and Diana's deaths, two years before. There were childhood images of JFK and a demolition job by Martin Amis of Thomas Harris's *Hannibal*. Stoppard's photograph was taken by David Bailey. The whole affair was as fashionable as could be. The magazine was launched on Liberty Island, where – as the papers would say – a 'star-studded event' was attended by the likes of Madonna, Demi Moore, George Plimpton, Harvey Weinstein and Salman Rushdie. Eight hundred guests arrived by barge for a picnic dinner under the Statue of Liberty lit by thousands of Japanese lanterns and a lavish fireworks display.

Right in the centre of this glitzy product was Stoppard's thoughtful and moving piece about his family's history. That combination of high glamour and reflective inwardness was a feature of his life.

He began the piece, at a pitch of strong emotion, with a family photograph. 'Here, now – here and now in this room in the only country that is my country and among books in the only language I can remember speaking – the English writer who is myself considers the Czech family Beck in 1908.' It shows Rudolf and Regina Beck, his four aunts, and his uncle Ota as a little boy in a sailor suit. Another picture of the family includes his mother, a dark little girl in a pinafore, looking sweet and bold. 'They stare back across 90 years of war and peace and war and peace.' It is a photograph which has many parallels, 'the family group who never made it together through the Holocaust'. Then there were photos of Marta (here spelt Martha) and Eugen, and of Peter and Tom as small boys in Singapore. He had asked his mother, he says, when she was seventy, in 1981, to write him the story of her life. Now he realises how much that account kept back. When they were young he used to ask her if they were Jewish; and she would respond dismissively, with an irritated sound: 'tsk'. He didn't know that for the last eighteen months of her life she had been corresponding with Emil Máčel about the story of the Bata Jews. He noted that Jewishness had not played an important part in her life until 'Hitler made her Jewish in 1939'. He told the story of their journeys to Singapore and India, her remarriage, and the character and opinions of his stepfather. He described her 'engaging foreignness', her anxieties and care for them, her death and her last words.

Then he described how he had learned, first from Alexandr Rosa, then from Sarka, in London and Prague, of the fate of his Jewish father's and mother's parents and sisters. He described going to the Pinkas Synagogue and finding the names of the Becks and the Sträusslers. But he set these discoveries against the admission that he had never had a 'special feeling' for his birth country, even when Russia invaded Czechoslovakia in 1968. 'I knew I was – used to be – Czech, but I didn't feel Czech . . . I felt about as English as you could get.' And, though he had known his father was a Jew, Jewishness had not meant much to him. When he got involved in the cause of Soviet Jews and first went back to Czechoslovakia, in 1977, he would regularly say to interviewers that he was not Jewish, or not *really* Jewish. Looking back, he thought of this as a 'willful purblindness', arising from his desire not to upset his mother by questioning her – even after his meeting with Sarka. And his new discoveries did not mean that he suddenly felt a strong sense of Jewish identity. 'I feel no more Jewish than I felt Czech when, 22 years ago, I went to Prague for a week to do my English bit for Charter 77.' He was as uneasy as he always had been with Jewish orthodoxy – and with the situation of the Palestinians.

The deepest emotions are about his parents and their families. Turning from his mother's to his father's story, he told what he knew about him and his work for Bata. He described his meeting with Mrs Albertova, and her daughter Zaria's memory of Dr Sträussler having stitched a cut on her hand. The essay pauses on this moment.

Zaria holds out her hand, which still shows the mark. I touch it. In that moment I am surprised by grief, a small catching-up of all the grief I owe. I have nothing that came from my father, nothing he owned or touched, but here is his trace, a small scar.

Then he returns to his mother's memories of their life in Singapore and their journey to India, and to his own memory of being told that his father had died. He jumps back from that to his mother's death, and tells the story of Ken Stoppard asking him, immediately after she died, to stop using his surname. It seemed ironic to him now. Ken Stoppard had been angry with him for not coming up to scratch, in his view, as an 'honorary Englishman'. But now that he had returned to his birthplace and learned his whole story, he realised that the claims of the past were 'all too late'. These remains of his past 'have the power to move, but not to reclaim. Englishness had won and Czechoslovakia had lost.' In the same breath as describing these dramatic revelations, he also held them at bay. But they would return.

This essay became one of the best known and most often cited of his writings. Reactions were strong and various. Madeleine Albright, then Secretary of State under Clinton, who had had similar late revelations about her Jewish Czech family, claimed kinship. Some of his Czech connections, with their own histories of silencings, thought perhaps he had said too much. Many of his friends – including Vera Somen – were astonished to find out what he had not known. Some, especially his American Jewish friends – Steven Spielberg, Manny Azenberg, Mike Nichols – thought it provided a key to his character. Spielberg was surprised, at the time, that he did not go on to write a play about his discovery. His brother Peter was not convinced that all this mattered so much. And certainly he did not suddenly become interested in or committed to Judaism or Jewish political issues.

All the same, this moment marked a change in his relationship to his past and his sense of himself, which, long-term, would profoundly affect his writing. And he had done something he had hardly done before, except in 'Going Back', his 1991 piece about his return to India. He had written revealingly and publicly about his private feelings, his family history and his mother's secrets. It foreshadowed a move, in plays to come, towards a more intense concentration on history and its outcomes, both public and private. 'On Turning Out to Be Jewish' coincided with the start of his next and biggest work, a historical trilogy of revolution, exile, loss, hope and change.

PART FIVE

PART TWO

28

Sir Tom, OM

> He's a free man because he gives away freely . . . Every giving-up has
> to be self-willed, freely chosen, unenforceable . . . What is the largest
> number of individuals who can pull this trick off? . . . I would say the
> largest number is smaller than three. Two is possible, if there is love, but
> two is not a guarantee.

Stoppard's millennium was marked with rehearsals at Philadelphia and
San Francisco for *The Invention of Love*, which a few months later opened
in New York, in Jack O'Brien's production, overlapping with the run of
David Leveaux's *The Real Thing*. *Rosencrantz* was chosen as one of the
hundred best English plays of the century by the National Theatre, and
there was a reunion of members of the first cast on the stage, on 23 May
1999, at which Stoppard read some of the Player's speeches. He was finishing off the last bits of the screenplay of *Enigma*, which finally came
out in 2001, and for which large payments arrived ($100,000 on the first
day of shooting, $100,000 on determination of credit, and then a further
$200,000), as they had for *Shakespeare in Love*. He helped with Disney's
102 Dalmatians. He was writing uncredited lines for Tim Burton and Scott
Rudin's gothic horror film *Sleepy Hollow*, loosely based on Washington
Irving's story, which came out in the UK, starring Johnny Depp, in 2000.
He did an adaptation for Roland Joffé of *Vatel*, a French story about a chef
(Gérard Depardieu) at the court of Louis XIV, a riot of highly costumed
decadence which got a lukewarm reception at Cannes in May 2000. ('The
to-ing and fro-ing over *Vatel* with Joffé at one point got so exasperating that
he wrote on a memo about it to the long-suffering Jacky, 'Don't resign.')
Early in 2002 he responded to an invitation from John Madden to work
with him again, on a film adaptation of Deborah Moggach's novel *Tulip
Fever*. Other film approaches were quickly dismissed. Sydney Pollack sent
him a script which Stoppard disliked, and he said so firmly, as in: 'What
am I being told here? I don't know' . . . 'A confused aim hoping to pass

for psychological complexity.' He turned down Francis Ford Coppola's suggestion of a science-fiction book adaptation: 'I'm afraid I have a blind spot for S.F.' Harvey Weinstein, wanting approval for a screenplay from a popular novel about running, was given a no: 'So, Harvey, don't ask me again! . . . I'm the wrong person for this, I can't tell you what you want to hear. I'm very *pedantic*, perhaps about things which simply don't worry movie audiences in general . . .' He turned down a suggestion from Matthew Warchus of a theatrical adaptation of Bulgakov's *The Master and Margarita*.

That was one of many 'no's to the requests that came in while he was writing *The Coast of Utopia*. No to a new BBC Radio 4 series on 'writers who have moved away from their country of birth'. No to *Nova* magazine asking him for an interview on 'What do you know now that you wish you'd known at twenty?' No to American PEN inviting him to a Town Hall event in New York: 'My life simply doesn't work that way – crossing the Atlantic for dinner – and simply cannot, even for such a good cause.' No to sitting on the jury of the Milan Film Festival. No to a Croatian interview: 'You are asking for *hours* of my time, and I don't have minutes.' No to an old acquaintance, Homer 'Murph' Swander, theatre professor at Santa Barbara, to give a lecture: 'At the moment I'm dropping things all around like an overloaded waiter.' No to the Harbourfront literary festival in Toronto, and to giving the prestigious Blashfield address at the American Academy of Arts and Letters. It was 'deplorable' to turn this one down, but 'really I think writers should write and I hope to be forgiven'.

But he also, often, replied positively to invitations and queries. Yes to a discussion on Beckett at the Barbican, chaired by his fellow Zlínian, John Tusa. Yes to choosing a favourite poem suitable for an anthology to raise money for refugees: his choice was Larkin's 'The Trees'. Yes to writing in support of Trevor Nunn and John Tydeman for honours. Yes to defending the Net Book Agreement at the High Court against a move to abolish it, alongside Auberon Waugh, in 1997. He argued in court that if independent bookshops, and publishers who were helped by the agreement, ceased to exist, then some authors might never be published, and it would be a great misfortune for readers who value independent bookshops. He responded, if somewhat impatiently, to a series of questions about how to write film scripts: Do prospective buyers prefer originality or familiarity? 'Familiar originality.' Any advice? 'Persist.' He told the National Theatre, for a questionnaire, which he thought were the ten most significant plays in the English language of the twentieth century: his first choice was *Waiting for Godot*, and after that came *The Birthday Party*, *Look Back in Anger*, *Heartbreak House*, *Oh! What a Lovely War*, *The Front Page*, *A Day in the Death of Joe Egg*, *The Zoo Story*, Odets's *Waiting for Lefty* and Priestley's *When We Are Married*.

When he wanted to keep his options open, he scribbled 'Yes-ish', for Jacky's benefit, on the invitations. But usually his responses were more definite. He said yes to Julian Barnes, now becoming a friend, to read for Barnes's Victims of Torture evening, and whose invitation read: 'A quick No is better than a slow Maybe; but a Yes would be wonderful.' He responded to a journalist from the *New York Times* who wanted to know the source of Joyce's line in *Travesties* (in response to being asked what he did in the war), 'I wrote *Ulysses*.' 'No source,' replied the playwright, 'I made it up.' He helped a young director and actor in LA who had made a film of *The (Fifteen-minute) Dogg's Troupe Hamlet*, and who wrote in thanks: 'Whenever I think about your generosity I'm overwhelmed. I wanted to let you know how much I appreciate the opportunity you gave me. It is extremely rare in this day and age that an artist of your reputation will help a younger artist (?) in the way that you have.'

There were more honorary degrees to accept, at Cambridge and at Yale in 2000. In April 2000, he was made an Honorary Member of the American Academy of Arts and Letters, but couldn't attend the ceremony in Cambridge, Massachusetts. In May 2000, to his great delight, he was awarded the Order of Merit, one of the highest honours in this country, limited to twenty-four very distinguished people at any time, chosen by the Queen. (The medal has to be returned after they die.) He was made an OM in the same year as Roger Penrose and Anthony Caro; other then members of this very exclusive club, who, once they had been honoured, lunched with the Queen every two years, included Norman Foster, the historian Michael Howard, Margaret Thatcher, Lucian Freud,

Joan Sutherland, the chemist and biophysicist Aaron Klug and the mathematician Michael Atiyah. The theatre had not, historically, been much represented, with the exception of John Gielgud. The lunch would occasion an urgent phone call to his hairdresser: 'I've got to have lunch with the Queen and there's only twelve of us, could you quickly come over and do my hair? Don't make me look *too* tidy!' Jacky made an excited entry in his appointment diary: 'June 14 2000: OM award, 11.50 am. Morning dress. 11.50 to 12.15: Audience with the Queen. Photographer, then entirely private. 12.15: all over – back to Chelsea! 13.00: lunch at Chelsea.' At the lunch party at Chelsea Harbour afterwards, he changed into a white linen suit and celebrated with his team – family, Faber people, Jacky and Dave, the agency. The flat was full of flowers.

Other engagements in 2000 and 2001 were a perfect fit in the life of a much-honoured, very well-connected public figure: a private view of Lord Snowdon's photographs at the National Portrait Gallery, a dinner for Princess Margaret's seventieth at the Ritz, a black-tie party in honour of David Cornwell at the Connaught, invitations from Paul Getty to watch cricket at Lord's and at Wormsley, his estate in the Chilterns, repeated friendly invitations from the Devonshires at Chatsworth, a return as a 'famous Old Boy' to Pocklington School to open an arts centre named after him, a talk at the Athenaeum Club on 'Writing Plays for Fun or Money'. He supported the Countryside Alliance, though he didn't have time to go to their meetings. He would oblige Prince Charles, in 2002, with an appearance at the prince's new project, an Education Summer School at Dartington for teachers, intended to tackle the underlying problems of education in the country and to help children understand literature and history.

He wrote a short piece in 2001 about having two unconventional portraits of him painted by Anthony Fry, in Cochin. These weren't the only images of him in existence. In the 1970s he (and Miriam) had been painted by Ottilie Tolansky and by Glynn Boyd Harte. John Bratby also did oil versions of him, in the 1970s, rapidly painted in his Sickert-like studio-kitchen, and told him he had 'a splendid face'. There was a charcoal portrait by Howard Morgan, and a bronze bust by Angela Conner for the grounds of Chatsworth. Most of the images of him in the National Portrait Gallery are photographs, including a double portrait of him and Pinter in the empty Haymarket theatre. He remembered anxiously trying to work out which the most modest position would be to take up: should he sit, or stand deferentially and let Pinter have the chair?

That close friendship continued, in spite of their differences. He was at odds with radical movements arguing for special treatment for writers. He had not supported a 1990s organisation called the Theatre Writers Union, which argued that there should be a 'Dead Writers Levy' whereby copyright fees would be reintroduced on long-dead writers (like, say, Shaw or Sheridan), so that theatre managers would have an incentive to put more new plays on by living writers, and the money could go to Equity to support actors. He thought it a recipe for 'dead theatres'. Small venues would struggle and close. And 'there is no special virtue in more new plays unless they are good plays', he wrote to Pinter, who supported the TWU. He chose his words carefully, in case of an eruption. But Pinter replied mildly that he completely saw his point.

He resisted an invitation from Adrian Mitchell and Michael Kustow to send in ideas for a 'grass-roots' movement manifesto called 'The Charter for the Arts'. Ideas already mooted proposed that 'serious artists' should not pay income tax and that Arts Council decisions should be made by artists not managers. Count me out, Stoppard replied. The document was 'catnip' for anyone who thought that artists were self-important whingers and wankers. The last thing he thought artists should go in for was 'special pleading for special people'. Why should artists stop paying income tax, but not doctors, teachers and builders? On the other hand, he put his name to a group of sponsors in the music, art and theatre worlds, fronted up by Peter Hall, who decided to set up a 'Shadow Arts Council' to act as a pressure group on behalf of resources for the arts, arts policy, and arts education in schools.

Given the conservative aspects of his public life, there were plenty of commentators eager to weigh in when he made a speech about art at a Royal Academy dinner on 30 April 2001. His 'theme' was that 'a fault line in the history of art had been crossed when it had become unnecessary for an artist to make anything, when the thought, the inspiration itself, had come to constitute the achievement'. The ancient idea of an artist was identified with 'the sense of skill, manufacture, technique, expertise . . . From Praxiteles to Pollock, the artist was somebody who made something.' This idea of the artist as maker, he said, 'has now been jettisoned'. 'At its present extreme, a work of art may be no more than a mental act, complete at the moment of inspiration – "Eureka! An empty room painted green!" . . . "Eureka! Framed tinfoil!"' But he added that the conceptual artist would argue that this was simply a realisation that the essential purpose of art – looking at things in a new way – could now be achieved differently. Now, 'an object can be a work of art just because the artist says it is'.

He was trying to be objective, and to keep value judgements out of it. But his speech was reported simply as an attack on modern conceptual art. Perhaps some of his listeners remembered a very similar debate between Tzara and Joyce in *Travesties*, in which Joyce unquestionably has the last word. The *Daily Telegraph* ran a headline on Stoppard's 'denunciation of modern art', with a cartoon of him daubing 'Rubbish!' on a work by Damien Hirst – whom he hadn't mentioned. Janet Street-Porter joined the attack by calling it 'an outburst provoked by pique at theatre's not being "incredibly popular" like modern art'. Stoppard wrote a rueful piece, published in the *Times Literary Supplement* and the *Telegraph*, about this little firestorm, acknowledging that he did have a bias, but wishing that his speech had provoked a debate about the nature of conceptual art, rather than an attack on him for being a conservative fogey. In 1989, in a speech at Duke University, he had made the same point more bluntly, echoing lines from *Artist Descending a Staircase*: 'Talent without imagination: wicker baskets. Imagination without talent: modern art.'

Try as people often did – from Kenneth Tynan to Royal Court playwrights to academic critics – to box him in as a conservative, establishment figure, there were always contradictions. In the theatre, for example, he admired the radical, challenging work of Sarah Kane, and paid attention to the production of *4.48 Psychosis* at the Royal Court in 2000, performed by actors he knew. He was a friend to younger playwrights such as Patrick Marber. A reminder of his own involvements in experimental theatre came in a wistful letter from Ed Berman, who had fallen on hard times. Watching him now from a distance, Berman imagined Stoppard as always having to do things he didn't want or need to do. But he still thought of him, with friendly admiration, as 'the most important talent in the English-speaking theatre – and probably the rest'.

Among the things he didn't need to do, but felt a duty towards, was his work for PEN, now chaired by Victoria Glendinning, who often asked him to read and to appear at their galas. He was reluctant to ask wealthy acquaintances like Paul Getty or Drue Heinz for money for an Amnesty Human Rights Centre in Europe or for a PEN Writers' House in Portland Place, because he had already approached them on behalf of the National Theatre (and would, again, for the London Library). But he made his own donations, and regularly gave his South African royalties, or first editions for auction, to Index on Censorship. In a few years' time he would become deeply involved with the Belarus Free Theatre movement.

His plays went on travelling all over the world. *Arcadia* went, in translations, to Russia, France, Latvia and Germany. *The Invention of Love* went to Gdańsk in Polish. *Albert's Bridge* turned up in France as *Albert et son pont*. *The Real Inspector Hound* and *After Magritte* were put on in Melbourne. *Rosencrantz* was done in Mexico (not to mention Tokyo, Pittsburgh, Bologna and Siena), in a production which had Rosencrantz, Guildenstern and Hamlet all played by women.

He did as many events as he could in support of his plays and the people working on them, helping with publicity – as for the New York *Invention of Love*, and a new *On the Razzle* in Chichester in 2001. One such event was a packed reading at the 92nd Street Y in New York, a big, welcoming venue for artists and writers, on 27 March 2001. He joked with the adoring audience. He had thought that a reading would be a soft option, but then realised he couldn't do voices – unlike Eliot's narrator, quoting Dickens in the manuscript of *The Waste Land*: 'he do the police in different voices'. ('I'll explain that at the reception,' he added.) So he might be in trouble. 'The period for questions will be either forty minutes, or five.' He told them he would give them some of his 'album of greatest hits, like a saloon singer'.

He read to them from *Cahoot's Macbeth*, the chillingly funny speech of the police inspector who breaks in on the private performance of *Macbeth* in Soviet-run Czechoslovakia. The problem with the play, he said, had been too much *Macbeth* at the start, before the inspector arrived. 'After about ten minutes, the carpet began to touch the floorboards.' He meant that a too-long attention span in the theatre is like two men carrying a long carpet: the middle starts to sag. He read from *Night and Day*, noting that he was still a newspaper junkie, and wanted to write another play about journalism, but that his feelings about the press had become more complicated. He read from one of his 'greatest hits', *Arcadia*, saying how touching the play's popularity in America was to him. Then, with a warning to them not to transcribe it, as it was something he'd written 'the night before', he read a short section from work in progress, a speech by the Russian philosopher Alexander Herzen from *The Coast of Utopia*. He'd had to correct a reporter who had him down as writing about 'nineteenth-century passions', not 'nineteenth-century Russians'. Delighted laughter and applause embraced him.

In his private life, one of the joyous events of the early 2000s was his youngest son's marriage. Ed had decided to become an actor after he finished his degree at Edinburgh, and went to learn his trade at LAMDA. Miriam was delighted about this, but his father was more circumspect. He told Ed that in over thirty years in the business he had watched many good actors come into the room for an audition and walk out without a job. For Ed, his father's fame and success and, as he quite simply called it, 'genius', were an inspiration to him, but also something to live up to. He thought his life as an actor would have been less 'angst-ridden', in its early stages, if his father had not had such a heroic status. Ed Stoppard was often called Tom, at work. At first this upset him; later on he just found it funny. And he soon began to have his own success, in film (in 2002, in Polanski's *The Pianist*), on TV (in 2003, as Monsieur Heger in a series on the Brontës) and in theatre, at Chichester and the Richmond Orange Tree, with admired performances as Konstantin in *The Seagull* and as a young gambler in an eighteenth-century comedy, *The Road to Ruin*. At twenty-seven, in February 2001, he married

Amie Stamp, the niece of Terence Stamp. The invitation to the prenuptial dinner and to the wedding was sent to Tom and Sinéad.

Just at that time, in January 2001, Stoppard's old Bristol friend and landlady Val Lorraine died. Characteristically, he had kept in touch with her for nearly fifty years. When he heard she was dying, he went to Bristol, meeting up with Anthony Smith. They went in to see her together. After they came out, Stoppard said he wanted to go back in to be with her for a few minutes on his own. At the gathering to celebrate her, after her death, he spoke movingly. The house, as warm and messy and bohemian as it always had been, was full of his traces – cards, gifts, mementoes. She had followed his success with loving attention. He would always remember her encouragement to him, when he most needed it.

Now that he was in his sixties, and some of the people he knew were dying, and his sons had started their own families, and he had two houses and a large income, he made a will, in 1999. He carefully allocated legacies that would suit them and answer their needs to all his nearest and dearest, including Miriam, Felicity – and Sinéad. Now, and for most of the 2000s, she was at the heart of his life. He was with her while he was writing *The Coast of Utopia*. He would write the play after that, *Rock 'n' Roll*, and his next adaptation of Chekhov, with her in mind. From the outside, his relationship with Cusack might have looked something like his partnership with Kendal, by then at an end. Both were famous actors from theatrical families who had started young in the theatre, and whose work he greatly admired. Both inspired him to write plays for them. Both had complicated personal lives and were devoted to their sons. Both relationships lasted for about ten years, without leading to permanently shared homes or marriage. Both love affairs grew out of friendships, and continued as friendships after they went their separate ways. But in actuality the two relationships, and the two women, were very different.

He and Kendal had had a working relationship for many years before they fell in love. The connection to Sinéad Cusack was not like that. Of course he knew of her, before they came to know each other. She was the daughter of a famous Irish theatrical family. Her father, Cyril Cusack, was a renowned actor, famed for his subtle, winning, witty performances in

Synge, Shaw, Boucicault and Chekhov, and equally famed for his rascally upstaging of other actors and his heavy drinking. Her mother, Maureen Kiely, had been an ingenue for the Gate Theatre's legendary director Micheál MacLiammóir, until her marriage to Cusack swallowed up her career. Her sisters, Niamh and Sorcha, and her half-sister Catherine, were actors, her brother Paul a TV director and her brother Pádraig a theatre producer. She went to a convent school, and joined the Abbey Theatre in 1965, at seventeen, after a false start reading English at University College Dublin. Her mentor at the theatre was Joan O'Hara, mother of the future novelist and playwright Sebastian Barry, with whom Sinéad would work closely, decades later. It was not public knowledge that while she was at the Abbey Theatre, she had a relationship with a much older, married actor, Vincent Dowling, and had a child by him, a son, who was placed for adoption when she was nineteen. It was 1967, the very end of the period in Ireland when children born out of wedlock or from adulterous relationships were given up through the agency of the Church, and when to have an illegitimate child was a matter of shame and disgrace.

Cusack moved to London in the 1970s, keeping her secret, and soon joined the RSC, where she played most of the leading Shakespearean heroines. A beautiful, passionate and lyrical actor, with a quality of quietness as well as power and intensity, she was hugely admired. In her private life, there was some brief, excited publicity around her short affair with the self-destructive football star George Best. Her mother died in 1977; her father remarried not long after. She married Jeremy Irons in 1978, and they had two sons, Sam, born that year, and Max, born in 1985. Irons leaped to fame soon after they got married, with *Brideshead Revisited*. They acted in films together, and they both supported the Labour Party. They were classic 'luvvies', she would say wryly, canvassing for the party at elections and donating funds. Their marriage was turbulent and dramatic, and Irons's escapades were often picked up by the tabloid press. When he played Henry in the New York production of *The Real Thing*, tabloid gossip linked him to his co-star Glenn Close.

Cusack got to know Stoppard through his work. Because of *The Real Thing*, they met in 1984. She had seen the play first in London with Kendal and Rees. When Jeremy Irons was cast as Henry, the Stoppards invited them both to dinner at Iver, and they had a convivial evening. Cusack had already gathered a strong sense of him from his play, and at this first meeting, as she put it, 'he came up to expectation'. She sat in rehearsals in New York, watching him work on the play with Mike Nichols and with the cast, with admiration and awe. *The Real Thing* opened a window, for her, on the nature of the person she would come to know intimately. She summed up the ingredients of that nature, as revealed in *The Real Thing*, as his playfulness, his passion, his amatory nature and his understanding of pain. She recognised, too, his tough intellectual rigour and his constant interrogation of others and of himself. There was a strong affinity between them from the start. They always had a great deal to talk about, and they liked each other very much. She found him, always, as she said, 'a delight to be with'. 'I loved Tom from the first day I met him, I think.'

But their paths were separate. He was with his wife and his boys, and then with Kendal. Cusack was very much married, with two sons. They existed in parallel universes, and it never occurred to her that it might ever be different. They met socially, with their partners: for instance, in 1988, the Stoppards were invited by the Ironses to a dinner to celebrate Jeremy's fortieth birthday. She was a close friend of one of Stoppard's favourite designers, Bob Crowley, and of his old friend John Boorman. And of course they knew many of the same people in the theatre world. She was much in demand: two of the peaks of her career, in the 1990s, were her performance as Masha, in Frank McGuinness's version of Chekhov's *Three Sisters*, at the Gate, for Cyril Cusack and three of his daughters (with stormy times backstage), and as Mai O'Hara in Sebastian Barry's *Our Lady of Sligo*, directed by Max Stafford-Clark. Her character was based on the mother of Joan O'Hara. Stoppard came to see it. It was extremely demanding to be, for two and a half hours, an old woman dying of cancer in hospital. She told Barry, who sat in rehearsals of his plays every day, as Stoppard did, that she didn't think she could do it. My play will give you grace, he replied. She was the kind of actor – tough and romantic, emotional and humorous, intensely responsive – for whom the remark was helpful.

In 1997, Jeremy Irons bought a castle on the coast of West Cork, in Ballydehob, near Macroom, and started to renovate it, a project which absorbed him from 1998 to about 2004. (They also had houses in Dublin and Oxfordshire.) Somewhere around this time, something changed in her relationship with Stoppard, or, as she put it, 'a window opened'. It had been a love affair a long time in the making. For years they had known each other well and taken pleasure in each other's company. She described him as bringing a shade of colour into her life, strongly felt always, but now changing, because of their circumstances. Her marriage was under great strain; his own relationship was ending. And, as she would put it: 'a different shade entered the colour'. If you imagined it as the colour red, the red now darkened and strengthened.

In November 1997, a card to Stoppard from Mike Nichols sent love to Sinéad. In May 1998, Cusack's name first appeared in Stoppard's appointment diaries, booked to travel to Marseilles on the same day but on a separate flight from him. That autumn, he bought the house in Lacoste, and there was some belated press coverage of his break-up with Kendal. From then on, there were many references in the appointment diaries to Cusack's birthdays, performances and flights to and from France. He began work on *The Coast of Utopia*. And she was always busy. Over the next few years, *Our Lady of Sligo* was done off Broadway, and she played in Sam Shepard's *A Lie of the Mind* at the Donmar. In 2002 she was playing Cleopatra at the RSC ('Send SC flowers, first night', noted his appointment diary) with what Michael Billington called 'quicksilver energy, boundless curiosity and emotional volatility'.

Their lives were full and not without problems. At the time they acknowledged their attraction for each other, her marriage was unhappy, but also unbreakable, and her sons, then at school, were all the world to her. This was all the more so because of her history. The scar of having given away her first child for adoption affected the rest of her life. It meant that she never quite got over the fear of having her children taken away from her. From the time they became lovers, Stoppard understood all this completely. He was, as she said, an 'empathetic' person, and a person of honour. They respected each other's responsibilities, and gave each other the kind of 'unenforceable' freedom of which Herzen speaks, in the play Stoppard was writing when they were first together.

Politically, they were very different. As in his plays, where she felt he examined issues even-handedly, without being dogmatic, so in his life. Their discussions took the form of his listening, rationally interrogating, and trying to understand another point of view. By the time they were together, he had moved away from his earlier attachment to Thatcherism. Unlike many people who get more right-wing as they get older, with him it was rather the reverse. Even so, Cusack's support for the radical left was very far from Stoppard's views. But possibly her opinions influenced his. She was struck by his open-mindedness.

He knew that her marriage and family life, even though in trouble at the time, was crucial to her well-being. He did not want to disturb that. He knew too that she was looking for her lost son, and had been doing so since 1990, when he would have reached his early twenties. There were no secrets, except from the outside world. Her boys had known from early on about her first child. She told her husband about her new relationship as soon as it began, and she also told her sons. Friends like Bob Crowley knew what was happening, but also knew that it was not for public consumption. John Madden, for instance, was aware that they were together at the time *Shakespeare in Love* won its Oscar, but that it was 'off the record'. Stoppard's women friends, like Teresa Wells and Antonia Fraser, always concerned for his happiness, liked Cusack very much, and also saw, over time, that she was not going to leave her marriage. Richard Eyre remembered going to a party at Stoppard's flat when Cusack was, as he put it, *maîtresse en titre*. Jeremy Irons was there, and Eyre thought, with some admiration and surprise, 'how modern!'

She never talked about her private life in public, and neither of them ever spoke about their relationship to the press. Lacoste was their refuge and they spent a great deal of their time there. They did not go out on the town together in London. There was much less press attention paid to this relationship than there had been to his life with Kendal. The tabloids concentrated on Jeremy Irons's adventures.

In France, Stoppard read and wrote, and she worked on her roles. In London, their time was divided up by work, family and social commitments. Whoever he was with, he always needed to have time and space to himself while writing, though he never managed to regularise his working day or keep writing time sacrosanct. In his sixties, as in his twenties, he was forever writing against the clock. And, as ever, he needed solitude in order to write, to keep the bubble unpricked, the train of thought undisturbed. All the women who shared his life understood this.

He would write for her twice during the 2000s. As he had for Kendal in *Hapgood*, he wrote a big double role for her in *Rock 'n' Roll*. As Kendal was in *The Seagull*, Cusack was the star of his *Cherry Orchard*, in 2009. But by the time of that production, their lives would have changed again.

29

Utopia

Don't look for solutions in this book. There are none.

'History is all improvisation.' So thought Alexander Herzen, the presiding spirit of *The Coast of Utopia* – the overall title of the three linked plays, *Voyage*, *Shipwreck* and *Salvage*, which Stoppard wrote between 1998 and 2002. This epic trilogy was itself a kind of historical improvisation on the lives of a remarkable group of nineteenth-century Russian writers and activists. All born in the 1810s, they lived, in Russia or in exile, through the oppressive regimes of Tsar Nicholas I and his son Alexander II. Some of their thinking and writing led, eventually, to the Russian Revolution. They were all committed to an idea of freedom, though this took different forms.

The Coast of Utopia spans thirty-five years, from 1833 to 1868. *Voyage*, the first play, covers eleven years, from 1833 to 1844. *Shipwreck*, the most compressed in time, runs from 1846 to 1852. *Salvage* spreads over fifteen years, from 1853 to 1868. The trilogy is essentially about six men, all closely linked, who are very young when the plays begin, and in their fifties – or dead – by the end. They are the philosopher and journalist Herzen (1812–70), his close friend the editor and poet Nicholas Ogarev (1813–77), the novelist Ivan Turgenev (1818–83), Mikhail Bakunin the revolutionary activist (1814–76), and two short-lived influential thinkers, Vissarion Belinsky, critic and editor (1811–48), and the philosopher Nicholas Stankevich (1813–40). Each play shifts the emphasis between them. Playing crucial parts in their lives are wives and lovers and family and children. Around these central figures are a host of journalists, fellow revolutionaries, international conspirators, cavalry officers, ambassadors, spies, mistresses, poets, printers, philosophers, historians, serfs, servants, beggars, and émigrés of all kinds. Not to mention Pushkin, Marx, Mazzini and an ominous six-foot-high Ginger Cat.

His own story lay deeply under the story of this group of 'Russian Thinkers': his childhood escape from Nazi Europe and Communism in

Czechoslovakia to the liberty of post-war England, his lifelong sense of his good fortune in comparison with his Czech and Russian writer-contemporaries, his visceral dislike of Marxism and Communism. At the heart of the play is a resistance to totalising solutions, as he said in an interview:

> Utopia is not an optical illusion, but a logical illusion. It's like trying to 'square a circle', as somebody says in the play. You cannot actually, even in your mind, construct an ideal society, in which everybody's take on what is equality, what is liberty, what is justice, what is mercy, is the same – where you can take an absolute position on any of these ideas, and hope for them to stick together like Rubik's cube. They just won't do it.

There is a strong link between Lenin in *Travesties* and Marx in *The Coast of Utopia*. His Eastern European involvement in the 1970s and '80s, and his plays of that time, connect to his interest in these nineteenth-century Russians. His passionate belief in the importance of a free press, the subject of *Night and Day*, is a big subject here, too. His opposition to totalitarianism is voiced through the character of Herzen, and would return again in his next play. He was never done with this subject.

Part of the argument of *Coast*, a very argumentative trilogy, is about what a writer can or should do in response to political demands. Turgenev is the spokesman for Stoppard's resistance to art as polemic. As Stoppard says: 'Perhaps it is the artist after all, rather than the three publicists of genius [Herzen, Bakunin, Belinsky], who is the true hero of *The Coast of Utopia*.' It is in Turgenev's character, as in Stoppard's, not to use his writing for providing solutions, or for manning the barricades.

The debates in *Coast* act out his belief that political positions are also matters of character – a point made twenty years before by Henry in *The Real Thing*: 'Public postures have the configuration of private derangement.' And there is plenty of private derangement in *Coast*. But there is also ambition, endurance, friendship, love, optimism and brio, under very harsh circumstances. As Herzen says, 'Wit and courage would be needed.'

As usual he did a huge amount of reading. He knew it was his 'killer neurosis', the fear that if he didn't read just one more book, he might miss a crucial piece of information which would be the key to the play. He knew he didn't really have to bury himself for months in yards of Hegel, or read most of Herzen in translation, or ('no fun at all') the whole of Belinsky. But he was educating himself about a group who fascinated him. He found in his reading portrayals of men who 'dedicated their lives to rebellion against every form of oppression, social and political, public and private, open and concealed'. He found, too, ruthless extremists, weak, posturing men of straw, disillusioned liberals, nihilists and hard men of the revolution. And he found heartbreaking stories of disintegrating marriages, reckless affairs, rocky attempts at open relationships, premature deaths and lifelong partings. These people were often frustrated, defeated, muddled or ridiculous. Some died young, and some went into exile, where they spent their lives trying at a distance to influence the future of the country they had had to leave. Most of them counted as failures. But, in the eye of history, they mattered.

He was deeply interested in the choices they had to make between home and exile, having always been 'a moth to the candle' for stories of émigrés moving through Europe in times of upheaval. The trilogy began as a play about the literary critic Vissarion Belinsky, who left Tsarist Russia for Paris but was determined to return home, even though he would be at risk, because where writers lived under punitive censorship they were also taken seriously. Belinsky's choice reminded him of Czechoslovakia during and after the time of Charter 77. When he went back to Prague after the end of the Communist regime, he had the sense that, for all the relief, there was also nostalgia for the time when writers mattered. No one was in favour of a police state where writers were put in prison. But because of those terrible conditions, the significance of writers became enormous. That resemblance between Russia in the mid-nineteenth century and Czechoslovakia in the 1970s and 1980s was what first sparked off *The Coast of Utopia*: 'I was interested by the idea that artists working in a totalitarian dictatorship or tsarist autocracy are secretly and slightly shamefully envied by artists who work in freedom. They have the gratification of intense interest: the authorities want to put them in jail, while there are younger readers for whom what they write is pure oxygen.'

Having started with Belinsky, he then saw that he needed another play to do justice to Herzen. Then he realised he needed a play about Bakunin. At the point when the first play was called *Belinsky*, he sent it to Kenneth Ewing, telling him it was probably going to turn into three plays. Ewing wrote back encouragingly: 'I'm having a great time with "Belinsky" . . . I look forward greatly to "Part 2". But see already that it must be a trilogy.' Soon after that Stoppard told Trevor Nunn, who was to direct: 'I'm writing three plays called *Bakunin*, *Belinsky* and *Herzen* – I think.'

One of his main sources was Isaiah Berlin's essays: his 1978 *Russian Thinkers*, his introductions to Herzen's memoirs and to Turgenev's *Fathers and Sons*, his famous essay on Tolstoy, 'The Hedgehog and the Fox', and his writings on liberty and Russian intellectual history. Stoppard described himself as 'infected by Isaiah Berlin'. Because of Berlin's writings on these people, 'the simplest way to put it is that I fell in love with them – at first, intellectually, but as my reading expanded, I felt an emotional engagement with their stories'.

He admired Berlin greatly and knew him slightly. Though of different generations (Berlin was born in Riga in 1909), they had a lot in common. When Stoppard read Berlin's obituaries he recognised his saying that all his life he felt 'over-esteemed'. Berlin, too, was a Jewish intellectual, a childhood émigré from Eastern Europe to England, a man of ideas and of the world, immensely loquacious, with a gigantic appetite for knowledge, a quicksilver brain, passionate cultural interests and insatiable curiosity. His twentieth-century experiences – of the Russian Revolution, of the First and Second World Wars, of Nazism, Communism, Stalinism and the Cold War – gave him a profound aversion to totalitarianism and a lifelong commitment to pluralism and liberty. Berlin made friendly overtures to the playwright, but Stoppard was too much in awe of him to respond: 'The idea of occupying his mind for an hour or two just struck me as being out of my reach.' They met socially a few times, and Stoppard also got to know Aline Berlin a little. Had Isaiah Berlin not died in 1997, just before Stoppard started work on *Coast*, there might have been an interesting exchange between them about Herzen. As it was, *Russian Thinkers* became his guide. It gave him vivid portraits of this 'Westernised intellectual élite' and of their historical context.

Russia was viewed in the mid-nineteenth century by democratic Western nations, Berlin wrote, as 'the arch-enemy of freedom and enlightenment, the reservoir of darkness, cruelty and oppression'. Tsar Nicholas I's autocratic regime, enforced by a police state of surveillance across the vast country, and buoyed up by nationalist fervour after the defeat of Napoleon; the wretched servitude of the peasant class, living in 'a feudal darkness', victims of Orthodox religion and serfdom; the moribund bureaucracy of petty officialdom: all this seemed to the young radicals of the 1840s stiflingly corrupt and unjust, a 'gigantic straitjacket of bureaucratic and military control'. (Though set later in the century, Conrad's *Under Western Eyes* (1911) gives a savage picture of this atmosphere of fear under an oppressive regime, and of the conspiratorial, futile lives of the revolutionaries in exile.)

The educated 'Westernised elite' felt profoundly alienated from this environment. As Berlin puts it, they 'were reduced either to an easy-going quasi-Voltairean cynicism, at once subscribing to liberal principles and whipping their serfs; or to noble, eloquent and futile despair'. These were the melancholy, ineffective, neurotic 'superfluous men' who appeared in Lermontov and Turgenev and, later, Chekhov's plays. But the ardent revolutionary philosophers refused to sink into gloom or passivity. They wanted to take action, even if they couldn't agree on what it should be. The Berlin scholar and Herzen biographer Aileen Kelly, also a useful source for Stoppard, said they were 'torn between their suspicion of absolutes and their longing to discover some monolithic truth that would once and for all resolve the problems of moral conduct'.

For Herzen and Ogarev, the hopeless and harshly punished 1825 uprising of the officer-class 'Decembrists' was their inspiration. As schoolboys they dedicated themselves to resistance, to the emancipation of the serfs and the overthrow of the Tsar. Unable to speak out, they channelled their radical ideas into literary essays. (Even that could get them arrested and exiled.) They and their companions became known as the 'intelligentsia', at first a specifically Russian term. It meant more than 'intellectuals'. Its members 'thought of themselves as united by something more than mere interest in ideas; they conceived themselves as being a dedicated order, almost a secular priesthood'.

But though united in their loathing of the status quo, they were divided on almost everything else. They argued over whether the Decembrists had been quixotic failures or inspirational models; whether Pushkin was really a great national literary hero; whether Hegel, Fichte or Schelling was the philosopher to live by; whether the future lay with a Slavophile belief in Russian traditions and peasantry, or a Western model of democracy and revolution.

Berlin brings them vividly to life. He reveres poor, awkward, consumptive Belinsky, a 'burning moralist' who went through 'violent changes of position' and whose states of mind amounted 'to a kind of moral frenzy'. Belinsky, to whom Turgenev and Herzen were devoted, was an extremely influential writer – though not much heard of outside Russia. His secretly circulated 1847 attack on Gogol as a reactionary had a huge impact, and after his death he 'became the very embodiment of the committed man of letters'. Berlin dramatically captures his strange, intense personality:

In the heat of a literary or philosophical discussion his eyes would shine, his pupils dilate, he would walk from corner to corner talking loudly, rapidly and with violent intensity, coughing and waving his arms. In society he was clumsy and uncomfortable and tended to be silent, but if he heard what he regarded as wicked or unctuous sentiments he intervened on principle, and Herzen testifies that on such occasions no opponent could stand before the force of his terrible moral fury.

Nicholas Stankevich, by contrast, a metaphysical philosopher and a kind of genius, was 'a gentle and idealistic personality' of 'exceptional sweetness'. His transcendent belief (shaped by German philosophy) in eternal peace and inner harmony under the appearances of the material, empirical world, to be attained through intellectual effort and strength of mind, was influential even on a sceptic like Turgenev. His friends 'idolised him in his lifetime, and after his death worshipped his memory'.

Berlin takes a different tone about Bakunin, whom he describes as the spoilt, high-spirited, reckless son of a wealthy landowner, 'intellectually irresponsible' in his coldly destructive drive for violent revolution at any cost, his path strewn with 'victims and casualties'. 'There are no coherent ideas to be extracted from his writings . . . only fire and imagination, violence and poetry, and an ungovernable desire for strong sensations . . . for the disintegration of all that is peaceful, secluded, tidy, orderly, small-scale . . . moderate.'

Berlin keeps returning to the war of ideas and personalities between Bakunin and Herzen. This will be one of the main stories of *Coast*. Herzen was fond of Bakunin, but profoundly suspicious of his ideas. He hated his Hegelian commitment to ultimate ends at any cost. In Bakunin, Herzen saw ('rightly', Berlin comments) 'a cynical indifference to the fate of individual human beings'. For Herzen – as for Berlin and Stoppard – the Hegelian or Marxist concept of a totalising solution to the world's problems was anathema. When Berlin writes about Hegel's 'vast unitary system', his dialectical 'thesis and antithesis' whereby, through the 'march of history', out of perpetual conflict ultimate solutions will be reached, he writes with a kind of fear and horror. When he writes about Herzen's opposition to that 'great despotic vision', his tone is heartfelt and admiring. Berlin is always reminding us that for Herzen 'personal liberty' comes first, 'liberty today, the liberty of living individuals' as 'an end in itself'. Often a scathing writer, Herzen was contemptuous of those who were prepared to sacrifice present happiness and liberty for the sake of 'some remote and intangible Utopia'. In his essay *From the Other Shore* (on the events of 1848), a major source for Stoppard, Herzen says:

> If progress is the goal, for whom are we working? Who is this
> Moloch who . . . as a consolation to the exhausted and doomed
> multitudes . . . can only give the mocking answer that after their
> deaths all will be beautiful on earth? . . . If humanity marched straight

towards some result, there would be no history, only logic . . . History
is all improvisation, all will, all extempore.

For Herzen, 'nature obeys no plan . . . history follows no libretto'. Berlin
celebrates his gaiety, his wit and the delight he took 'in independence,
variety, the free play of individual temperament'. This, Stoppard says,
is 'what bound Isaiah Berlin to him heart and soul'. It is at the heart of
Herzen's political philosophy, of Berlin's writings, and of Stoppard's play.

Herzen's path through life was hard. In 1847 he went with his family
into exile – to Paris, the Promised Land for all hopeful revolutionaries –
where he and his fellow radicals had great hopes of the 1848 Revolution.
But Herzen watched with dismay and profound disillusionment, in
Stoppard's phrase, 'the events which were to transform the brave new
Second Republic into the Empire of Napoleon III'. Travelling from France
to London to Nice to Geneva, embroiled with messy personal affairs and
family tragedies, Herzen did have a phase of success and influence, in the
early 1860s, with his magazine *The Bell*. This reformist journal-in-exile
was extremely important to Russian radicals at home and abroad. For a
time, in London, Herzen was at the centre of the expatriate Russian community, and their beacon of hope. But *The Bell*'s willingness to give Tsar
Alexander's reforms the benefit of the doubt, after the emancipation of
the serfs in 1861, brought him into conflict with the 'new men', anarchists,
nihilists, Marxists, writers like Chernyshevsky and Dobrolyubov, grimly
committed to violent revolution. For them, Herzen was one of the redundant liberals of the 1840s. As for Turgenev, the darling of the West – he
wasn't even worth speaking to.

Herzen and his friend Turgenev embodied for Isaiah Berlin the insoluble 'dilemma of the liberals':

They wished to destroy the regime . . . They believed in reason,
secularism, the rights of the individual, freedom of speech . . . above
all in the rule of justice . . . But they feared that the losses entailed
by terrorist or Jacobin methods might be irreparable, and greater
than any possible gains; they were horrified by the fanaticism and

barbarism of the extreme left . . . by its blind faith in what seemed to
them Utopian fantasies, whether anarchist or populist or Marxist.

Speaking from the heart, Berlin notes: 'The middle ground is a notoriously exposed, dangerous and ungrateful position.'

Turgenev brings out Berlin's warmest tone. He shared his friends Herzen's
and Belinsky's hatred for 'every form of enslavement, injustice and brutality' but, as Berlin puts it, 'he could not rest comfortably in any doctrine
or ideological system'. Turgenev exasperated his revolutionary friends by
never committing himself. Though his subject was Russian peasantry and
provincial life, he was thoroughly Westernised and lived mostly in Europe,
following the love of his life, the married opera singer Pauline Viardot. In
the West he was admired and loved, but in Russia he was criticised by the
progressives for not taking up a stance – particularly in his portrayal of the
nihilist Bazarov in *Fathers and Sons* (which he dedicated to the memory of
Belinsky). He shared the revolutionaries' hopes of freedom, but could not
bear 'their dogmatism, their arrogance, their destructiveness', their ignorance of all he valued in European culture, and their reduction of human
beings to 'agents of impersonal forces'. In his novels, he drew out 'the multi-
plicity of interpenetrating human perspectives'.

> For Turgenev [Berlin wrote] everything is compounded of
> characteristics in a perpetual process of transformation, infinitely
> complex, morally and politically ambivalent . . . Turgenev's liberalism
> and moderation, for which he was so much criticised, took the
> form . . . of remaining outside the situation in a state of watchful and
> ironical detachment . . . an observer in a state of cool, emotionally
> controlled doubt before a spectacle of life where nothing is quite what
> it seems.

Berlin's view of Turgenev, and Turgenev's own work, ironical, minutely
observant, subtle and humane, had a profound influence on *Coast*. The
story of the battle between the generations, and between the liberal and
the nihilist, in *Fathers and Sons*, the futile lives of the 'superfluous men'

in *A Month in the Country*, his fictional versions of the radicals he knew well, in novels like *Rudin*, *Smoke* and *On the Eve*, the painful, hopeless love affairs he wrote about and his vivid 1860s reminiscences, humorously describing his contemporaries, all coloured Stoppard's trilogy. In interviews, he admitted to some fellow feeling:

> He identifies with Turgenev, who said, 'I'm not pure spirit, but I'm not society's keeper either.' 'Alas, yes, that's my temperament,' Stoppard says. 'I felt close to his character when I was writing the play in ways which made me feel better – and worse – about myself. He had a terror of violence, and didn't consider himself to be a revolutionary, but in the movement of history, he knew which way he wanted the river to go.'

Another crucial source for him was the historian E. H. Carr's racy account of the lives of Herzen and his group, *The Romantic Exiles* (1933). Here he found the intimate story of their personal lives, closely based on Herzen's astonishingly candid memoirs. Carr (who also wrote a life of Bakunin) was light stuff compared with Hegel or Belinsky. Stoppard told the American cast of *Coast* they could easily read *The Romantic Exiles* in an evening – which they affectionately took as an example of his gigantic braininess.

Carr begins his story with the Herzen family leaving Moscow – as it turns out, for ever – in January 1847. The dramatic start sets the tone for a story of romantic idealism shipwrecked by political disillusion and personal tragedy. Carr's Herzen is both a romantic and a realist. Arrested and imprisoned as a young man, he put on a 'mask of irony' and rapidly became caustic and embittered, especially after the events in Paris in 1848, which filled him with 'agonised disgust'. In exile, he found the English cold and unfriendly, but was amazed at their freedoms and their openness to political refugees. One of many details Stoppard takes from Carr and Herzen is his astonishment at the role of the English police, there not to arrest you but to keep you safe and show you the way. Carr describes Herzen's resurgence as a leader of the refugees and editor of *The Bell*, the hopes aroused by the death of Tsar Nicholas, and then his dismissal by the younger revolutionaries as a has-been. He gives a darker version than Berlin of Herzen's late life, his growing distaste for Europe and homesickness for Russia, and his belief, in the end, that change could only come from the Russian people.

Like Stoppard, Carr believes that 'a man's political convictions reflect his intimate personal experience'. And what dominates *Romantic Exiles*, and gave Stoppard the plot of *Coast*, is the story of Herzen's personal life. Carr brings the women into the forefront of the story – and gives vivid accounts of Herzen's quarrels and rivalries with his friends. These 'romantics', however politically resolute, are also self-absorbed, volatile and emotional. Herzen was illegitimate, and so was his wife Natalie (who was also his cousin). They eloped; but their story curdles. In Germany, with their children, they become friends with a popular German poet, George Herwegh, whom Carr sums up as 'a dilettante of many parts', and his doting wife Emma. Natalie, inspired by Rousseau and the high-minded romances of George Sand, falls in love with Herwegh. The painful public drama which ensues leaves Herzen humiliated. Tragedy follows. Natalie and Herzen's deaf-mute son, Kolya, dies in a shipwreck. Natalie dies soon after, described by Carr as 'child and victim of the Romantic age'. The children are looked after by a well-organised German governess, Malwida von Meysenbug. The Herzen menage moves to London. Herzen's old friend Ogarev, now a physical wreck, an epileptic and an alcoholic, and his wife, another Natalie (Natasha) join the ménage. Herzen and Natasha have an affair. The three of them live together, while a daughter and then twins are born, who are officially identified as Ogarev's children. The twins die young; Natasha falls apart; the daughter will later kill herself. Herzen dies in Geneva, having 'outlived his political influence'.

It is a tragic story. But Carr's tone is often light and sardonic, and Stoppard draws from him the chaotic comedy of these Russian exiles. Ogarev wrote a one-scene play, which Carr reprints, caricaturing the irritability and hysteria of the Herzen ménage in England, a bit in the style of Goncharov's *Oblomov*, the classic Russian comedy of the 'superfluous man'. It is called 'Bedlam: Or a Day of Our Life (1857–1858)', and begins with Ogarev wondering whether to get out of bed or not. It continues with squabbles between the three of them, and Ogarev's musings on his everlasting predicament: 'Ah, these amorous–hostile relations between two beings whom I love more than anything on earth . . . I must get away or I shall be stifled.' The tone of this absurd little sketch may have played into *Coast*.

Stoppard was, after all, a playwright, not a historian, a biographer, an essayist or a philosopher – though he feeds off all those genres. All this material had to be turned into a drama that would make people laugh and weep, as well as think. He had some Russian plays in mind as models. Turgenev's *A Month in the Country* beautifully showed the gentry frittering away their lives on their country estate in the 1840s. Gorky's 1904 *Summerfolk* gave a harsher tone to a pre-revolutionary story of marital discord, family tensions and political arguments. An evocative production by Trevor Nunn at the National in 1997, with fine performances by Simon Russell Beale, Michael Bryant and Jennifer Ehle (later to be cast in the American production of *Coast*), greatly influenced him. Above all, Chekhov was his model. *Coast* partly came out of working on *The Seagull*, which he would follow a few years later with *The Cherry Orchard* and *Ivanov*. Chekhov influenced his desire to write a play in which people were not 'making smart remarks all the time'. He had found the story he needed of 'Russians of a certain period, in which the intelligentsia had a predicament of great interest'. And he wanted to recreate a Chekhovian mood of interrupted conversations, inconsequential talk, inconclusive scenes, characters caught in inertia, frustration and disappointment, crises of intense emotion, and a fast light pace for the heartbreaking comedy of people's ordinary lives. His son Ed remembered his saying that the wonderful thing about Chekhov was that 'nothing seemed to be happening . . . but it's absolutely riveting'. He told Ed that he wanted *Coast* to have 'a Chekhovian feel'. To signal his debt, he even has a brother and one of his (four) sisters cry out, in *Voyage*: 'Yes – we must get out – out! – to Moscow!' 'Moscow . . . !'

Voyage starts like a Chekhov play, in high summer, in 1833, in Premukhino, the country estate of the Bakunin family. The characters are serf-owning, Westernised bourgeoisie. It's a family scene, with servants; there's a hammock and a garden and a lake, and there's going to be cigar-smoking

and champagne-drinking, eating and fishing, laughter and tears, arguments and thwarted love scenes. Everyone is rushing in and out, excited,
despairing, hopeful, talking all at once, speechifying, misunderstanding
and interrupting each other. The trilogy's opening line is: 'Speaking of
which . . .' Premukhino is overseen by a benign, liberal–conservative
father, for whom serfdom, the honour of the army, patriotism, family
reputation and the rule of the Tsar are givens, but who has educated his
daughters, is decent to his servants and has Western sympathies. He is
what is best about the older generation – and what will be eradicated
in the cataclysms to come. There is a bevy of young daughters, '*jeunes
filles en fleur*' on the brink of adulthood, an English governess, a foolish, fussy mother (who treats her serfs with unthinking cruelty), and a
beloved wayward brother, home from the army, full of idealistic notions
and arguing violently with his exasperated father. This is Bakunin, here
dramatised as a ludicrously excitable, feckless young egotist, a comical
character, but one of unstoppable energy.

The scenes at Premukhino are counterpointed with the life of Bakunin's
contemporaries in Moscow. Like the Bakunin sisters, these students and
philosophers are all very young, setting out on their voyages of discovery.
They are struggling to make their way as journalists, translators, editors,
critics, poets, reviewers, essayists – whatever outlet they can get, under
conditions of rigid censorship. They argue passionately over philosophical ideas and ultimate ends. Like all intense young men who take themselves extremely seriously, they are often silly. Stoppard has fun with their
intense debates over the relative merits of Fichte and Schilling and Hegel,
their discussions on the nature of reality and the importance of literature,
and their arguments over reform. But we are meant to see that they are
also remarkable.

The play has to sort them out for us quickly and vividly. On they come,
these people from history, with all the traits he had read about in his
sources, now turned into Stoppard characters: Belinsky, awkward and
clumsy, inarticulate till provoked, then bursting out with manic eloquence;
Stankevich, star of the Moscow philosophical circle, gentle and idealistic,
beautiful and consumptive, and ludicrously bashful with women; Ogarev

the would-be poet, devoted to Herzen, desperate (as his author once was) at the thought of not having achieved anything at twenty-one; large, laconic, charming Turgenev, loitering on the fringes, a sportsman from a wealthy family who might one day be a writer; Herzen, at twenty-two already the dominant voice, the caustic realist, the person who takes the long view. Bakunin, quarrelsome, predatory, conspiratorial, domineering, is regarded by them all with affection and dread. Around them are the editors, the publishers, the censors, the secret police and – an unwelcome guest at a fancy-dress ball – the Ginger Cat, keeping watch over his future victims, emblem of 'the Moloch that eats his children', of fate and doom.

Voyage at first has an ebullient tone, shading into melancholy. Bakunin's sisters and friends start falling in love. The eldest sister, Lyubov, doomed to die young, refuses a good match and falls for Stankevich, who is too shy to respond. Varenka, the second sister, is suitably married off and has a child, but after Lyubov's death she goes off with Stankevich, until he too dies young. She becomes, offstage, a pioneer for a freer life for women. Tatiana, the closest to her brother, as ebullient and endearing as Thomasina Coverly, has a crush on Turgenev. The youngest sister, Alexandra, worships Pushkin, the romantic hero of the age, like Byron in *Arcadia*. His death in a duel is felt as a major tragedy.

By the end of *Voyage*, darkness is falling on the 'paradise' of Premukhino. Death was always in the picture. Lyubov and Stankevich have gone, Bakunin has been sent into exile, Herzen imprisoned, and a saddened Tatiana is left with her dying father, rather like Sonia and Uncle Vanya at the end of Chekhov's play. The sun sets. And then the enchanting Bakunin sisters disappear and are never heard of again in the next two plays. The curtain has been rung down on that kind of Russian story.

He had meant to start the second play in exile, but then realised he needed a scene set in Russia ('after much struggling to accommodate this retrospectively in France'). *Shipwreck* opens, in the summer of 1846, on another Russian country estate, Sokolovo, but with a very different atmosphere. There are no parents, no old guard, no innocent young girls. Our Russians are now turning thirty, bringing up families. 'Grown-upness has caught up with' them. Herzen is at Sokolovo with his wife Natalie, their children, Sasha (seven at the start of the play, eleven by the end), Tata, aged three, offstage in this play, and their deaf son Kolya, a two-year-old at the start, a cause of loving anxiety to them all. Ogarev is there, by now unhappily married and ill, and Turgenev, as detached as always. There are new characters, a historian, a translator and a nationalist Slavophile, all squabbling in temperamentally comical 'Russian' fashion over coffee and revolution. Herzen, who has most of the big speeches in *Shipwreck*, speaks out against utopian solutions ('Spare me your conceit that we're all acting out the destiny of an abstract noun!'), but has high hopes of a European revolution. Aksakov the Slavophile and Herzen the Westerner are irreconcilable: 'You that way, we this way,' says Aksakov (one of Stoppard's favourite lines of Shakespeare), as they all get ready to leave. A storm is brewing.

Into exile they go. We see Turgenev and Belinsky, now very ill, in a German spa, arguing over Belinsky's scathing letter to Gogol and Turgenev's evasiveness. The novelist defends himself crossly: 'I'm not pure spirit, but I'm not society's keeper either . . . People complain about me having no attitude in my stories. They're puzzled. Do I approve or disapprove? . . . My readers want to know where I stand. What has that got to do with my readers? How would that make me a better writer?' The two friends are next seen in Paris, where Belinsky is unimpressed by the sights. The Herzens, their children and his mother have set up house as Parisians, with fancy French servants ('nothing prepares you for their natural condescension') and with their new friends, the preciously sensitive Herweghs. In exile, Bakunin and his fellow conspirators continue to plot the coming revolution.

Belinsky chooses to return to Russia, because 'at home the public look to writers as their real leaders'. His choice is the seed from which the whole trilogy sprang. Herzen is much moved by Belinsky's decision. He, meanwhile, is locked in arguments with Bakunin over the revolution, which Bakunin, as always, thinks is imminent, and over the meaning of freedom. Bakunin and Turgenev encounter Karl Marx, in a satirical scene in which Marx speaks in slogans ('Victory will be decided between the proletariat and the bourgeoisie!') and Turgenev searches for the right translation of Marx's phrase 'the spectre of Communism'. He comes up with the word 'hobgoblin'.

The 1848 Revolution unfolds, with a roll of thunder and drums, red flags and the singing of the Marseillaise, the only time in the trilogy that world events edge their way onstage. Herzen watches in horror as the proletariat are betrayed and imperial rule is resumed: 'Broken promises, broken heads, the red flag torn down by the police, and the tricolour flying from the flagpole, saying "business as usual".' A silent beggar on the stage stands in for the fate of the ordinary people, sacrificed to history. Herzen tells him his fate according to Hegel and Marx: 'History itself is the main character of the drama, and also its author. We are all in the story, which proceeds by zigzags, or, as we say, dialectically, and it ends with universal bliss. Perhaps not for you. Perhaps not for your children . . . Till then, as luck would have it, you're the zig and they're the zag.' A disillusioned Herzen argues with Turgenev over his detachment, but their conversation is cruelly interrupted when they hear of the death of Belinsky.

In the second act, still in Paris, Natalie Herzen is falling sentimentally in love with the spoilt, vain and ridiculous George Herwegh. Their liaison causes anguish to Emma Herwegh (who confides in Turgenev, just now writing his play about futile love affairs – everything he sees is useful to him). Herzen is jealous and ashamed. And his argument with George Herwegh is not only over Natalie. He takes issue with Herwegh's passive belief that 'apathy' is a kind of freedom, 'the freedom that comes from accepting that things are what they are . . . that history . . . is more like the weather: you never know what it's going to do'. Herzen is arriving at his own very different interpretation of freedom, which links the private to the political life:

> I'm beginning to understand the trick of freedom. Freedom is what
> we give each other, not what we take from each other like a fought-
> over loaf. We balance what we give up against our need for the
> co-operation of other people . . . What is the largest number who
> can pull this trick off? I would say it's smaller than those utopian
> communities . . . I would say the largest number is smaller than three.
> Two is possible, if there is love, but two is not a guarantee.

The political and the personal continue to intertwine, and in both realms, freedoms are at risk. Ogarev's estranged wife refuses to divorce him so he can marry his new love, Natasha Tuchkin (once a bosom friend of Natalie Herzen). Bakunin has been thrown in prison. The exiles move to Nice, where Natalie Herzen has a daughter, Olga: we're not sure if she is Herwegh's child or Herzen's. The crisis comes messily to a head between the Herzens and the Herweghs. Herzen is told by the authorities that he is free to return to Russia, but chooses to stay in Europe. The dreadful news comes of seven-year-old Kolya's death at sea, with Herzen's mother and a tutor. Herzen has an imaginary meeting, in a kind of dream sequence which is at the heart of the trilogy, on a cross-Channel steamer, with Bakunin (in reality in prison in Russia). Natalie has died. He tells Bakunin what he thinks the meaning of Kolya's short life was. In a wistful coda, we jump back to the happier time in Sokolovo, before they all left Russia, with the storm passing them by, and Kolya still alive.

Shipwreck is lavishly (and riskily) argumentative. It holds in parallel the loss of faith in a European revolution and the loss of idealism in love. Herzen dominates throughout, but Turgenev, Belinsky and Bakunin are also crucial presences. The Herweghs provide a dark comic subplot. And three people we have come to mind about are lost to us: Belinsky, Natalie and the boy Kolya.

Salvage, the third play, is essentially about political refugees in England. It starts a year on, in 1853, and takes us from Herzen at forty to Herzen at fifty-six, two years before his death. The exiles are clustering together in the baffling, chilly English social landscape of the 1850s. Here, no one is friendly, but people are free to speak their minds. The class system is entrenched, poverty is abysmal and people are dying of starvation, but demonstrations are allowed on the streets and newspaper editors can report what they like without being arrested. As Ogarev says: 'It's not just liberty. You never saw so many eccentrics, human nature tolerated in all its variety.' In nineteenth-century England – and, for that matter, a hundred years on, during Stoppard's youth – the doors are open to political refugees from all over the world. As the Herzen family moves around the outskirts of London, the stage fills up with a drifting crowd of bad-tempered émigrés, sometimes in Herzen's dreams, sometimes in reality, all feuding and conspiring. It is a 'theatre of political exile'.

Everyone makes their way to Herzen's house: the Germans, the Poles, the Hungarians, the Italians, the French; printers and ambassadors, journalists and spies, socialists and bourgeois republicans, Communists and anarchists. There are walk-on parts for Mazzini and Kossuth, and implacable appearances by Karl Marx, preaching of bloody revolution to come. Herzen explains why England allows this 'flotsam' of Europe and Russia to make their home here, 'under Western eyes'. It is one of the key moments in the trilogy: 'They don't give asylum out of respect for the asylum-seekers but out of respect for themselves. They invented personal liberty, and they know it, and they did it without having any theories about it. They value liberty because it's liberty.'

But what is to be done in exile? While the great events of history roll on – the Crimean War, the death of Tsar Nicholas I, the emancipation of the serfs, the attempted assassination of Tsar Alexander II – the exiles continue to publish and plot. Bakunin returns, the same as ever, planning world conspiracies that go disastrously wrong, and still arguing with Herzen over different versions of Utopia. Turgenev, now a well-known novelist, maintains his role of ironical ambivalence. Herzen (who has got his money out of Russia) is roped in to fund a Polish free press. The Poles get a sympathetic treatment in the play, especially the old exiled nationalist Worcell, who, like Bakunin's father, embodies the dignity of a vanishing generation. His wry, sad exit line – 'It's all downhill' – sums up his view of the future.

Herzen's involvement with the Polish press leads to his editorship of *The Bell*, and *Salvage* is full of excitement when the magazine becomes a rallying point. Herzen is increasingly coming to believe that revolution will come, gradually, from the Russian people. But Marx and the hard new men of the 1860s, like Chernyshevsky, are beginning to dominate. They think of Herzen's generation, dismissively, as 'the romantics'. Bakunin's optimism is sidelined by Marx's ruthlessness. The word 'liberal', Turgenev says, 'has entered the scatological vocabulary, like "halfwit" or "hypocrite"'. Herzen's 'gaiety' is being overtaken by Chernyshevsky's 'grimness'. He and Herzen argue bitterly.

Herzen: There's no such thing as 'everyone everywhere'. For Russia –
now – the answer is the socialism of the commune.

Chernyshevsky: Not *communal* socialism, but *communistic* socialism,
with millions sharing the labour and the harvest—

Herzen: (*angrily*) No! No! – we haven't embarked on this long journey
only to arrive at the utopia of the antheap.

The Russians all go on holiday to the Isle of Wight – it's a comedy of
'little Russia' in the south of England – where, in a strange encounter,
shadowed by the terrifying atmosphere of the island's shipwreck point,
'Blackgang Chine', Turgenev encounters a grim, steely character, a doctor
who says his name is – Bazarov. He will be Turgenev's nihilist in *Fathers
and Sons*. They have a telling exchange:

Turgenev: You don't believe in progress, or morality, or art?

Doctor: Especially not in progress or morality or art. Only the
authority of facts. Everything else is sentimentality.

It seems that the 'romantics' are on the way out. Herzen and Bakunin
quarrel, *The Bell* is rejected by the younger generation, and Herzen,
ending his days in Switzerland, is told that he is a failed prophet, a dead
man.

There are no solutions or successes in Herzen's personal life, either.
In mourning for Natalie and Kolya, he is trying to bring up Sasha, Tata
and Olga with the help of a nanny, and then of the formidable Malwida
von Meysenbug, who, like a German Mary Poppins, breezes in, puts the
household to rights, but steals the children's affections. Her regime is sub-
verted by the chaotic arrival of Ogarev and Natasha, soon to be Herzen's
mistress. Ogarev, a sick man and an alcoholic, consoles himself with a
working-class Englishwoman. Their muddled emotions, the deaths of
Herzen's and Natasha's young twins, her rage at Herzen's idolisation of
his dead Natalie, and the gradual estrangement of the children, keep pace
with Herzen's political decline. The string of a child's kite, at the start of
Salvage, breaks and the kite floats away; at the end of the play, a cow's

is too late. Where is the song when it's been sung? The dance when it's been danced?

We are wrong, Stoppard's Herzen goes on to argue, to imagine an ultimate destination. 'There is no such place, that's why it's called utopia.' The only question that matters is, 'Was the child happy while he lived?' We should not be trying to arrange 'the happiness of those who come after us'. It is the key speech of the trilogy. And it draws closely on his sources. Herzen writes in *From the Other Shore*:

> Life pours the whole of herself into the present moment . . . But human beings are not satisfied with this. They want the future to be theirs as well . . . And what, pray, is the end of the song that the singer sings? . . . The sound that bursts from her throat, the melody that dies as soon as it has resounded? If you look beyond your pleasure in them for something else, for some other end, you will find that the singer has stopped singing, and then you will have only . . . regrets.

In another section, Herzen uses a different image for life's immediacy: 'We believe that the aim of a child is its coming of age, because he does come of age; but the aim of a child is rather to play and enjoy himself, to be himself. If one looks for the final aim, then the purpose of everything living is – death.'

In *Russian Thinkers*, Berlin runs those two separate passages together, in order to show that this is 'Herzen's central political and social thesis'. This is Berlin's version:

> Who will find fault with nature because flowers bloom in the morning and die at night, because she has not given the rose or the lily the hardness of flint? . . . What is the purpose of the song the singer sings? . . . If you look beyond your pleasure in it . . . for some other goal, the moment will come when the singer stops and then you will only have memories and vain regrets because, instead of listening, you were waiting for something else . . . We think the purpose of the child

is to grow up because it does grow up. But its purpose is to play, to enjoy itself, to be a child. If we merely look to the end of the process, the purpose of all life is death.

Clearly Stoppard has taken Berlin's version as his basis for Herzen's moving speech. But the difference is that Stoppard makes the speech refer directly to the death of Kolya (which it doesn't, in his sources). That change is at the heart of what he does with his materials. Private lives, families, children and love are what matter. Political theories must take notice of individuals and not sacrifice them. How we behave in our personal lives raises the question which is deep inside the play, and in his mind: whether we're *good* or not, and what happens to 'goodness' in the public realm. That is why the death of the deaf child, or the hopes of the young Bakunin sisters, or the disappointments of the two women who are in love with Herzen, or the lifelong friendships between men who may violently disagree, are at the forefront of the trilogy. It isn't a sentimentalising of history, it is a firm belief that personal behaviour counts more than abstract theories. It's also a satire on ideologues who think they can organise the future of the world, but whose private lives are in chaos.

David Hare, after seeing *Coast*, indignantly objected to Herzen's speech. He told Stoppard he thought it was a disgusting attitude to the death of a child, and that it had spoilt the play for him. Stoppard explained that the speech was there because that was what Herzen actually said. Hare crossly responded: 'Oh, it's a verbatim play, is it? Nobody told me!' He felt an idiot. He knew that characters don't necessarily voice the playwright's opinion – but the speech had been so powerful it had made him think, 'My God, Tom Stoppard's a callous bastard!' All the same, he had a point. Stoppard's own feelings and views did find their way into this historical drama.

Making the link between the personal and the political was one challenge he had set himself in writing the trilogy. That was not the only one. *Coast* covers thirty-five years across nine hours (eight in New York) of theatrical time. It has a cast of about thirty, with lots of opportunities for double and triple casting. It requires a stage area which must become, at the drop of a hat, Moscow or St Petersburg or a Russian country estate, Paris, Hampstead, Richmond, Geneva or Nice, a cross-Channel ferry, a cafe, a nursery, an urban revolution, a fancy-dress ball or a dream. There is an enormous amount of conversation. There are also love scenes, quarrels, mishaps, domestic ménages and big social gatherings. Children are everywhere.

There are very few onstage scenes of action, but historical events are glimpsed: corpses piled onto buses in Paris, the sound of a shot fired by the Tsar's would-be assassin, Bakunin leaving Russia in a storm, a sighting of a haughty, glowering Pushkin. Real history keeps dissolving into phantasmagoria. Herzen often seems to be dreaming: one stage direction describes him as 'attended by dreams'. (In the New York production his dreaming dominates the stage.) He summons up encounters with figures who are dead or absent. Turgenev's encounter with 'Bazarov' feels half real, half fictional. The Ginger Cat is a figure from our nightmares.

As if all that weren't enough, the trilogy also plays fast and loose with time. There are flashbacks and reprises, jumps across time gaps, scenes in parallel time zones. Natalie sums up the point of this, in *Shipwreck*. 'But don't you ever have the feeling that while real time goes galloping down the road in all directions, there are certain moments which keep having their turn again . . . ? Like posting stations we change horses at . . .' Little pieces of plot – a lost penknife miraculously re-found, a child's single glove kept in a pocket – are strung through time, and detonate their charge long after we first hear of them. Characters disappear and reappear years later. Motifs, phrases and themes echo across all three plays: 'Who is this Moloch?' 'What is wrong with this picture?' And, alluding to Tolstoy: 'What is to be done?' These details show that though *Coast* is on a huge scale, its methods are delicate and fine-tuned, subtly netting the past and the future together.

Turning his historical sources into dramatic dialogue was something he loved doing. He could be as anachronistic as he liked. As he said of the play: 'All those people are still, in a sense, continuing a conversation, or you're continuing it for them.' The characters have to be historically true, and intelligible, but they also talk as though they are living people. He was horrified when he saw that an American reviewer had advised audiences to do their homework ('Required Pre-Theater Reading') before they saw the play. That was just what he did not want them to feel. 'What kind of madman would write a play that requires the audience to read a dozen books in advance? Come as you are, you'll be fine.'

He wanted his audience to be entertained; and *Coast* is often funny. When Kenneth Ewing wrote to congratulate him on the first draft, he praised the 'Stoppardian wit' and the 'Russian absurdities' and said that there were 'a lot of laughs' already. And so there are. The English view of 'Russian absurdities' is indulged, and there is plenty of Slavic temperament on show: 'I demand that you finish what you were going to say!' 'It's all over between us. I'm going back to Moscow.' 'I'm going to be an artist, my whole life is at stake!' Character traits are pumped up for comedy: Bakunin is always borrowing money from his friends, Belinsky is forever falling over chairs and mortified because he doesn't have any foreign languages, Marx has never met a working-class person. ('What are they like?') Turgenev's ambivalence is often comical:

Turgenev: I'm agreeing with you.
Herzen: You agree with everyone a little.
Turgenev: Well, up to a point.

As in *On the Razzle* or *Rough Crossing* or *Dirty Linen*, there are lots of farcical misunderstandings and double entendres, like the two ladies admiring Herwegh's flannel waistcoat. ('Don't scream when he pulls it out.' 'Can I hold it?' 'Oh!') And there are plenty of dry one-liners. This was what audiences would expect of him, and, in the middle of all the political arguments, would be longing for. A newspaper editor asks a philosopher whether he's read the latest Russian play, *The Hand of the Almighty Saved the Fatherland*. No, he replies, 'I started to read it, but after a while I seemed to lose interest, and I was still on the title.' Herzen complains he is finding a funeral depressing. 'That's all right,' says his companion, 'you don't have to be a controversialist all the time.' In Herzen's dream of meetings between

political exiles, they are all politely bowing, but, in asides, ferociously insulting each other: 'So you're still keeping in with that great flatulent bag of fes-
tering tripe? . . . What a charlatan! . . . Unctuous jackass . . .' There are little
spoofs of biopic clichés, as when Bakunin bumps into Marx in Paris, holding a copy of the *Communist Manifesto*, and exclaims: 'Marx! Who'd have
thought it?!' When Turgenev encounters the grimly fact-driven Doctor
'Bazarov' in the Isle of Wight, they have an exchange about the usefulness
of art. For a *useful* book, says the Doctor, 'give me Mackenzie's *No More
Haemorrhoids*'. Turgenev agrees enthusiastically – it is indeed an excellent
book. But, he adds: 'Here's a tip. I found that reading Dr Mackenzie made
me very aware of [my haemorrhoids]. Whereas reading Pushkin, I quite
forgot them. Practical utility. I believe in it too.'

Still, *Coast* isn't generally described as a dazzling comedy, as *Travesties*
was. Many of his theatre friends – Richard Eyre, Carey Perloff, David Hare
– thought of it as deeply personal and emotional. Ed Stoppard could see
that the actors needed to find the key to it – as often in his father's plays
– through the emotions, not the 'cerebral' side. Every so often, Stoppard
drops in an echo of an earlier play, like a signature: a discussion of how
impossible it is to 'square the circle', an orchestra used as a metaphor for
the relation between individuals and organised groups. And there are
many links to his past work: the long-ago play he had thought of writing of
ageing White Russian exiles-in-waiting in London; young characters challenging conventions, as in *Arcadia* or *Travesties*; historical figures turned
into fictional characters, as in *Invention*; arguments between opposing
views, like George versus Archie, or Joyce versus Tzara, or Housman versus Wilde. And in its story of people caught up in processes which they
can't control, who can't find their way back home, and who spend their
time trying to understand how best to play their parts in history, there is a
touching echo of the two famously bewildered characters in the play that
had made his name, thirty-five years before.

Coast seems to be the most historical and least personal of all his plays.
But it is full of his concerns. There are moments in the trilogy where we
seem to hear his own voice, as when Herzen is explaining that the English
welcome refugees out of respect for themselves, or when Belinsky makes

a comically uncontrolled, passionate speech about the difference between art and propaganda:

> A poem can't be written by an act of will. When the rest of us are trying our hardest to be present, a real poet goes absent. We can watch him in the moment of creation, there he sits with the pen in his hand, not moving. When it moves, we've missed it. Where did he go in that moment? The meaning of art lies in the answer to that question.

These nineteenth-century Russians are talking about issues which mattered to Stoppard and which matter to us: how do ideologies relate to individual lives, how can you live in a repressive system, what is freedom, what is the role of the artist? In the end it is Turgenev, as he acknowledges, who speaks for him most closely. Here, he is accosted at Herzen's house by one of the émigrés (in fact a spy), who is asking him about *Fathers and Sons*.

> Perotkin: And what was your attitude really?
> Turgenev: My attitude?
> Perotkin: Yes, your purpose?
> Turgenev: My purpose? My purpose was to write a novel.
> Perotkin: So you don't take sides between the fathers and the children?
> Turgenev: On the contrary, I take every possible side.

The Coast of Utopia was a huge project for any theatre to take on – and it could only be done in a subsidised theatre. The National, and Trevor Nunn, were committed to it even before they knew how big it would be. Stoppard started to think about it while *Invention* was running, in 1997, and it was put on in the summer of 2002. The first preview of *Voyage* was on 27 June, of *Shipwreck* on 8 July and of *Salvage* on 19 July. In the middle of those first nights he had his sixty-fifth birthday.

In those five years of work – 'by far the most arduous thing I've done', he told journalists – there were some fraught moments. The National was hoping to stage *Coast* in 2001. But by the end of 2000 he had one play written, a second drafted and the third play not yet done. He had to tell them that it wasn't ready. In December 2000 he and Nunn had a long discussion. There were two possibilities. They could stop thinking of it as a trilogy, for the moment, and put on two of the plays in the summer of 2001, with the third to follow later. Nunn was constrained by his existing schedule – his production of *My Fair Lady* was opening in the spring, and he had *South Pacific* booked after that. The better choice, they decided, would be to put off *Coast* until the following year – even though, Nunn told him, 'the National really needs the excitement of two new plays by you in the 2001 season'. That meant Stoppard could spend 2001 writing Play 2 and Play 3 and revising the whole trilogy. 'I ended up', he said, 'writing the third play more or less to a newspaper deadline.' *Salvage* was still being completed when *Voyage* opened.

The delay of a year, though not ideal, might make some exciting casting possible. Names being floated were Simon Russell Beale for Herzen and Alex Jennings for Turgenev. Russell Beale very much wanted to do it, and was heartbroken that in the end it did not work out. (So much so that he never went to see *Coast*.) But it was hard to capture specific actors if their parts in the three plays hadn't yet been fully written. Stoppard agreed that they should delay, disappointed with himself for not being ready. But he wanted the three plays to come out as one story. For Nunn, the change in scheduling was difficult: it meant that he had to do *South Pacific* earlier, in the slot he had been reserving for *Coast*. It wasn't so long since he had put on *Oklahoma*, and as a result there was much raising of eyebrows about his lowering the tone of the National and his 'excessive dependence on the musical'.

As soon as the second play was ready, in the autumn of 2001, they 'workshopped' it in the National's rehearsal studio, with actors reading their parts. Trevor Nunn would vividly remember coming out of the workshop on 11 September and seeing people clustered around a radio as the terrible events of 9/11 unfolded. In his memory, he and Stoppard and the cast conferred, in a shocked and anguished conversation, about whether to break for the day, but decided it was important to go on working. Stoppard had no memory of such a conversation, but recalled a note being brought in for Nunn during the workshop – it was the news of the second plane – and he calmly set it to one side and carried on with the workshop. When the day's work was over they all went home and switched on the television.

Nunn, a master of crowd control and big-scale action, decided to give *Coast* a cinematic feel on the big Olivier stage. He and his designer, Bill Dudley, who was fascinated with finding ways of making theatre more filmic, used video projections to create a kaleidoscopic sense of atmosphere, and to avoid, as Nunn said, its all being 'about scenery, scenery, scenery'. Stoppard was keen. Dudley created a series of 3D computer-animated videos, projected onto seven screens, which merged fluidly from one setting to another – from a birch wood to a Moscow street, from a London skyline to a lakeside villa in Geneva – with music covering each scene change, while the characters walked along the revolve from one scene to another, or seemed to emerge from invisible doors. The videos had to be in place before rehearsals even started, so Nunn had the challenge of blocking the actors' movements to fit with the videos. It was technically immensely complex. At the same time the argument, the emotion, the drive and the clarity had to be kept up over many hours. Because the effect of the projections was so sensational, the actors had to give big performances to match. There were thirty actors playing over seventy parts – for which 169 costumes had to be designed. In a strong cast, there were especially arresting performances from Douglas Henshall as Bakunin, Raymond Coulthard as Stankevich and Herwegh, Will Keen as Belinsky, Guy Henry as Turgenev, and John Carlisle as the two old men, Bakunin's father and Worcell. A fine team of young actresses – Eve Best, Charlotte Emmerson, Lucy Whybrow, Anna Maxwell Martin doubled as the Bakunin sisters and the Herzen/Herwegh women. Interviewed together, they said, charmingly, of the author: 'We're all in love with him.' Stephen Dillane, Henry in the Leveaux revival of *The Real Thing*, was cast as Herzen, and gave an introverted, edgy performance. It was a very difficult part to sustain. He told Stoppard that he was terrified.

Stoppard was anxious that there wasn't enough rehearsal time – four weeks for each play – and that they had to be worrying about the next play before the current one was fully taken care of. But Nunn's mighty will drove it along. Stoppard worked alongside him and gave three months of his life to casting and rehearsals, constantly tweaking the script in the process. He loved the design, and the company, and was in awe of the skill with which Nunn controlled the logistics of it all.

Audiences flocked to this big event, which, five years after *Invention*, was seen as a major landmark. Reactions were very mixed, ranging from excited admiration, interest in the subject and pleasure in taking on the challenge, to feelings of being exhausted, bored, overloaded and over-informed. There were, as Ewing had foreseen, 'lots of laughs', and tears too: everyone was moved by the death of Kolya. Some were drawn into the story; some felt there was too much homework showing; some thought its personalising of grim political history sentimental.

The reviews wavered. 'There are no dramatists for whom I'd rather risk deep-vein thrombosis than Tom Stoppard, but his nine-hour flight through . . . Russian history isn't the easiest ride . . . You leave sated, exhausted, impressed.' 'Long stretches of *Coast* appear to have been written with perspiration rather than inspiration.' One review said that 'nothing of such intellectual ambition, such daring or epic scope has marked the National Theatre's 38-year-history as this brain-storming trilogy of plays . . . a breath-taking, back-straining nine hours'. But it complained of too many lengthy monologues and an unclear sense of where the plays were going. Michael Billington called it 'heroically ambitious and wildly uneven'. There were criticisms of Dillane for being 'passionless', or for being an Englishman playing a Russian without enough 'fleshly charisma'. John Lahr, visiting London for the *New Yorker*, complained that all the drama was in the wings, and what was on stage was 'just talk'. But others called it 'thrilling' and 'unmissable', 'the type of drama that could change your life'.

There was some right-wing appropriation of his arguments. Paul Goodman, a Tory MP writing for the *Telegraph*, in a piece called 'The Police Used to Carry Gazetteers Rather than Guns', said that Stoppard has 'a Utopia all of his own, Britain, or rather not Britain but England, the England of freedom in which . . . Herzen finds asylum'. The piece was illustrated with a cartoon by Steve Fricker, which has Stoppard pointing up at a statue of Britannia and 'British Freedom', a copy of *Arcadia* under his arm, with a group of puzzled Russians at the side. Stoppard was happy to be enlisted by Charles Moore, the editor of the *Telegraph*, for a conference on 'Liberty' ('to take away freedom is to take away humanness', he said in his speech), among the many interviews, features and lectures he agreed to do for the play.

Personal responses were mostly enthusiastic. A relation of Herzen wrote to say he and his family had enjoyed it but were worried about the inclusion of fictional scenes with Marx in the midst of the historical realities. Friends, fellow playwrights and fans wrote with admiration. Michael Frayn was amazed by Stoppard's courage and by the play's 'heroic scale and sweep . . . I still can't imagine how you ever undertook it.' Simon Gray told him, touchingly, at the end of the run, that it would leave a gap. 'So they're gone. I shall miss them. Very hard for you, I should think, that they're not there for ever, peopling the world.' Pinter liked the play but not the videos. David Leveaux found himself at an uncomfortable dinner at the Ivy with the Pinters and Stoppard, after watching a preview next to a jumpy Trevor Nunn. At dinner, Pinter said he didn't think the play needed so much 'set', and Stoppard replied that he always felt, in a subsidised house, that the audience should get their money's worth. Pinter turned to Leveaux and asked for his view. Panicking slightly, Leveaux replied: 'The problem here is that I'm sitting between the sun and the moon.' Which is which? Stoppard asked him. Leveaux said something about how Pinter could take an empty room and imply the whole world, and Stoppard could take an empty room and stuff the entire world into it. He meant – but didn't say – that Pinter was the moon and Stoppard was the sun.

Jack O'Brien and his friend the designer Bob Crowley went to one of the all-day performances, with a view to staging it at the Lincoln Center. They watched with sinking hearts. To their eyes it was a spectacular, jaw-dropping marathon which ran out of steam towards the end. Stoppard had sent a cab to bring them to a very late dinner at Chelsea Harbour after their nine-hour endurance test. In the cab, they said to each other, we vow that we are not going to do this. It will kill us! It will be a year out of our lives! They arrived in a state of dread, feeling they were being hijacked. Sinéad

Cusack, Bob Crowley's dear friend, was there at dinner: he thought she had been enlisted to seduce them into saying yes. And sure enough, they were charmed into agreeing. André Bishop, the Lincoln Center manager, who also saw it in London, was very nervous too. Perhaps, he suggested, the Lincoln Center could just do two of the plays? No, said Stoppard, that is not what I had in mind.

Bishop was daunted, but he put his faith in Jack O'Brien – and with good reason. O'Brien and Crowley made each of the three plays feel distinctive by bringing a second designer on board. Crowley had experience of working on big projects (the Plantagenets at the RSC, David Hare's trilogy) and of Russian drama: 'I'd done my Chekhov and Ostrovsky.' O'Brien created a much warmer, more vociferous atmosphere – as Crowley put it, 'romantic, beautiful people falling apart . . . a very jolly and happy experience'. Herzen starts the plays suspended, spinning in a chair over the scene, as if everything is his dream. But within the dream there are full-blooded realities. In O'Brien's instructions to the cast, he always emphasises the human elements: the house servants mustn't make eye contact with their owners, Marx must speak of bloody revolution with 'horrifying jocularity', the exiles should be 'waiting in a weary posture – thinking, "how the hell did I get here?", looking back towards "the other shore"'.

There were many problems. The grand old actor Richard Easton, playing the Bakunin father, was unwell before the first night and they had to open with the understudy. There were times when Stoppard didn't like what he saw on stage. O'Brien was aghast when Stoppard gave a particularly savage note to Ethan Hawke, playing Bakunin: 'Yesterday when you did that speech it was one of the most moving moments of my life – I've never heard it done better. It was gorgeous. This afternoon it was as if we opened the door to 10th Avenue and *anybody* walked on the stage and did it.'

He could be equally caustic in the notes he sent to O'Brien, meant to be more gently relayed to the cast. The notes were always to do with audibility, clarity, timing, 'landing' a line so that it got its effect, and not overacting:

I'm not laying down the architecture for the speech, but at the moment it has no architecture . . .

I'm not saying change it. I'm only saying I don't actually need all that help. The car will steer. I know how to make cars. It will steer with one finger on the wheel, the driver doesn't have to fling himself around to get the car round the corner.

Stoppard told his New York interviewers that it 'wasn't a polemic', 'it's about a family, and brothers and sisters and struggles between lovers, and parents and children'. He told the actors it was about love affairs, family and friendships, so that they didn't feel overwhelmed and could 'find their characters'. O'Brien and Crowley worked their magic. The company became very close and were happy doing this big ensemble work, joking with each other about whose character got killed off soonest.

Simon Gray, whose play *Butley* was in previews while Stoppard was in rehearsals for *Coast*, was impressed by his steadiness, when they met up in the only restaurant in New York where you could still smoke. Gray wrote: 'I find his calm in these situations almost preternatural, as if, a benevolent man himself, he has become used to benevolent outcomes in his journey through life.' Gray had once asked him if he thought he was a lucky man. Yes, I think I am, he had replied, to Gray's delight. Somehow one couldn't begrudge him his good fortune: 'It is actually one of Tom's achievements that one envies him nothing, except possibly his looks, his talents, his money and his luck. To be so enviable without being envied is pretty enviable, when you think about it.'

His luck held for this production. The critics enthused, in a spirit of self-congratulation for having survived it, describing it 'as this season's required heavy lifting for Stoppard fans'. The *New York Times* wrote, somewhat snidely: 'Despite its status as the season's ultimate snob ticket, a concert of clever historical name-dropping orchestrated to give middle-brow audiences the illusion of a brow lift, *The Coast of Utopia* is as hot-blooded and teary-eyed as your average afternoon soap opera.' Audiences loved it, especially the marathon three-in-one days. It was garlanded with seven Tony awards, for best play, director, designers, costume and lighting, and for the performances by Jennifer Ehle and Billy Crudup as Belinsky. He was fascinated by the different reactions in New York to particular lines. When

Herzen is talking about his name being German, he says: 'Being half Russian and half German, at heart I'm Polish, of course.' 'In New York', Stoppard said, 'that gets a big laugh. In London it's not anything like that . . . In New York it seems to be a joke about almost a third of the audience.'

Coast worked so well at the Lincoln Center partly because it was much tighter and leaner. Coming back to the plays four years on, Stoppard felt they were much too prolix. There hadn't been the time, or the distance from the writing, to shorten them for the National Theatre production. Now he cut fifteen minutes out of each play, shortened many of the big speeches and did a lot of rethinking. For instance, he felt he had 'let Bakunin down' by always giving him the worst of it in argument with Herzen (rather like Billy with Henry in *The Real Thing*). Watching Ethan Hawke's performance – even when he was steering the car too hard – made him fall in love with Bakunin. Bakunin's first appearance in *Salvage* was rewritten so as to give him the last word. 'You're not always right about everything,' he now tells Herzen.

Such radical changes meant that the 2002 Faber first editions of the play and the Grove editions of 2007 and 2008 were extremely different. It was nothing new for him to make big changes between his first and second editions, but this play was one of his most revised. In the introduction to the American second edition, he explained:

> In London, as far as I remember, I adjusted the text as we worked
> on it . . . This edition . . . closely follows the New York text. It
> differs . . . from the London text in many places: it is swifter and
> clearer . . . I wish I'd written it this way first time round, but I didn't
> know enough then.

The Faber 2008 one-volume edition of the trilogy describes itself as 'brought into conformity with the text as performed in New York in the Lincoln Centre production (2006)'. *Coast* was rarely performed after that, but when it was, this was the text that was used.

The place where *Coast* did get a new production was Russia. Stoppard's involvement with the Russian *Coast*, which opened in Moscow in 2007, involved him in some remarkable journeys and in a new political cause. Before that, and overlapping with the production of *Coast* in New York, his next play, *Rock 'n' Roll*, opened in London in 2006. A hundred years had passed between the last date mentioned in *The Coast of Utopia*, 1868, and the date of the opening scene of *Rock 'n' Roll*, 1968. One play connects to the other over that century. In *Rock 'n' Roll*, Stoppard's own life story, so deeply shaped in the twentieth century by what was happening in nineteenth-century Russia, came into the foreground at last.

30

Commitments and Engagements

I think it's also a play about the fact that we don't die. That something of
us continues, even if it's just somebody's memory of us.

On 29 December 2002, Jose Stoppard died suddenly of a heart attack. She
was sixty-two. A heavy smoker with a history of alcoholism, for many years
she had had serious health problems. She had spent time in mental institutions and had regular contact with a psychiatrist. She had become very
religious, and had got to know the nuns in a convent in Hemel Hempstead
near where she lived. Oliver and Barny, now bringing up their own children, had visited her regularly, and Stoppard had continued to support
her financially. On 19 April 2003, thirty-one years after their divorce, her
ashes were scattered in the convent grounds. There was no tombstone: she
was, as Barny put it sadly, 'lost to the winds'.

In his mid-sixties, hugely in demand, happy in his personal life and
full of undiminished energy, Stoppard was, also, strongly aware of time
passing. He never stopped hearing the 'unceasing ticktock of the universe',
as in this interview:

When you take away everything plays think they're about, what's
left is what all plays – all stories – are really about, and what they're
really about is time. Events, things happening – Ophelia drowns!
Camille coughs! Somebody has bought the Cherry Orchard! – are
different manifestations of what governs the narrative we make up,
just as it governs the narrative we live in: the unceasing ticktock of the
universe.

At the beginning of 2003, he wrote to his old friend and hero Václav
Havel, who resigned as president of the Czech Republic in February 2003.
Havel was in very poor health, with his authority and popularity much
diminished since the splitting of Czechoslovakia into Slovakia and the

Czech Republic in 1992, which had been a terrible political defeat for him. He had kept his international reputation as an inspiring figurehead for human rights and democracy, with initiatives like his annual global 'Forum 2000' – the last of which, featuring appearances by Stoppard and by the Plastic People rock band, would take place in October 2011, two months before Havel died. But at home, his era of revolutionary idealism (rather like the era of Herzen, which Stoppard had just been writing about) was giving way to the rule of 'pragmatists, political managers and media experts'.

Stoppard wrote to him on 29 January 2003. A production of Havel's version of *The Beggar's Opera* – banned in Czechoslovakia in 1975 – was being staged by Sam Walters at the Orange Tree Theatre in Richmond, which had often put on his plays, to mark the end of his presidency. Stoppard introduced the performance on 22 January in aid of PEN's Writers in Prison fund. So the practical purpose of his letter was to tell Havel how the production was going. But he used that excuse to say to him what he would normally be shy of saying. He wanted 'to congratulate you, first, on surviving, and on – well, surviving in soul and body. I won't embarrass you – unduly – by dwelling on this. But some things should be said, even among friends, and your three careers, as writer, Chartist and President, constitute a rare flower, a phenomenon, in the modern history of national cultures.' Twenty-six years before, Stoppard had thought about their two lives as playwrights in the West and in the East, and had imagined writing something based on that contrast: 'Perhaps a play about one man with alternative lives, mine & his. The Double Men.' Now, thinking about the end of Havel's career, the idea began to come back to him.

In 2001, he had done some work on a screenplay of Beckett's *Ohio Impromptu*. This was part of a project thought up by Michael Colgan, the director of the Gate Theatre in Dublin, to film all nineteen of Beckett's stage plays, with playwrights among those doing the adaptations and the direction of the films. *Ohio Impromptu* is a mysterious twelve-minute exchange between two characters, a Reader and Listener, who seem to be each other's doppelgänger, two in one, the Reader speaking in the third person of the Listener's thoughts and feelings. Phrases of loss and regret and thoughts of the past echo through: 'As when his heart was young'; 'Little is left to tell'; 'What he had done alone could not be undone'; 'So the sad tale a last time told they sat on as though turned to stone.' They seem to be in Paris, and Stoppard wanted to set the film, realistically, in a room looking onto the Ile de la Cité. But the Beckett estate was immovable about not changing the abstract 'otherworld' of the original text. He pulled out, and in the end Charles Sturridge directed it, with Jeremy Irons playing both characters. But the idea of the two-in-one characters (always interesting to him), thinking back over their past, stayed in his mind.

History came pressing in on him with the impact of 9/11 in 2001 and of the Iraq War in 2003. The transfer of the 2003 revival of *Jumpers* to the Piccadilly Theatre in the West End, on 20 November 2003, was accompanied by the noise, outside the theatre, of thousands of people protesting against George Bush's state visit. He did not join in the anti-war protests, writing in 2005 to David Wilson, an old acquaintance from the War Child charity, now collecting signatories for the Stop the War Coalition: 'I just don't want to be on a list with George Galloway [an exhibitionist left-wing politician expelled from the Labour Party in 2003].' But he brooded on what these historical events meant for writers, as in an interview with Adam Thirlwell, in 2005, where they talked about whether pure art forms (like sonnets) were affected by such major historical points of change. Thirlwell kept in Stoppard's unfinished sentences in the published interview, so he seems to be thinking aloud:

> 9/11 and the Iraq war are events which . . . You can't behave as though they changed nothing, you know? [. . .] I kept very quiet after 9/11. Everybody sort of bounced into print in a self-questioning way – and I can understand why, I felt much the same – but I thought, 'Don't say anything because the times are distorting: they're distorting your ability to think clearly at the moment.'

He felt 'completely drained' by his five years' work on the trilogy, but at once started worrying about not having another play in mind. As always he felt the pressure of time. He liked the thought of a play that didn't need a lot of research, didn't 'require me to read for two years before I can start!' He had a fantasy of writing while 'nobody's waiting for it'. But he knew that someone would throw him a deadline and there he would be, 'missing Wimbledon, missing going fishing, missing going to the theatre, missing dinner, because of this idiotic commitment I've let myself in for . . .' He knew it was 'a clinical condition'. But surely, people would say, he didn't need to worry about what came next or how long it took: look at his achievements! No: 'It doesn't seem that much to me, when you think how many years have gone by. I mean there are people who write a play every eighteen months, and I don't know why I'm not one of them, I'd like to be . . . My life is too crammed with commitments and engagements.'

Revivals or reissues came back to remind him of the past; he was pleased when old work took on new life. The poet and editor Craig Raine printed *Galileo*, Stoppard's never-produced screenplay of 1970, in the Spring/Summer 2003 issue of his magazine *Areté*. In June 2003, there was the much-praised National Theatre revival of *Jumpers* by David Leveaux. There had been two 1980s revivals, Nicholas Hytner's in Manchester with Tom Courtenay and the Aldwych Theatre revival with Felicity Kendal and Paul Eddington. This was the first major new production since then, over thirty years after its first staging with Michael Hordern and Diana Rigg.

Stoppard loved being in rehearsal, watching his play being brought back to life. For Simon Russell Beale, playing George, it was as if Stoppard was revisiting an 'old friend, or an old child'. For him, *Jumpers* was a mighty challenge (more so than playing Guildenstern in 1995). There were practical difficulties: the production got behind schedule, Vicki Mortimer's revolving set with its tatty art deco ballroom was complicated, there was a terrible tech rehearsal with doorknobs falling off, keeping the shaving foam on his face under the hot lights was a problem, and so on. The huge monologues were hard to learn, but that, as he said, was just a matter of logic: if this, then that; on this word I pick up a glass; now for the next step in the thought process.

He had the shade of Hordern to contend with. Hordern's widow, Patricia England, wrote to Stoppard: 'I am bound to feel Michael was the only George in the world but I thought it a splendid evening . . . it brought back so many memories of Michael anguishing over the lines . . . he said he finally understood it by the last night.' Many of the reviewers, too, had ineffaceable memories of Hordern. The first play Russell Beale ever saw, as a young man, was Peter Wood's production of Sheridan's *The Rivals*, in which Hordern ate a boiled egg on stage, at great length. He was enchanted. And he worried that Stoppard was finding him a bit dull and low-key in rehearsals by comparison with Hordern's George, especially next to his co-star Essie Davis, who dazzled from day one. Russell Beale needed an audience, and when he got one he addressed them directly on God and the meaning of good, as though he were doing a Shakespeare soliloquy. He wanted to convince them. No audience of *Jumpers*, he thought, would ever understand every word. But, as Stoppard once said devastatingly to an actor: 'It's not so much that I can't hear you, it's that you're not compelling me to listen.' That was what Russell Beale had to do as George. And he wanted to tap deep feeling. 'George's quest is an emotional quest, in my book. To the outside eye it might look as if he's talking in abstractions, but for George it's not. Or for me. That's why Stoppard's plays are emotional. We're looking for something.'

Reviewers were moved by his anguished, clumsy, pompously donnish George – and most agreed that the play now felt more emotional. Mark Lawson was struck by how much it now reminded him of *The Real Thing*: a play about a breaking marriage. The general view – as so often, since the 1980s – was that Stoppard was 'shown to have a heart all along'. In interviews for the revival, he said that Peter Wood had complained, when first directing the play: 'This is so awfully cold, can you put in some human background?' He had been wary in those days of exposing his feelings, and he still thought of himself as shy and 'timid'; but 'the older he got, the less he cared about self-concealment'.

Jumpers went on tour, transferred from the Lyttelton to the Piccadilly Theatre in November 2003, opened in New York in April 2004, where it was welcomed warmly, ran for four months and was nominated for a Tony award for best play revival. The production marked the beginning of a close friendship and working relationship with the producer Sonia Friedman. It was twenty years since an eighteen-year-old Friedman had dropped the follow-spot on Felicity Kendal as she swung on her trapeze in the 1985 *Jumpers*, and been sacked for it. Since then she had worked at the National again, from 1988 to 1993 (though she never met Stoppard there, who was a living legend to her), founded the Out of Joint company with Max Stafford-Clark, worked as a highly effective producer with the Ambassador Theatre Group, and, in 2002, launched her own production company. The 2003 revival of *Jumpers* directed by David Leveaux (with whom she'd been in a relationship) was her first success with Stoppard. After that she would finance and produce *Rock 'n' Roll*, the 2009 revival of *Arcadia* (Leveaux again), Lee Hall's stage version of *Shakespeare in Love* in 2014 and Patrick Marber's *Travesties* in 2016, through its transfers to the West End and to Broadway. When she first met Stoppard, she realised he'd been expecting to meet a wealthy lady producer, probably middle-aged, with furs and a chauffeur. Instead he met a feisty young woman with bovver boots and a cap, as keen as he was to go outside and have a smoke. (In her memory, this first meeting was at the back of the stalls during rehearsals of the 2003 *Jumpers*; in his, it was in the foyer of the Ivy restaurant.) They bonded immediately. Stoppard loved Friedman's courage, energy, appetite for life and complete commitment to everything she took on. She thought of him as one of the greatest playwrights of the time, always exploring, forward-looking and curious. But she also found him modest, encouraging and never condescending. Long before she became one of the theatre world's most powerful impresarios, he listened to her, gave her confidence and took pride in her successes. She thinks she would not have become the producer she is, had it not been for him. After he saw Jez Butterworth's *Jerusalem* at the Court in 2009, for instance, he texted her: 'You cannot call yourself a producer if you don't transfer this.' (In his memory, his message said: 'If you can't transfer a play like this, then we don't deserve to have a West End.') Professionally, she admired his dedication to his work, his integrity and his insistence that writers should be treated well financially (as they increasingly were not, on Broadway). She also felt that he should have complained more when productions of his plays disappointed him. He came to confide in her, calling her often, from all over the world, frequently texting her (with Stoppardian literary eloquence), and always wanting to know how she was getting on. It was not a love affair, and he was not a father figure to her. But they were very close friends, and over time their relationship became almost domestic: she was one of the Stoppard family.

One of the ways Stoppard tried to get round his 'commitments and engagements' was to spend as much time as he could in France, with Cusack. The other was to bring all his social obligations together in one big, regular event, so as not to feel guilty about the many people he didn't see enough. He and Miriam had had their summer marquee parties at Iver Grove. When he was in New York, he regularly hosted an English tea party at the Grolier Club. He mixed up old friends and colleagues (Jack O'Brien, Manny Azenberg, André Bishop, Mike Nichols and Diane Sawyer, Kathy Kennedy) with writers, journalists and artists (Stephen Sondheim, Peter Shaffer, Tony Kushner, Harold and Tina Evans, Martin Amis, Nora Ephron, Anna Wintour) and a few superstars, who might include Yoko Ono or Sting. But the London gathering was a much bigger affair. It became a legendary event, a kind of theatrical production in its own right: Tom Stoppard's Chelsea Physic Garden Party.

The Physic Garden, one of the oldest botanical gardens in England, dating back to the seventeenth century, is hidden away behind brick walls near the Embankment: three and a half acres of rare plants, herbs and trees, formally laid out with statues, paths and hedges. It was conveniently near Chelsea Harbour, and it also had a nice literary association for him. The first party was on 13 September 1997, the year of his sixtieth birthday. At the time, he was rewriting the shooting script of *Poodle Springs*, and he found out that Raymond Chandler had lived in Swan Walk. 'I gave a party in the Chelsea Physic Garden where the mulberry trees throw their afternoon shadows into Swan Walk itself. I must have parked my car outside Chandler's house.'

From 1997 onwards the party was held every two years, from noon till dusk, always on a Saturday, sometimes in early September, more often in early July. In 2007 and 2017 the parties again coincided with his important birthdays. But each one was celebratory – and the sun always seemed to shine. It was a lavish, convivial expression of good will. Under Jacky's supervision, the garden was turned for the day into the setting of a *fête champêtre*. There were jugglers, and stilt-walkers dressed as flamingoes or clowns, a moving tree, face painters and a Punch and Judy show. There was a jazz band and a string quartet and a trumpeter. There were long tables all up and down the sides of the garden walks, manned with waiters and cooks: barbecue stands, seafood stands with oysters, a spit roast (with crackling) and a hamburger stall, cake tables and ice-cream bicycles, crêpes and cakes and fruits, all kinds of drinks. The stage set featured a marquee and awnings, rugs and bamboo chairs and sunshades. Older people sat in the shade, children ran round everywhere, groups of nicely dressed guests with lots of sunhats drifted and chattered all day long. Somehow he managed to keep the place free of reporters, though a small group of paparazzi would stake out the entrance. Some guests just dropped in for a couple of hours – the actors before their matinee or an evening show – and others made a day of it, with their families. He told Antonia Fraser that in the first year he asked four hundred guests, the next year he asked the same people and twice as many came, and so on. Jacky's annotations of the guest list would often include phrases like 'probably with entire family', or 'bringing newish baby'. Over the years the parties grew to include not only family, friends and colleagues but patrons of his causes and people he felt indebted to or missed seeing. He came to feel it was his 'social duty' to go on hosting them – though they didn't solve the problem of 'too many commitments and engagements'. And they were expensive. The total cost for the 2013 party, for instance, on the basis of 650 guests and 150 children, was about £118,000, including the hire of the garden, the food, the staff, the marquee, the entertainers and the wine. One cynical publishing friend thought he must have been wondering what to do with all his money.

Truckloads of heartbroken refusals, happy acceptances and ecstatic thank-you cards poured in, and they all used the same words: enchanting, abundant, joyous, magical, dreamlike, generous. One word came up frequently: 'Do you think heaven is like this?' 'Our boys thought they had arrived in heaven.' 'It had a "we've gone to heaven" quality about it.'

He replied to most of these notes in detail, as to Antonia Byatt in 2003, who wrote to say she was sorry she couldn't come, and asked (having just seen *Coast*) if he'd ever read Henry James's novel about revolutionaries, *The Princess Casamassima*, in her view not as good as *The Bostonians*. He replied: 'I might die before reading the Princess C! – though I'll now – though not *now*, of course – get round to The Bostonians.'

Everyone remarked on the party's openness. Theatre and film people, stars and royalty, writers and musicians were mixed up with his family and his 'team' (publishers, agents, helpers, lawyers, accountants). People wandering about might bump into Mick Jagger or Twiggy, David Bailey, Johnny Dankworth and Cleo Laine, Paul Simon, Pete Townshend, the Duchess of Devonshire, Harrison Ford, Keith Richards or Princess Margaret. Nicholas Hytner wrote: 'Any garden that contains Ronnie Wood *and* Alfred Brendel is one I want to be in!' Teresa Wells loved 'the generosity and imagination of inviting *everyone*. A grand-daughter being able to meet Florence and the Machine, or discuss the Harry Potter film with Michael Gambon.' Anthony Smith, who brought his family with him from Bristol, reported: 'At one point my 9-year-old grand-daughter Inez grabbed my hand and said, "I've just talked to Stephen Fry, now introduce me to someone else famous."' Martyn Fletcher, who did Stoppard's hair, was nervous the first time he and his partner were invited, but didn't feel it was at all snobby. He knew that Stoppard never said to himself: 'I don't think I can invite you because you're only a so-and-so.'

Elderly friends hobnobbed with small children. 'So many generations having such fun,' said the guests. 'Nobody's left out. He's very nice to old people.' Drue Heinz, coming to the party at the age of over a hundred, looked around and said wistfully and happily: 'So many children!' For the theatre people, it seemed as if their whole past was in that garden. Tom Hollander said: 'People feel as if they are part of some huge continuing family.' Michael Blakemore described it as 'a graph of practically my entire working life'. Some guests, like Bamber Gascoigne, thought that the parties 'deserve a place in social histories of post-millennium Britain'. Rose Cobbe saw them as an expression of character: 'You are such an extraordinary host, Tom. No attention or detail that could enhance the pleasure of the day is lacking – perhaps it's your upbringing – but I think it's more nature than nurture.'

Among the 'commitments and engagements' which the party didn't help to reduce was, from 2002 onwards, the London Library. It had been his major research resource, and his favourite place in London, ever since 1967 when he became a member. In 1989 he was made a trustee. In October 1997 he gave the London Library lecture, on 'Biographical Fiction'. ('Princess Michael there!' he noted: she had been a friend since the mid-1980s.) In 2000 he became a vice-president, and in 2002 he agreed to be president, and was duly elected on 11 November. His predecessors included John Gross, Kenneth Clark and, from 1952 till his death in 1965, T. S. Eliot, a main reason for doing it. He did this for the next fifteen years, retiring on his eightieth birthday. It was a time-consuming and sometimes irksome public role which he carried out loyally and energetically. The other advisory roles he took on over the years – the Board of the National Theatre and (for a few years in the 2000s) of the Donmar Warehouse, Index on Censorship and PEN, on the masthead of the Society of Authors and the *Salisbury Review* – were none of them as onerous as this. But he was honoured to be asked. He did it for the love of books. His idea of a good death, he once said, would be to be killed by a falling bookcase while reading.

The Library, founded in 1841 by Carlyle, Macaulay, Gladstone and other Victorian sages, with Dickens as an early member, grew from 2,500 books to a million, which can be taken out (ten at a time, or more for non-Londoners) or mailed to members. Since the 1840s it has occupied a tall nineteenth-century stone house in the corner of St James's Square, just off Pall Mall. It looks like a gentleman's club at the heart of the London establishment. Inside there are old portraits, wood panelling, leather chairs, long stacks with steel grille floors and ceilings, and seven floors of narrow staircases. Books are arranged by subject and theme. Stoppard often told a story about this, which he heard from his friend John Wells, as an example of why he liked the Library so much. Arthur Koestler had to write a piece on the Fischer–Spassky chess match in Reykjavik. He went to the London Library to do his homework. In the entrance hall he hesitated. Chess first or Iceland first? Chess was nearer. On the Chess shelf the first book that caught Koestler's eye was *Chess in Iceland*.

The seven or eight thousand members include a great many well-known British authors. The Library arouses feelings of devotion and possessiveness, and describes itself as 'a university library for people who are no longer at university'. It is a traditional institution. The practice in the Reading Room was to have special shelves where members could leave books, marked with their names, if they were going to return shortly. A member once saw a slip of paper on a pile of books reading 'Kingsley Martin'. He had been dead for two years.

Stoppard called its existence 'an existential fact of culture'. It was one of the 'old English institutions' that, 'as a fake Englishman', had a strong pull on him. And it was 'the library I love'. Books were mailed to him, and he went in to exchange one pile for another, and was often to be seen browsing the shelves. But he didn't write there, of course, because he needed to smoke while he worked. *Jumpers, Indian Ink, The Invention of Love* and *The Coast of Utopia* – among other plays – drew heavily on the Library's resources. He liked describing the link, which he found moving, between Isaiah Berlin's reading Herzen there in 1930 and his own discovery of Berlin's books, on the same shelves, seventy years on.

In 2004 the Library bought up a 1970s office block next door, Duchess House (renamed T. S. Eliot House in 2008), which gave it much more space. That purchase, and further refurbishments and extensions, meant a £25 million fundraising campaign, launched in 2005. He set to with a will. 'If I take something on, I don't like to hang about on the sidelines.' He did an enormous amount of speeches, hosting, AGM meetings and private tours of the Library for potential donors. He donated his manuscript of *Arcadia* to the London Library so that they could sell it (for £20,000) to the British Library, and gave them memorabilia for their auctions. He made promotional films from the book-lined balcony of the Library's main room. He hosted donor dinners in London and New York, and fronted up the Library's summer and Christmas parties, luring big-name actors to read at them. He created an award which linked the Duke of Devonshire's Heywood Hill prize to the Library.

His friend Max Hastings has noted his powers of persuasion: 'Whatever he wants you to do, you want to do it for him.' Lottie Cole, the Library's development director, with whom he worked closely, said: 'Most people, when you ask, "Would you come and have lunch with Tom Stoppard?" would find it hard to refuse.' She was surprised how unconvinced he was himself about the pulling power of his name. But with his charm, his fame, his contacts and his eloquence, he was the most effective of fundraisers. And he was successful, she observed, because it was a cause he cared about. He wrote elegantly flattering letters (which he would not let Lottie write for him) to culturally inclined millionaires, the likes of Maurice Saatchi, Lady Rothermere, Lady Hamlyn, George Soros, Sigrid Rausing, Evgeny Lebedev or Leonard Blavatnik. He jumped at all opportunities, writing here to a banker who had brought colleagues to the revival of *Every Good Boy* in 2009:

I have another thought for the intersection of bankers and culture . . . I wonder whether you, perhaps with one or two colleagues, might like to visit us for tea-and-tour one day soon. We are engaged in expanding and improving the fabric of the Library for future generations . . . You may like to be associated with this particular contribution to our culture – or may not – but either way it would be pleasant to see you and show you round.

When the donations came in, he wrote again, by hand: 'What a joy to be in the position of writing to you in such circumstances! . . . Your magnificent gift means so much to all of us – but let me thank you in my own name, because I love the Library and your sympathetic and generous expression of support has brought sunshine into this rather grey day.' Thanks to his efforts, Eliot's widow Valerie gave £2.5 million for the extension in 2008, and his friend the philanthropist Drue Heinz became closely involved with the Library and left it a legacy.

Rather as the gentlemanly exterior of the building concealed a steel structure within, he had no illusions about this whole process. Writing to a fellow supporter of the Library during the run of *Rock 'n' Roll*, he said: 'I'm wondering how I might do something useful for the Library by exploiting my play . . . a small gathering of billionaire bibliophiliacs is my fantasy. I'll work on it – play – supper – cheque books.' Teresa Wells helped him dine some potential donors, and was impressed to see him charm a few thousand out of a very rich lady. That's brilliant, said Teresa. No, it's not, he replied, it's pathetic, not nearly enough.

At the end of 2007 his presidency ran into trouble. Because of the purchase of the new building, the Library needed to hike up the subscription fees, which by no means covered the running costs. (It has no government subsidy.) The trustees, without consulting him, raised the subscription in one fell swoop, by eighty per cent, from £210 a year to £375. Many members left, there were angry public statements and over 1,500 letters of complaint, especially from the long-standing members, some of whom were his friends. It was a major storm in a London teacup. The governance of the Library was questioned at the Annual General Meeting of members on 1 November. Stoppard was away, but sent a message, which was read out, asking members to support the change. The decision had not been his choice, but he had to defend it. In a message to all members, on 21 November 2007, he took a firm tone. He understood the feeling that the trustees had acted in a 'high-handed way'. He was sorry that he had not been at the AGM: he had been rehearsing a play in New York. 'For that, I put on the presidential sackcloth.' It was a mistake to have raised the subscription all at once. And he ought to have written to them 'in advance and not in arrears' of the fact. Otherwise he was unrepentant. Members needed to understand that decisions were devolved to the trustees; that the rise had been agreed by a clear majority at the AGM; that the much-needed expansion of the Library had also been agreed by members; that the Library's reserves had been subsidising subscriptions to the tune of about fifty-five per cent; and that there was a separate fund for those who could not afford the full subscription. And he concluded: 'To be a member of the greatest independent open-stack lending library in the land for just over a pound a day is not an offer for which we should apologise.'

Reproaches continued to flow in, some taking offence that a rich famous writer should tell other people that they had to pay more. He felt pressured, cross, exasperated and a bit guilty. Some of his support team thought his involvement with the Library overburdened him and got in the way of his writing in the late 2000s. But he took the flak, did not resign, and stayed on as president for another ten years. He was in the habit, in interview, of playing down his lasting commitment to his good causes. 'My life as a do-gooder', he would say, 'tends to have no second act, let alone a third act.' But in this he did himself an injustice.

The presidency of the Library, like the giving of the annual summer party, was a much-loved public performance. He was, as David Cornwell observed, always putting his head above the social parapet. His friend Jack O'Brien said, of this social self: 'Tom unedited is something socially we rarely see . . . He's a *benign pachyderm*. He masks himself . . . He wants to be adored. And he's good at being adored.' Stoppard was aware of his own doubleness – and not only as a fundraiser. In the last year of his presidency, during the Library's 2016 'Words in the Square' festival to celebrate its one hundred and seventy-fifth anniversary, he made some wry, candid remarks about himself. He was aware of the effect he had on people, he said, and he was not careless about it. But he was not as nice as he seemed. The audience laughed in disbelief – but he meant it. Expanding on this later, he said that he often had a five-minute conversation with someone he was meeting for the first time, when he would be pleasant and agreeable – because it was easier to be pleasant than not – and knew that he was leaving behind him an impression of vivid attention. But he was quite capable of not recognising that person the next day. It was 'a sort of five-minute performance for the public good'. On the other hand, if he met someone whose work or ideas interested him, the attention would be entirely genuine. He had a high degree of self-sufficiency. In truth – he said emphatically – he didn't need to talk to anybody.

But for his close friends and family there was very little he would not do. In 2000, Jack O'Brien's long-term partner suddenly died. Without alerting him, Stoppard crossed the Atlantic for the memorial service. 'You don't mistake that for something else,' O'Brien said. When Andrew Cavendish, the Duke of Devonshire, died, he wrote kind consolatory letters to his friend Debo. She responded in character: 'All understood and accepted as proper good thoughts, appreciated and taken in.' When Manny Azenberg reached seventy, the family asked his friends for their first recollections of him, for a scrapbook. 'I can't remember last week,' he replied, but 'my recollection of Manny from those early days is . . . warmth, naturalness, kindness, twinkle in eye, moustache, independence, not necessarily in that order.' In the summer of 2002 he flew to Munich to be best man at André Previn's fifth wedding, to Anne-Sophie Mutter, a romantic occasion involving sleigh rides through the German countryside.

On 7 December 2003, Mike Nichols was awarded the Kennedy Center Honours at a black-tie gala in the JFK Center for the Performing Arts in Washington, an event of Oscar-style proportions, with George and Laura Bush as guests of honour. Striding onto the big stage, looking very grand and sounding at first a little nervous, Stoppard gave a funny speech which was greeted with huge laughter and applause. He described himself as a member of MNEMONIC, the Mike Nichols Every Medal or None International Committee, who had awarded him prizes in every medium, 'through his vinyl period, his early 9 millimetre masterworks in German, and the rare wax cylinder of farmyard animal impressions'. Like the slave who would follow a Roman general around to remind him he was human, MNEMONIC would periodically remind Nichols that he 'made that Garry Shandling movie' (a disastrously embarrassing, unfunny comedy, *What Planet Are You From?*, about an alien with no genitals). He would not have mentioned MNEMONIC, he added, had not 'the President of the American branch only a couple of days ago removed the tariff on irony imports'. This was an ironic reference to Bush having just lifted the tariff on steel imports, generally regarded as a victory for Europe. The camera panned to the president smiling uncomfortably. Stoppard continued: 'It's time to put my cards on the table and my heart on my sleeve.' In the same phrase he had used at Tynan's memorial, he said: 'Mike is part of the luck I've had.' He went on: 'He's good at comfort and joy, at improving the shining hour and lighting the dark one, and of course he's superlative fun . . . To me . . . he's the best of America.' In the context of the George Bush joke, this had a strong ring. Nichols wrote to thank him, saying how proud he was of his friendship. 'What you did in that complex situation was beyond imagining. You told the truth and were so funny doing it that it was a lesson in both truth and humor not to mention courage . . . You raised the level of discourse . . . As always you make it seem easy. I know better.'

A few days later Stoppard was on a plane to Australia, invited by the premier of New South Wales, Bob Carr, to attend the opening of a new theatre on Sydney Harbour and to take part in the Sydney Literary Festival. He liked going there, though he disliked planes and travelling, and made the journey several times in his life, in 1979 to the Perth Literary Festival, in 1994 for productions of *Arcadia* and *Rock 'n' Roll*, and again in 2007 and 2011. This month-long trip to Melbourne and Sydney included a British Council brunch with Ian McKellen (there doing *The Dance of Death*), the first night at the new theatre, fundraiser lunches on its behalf, parties for the Sydney Festival, a harbour cruise, numerous press interviews and the main event, a Town Hall conversation with Bob Carr, at which, as ever, he charmed and engrossed a huge audience.

Back home, family meetings, new productions needing his input, parties, weddings, birthdays, funerals, receptions, fishing days, cricket matches (as spectator, now) flowed on. There were public events like return visits to Chatsworth for the Heywood Hill prize, or to the Prince's Educational Trust, or getting the Bodleian Medal in Oxford in November 2004 alongside Richard Attenborough and Seamus Heaney, or going to drinks at Downing Street, on 23 November 2004, where Sabrina Guinness was also present – her first appearance in his appointment diary. In between, he escaped to Lacoste.

One of the most demanding invitations, which arrived in 2002 for a date in 2004, was to give the Isaiah Berlin Lecture at Wolfson College in Oxford (a large graduate college founded by Berlin). There was a suggestion he might talk about Herzen. His reply was typically mixed.

What a compliment. Frankly, it scares me and I wish it would go away, because part of me says I shouldn't funk it. Do you mind if I stall? . . . The other thing is – I've rather *had* Herzen, if you see what I mean. I'll always love him, but not necessarily wish to work for him, especially because by 2004 my head will be full of someone else, probably.

Nervous about the event, he went to the college in the summer of 2003 to hear the lecture before his (John Pocock on the Enlightenment), an indication of how much he revered Berlin, and how unconfident he could be in that context. This was a lecture he needed to write, rather than improvise. His talk, given on 10 June 2004, was called 'Drawing on the Wall of Plato's Cave'. It was a defence of the artist against Plato's attacks and a meditation on what the artist is for. (Stoppard used the pronoun 'he' throughout the lecture, not wanting, he said, to have to 'double de-clutch' on every pronoun.) He used some of his own favourite passages – Joyce on Homer, the artist as the 'lucky bastard' with the chit from Matron, from *Travesties*, Belinsky in *Coast* on the mystery of writing – to argue that the artist is more than just a craftsman, or an inadequate imitator of reality, as Plato maintained. Stoppard liked to think of himself 'as a practitioner of a storytelling art form which is nothing without craft, and as being too occupied with it to entertain general theories about it'. But he recognised this as an affectation. He needed to ask where inspiration, imagination and aesthetic emotion come from. Scientists would argue that it's nothing but 'an excitation of neurons', but, he noted drily, 'as an account of . . . inspiration it does seem incomplete'. The unknowable is built into art. 'Like a saxifrage blindly seeking the light and not to be denied, the artistic impulse, in pursuit neither of facts nor food, or efficiency or survival, splits the rock and breaks out into flower.' No wonder it has been feared, from Plato onwards. But Plato, he maintained jauntily, was in a muddle, which he wanted to try and sort out. 'There's an itch there which hasn't had a proper scratch.' Why would Plato praise Sappho and Homer, yet banish poets from his Republic and dismiss theatre as vulgar and meretricious? (Plato would probably have had the same complaints about a *Carry On* film as about Aristophanes.) The trouble for us is that Plato didn't have a separate word for 'artists': he lumped them together with craftsmen. But artists are more than that. Of course (narrowly resisting a dig at conceptual art here), they do have to be craftsmen with technique, constructing something that works, like a 'well-made play'. Running lightly through contrasting examples from Shelley, Van Gogh, James, Brodsky and Beckett, Stoppard ended up with a confusion not unlike the one he attributes to Plato. Do we think of the artist as 'a worker trained to take on a social responsibility', or 'a seer, a visionary . . . a village magician, an outsider?' Does he belong to Caesar, or to God? He answers the question more firmly than he had long ago in *Jumpers*, where he had quizzed the idea of the artist as a special being. Now he says: 'Our heart belongs to the outsiders, the madmen, the visionaries, the prophets, the ruffians on the stair who just possibly are coming down from seeing God.' Berlin's own work (which he comes to at the very end of the lecture) on the Russian poets and writers who, under the Tsars and under Communism, were so persecuted and feared by the authorities, and at the same time so venerated, suggests there is more to them than civic accountability.

The lecture, though much admired, was somewhat jinxed by an unreliable microphone, and by the fact that, on his way out of Oxford, he picked up a speeding fine – not his first – which meant he had to attend a speed awareness course in September. When asked to do another lecture in memory of Berlin, he said no: 'My last Isaiah Berlin lecture took over my life for many weeks and I simply can't rise to the occasion again.'

The Berlin lecture shows the first seeds of *Rock 'n' Roll* (and of *The Hard Problem*), with its thoughts about scientific accounts of consciousness and its references to the surviving fragments of Sappho. But he had a lot of other things to get through before the next play could rise to the top of his mind.

In the summer of 2002, he agreed to write a screenplay of Philip Pullman's trilogy, *His Dark Materials*, which, published between 1995 and 2000, became a worldwide hit and was the first children's book to win the Whitbread Prize, in January 2002. Pullman was enthusiastic about his involvement. This was a lucrative contract for a high-profile project: $1.6 million for the first draft, $350,000 for revisions, $150,000 for the 'polish' and $250,000 for a possible second and third film. Once he started reading, it became very interesting to him, though it might not look like natural Stoppard territory. *His Dark Materials* is, famously, an epic story of two resourceful children from different worlds, Lyra and Will, on their quests for knowledge, pursued by enemies, and helped by an assortment of witches, shamans, armoured bears, scientists, boat-people, angels and the 'daemons' who are the animal alter egos of the humans in Lyra's world. It is a fantastical adventure story grounded in a deeply serious opposition to religious doctrine, social hierarchies and repressive authorities, and much concerned with our destruction of the planet: the opposite of Tolkien or C. S. Lewis. Milton and Blake are its literary parents. It uses images of 'Dust' (particles of dark matter which are the material embodiment of consciousness), and of multiple universes, to show that knowledge, disobedience, sexuality and sin are desirable and necessary, and that the myth of an Authority as Creator, who tells us what we should and shouldn't do, is bogus and oppressive. Though Lyra doesn't know it, she is a second Eve, child of a rebel angel, born to make choices that will lead this world towards its own 'republic of Heaven'.

Stoppard started to sink his teeth into all this, first with a meeting at Pullman's house in the autumn of 2002. (The Pullman household didn't have an ashtray; after his visit, when he had talked and listened and smoked for several hours, they invested in one, which they called the Tom Stoppard Memorial Ashtray. But no other smokers ever came to the house.) Some of the producers seemed to see the project as 'a family fantasy with talking animals'. They agreed this was to be avoided, and discussed the meaning of the book at length; it was clear to Pullman that Stoppard was interested in its philosophy and its metaphors. They got on well. Through 2003, Stoppard wrote the screenplay of the first volume, *Northern Lights* – which in the States had been titled *The Golden Compass*, hence the name of the film. He also did film treatments of the second and third books. In interviews he said he was writing a fantasy film about a twelve-year-old girl.

He sent Pullman his basic outline of the story. His concern was to make the screenplay as coherent as possible, and his central question was, 'What is at stake?' Pages of detailed questions followed. Does the Church change its mind about Lyra, and only gradually realise she is a threat to its established order? Was Asriel, her father, contradictory in his view of Dust? How was

Lyra's friend Roger murdered? 'I think the audience needs to know more than the reader needs to know regarding the nuts and bolts of severing Roger and his daemon.' Do daemons grow up? Could Lyra's wicked mother Mrs Coulter be a witch? 'What can Asriel do *that a film can show him doing?*' At one point he told Pullman he felt he was 'trapped in a Möbius strip'. One set of questions concluded sweetly: 'Write on one side of the paper only and put your pen down when the bell rings.' Pullman replied that the Möbius strip was like a Gordian knot, and could only be resolved by surgery. He sent Stoppard a precis of his mythology, tried to sort out the contradictions and offered some rewritings. He couldn't always answer questions about his characters' behaviour. In one response, he said: 'But what do I know?'

Pullman thought Stoppard's first draft read like an interesting unperformed Stoppard play. It was too much about fate, free will and consciousness, and not enough about Lyra. Pullman told him that it had taken him ages to understand the book's popularity:

I have realised why they're willing to follow a complicated story through 1,300 pages and all kinds of theologico/philosophico/scientific speculation-cum-gobbledygook, and the reason is this: they don't *mind* being in the dark about what's going on, because Lyra is also in the dark, but she's trying to find out, and they trust her to do it . . . So if we establish Lyra as our centre right from the start, the fact that she's surrounded by adults doing mysterious things is perfectly OK, because all children feel like that anyway.

'Yes, yes,' Stoppard replied, Pullman was being 'patient and tactful': 'The first draft was too plot-driven, not enough Lyra-driven. I'm afraid I was focussing on the metaphysics and the science, which interest me . . . I stripped the book down too much before, to fit all the bits together in the space.'

Pullman knew that condensing his book was challenging and that it had to be translated into what would work visually. He appreciated the application of Stoppard's 'daemonic shimmer' to his work, and was grateful for 'the enormous care and the sheer weight of analytical power you're

The script he wrote was a long way from the novel, and looking back, he thought he and Madden had not done a good job. Others too thought it confused the storyline and was cerebral when it should have been emotional. In a crucial scene in the novel, the rare and expensive tulip bulb on which the lovers' fate depends is eaten by a drunken servant. Stoppard thought, instead, there should be an Aristotelian version of the plot in which their destinies are caught up with the implosion of the financial world. So the tulip bulb is eaten by a dog, a minor incident compared with the financial crash. In the novel, the artist, while painting the young married woman, expresses his passionate love to her. In Stoppard's script he gives her a lecture on ultramarine pigment.

In February 2004, eight weeks before shooting started, with the set built and the cast nearly lined up (Jude Law, Jim Broadbent, Keira Knightley or Natalie Portman), Gordon Brown, then Chancellor of the Exchequer, closed the tax loophole which had allowed investors to form partnerships with film companies and pour large sums of money into the cash-strapped British film industry while taking advantage of tax breaks. Getting rid of that loophole immediately wiped out £600 million worth of investment on which producers were depending. *Tulip Fever* was one of the most high-profile of the forty or so British films which were the victims of what John Madden called the 'Black Friday' of the film industry. An investment company called Ingenious, via its 'Inside Track' scheme, had put £12 million into *Tulip Fever* – thirty per cent of the film's funding – which would now be written off. Dreamworks pulled out, 'greatly regretting', etc. An entire recreation of seventeenth-century Amsterdam, built at Pinewood Studios, complete with twelve thousand tulip bulbs, was demolished immediately. 'TF shooting starts' was crossed out of Stoppard's appointment diary for the date of 26 August 2004. Madden noted that he behaved 'impeccably' throughout.

Almost ten years later, Harvey Weinstein acquired the rights in the film, dropping John Madden and making his own choice of director, Justin Chadwick. Stoppard got wind that *Tulip Fever* had come back to life, and asked his film agent Anthony Jones to make enquiries. If his name was on the script, he wanted to know what it was like. And when he saw it again – with the mark on it of numerous other writers along the way – he wanted to put it to rights. He liked Chadwick, offered to help him, and came on board again. The new script was closer to the book. Through much of 2014, he was tweaking it, especially at the 'ADR' or post-synch stage, when significant changes can be made to the tone and feeling of a film. (Stoppard describes it as when the editors are 'making a character say things when the character's mouth is not on camera'.) Moggach was asked, separately, by Weinstein, to help. She felt she was brought back to make more sense of the film's emotional narrative. In the credits for the screen-play, she appeared as first writer, and noted Stoppard's gentlemanliness about this. *Tulip Fever* was shown at Cannes in 2015, but there was then a long delay before it was generally released: it seemed that Miramax did not have confidence in its success. It finally came out at the end of 2018, and then vanished from cinemas extremely quickly. Reviewers thought it handsome, old-fashioned, dull and cold.

A quicker, jollier piece of work for him in the early 2000s was a short version of Shakespeare for schoolchildren and young actors. He went to a lunch at 10 Downing Street in November 2003, when Tony and Cherie Blair launched a three-year 'Shakespeare Schools Festival' (now known as the Shakespeare Schools Foundation), a project involving hundreds of schoolchildren between eleven and fifteen, all over the country, in pro-ductions of abridged Shakespeare plays. Some extracts were performed at the launch, and he was impressed: 'There was real engagement between the mind and the ability of the children and this long-dead genius, and it was very moving.' He undertook to do a thirty-minute version of *The Merchant of Venice*, ruefully recalling his embarrassing reading of Nerissa at Pocklington School, and wrote it in the autumn of 2004. A more seri-ous project than his long-ago *(Fifteen-minute) Dogg's Troupe Hamlet*, it raised the same problems of sorting out a large cast of characters very fast, so that audiences wouldn't be going: 'Who? What? Where? When?' But he didn't want to oversimplify: he told the young company that 'I have this habit of not wanting to make things easy.' With some anxiety, he cut chunks out of 'very famous speeches', left out a lot of Shylock, but kept in the Gobbos, in the belief that their comedy was an essential part of the play. A delighted cast of schoolchildren and National Youth Theatre members performed his version, set by the producers in 1930s Mussolini-era Italy, at the Linbury Theatre at the Royal Opera House, in October 2005. The BBC Learning Zone made a documentary of the production, and the NYT then took it to Beijing, and kept it in their repertoire.

Shakespeare was in his head at this time, too, because of an interesting approach from a director and a theatre he admired, Michael Grandage at the Donmar. Grandage, who took over the Donmar in 2002, was inviting major writers to do new versions of the European repertoire. He asked Stoppard to take on Pirandello's *Henry IV*, first staged in 1922. Stoppard agreed at once, without even having read the play. It was a good match. *Henry IV* was much inspired by *Hamlet*, and *Rosencrantz* was often compared to Pirandello's most famous play, *Six Characters in Search of an Author*. Like early Stoppard, Pirandello had darkly comical fun with reality, enjoyed wordplay, broke the fourth wall, upended theatrical conventions and liked his characters to meditate on truth and mortality. *Henry IV* is a play about madness and sadness, written soon after Pirandello's wife was committed to an asylum.

A twentieth-century Italian aristocrat has been concussed by a fall from a horse during a historical pageant when he was dressed as the eleventh-century anti-papist German emperor, Henry IV – and has got stuck in his role. For twenty years he seems to have gone on thinking he *is* Henry IV. His rich relations, to keep him pacified, have kept him in a 'medieval' castle with fake portraits, courtiers dressed in period costume and visitors all adopting historical roles. The play begins with a baffled new employee (a Rosencrantz/Guildenstern type) being inducted into the charade, on the day that 'Henry''s nephew, the woman he once adored, her lover, her daughter and a psychiatric doctor all arrive to try and shock 'Henry' out of his delusion, with a lot of Pirandello-ish family agitation and argument. But the joke is on them. For the last eight years, it turns out, 'Henry' has only been pretending, Hamlet-like, to be mad, as a refuge from the real world. He points out that they are all as trapped in their roles as he has been pretending to be. Who is truly insane, the false madman or the society that confines him? 'I'm cured, gentlemen,' he concludes, 'because I've woken up to my madness . . . Your problem is that you haven't woken up to yours, so you toss and turn your whole lives through.'

Reworking Pirandello wasn't easy. 'Off virtuously to bed you go, a good and faithful servant of Pirandello – and then you get up in the morning and it's as if the Portuguese au pair had been at it and done her version. You think, but this is gibberish – and go back to work on it again and again.' It was a garrulous play, and he sharply tightened it – even more so after he had seen it in rehearsal, when, as Grandage put it, he clipped a wayward hedge into a more shapely form: 'great topiary'. As with *On the Razzle* or *Rough Crossing*, he made it as colloquial as he could. When 'Henry' suddenly turns on the people he's been hoodwinking, which in one translation reads: 'The clowns! Buffoons!' Stoppard has: 'What a bunch of wankers!' He has fun with the psychoanalyst's lingo. 'He can't quite find the point of equilibrium between ego and super-ego' is his version of (in another translation): 'He is slowly readjusting himself beneath his outer personality.' 'Henry''s lamentation on the condition of masquerade and solitude to which we are all condemned, whether mad or sane, is movingly phrased: 'Pray God you don't find out the thing that'll drive anyone crazy: that when you see yourself reflected in someone's eyes – as happened to me once – you see a beggar standing at a gate he can never enter. The one who goes in can never be you, in your closed-off, self-created world.'

His version was praised as 'true-spirited and boisterous', 'snappy-clever and inventive'. One reviewer compared the sad human story coming through the wit and cleverness to the recent revival of *Jumpers*. And a 'gale-force' performance by Ian McDiarmid in the title role was praised as 'a master-class in the grandeur of delusions'. When the play was published, he made sure Pirandello got bigger billing than he did in the blurb, and reproved his editor at Grove Atlantic, Eric Price, for inflating his reputation: 'I don't like being called one of the 20th century's greatest playwrights. It's too soon to tell!'

He was asked to adapt another European play in the mid-2000s. This was also about delusion as a refuge from the outside world – faintly echoing his television play of 1966, *A Separate Peace*. The play was by a French actor-writer, Gérald Sibleyras, twenty or so years his junior. *Le Vent des peupliers* had a big success in Paris in 2003. Stoppard's version, put on at Wyndham's Theatre in October 2005, was renamed *Heroes*, to avoid any confusion with *The Wind in the Willows*. (He'd have liked to use *Veterans*, but Charles Wood had got there first.) Three old First World War soldiers are spending what's left of their lives in a Catholic retirement home for military men. Gustave, a one-time war hero, grumpy and antisocial, has wild plans for them to make their escape to Indo-China, but in fact can't get beyond the gate of the home into the outside world. Henri (René in the original), lame, short-sighted, easily discouraged, doesn't want to plan anything more ambitious than a picnic – if possible as far as the line of poplars on the horizon. Philippe (originally Fernand) is musical and neurotic, always passing out because of shrapnel in his skull, convinced that the head nun of the home is planning his murder, and reluctant to quarrel: 'Don't make me take sides, I can't stand it.' Each of them thinks the others are batty. A stone dog, which seems almost human, is their only witness. It's a geriatric version of *Three Men in a Boat*, except that, like Beckett characters, the three men do nothing but talk, bicker, fantasise, plan their escape like a military campaign – and stay put.

Stoppard found the play humane, truthful and oddly consolatory: 'I think it's a play about the fact that we don't die. That something of us continues, even if it's just somebody's memory of us.' He enjoyed working with Sibleyras, who happily accepted Stoppard's ruthless cuts, which got an already short play down to ninety minutes' running time. He was on the lookout, Stoppard explained to him, for things 'that might slow things down at the wrong moment'. 'I have cut the script as I would if it were mine – to make it faster.'

He was always pushing for lightness, speed and colloquialism, as tiny comparisons between his first and last versions show. 'Still, one couldn't say you're in the best of health' turns into 'not that you're in the pink yourself'. 'Can't you see how pleased she is with herself? Stuffed full of her own benevolence' becomes 'puffed up with her own do-gooding'. 'We should take care of our little retreat' is changed to: 'Must keep the place in good order.' Towards the end, an insulting diary entry is read out: 'September 20th. Two of you are barking and the third's petrified, so why don't you go and fuck yourselves?' This became: 'You're all barking, except the dog.'

Both writers relished the richly comical trio of performances from Richard Griffiths, John Hurt and Ken Stott in Thea Sturrock's production, which opened in October 2005 and won the Laurence Olivier award for best new comedy in 2006. Stoppard, always careful to maintain the status of the author in commercial theatre, took care not to benefit the most. He was a much better known playwright than Sibleyras, and when he was first approached, the producers began by saying that, of course, it would be a fifty–fifty cut for the two authors. No, said Stoppard, he was translating someone else's work, and it ought to be divided sixty–forty between original writer and translator. His agents noted, with admiration, that he lost out on a point of principle.

While these European plays were in his mind, and while he was partly living in France, he was also much involved with Eastern Europe and Russia. His very English public life was never the whole story. Five years in the company of his 'Russian Thinkers', his continuing attachment to Havel, his thoughts about his birthplace and his history, especially since the death of his mother, all profoundly affected him. Ideas about nationality, origins, exile and historical identity kept coming back to him.

His work had been banned in Russia since 1977; but in 2001 it became known that copies of his work had secretly been kept in the Russian State Library. In October 2002, the possibility arose of having *Coast* translated and put on in Russia. The Bolshoi Drama Theatre in St Petersburg (who had had a success with *Arcadia*) were interested, but got cold feet about staging it in what they called 'the current cultural context'. They explained that the nineteenth-century revolutionaries were now anathematised in post-Soviet Russian history lessons, and 'a Russian will see Herzen differently from what an Englishman will see'. The Russian Drama Theatre in Riga declared itself 'too provincial for such an avant-garde project'. Then Stoppard was approached by Arkady Ostrovsky, the Moscow correspondent at the *Financial Times*. Ostrovsky was also a specialist in Russian theatre history, writing a book at that time about Gordon Craig's co-production of *Hamlet* with Stanislavsky in 1911. (In 2015 he would write an invaluable book on

post-Soviet Russia, with a Stoppardian title, *The Invention of Russia*.)
Ostrovsky's colleague, the *Financial Times* theatre critic Alastair Macaulay,
a great Stoppard admirer, invited Ostrovsky to see *Coast*, and as he watched
it, he became fired up with the thought of how it could play in Russia. He
immediately wrote to Stoppard, and was astonished, a few weeks later, to
get a phone call which began: 'Hi, it's Tom here.' He thought one of his
friends was playing a joke on him. Stoppard invited himself round and they
talked intently about Russian theatre and how *Coast* might get to Moscow.
Ostrovsky was just about to move there from London with his family as
the *FT*'s foreign correspondent. He started work with his brother Sergei
(a theatre historian and dramaturge) on translating *Voyage* and *Shipwreck*.
Stoppard went to Moscow in May 2003 and Ostrovsky was his guide there.
He introduced him to the Russian theatre historian Anatoly Smeliansky
and to Oleg Tabakov, famous actor and artistic director of the Moscow Arts
Theatre, who at first seemed enthusiastic.

Ostrovsky took Stoppard to the Bakunin family estate, Premukhino,
where *Coast* begins. Ostrovsky observed him closely on this trip, and felt
that he was moved by being there. On the way, Stoppard asked to get out
of the car for a moment to get some air, and perhaps to have a moment to
himself. Premukhino was in disrepair, an overgrown ruin, a place where
young anarchists would come out at night and camp. A caretaker turned
up, whom Ostrovsky had contacted beforehand. Stoppard told him that
he had written a play about Bakunin. The caretaker replied, 'I also wrote a
play about Bakunin.' They drank some vodka, and Stoppard showed them
the lake and where the family would have fished for carp. He seemed
to take possession of the place, as if, Ostrovsky thought, he were taking
them into his imaginary world, *his* Premukhino. In Moscow, they went
to Herzen's museum and saw his personal relics, including Kolya's glove.
They went up to the Sparrow Hills, where the young Herzen and Ogarev
made their revolutionary pact together. Ostrovsky asked him if he wished
he had been to these places before writing his play. No, Stoppard said, I
had all my London Library books, I didn't need to be here.

For Ostrovsky, the seriousness and scope of *The Coast of Utopia*, its
attention to Russian history and its strong moral themes were an antidote

to the Russian narrative of the times. He saw Moscow in the early 2000s as a centre for oil-rich hedonism, fashionable nouveau riche lifestyles and light entertainment. It wasn't in the mood for long serious theatre about the past. It was precisely because *Coast* was so remote from the mood of the times that Ostrovsky wanted to see it put on. But the Moscow Arts Theatre weren't persuaded. Tabakov, who had canny commercial instincts, took fright: he thought it was too long and too intellectual. Both Ostrovsky and Stoppard were upset by this change of heart.

But the translating went on, and so did the friendship. Two years later, in 2005, Ostrovsky talked to Alexei Borodin, the artistic director of Moscow's Russian Academic Youth Theatre and professor at the Russian Academy of Theatre Arts. Borodin, a cultured and courageous theatre grandee, sat up all one night reading *Coast* and decided that, as Ostrovsky put it, 'he could not *not* do it'. In 2007 – soon after the trilogy won seven Tony awards in America – Stoppard went to Moscow to work with the cast, watching his play and his exiled characters coming back to life in Russian, a language he couldn't speak. In the programme note, he said how strange it would seem for a British audience to watch a play about nineteenth-century British radicals written by a Russian playwright who knew no English. Yet, in his own defence, he said he had always felt an 'emotional entanglement' with the whole story of Russia. 'When I was born, the Russian Revolution was only twenty years old . . . by the time I myself was twenty years old, the USSR seemed to have become a permanent fact of life . . . When I was fifty, that permanence seemed to stretch towards a future without end . . .' Looking back now, post-1990, one could see that 'at the centre of that [Russian] story has always been the individual spirit expressing itself in the vast intimidating shadow of impersonal authority'.

His presence, over several weeks of rehearsals, was closely observed by two people, Ostrovsky and the young playwright-director Nina Raine (grand-niece of Boris Pasternak), who was writing a piece on the event. As Raine observed, the difficulty was to keep Stoppard's essential mixture of weightiness and lightness. 'The dramatist is here to ensure, in his gentle way, that . . . the production stays air-borne.' As he smoked, ate sweets, drank endless coffee and gave patient, tactful notes through a translator to a very serious cast, all questioning the emotions and psychology of their characters, Raine saw him trying to make sure of comedy, clarity and irony, through the sound and feel of what they were doing. His own conceptions of the 'Russian soul' and 'Russian acting' were being challenged, while the actors were having to learn how to take him less seriously. 'And lightness', he told them, 'is not a bad word, because this is *not* a polemical play.' There were moments of lightness, too, for them all. At lunch, he asked what a plate of pink sliced meat was. 'That is' – an actor hunts for the word – '. . . language.' 'Language! I love it!' said Stoppard. It was tongue.

Outside the rehearsal rooms, he was bombarded with interviews, where he was repeatedly asked about the condition of Russia today and how his play applied. *Coast* opened in Moscow in October 2007, in a very different Russia under Putin than in 2003. In Ostrovsky's view, 'everything that Herzen detested [was] being resurrected – censorship, the autocracy of the Russian state, a macabre union of Orthodoxy, nationalism and authoritarianism'. Putin was moving Russia into confrontation with the West, and the Moscow audiences of *Coast* applauded the characters' speeches about Russian oppression versus Western liberalism. (Significantly, Gorbachev would later go to see *Coast*; he and Stoppard got on well.) The day after it opened, rival demonstrations in Moscow protested against the murder the year before of the journalist Anna Politkovskaya, and celebrated Putin's birthday. In that context, Borodin felt that 'he needed this play like air, with its heightened sense of justice and his uncompromising, rebellious characters'. Ostrovsky saw the production as 'an antidote to the poisonous atmosphere in Russia's public life'. It went on being part of the theatre's repertoire for years. Large, brightly coloured framed posters of the Russian *Coast* hang on the walls of the top floor of Stoppard's home, next to his study. *Coast*'s journey, bringing his exiles back to Russia, was very important to him.

But before *Coast* reached Russia, there was another kind of involvement for Stoppard with Eastern Europe. In late July 2004, just over a year after the first trip to Russia, he was invited to a big annual Czech film festival in Uherské Hradiště, a Moravian town near Zlín. The theme that year was 'Film and Childhood', and he was asked partly because they knew he was working on *His Dark Materials*. He built another trip to Zlín around it, with Peter, Richard and Fiona. His half-brother and sister were very moved to see their mother's Czech home with him. That return fed into his thoughts about his next play. So did an approach, some months later, from a group of Eastern Europeans who were to become insistent presences in his life.

There was one country in the former 'Soviet bloc' where an autocratic regime still held sway. This was Belarus, which, having suffered horribly under Stalin's purges, declared its independence from the Soviet Union in 1990, but in 1994 fell under the repressive rule of Alexander Lukashenko. Belarus was returned to Soviet-style brutality, censorship and surveillance. Political dissent was harshly punished with sackings, imprisonment, harassment, torture, labour camp sentences, disappearances and killings. The media was controlled, living conditions were poor, artistic life was stifled. And so it continues. Belarus was not much taken up as a Western cause, though Amnesty International was working on its behalf, identifying human rights violations and 'prisoners of conscience', and a 'Free Belarus' coalition had been set up in 2003. In 2005 a small intrepid group of players founded the Belarus Free Theatre.

The leaders of BFT were Natalia (or Natasha) Kaliada, an unstoppable force of nature, her husband Nikolai (or Kolia) Khalezin and the playwright Vladimir Shcherban, with other actors who had been sacked from their official jobs or been detained or arrested. They staged short, stripped-down productions of European and Belarusian plays at secret venues all over Minsk, at great risk to themselves and their families, with audiences alerted at the last moment. They mounted workshops and competitions. They had ambitious plans for international recognition. Their voices came, as Kaliada put it, from a zone of silence.

Early in 2005, they wrote to a number of Western writers asking for a message of support. Among the few who responded were the writer Mark Ravenhill and Stoppard. He replied in March 2005, giving them a statement and undertaking to go and see them. As he said to Ostrovsky, he could just have asked Jacky to 'give these people my message of support', and then gone to lunch and left it at that. But their plea got through his defences. This was an ostracised theatre group trying to maintain the work and the culture it cared about in conditions of vicious repression. It was *Cahoot's Macbeth* or *Every Good Boy* all over again. Living in the semi-detached way that he did, he was a free agent, and could get on a plane to Minsk whenever he liked. He decided to go and meet them. You have my support, he told them; what else can I do? David Hare, who greatly admired this side of Stoppard's life, compared it to Chekhov going to Sakhalin to report on the penal colony. And it fired up his imagination.

In September 2005, he flew to Minsk, with Arkady Ostrovsky as his translator. He described being met by 'hefty Kolia with his fair hair pulled back into a ponytail' – wearing, rather to his alarm, an anti-Lukashenko T-shirt – and 'dark gamine Natasha, smiling and waving'. He was caught up in an intense few days of discussions about the purpose of theatre in repressed societies, seeing their production of Sarah Kane's *4.48 Psychosis* in a tiny bar, and meeting relatives of the 'disappeared'. Ostrovsky heard him saying to the young Belarusian actors that they had to have talent, but that bravery was as important: 'Of all aspects of life art brings to the surface, the part of it which expresses us at our most intense is that part where we have to show just a little courage.' He listened intently to their stories, and told them: 'I can't teach you anything because I'm still learning.'

He talked to Kolia about his play *Generation Jeans*, in which rock music and long hair and the wearing of jeans were expressions of freedom for youth in Belarus, and to Ostrovsky about *Rock 'n' Roll,* in which alternative lives lived under Communism and Western freedoms are pitted against each other. Kolia and Natalia and Ostrovsky all felt that he had found another country where the story of his new play was still unfolding. 'Now I understand why I'm here,' he told them. And Minsk, with its Soviet architecture, *samizdat* theatre, rock concerts, beautiful women, cafes where everyone smoked, and KGB men staking out the hotels, had the kind of impact on him that Prague had once had.

Throughout the visit, he was practical. What do you want? he asked them. We need a good computer and a camera, they said; he bought them at once. He told Natasha and Kolia, on his return, that it had been 'a very interesting and important experience for him'. He wrote a big piece about Belarus for the *Guardian*. So, later, did Ravenhill, who had asked the group whether they could be optimistic about the future. Shcherban replied: 'These words don't apply. There is no optimism or pessimism. We are living in hell and we are doing the best we can.'

Stoppard's piece aroused interest, including an upset letter from a Russian lady in Ireland, who objected to his Western misunderstandings. He wrote back politely, and personally:

My mother, who died about ten years ago in her eighties, used to upbraid me when I wrote in support of dissidents in Eastern Europe. She would tell me that 'ordinary people' were quite happy to get on with the only lives they knew. Western 'freedoms' did not concern them . . . So I read your letter with some understanding. I wrote a play this year in which a Czech character, during Communism, says: 'All this human rights is just foreigners thinking they're better than us. Well, they're not better than us.'

For some years, a large chunk of his life went into his support for the Belarusians. He spent time and money helping them with contacts for their theatre tours abroad, rousing up starry support (from Jude Law, Kevin Spacey, Mick Jagger, Steven Spielberg), introducing BFT productions and film screenings, making speeches and writing letters on their behalf. He liaised with human rights organisations in the cause of Belarus's political prisoners, took part in public protests and led delegations to the Belarusian Embassy and the House of Commons. Natalia and Kolia poured out their gratitude and enlisted him in all their plans.

Havel and Pinter (who allowed them to perform any of his plays free) were already on board. The BFT created a play which intercut scenes from Pinter with statements from Belarusian detainees, *Being Harold Pinter*. In April 2007, they performed it at Leeds University, on the day that Pinter was given an honorary degree. Stoppard went with him and introduced the performance. It was to be their last outing together: Pinter died at the end of 2008.

Things got much worse in Belarus. On 19 December 2010, a fifty-thousand-strong peaceful protest against Lukashenko's rigged elections ended in a violent clampdown, with hundreds of people beaten up, arrested and imprisoned. Leading opposition figures were incarcerated and their families threatened. Natalia was arrested and released; she and Kolia and their two daughters had to flee Belarus into exile in London in 2011. No one was wearing jokey T-shirts any more. 'Free Belarus' worked with Index on Censorship, Amnesty International and PEN for the political prisoners and their families. Stoppard, as Natalia put it, 'organised the whole world to notice' what was happening. In February 2011, he helped to set up and fund a Belarus Committee in the West, asking Havel to be its president. With so many groups working under such difficult circumstances, there were inevitable tensions. At one point, during a heated misunderstanding between one of the Belarusians and Index's legal team, Stoppard calmed everyone down: 'Self-justification on either side would merely extend the moment, and is essentially irrelevant. What is required instead is a contest of generosity. From this point on, ladies and gentlemen: empathy, patience, kindness, action, communication – followed by more of the same.' It could sum up his own life's policy.

He knew very well that Belarus was only one of many causes out there, and continually tried to keep it in people's minds:

> You could be forgiven for asking: set against the scale and violence of the retaliation by autocracies in North Africa and the Gulf, don't we have worse things to worry about than the crimes of Alexander Lukashenko and his bully boys? It's the wrong question. Better to ask: are we going to let this village tyrant enjoy a respite from scrutiny and accountability because, for the moment, our attention is engaged by larger, louder, more sensational and more photographable news elsewhere?

There were times when it took over his life. On 19 January 2011, while he was in New York with a production of *Arcadia*, he helped to promote a BFT performance at the Under the Radar alternative theatre festival in the East Village, rousing up support from Don DeLillo and E. L. Doctorow. He flew home three days later, and went to a Belarus Committee meeting the next day. In March he made a quick work trip to LA, and on the day after he got back to London he gave out an Index on Censorship prize on behalf of Belarusian prisoners of conscience. The next day, 25 March, he went to Brussels on the dawn Eurostar to present their case in a short speech to a European Forum. A journalist interviewed a bleary-eyed, jet-lagged Stoppard on the train. He told her it was his 'fifth straight day on the Belarus trail', and that he was half wondering what on earth he was doing. He also said he was amazed that 'having seen the Wall fall, and much of the old eastern bloc become part of the EU, he'd still be fighting the same old battles'.

That level of commitment couldn't be sustained. He retreated from the Belarusians over the next few years, but continued to back them. Looking back on his involvement and its limits, he said, rather sadly, that there were 'only a given number of slices you can cut yourself into'. But their gratitude for him never lessened: Kolia Khalezin and Natalia Koliada call him their 'third father'. She says he has taught her one of the great lessons in life, that – in his words to her – 'dictatorship isn't a political issue, it's a moral issue'. And their cause has been important to his life and work. Whenever he wrote about the Belarus Free Theatre, he always raised their particular predicament to a matter of first principles:

> The necessity of freedom, autonomous freedom, the freedom of the individual, is an innate, unerasable condition of the wholly lived life, and that condition holds true on every scale. The rights of the individual underpin the rights of populations. It is the same right. If, in the face of huge collective enormities, we sideline what seems relatively slight in scale and acuteness, we break the connection between 'rights' and rightness.

31

Rock 'n' Roll

We have to begin again with the ordinary meaning of words.

Strange for you, coming back. A little English schoolboy.

Rock 'n' Roll was researched and written through 2004 and 2005, much of it in France. The Belarus cause, his 2004 return to Zlín with the family, his Isaiah Berlin lecture, all fed into it. And his continuing work on *The Coast of Utopia* for the American and Russian productions kept the trilogy at the front of his mind. *Rock 'n' Roll* was, in a way, the sequel.

The new play connected that history of the origins of the Russian Revolution to his own life. In *Coast*, he had lent some of his emotions and beliefs to Herzen, Turgenev and Belinsky. *Rock 'n' Roll* played out his own relationship to Communism, in the East and in the West. His friend and hero Havel was one of the presiding spirits of the play. Its story of dissenters in Czechoslovakia under Communist rule, and of Western attitudes towards Communism, took him back to his political plays of the 1970s.

As in *Arcadia* and *The Invention of Love*, he gave a long view of time by bringing classical fragments, relics of the distant past, into a historical play. Classical survivals were one of his favourite subjects. So was rock 'n' roll. He'd had a lifetime of loving rock music, involving his friendships with Jagger and Bowie and, later, David Gilmour and Pete Townshend. He loved going to rock concerts, especially the Rolling Stones. He had a habit of listening obsessively to one rock music track while writing a play, like John Lennon's 'Mother' for *Jumpers* or Paul Simon's 'Graceland' for *Hapgood*. He was always delighted when Peter Wood found a perfect piece of music for a play – William Bolcom's 'Graceful Ghost Rag' (for *Travesties*) or Keith Jarrett's 'The Köln Concert'. But this was the first time, since Henry's choices for *Desert Island Discs* in *The Real Thing*, that he put this passion onto the stage. Rock 'n' roll is the hero of a play which doesn't quite have heroes.

The nearest thing to a hero is Jan, the Jewish boy from Zlín who left Czechoslovakia in 1939 as a baby when the Nazis came, spent the war (when his father was killed) in England, and in 1948 went back to Zlín – then Gottwaldov – with his mother. Jan is 'a little English schoolboy', a Czech with a childhood love of England, who becomes a student, then a writer and teacher – and then a baker – in Prague. Stoppard spelt out the similarities, and the differences, between them in his introduction to the play: 'He was born where I was born, in Zlín, and left Czechoslovakia for the same reason (Hitler) and at much the same time. But Jan came directly to England as a baby, and returned to Czechoslovakia in 1948, two years after I arrived in England having spent the war years in the Far East.' In the first draft of the play, Jan is called Tomas: 'my given name which, I suppose, is still my name'. (The name Tomas stays in the play: it's given to an offstage English Czech, the 'go to' man for dissidents in England.) In his early notes, he makes an entry: 'T.S. parallels'. This is not an auto-biography, but it was closer than he had come yet to writing one. Carey Perloff, who directed it for A.C.T. in 2008, thought that 'in a way this play is . . . "There but for the grace of God go I."' He said similar things himself: 'I've often thought of writing an autobiography set in a parallel world in which I did go home to Czechoslovakia after the war. But I never started it. Jan . . . is a vestigial gesture towards that.'

His imaginary other Czech self was one of the play's alter egos; another was Havel. Finally he would use the idea first noted down in 1977 of a play about 'alternative lives', his and Havel's: 'Double Men'. Like so many of his plays, *Rock 'n' Roll* is full of parallel lives and duologues of opposing views. The idea of 'alternative lives' made him think again about what *he* would have done in another's circumstances. Would he have spoken out, signed petitions, been imprisoned and lost his job? Would he have been too much of a coward to be a dissident? Would he have 'shut up and eaten shit'? Would he have gone into exile, or found himself unable to write? These life-questions are part of the plot of *Rock 'n' Roll*.

But he always disliked the idea of writing about himself, and he moved the play away from being his own alternative life story: as he put it, 'the degree of self-referential conceit got to me'. He read back into the history of Eastern Europe – which he already knew well. In the late 1980s and early 1990s, Havel had published several collections of his writings: *Letters to Olga*, *Open Letters*, *Disturbing the Peace*, translated by Paul Wilson, one of Stoppard's advisers on the play. Wilson was additionally useful to him because in the early 1970s he had been a member of the Czech rock group the Plastic People of the Universe, whose story is central to the play, and whose manager, Ivan Jirous, he also talked to. As ever, he picked a lot of brains and did a lot of homework. He said to one of his Czech correspondents, the counterculture expert Jaroslav Reidel: 'The trouble is I feel I have to know *everything* (impossible) just to use the tiny bit I need.' It was his usual problem.

He reread essays by Havel which he had been moved by long ago. One of them, the lecture on 'Politics and Conscience', he had delivered himself, standing in for Havel for his honorary degree in Toulouse in 1984. That essay, with its plea for 'anti-political politics', 'politics as practical morality', got into his notes for *Rock 'n' Roll*. He was also reading Havel's more recent essays. In *Disturbing the Peace* (1990), Havel looked back on the origins of Charter 77, which he had written about in his 1976 essay 'The Trial', an important source for Stoppard. He retold the story of how Ivan Jirous introduced him to his 'non-conformist rock group' and how their trial seemed to Havel 'an attack by the totalitarian system on life itself, on the very essence of human freedom and integrity'. He recalled his fellow dissidents dismissing the Plastic People of the Universe as a bunch of long-haired hooligans, but that he had seen that 'the truth was on their side'. The story of how that trial led to the founding of Charter 77, which had gripped Stoppard at the time, became the central pivot of *Rock 'n' Roll*. The point of the story, as Stoppard said, was that 'in the logic of Communism, what the band wasn't interested in and what the band wanted could not in the end be separated . . . What could not be separated were disengagement and dissidence . . . Culture is politics.' What looked like art for art's sake 'became a rebuke to the established structures of society'. The Plastics would not conform, would not change their name, would not cut their hair, and didn't care about politics. They just wanted to be left alone to do their thing. That made them much more threatening to the regime than any dissident. 'Actually', Jan says to an English journalist, 'the Plastic People is not about dissidents.' The journalist replies: 'It's about dissidents. Trust me.'

Rereading Havel gave Stoppard his arguments for the play, and also reinforced his admiration for him. He felt an 'overwhelming sense of humility and pride in having a friend of such bravery, humanity and clear-sighted moral intelligence'. He dedicated the play to Havel, the second time he had done this. Havel, who used the word 'truth' very often in his writings, was acutely conscious of the misuse of words by totalitarian regimes and how easy it was for civilians living under such regimes to lead double lives, giving way to inertia and self-deception. Many of Stoppard's notes for the play mark up such passages in Havel's essays, and some of his characters quote them directly. For instance, Havel's 1987 essay 'Stories and Totalitarianism' describes (in terms very like Czesław Miłosz's *The Captive Mind*) a kind of doublethink where in public life history is replaced by the 'pseudo-history' of heroic anniversaries and mass celebrations, and in private life individuality is suppressed and people become 'nihilised', cautious, helpless and apathetic. 'Pseudo-history' and inertia get into Jan's speeches.

In the late 1960s, there had been a public altercation between Havel and the novelist Milan Kundera about the virtue of signing petitions for political detainees, an argument which Kundera, in 1984, by then self-exiled in France, put into the mouth of his character Tomas in *The Unbearable Lightness of Being*. That was another reason for Stoppard's initially calling his Czech character Tomas. Havel returned to the argument in *Disturbing the Peace*. Kundera, and his character Tomas, think that signing the petition is a form of 'moral exhibitionism'. Havel believed that signing was helpful to the prisoners even if they weren't immediately released. Signing marked the moment at which 'people's civic backbone began to straighten again'. In the play, Jan also uses the phrase 'moral exhibitionism', and starts by arguing Kundera's case against his friend Ferdinand, a dissident who represents Havel's views in the play. But Jan moves from Kundera's to Havel's position, and his change of mind is one of the play's crucial stories. Stoppard had thought of giving Ferdinand the surname 'Vaněk', after one of Havel's recurring characters, only to find that three other playwrights had got there before him.

Rock 'n' Roll, under Havel's influence, is a play which is partly about having the courage of one's convictions and using words truthfully. Jan, who for a time seems to be suppressing his individuality in the interests of a quiet life, speaks of reclaiming the meaning of words and of the need for truth. In England, he says bitterly, 'Words mean what they have always meant. With us, words change meaning to make the theory fit the practice.' He comes to realise that 'we have to begin again with the ordinary meaning of words. Giving new meanings to words is how systems lie to themselves.'

Jan says this to Max, a diehard English Communist academic who feels furiously betrayed by what has happened to the old left. Stoppard read up, for his character, on the twentieth-century history of the British left. He knew of good examples of English intellectuals, like Arnold Kettle or Eric Hobsbawm, who had hung on to their Communist Party membership for life. In an early draft, Max was called Eric – and Eric Hobsbawm became a friend through the play.

Rock 'n' Roll is as much about Britain as it is about Czechoslovakia. When Jan takes exception to Max's attacks on England as a land of political and social injustice, he echoes Stoppard's own impatience. Ostrovsky, talking to him in a bar in Minsk, told him that when he first came to England, he didn't take kindly to 'champagne liberals' telling him how terrible their country was, and how wonderful it must be to live under Communism. Stoppard replied: 'That's what my play is about.'

He often spoke about being embarrassed by the student protests of 1968, the 'slogans and postures of rebellion' in a society which seemed to him, as an adopted Englishman, 'to be the least worst system into which one might have been born – the open liberal democracy whose very essence was the toleration of dissent'. He was well aware that he was 'much more disposed to champion' the country that had taken him in than 'to find fault with it'. But the play is partly about how that democracy is changing.

Freedom of speech, and the state of the media, is a major theme. Lurking inside *Rock 'n' Roll* was the play about newspapers he had been wanting to write again since *Night and Day*. In an interview begun in autumn 2004 for the *British Journalism Review*, he talked about the Fourth Estate. He still felt that the freedom of journalists in the West to tell the truth is the 'freedom which made all the other freedoms possible'. But there is a fierce debate in the play – and in the interview – about whether tabloid cruelty and sensationalism is worth it as the price of a free press. A piece about free speech for *Index on Censorship*, published in 2005 (at a time when hate speech, offence and identity rights, post-9/11, were intensely debated subjects) also coincided with the writing of *Rock 'n' Roll*. It argued that we can't say that free speech is an absolute human right, but we can argue that it is 'good in itself'. He endorses Voltaire's position: 'I disagree with what you say but I will defend to the death your right to say it.' And he gave a personal view:

I was proud to be British before I was British. I arrived in 1946 when I was eight, and that was that. Czechoslovakia, which I couldn't remember, Singapore, which I could barely remember, and India, which I enjoyed, fell away like so many ladders. It was a love affair, and I was not very much older when I first articulated to myself what it was that was the foundation of my anglophilia. It was the Voltairean credo, enshrined in my adoptive country.

He told Adam Thirlwell in the summer of 2004 that he had 'at least two subjects for a play':

[One is] to do with what's called 'the problem of consciousness' . . . And then there is Sappho . . . fragments as an art form . . . it's just I have no idea what the story will be . . . There are three or four things I thought, you know, might justify writing a play. I mean, they're all quite interesting . . . but I have no idea of any kind of narrative or characters . . . I decided to jam them all into the same narrative like cats in a bag fighting.

'I never quite believe I've got a play to write', he told Mark Lawson in 2007, 'unless two or three different plays turn out to be the same one.'

That richness of possibilities could be inhibiting, too. In a spoof interview with himself, done for the Royal Society of Literature in 2004 soon
after they had made him a 'Companion of Literature', their highest honour, he talked to himself about this problem:

> I don't know how I write plays. At the moment (I hope this changes
> by the time you're reading it) I'm failing at getting into a new play,
> and I'm not aware of any technique that might help me. It's like trying
> to pick a lock without thinking about the lock. I have a topic, more
> than one, but I can't find a way in . . . When I was busy failing (this
> has been going on for a couple of months) I was reduced to reading
> my own work, trying to remember how I did it, what I did, how I got
> in, but there didn't seem to be anything to remember. Previously, after
> – sometimes – a lot of preparation . . . I took the cap off my pen and
> suddenly I was in, I was off, like the daring young man on the flying
> trapeze. So it's a sacred mystery, near enough.

In his first notes for the play, he wrote down long lists of keywords and
topics, including:

Rock 'n' Roll
Pan
Consciousness
Theory and Practice/New Left
Sweet Bitter/Sappho
Censorship
Capitalism/Freedom/Market
Hymn to England
James Joyce
Barrett
Memories of hippies
Greed is Good
Plutarch. On the Decline of Oracles.
Vera/Mrs Thatcher

Havel '97

TS parallels

Interrogator?

What happened to England

What happened to Communism

Consciousness and Idealism/Beauty/Love/Sappho

Counter culture/Plastic People

The End of History – 9/11

Press – Privacy

Mystery of Consciousness

Duologues

'Pan is Dead'

'The End of History'

Three of these items, 'Pan', 'Barrett' and 'James Joyce', belonged together. One of his starting points was a photograph of the legendary Syd Barrett, once the wild, glamorous, druggy lead singer and 'dark angel' of the rock group Pink Floyd, dropped by the band in 1968 for being a hopeless mess, who by the 1980s had turned into a recluse called Roger, living with his mum, a bald-headed, middle-aged, heavy-set man taking his groceries home in the basket of a bicycle down a suburban Cambridge street.

Barrett's story gave him 'the shimmer of a play asking to be written' – a play that turned out to be 'partly about Communism, partly about consciousness, slightly about Sappho, and mainly about Czechoslovakia between 1968 and 1990'. He had not been a big fan of Pink Floyd in their heyday. When the photographer Paul Joyce told him, in 1973, that he ought to write a play based on their new album *The Dark Side of the Moon*, he paid no attention, taken up as he was with *Travesties*, and it would be forty years before the suggestion paid off. But he came to know and love their (post-Barrett) music through his sons, in the 1980s. The most embarrassing moment of his life, he once joked, was when their star David Gilmour came to his party and asked him which was his favourite Pink Floyd track:

though he had been listening to them avidly for years, his mind went
blank and he couldn't think of *a single one.*

What struck him about the Barrett photograph was partly its sadness. It
filled him with a powerful sense of mortality, Virgil's '*sunt lacrimae rerum*',
'the tears there are in things'. And it also shocked his settled ideas of identity. We think of ourselves and of other people as somehow continuous,
even through great changes. 'The reason I was so fascinated by Barrett on
his bicycle was that for a mind-wrenching moment he was – literally – a
different person.' This fitted well into a play that was partly about the passage of time and how much people can change – as well as being about rock
music as an expression of freedom and inspiration. Pink Floyd (in their
Syd Barrett days) called their first, 1967, album *The Piper at the Gates of
Dawn.* They took the title from a chapter in Kenneth Grahame's children's
book, *The Wind in the Willows*, in which Pan appears and plays his pipes
to the story's animal characters. So late-nineteenth-century English neo-
paganism got picked up by a 1960s psychedelic, anarchic rock group – and
was picked up again by Stoppard in his play. Rock music works to point up
East/West differences. The rock music of the free West – Pink Floyd, the
Stones, Dylan, the Beatles, the Grateful Dead, the Velvet Underground –
is set against the rock bands of Eastern Europe, as part of the arguments
about freedom. Syd Barrett opens the play, the Plastic People are its offstage heroes, and it ends with the Rolling Stones in Prague.

Pink Floyd's neo-paganism makes a startling link to his fascination
with the erratic survival of classical texts. As part of his research, he consulted a Sappho scholar and went to look at the fragments of papyrus in
Oxford's Sackler Library, all that are left of Sappho's poems. He thought
they looked 'like a box of cornflakes'. Perhaps he would write the play as
fifty fragments which the audience would have to interpret. He made one
of his characters an expert on Sappho. The libido and freedom of rock
music link to the erotic poetry of the distant past. Pan and Sappho tie in
with Syd Barrett and the Stones.

The themes of imagination and inspiration connected, in another leap,
to his interest in consciousness. That interest went back to *Jumpers*, and
would return in *Darkside* and *The Hard Problem*. Now he boned up on

brain science, had some discussions with Richard Dawkins on biological evolution and read Richard Rorty on the mind's relation to reality.
Characters argue about whether there is anything beyond a mechanistic brain function, whether identity consists in individual consciousness,
whether we have such a thing as a soul. And the question of individualism
came round again to politics. Carey Perloff noted that 'what he is really
interested in is our relationship as individual people to enormous shifts in
history'. With so many ideas jostling for precedence, he had to warn himself in his notes to keep focused: '*Remember what this play is about – it's
not about everything*'.

He started the first drafts of *Rock 'n' Roll* on the back of his typed script
of *His Dark Materials*, and worked on it for almost two years. In August
2005 he sent it to Trevor Nunn, who was going to direct it, and who told
him it was 'absolutely sensational'. By November 2005 it was done. It went
into rehearsal in April 2006, had its first preview on 3 June 2006 and its
first night on 14 June.

2006 was the tenth anniversary year of his mother's death. For a time,
he avoided saying that her death had enabled him to acknowledge his
Czechness. But, talking to Mark Lawson in an interview for his seventieth
birthday, he said: 'I wonder whether her death somehow gave me permission to be Czech again . . . I probably began to feel more Czech since
then . . . Somewhere working within me quite deep was the sense that I am
Czech, I was Czech, I'm English now but I haven't stopped being Czech –
and that's that.' Teasing Lawson for having elicited this confession, he said
– very Englishly: 'It's a fair cop, guv.'

Rock 'n' Roll is a time-travelling play about change, optimism and disillusion, hope and regret, and the possibility of individual happiness in the
teeth of historical circumstances. Dates pop up like headlines at the top
of each scene, with a music track which fits that scene and that moment.
Scenes change abruptly between Cambridge and Prague, and from one
date to another, through a series of 'smash cuts', abrupt changes of set and
lighting. (That was what was left of the original idea of fifty Sapphic fragments.) In Act One, the 'smash cuts' jump through almost every year from

1968 to 1976. Act Two starts after a five-year gap and jumps from 1982 to 1987 to 1990, when the characters reminisce about the late 1960s – so it feels as if we have circled round.

It starts in 1968 with a misfit rock star singing to a teenage flower child over a garden wall in Cambridge; it ends with the soundtrack of the Rolling Stones playing Prague in 1990, with the same girl, now in her thirties, in the audience. In between these dates, the history of twentieth-century Communism and its effects come at us through the lives of two Czech friends in Prague and an English academic family in Cambridge.

The flower child is Esme, daughter of the Cambridge philosopher Max Morrow and his wife Eleanor, who teaches classics, and who is dying of cancer. Max, combative, loud and fierce, is the Communist who still believes in a workers' state and a socialist future, in a theory that fits the practice: 'From each according to their abilities, to each according to his needs.' What happened under Stalin, what happened in Hungary or what is happening now, with the tanks rolling into Prague, shouldn't, in his view, overshadow the essential value of the *Communist Manifesto*. The Communist defeat of Nazism and fascism should never be forgotten: 'Was there anything more unbelievable, more heroic, in my lifetime?' Max says in an early draft of the play. He believes in collectivity: 'To be human is to be joined together. Society!' It's the collective mind, not individual consciousnesses, that interests him. He marks the end point, a hundred years on, of the utopian socialists of *Coast*. And he's a good example of Stoppard making a persuasive, even sympathetic character, out of what he himself thinks of as untenable opinions.

Max thinks that cognition, experience, bodily sensations and feelings are 'so many neuron-firings whizzing about the cortex' and that there is no such thing as 'consciousness' beyond that mechanical process. But Eleanor knows different. Agonised with fear and pain, she is there to tell him, for what's left of her life, that there is a 'self', a consciousness, that is 'undiminished'. 'I'm exactly who I've always been. *I am not my body.* My body is nothing without *me*, that's the truth of it.' Eleanor's rage, desire, horror at what is happening to her body and terror of death are more powerful than any political discussion.

Eleanor teaches her students (one of them a sexy, clever Czech called Lenka, who has designs on Max) to translate Sappho. These tiny fragments, which have miraculously survived through time, speak of love, desire and jealousy; the voice of the poet conjures up Eros, the 'sweet-bitter' god of love, from centuries ago. Sappho makes us think about inspiration – something beyond Max's idea of the mechanical brain. We used to call it the Muse. Whatever we call it now, it's where poetry and music come from. Sappho's erotic fragments link to the music of desire that fills the play, from Syd Barrett to the Stones. When the beautiful, mysterious rock star sings to Esme his haunting version of Joyce's poem 'Lean out of the window, Goldenhair', to her he seems like 'the Great God Pan'. But 'Pan', in this case, ends up as an old baldy with his groceries on a bike. In the play's last scene, another classics tutorial is taking place, in which we hear a translation of Plutarch's famous legend about the vanishing of the old Gods. An Egyptian helmsman calls out from his boat the news to the Greeks that 'the Great God Pan is dead'; lamentation and wailing are heard from the shore. But perhaps, the play romantically suggests, Pan lives on in the pagan recklessness, anarchy and passion of rock music.

The most dedicated rock 'n' roll fan in the play is Max's summer-school visitor from Prague, Jan, who comes to study with him and falls in love with the whole family. He is given Stoppard's own early memories.

I love England. I would like to live for ever in my last English schoolboy summer. It was exceptional, you know? 1947, endless summer days, I collected birds' eggs, and the evenings so long you couldn't sleep for the light, listening to the farmer's boy calling the cattle home. And the winter was amazing that year. A Christmas card winter. My mother knew all the songs. She baked *svestkove buchty* for all my friends, and sang 'We'll Meet Again' in a terrible accent over the washtub. I was happy.

When he says goodbye to people, Jan always says: 'Some sunny day'. Vera Lynn, the English countryside, family Christmas: it's all part of the nostalgia he feels for the free country which took them in. He won't accept

Max's attack on English injustices – compared with his own country, they aren't worth consideration. England is his ideal. (Their duologues, Max roaring and fierce, Jan quiet and ironic, might be a bit like arguing with Pinter on this subject.) Jan – unlike Max – can see the funny side of all this. And his 'hymn to England' gets a number of laughs from audiences, especially on the words 'philistine', 'superior' and, most of all, 'moderately':

> If I was English I wouldn't care if Communism in Czechoslovakia reformed itself into a pile of pig shit. To be English would be my luck. I would be moderately enthusiastic and moderately philistine, and a good sport. I would be kind to foreigners in a moderately superior way, and also to animals except for the ones I kill, and I would live a decent life, like most English people.

When Jan decides to go back to Czechoslovakia after the invasion, instead of staying on in Cambridge, because the tanks have rolled in and he is worried about his mother, Max is bitterly disappointed in him; he thinks he's a feeble traitor to the cause of true Communist values. The stand-off between them is personal as well as political; it's like a failed father–son relationship. There is weight on both sides: Stoppard gives as much power and conviction to Max's arguments as to Jan's. And the relationship between them is more complicated than it seems.

It turns out that Jan isn't quite the eager young Communist Max takes him for. He doesn't care about politics much; he cares about England, intellectual study, his mum and his records. His trip to Cambridge that summer was paid for by the Czech authorities in return for a dossier on the well-known English communist Max Morrow. When he returns to Prague, his precious rock 'n' roll records are confiscated and he is interrogated. He gets his records back in exchange for giving some rather vague information on Max. But he is not the only one spying. We find out, later, that Max too has been a source of information to the Czech authorities, and he too has been asked to spy on Jan by the secret police.

Jan starts out as a hopeful socialist who believes in Dubček as a reform Communist. Once back in occupied Prague, he still thinks that reform will continue under Husák's 'government of normalisation'. Unlike his friend Ferdinand, he takes the new situation lightly. The play catches the 'bittersweet' black humour of the occupied Czechs, something Stoppard knew well from his time there in the 1970s, from his friends Havel and Pavel Kohout, and from reading Kundera. *Rock 'n' Roll* is often painful, but it also has a bleak, dark playfulness. The Interrogator says to Jan: 'We're supposed to know what's going on inside people. That's why it's the Ministry of the Interior.' Jan tells Max that the Plastic People are treated as 'undesirables'. Undesirable how? asks Max. 'Their songs are morbid, they dress weird, they look like they're on drugs, and one time they sacrificed a chicken on stage, but otherwise it's a mystery.' Max explains in 1990 why he's given up on *Marxism Today*: 'It's not so much the Euro-Communism. In the end it was the mail order gifts thing. I couldn't take the socks with the little hammers and sickles on them.' Jan has the chance of going into exile in Frankfurt – 'but I don't know . . . German rock bands . . .'

At first Jan doesn't realise how bad it is going to get. Gentle, ironical, thoughtful and courteous, he just wants to get on with his own life – and to look after his mother. (Stoppard gave a note to Rufus Sewell, as Jan, pointing out a similarity between Jan and Syd Barrett: 'You and Syd love your mothers.') But Ferdinand knows this is the end of individual freedom. Years of persecution, from the petty to the catastrophic, teach Jan the hard way that Ferdo is right. In Jan's first interrogation (straight out of *Every Good Boy*), we see more clearly than he does that the totalitarian system involves gradual, almost unconscious compromise. The interrogator invites Jan to eat a biscuit even though he doesn't really want one: but hey, eating a biscuit is no big deal. At least, not at first.

In every scene after that we see his situation getting worse (and his hair getting longer): he is spied on, forced out of work and, like many of his friends, put in prison; his precious record collection is smashed to pieces – just to show him what they can do – and he spends years working in a bakery. (Kundera's Tomas, a surgeon, spends his years under 'normalisation' working as a window cleaner; Havel and his fictional character Vanek worked in a brewery.) Gradually Jan changes his mind and his life. He starts by thinking: 'They think they're using you, but really you're using them.' In the end he finds out the reality of 'who was using who'.

Others change, too. In 1971, Max visits Prague for a philosophy conference (like the philosopher in *Professional Foul*). He and Jan have a bitter argument over the realities of Soviet Communism: Jan is now standing up to him. In 1977, Max is back in Prague, being urged to spy on Jan by the secret police; he declines. The balance shifts, too, in Jan's arguments with Ferdo, moving from Jan's Kundera-like refusal to sign petitions to his realisation that the trial of the Plastics means he should sign up to Charter 77 and commit himself, Havel-style, to opposition. In doing so he finds a kind of calm sense of independence, or authenticity.

Rock 'n' roll is at the heart of the play's political argument. In the capitalist West, in the late 1960s and early 1970s, when Stoppard and his generation were in love with Anglo-American rock music, it seemed part of the 'liberation' of the times. (To an old Commie like Max, that time was, politically, a wasted opportunity, middle-class social libertarianism instead of a workers' revolt.) In Eastern Europe, those cultural freedoms, harder to access, were desired and imitated. 'Generation Jeans' (the title of a Belarus Free Theatre play) loved the music of the Anglo-American bands. Rock groups in Prague, or Minsk, played their own punky, grotty, anarchic versions of the Stones and Frank Zappa and the Grateful Dead.

Under a totalitarian regime, as Jan comes to realise, there is no such thing as living outside the system. The Plastic People's indifference to politics is a threat to the authorities because they are 'uncontrollable', like the old Gods, Pan or Eros. 'They're unbribable,' says Jan. 'They're coming from somewhere else, from where the Muses come from. They're not heretics. They're pagans.' The speech goes straight into the Stones playing 'It's Only Rock 'n' Roll'. In the first draft, the argument is even more emphatic:

The Plastics and the tribe of drop-outs, rockers, punks, poets, piss-artists . . . they just don't care at all. They're not heretics. They're pagans. They believe in strange gods. They reach back to something before politics, before the polis, the deep hidden springs of the earliest consciousness where singing came from, and Eros and Dionysus were as real as nature. They are an affront to the very basis of society, which is at war with consciousness.

'Or something like that!' he added to himself at the end of this draft. And 'something like that' is at the heart of the play. After Jan's record collection has been trashed and he finally signs up to Charter 77, he says, jokingly and consolingly to Ferdo: 'Hey, Ferdo, it's only rock 'n' roll.' That ends Act One. Stoppard told Sewell he thought it was one of his best curtain lines ever.

Act Two starts in 1987. Eleanor is long dead. Her daughter Esme was last seen saying a fond goodbye to Jan – she offered him her virginity as a parting gift, but he took her Velvet Underground record instead: 'How bourgeois of him,' scoffed Max. A teenage runaway from home, she left school with two O Levels, had a baby, lived in a commune and got married to the English journalist, Nigel, who is now with someone else. (Esme's character, sweet-natured, generous, anxious, truthful, unworldly and unintellectual, has a recognisable trace of Fiona Stoppard.) Esme's teenage daughter Alice has inherited Eleanor's brains: she is a clever classics student.

Max too has changed. After Eleanor's death, he had an affair with Lenka – grief takes unaccountable forms, he says. He is seventyish, unfit and as grumpy as ever. The old bruiser has finally left the Party, utterly disappointed with Labour's move to the centre and with the sell-out of the workers to Thatcherism. 'The working-class vote could make this a socialist country *permanently*, and they voted in millions for the most reactionary Tory government in modern times.' In the penultimate scene, set in 1990, which brings most of the characters together, Jan returns to England to show Max his secret police files. Only now has he realised that it was Max who got him out of prison and helped him get work – and only now does Max tell him that he did so because Esme was always urging him to. Only now does Jan tell Max that he had been sent to spy on him in 1968. In his own rough manner, Max gives him the forgiveness he has come to seek. Neither of them is all good or all bad.

The reunion between Jan and Max is not the climax of the play, though we might have expected it to be. Jan's return coincides with Nigel's new

Another small commission, which he clearly enjoyed, was a Toronto theatre director's idea for 'Three Plays in a Day'. Three playwrights were given the same opening line and twelve hours later the company put on the resulting twenty-minute plays. Stoppard, asked to provide the opening line, gave them this: 'Don't anybody move – there was an asp in that basket of figs and the little bastard is somewhere in this room!'

His work was continually in demand. A sample of what his agents were dealing with in the summer of 2007 included (quite apart from multiple productions of *Rock 'n' Roll*) *Heroes* opening in Australia, New Zealand and Florida, a new French translation of *The Real Inspector Hound*, *Rosencrantz and Guildenstern* in Hebrew in Tel Aviv and in a puppet production by a Polish company, *Coast* in Rome and Japan, a Spanish *Arcadia* in Barcelona, *Every Good Boy* coming to Salt Lake City and *The Real Thing* done by a youth theatre group in Tokyo.

He was travelling too. One trip, in May 2007, was to Brno, for an honorary degree from the Janáček Academy of Music and Performing Arts, where he spoke movingly about his parents (and about the relationship between 'virtue and aesthetics'). He said he had been thinking about them a lot, and knew they would have been proud of him on this day: 'I am here, honoured by the city which sent my father out into the world as a young doctor, so . . . this seemed to me a good moment to . . . try to convey something about him which might last a little longer as a memory of a memory among the stones of Brno.'

There were journeys, also, to Prague and to Russia, to the States (often), to Sydney for a guest-of-honour interview at the Opera House in December 2007, to Dublin for a Writers' Festival in June 2008, to Brazil for a week in July 2008 for the Paraty Literary Festival (founded by the publisher Liz Calder), to Mick Jagger's birthday party in St Petersburg, where the Stones were on tour, and to numerous Belarus events in Europe. In May 2008 he went to Tel Aviv University to receive a prize from the Dan David Foundation. Looking elegantly ruffled, wearing pale-coloured linens and cream shoes, running his hands through his untrimmed mane of grey hair, and with a very bad cold and cough, he performed his usual riffs on 'clarity of utterance', on how everything changes in rehearsal, and how,

Working with Mick Jagger on *Enigma*, September 1995.

Jacky Matthews in July 1997.

With brother Peter and their guide, Emil Máčel (*l*), outside the family home in Zlín, May 1998.

Outside the theatre where Ed Stoppard was playing Hamlet, 2006.

The Invention of Love, 1997, Paul Rhys and John Wood as young and old A. E. Housman.

Rock 'n' Roll, Faber cover; Sinéad Cusack and Alice Eve in *Rock 'n' Roll*, Royal Court Theatre, 2016.

Stoppard's *Cherry Orchard*, 2009, with Sinéad Cusack as Liubov Ranevskaya and Simon Russell Beale as Lopakhin.

The Coast of Utopia, Russian style, 2007.

The Coast of Utopia, English cartoon, 2002.

With agent Kenneth Ewing at his retirement party, 28 June 2007.

Tony Award winner, 10 June 2007.

Among the O.M.s at Buckingham Palace, 20 May 2009.

In Tokyo, meeting Japanese
actors, for the Praemium
Imperiale Prize,
22 October 2009.

Cartoon-fodder:
Private Eye, 2017.

Visiting the refugee camp
The Jungle at Calais, with
others, 23 February 2016.

H. D. HERNEMAN

"Look at the Joneses pretending to get all the jokes in a Stoppard play"

Tom and Sabrina on their wedding day, Dorset, 7 June 2014.

The Hard Problem at the Wilma Theatre, Philadelphia, with Sarah Gliko and Michael Pedicin, January 2016.

Leopoldstadt, Wyndham's Theatre, January 2020: Scene One, the company.

Stoppard during *Leopoldstadt* rehearsals, 19 January 2020.

when you are writing, 'you make your own luck': 'when something works out really well, you don't actually feel clever, you feel lucky'. And he talked movingly – as he did freely now – about his mother's death releasing him to speak out about his identity. But: 'I don't ever quite understand myself to what degree I feel Czech.'

At home, he accepted the Critics' Circle award for Distinguished Services to Literature and the *Sunday Times* award for Literary Excellence. His work continued for the Belarus Free Theatre, and he joined human rights protest meetings and marches about the war and the refugee crisis in Darfur. His public platforms weren't predictable: in July 2007 he joined a session on 'Theatre in Revolt' for the Marxism 2007 festival, and in November 2008 he shared a platform with Derek Walcott at the Graduate Centre in New York on 'Cultural Power'. Two well-received revivals – of *Hapgood* in Birmingham, with Josie Lawrence, in April 2008, and of *Every Good Boy* at the National in January 2009, with Toby Jones and Joseph Millson – involved him in rehearsals and publicity. The coverage talked about how well these two 'Cold War' plays had lasted.

In 2007, his personal life altered. Since 1990, Sinéad Cusack had been searching for the boy she gave up for adoption in 1967. (She waited to start looking until he was an adult.) After a change in the Irish law in 2005 which created a register for questing parents and adoptees, she was at last reunited with her son, Richard Boyd Barrett, a left-wing, anti-war Irish politician. From 2005, Cusack spent as much time as she could with him in Dublin and worked with him on his 2007 election campaign.

The effect of finding him was, as she put it, 'seismic'. She had lived all her adult life with feelings of guilt and loss. The reunion took her back to times of sadness, but it also felt like a second chance. She wanted to get to know him and to integrate him into her life and with her family (who had always known about her quest). It was a time of intense joy. Her dear friend Bob Crowley remembered her proudly saying to him, at a matinee of *Rock 'n' Roll*, 'meet my boy!' But there was also great stress. She had her marriage and her two younger sons to look after, and her work to do, and her relationship with Stoppard. She was pulled in contrary directions; the 'tissue of her life' felt stretched too thin. The time that she would have been spending in France with Stoppard she now needed to spend in Dublin. She felt that she was letting him down, and that she could not be for him the person he needed her to be. And so their relationship came to an end. She saw that he was bewildered and sad. But from his point of view what happened was natural, and, he said, not painful. He understood it entirely: he could see that at this point 'the love of her life was Richard'.

Her marriage continued, and so did their friendship. Her birthdays stayed in his appointment diary (to be joined by Boyd Barrett's). He sent gifts for her first nights, she came to his parties, they went on working together and they remained close. A while later, he asked if he could draw, very indirectly, on her search for her son for *The Hard Problem*. She trusted him to do this honourably, and readily agreed. She was deeply sad, over many years, about losing him from the heart of her life. But her feeling for him remained. It was, as she put it, a vivid strand of colour, from 1984, when they first met, and for the rest of her life. 'The shadings changed in all those years' but the emotion never went away. It was, simply, love; in her words, 'extraordinary and wonderful'.

The house at Lacoste was sold in 2007. This was something of a relief. He told Isabel that he was glad not to have Provence any more. He wasn't spending enough time there, and was happy not to be getting the kind of phone calls that went: '*Monsieur, le jardin est tombé dans la rue!*'

There were other losses and changes. His agent and friend since 1962, Kenneth Ewing, died on 14 April 2008. Mainly retired by then, he had still been living, with Gordon Dickerson, in the big house in Clapham where the first-night party for *Rosencrantz* had been held in April 1967. Stoppard gave the address at the memorial on 19 June, at St Paul's Church in Covent Garden. The service included a scene from *Rosencrantz*, performed by Edward Petherbridge and John McEnery, a scene from *Noises Off* (years ago, Stoppard had sent Frayn to Ewing) and readings by another client of Ewing's, Tony Harrison. Then they all went across the road and raised a glass to him at the Garrick Club.

Stoppard said in his speech that he needed to guard against hyperbole, 'because Kenneth never gushed and never exaggerated'. Sometimes he had wished Kenneth might have gushed a little, and given him the praise he was craving. But for Ewing, 'accuracy was morality'. His avoidance of proclamations was his form of 'courtesy'. What Stoppard most associated with him was an expression of 'bemusement', as when they drove around Los Angeles after *Shakespeare in Love* won the Oscar: 'I've had dentists who were more showbiz than Kenneth.' (Though he also associated him with a keen happiness in travel and history, as when they went to visit the battlefield of Waterloo together.) That unexaggerated manner cloaked a person of wisdom, reason, honesty and kindness. 'His kindness defined how others dealt with him, personally and professionally.'

At the end of Ewing's life, an ugly break-up was going on at Peters Fraser and Dunlop, which led in 2007 to the splitting away of Stoppard's team – Rose Cobbe, St John Donald, Anthony Jones and the literary agent Pat Kavanagh (who placed his printed pieces) – to found a new agency, United Agents, in 2008. They took with them many of the authors who had been with PFD, including Stoppard. He was steely about protecting his interests, but took a regretful and dignified tone on what was a painful situation. In his leaving letter to the PFD management, he wrote: 'I won't deny that I am saddened: I believe it's 47 years since I joined Kenneth in his tiny office at the top of 91 Regent Street.'

Pat Kavanagh, Julian Barnes's wife, died in October 2008. Stoppard took care to be in touch with him, and they became closer friends over the next few years. Barnes noted, of their meetings: 'All the time he is with you, whether he is talking or you are talking, he gives you his entire attention and never looks other than at you.' The affectionate, humorous relationship between them is nicely captured in an account by Barnes, in his diary, of a lunch Stoppard gave on 16 July 2010 for him, Arkady Ostrovsky, the film and TV producer Susanna White and the then Czech ambassador Michael Žantovský and his wife Jana.

> Lunch at Tom Stoppard's 'penthouse apartment at luxury Chelsea Harbour' (i.e. instead of getting planes overhead like the rest of us, he gets regular very loud helicopters landing at the nearby pad) . . . He offers us white burgundy or pink champagne. After a bit, Mick Jagger's

name comes up. 'This white burgundy comes from Mick,' says Tom with that air of mild puzzlement. 'He sent it to me for Christmas.' An hour or so passes. There is cheese. 'Would anyone like some claret?' I say, 'Only if it comes from Paul McCartney.' He says, 'You won't get any for that remark.' We have claret – 98 Mouton. After a bit, musingly, he says, 'Philippine de Rothschild sent me three bottles of this, I don't know why.' He is, of course, wonderful: utterly courteous, bringing everyone in, and (for a good change) preferring general conversation round a table of 8 to the usual 4 × 2 gabble. Still smokes like a chimney at 73.

In his seventies, newer friendships, as with Barnes, were set against the loss of old friends. Harold Pinter died on 24 December 2008. Their friendship had been continuous and strong. When Pinter got the Nobel Prize (hardly ever awarded to dramatists) in October 2005, there was no tinge of jealousy in Stoppard's reaction – unlike some other playwrights, Richard Eyre noted. Antonia Fraser, though, has a mischievous story she likes to tell about this. The week before the Nobel was announced, Pinter, who was very unwell, had been in Dublin for a celebration at the Gate Theatre for his seventy-fifth birthday. While there, he had taken a bad fall and injured himself. Stoppard had been away, and, when he got back, he heard the news of the fall before the news of the prize. He rang up Antonia, very concerned: 'Antonia, I've just heard the news and I'm horrified, I'm absolutely horrified, I just thought I should ring you straight away.' Antonia said: 'Oh, are you *very* upset?'

After Pinter got the Nobel, the journalist Christopher Hitchens described him as a 'thuggish bigmouth' of dubious artistic merit. Stoppard, who liked Hitchens and usually read him with interest, wrote him a long letter. He made it clear, as he always did when he had an argument with someone he respected, that this was not a falling-out but a disagreement. (When Hitchens died young in 2011, Stoppard went to his memorial in New York, alongside Martin Amis.) He told him that in the Stoppard family all new plays had to pass what was called 'the William test'. If a play couldn't overcome Will's general indifference to the theatre, then it failed. And the biggest success he ever had with Will was *The Birthday Party*. What could that mean about Pinter? He knew he couldn't just say to Hitchens, Pinter's plays are masterpieces, 'and if you don't get it, bad luck'. He needed to make the critical argument. So, Stoppard told Hitchens, here it is: When he first saw *Godot* or *The Birthday Party* (unlike when he first saw *Look Back in Anger*), they were 'utterly bewildering'. Pinter – and Beckett – weren't like the other playwrights of their time. Pinter did 'something amazing'.

> It was – at the time – counter-intuitive to see that a shortfall of information, rather than surplus, is what can make theatre hold up the mirror, and that the effect is dramatic – funny, disturbing, fascinating . . . and not because the writer is withholding information tactically, but because he doesn't know the answers. Not knowing the answers is the modus vivendi . . . It opened up a different street.

He had said similar things about Pinter in public and would do so again. But that he took the trouble to send a four-page handwritten letter in Pinter's defence shows how much he meant to him.

Two days after Pinter's death, he wrote Antonia Fraser a moving letter. They are the words of a fellow writer, a loyal friend and a kind consoler.

> I hardly understood my own dependence on Harold's existence, I miss him so much now, and feel so sad at the wrench of your loss. It was clear that your love for each other was his anchorage for half his life, so we all owe you something too . . . There has never been a death near me which caused so much commiseration between so many people, in phone calls and textings and encounters, some in tears and all in shock, in several countries.

A year later, he wrote a poem in humorous and admiring memory of Pinter, titled 'Another Time' – the title of one of Pinter's own (notoriously short) verses. One of Stoppard's rare published poems – there were many unpublished ones – it used the word 'pinteresque', but had a lot in it, too, that was Stoppardian.

another time
> he was rehearsing
> he said any time you're passing
> drop in do any time
> so one day when I was passing
> well not exactly passing
> but yes there they were rehearsing
> he and friends of mine
> at the bottom of the long slope
> of stalls and I at the top
> so naturally they stopped
> looked up and looked up the slope
> oh I say I hope
> into the glare of his glasses
> hello you remember the occasion
> of your open invitation if I were passing
> well I was passing
> though not exactly passing
> so anyway how's it how's it
> so how's it all going Harold
> he let me have both barrels
>
> *was it? was it?*
> was it what for fucksakes
> oh open yes I see yes
> how very pinteresque
> but haroldly he broke for tea
> for he was always kind to me
> I wish I'd brought a cake.

Watching him working with the Russians on the Moscow production of *Coast* in October 2007, Nina Raine noted that they had difficulties with the interplay between 'laughter and lament, poking fun and pathos' in

Stoppard's work. 'Which requires . . . considerable dexterity of tone. *Just like Chekhov.*' She was amused by the fact that this Chekhovian quality in Stoppard was particularly difficult to get across to Russian actors.

While *Coast* was playing in Russia in the late 2000s, Stoppard went back to Chekhov. His next works for the stage after *Rock 'n' Roll* were two new versions: *Ivanov* for Michael Grandage in September 2008 and, a year after that, *The Cherry Orchard* for Sam Mendes and his new Bridge Project, a company which mixed American and British actors and played at the Old Vic and at the Brooklyn Academy of Music.

Grandage asked him to do *Ivanov* four years after their work together on Pirandello's *Henry IV*. The Donmar Theatre under his regime had become so successful that Grandage had decided to move the company for a season into the West End, at Wyndham's Theatre, keeping the same policy of cheap seats all through the house and new productions of foreign plays. He needed big star names, and Stoppard's was one of the few which were, as he put it, 'selling points in their own right'. He matched that by casting Kenneth Branagh as Ivanov and an intense Tom Hiddleston as the play's puritanical young doctor.

Ivanov was Chekhov's first full-length play, written in his twenties, a flawed and awkward tragicomedy of the 'superfluous man', with dying wife, tiresome neighbours, nagging doctor, debts, self-loathing, a young girl who thinks she loves him, and no purpose to his life. It's an early version of the theme of the self-lacerating, ineffectual landowner, which he does more richly and subtly later in *Uncle Vanya*. Using a literal translation by the Russian scholar Helen Rappaport, Stoppard made a sharp comedy out of it, praised by critics as biting, punchy and witty. As with his 1997 *Seagull*, he didn't want his Chekhov to be gently melancholy. Ivanov's perpetual gloom is given phrases like 'I'm a bag of nerves', 'down in the dumps', 'it's all getting you down', 'I feel I've eaten the wrong kind of mushroom'. He describes himself as 'a sort of hangdog parody of a literary cliché – the superfluous man!' Every so often the characters spoke directly to the audience, breaking the Chekhovian fourth wall. When Ivanov is going on endlessly and repetitively in the last act to his friend Lebedev, Stoppard had Lebedev interject comments and then, exasperated and bored with this endless diatribe, leave the stage and come back, while Ivanov moans on, not even noticing that he's left. It was cheeky, he thought – but would be perfectly realistic 'in an Ayckbourn play (or a Stoppard)'. Grandage thought this very bold, and noted Stoppard's delight at this wheeze, which got big laughs.

Stoppard was less delighted, in rehearsal, by Branagh's wild inventiveness. Grandage was used to Branagh, and knew that he was in the tradition of actor-managers who liked to make their own decisions. He also knew that Branagh had unerring theatrical common sense and would find out quickly when something didn't work. So at moments in rehearsal when Ivanov did a whirling dervish dance all through a long speech, or hid under a table in tears, Grandage was less perturbed than Stoppard, prepared to wait until Branagh would know whether to drop that experiment or keep it. By the first preview, Stoppard was won over. He turned to Grandage and said: 'You've got to hand it to him, haven't you.'

Grandage particularly remembered two moments during their work together. At the end of one rehearsal (in the Jerwood Space, south of the river), when only he and Stoppard were left in the room, the door opened and in came a very frail Harold Pinter, who was working in the rehearsal room next door (with Rupert Goold on his production of *No Man's Land*). Grandage sat and watched while the two great men, who he could see had enormous affection for each other, talked about their day: 'How's it going for you in your room?' It was the summer of 2008, a few months before Pinter's death. He remembered vividly, too, Stoppard's words to the company, before the play opened, words said, as Grandage put it, 'without a whiff of arrogance': 'As a seventy-year-old playwright who has learnt a thing or two, I hope I can help this young playwright at the start of his career.'

The last of Stoppard's three Chekhovs, *The Cherry Orchard*, was done for an exciting new organisation. Sam Mendes set up the Bridge Project with a company which included Simon Russell Beale, Rebecca Hall and Ethan Hawke, to do *Cherry Orchard* and *The Winter's Tale* in their first season. Sinéad Cusack, a passionate Chekhovian, was longing to play Ranevskaya. Mendes originally had Judi Dench in mind, whom he had directed in 1989 in Michael Frayn's version. But the thought of combining Cusack as Ranevskaya and a Stoppard version was highly appealing. And it was a pleasure for Stoppard to 'do' Ranevskaya for her, as he had done Arkadina for Kendal in his *Seagull*. Cusack relished the 'sprightly' word-play of his version. 'He gives actors the gift of his gift for language,' she would say. As with *Ivanov*, he worked from a literal by Helen Rappaport. He wrote it from March 2008 onwards; rehearsals started in the autumn. The production went first to Brooklyn, opening on 3 January 2009 (the day after Pinter's funeral), and then to the Old Vic in May 2009.

It seems almost uncanny that he didn't work on *The Cherry Orchard* until after *The Coast of Utopia*, so close in tone is Chekhov's student revolutionary Trofimov to the utopian idealists in Stoppard's play, so 'Chekhovian' in feeling are parts of *Coast*. But by 'Chekhovian' Stoppard did not mean melancholy or elegiac. He thought of *The Cherry Orchard* as a comedy. The merchant Lopakhin, who will take over the estate where his family were serfs, has a comical bullish energy about him, and is also harshly self-critical. He calls himself 'an ignoramus and a clod' and has no time for sentiment or repining:

Gaev: I'm fifty-one years old, hard to believe.
Lopakhin: Yes, time passes.
Gaev: What?
Lopakhin: Time. I said it passes.

Everyone's silliness is played up. The language is sharp, quick and collo-quial. The manservant Yasha, full of scorn for the peasants around him, is in Stoppard's version a smart, modern act: 'You can see for yourself – this country is so backward, and the *people!*' 'Peasants . . . they're just a bit thick.' The bumbling, unfortunate clerk, Yepikhodov, known in most pro-ductions as 'Twenty-two Misfortunes', is here called 'Catastrophe Corner'. Russell Beale, who played a magnificently angry, resentful Lopakhin, half in love with Ranevskaya but determined to take his opportunity, thought it was the most cruel, unfeeling Chekhov he had ever been in. To him, these damaged characters seemed only to live in the moment: their emotions lead nowhere, nothing has any consequence. 'They don't give a fuck about the cherry orchard, not really.' But with all that harshness, Stoppard's *Cherry Orchard* is also moving, especially with performances like Russell Beale's, Rebecca Hall as Liubov Ranevskaya's stoical daughter Varya, and most of all Cusack's radiant, brittle, childish, imperious, self-deceiving Ranevskaya.

Here, she has just come back with her brother to the estate where she grew up, and where her little boy was drowned. In the next breath, she will have moved on, volatile and contradictory, to another mood. But it's in such moments that Stoppard's Chekhov could – like his own comedies – have heartbreak in it.

> Gaev: The orchard is all in white. Do you remember it, Liuba? – The long avenue as far as you can see, straight as a ribbon, do you remember how it shines on moonlit nights? You haven't forgotten?
>
> Liubov (*looking out of the window at the orchard*): Oh, it's my childhood come back! – innocent days! – when I slept in the nursery and woke with happiness every morning and looked out at the garden. It was just the same, nothing has changed. (*Laughs with joy.*) White everywhere . . . my orchard! . . . Oh, if only I could lose the weight of this stone I carry in my breast. If only I could forget everything up to now.
>
> Gaev: And now the orchard is going to be sold to pay our debts, hard to believe.
>
> Liubov: Look! – there's our darling mama, dressed in white, walking in the orchard! (*Laughs with joy.*)
>
> Gaev: Where?
>
> Varya: Bless you, mama.
>
> Liubov: She's gone. It only looked like it for a minute. There, look, on the right, by the turning towards the summer house, that branch bending over like a woman in a white dress.

32

Parade's End

The only thing that matters is to do good work.

Well, there'll be no more parades for *that* regiment. It held out to the last man, but you were him.

By 2007, when Stoppard was seventy, he had seven grandchildren; before long there would be eight. His sons were in their mid-thirties and early forties. Oliver, still living with Marie in Norfolk and working as a postman, had two daughters, Catherine and Sarah, born in the mid-2000s. Barny, who tried the restaurant business and then went into post-production film work, had two children by his partner Ashleigh, Eden, born in 1999 (the oldest Stoppard grandchild), and Brodie, born in 2001. Will was a manager in the music business; in 2004 he married Linzi, a model and a rock violinist, and they would have a baby, Poppy, some years later. Ed, who married Amie Stamp in 2001, had three daughters, Esmé, born in 2004, and the twins, Maggie and Evie, born in 2006.

He was a benign and willing grandfather, though (as when the boys were young) he didn't get involved, hands on, in his grandchildren's playtime. But he would go round or visit at a weekend and spend tea-time and bathtime with the children, and they would ask him to read to them, which he liked doing. Occasionally he'd be asked to babysit; on one occasion, as they left him to it, Ed and Amie asked if he would be all right. He gave them a look, as if to say: 'What do you mean, of course I'll be all right! Give me a break!' Birthdays were never forgotten. Financial help and support were always there, for all his sons and their families, as for his sister Fiona and her two children. When Oliver was having personal difficulties, which eventually involved the break-up of his marriage – though he then settled into a happier new relationship and second marriage – his father regularly visited him in Norfolk. He spoke on the phone to his sons all the time. Ed and Will had used Chelsea Harbour as their base for years, before they married. Many affectionate, humorous, grateful notes were sent over the years from the sons to their father, like a birthday card Oliver gave him, probably in the early 2000s, covered in quotations about fishing: 'You will search far to find a fisherman to admit that a taste for fishing, like a taste for liquor, must be governed lest it come to possess its possessor'; 'Angling may be said to be so like mathematics that it can never fully be learnt.'

'I worry about them all,' he said once in interview, sounding rather like his mother. 'Some parents take it as an axiom that their child will be the best pianist or cook. To my discredit, I'm sceptical.' But this meant that their successes delighted him. Sometimes there were tensions, as with all grown-up children and their parents. Will knew his father was wary of nepotism, and that even if he opened doors for them, it was up to them what they made of that. With Will and Barny's involvements in the film world, he would help out sometimes as an adviser, but he never interfered with or passed judgements on what they were doing. Barny sometimes found his father's fame a challenge, and would say that if any of the next generation were to be writers, they might do well to change their surnames. Will, always very close to his mother, occasionally felt that he was not on his father's wavelength. On one family outing in the early 2000s, when they had been to see an Andrew Lloyd Webber musical (probably *Love Never Dies*) along with Linzi, Fiona, Miriam and others, Will made an unthinking remark about the show which irked his father, who rapidly corrected him, as if he should have known better. Over dinner afterwards at the Wolseley, Will was a little assertive about the choice of wine, as if reminding his father that he had his own kinds of expertise. A week later, Will had a long letter from him, acknowledging that he hadn't always recognised the value of Will's different interests and areas of knowledge. Will saw it as a shift in the relationship and an admission of fault. Certainly it shows how carefully Stoppard treated his grown-up sons.

He took great pride in Ed's successful career as an actor. In 2009 David Leveaux directed the first major revival of *Arcadia* at the Duke of York's Theatre in the West End, in which Ed was cast as Valentine – with Samantha Bond as Hannah, Neil Pearson as Bernard, Jessie Cave as Thomasina and

Dan Stevens as Septimus. Previews started in May, and it ran from June to mid-September. In the spring of 2011, Sonia Friedman took the production to New York with a different cast, which included Lia Williams and Billy Crudup, a favourite actor of Stoppard's, who had played Belinsky in *Coast* and Septimus in the 1995 Lincoln Center *Arcadia*, and now played Bernard.

When Ed was being considered for *Arcadia*, Stoppard withdrew from the casting process. But David Leveaux had no doubts. A few years earlier, while Ed was still a student at LAMDA, he had auditioned him for Billy in *The Real Thing*. And Stoppard was professionally impressed by his son: he told Leveaux, once rehearsals were underway: 'I've got to say, Ed is brilliant.' There was naturally some interest in what it was like for Stoppard's son to act in one of his father's best-loved plays. In numerous interviews Ed politely put up with questions about whether the family in *Arcadia* resembled the Stoppard family, or whether his father's fame had been an advantage or a disadvantage. When playing Hamlet, he had had to tell interviewers that he wasn't in an Oedipal relationship of rivalry with his father: he was his father's 'greatest fan'. But 'hero worship could be an inhibitor as well as an enabler'. In school plays at Stowe, or at LAMDA, and in the early days of professional work, Ed had suffered badly from stage fright. At moments he had thought the family name 'might be more of a hindrance than a help'. Perhaps he should rename himself Ed Sträussler? In due course his successes cleared away those anxieties.

He didn't get any 'special treatment' from Stoppard during rehearsals. 'When we walked away after the first read-through . . . I said to my dad, "That was a bit odd, wasn't it?" He said, "Really? I didn't think so." And I thought: "Oh, I see, I'm not going to get any help or sympathy here . . ."' Leveaux noted that Stoppard treated his son exactly the same as everyone else, though the affectionate bond between them was clear. It amused Ed that when his father wasn't in the room, the other actors would sometimes ask him to explain a line: 'I don't know what this means, Ed, do you?' To which he would reply: 'Don't look at me, *I* don't know!' Like all actors who worked with Stoppard, he was struck by how open to making changes he was. Sometimes at the end of the working day when they shared a taxi,

Ed would ask him if he thought they were doing it right, and he might reply that it was not what he had originally had in mind, but that now, 'it's theirs'. One thing he was adamant and precise about, though, was the timing of the jokes. Ed learnt from him: 'you either land it or you don't'.

They had fun working together. While *Arcadia* was in rehearsal, Stoppard was doing (uncredited) rewrites for the screenplay of Ridley Scott's *Robin Hood*. At the same time, Leveaux was asking him for small rewrites for *Arcadia*, often by text. One night he received a text from Stoppard, reading: 'Robin: May the lord and all his bishops protect thee.' Leveaux texted back: 'Is this before or after Bernard gets back from the crusades?' The next day in rehearsals, Ed and his father were laughing about it, imagining the film people at Shepperton being sent baffling lines from *Arcadia* to go into *Robin Hood*.

Leveaux thought *Arcadia* a deeply beautiful play, a play about awe and wonder. He felt acutely aware, as he was directing it, of the rise of fundamentalism in the world around them, a very different environment for the play in 2010 than in 1993. *Arcadia* seemed to him to express a profound scepticism about absolutes; it 'restored to the secular a traditional sense of wonder'. The reviewers agreed with him. Billington said that the excellent production 'reminds us there is poetry and passion behind the mathematics and metaphysics' and that the play 'intensifies our awareness of what Lear called "the mystery of things"'. Leveaux's work was praised as lucid and intelligent; it brought audiences back, reviewers agreed, to what was probably Stoppard's 'finest play'. And Ed Stoppard's 'gripping', 'other-worldly' Valentine was much admired.

There was no shortage of Stoppard in the theatres. *Arcadia* and his *Cherry Orchard* were overlapping through 2009, soon after the revival of *Every Good Boy* at the National (which came back again early in 2010). In the late spring of 2010 there was a well-received revival of *The Real Thing*, directed by Anna Mackmin at the Old Vic, with Toby Stephens and Hattie Morahan. A year later, Trevor Nunn did a new *Rosencrantz* at Chichester and at the Theatre Royal Haymarket.

In May 2010 he contributed to the Royal Court's 'Cries from the Heart' series, mounted on behalf of Human Rights Watch. This one, under the general title *The Laws of War*, was put together by Richard Bean from disparate short pieces by Stoppard, David Grossman and others. Stoppard's ten-minute two-hander, rehearsed and performed by Emilia Fox and Bill Nighy over a couple of days, was a sinister interrogation scene, in which the suave, menacing interrogator forces a terrified woman to replace the word 'torture' with the word 'pizza', and to agree that no harm is being done to her. As in the interrogation scenes in *Every Good Boy* and *Rock 'n' Roll*, the oppressor is bending language to control dissent: one of his perpetual themes.

But, from 2006 to 2015, there was no new Stoppard play. He didn't use the phrase 'writer's block', but he voiced some despair about this in the early 2010s, in private to friends such as Isabel, in public to a probing interviewer such as Mark Lawson, to whom he said he was 'craving' a new play, but that inspiration was only intermittent. He sounded frustrated and impatient with himself:

Writing a new play shouldn't be seen as a mystery belonging to a priesthood, but as a . . . technical challenge, just to get into it . . . If I had been asked to write 1,200 words for a newspaper tomorrow, on any subject, I would just do it, rather than leave a white hole in the page. And I think it's a very healthy attitude to take to writing anything . . . a corrective to the view, which I tend to flinch [at] when confronted with: that it's all rather deep and mysterious and special and privileged. Sod that!

There were plenty of possible ideas. For some time he had been mulling over ideas about consciousness, altruism and evolution. He thought of writing a play about the financial crash of 2008, or (still) about newspapers, or about a mathematician. He was interested in William Hazlitt's extraordinary 1820s piece of confessional romantic autobiography, *Liber Amoris*, about Hazlitt's obsessive love for his landlady's daughter, and thought of making something of it, possibly for radio. Ideas were always being put to him for television or film adaptations, such as George Eliot's *Middlemarch* or Edith Wharton's *The Age of Innocence*.

Interruptions to writing were always available. Jacky, and his team at Faber and at United Agents, noted that he was more easily frazzled by distractions and demands in the years when he was living alone. (He was also having some eye problems, for which he had laser treatment in 2010.) Now that the house in France was gone, it was much harder to decline requests. 'Terribly sorry, would have loved to, but I'm in Chelsea,' didn't quite work as an excuse. So, in the summer of 2010, he rented a country retreat, an idyllic-looking thatched cottage (he called it his 'Goldilocks Cottage') in the village of Shalden, near Alton, about an hour and a half's drive from London. This never became a place close to his heart, like Iver or Lacoste – or his first house, River Thatch – but for a while it served as a retreat. The plan was to write the next play there.

But the usual invitations came pouring in. In 2009 – to give a very few examples – he went to Barcelona to accept a prize, was nominated Honorary Patron of the University Philosophical Society of Trinity College Dublin (but 'I'm concerned about my New Year resolution to stop travelling and start writing'), judged the PEN Pinter Prize (awarded to Tony Harrison), attended Prince Charles's Dimbleby Lecture at St James's Palace about climate change and the environment, and declined being Chancellor of Leicester University or a visiting professor at Cornell ('I can't, I really can't'). He went back to Prince Charles's Teaching Institute summer school, this time in Cambridge, but preferred not to be an ambassador for the institute: 'How are you to know that I'm in a constant losing battle trying to defend my shrinking writing time? . . . I'll be an Ambassador when I retire! But you may have to wheel me round in a box.' He accepted Japan's Praemium Imperiale, a lucrative and distinguished award, drawn from international recommendations in different artistic fields, for which he went to Tokyo, amid much ceremonial and publicity, alongside Alfred Brendel, Richard Long and Zaha Hadid. He made a more relaxed and enjoyable guest appearance at the Salzburg Theatre Festival (in August 2009), where he shared a platform with Adam Thirlwell and Daniel Kehlmann.

Kehlmann, a bestselling Austrian–German novelist and playwright in his mid-thirties, had been invited to be writer in residence at the Salzburg Festival, a big programme of opera and theatre on a huge stage. This involved choosing some events for the festival. An admirer of Stoppard's since seeing *Invention* on Broadway in 2001, he knew that *Coast* had not been staged in Germany, and suggested a semi-staged reading. Stoppard agreed to come to watch this and do an interview, partly because he had already read a good piece by Kehlmann, in translation, about *Coast*. During the interview, Kehlmann was nervous, and often paused before his next question; at one of these pauses, Stoppard, smiling wickedly, said, 'Do I see panic in your eyes?'

At Salzburg, Kehlmann launched an attack on the cult of 'director's theatre' in Germany, *Regietheater*, in which the writer's meanings and intentions were often overridden by the director's ideas. This got him into some trouble. Stoppard said, teasingly, that his association with Kehlmann would ruin his own career in Germany from then on. The younger playwright viewed Stoppard, with awe, as a supremely intelligent person who was impatient with slowness and sharp with mediocrity. But he also experienced his generosity. Later, Stoppard would adapt a play of Kehlmann's for the radio. Himself a writer deeply immersed in ideas and philosophy, Kehlmann felt that Stoppard was helpful to him 'simply in the fact that his work exists'. One play of his in particular was influenced by Stoppard, called *Ghosts in Princeton*, translated in 2012. It was about Kurt Gödel, the Czech–Viennese mathematician of genius who fled the Nazis in 1939 to join Einstein in Princeton. Stoppard saw it, said rather little, and asked to see the manuscript. The subject would remain in his mind.

Even if German directors and theatres, according to Kehlmann, underrated Stoppard, calling *Arcadia* a piece of light boulevard entertainment whenever it was put on, Stoppard was in demand elsewhere in Europe. In 2010 he attended a 'Tom Stoppard Festival' in Madrid, alongside a Spanish production of *The Real Thing*, but warned the organiser about being over loaded: 'Past experience makes me cautious . . . I arrive somewhere thinking I'm coming for a treat in a nice place, and find myself locked into a solid programme of interviews, formal engagements etc, so the whole thing becomes exhausting.'

At home, in May 2011, he gave the Richard Hillary Lecture at Trinity College Oxford, in the Sheldonian, on 'Pragmatic Art'. (He was still writing it, smoking and sitting in his car in Trinity, scribbling on small cards, ten minutes before the lecture was due to begin.) In June he lectured on 'The Privilege of Artists' in St George's Chapel at Windsor Castle for the St George's House Annual Lecture, to an audience which included the Duke of Edinburgh and the Dean and a Canon of Windsor. When the alarmingly formal invitation arrived, he felt he had to say yes, but said to Jacky ruefully: 'I should have turned down my OM!' He took Will with him as his guest, and 'tried to live up to the occasion'. He talked again about the value of what an artist does, the relation of aesthetics to morality, and where the artistic impulse comes from, with some of his favourite quotations from *Travesties* and *Coast*. He asked his audience to 'make a thought-experiment' in which they imagined a world 'in which every manifestation of the artistic impulse, good or bad, is removed; and then to meditate on what's left. What's left is dystopia.'

Meanwhile, his work went on for the Belarusians, for the London Library and for the Donmar Warehouse. He still took the trouble to explain, via Jacky, why he was saying no to a million other things, like an invitation to attend a five-day Italian retrospect on his work ('It's high time I tried to get into a new play, and talking about my past work is a bad reason for more delay and interruption, from which I suffer continually!') or a request from Havel's agent to read a book for a recommendation: 'I'd have to empty my head of what I'm trying to keep in it, probably for a week, and I can't do it . . . there's water slopping into my boat from every side every day. I have to change my life!' To his new friend Daniel Kehlmann, who asked him for a blurb, he gave a truthful account of why this, at least, was one thing he always said no to:

> I boxed myself in years ago by telling publishers I never do it. Yours is the second one this week and it's only Wednesday. I recommend this policy to you. Firstly, it enables you to respond to friends' books without looking over your shoulder. Secondly, it gets you out of a difficult situation with friends who write ordinary decent books or mediocre or rotten books.

Very occasionally, he would find himself with a day where he could just please himself. He wrote a short piece about this, commissioned for a 2010 Faber collection called *Modern Delight*, inspired by J. B. Priestley's idea of writing about what gave him 'delight', and published on behalf of Dyslexia Action and the London Library. (Other contributions included Clive James on second-hand bookshops, Richard Eyre on the perfect vodka-tonic, and Christopher Ricks on misquotes and mistakes.) A day of 'Undelight' was when he had to be woken up too early by the alarm clock, get on a plane or go to a meeting, deal with his in-tray and try to write while feeling tired. A day of 'Delight' was when he woke up alone and late, and then spent ninety minutes with two newspapers (delivered to the door of his flat six floors up) with 'tea, toast, four choices of orange marmalade, and the first cigarettes of the day': 'complete delight, completed by not having to speak, listen, wash up or put the cap back on the toothpaste'. If that beginning could be followed by uninterrupted work, starting 'no earlier than noon', possibly delayed by looking at a periodical or two and by anything in the post with a handwritten envelope, and then some afternoon reading and perhaps a nap as the sun set, and then something 'delightfully micro-waved', and then working till one or two in the morning and reading until sleepiness set in, 'not having spoken to or seen a living soul', that would be 'unadulterated delight'.

In these years when he wasn't writing a new play, he embarked on one major project which he found deeply interesting, an adaptation of Ford Madox Ford's *Parade's End* for television. This wasn't initially his own idea. It was suggested to him by Damien Timmer at Mammoth Screen production company, who thought it might make a good TV series – if written by Stoppard. He had been interested in Ford since reading Hemingway's account of him in *A Moveable Feast*, and he already knew and admired *The Good Soldier*, Ford's great modernist masterpiece of deception, desire, love and sadness. Now he read *Parade's End*, and was fired up by it. He began work in July 2008, in, of all places, the Copacabana Hotel in Rio de Janeiro (while visiting the Paraty Literary Festival). It would be another four years before the completed series was aired, in August 2012.

Ford Madox Ford was an appealing figure to him. Wherever you look in the international world of modernism between the 1890s and the 1930s, a period that fascinated Stoppard, Ford is there, playing a vital part. He had links to Stoppard's great literary heroes Eliot and Hemingway. He collaborated for years with Conrad. Beyond that, his cultural connections stretched from the Pre-Raphaelites and Henry James to Pound, Joyce, Wells, Lawrence, Allen Tate and Caroline Gordon, Jean Rhys, the Garnetts and their Russian anarchist friends. One of his admirers was the poet, critic and art historian Herbert Read, whom Stoppard had met in the 1960s through his son Piers Paul Read: a tangible link.

Ford (not unlike Stoppard) was a major English literary figure who wasn't entirely English, and who had a changed name. He was born Ford Hermann Hueffer in 1873. His father was a German Catholic Anglophile music critic who died when Ford was fifteen, and his mother was the daughter of the painter Ford Madox Brown. He renamed himself Ford Madox Ford in 1919. Like Stoppard, he left school at seventeen to live on his wits. He thought of himself as an outsider, a 'lonely buffalo', even a 'pariah'. He travelled widely, and had a scandalous and complicated marital and love life. Large and red-faced, he was attractive to women because he was interested in them. He was the author of seventy books, a novelist, poet, critic, historian and editor of two important short-lived literary magazines, the *English Review* and the *Transatlantic Review*. He was a generous encourager of younger writers, and a self-educated expert on literature, art, music, cookery, agriculture and all things French. A person of contradictions, he was a country-loving cosmopolite, an anarchist-socialist-Tory, a wobbly Catholic, and a patriotic Anglophile who left England to live in France and who had his biggest following in America. He was expansive and gregarious, reticent and private, an untruthful fantasist and great exaggerator, neurotic, sensitive and depressive. He had several breakdowns, and thought about suicide. The Great War, in which he enlisted at forty-one in poor health in July 1916 (partly as an escape from impossible personal and financial problems), broke his life in two.

As a writer he was a stylist of great originality, who wanted to communicate experience as vividly as possible, using techniques drawn from painting which he called 'impressionism'. 'Consciousness' was his subject. Especially in *Parade's End*, he is a brilliant and disturbing writer of war. But *Parade's End* was also about Ford's favourite subjects of honour, betrayal, obsessive love, class, religion and repressed emotions. It's told with Ford's typically complex jumps through time, recurring motifs and broken phrases of speech. These often confusing modernist effects try to mirror (like Eliot's fragmentary lines or Conrad's time shifts) the unaccountable ways in which perception and memory work. The tetralogy owes something to Proust's minute, epic account of French society in the years leading up to the war, to Tolstoy's *War and Peace* and to Dostoevsky's intense extremes.

The hero of *Parade's End*, Christopher Tietjens, is both like and unlike Ford. He was partly based on his friend Arthur Marwood, a Yorkshire Tory squire with, as Ford put it, 'the clear, eighteenth-century English mind which has disappeared from the earth'. But Ford also gives Tietjens some of his own experiences: of shell shock in the war, of being caught between a vengeful ex-mistress and a new, younger love, of feeling alienated from his English society.

Tietjens can be unbearable, which adds to the challenge of an adaptation. Like Marwood, he is a dinosaur, an old-school Tory English gentleman nostalgic for the feudal era. He despises the modern world of bankers, stockbrokers and string-pulling, incompetent politicians and bureaucrats. He is a brilliant mathematician working for the 'Imperial Department of Statistics', and his favourite hobby is annotating the errors in the *Encyclopaedia Britannica*. He believes in honour, courtly love and integrity, while living in a society riven with corruption, scandal and ineptitude. He is emotionally repressed and socially awkward. He allows himself to be slandered, out of scorn for the slanderers – as a result of which his father kills himself on hearing vile, and false, rumours about his private life. He goes to war when he doesn't have to. Out of chivalry and self-blame, he is passive about his wife's infidelity, even though his son, whom he loves, may not be his. He is devoted to his ancestral Yorkshire house, Groby, with its old farming methods, its deep well and its Great Tree, a relic of pagan England. He loves England, horses, children, his employees and his soldiers, and seventeenth- and eighteenth-century art, music, poetry and furniture. He is the one good man, the 'lonely buffalo'. But we can see how intolerable his high-mindedness can be, particularly to his wife.

The beautiful and self-hating Sylvia, an unhappy Catholic, perverse and manipulative, is driven mad by Tietjens's passivity and saintly chivalry ('you forgave without mercy,' she tells him). Brought up to believe she can only wield power through attracting men, she is a victim of her times, as well as a monster. Her savage need to keep his attention, which sours into vengeful malevolence, is one of the driving forces of the plot. By contrast, the young woman Tietjens falls silently in love with, Valentine Wannop, offspring of a Latin scholar and a lady novelist, is a modern independent girl with a strong work ethic, a suffragette and a pacifist, athletic, passionate, virginal and true-hearted. This triangle of frustration is embedded in its social world. There's a lot of comedy in Tietjens's intractable relations with his government employers and his aristocratic and military family connections (especially the ever-indignant General Campion), and with his friend the aspiring literary critic MacMaster and his aesthetic mistress Mrs Duchemin, the ambitious wife of a dangerously unhinged vicar with Tourette's syndrome.

The war smashes across personal lives and social traditions, though it also magnifies, rather than distracting from, private anxieties. Ford used elaborate experimental techniques to give the sensations of a person in a war zone, as if we were there with him. In Tietjens's shattering experience, which begins with concussion and shell shock, undergoes the endless bureaucratic demands of the work at base camp and ends with being blown up in the trenches, he is tested to extremes. In what Ford called that 'Hell of fear', Tietjens tries to behave courageously and decently. But, as in civilian life, he is dogged by bad luck, misrepresentation, Sylvia's vendetta and the chaotic incompetence of the War Office.

Tietjens survives the war and, on Armistice Day, finally comes together with Valentine. In those scenes, and in the final novel, *Last Post*, set in rural England a few years after the war, with Valentine pregnant and Sylvia despairingly excluded, some happiness is rescued from the wreck.

'Reconstruction' is the theme, even though the traditions of Groby, and the England it stood for, have been burnt away. But in most of *Parade's End*, Ford, through Tietjens, expressed his horror of the war and his conviction that the soldiers were betrayed to their deaths by the incompetent ruling classes. Long after it was published, he said he had written it 'with the intention of . . . bringing about such a state of mind as would end wars as possibilities'.

Parade's End was greeted with admiration, if also some bafflement and shock, when it came out in the mid-1920s. By the 2010s, it was no longer much read (its afterlife not helped by Graham Greene's omitting *Last Post* from his 1963 reissue of the book), and Ford was remembered above all for *The Good Soldier.* Stoppard sank his teeth into the challenge of bringing the novels back to life for a general audience. It was a process of double ventriloquism: Stoppard turned himself into Ford, as Ford had turned himself into Tietjens.

He wanted to be true to the book's deep meaning, its sense of an ending, of the passing away of an English tradition and a kind of English behaviour, and he also needed to make it accessible. He had five one-hour episodes – though he would argue, unsuccessfully, for more air-time. 'I did have to unravel it all', he told an interviewer, 'and also invent a lot, as the book doesn't actually provide the action that five hours of television requires.' He created a chronological structure running from 1908 to 1918, and unpicked Ford's narrative complexity to make the story easier to follow. For instance, the first novel, *Some Do Not*, starts with a prolonged series of flashbacks spooling back from Tietjens and MacMaster going on a train to Rye to play golf. Through their interior monologues we find out about their friendship, Sylvia's infidelity, the probability that their child may not be his ('She's bitched me'), and Sylvia's request to come back to him after her latest escapade. Stoppard gets rid of all that and starts with Sylvia having wild sex with her lover the night before her wedding to Tietjens, then the wedding, then their intolerable home life. As the director Susanna White put it, he 'filleted out' the love triangle from a huge, sprawling series of books. He gave a lot of time to the pre-war social and personal narrative, and condensed the war sections into parts four and five of the series. He made minimal use of the final post-war novel, *Last Post*, just taking from it a few crucial events, like Sylvia having Groby Great Tree cut down, or her last encounter with Christopher and Valentine on Armistice Day, and putting those back into the chronological sequence of events.

He was 'partly proud and partly embarrassed' that he had written a lot of scenes which didn't exist in the book. He sometimes couldn't remember what was Stoppard and what was Ford. He provided some dramatic additions, like a suffragette slashing Velázquez's *Rokeby Venus* in the National Gallery, or an Eton–Harrow cricket match where Valentine is insulted by Sylvia's posh friends. To emphasise Valentine's emancipation, he invented a scene in which the schoolgirls she is teaching are secretly reading Marie Stopes's *Married Love*, and she defends them to the other teachers.

But he wanted to be true to the tone and style of the books. So he did keep in some flashbacks, as quick surreal images breaking up the screen, like Tietjens's first love-making with Sylvia on a train, just after they meet. (Ford loved trains, and so does this TV adaptation, with lots of scenes shot, entirely out of sequence, at St Pancras Station.) He used some of Ford's recurring images and motifs: a door handle slowly turning in a hotel bedroom, or the Edwardian turn of phrase used for Sylvia's tricks, 'pulling the strings of the shower bath'. Though he made the war scenes less hallucinatory, he tried to keep their sense of unreality. He was helped by the strong visual allusions – to Paul Nash, Ravilious, Christopher Nevinson, Vorticist photography – which Susanna White encouraged in Martin Childs's production design. And he kept key scenes in the book, of Tietjens's night ride in the mist through the English countryside with Valentine, or Sylvia's destructive visit to the base camp at Rouen.

He piled on the comedy, especially with the Duchemin–MacMaster scenes, the novelist Mrs Wannop's self-promotion, and General Campion's baffled exasperation at Tietjens's behaviour. There are jokes that are more Stoppardian than Fordian, as when Sylvia's socialite friend uses a holy water scoop in Sylvia's religious retreat as an ashtray, or Valentine mishears Mrs Duchemin ('I run a bath and think of Browning' – 'Drowning?'), or General Campion makes a category error:

Campion (*angrily*): How dare he not get divorced! He told me his wife
was co-habiting with – an Egyptian, wasn't it? – some sort of dago
anyway.
Colonel Levin: No, sir, an Egyptologist.

One joke seems made for his own private satisfaction: in a 1912 scene in
the MacMaster–Duchemin salon, part Pre-Raphaelite, part Bloomsbury,
the action direction reads, as if straight out of *Prufrock*: 'Two women come
and go, talking of Michelangelo.' And some of the comedy of the series
owes its atmosphere not so much to Ford as to a satirical show he had
hugely admired in the 1960s, Joan Littlewood's *Oh! What a Lovely War.*

Ford's novel, like many great modernist fictions (*Ulysses, Mrs Dalloway*),
is written in 'free indirect speech', a flexible third-person narrative that can
roam in and out of people's minds and incorporate snatches of speech and
allusions. All that had to be turned into dialogue. And so a character who
doesn't like self-revelation has to speak out about his own beliefs, and say
things like: 'We've seen the last of England . . . we're all barbarians now.'
Stoppard got round this, cunningly, by making Tietjens's expressions of
faith often hesitant or incoherent, and by having other characters tell him
what he's like:

Christopher: Yes . . . but still, there is . . . or used to be . . . among
families of position . . . a certain . . .
Campion (*stops*): Well?
Christopher: On the part of the man . . . a certain, call it, parade!
Campion: Was there! Well, there'll be no more parades for *that*
regiment. It held out to the last man, but you were him.

Changing Ford's complex narrative into concise, direct speech, while
trying to be faithful to the tone of the book, was a task which he found
both arduous and enjoyable.

But turning a complex narrative into an accessible, dramatic screenplay was not the only challenge. Getting *Parade's End* from the page onto
the air was a long, frustrating process. The BBC commissioned the script

in co-production with Mammoth Screen. Once the idea had been suggested to him, he took fifteen months to write the five episodes, between
2008 and 2010. In 2010, his diary notes numerous meetings with the production team. In February he told Isabel that his *Parade's End* was looking for a director.

Over the year, he sent his five episodes, one at a time as he wrote them,
to Mammoth. To fund the film, which would have 110 speaking parts and
146 locations and cost £12 million, the BBC needed a co-partnership with
an American broadcaster. So the giant corporation HBO came on board –
with strings attached, including demands for 'star directors' and big-name
actors. Luckily, Susanna White, who had done a good *Bleak House* for the
BBC, agreed to direct. She was gripped by Stoppard's screenplay and rapidly became a devoted Fordian. Through late 2010 and 2011, Stoppard was
involved in pre-production, auditioning, recce-ing locations and shooting. From August 2011 onwards, his appointment diary began to contain
entries like: 'Shooting hay-making, Salisbury Plain'.

But during this process, HBO pulled out, and the BBC, through its
global arm, BBC Worldwide, had to raise international funding by selling
the series before it was made, to European and Australian channels, while
Mammoth looked for cuts in the budget. There were moments when the
entire project looked vulnerable. Stoppard wrote strong letters to the BBC
and Mammoth producers, Damien Timmer and Piers Wenger, resisting
demands that would 'disembowel' his script for financial reasons. ('To quote
P. G. Wodehouse, though not disgruntled, I am far from gruntled about the
hoops we are going through.') He went for advice to his film-making friends,
Kathy Kennedy and Mike Nichols, and he got involved with the fundraising,
which he hadn't had to do since the making of the film of *Rosencrantz* in the
late 1980s. He was listed in the credits as a production executive, as well as
'writer'. David Hare (who was fundraising for his own BBC project, the spy
film *Page Eight*, at the same time) noted how frustrating Stoppard was finding it. Hare thought that he was used to being under the wing of the likes of
Kennedy and Spielberg, and hadn't realised how tough the money-raising
climate in the film world had become. And, as Susanna White observed,
'five hours of modernist drama was not an easy sell'.

Throughout, he was completely supportive of White. When she was sent by Mammoth to look at cheaper, and less suitable, locations in Northern Ireland, he supported her refusal to shoot there. They both knew it had to be a portrait of England, with English settings: the golf course at Rye, the Kent marshes, Gray's Inn, the North Yorkshire moors. (Groby was mostly filmed at Duncombe Park.) The war scenes were filmed in Belgium.

They agreed on casting, too. Stoppard had visited the set of Spielberg's *War Horse* in 2010, while the finances for *Parade's End* were looking shaky, and seen Benedict Cumberbatch – not as yet famous – in an officer's uniform. '*That's* what I want,' he thought, before there was even a series ready to cast him in. By the time *Parade's End* was ready to shoot, *Sherlock* had made Cumberbatch a superstar. Luckily for them, he was steadfastly committed to Tietjens, which made the money flow in much more easily. Stoppard and White both wanted Rebecca Hall as Sylvia, and they were right: her intelligent, sensual performance made the character pitiable and magnetic. Around them was a terrific cast of English actors: Roger Allam magnificently comical as General Campion, Rupert Everett as a sombre Mark Tietjens, Anne-Marie Duff an edgy, hysterical Edith Duchemin, Stephen Graham funny, touching and vain as MacMaster, Miranda Richardson a forceful Mrs Wannop, the great Alan Howard making his last appearance as the troubled, haughty Tietjens senior, and a hilariously sinister cameo by Rufus Sewell as the mad Reverend Duchemin.

The most daring piece of casting was of Adelaide Clemens as Valentine. A young, little-known Australian actor, she was in competition with a number of more experienced names, and she had to fight for the part, flying over from LA and impressing Stoppard, especially, by 'intelligently' wearing Edwardian clothes for the audition. He thought she was a 'heart-breaker'; and both he and White loved her quality of fresh intense beauty and seriousness. White set up a 'chemistry read' between her and Cumberbatch, which worked perfectly, and Stoppard drilled her on every word for pronunciation. He hugely admired her performance – and she would return as the heroine of *The Hard Problem* in its 2018 New York production.

By choice, Stoppard invested a great deal of time in *Parade's End*. It was the main focus of his working life for four years. He was possessive and defensive of it, almost as if it were his own original play. This was the first time he had felt 'as involved in film as in working in theatre'. Some of his team worried that *Parade's End* was sucking the juice from a possible new play. Looking back, though, he would firmly resist the notion that *Parade's End* was a form of displacement activity. It was something he passionately wanted to do.

He was on location regularly, whether in London, Rye or Belgium, in his long camel coat, chewing sweets, smoking, listening and watching carefully and thinking fast. He and Susanna White worked trustingly together. She found him extremely precise about dialogue, diction and physical gestures. It was he, for instance, who suggested that Janet McTeer, as Sylvia's snooty mother, should hold up her teacup impossibly high, a perfect gesture for her imperiousness. If a few lines were suddenly needed to fill an awkward hiatus, he would scribble them there and then and give them straight to the actors. Sometimes he was exasperatingly perfection-ist, trying to change bits of dialogue just before they were going to be shot, and White would have to keep him away from the actors. But Rebecca Hall, writing to thank him for Sylvia, told him it was a 'godsend' that he was there on set. He would come away at the end of each day wishing they had had more time, or had been able to spend more money on the set-dressing. But in the end he was amazed by how well it worked on screen.

At every stage, he stood for the writer's integrity, for fidelity to the spirit of the book and for aesthetic values, against financial imperatives, corpo-rate decisions and underrating the audience's intelligence. While the series was being cast, HBO came back on board. This was a relief, of course, but it also meant that in post-production – when he spent almost every day in the cutting room – he had to defend his script against requests for it to be made simpler and more intelligible.

He was always arguing against over-signalling. Groby Great Tree has mysterious pagan objects hanging from its branches, put there by gener-ations of locals. Stoppard resisted this being laboriously set up: 'the shot is better when the explanation is unknown and mysterious. We really, really, must resist the pressure [in exasperated caps] TO PREPARE THE AUDIENCE IN ADVANCE . . . The Explaining/Preparing Tendency tends to flatten out the intrinsic nature of the play. I have been fighting this for 45 years – but mostly in the theatre, where the writer has the casting vote!' He didn't want to be constrained by what viewers might know or not know: 'I don't care about any audience who don't know what *le bon Dieu* or *amour* means.' He was constantly telling them that *Parade's End* was not a conventional story of a love triangle: it was 'an oddity', and should be kept that way: 'The main character's behaviour baffles and infuriates the people around him . . . Lovers don't declare themselves. Characters are kept apart. And so on. That's why it's special. It's not a "normal" story.'

Sometimes the demands for clarification, handed down from the money men, were helpful to him. More often they weren't. There were many times when he dug his heels in, usually from a horror of over-explicitness. And there were times when he didn't, but felt he should have done. Tietjens senior, before the war, gazing from Groby terrace at the fields where a horse-drawn plough is working, says: 'The motor-plough didn't answer.' This was exactly what Ford wrote. (When Christopher goes back to Groby after the war, we see a motor-plough in action in the fields: the old ways have gone.) He was told that this word wouldn't be understood, and reluctantly agreed to change it to 'The motor-plough didn't serve.' 'I loved "answer" for being precise to the old-school ways of the character, but I got tired of fighting for it.' And for him to say to the producers, 'I know half the audience may not understand this, but I'm writing for the other half,' was perhaps not even a respectable view to take. Another writer might just have told them to fuck off. But that didn't occur to him, because he was not that kind of writer, or that kind of person. Sometimes he thought he should have been.

He was profoundly committed to the fortunes of *Parade's End*, and did a lot of publicity for it at the time of the first screening in February 2012. The series was aired between 24 August and 21 September 2012. Some critics wondered why on earth the BBC chose to put it out in the dog days of summer, but he kept his counsel. He held a celebratory party at Chelsea Harbour for everyone involved when episode five was screened.

Stoppard's 'return to television after thirty-five years' was celebrated, and *Parade's End* was a big critical success, generally acclaimed as 'something rare and wonderful'. The first episode had 3.5 million viewers, a figure which dropped off during the course of the series, with some complaints about inaudibility. '*Parade's End* Loved by Critics, But Viewers Switch Off', one headline read. Coincidentally, by the time it came out, *Downton Abbey* (which didn't exist when Stoppard had begun work on Ford) was having its third series. So everyone compared *Parade's End* with it, along the lines of 'the thinking person's *Downton Abbey*' or, more positively, 'Stoppard's glorious gem puts *Downton* to shame'. Exasperated with the assumption that *Parade's End* was just another cosy Edwardian costume drama, Susanna White said that viewers could go and make themselves a cup of tea during *Downton Abbey* and come back and pick it up easily, but that if you went out to make a cup of tea during an episode of *Parade's End*, you'd be lost. (She also said that it was like *Downton Abbey* crossed with *The Wire*.) In terms of popular success, *Downton Abbey*, targeted at a mass audience and averaging about 13.3 million viewers a week, made mincemeat of *Parade's End*. But in terms of critical reputation, *Parade's End* left *Downton Abbey* nowhere.

He was especially pleased to get approval from a devoted and knowledgeable Fordian such as Julian Barnes. On 11 September 2012 Stoppard wrote to Barnes from his 'thatched bolt-hole' in Shalden, thanking him for his phone call about the series. 'You probably don't know how much your message meant to me and to Susanna,' the playwright told the novelist. 'We outed each other afterwards as highly Barnes-sensitive about *Parade's End*, each silently anxious about whatever opinion you might have about it.' And he sent him the published screenplay with the inscription: 'To Julian – my *Parade's End* conscience – with love, Tom'. He was pleased, too, that Max Saunders, Ford's latest biographer, admired his version and thought that he had reintroduced 'a new generation of readers to this amazing, expansive, and deeply moving work'. Thanking Saunders for his advice, he told him: 'I loved the job but I think it was the most difficult job I ever had to do.'

In the spring of 2013, five years after he first read *Parade's End*, Stoppard attended a TV film festival in Paris, Séries Mania, at which the first two episodes of the French TV version of *Parade's End* were shown. Here he had a horrid surprise. He was enraged to realise, belatedly, that BBC Worldwide had sold the series to European and Australian TV without regard to the fact there was no drama slot longer than forty-five minutes on those channels. The five hour-long episodes he had written had each been carefully structured to contain one coherent part of the story, with time lapses between each episode. But in the French Arte version the episodes had been sliced, arbitrarily, into six forty-five-minute slots. He felt at that moment it would have been better for *Parade's End* not to have been made at all, rather than having been 'butchered' for demeaning financial imperatives. Interviewed by French reporters at the festival, under the shadow of this upsetting discovery, he struck an unusually gloomy note. He might write one more play and give up, he told them, because he was very slow. 'I am seventy-five, I am seventy-six in a minute . . . My brain cells are dying in their trillions.' After a while, his fury wore off. Generally stoical rather than excitable, 'I shrugged, and got on with my life.' Perhaps, he thought later, he might have done better to have written it and then finished with it, fatalistically saying to himself, 'Let whatever will be, be.' After all, though two or three million people watched it, it then vanished from sight. (Except, that is, on DVD and Netflix.) No one would ever set it alongside *The Real Thing* or *Arcadia* in a history of his work. Nevertheless, he minded about *Parade's End*, and was rightly proud of it.

Just after he finished writing *Parade's End*, he was asked to do a screenplay of Tolstoy's *Anna Karenina*, at the suggestion of the director Joe Wright, who had adapted *Pride and Prejudice* and Ian McEwan's *Atonement*. Keira Knightley starred, as in those films, with Jude Law as Karenin. The two film projects overlapped: for instance, on 30 August 2011, there was a read-through of *Parade's End* and a rehearsal of *Anna Karenina*. Both were adaptations of big, classic novels about society, adultery, marriage and, above all, love. But the resemblances stopped there. This was a very different level of involvement for him. He did his homework, of course, watching the many film versions of *Anna Karenina*, rereading the novel in the Penguin translation and drawing clear lines between the three main plots: Anna's passionate, doomed adultery with Captain Vronsky, which wrecks her loveless marriage to the chilly bureaucrat Karenin, divides her from her beloved son and leads to her tragic suicide; her worldly brother Oblonsky's casual infidelities in his marriage to the long-suffering Dolly; and the deep, slow-moving relationship between Dolly's sister, the innocent Kitty, and the idealistic landowner Levin. His script concentrated on the novel's different versions of love, rather than on its political and philosophical side, though he gave space to Levin's revolutionary brother, who accuses the serf-owning Levin of being 'on the wrong side of history'. He had a fondness for some of the minor characters, like Princess Betsy's husband, whom he turned from a collector of etchings to a specialist in antiquarian books, because 'I prefer antiquarian books to etchings'. He gave strong, modern expression to Anna's social imprisonment within the double standards of her time and to the predicaments of all the women characters. Speaking of her own scandalous love life, Vronsky's mother says to Anna: 'I'd rather end up wishing I hadn't than end up wishing I had.' Anna says to Vronsky, when she knows she will lose her son if she runs away with him: 'The laws are made by husbands and fathers.' And a friend of Vronsky's explains to him why he can't acknowledge Anna in public: 'I'd call on her if she'd only broken the law. But she broke the rules.' There are feminist sympathies in both these adaptations.

He had no idea what Joe Wright was going to do with it, and nor did Wright, at first, who spent a long time in Russia looking for suitable locations. In the end Wright got impatient with the conventional precedents and decided to stage it in a dilapidated 'Russian' theatre, built in Shepperton, and to have most of the action (apart from the rural scenes) take place in different areas of the theatre, with mannered, co-ordinated choreography and almost continuous 'Russian' music, so that at times it's more like a musical or a ballet. This decision had nothing to do with Stoppard, and came as something of a shock to him. 'I wrote it "straight",' he told his friend the dance critic Alastair Macaulay, 'the modernist narrative-frame being imposed on it later.' But he called Wright's conception bold and rewarding.

He showed up very occasionally on the set. He was there for the filming of Anna throwing herself under the train, and suggested one new line to Knightley in mid-shoot, which she accepted. The film was released to moderately good reviews in September 2012, just as the *Parade's End* airings were ending. Some critics found what Peter Bradshaw called the 'semi-permeable fantasy theatre' a problem. Philip French thought the film 'only occasionally touching, and rarely truly moving'. The *New Yorker* critic called it banal, fussy, flat, 'simultaneously simplistic and overdone'. Stoppard passed no judgement, but said in interview that compared with *Anna Karenina*, *Parade's End* felt much more like his own work.

The years of *Parade's End* took him into his mid-seventies. He was living alone, working with unremitting energy, always in touch with family and friends, looked after by his faithful team, hugely in demand, greedy for quiet thinking time, at once private and famous. Younger friends and colleagues, like Sonia Friedman, Patrick Marber, Daniel Kehlmann, Adam Thirlwell or David Leveaux, brought new interests into his life; his established friendships, as with Antonia Fraser, the Johnsons, Mike Nichols, Jack O'Brien and very many others, were steadily and affectionately sustained.

His favourite actor and long-time collaborator John Wood died at eighty-one, in August 2011. He spoke humorously and lovingly at his memorial (a major theatrical event in the 'Actors' Church' in Covent Garden in July 2012) about his haughty and ascetic character, his fearsome cleverness and scathing wit. Wood, he said, seemed to know something about everything and everything about something. He was a fanatical perfectionist, often giving notes to other actors, sometimes while they were on stage, as to Rosencrantz when Wood was playing Guildenstern. Nicholas Hytner recalled that at one performance of *Travesties* to a dozy matinee audience, Wood turned to them and expostulated: 'Oh, do keep up!' Simon Russell Beale read a speech from that play; and at the end of the ceremony they listened in awe to Wood's recording of Prospero's farewell 'in which', as one listener described it, 'that mighty, metallic voice let rip over several octaves'.

He was moved in a different way by an expected, but desolating, loss. On 18 December 2011, Václav Havel, who had been ill for some time, died in Prague. There was worldwide mourning. The state funeral was on 23 December at St Vitus Cathedral in Prague Castle, attended by leaders from all over the world and about two thousand mourners. Speeches were made about his legacy and the freedoms he stood for. In the evening, in the Great Hall of the Lucerna Palace, there was a celebratory session of music and performance, with the Plastic People of the Universe as the grand finale.

Stoppard, to his distress, could not get to the funeral – he was in Sri Lanka – but he had been in continuing touch with him in his last years. After Havel came to the starry first night of *Rock 'n' Roll* in June 2006, Stoppard went to his seventieth birthday in Prague in October 2006, and was back in Prague to see him again in November 2009. In February 2011 he did an interview about Havel at the Czech Centre in London, and in August 2011 he was at the opening of the Orange Tree Theatre's production of *The Conspirators*. He saw a good deal of Havel's close friend, colleague and biographer Michael Žantovský, Czech ambassador in London from 2009 to 2015. He wrote his condolences to Havel's widow Dagmar (his first wife, Olga, had died in 1996 and he had remarried in 1997). On 29 February 2012 there was a tribute to Havel in London, held at RIBA, with Prince Charles in attendance, hosted by Žantovský, with readings and film extracts and songs. The programme contained a photo of Havel and Stoppard smoking and talking happily together, and described Stoppard as having written several plays influenced by Havel and Czech dissidents, and as having been a 'close friend of the late President'. He made the main speech, in which he quoted John Motley's eulogy of William of Orange: 'As long as he lived he was the guiding star of a whole brave nation, and when he died the little children cried in the street'. But, true to the ironical honesty which was one of the things he shared with Havel, he also warned against 'sentimental hyperbole'. Dagmar thanked him afterwards for his dignified and measured eulogy. He had been right to suspect that Havel would have chided him for sentimentality. 'But sometimes our own emotions count as well.'

He felt it as a great loss. They were almost the same age, and the contrast between their lives was always sharply in his mind. He often set his luck, his chance, his fate, against that other Czech writer's life. There was more good luck to come.

33

Circumspice

What is the Good?
It is nothing but a contest of kindness.

Stoppard had known Sabrina Guinness since the 1990s. She seemed to know everyone. She had friendships, contacts and family links which spanned film, rock music and media people, the British royals and Hollywood royalty. They met first through Mick Jagger and Jerry Hall, but they had many other links too. Born in 1955, she was a Guinness of the banking, not the brewing, branch of that large, high-profile, wealthy Irish dynasty. She was one of five children of the merchant banker James Guinness and his wife Pauline Mander, often referred to in her youth as a 'society beauty', in later life not the easiest of mothers. Sabrina had a typical upbringing for the daughters of upper-middle-class, well-off British families in the 1950s and 1960s: nannies and au pairs, parents often absent, girls' boarding schools, where she learned to arrange flowers and cook but didn't do A Levels (she was booted out for breaking rules), a Swiss finishing school, training as a Montessori nursery teacher, a flat bought for her in West London, and expectations that she would marry early and settle down.

A chance encounter in the mid-1970s, while playing frisbee with friends in a park in South London, led to her going to Los Angeles for a summer job, when she was eighteen, as nanny to Ryan O'Neal's daughter Tatum. She started to work in Hollywood as a production assistant and her life became more adventurous and various than the one she had been expected to lead. She was charming, attractive, sociable, independent-minded, eager for experience and delighted to be finding her own way. 'America allowed me to escape and to get to know myself,' she would say. Doors opened to her partly because of her famous surname, which she thought of as a brand, and nothing much to do with her real self.

Over the next twenty years she would come and go between the West Coast and her London life. For most of 1979, she was Prince Charles's girlfriend, and talked of as a possible royal bride. (A senior member of the royal family was said to have remarked, with mild surprise: 'We thought we were quite well connected until we met Sabrina.') She escaped that net, just as Diana came on the scene, though she and Prince Charles remained friends. But it meant that she came in for a lifetime of unwelcome attention from the tabloids, who nicknamed her 'Goldilocks' and tracked her love life greedily, under labels like 'the most eligible woman in Britain'. Any famous person she was ever seen out with was fodder for another story. In the early 2000s, when she was being referred to as 'the queen of Ladbroke Grove's boho Anglo-Irish contingent', she was linked with Paul McCartney, as his marriage to Heather Mills broke up. Her friends included Jagger and Jerry Hall, the tycoon Arki Busson, Bono and Bob Geldof (Pixie Geldof is her god-daughter). She also had a team of close girlfriends, among them Geraldine Harmsworth of the Rothermere family. But with all her romances, real and supposed, her varied friendships and her busy social world, she never lived with anyone and, unlike most of her friends and family, didn't marry or have children.

The Guinness siblings, who included two sets of twins, got through their childhood together, then mostly went their own ways, though their social lives overlapped. Sabrina's twin Miranda, who worked for Mick Jagger for a time, married Keith Payne, who designed sets for the Rolling Stones. Her younger sister Julia married one of the Samuel banking family, had four children, worked as a bereavement counsellor, was a friend to Princess Diana and is godmother to Prince George. Julia's twin, Hugo, potter, screenwriter, reformed addict and glamorous man-about-town, moved to America and married the artist Elliott Puckette. The third sister, Anita, married Amschel Rothschild, and, after his tragic death, the horse breeder James Wigan. Anita's Rothschild daughters married Goldsmith brothers, Ben (that marriage didn't last) and Zac. Her son James married Nicky Hilton, sister of Paris.

But Sabrina Guinness was not a millionaire's heiress. She wanted to work. In 1994, she founded a media charity which drew on her contacts, her administrative skills and her interest in the arts. Youth Culture Television was set up to train children from deprived backgrounds in TV production skills and to give them professional advantages. It was supported by the BBC, Carlton TV and Channel 4. Anneka Rice, in her 1990s BBC reality show *Challenge Anneka*, was set the task of building a studio for YCTV, and Greg Dyke was persuaded to be chairman. YCTV ran for about fifteen years and had some notable success stories. After it came to an end in the late 2000s, she worked for a time as a PA and organiser for the Anglo-Russian newspaper magnate Evgeny Lebedev, in charge of his foundation's charitable giving.

At YCTV, she would ask media figures and writers to give visiting workshops. In 2003 or 2004 she invited Stoppard, whom she knew from public encounters, dinners and parties. (Amie Stoppard, Ed's wife, had worked for YCTV for a time.) She was rather in awe of him, as well as thinking he was 'drop dead gorgeous'. He came and talked about *Shakespeare in Love*, and afterwards they went for a plate of pasta and a chat. The young members of YCTV were very struck, she wrote in an admiring thank-you letter: 'They were particularly impressed that you really listened to their questions, and answered them with such embellishment.' She signed off, with much love: 'Many thanks – you're great!'

Their paths continued to cross, and he included her occasionally in the small lunches, of eight or so people, that he liked to host at Chelsea Harbour. At one of these she sat next to a charming old man called David, but had no idea until he'd left that he was John Le Carré. At a big public event with the Jaggers and other stars, where Stoppard was much in demand, he made his way through the throng, looking for her. He told her he had asked Sinéad if he could take her out, but that Sinéad had said she would rather he didn't. But after the time of Sinéad's reunion with her son, from 2005 onwards, he took Sabrina to the theatre now and then. These invitations would make her heart flutter, but she thought he was entirely out of her reach and could not possibly be interested in her.

By 2009, their outings had become quite regular. They went together to David Hare's *Gethsemane* in January, and to see Helen Mirren as Phèdre in July. On 27 October 2010, he invited her to go with him to Nina Raine's play *Tribes*, at the Royal Court. What was she doing the next day, he asked her. If she had no plans, 'I thought I might take you to the country tonight.'

But at the theatre they found Nina Raine and her family, and Susanna White and her husband, so they all ended up having dinner together, while Sabrina was completely distracted from Raine's excellent new play and from the dinner-party conversation, for thinking: 'I'm going to the country tonight!' It seemed very romantic to her, and from that point on she felt sure that they would be together. 'The country' was another of their overlaps: Stoppard's Hampshire cottage at Shalden was twenty minutes away from the cottage she had on her parents' farm in a nearby village. All through 2011, they spent time in one or other country hideout while he was working on *Parade's End* and *Anna Karenina*.

In London, they went out to plays and parties and dinners, but didn't want to advertise their relationship: they both had all too much experience of press intrusion. In September 2011, Piers Paul Read observed her going up to Stoppard at his Chelsea Physic Garden Party with 'proprietary body language', and heard Stoppard asking her how long she had been there, as if to make a point to listeners that they had not arrived together. Read asked her if she was 'seeing' Tom Stoppard. 'From time to time,' she replied. Her old friend the director Michael Grandage, who had often had conversations with her about finding the right man, had the sense, too, that something was going on.

At the end of December 2011, he was invited to Australia, and then to the Jaipur Literature Festival. He invited her to come on a two-week holiday with him in Sri Lanka in between those commitments, away from any press intrusion. She flew out to join him, feeling extremely nervous. It was some time since she had had a close relationship. She was anxious that, together alone for any length of time, he would think she was dim. But it wasn't like that at all. They had an easy, loving, companionable and comfortable time. She was touched by his thoughtfulness, the little presents that kept appearing, the care he took. She felt that they trusted each other. As they began to consider the future, he was worried that he was so much older, that he needed solitude and concentration for his work, and that she might get bored or feel neglected. But she had no doubts. She was used to living alone and being independent. She wanted to look after him, but she had her own resources for solitude.

On 9 January 2012, her birthday was entered into the diary for the first time. They became a public couple, and made plans for their life together. Family and friends were largely delighted, and a chorus of approval went up from all who minded about him. Her own family fell in love with him, and were brought more together. He was very good with her mother, now in her late eighties. His sons, he noted with amusement, were relieved. Now they wouldn't have to take care of him in his dotage. Not that they wouldn't, but it took the heat off them, he thought. Sabrina, who would have liked to have her own children, welcomed the grand-children. Miriam was kind to her and gave her advice about the family dynamics. His brother Peter was tickled when he said he was 'walking out with Sabrina Guinness'. It should be 'stepping out', Peter told him. Many of his friends had known her socially for years. 'Lucky chap!' thought Tim Rice. David Cornwell saw that she would 'adapt herself around him' in a way that previous partners hadn't. All who knew him could see that he was very happy and in love; Sabrina told everyone she couldn't believe her good fortune, and that, in all her life, she had never loved anyone as deeply before. His women friends soon realised that they wouldn't need to feel threatened (as can happen when a new lover enters a long-established network), because she was not possessive or excluding. She had no jealousy about his past, and she was friendly and adaptable. Sonia Friedman called it 'a beautiful late romance', for which Sabrina had waited all her life. Sonia thought her 'smart, wise, and self-effacing'. Oliver's new partner Evonne, also a newcomer to the Stoppard family, thought that Oliver's father and Sabrina were rather alike, both 'kind, amiable and considerate'. It was a nice change for him to be looked after, and, as Diane Sawyer, one of his closest female friends, said, 'I'd like to have Sabrina look after me.' He took to referring to her, not entirely to her amusement, as his handmaiden, or carer.

She and Jacky got on well from the start, and they agreed a new arrange-ment between them. Jacky wanted to retire, to spend more time travelling with Dave and looking after her grandchildren. Sabrina had worked as a PA and was a good organiser. She took over the diary, the timetabling, the travel, the meetings, the invitations, the correspondence, the parties, the whole big operation that was his working and social life. He never did his own emails, as he knew he would drown in them (though he had taken avidly to texting), so, just as Jacky had done in the days of faxes, Sabrina received them, printed them out and replied according to the notes he scribbled on them. Jacky went on doing the finances and typing the scripts. He said, wickedly: I have two secretaries and I sleep with one of them. Sabrina's vast network of contacts became very useful to him in his fundraising work at the London Library. Lottie Cole at the Library said, with awe: 'She has an address book like no other address book.'

Through 2012, his public life was often shared with Sabrina. In the spring, there was the tribute to Havel at RIBA, and a ceremony at Windsor for the Queen Mother (where Stoppard was filmed leaving, chatting affably with Kendal), a rapid trip to New York for Christopher Hitchens's memorial, presenting the South Bank Awards, and hosting the Duchess of Cornwall at a London Library dinner. In the summer he held a party at Chelsea Harbour to watch the Queen's Diamond Jubilee flotilla go past in the pouring rain, went to the Prince's Institute patrons' dinner at St James's Palace and to Jade Jagger's wedding, celebrated his seventy-fifth by going to see *Uncle Vanya*, attended John Wood's memorial and Prince Michael's seventieth. There was a lot of publicity for *Parade's End.* They had a weekend in Pescara where he was given the Italian Flaiano cultural award, and spent a quiet month together in a house near Cartmel, in Cumbria, where he started to write *Darkside*. In the autumn they went to New York for him to chair a platform event at MOMA with the Rolling Stones, to an enraptured audience, to go with showings of *The Rolling Stones: 50 Years on Film*. He was nervous about it – he thought his questions were 'Rock 'n' Roll 101', like asking Jagger what kind of harmonicas he used – till he realised the Stones were even more nervous. The difficulty was to stop it being just a Mick-and-Keith show. Around that time, he and Sabrina made their first deliberate appearance in front of the press, at the red carpet opening of *Anna Karenina*.

John Boorman saw his old friend Sinéad Cusack at the Abbey Theatre, where she was giving a moving performance in *Juno and the Paycock*, soon after the new relationship became known. She said to him: 'You know,

Sabrina has always been looking for a good man; and now she's got the best man in the world.'

In 2013 they decided to find a new home and to change their lives. That year included trips to LA, Paris, Cologne and Tallinn (for a performance of *Coast* in Estonia) as well as all the usual London events. He was desperate to get started on the new play which he had been thinking about, now, for at least two years. They wanted a house far enough away from London to avoid constant interruptions and quick trips to town. They had another Cumbrian holiday, in March, and then Sabrina started house-hunting. She found them a fine home in deepest Dorset countryside. It was a Grade II listed 1790s house, once a parsonage, hidden from the road behind trees and a curving drive, built from the materials of a demolished Vanbrugh house. The outside walls were made of 'banded flint and ashlar', which give a black-and-white stripy effect. There were handsome steps up to the gabled entrance porch, a stone-flagged kitchen, high ceilings in the light downstairs rooms, with tall windows looking out onto a landscaped garden, and open fires in marble fireplaces. There was a stone stairway to the first floor and above that a wooden staircase, with elegant banisters, going to the two upper floors. There would be room for two studies and for visitors and grandchildren. Jacky thought it was a good thing that the sons would be able to come with their families for birthdays and Christmases, which hadn't been possible in London.

After twenty-five years of living there mainly on his own, he left Chelsea Harbour and his view of the Thames. It was rented out, and they kept Sabrina's West London flat for their London base. He ended his Shalden tenancy, and Sabrina rented her cottage to Sonia Friedman. He spent the summer of 2013 going through his papers and throwing things away, picking out materials that would go to his archive at the Harry Ransom Center in Texas, where he had sold regular tranches of his manuscripts and professional letters since 1993. In the middle of this discombobulating process of sorting and packing and moving, they went to Oxford on 19 June, where he was awarded an honorary degree. He was very pleased: 'I like tradition, heritage, dressing up,' he said, 'and I've always had an attraction to

Oxford.' There was much dining and ceremony, and Mark Damazer held a tea party for him at St Peter's College, where he made a point of talking the most to the least well-established people in the room, the young students who were putting on one of his plays.

A few days after the removal vans went to the new house, he gave his summer party on 6 July, as joyous and lavish an event as ever. As part of this tidying-up process in his seventy-sixth year, he selected his biographer. He had never got round to reading Ira Nadel's 2002 biography, and since then had politely turned down two or three approaches. Around that time, perhaps with biography in mind (and by way of a warning to any biographer), he gave a talk at the Dorset Chalke Valley History Festival on 'Live Theatre and Dead People', in which he considered, as in his 1997 London Library lecture, the thin divide between historical or biographical truth and the kind of truth there can be in fictional drama. Biographers and historians are obliged to be accurate, but 'the interpretation of historical events is constantly shifting', and biographers have to tread warily with the apparently 'irrefutable' facts provided by documents. But an imaginative writer, like himself, who 'makes things up', may be able to create a more 'persuasive' version of the truth – in, for instance, the lines he gives Wilde and Housman to say in *The Invention of Love*. Not for the first time, he proposed the nice paradox that there can be a 'relative instability of truth in history as opposed to the unchallengeable truth of fiction'.

By September, they were well settled into the house, and the phase of having books in boxes and not knowing where to find anything was over. Sabrina gave the house a comfortable, luxurious, friendly air. His first editions were ranged behind glass-windowed cupboards downstairs, his books and runs of literary magazines filled the wide landings and the upstairs shelves, his Russian posters for *Coast* hung outside his study, his framed writers' autographs were up in the bathrooms, his collection of British art – nineteenth-century watercolours, David Inshaw, Sarah Chatto, Craigie Aitchison, Mary Fedden, Alec Cobbe (Rose Cobbe's father) – hung in the downstairs rooms. A cavernous basement held their wine and his archive boxes and his fishing gear. Much of the life of the house took place in the ground-floor kitchen, with an Aga and a round table and a window seat, everywhere covered with newspapers and ash-trays, the Channel 4 news on every evening, high dressers overflowing with colourful kitchenware. Visitors would be settled down with the good wine which he hardly drank himself, in front of a log fire in the big sitting room and in an opulently welcoming guest room. David Cornwell and his wife thought it an 'enchanting' vision of country-house life, almost too good to be true. At first he worked in the downstairs front room, then moved up to the top floor, where, provided with a microwave and a kettle, he could hide away from the domestic and social life of the house. There were grand plans for the garden, where resident owls hooted on summer nights. They began by renting the house, but they were hoping to stay there forever, and by 2017 they owned it.

While they were moving, he asked Sabrina to marry him, and at the beginning of December 2013 they announced their engagement. The papers reacted predictably – 'It Girl and the Egghead' – as though they were talking about Arthur Miller and Marilyn Monroe. The next summer, on 7 June 2014, they were married in the local registry office, with family and close friends at the wedding, and a hundred guests at the party after-wards. Jacky helped with the planning. The flowers took five days to set up, the three-tier cake was decorated in summer blooms, rose petals were thrown, there was a marquee at the house, the sun shone, and Sabrina per-suaded him into an elegant new dark blue suit with waistcoat, a salmon-pink striped silk tie and a blue flower in his buttonhole. In the registry, under occupation, Sabrina wrote: 'housewife'. No journalists were invited, but two or three turned up and took photographs on the steps of the reg-istry office. They made albums afterwards of their own pictures. Both of them were beaming with happiness throughout.

Settled into his marriage and his house, he wanted to get on with the next play. Conditions weren't always perfect, of course. Sometimes there were too many interruptions, sometimes he felt he was having to go to London too often. In the autumn of 2014 he was diagnosed with Type 2 diabetes. It was a manageable condition but needed attention to diet (Sabrina took great care) and meant he got more tired, for all his inbuilt stamina and strong constitution. He still smoked.

But, broadly speaking, life in his late seventies was good. Living in the sort of country house he had dreamed, as a young man, of ending his days in; happy in a late marriage to a person who brought him comfort and companionship and many new friends; honours and titles lavished on him; and, above all, still working: all this gave off a settled, secure air. He often spoke of having a temperament which wanted to 'conserve' values and traditions, and a passionate feeling for England and Englishness. But, as he said, not for the first time, at his Chalke Valley lecture: 'Truth is a complex thing, not a simple one.' His voting patterns, for example, have not been predictable. He had voted for Harold Wilson, as well as for Margaret Thatcher. After his dedicated Thatcherite years in the 1980s, he voted New Labour in the 1997 election, Green in 2005, after the Iraq War, and Liberal Democrat in 2010. In 2019, he did not rule out ever voting Labour again, if Labour had a different leader.

His political acts – supporting the Soviet Jews, or the Czech dissidents, or the Belarus Free Theatre – had to do with the possibility of 'good'. Whether there *was* such a thing as 'good' was again preoccupying him in his new play. He took note of public situations where morality, decent or good behaviour, seemed to be under threat. His love of England increasingly took the form, not of complacent identification, as an outsider who had found his rightful home, but of anxious watchfulness. One channel for this anxiety was the current state of British newspapers. He never lost his romantic involvement with journalism, or his hopes of writing another play about it. But he observed with dismay and disgust the News International phone hacking scandal and its aftermath. When the scandal was at first attributed by News International to a single 'rogue reporter', he knew 'this wasn't a bad cough, it was cancer'.

The Leveson Inquiry was set up in 2011, exposing a shocking history of press intrusion into the lives not just of royalty and celebrities but also of ordinary people like the McCanns or Milly Dowler's family. In 2012 Leveson recommended an independent body for press regulation, which, as Stoppard saw it, would be a more 'disinterested version' of the discredited Press Complaints Commission, with some form of oversight which would require legal backing. Hacked Off, the protest movement for victims of press abuse, which had been formed in 2011, called for full support of Leveson in December 2012, with large numbers of signatories, including Stoppard. David Cameron, then prime minister, undertook to implement Leveson, but then reneged on his commitment. After much debate in parliament, in March 2013 a Royal Charter on the self-regulation of the press was approved, which eventually, in November 2014, set up an independent Press Recognition Panel to oversee press regulation. But most newspaper publishers, especially Murdoch's News International, were as vociferously opposed to the Royal Charter's PRP as they had been to Leveson, arguing that it introduced the threat of state regulation and censorship. Their preferred alternative was IPSO, the Independent Press Standards Organisation, which was set up in September 2014. IPSO's supporters argued that any criminal actions on the part of rogue reporters could, and should, be punished by the law of the land, not by the PRP, which, they argued, curtailed human rights to free speech.

Stoppard was disconcerted, if also flattered, to find that lines spoken by his idealistic young journalist in *Night and Day*, thirty-five years before, were being cited by opponents of Leveson. Writing in the *Independent* in March 2013, he said that such journalists had him down as 'an all-or-nothing man on press freedom'. '"No matter how imperfect things are," says my young reporter, "if you've got a free press everything is correctable, and without it everything is concealable."' As for what he calls 'junk journalism', that's 'the price you pay for the part that matters'.

But things had changed since *Night and Day*. His young reporter Jake was thinking of 'tabloid nonsense'. Jake 'isn't thinking of what happened to the McCanns, to Charlotte Church, or to hundreds of victims of phone-hacking, chicanery and outright lies by monstering journalists. Was it ever thus? It was not, not in the journalism I thought I was writing about in 1978.' In 2018, he would write to the *Guardian* making a similar point about the BBC's filming of the police raid on Cliff Richard's home. Stoppard noted that in his day as a journalist, if you named an as yet uncharged suspect 'you were in deep trouble'. 'American journalistic practice we considered a bad joke and an offence to legal process. We're catching up fast.'

He admired *Great Britain*, Richard Bean's 2014 National Theatre show about the phone-hacking scandal. And he argued over Leveson and the Royal Charter, amicably, with his journalistic friends. Max Hastings, who opposed the statutory regulation of the press, was surprised that a person with such profound liberal instincts should support it and attributed this to his having suffered from press intrusion into his own personal life. Bill Hagerty, editor of the *British Journalism Review*, to which Stoppard had contributed, understood that Stoppard was not *against* the press but was deeply concerned that it had got out of control. Stoppard reiterated his position at the *BJR* conference on 14 June 2016, organised by Hagerty, in memory of Charles Wheeler. In his speech to the conference, he admitted readily that he understood the argument for a libertarian press, but the problem was the collateral damage to the victims. He had been collecting materials to do with Leveson for several years, he told the audience, and he had read all the small print of the Royal Charter, to see exactly how the Press Recognition Panel would be arrived at. It seemed clear to him that this committee would be far more independent of parliament than IPSO was of the newspaper editors. It was no longer possible, in his view, to say that rubbish journalism was the price you pay for the part that matters. What was under consideration was behaviour which, even if not criminal, was damaging, irresponsible, indiscriminate and malicious. He took a moral view of the question.

In 2013, he was awarded the PEN Pinter Prize, which had been set up in Pinter's memory in 2009 to be given to a writer of distinction who (in the words of Pinter's Nobel speech) cast an 'unflinching, unswerving' gaze upon the world and showed a 'fierce intellectual determination . . . to define the real truth of our lives and our societies'. Accepting, with pride, the award from his old friend Antonia Fraser on 7 October 2013, he gave a talk called 'Circumspice'. The Latin motto in full, '*Si monumentum requiris circumspice*' – as on Christopher Wren's tomb in St Paul's – traditionally means, Look around you (with admiration and awe) and you will see my monument. Stoppard changed the inference of the word from eulogy to warning.

He spoke of what he had so often called 'his charmed life', having arrived in England when he was eight, the land of 'tolerance, fair play and autonomous liberty, of habeas corpus, of the mother of parliaments, of freedom of speech, worship and assembly, of the English language'. By the age of eighteen he added to that list 'the best and freest newspapers, forged in the crucible of modern liberty, and the best theatre'. Since then, reading Isaiah Berlin had taught him to think in terms of 'positive and negative freedom'. He had little reverence for 'positive' freedom, of the sort promised by a 'centralised state'; he minded much more about 'negative' freedom, by which Berlin meant 'the freedom to think for oneself . . . to name things for what they are and not for what they purport to be, to apply common sense, and common humanity'. The horror of the Soviet Union was 'the loss of autonomy, of the freedom to move freely'. By contrast to that, Stoppard had always had a sense of 'comfortable national superiority'. But he didn't have it any more. He was beginning to feel the need to write 'obsequies for the England we have mislaid'. What did he mean? He offered a random list:

Surveillance. Mis-selling pensions and insurance. Phone hacking. Celebrity culture. Premiership football. Dodgy dossier. Health and Safety. MPs' expenses. Political correctness. Internet porn. Targets as in the NHS. Managers as in the BBC. Bankers' bonuses.

Circumspice.

We are selling the family silver, by which I mean the family honour.

And he went into a long and anguished riff about what had happened to the free press in the era of the phone-hacking scandal. 'The nexus of politicians, police and newspaper executives, the poison fruit of, respectively, fear, corruptibility and remorseless commercial competition, was a fall from grace at the very heart of the freedoms hard-won long before I was a schoolboy agog with pride at being British.'

The PEN Pinter prize-winner is invited to give a subsidiary prize to a writer of their own choice. To mark his point, he gave this to Iryna Khalip, a courageous Belarusian journalist whom he had first met in Minsk in

2005, supporter of the late Anna Politkovskaya and wife of the Belarusian opposition politician Andrei Sannikov. She and her husband had both undergone arrest and surveillance. She was a reminder to him, and to the world, of 'honest and brave journalism'. 'She is the reporter I wanted to be.'

There are other examples from the late 2010s of political acts of his which link back to '*Circumspice*', relating to two of the most terrible aspects of the modern world, the refugee crisis and terrorism. He often accused himself of 'timidity': not putting his head above the parapet enough, avoiding confrontation and involvement. He was aware, too, that one could be over-praised and over-credited for making gestures of solidarity for those less fortunate, without putting oneself at risk. But he was harsh on himself.

7 January 2015 was the day of the assassinations at the *Charlie Hebdo* office in Paris. He happened to be in Paris on the following weekend, for Sabrina's sixtieth birthday. On 11 January, he joined the march of millions of Parisians protesting against the atrocities. It was just before the opening of his new play, *The Hard Problem*, and a week later he gave an interview in which he talked about those events. Of course he condemned the murders as indefensible atrocities carried out by 'deranged criminals'. But he could not associate himself entirely with the magazine. He didn't agree with making aggressive scatological jokes about Islamic beliefs. And he thought the slogan '*Je suis Charlie*', which was 'supposed to be a statement against extremism', was actually 'a gratuitous swipe at the entire population of Muslim countries'. What we have to do, he said, faced with extremism and violence, is 'demonstrate by our behaviour that our values are better than theirs'.

A year later, on 21 February 2016, he was one of a group of theatre people who went to read and perform at the refugee camp, the 'Jungle', in Calais, as it was being threatened with demolition. Sonia Friedman and Natalia Kaliada were both involved, and urged him to come. The visit was under the aegis of Good Chance Theatre, an organisation which creates pop-up theatre performances in areas of need, and Letters Live, for which actors read in support of causes and charities. There were pictures of the seventy-eight-year-old playwright, in Barbour and wellies, smoking, and tramping through the camp alongside Jude Law, Juliet Stevenson, Toby Jones, Kaliada and others. He knew very well how some of the press would treat this expedition of luvvies to read to refugees from Africa and the Middle East. And he didn't consider it a major action on his part: all he had to do was turn up, and then go home. Still, he thought it was the right thing to do. For him, he said to reporters, the question was moral rather than economic.

> This discussion is like peeling an onion. There are all these arguments and counter-arguments, but finally you have to go with something deeper: what do you feel is right? What would you feel more or less ashamed of? I would rather be wrong this way . . . I don't sneer at people who are worried about the infrastructure in England, [but] that's just not the strong argument. The strong argument is to behave decently before you try to do the arithmetic, because the arithmetic is never going to be that bad. There is a lot of space, money and goodwill in England.

David Hare, reading this interview, thought: "This is why I love this man. It so perfectly expresses the way he thinks."

The refugee crisis, the war in Syria, the acts of terrorism in Europe, the rise of UKIP, which he found 'scary and depressing', made him feel, as he had felt after 9/11, that world events were too monstrous and bewildering for him to write about directly. A few months after his visit to the Jungle came Brexit. He voted to remain. As usual, he had listened to both sides of the question, and understood the concerns about an over-bureaucratic, expensive and inefficient European apparatus. But he soon came to feel, as the debate progressed, that 'something unpleasant had been unleashed'. The bitterly divided aftermath of the vote bore out his feelings in '*Circumspice*', three years earlier, that something was going profoundly wrong with the England he had loved.

Later that year, in December 2016, he had a long conversation with Arkady Ostrovsky. Ostrovsky said to him that when he came to England as a young man, that was the country he wanted to belong to; but now, in his forties, he felt that it had changed into another country, about which he didn't feel the same. It reminded Stoppard of Herzen's words, which he put into *The Coast of Utopia*, about the English giving asylum to Russian exiles, not out of respect for them, but 'out of respect for themselves'. That, he thought, was what we have lost. When did that go? Why did that go? *Circumspice.*

In the five years since *Rock 'n' Roll*, and while he was absorbed in *Parade's End*, there was no new play. He had been collecting materials: about newspapers, about the financial crash of 2008, about neuroscience and consciousness, about belief. He had got interested again in moral philosophy and ethics. Interviewed by Mark Lawson in the summer of 2013, he said, in tones of quiet desperation, that this long gap was 'horrifying' to him, and he was *determined* to write another stage play. He thought of himself, always, as 'a theatre writer who does other things in between'.

One of those 'other things' came out of an approach from a young producer at BBC Radio 2, James Robinson, an idea for marking the fortieth anniversary of Pink Floyd's 1973 album, *The Dark Side of the Moon*, with a radio play. It appealed to him because it linked back to the appearance of Syd Barrett in *Rock 'n' Roll*, and also for the chance of writing again for the radio. It was a medium he loved and was loyal to. Briefly involved in 2010 in a controversy about the status of plays on the BBC, he told the controller of Radio 4, Mark Damazer, that he thought BBC radio drama was 'a national treasure'. It was coming up to his own anniversary of nearly fifty years since his first radio plays, *The Dissolution of Dominic Boot* and *'M' Is for Moon*.

The Dark Side of the Moon, one of the most influential and bestselling rock albums of all time, was recorded a few years after Barrett had fallen out of the band into the dark side of his mind. It is a continuous flow of songs with a complex underscore of interpolated voices, laughter and sound effects like ticking clocks, a heartbeat, a tolling bell and the tinkle of cash registers. In an obscure and surreal way (food for a thousand 'disambiguations'), the album told a story. The songs were about madness and those on the edges of society, about time and its terrors, about the haves and have-nots, and about the sense of our little lives flowing through the vast universe. It was written at a time when the alternative psychoanalyst R. D. Laing was a force; the band was said to have consulted Laing about Barrett's mental state. Laing's opposition to conventional treatments of schizophrenia and his work on madness as a kind of shamanic journey of revelation is one of many influences that underlies the album, and it gets into the radio play.

Stoppard set out to use the album 'in a loose sort of way'. But the structure was very precisely worked out. There were fifteen minutes of the vocals, played straight with no interruptions, and forty-five minutes of play, twenty-five of which were underscored by non-vocal sections of the album. He assured the members of Pink Floyd, who were happy with what he wanted to do, that he would not write his words over their lyrics. He didn't try to make a story directly out of the songs, but rather to 'invent a little story, in the spirit of the album'. It wasn't realistic, he warned the producer, 'more like magic realism'. He got annoyed when the producer tried to 'clarify the story'. Don't impose a logical structure on what is dreamlike, don't make it ordinary, he told him. And then, apologetically: 'My entire career seems to have been a campaign against over-explicitness.'

In his notes to himself, he identified the essence of each track, mixing his own language with Pink Floyd's phrases. The theme of the song 'Breathe' was 'keep running, keep working, grafting to your grave'. 'Time' told you that 'you fritter your life away thinking there is lots of time . . . You try to catch up, but fall further behind . . . you hang on in quiet desperation . . .' The essence of 'Money' was: 'Me. Mine. Hands off!' 'Us and Them' reminded him of Lenin's slogan, 'Who whom?', which he had used before as a shorthand for power struggles: who does what to whom, who prevails? 'Let the weakest go to the wall.' 'Brain Damage' spoke of the unworldly, the unstable: 'If you feel powerless, overwhelmed, intimidated, you're not alone – I'll see you there.' 'Eclipse' made him think of 'No man is an island. The bell tolls for you.'

Out of these jottings he devised a story which took shape around the tracks, in their order as on the album. Working this out was the kind of puzzle-problem he enjoyed, like matching the rock music to the scenes of *Rock 'n' Roll* or creating a story around the songs in *Cats*. At first he thought of beginning with a voiceover about the dawn of time, written in the tone which he developed for the whole play, as if telling a magic fable for children. 'Once upon a time there was nothing. Only, it wasn't nothing, it was nothingness. Lots and lots of nothingness. Only it wasn't exactly nothingness, it was nothingness with things . . . Then a long time went by.' (He said in a lecture in 2011 that what he liked about radio was that, unlike in any other medium, you could start a play: 'Scene 1: A billion years ago; Scene 2: A week later.') Then he abandoned this idea and plunged in with the alarming soundtrack of the start of the album: a heartbeat, a helicopter, machine-gun fire, screaming. It was like the dream of war at the beginning of *Night and Day*.

In the end the story of *Darkside* had as much to do with his own interests as with Pink Floyd. He had been reading about thought experiments (in physics and in philosophy) and he liked the idea of a play full of characters from thought experiments: the Fat Man who has to be thrown from the leaking hot-air balloon, the boy who is on the railway track when the points are switched to save the lives of the people on the train. Emily McCoy, the young heroine whose surname tells us she's the real thing, is a moral philosophy student; she's also a patient in a mental hospital who hears voices. What better medium for the idea of hearing voices than a radio play? The play switches tracks unpredictably between her 'mad' dream world, her classroom and the mental ward. The philosophy teacher, in her dream world, is Ethics Man (a suave Rufus Sewell), the Superman who runs the thought experiments. (In the classroom world, there is a nice joke about him not being able to spell Nietzsche: 'Hang on, that doesn't look right – I think I've got the "z" in the wrong . . .') The mental doctor, the lobotomist, is also a witch finder (played with lovely malevolence by Bill Nighy). Fat Man speaks entirely in famous lines from famous movies. Emily and the boy from the tracks and Fat Man, like travellers in Oz or the innocent children on the run in Pullman's *His Dark Materials*, seek the wise man up a high mountain to tell them the secret of life, which turns out to be: 'This is not a drill.' 'That was a little disappointing, I thought,' says Emily. They flee their enemies, who are the men in charge of the world, logicians, bankers, politicians, mental doctors. They risk being burnt at the stake as witches (a touch of Shaw's *St Joan* here), lose and find each other again. The boy is only in her mind, but he is also real, like 'the juggler on the radio' he knows is there, even if you can't hear, see, smell or touch him – an image which makes a brilliant radio-play-within-a-radio-play device. The world they travel through is a blighted wasteland of green river valleys turning to dust and bones. This is Stoppard's only ecologically-minded play, in which climate change and man's spoiling of his own environment are part of the problem. ('We consume everything. We're dying of consumption. Hardwoods are toppling for dashboards . . . The last swordfish is gasping beneath a floating island of plastic as big as France.') If only Emily could find the words, she could tell everyone how to save the world. And her message is:

> The earth is a common.
> You can't save it for yourself but
> you can save it for others, and
> the others will save it for you.
> The other is us, and we are the
> other. We are of a kind, we are
> natural born to kindness, which
> means to act as to our kind, as
> kin to kin, as kindred, which is
> to act kindly. What is the Good?
> It is nothing but a contest of kindness.

Emily's message doesn't save the world, needless to say, but it does tell us what is preoccupying her author. Isn't there more to reality than materiality and machines? Isn't there a spiritual domain? – 'more to us than meets the scanner', as he put it in interview. And isn't there such a thing as 'the good', borne out by our essential need for kindness and altruism? The juggler on the radio is as ineffable as the presence of God in *Jumpers*, the play that came out a year before *The Dark Side of the Moon*, and which this little radio play, with its mad girl and its philosopher and its questions of belief, strongly echoes, forty years on. And it looks ahead as well as back. *Darkside* humanises thought experiments, questions materiality and proposes kindness and altruism as evidence for 'the good' in exactly the way that *The Hard Problem* will, two years on. He spoke of it as a minor work. 'It's light,' he told Alastair Macaulay, 'fifty-five minutes including the whole album.' And 'it helps if you like Pink Floyd'. He had wondered whether Radio 2 (usually the channel for popular music, not plays) was the right place for it, but was delighted that he would get an audience probably 'as large as all my other audiences put together'. It was greeted with respect and bafflement. But, for all its oddity and slightness, it carries the weight of his deepest concerns.

34

The Eightieth Year

We're dealing in mind stuff that doesn't show up in a scan –
accountability, duty, freewill, *language*, all the stuff that makes behaviour
unpredictable.

The summer of 2014, the summer of his marriage and of finishing *The Hard Problem*, also involved discussions about turning *Shakespeare in Love* into a play. He had been asked more than once by Sonia Friedman to do this, and had made a reluctant start. Her argument was that the film was based on a play that was yet to be written. But he wasn't convinced by the need for a stage version of what had been such a successful film. And it bored him to go back over old work. Though he abandoned the idea of adapting it himself, Friedman did not give up on it. Lee Hall, of *Billy Elliot* fame, was asked to do it, and Friedman nudged Stoppard into taking a benign interest. He sent Lee Hall encouraging messages ('out of the frying-pan into the clover is how I see it') and his own unfinished draft, which gave more stage time to Christopher Marlowe. There were meetings with Hall and Friedman during 2012 and 2013, and Hall gave him careful updates: 'No one writes such coruscating dialogue with such a lightness of touch, so it is with great trepidation that I send this to you.' It opened in July 2014 at the Noël Coward Theatre, with a huge cast, directed and designed by the Cheek by Jowl partnership of Declan Donnellan and Nick Ormerod, who conjured up strong theatrical magic from the film. Boisterous, fast-moving, touchingly acted and good-looking, it was a hit. It ran on into the spring of 2015, transferred to the States and went on tour. Stoppard thought it was 'very nice'.

In the early autumn of 2014 two revivals in the States, both Roundabout Theatre productions, were also taking up his time. *Indian Ink*, directed by Carey Perloff, opened in September 2014 off Broadway, in a delicate production. The veteran Rosemary Harris played the Peggy Ashcroft/ Margaret Tyzack part of Eleanor Swan, there was a masterly Firdous Bamji as Nirad Das, and Romola Garai was a sharp, mannered Flora. As the New York audience settled into their seats, Stoppard's voice came over the house speakers: 'Unwrap your candies now!' A new Broadway production of *The Real Thing* started rehearsals as *Indian Ink* opened, directed by Sam Gold, with some big stars, Ewan McGregor, Maggie Gyllenhaal, and Cynthia Nixon, of *Sex and the City*, who had played the daughter in the first New York production, as Charlotte. He went over for both productions. *Tulip Fever* had also come back, and he spent some days in the cutting room and working on new bits of dialogue for this ill-starred venture. In November 2014, he was given an accolade he didn't relish, the Lebedev Award for 'Greatest Living Playwright' at the *Evening Standard* theatre awards. The description profoundly embarrassed him.

That autumn, two deaths touched him deeply. His great friend Debo, Duchess of Devonshire, died on 24 September 2014. On 19 November 2014, Mike Nichols died. He had been one of Stoppard's dearest people, and his tributes to him were grief-struck. 'He was my hero . . . to have been his friend was a blessing.' A year on, he spoke of it as 'the most wrenching bereavement I can ever remember experiencing. I'm not reconciled to it yet.' He never stopped missing him.

Towards the end of 2014, he finished *The Hard Problem*, which was dedicated to Sabrina. It went into rehearsal in December 2014 and opened in January 2015. Ten or more years' worth of yellowing clippings fed into it, going back to the financial crash of 2007–8, and before that to debates in the mid-1990s between the philosophers John Searle and David Chalmers on the mystery of consciousness, and to his reading for Mosley's *Hopeful Monsters*. It linked further back, too, to his philosophical homework for *Jumpers* in the 1970s. He had tried out versions of its ideas in *Rock 'n' Roll* and in *Darkside*. At one point he thought of it as a play about the financial market. Another idea, long in his mind, was to write a play about an American population geneticist called George Price, who worked on altruism and coincidence, suffered from depression and killed himself in London in 1975. And he had always wanted to write a play about a mathematician. Those unwritten plays lurk behind this one.

The Hard Problem is a short argumentative play about very large subjects: how consciousness works, whether altruism and goodness are innate human qualities, whether God exists. The venue for these discussions is a Brain Science Institute founded by Jerry Krohl, a 'squillionnaire' hedge-fund manager. The financial market provides parallels, or metaphors, for the play's arguments about consciousness and the brain. He told the National Theatre cast – to their amusement – that he had a tendency to write plays that have two or three things in them which at first glance don't have much to do with each other.

Computers, mathematics, thought experiments, psychological investigations, evolutionary examples and statistical data are used as tools for arguments: this allows him to have fun with specialised jargons. The characters are mainly young professionals – it is an old writer's play about the confusions and ambitions of youth – who are competing and partnering and jostling for their place in the ruthless fields of science, sex and finance. Through the rapid, time-jumping scurry of debate and information, certain words ring out quietly: 'coincidence', 'outlier', 'prayer', 'good'. The play's urgent, anxious questions circle around a central story, as grave and simple as a fairy tale or a late Shakespeare romance, of a young woman who has lost her daughter and finds her again.

This being a Stoppard play, not a play by Shaw or Ibsen or Hare, no one gets the last word. As usual, arguments which the author doesn't find sympathetic are forcefully made. Because this is a concentrated piece of minimalism, relationships are condensed and only essential background for the characters is given. Yet there is love and sorrow, friendship and longing, in the play. And there is a strong emotional preference for some choices over others, as to how you might want to live your life or what you might want to believe. Most of these are voiced by the young woman, Hilary Matthews (her surname another private tribute to Jacky), who – like the heroine of *Hapgood*, or *Indian Ink*, or *Darkside* – carries the play.

The 'hard problem' was a term coined by Australian philosopher and scientific materialist David Chalmers to apply to the intractable question of what consciousness consists of. Why do we have subjective 'first person' experiences? We know everything about the physical composition of the brain, but very little about why we have certain emotions in response to the colour blue, a sunset, the smell of hot buttered toast or a Rolling Stones song. Chalmers says that consciousness is 'the thing in the world that we know the best and understand the least'. He asks: 'Why do we experience our lives the way we do? Why are we self-aware?' The missing ingredient in empirical explanations of consciousness is: 'How does objective reality relate to subjective reality in the world of science?' 'The hard problem is the seemingly unanswerable question of how a physical, objective brain can create the ineffable, subjective experience of consciousness.' Chalmers calls it the 'hard' problem, as opposed to the 'easy' problem of understanding the physical components of the brain. Stoppard spent some time in rehearsals for the first production nudging the cast to say 'the *hard* problem' and not 'the hard *problem*'.

The 'hard problem' is summed up in an argument about computers and the brain between Hilary, a psychology student, Amal, a mathematician turned biophysicist, both in for a job at the Krohl Institute, and Leo, the psychologist at the institute, who will hire one of them. Amal argues that the human brain doesn't 'come close' to what a computer can do. Hilary isn't interested: to her the concept of a computer thinking isn't 'deep'.

Leo: So, what would be your idea of deep?

Hilary: A machine that minds losing . . .

Amal: If I made a computer simulating a human brain neuron by neuron, it would mind losing.

Leo (*to Hilary*): Do you agree?

Hilary: No.

Leo: Amal's machine wouldn't be conscious?

Hilary: No, but how would you tell? You can't tell by watching the wheels go round. Just like with a brain. I couldn't tell what you're thinking by watching what your brain is doing, or even that you're thinking.

Amal: I'll tell you what I'm thinking. There is overwhelming evidence that the brain causes consciousness.

Hilary: There's overwhelming evidence that brain activity correlates with consciousness. Registers consciousness. Nobody's got anywhere trying to show how the brain is conscious.

Amal: This is sophistry! [Changed from the original line: 'This is
    mysticism!']
Leo (*to Hilary*): So, how would consciousness come about?
Hilary: I have no idea, and nor does anyone else. I thought that's why
    we're here. To crack the Hard Problem.

There is another version of the argument in the opening scene in
Hilary's bedroom, where her tutor, Spike, is spending the night ('an abuse
of trust without precedent in higher education'). Explain consciousness,
says Hilary to Spike, who is impatient with the question. Shockingly, he
holds her finger to a candle flame and she starts back.

Spike: Flame – finger – brain; brain – finger – ouch.
Hilary: Brilliant. Now do sorrow.

The issue of consciousness cuts across different fields of enquiry: that
was one of the things that interested him about it. In an early clipping,
from a 1995 *New York Review of Books*, John Searle observed that 'the most
important problem in the biological sciences is one that until quite recently
many scientists did not regard as a suitable subject for scientific investigation at all. It is this: How exactly do neurobiological processes in the brain
cause consciousness?' *The Hard Problem* reflects that cross-disciplinarity
by having the Krohl Institute (complete with Pilates studio, gym and
organic vegetables) hire evolutionary biologists, neuroscientists, mathematicians and psychologists – everything except philosophers. When Hilary
leaves the institute she goes to America to study philosophy – perhaps,
who knows, with Thomas Nagel, the philosopher whose argument for a
subjective aspect to consciousness was one of many influences on the play.
    By sleight of hand, the play links together arguments about con-
sciousness and about altruism. Is everything evolved for survival? Or are
there innate, irrational emotions that aren't about self-preservation? The
Chalmers-derived title (which he was a bit worried about in case people
might think it was a play about erectile dysfunction) makes it look as if
the play is all about consciousness. But it could also have been called,

after George in *Jumpers*, 'Is God?' or, after Emily in *Darkside*, 'What is the Good?'

In the opening scene, Spike, an aggressive believer in the brain as a machine and a Dawkinsian advocate for 'selfish gene' evolutionary science, is testing Hilary out on the game theory thought experiment of the Prisoner's Dilemma, which is so banally familiar to her as to bring on nausea. Stoppard, when asked to sum up this thought experiment for the lay people to whom it *isn't* banally familiar (which he reckoned made up about half his audience), explains it thus:

Two prisoners, held incommunicado, are being questioned by the police about a crime they've collaborated in (a jewellery robbery, say). If they both remain silent (the technical term is 'co-operate'), they can only be charged with a lesser offence, carrying a maximum sentence of one year. But this depends on their trusting each other. If one of them betrays the other (technically, 'defects'), telling the whole story, that prisoner will go free and the other one will get ten years. So one prisoner is sitting there, thinking: 'If I can trust him, or her, we'll be out of here in a year. But if she's shopping me, then I'd better shop her back, to protect myself.' And if they both shop each other, they both get five years. The prisoner is thinking: 'Christ, I could be locked up for ten years, but if I betray my partner, it'll only be five. If I can trust my partner and stay mum (and trust her to stay mum), it would only be one year.' In short: two rational prisoners will betray each other if they act rationally, although they know that by trusting each other they'd have been better off.

One of his experts on the Prisoner's Dilemma, Ken Binmore, says that it 'represents a situation in which the dice are loaded against the emergence of co-operation'. 'The dilemma is that mutual co-operation yields a better outcome than mutual defection, but is not the rational outcome, because the choice to co-operate, from a self-interested perspective, is irrational.' (Stoppard's characters talk about the Prisoner's Dilemma as a 'one-off' situation; game theorists note that outcomes are different when the game is played repeatedly – 'iterated Prisoner's Dilemma' – because the players learn to second-guess each other, and, over time, 'reciprocal altruism' may emerge as the best form of self-preservation.)

Who whom? Who rats on whom in Spike's scenario, 'Bob' or 'Luanne'? ('*Luanne?*' says Hilary disbelievingly. Spike: 'There's never been a smash-and-grab jewellery raider called Hilary.') But Hilary says that, as 'Luanne', she loves 'Bob' and will take the rap for him. It wrecks the game, because the Prisoner's Dilemma can't do love, or empathy, or self-sacrifice, or kinship – any more than computers can do 'minding'. Later in the play, which is full of neat parallels, Hilary does just this – takes the rap for a colleague who loves *her*. As the witch finder in *Darkside* complains, when faced with prisoners A and B in the game of Prisoner's Dilemma who are 'making false confessions to sacrifice themselves, each for the other', this is not something he's ever come across: 'competitive altruism'.

Spike argues for self-interest as the evolutionary basis of all behaviour. Hilary argues for the possibility of innate good, and for something outside the machine. 'Who is the you outside your brain?' she asks him. She won't accept that science has all the answers. 'Virtue is not science. You can't get an *ought* out of an *is*. Morality is not science. So there must be something else, which isn't science. Which science isn't. What is it?' Their positions are exaggerated for a play that needs to get complicated arguments across in a fast, dramatic and engaging way: his favourite task. He told the actors that though the debates had to be understood, the play wasn't *about* consciousness; it was about people's actual lives.

As always he accumulated a huge base of information under the tip of the iceberg that was the play. If he had been writing an essay, he might have shown how his arguments evolved from centuries of debate, going back to Descartes ('I think, therefore I am'). But all that had to be buried. His process was always the same. He read and read till he had taken on more than he could handle. Then he plunged in and made it up as he went along. There had to be a point where he stopped beating himself up for not knowing X, Y and Z, and began writing *without* knowing X, Y and Z. It was a lesson he had found hard to learn.

He consulted leading philosophers and scientists, including Richard Dawkins, whom he asked whether 'virtue' can always be reduced to Darwinian utility. Dawkins argued that 'sympathy, pity, empathy, warmth' are 'natural selection's way of seeing to it that we do the right thing by our genes'. 'Who believes this really and truly?' Stoppard responded. Part of this exchange was printed in the programme. He got help from the evolutionary biologist Armand Marie Leroi on how game theory can support an argument for an evolving society where co-operation may arise out of self-interest as a mode of survival: 'reciprocal altruism', colourfully demonstrated in the play by the behaviour of vampire bats. Leroi read and annotated the first draft of the play.

He talked to the American evolutionary biologist David Sloan Wilson, whose book *Does Altruism Exist?* came out around the same time as *The Hard Problem*. Wilson challenged Dawkins's view of genetic evolution as a form of selfishness, arguing that in evolutionary terms 'altruistic groups' beat 'selfish ones'. Stoppard debated with him in public after *The Hard Problem* opened. He argued, like Hilary, that a scientific analysis of the evolutionary functioning of groups can't account for our everyday meaning of altruism, 'selfless behaviour that benefits others and involves personal sacrifice'. Without describing himself as particularly spiritual, there was something he wanted to call 'transcendence'. (As he put it in an interview: 'I just instinctively don't feel that consciousness is the product of a biological computer.') Wilson noted that in *The Hard Problem*, 'consciousness and altruism are thoroughly intertwined'. Yes, Stoppard replies, 'I think altruism is unintelligible without consciousness in the way I'm using the word.' His feeling is that altruism is demonstrated on a 'one-to-one', family level. It was in his nature to put the argument in terms of family, or what Emily in *Darkside* calls 'kin'. 'Altruism is what you do for someone you love.'

In these conversations, it amused him to define himself as 'a dualist by default' or a 'naive sceptic', an 'ethical realist' or an 'intuitionist'. Whatever the technical term, he belongs to the category of those who believe there is some divide between mind and body – or *soul* and body – and that not everything can be collapsed into the physical realm. His own views and feelings are part of the play but not the message of the play. All the characters have a point of view, and some of them change their minds. It's nice, he told the first cast, if the characters have a learning experience.

Amal, Hilary's rival, doesn't get the job at the Krohl, but he impresses Jerry, who employs him in his hedge-fund business. The unwritten play about finance edges in here. How can you predict the market? How is it that crashes happen? Five years on, Amal infuriates Jerry by second-guessing market fluctuations and giving out information which undermines their clients' confidence. Jerry, the big beast in the jungle, always supremely egoistical and aggressive (but, paradoxically, something of an altruist too in his personal life), needs always to be ahead of the game. He hires Spike because he likes his theory that you can predict poker players' (or stock-market traders') risk-taking and risk-aversion by analysing their saliva samples. Leo comments grimly that Jerry adores this, because it 'monetises the hormonal state of your trading desk'.

But not everything can be predicted. There will always be 'outliers'. The play implicitly draws on the financial crash as the catastrophic example of how the market at times behaves irrationally. 'In theory', as Amal says, 'the market is a stream of rational acts by self-interested people; so risk ought to be computable . . . But every now and then, the market's behaviour becomes irrational, as though it's gone mad, or fallen in love.' He begins to realise that his faith in computable systems may not be fool-proof. You have to allow for outliers.

At the institute, Hilary rediscovers (in one of the play's unlikely coincidences) an old school chum, now the Krohl Pilates instructor, and becomes friends with her and her brainy partner Ursula. Hilary does experiments to test empathy, and employs a young Chinese woman, Bo (this play has Stoppard's most multicultural casting), who carries out a statistical test for altruism in children of different ages. But Bo rigs the results of the test, in order to please Hilary, whom she loves. To prove her point about innate altruism, Bo gets rid of the 'outliers' in the experiment. Hilary takes the rap for Bo, and leaves the institute, much to Leo's regret. Leo's sad story – a middle-aged man struggling for the survival of his department and hopelessly in love with Hilary – is just touched in. The characters' relationships, briefly and sharply sketched, are all set up to illustrate the argument between egoism and altruism, materialism and metaphysics.

At the heart of *The Hard Problem* is Hilary's sorrow, *her* hard problem. As a fifteen-year-old schoolgirl, she gave up her baby, Cathy, for adoption and has grieved for her loss ever since. (She's twenty-two when the play starts, twenty-seven when it ends.) She believes that just by being 'good', behaving well, she might help herself and her daughter, and she thinks that praying is a good idea, and not just for her: 'Everyone should say a prayer every day, anyway, for who you love, just because it puts them in your diary.' This, of course, is anathema to Spike, who is as fanatically sceptical about the usefulness of prayer or the possibility of God as any religious fundamentalist. Hilary keeps trying to tell him it's not 'God' like an old man with a white beard 'who created the world in six days and then had a rest', it's 'God' standing for something outside what we know: 'otherwise we're just marking our own homework'.

The audience knows from Scene Four of the play that Jerry has an adopted daughter called Cathy who is the right age. But we, and Hilary, don't find out for sure until the end (spoiler alert, but it's not much of a spoiler) that Jerry's Cathy is her Cathy. The staggering unlikeliness of this coincidence may be a weak piece of plotting; it's also the point. But the argument between faith and materialism is not resolved:

Hilary: You know it's a miracle, don't you?
Jerry: A miracle? No. A long shot. A coincidence. I don't believe in miracles. As a matter of fact, I don't believe in coincidence either. You didn't have the information.

Nothing is concluded. But mother-love is strongly suggested as a proof of altruism. Spike won't hear of it. He calls Raphael's *Madonna and Child* 'Woman Maximising Gene Survival', which always gets a laugh. 'Do you know anyone who believes that, really and truly?' Hilary asks Spike – exactly as Stoppard asked Dawkins. Most of the play's audiences are likely to feel sympathy with her question. Most people, even if they aren't religious, have a vague idea that, individually, there are such things as goodness, altruism, empathy and generosity, even in a world of injustice, cruelty, competitive self-interest and conflict. And most people, according to Stoppard, 'would be surprised if they thought their behaviour derived from how we've evolved physiologically in response to our environment'. People feel they have moral autonomy. 'Some values haven't changed from

Homer and the Bible. There's a matrix which underlies the social behaviour that doesn't change as centuries go by.' But to others, these beliefs are sentimental illusions.

There is, as always, personal material buried in this play. Hilary's situation derives, much altered, from Sinéad Cusack's giving up of her son and her long quest to find him. And mother-love as the proof of altruism returned him to his feelings about his own mother, whose life story continued to be strongly in his mind. Those were not the things he said about the play in public, where he talked about its long gestation ('I didn't wait, I *procrastinated*'), its arguments and his own views, as when asked, 'For want of a better word, do you believe in God?' His reply: 'Is there a better word?'

He sent Nicholas Hytner, the director, a message at the end of 2013: 'It's about evolutionary biology and the banking crisis. Happy Christmas.' Hytner told the cast it was a beautiful, challenging, utterly original play that found new ways of looking at the world and who we are. But he would have liked there to have been more inner life for the characters. Stoppard wanted to keep it 'brisk', like a piano piece that had its own rhythm. He knew it was riskily short for a play that contained enough material for a *Coast of Utopia*-length trilogy. But he liked the hundred-minute length. He'd become envious of the recent vogue for short pieces played without a break. For one thing, it was a way of avoiding the curse of the playwright, people coming up in the interval and saying 'How do you think it's going?'

In rehearsal, he was keen to explain the play's ideas to the cast, less eager to provide them with back-stories or character notes. Why was Leo running late for his interviews, the actor asked. Hytner turned to Stoppard. 'Tom, do we know why he's late?' Stoppard said, mildly: 'No.' He didn't join in when the women characters were discussing why Hilary didn't go back to school after she'd had the baby, or how well Hilary and Spike knew each other before they got together. 'I was still trying to find that out as I went along,' he said.

He listened like a hawk for 'beats' and emphases, for 'speed bumps' and punctuation marks, for moments when lines or jokes weren't quite landing, for audibility and clarity. He made small changes willingly: 'I think I've got this sentence a bit wrong,' he would say, or 'I may have made things more difficult for you, the writing there is a bit stodgy.' He paid minute attention to the words, noting, for instance, that Bo, the Chinese-American, should say '*Re*search', and Amal, the Cambridge-educated British-Indian, should say 'Re*search*'. He frequently tried to explain why something in the play *wasn't* explained. 'I want the absolute minimum,' he would say, 'I don't want to write over-explicitly.' The acting notes he gave, which he put politely through Hytner, were always in the interests of understatement. The actors responded to his grace and warmth, though one or two of the younger ones would have liked more discussions about gender and race.

During rehearsals he makes a writer's nest of his corner table, listening hard, editing the layout of the programme, texting, reading the papers, occasionally snoozing, taking pencils out of his zip-up pencil case, ferreting in his beautiful old soft leather shoulder bag, cracking peanuts, clipping his nails and eating bananas and (diabetic) sweets. He turns up for work in a mixture of blue denim jacket over bulky pullover, green check tweed jacket, brown cords, baggy grey cardigan, lace-up leather shoes, orange socks, dark-coloured shirts. His hair a shaggy grey mane, his face a great lined map of thinking, he looks messy, grand, benign, idiosyncratic, sometimes weary, and not like anyone else in the world.

He told the company, on their first day, that he was extremely happy to be back at the National after so many years, all the more because the play had taken him a long time. He hadn't worked with Hytner before, so he felt inhibited, and didn't jump in freely in rehearsals as he would have done with Peter Wood or Trevor Nunn. But he never argued with him, and was impressed by his calm. This was Hytner's last production as director of the National Theatre. Many other things were going on outside the rehearsal room, but Hytner tried to keep all that at bay while they worked on the play.

There had been logistical problems at the National. The building works on the Dorfman Theatre, the newly revamped, former Cottesloe, were delayed. *The Hard Problem* opened there in January 2015, some months after it was originally scheduled. Anticipation was high. There were lots of preview pieces in the major papers, summing up his work, returning to the usual themes of emotion versus intellect, and using words like 'long-awaited' and 'major event'. It opened to eager audiences and packed-out houses. Bob Crowley designed a giant, glittering model of a brain, with multicoloured lights flashing through a cluster of rods and chains, like neurons zipping about, hanging above a spare, minimally realist set. Bach piano music covered the set changes. The effect was cool, objective, even abstract, though the actors, led by Olivia Vinall as Hilary, worked hard for passion and emotion.

But the reception was mainly negative. Reviewer after reviewer talked of 'a disappointing return from a great playwright', a dramatic 'dud', a 'strangely conventional' and 'tendentious' play from 'the great adventurer'. The play's big coincidence was thought unconvincing, its intellectual content over-taxing and its emotional life 'undernourished'. The production was described as elegant and uninvolving, not Hytner's best at the National. A general view began to prevail that *The Hard Problem* was a failure. It was as though critics had forgotten, over nine years, what a Stoppard play might demand of them or how to react to it, or even as though they were enjoying having a kick at the 'greatest living playwright'. A few lone voices stood out. Mark Lawson, writing after most of the other reviews, thought that 'excessive anticipation' had 'almost guaranteed disappointment', and argued that the play, compressed as it was, was moving, and displayed intact Stoppard's 'remarkable ability to synthesise complex knowledge into wittily metaphorical dialogue'.

Stoppard told Lawson he had been 'bucked up' by his piece. He took the critical reaction quietly and was cheered by the fact that audiences were flocking in, but it wasn't a happy moment. Matters weren't helped by the reporting of the National Theatre platform talk he gave with Hytner on 6 February 2015. In their conversation, Stoppard joked about how he had had to rewrite a line that was too oblique, during previews, because it wasn't 'landing'. After the rewrites, and with a new piece of action, by the fourth preview the line got a laugh. Hytner had foreseen that the line might be a problem, Stoppard hadn't. Teasingly, Stoppard said: 'And I *really resent* it!' A bit later, he talked about changes over the years in audiences' range of references. Everyone in the audience picked up a reference to Goneril in *Travesties* in 1974; by the time of the 1993–4 revival, he had noticed that many fewer did.

These two separate items were conflated in press coverage of the interview over the next few days. The *Independent* reported him as saying that audiences were getting thicker all the time and that he had had to rewrite a scene in *The Hard Problem* three times before the audience got it, and that he resented it. Stoppard wrote to the paper trying to sort out the misrepresentation ('We need a typeface for banter'). But by then other papers had picked up the story. Billington wrote a 'think piece' in the *Guardian* ('I would question Stoppard's assumption that theatre audiences are less clever than they used to be'), which also ran a 'Pass Notes' column on 'Sir Tom' complaining that he had to 'dumb down'. The *Telegraph* had a quiz headed: 'Are Tom Stoppard's Plays Too Clever for You?' Matt Rudd in the *Sunday Times* said that Stoppard had changed the rewritten line 'four times'. How did you get *four*, Stoppard asked the journalist bemusedly. It turned out Rudd had picked that up from the interview's original reference to the 'fourth' preview. Stoppard wrote another letter, and then let it go. But the notion that he had been snooty about the intelligence of contemporary audiences was now settled into the clippings. It was the sort of 'idiotic piece of flat-earth news' that both enraged and intrigued him.

He and Sabrina took a break in the spring of 2015, for a luxurious holiday in the Bahamas, where he started to turn his mind to other writing. But, as he moved on, *The Hard Problem* began to have a successful afterlife, with several new productions from 2016 onwards. It was done first in the States, in January 2016, by his friend Blanka Zizka at the Wilma Theater in Philadelphia, where he had so often worked. Her new production was prefaced by a platform conversation between him and David Chalmers, and by a tribute to Zizka at which he spoke of her admiringly and affectionately. Zizka brought in a saxophone player onstage, accompanying but not part of the action, which took place in a hard, bright white box, like a laboratory. She thought of this musician as Hilary's observer and inner voice, her consciousness. He very much liked the moment, near the end, when Hilary looked across at the saxophonist and briefly caught his eye, as if breaking through into a meta-reality.

Later that year, in October 2016, *The Hard Problem* opened at A.C.T., his home from home in San Francisco, in a typically intelligent production by Carey Perloff. Though by then he had other things on his mind, he went over to spend time in rehearsal. As always, that made him happy. 'Collaboration is a moving declaration of one's humanity,' he told an interviewer. They added some lines and switched a couple of scenes round. He and Carey did a platform talk on 14 October 2016, just before the play opened for a three-week run, a relaxed conversation between two people who knew and understood each other very well. The chair, Robert Semper, congratulated him on his lifelong interest in science, especially physics. Yes, Stoppard said, he read a lot of 'airport paperback science'. He talked about how, all his life, he'd been writing arguments, 'ping-pong games'. He thought it arose from his lack of security in his own views. He tended to agree with the last person who spoke. The conversation went on to his ways of writing, and he recycled a favourite saying: 'When you finish any play you see how things come out. It's very good news for the play if you feel lucky, but it's not very good news if you feel clever.' He said he wasn't as interested in characters as he was in ideas. 'No,' said Perloff, amiably contradicting him, 'you *are* interested in people. There's a reason actors have a good time doing your plays.'

In 2017, there were productions in Washington (from March to April 2017, directed by Charles Newell), at the Court Theatre in Chicago in April, and in Wiesbaden in Germany, in September. (He was slightly downcast that the German director got over one of the play's challenges, a time jump between the third and fourth scenes, by putting up a big sign reading: 'FIVE YEARS HAVE PASSED'.) As conversations about a New York production gradually took shape, after some delay in getting the Lincoln Center and Jack O'Brien into the same slot (October 2018 to January 2019), he took on board, warily, O'Brien's idea that the cast might spend the whole time on stage, observing the action. O'Brien, who always went straight for the heart in a Stoppard play, thought it was 'all about the daughter'. He found it tender and intimate; he knew it needed young actors. He used jazz for the scene breaks, and had the cast hang around, moving the furniture, having little jokes among themselves and giving the audience friendly looks as if inviting them into the discussion. His Hilary was Adelaide Clemens (the shining Valentine of *Parade's End*), who gave an intense, driven performance, almost ungainly in her concentration and trouble. In O'Brien's hands it became a much more emotional play about a private quest.

In 2019 the play moved from America to Russia, done – as *The Problem* – by his old team, Arkady Ostrovsky as translator and Alexei Borodin directing Moscow's Russian Academic Youth Theatre. He went over in October 2018 for the start of rehearsals. It was a difficult time for the theatre, whose managing director, Sofia Apfelbaum, had just been placed under arrest, collateral damage in the government's case against the theatre director Kirill Serebrennikov. He felt tired: the production overlapped with New York's, and another play was by now on his mind. And the actors were uncertain, to start with. But he felt warmly towards Borodin and the RAMT, and was pleased that the play kept taking on these new lives. He went back for the opening in the spring of 2019. Once up and running in Moscow, *The Problem* might run for years. *The Coast of Utopia* had just ended a ten-year run.

A leftover trace of *The Hard Problem* stayed in his mind in an idea for a play about artificial intelligence. He wrote a few pages of that early in 2018, while he was at the Jaipur Literature Festival. It has two scenes, one with a man and a woman ('Aleisha', a cross between Alexa and Ayesha), rapidly identifiable as a robot, who is playing the piano and holding conversation to order, but hasn't yet been fully programmed. Like Cecily in the library in *Travesties*, her topics for conversation haven't got beyond Aardvark and Aaron, and she utters logical but incoherent streams of information, like a crazed Wikipedia entry: 'Other empires include the British Empire, the Dutch Empire, the French Empire, the Hackney Empire, the Holy Roman Empire and the Ottoman Empire. The ottoman is an upholstered couch facing in all directions . . .' In the second scene, the programmer is discussing Aleisha with his wife (who also plays the piano, but is not so biddable) and his friend. Sounding a bit like Henry Higgins in Shaw's *Pygmalion* (he had Galatea as an early name for Aleisha), he airs the issues of racial stereotyping and sexism in creating a 'female' artificial intelligence. Their main dilemma is the hard problem of whether an organism cloned from *Homo sapiens* can have 'consciousness'. It would be a start, he says, if she could laugh at a joke, but she is locked in, for all the world like characters in a play, who – as in Oscar Wilde, for instance – don't find their lines funny. At that point he broke off, leaving poor Aleisha, with her potential unfulfilled, forever frozen in time. He wasn't happy with the tone, which he thought was arch. It was the only time in his life he had started a play and not finished it: perhaps fortunately, as AI became a popular subject for novelists in 2019.

As he waited for another play to 'arrive', there were other tasks occupying his time. At the end of 2015 there was a new production of *Hapgood* at the Hampstead Theatre by Howard Davies. Rather to his chagrin, he found he wasn't much wanted in rehearsals. Davies, whom he thought a superb theatre director, didn't want to discuss the production with him. Unlike most directors who worked regularly with Stoppard, Davies thought it was destabilising for the actors to hear from two people. So he ended up staying away. But he thought the production worked well. It was a snazzy, clear and stylish operation played against a bank of video screens, with a strong cast, including Lisa Dillon and Tim McMullan. And it was positively reviewed, even by those who still found the play puzzling. He told himself wryly that he should learn a lesson from this experience. Perhaps it was a delusion that he was necessary to the process; though that didn't stop him going back to rehearsals for his next revivals. In any case, he was pleased to see *Hapgood* put on again after so long, especially at Hampstead, where he had never been staged before. Howard Davies's death from cancer, a year later, came as a shock.

While he was on holiday in the Bahamas in March 2015, he started work on something he had long resisted. For many years, the film producer Scott Rudin had been asking him to write a screenplay of *Arcadia*. Just as he couldn't see the point of turning the film of *Shakespeare in Love* into a play, so he knew that *Arcadia* was essentially a theatre piece. But after much urging, he gave in, partly for the money, partly persuaded by the possibility (which came to nothing) that Matthew Warchus might direct it. He spent several months between 2015 and 2017 on this task. Much of it was straight from the play, but there was also – as with *Parade's End* – a great deal of narrative simplification and compression: more sex and less physics. In an early, discarded draft, Byron (always tantalisingly offstage, of course, in the play), makes a teasing appearance at a London party, saying one word: 'Albania'. Much that is imagined in the play becomes actual. We see the shooting of hares and pigeons, Bernard's red sports car racing towards the house, the grounds of Sidley Park before and after the improvements and in the 'present day', the peacocks on the lawn and the boat on the lake, the steam pump and the ha-ha. We see the sexual assignations all over the house and grounds, and Lady Croom cutting off a lock of her pubic hair to send to Byron. We see the hermitage and the hermit, the flames that consume Thomasina, and her memorial stone. He found it a hard and not altogether enjoyable task. He had an inner voice which kept telling him: 'The older you get the more important it seems not to go back over work you have done before, but to do new things.' After he sent off his final draft, Rudin fell silent; it seemed as if the project went into the Hollywood doldrums.

Overlapping with *Arcadia*, he embarked, surprisingly, on a screenplay of *A Christmas Carol*, for the director Bennett Miller, which he began at the end of 2015 and finished in the spring of 2016. He became absorbed by Ebenezer Scrooge's character, the London world around him, the Spirits and the sense of time passing. Stoppard poured his delight in family life into the Cratchit Christmas dinner. The little Cratchits made him want to weep. He planned for their goose to be carved and eaten in real time, which he much preferred, in a film, to 'trickery'. His version of the scene has all Dickens's rich sentiment – and all the vividness, too, of Gabriel carving the goose at the Christmas feast in Joyce's *The Dead*:

> Mrs Cratchit sights along a carving-knife, watched raptly by
> everyone, the Small Cratchits cramming a spoon in their mouths
> to stop from shrieking for goose while bouncing in their seats, and
> she plunges the knife into the goose breast bursting with stuffing,
> and out gushes juice and sage-and-onion, causing a murmur

round the table, and a little hurrah from Tiny Tim, banging his knife handle.

In REAL TIME (near enough) Mrs Cratchit carves the goose, to the company's fascination. She doesn't pause until she has separated every morsel from every bone and added it to the serving dish.

Mrs Cratchit: Plate.

IN REAL TIME.

The first plate is held out for her, loaded with goose and passed along for the addition of potato, apple sauce and gravy, and is set before Tiny Tim, by which time the second plate has received its share of goose, and is in transit. Everyone waits until everyone has been served. Then everyone takes the first bite of goose, and chews it luxuriously.

Bob (awed): I don't believe there was ever such a goose cooked.

Mrs Cratchit: I'll not gainsay it.

But, as with Scott Rudin and *Arcadia*, Bennett Miller went quiet after the script was finished. It remains to be seen if Stoppard's ghost of Christmas past will have a future.

At the end of 2016, he agreed to an interesting commission, out of affection for an old friend. André Previn had wanted them to collaborate again for ages, and suggested a 'monodrama' for Renée Fleming, Previn's 'muse'. Stoppard kept telling him he was musically illiterate, and he couldn't think of a subject. But he now started casting about for texts, at first thinking of American women poets, Edna St Vincent Millay or Emily Dickinson, and then going back to Homer for the story of Penelope. He liked the idea of, once again, putting a subsidiary character from a classic text centre-stage. And he liked the story: 'It had love, it had grief, it had drama, it had a happy ending.' He reread the *Iliad* and the *Odyssey* in different translations (delighted by the fact that the venerable classicist Peter Green published his new translations when he was ninety). He came up with a vigorous version, switching freely between grand Homeric idioms and racy modern language. Helen was kept as an offstage character, in case, he joked, Renée Fleming might feel competitive. Still, he put in glimpses of Helen dropping her shoulder-strap invitingly, or of her having 'a bottom like a cleft peach', or of her being begotten by Zeus 'swanning past Leda's defences'. We see all the action through Penelope's eyes. This Penelope, in his view, is in a state of some resentment that her reputation has come down to us just as the homely, faithful wife, doing her weaving and patiently waiting for her man to get back from the war. Here, she's a shrewd and feisty character, who describes her suitors as a 'rowdy mob of louts' and calls out to her absent Odysseus: '*Bastard!* What are you doing all this time?' But, after their suspenseful recognition scene, love triumphs, and a tender marital reunion in their 'good old bed' ends the piece.

He told Previn that he had no idea how to write for a singer, but Previn said: Do it as if it was a long speech in a play, and let me worry about how to make it sing. He scored the piece for soprano, string quartet (the Emerson) and piano. Stoppard's libretto was long, almost an hour, and he was surprised to find that a star like Fleming was daunted by this. The three of them worked together on it in Previn's New York apartment in the autumn of 2018, and decided to divide up the text between a singing voice and an actress. Previn was as inventive as ever, but crippled by arthritis and very frail. The piece was meant for his ninetieth birthday celebrations, part of the Boston Symphony Orchestra summer festival at Tanglewood, the orchestra's famous rural home in the Berkshires. But Previn died in February 2019. 'If there was a moment when he put down his pen,' Stoppard said, 'I missed it.' Previn's agent David Fetherolf finished the piece. The planned celebration was turned into a memorial concert, starring Fleming and Uma Thurman, held on 24 July 2019 at Tanglewood. Stoppard spoke about the making of *Penelope*, and their friendship. It was a bittersweet occasion.

New work continued; and past work stayed alive. All his plays were in print in the UK, apart from his long-ago translation of *Tango*, and *Enter a Free Man*, which he didn't like and didn't want produced, though acting editions did remain in print and it was very occasionally put on. His bestsellers were *Rosencrantz* and *Arcadia*, followed by *Coast* – though 'bestseller' is a relative term. For a playwright, to sell over two thousand copies of a play is unusual; for a popular novelist, that would be considered peanuts. But Stoppard was one of the rare exceptions. Worldwide,

Rosencrantz has probably sold over a million copies, *Arcadia* not much less, *Coast* just shy of 100,000. Quite a long way after come *The Real Thing*, *Travesties*, *Jumpers*, *Every Good Boy Deserves Favour* and *The Invention of Love*. Meanwhile, his highest-earning plays for production rights were the ones most put on by professionals and amateurs. These were, as ever, *Rosencrantz*, *Arcadia*, *The Real Thing* and *The Real Inspector Hound* (beloved of amateur theatre companies). *The Coast of Utopia* earned a lot if it did get staged, because it was such a big event, but, for the same reason, it was put on only rarely. *Rock 'n' Roll* brought in a large income because it was taken up for international productions after it first launched, but has not been revived in the UK or in New York. He often complained about how rarely he was 'done' in Europe, perhaps because of the difficulty of translating him.

Between 2016 and 2017, two remarkable revivals of his early plays had a huge impact, swept away the disheartening London reception of *The Hard Problem* and created a wave of new and resurgent interest in him. They brought into the theatre, as he neared his eightieth birthday, not only his dedicated followers but a new generation of Stoppard fans.

The writer, film-maker and theatre director Patrick Marber, nearly thirty years his junior, had been an admirer of Stoppard ever since, as a fourteen-year-old schoolboy, he saw his sixth form do a production of *Travesties* and thought: "That's the world I want to be in.' At nineteen he studied Stoppard at university, and when he was twenty-eight Stoppard came to his first play. He got to know him, went to him for advice and wrote him some heartfelt letters, as after seeing Leveaux's 1999 revival of *The Real Thing*: 'This is why I wanted to be a playwright – to write plays that might be half-decent . . . A great experience and a truly beautiful play in a terrific production.' In 2016 David Babani, the manager of the Menier Chocolate Factory theatre in Southwark, one of London's most exciting small venues for new plays and bold revivals, asked Stoppard if they could revive *Travesties*. Babani suggested Sam West as director. Stoppard asked Marber, who had worked with West, for his opinion, and Marber said that West was brilliant, but that if he wasn't free, he would love to do it himself; and so it fell out. For Marber it was a kind of miracle to be directing his lifelong hero, and they worked together well and easily. Because Stoppard liked Marber both as a playwright and a person, and because they recognised that they were both 'tinkerers' with their own texts, Marber could persuade him to go back and rethink the play. And Stoppard took pleasure, forty-two years after its first performance, in 'rebooting' this classic text.

The old problem with the intractable Lenins, Cecily's huge speech about the history of the Revolution, the Wilde parodies, the set-tos between Joyce and Tzara, Joyce's conjuring tricks, Carr's commentary on Lenin, were all revisited and some new solutions were found. There were lots of detailed textual changes; one robust example changes Tzara's insulting of Carr from 'You ignorant smart-arse bogus bourgeois Anglo-Saxon prick!' to 'You constipated sack of Anglo-Saxon horse dung!' Much tweaking went on during rehearsals, giving the actors the exciting feeling that they were at work on a new text hot from the press. If they asked for rewrites, Marber always referred them back to Stoppard. Sometimes he demurred, as when asked if they could cut the line about Lenin leaving Zurich for Russia in his hobnailed boots. No, he said firmly, he found it very valuable to have a concrete detail like that. He deflected them when they asked questions about their characters' motives or psychology. But most of the time he loved to watch them at work. 'Aren't actors wonderful,' he said fondly, as they made their way patiently through a long, slow, tedious technical rehearsal.

Marber poured song and dance and vaudevillian high jinks into the play and turned it, near enough, into *Travesties: the Musical.* At first Stoppard resisted some of his most outrageous ideas. Marber was surprised by his mixture of conservatism and experimentalism, something he hadn't perceived before they started working together. But mostly, Marber said, he 'tolerated' his innovations, if sometimes with scepticism. Marber and his designer Tim Hatley set the whole action in one space, in a set covered in paper and ghostlily grey, with a large stuffed beaver and a piano and a huge old chair for Carr, a space which could switch at the drop of a hat into a railway station or a library or a nightclub. Lenin came on in the first act in a ridiculous Elizabethan ruff and accompanied Gwendolen's Shakespeare sonnet with a lute. Joyce and the company burst into Irish song for 'Mr

Dooley', Cecily's stripper scene in the library came with flashing lights and full-on bawdy dancing, the two girls semi-sang their way through their competitive tea party, Lenin was seen off with a Russian revolutionary song, and everyone romped into a dance to end the show. Much care was taken with Joyce's lifelike rabbit, whom the actor fondly called Leopold. In what Stoppard drily described as his 'least defensible innovation', at the start of Act Two, Joyce, sitting at a table with Gwendolen, dictates to her the last lines of *Ulysses*, Molly Bloom's 'and yes I said yes I will Yes', to which Gwendolen responds with a little orgasmic cry. When Joyce leaves the room, Tzara emerges, surprisingly, from beneath the table and from under Gwendolen's skirts. Clearly it wasn't the dictation which produced her gasp of pleasure. This would get one of the biggest laughs of the evening. The whole production was full of joy, elan and silliness.

It was one of Marber's best ideas to have Carr get older and older, and more and more forgetful, as the play went on. So a play of high spirits, love, art and revolution also became, movingly, a play about ageing and mortality. As Marber said of it: 'If you're lucky you'll get old, and when you're old you don't remember so well as when you're young. And at the end of the play, everything he remembered he has now forgotten.' He kept in mind that Stoppard had written this play about freedom and youth when he was a mid-thirties father of four, as if looking back longingly on his own young life. Now he was coming back to it nearer to Henry Carr's age, closer to the time of remembering and forgetting and what Yeats fiercely calls 'bodily decrepitude'.

In public conversations together, Marber said he felt *Travesties* had much more chaos and anarchy in it than Stoppard's other plays. Stoppard said it now felt to him an extremely 'strange' play, unlike anything else he had ever written; but, he commented mildly, he didn't really have a subversive nature. Was it disconcerting to be looking back on a younger man's play? No, he replied, 'I feel like the same person, only later.' But he acknowledged that 'a play with a man at its centre who is all about forgetting and fantasising sits closer to me now than it did then'.

Between them they cast it superbly. Tom Hollander gave an enchanting performance as Henry Carr, quite different from Wood and Sher:

mischievous, charming, impish, angry and, in the speeches of life at the Front, heart-stoppingly quiet. The two 'girls', Clare Foster and Amy Morgan, were funny and clever, Freddie Fox was a wildly over-the-top Tristan Tzara, and Peter McDonald was a rivetingly plausible James Joyce. Audiences and critics alike adored it. Stars were showered on it, reviewers used phrases like 'mind-bogglingly entertaining', 'utterly engaging', 'scintillating'. Hollander was praised to the skies and Marber was congratulated for grasping that 'Stoppard is a more emotional writer than we commonly admit'. Friedman transferred it to the Apollo, in the West End, on 15 February 2017 (where Carr made his first entrance by knocking cutely on the 'iron', the stage curtain), and then to the States, keeping only Hollander and McDonald in the cast, where it was an uproarious success.

When the Faber text of the new edition was published in 2017, with most (though not all) of the new production's revisions, Stoppard added a preface about his rewritings. He spoke, again, of the provisionality and mutability of his plays. 'A playtext is not a piano score. It invited directorial invention . . . This reprint . . . is best thought of as a placeholder until the next time *Travesties* is being rehearsed in striking distance of my inclination to tinker. If the next gap is as long as the last one, I will be 103 and no doubt ready with blue pencil and blue-black ink as usual.'

A month after *Travesties* transferred to the Apollo Theatre, another hugely successful Stoppard revival opened at the Old Vic, to mark the fiftieth anniversary of *Rosencrantz and Guildenstern*, and his eightieth year. There had already been interest in the twenty-fifth anniversary of the film of *Rosencrantz*. His old friends, the producers Manny Azenberg and Michael Brandman, his companions in arms for the 1991 film, organised a Blu-Ray reissue of the digital film. Brandman did a long, nostalgic interview with Stoppard for the Blu-Ray package, in September 2015, asking Stoppard to look back on the film and on his career as a whole. Stoppard spoke vividly about the making of the film and paid particular tribute to Peter Biziou. But he resisted attempts to be drawn on what he thought his 'legacy' was. Asked by Brandman why there had never been an original Stoppard screenplay, he said that he had had a limited number of ideas – he didn't have a bottom drawer full of unused projects – and he never felt like wasting a new idea on a movie rather than a play.

In 2017, the play, which had been kept alive for half a century in productions all over the world, taught to generation after generation of schoolchildren and university students, and sold in its tens of thousands, returned to its London birthplace. Matthew Warchus, the artistic director of the Old Vic, asked one of Stoppard's favourite directors, David Leveaux, to do it. They cast Daniel Radcliffe as Rosencrantz, thereby ensuring packed houses and new young audiences (many of whom came only because they were Harry Potter fans, but who then got quite interested in the play). Rehearsals began in January 2017 and it opened in March, overlapping with *Travesties*. At a time of political derangement and economic uncertainty, London theatre was in a mood for revivals: that season saw new productions of *The Glass Menagerie*, *Who's Afraid of Virginia Woolf?*, *Angels in America*, Marber's *Don Juan in Soho*, *Young Frankenstein* and *Follies*. But the two Stoppard revivals, *Travesties* and *Rosencrantz*, attracted the most attention and the most rejoicing.

David Leveaux, who understood Stoppard's work well and brought to it a romantic intelligence and stagecraft forged through working with Beckett and Pinter, thought of *Rosencrantz* as a play of wit and youthful comedy but, at the same time, of fear, anguish and mortality. 'Death stalks the play,' he told the cast. He thought it had two different overlapping worlds, of speed and sound. Rosencrantz and Guildenstern are stuck in their clock-stopped limbo of waiting, which they fill up with rapid verbiage. But the *Hamlet* scenes burst into that stalled time. As Leveaux put it, Hamlet is 'busy busy busy', thinking, plotting, planning. The *Hamlet* scenes, inside the modern play, feel like a great flow of humanity, pouring on and off the stage, leaving Rosencrantz and Guildenstern high and dry every time. And, under all the movement and words and laughter, Leveaux hears an 'utter silence': the silence of death. 'The gathering pulse of mortality seems to surge up almost without warning, despite the sheer fun (and sometimes anarchy) of the hurtling, youthful comedy.' He saw Rosencrantz and Guildenstern as bewildered and afraid, characters made up of 'watchfulness, neutrality and fatalism'. He talked in rehearsal about power and helplessness. To the travelling Players, he said: 'Rosencrantz and Guildenstern are in your play, not the other way round.' He talked about breaking through the fourth wall or putting a hand through the looking glass. It fascinated him that once they have left the court and are on the boat, any 'domestic' or safe reality is gone. The boat is a move into an even stranger place: 'We're in another world, we've broken through,' Leveaux said to the cast.

Stoppard loved Leveaux's way of working and his ideas, and he liked the casting, too, especially David Haig. He had told Leveaux that he wanted to find a Player who was not the expected Henry Irving sort, grand, actorly, mellifluous. Haig played him as an East End mountebank, aggressive, demotic and sinister, but with sadness too. His desperate cry: 'We're *actors*, we're the opposite of people!' was powerfully startling. His Players were like a Fellini troupe of nomadic clowns, odd, strange creatures, all in thrall to him. It amused Stoppard very much when Leveaux said: 'I'll tell you one thing about this play, if you don't welcome the Player back, you're fucked.'

Most of the cast, apart from Haig and the Polonius, William Chubb (who had been in *Invention* long ago), were probably not even born when *Rosencrantz* was first produced. Yet here was the ageing playwright, fifty years on, sitting in the rehearsal room responding to queries from the young actors and – rather to their amazement – willingly making small changes. He had already done some rewrites before rehearsals started, in the interest of tightening things up. There was no such thing for him as a sacrosanct 'classic' text. Most of these changes (as so often) were made too late to be printed in the new 2017 edition. For instance, the 2017 edition has this famous exchange between Guildenstern and the Player:

> Guildenstern: We only know what we're told, and that's little enough. And for all we know it isn't even true.
> Player: For all anyone knows, nothing is. Everything has to be taken on trust; truth is only that which is taken to be true. It's the currency of living. There may be nothing behind it, but it doesn't make any difference so long as it is honoured. One acts on assumptions. What do you assume?

But what the actors read in the rehearsal text, and what the audience heard, was:

Guildenstern: We only know what we're told, and that's little enough. And for all we know it isn't even true.

Player: For all anyone knows, nothing is. Everything has to be taken on trust; truth is only a promise to pay the bearer. It's the currency of living. One acts on assumptions. What do you assume?

In rehearsal, a few more bits of Shakespeare were dropped in, to ease the transitions between the *Hamlet* scenes. Only now did it strike him that Gertrude needed more to say. In mid-rehearsal, they stopped to consult their *Hamlet*s (which all the cast had to hand) and agreed to put in her lines from Act Four, Scene One, 'Ah mine own Lord what have I seen tonight,' announcing the death of Polonius. Stoppard thought it would be nice to hear, offstage, 'a rat, a rat i'the arras', as well. None of this got into the printed text. Other changes came and went. He had cut into one long speech of Guildenstern's, but then put it back in rehearsal. He told the cast that he had been saying to himself: 'Get on with it, Tom.' Leveaux said, teasing him: 'Tom has been over-editing himself.'

Rehearsal notes switched between the metaphysical and the practical – the timing of an exit, the position of the barrels, the placing of the interval. They agreed, in the interests of speed, to turn three acts into two, with the interval coming as the king rises from the play and calls for lights. He was funny and generous in his tips to the actors. Rosencrantz's trousers falling down, he told Radcliffe, was like 'a Buster Keaton moment without Buster Keaton's genius'. Why were Rosencrantz and Guildenstern so aggressive with the Player? Josh McGuire and Radcliffe wanted to know. They suspect they are his playthings, Stoppard told them, it's a sense of insecurity about how solid the ground is under their feet. They run out of a store of moral courage quite quickly. How much does the Player know? Haig asked him. I don't think there's much you don't know, Stoppard replied, but you're presupposing foreknowledge on the play's part and you can't assume that. You may not know specifically what is going to happen, but your entire life's experience on the road with your gang is that everything ends in death – it's what you mostly do. The virtue, Stoppard told him, lies in being inexact. As soon as you start being exact, why should you be believed? Room for doubt is room for faith. The rehearsal room went quiet, taking that in. When they first met, Haig asked him if he thought more about death now than when he wrote the play. Well, Stoppard said, I quite look forward to awareness ceasing.

The *Travesties* rehearsals had started in August 2016, six weeks after the result of the Brexit vote. *Rosencrantz* rehearsals started in January 2017, coinciding with the inauguration of Donald Trump. (That day in the rehearsal room was filled with gloom and dismay.) Interviewers asked for his views on the political times, and whether they might be a subject for a new play. He explained that ideas didn't come to him like that (it would be another matter if he were writing TV documentary), and pleaded political naivety. He also noted how, over the years, people had suggested that *Rosencrantz and Guildenstern* might be a political allegory for whatever was going on at the time, from the Vietnam War onwards. He had always resisted such hypotheses, observing that if Beckett had explained who Godot was, the play would lose its force.

In the fifty years since the play first opened at the Old Vic and made him famous, he had been serially known as 'The author of *Rosencrantz and Guildenstern*', 'The author of *The Real Thing*', 'The author of *Arcadia*' and, for some, 'The [co]author of *Shakespeare in Love*'. Unlike some other long-lived world-famous writers who resent the fact that their names are forever linked to their first bestseller or to their early well-known work, he didn't mind these selective tags. And he was very happy to see the play back at its original home. One of his favourite lines was the Player's: 'Life is a gamble, at terrible odds – if it was a bet you wouldn't take it.' But occasionally you do win. 'I'm sitting in a room rehearsing a play which was first on 50 years ago. Who would have taken a gamble on that?'

The production was a hit, filled the theatre for months and only didn't transfer to the New York because of Radcliffe's other commitments. Faber published the fiftieth-anniversary edition, which sold over four thousand copies – unimaginable numbers for an 'old' play for most playwrights. While these two revivals were riding high and *The Hard Problem* was having its American afterlife, and as his eightieth birthday neared, awards and tributes were pouring in. There was nothing new in this. He was used to being a recipient of honours and to making modest and funny speeches in a black tie to adoring audiences. (As in: 'I'm speechless, and that's not a good position to be in when you're speech-less.') But, though he repeated anecdotes and favourite quotes, he gave each particular event its due. When he was given the American PEN/Allen Foundation award for services to literature in May 2015, lovingly presented by Glenn Close in New York, he spoke about why writers mattered. Sometimes he felt they were given too much importance. But 'the question isn't whether we deserve it; the question is how are we going to live up to it?' He went on to talk with passion about PEN and its service to writers.

In the spring of 2016 he was appointed a Visiting Professor in the Humanities at Oxford, as part of a series of 'Humanitas' Chairs set up by the publisher George Weidenfeld. He accepted because of his admiration for Weidenfeld. In his talk, he used some of his favourite examples (he called them his 'lantern slides') to discuss the playwright's voice and the relationship between drama and literature. He used, as he'd done before, Oscar Wilde's very bad first play, *Vera, or the Nihilists*, written before he'd found his 'authorial voice', to ask what was that 'elusive' thing, the 'voice' of the playwright? 'The idea that the writer subjugates himself to allow characters to speak is completely fallacious.' You would never confuse a play by Eliot with a play by Noël Coward. Eliza Doolittle's father is channelling Shaw just as much as Henry Higgins is, in *Pygmalion*. In Beckett, you can find the authorial voice in the astonishing 'control-freakery' of the stage directions to *Endgame*, as much as in the dialogue. He talked about cliché, naturalism and artifice in stage talk. 'Conversation is spontaneity. Dialogue is spontaneity worked on.' He mentioned famous bits of film dialogue which he wished he'd written. 'Forget it, Jake, it's Chinatown.' Or the final exchange between Harrison Ford and Tommy Lee Jones, his obsessive pursuer, in *The Fugitive*: 'I didn't kill my wife.' '*I don't care.*' Are those 'literature'? In the end the attempt to distinguish between what was literature and what was drama was 'demeaning'. Literature was not an island; it expanded outwards, like an infinitely wonderful cat's cradle. (That image would stay in his mind.) He could only explain what he meant by reading that much-cherished, deeply melancholy passage from James Saunders's *Next Time I'll Sing to You*:

> There lies behind everything . . . a certain quality which we may
> call grief. It's always there below the surface, just behind the facade.
> Sometimes . . . you can see dimly the shape of it as you can see
> sometimes through the surface of an ornamental lake the outline of
> a carp . . . It bides its time, this quality . . . you may pretend not to
> notice . . . the name of this quality is grief.

He had been quoting this for about fifty years; and when he first heard it, in 1962, he thought: 'Yes, this is more like it.' He learnt from Saunders that a) plays are literature and b) plays can do whatever they want.

A year after the Weidenfeld Professorship, he was back in Oxford as Cameron Mackintosh Chair of Contemporary Theatre, a post endowed by the theatre impresario, whom he knew well, and previously held by many people he'd worked with or was friends with. He gave his inaugural lecture on 11 October 2017 (taking time out that afternoon to visit an old friend in Oxford, the philosopher Bryan Magee, who was very ill). Hedging his bets, he called the lecture 'Professing'. The lecture covered familiar ground: the relationship between the event and the text, the authorial voice in the stage directions for *Endgame*, single lines from movies he wished he'd written. (This time one of his examples was the famous dying speech from Ridley Scott's *Blade Runner*: 'I've seen things you people wouldn't believe . . . All those moments will be lost in time, like tears in rain.') He talked about the strange translation of the private act of writing into the process of staging. 'The choice of words in the right order is what I do,' he said. The act of writing is as insulated as writing a sonnet. You don't need anything or anybody except you and what you draw on. But once the play is in rehearsal, this entire sense of self-sufficiency is 'blown away like a dandelion seed'. From then on, you and all around you are trying to control the physical reality, microsecond by microsecond. Everything is to do with physics: loudness, quietness, brightness and time. More than once, 'I've added a couple of words to an exit speech because the door was too far away.'

There were other public celebrations of his life and work in 2017. He was given a big send-off at the London Library, after his fifteen years of service, on 22 June, at which he said that words could hardly express his pride and pleasure in having done the job – and his relief at ending it. In July, he was made an honorary fellow of the British Academy, alongside A. S. Byatt, Graça Machel and George Soros. In November, to his delight, he was awarded the David Cohen Prize for Literature, which gives the biennial award, worth £40,000, for a lifetime's achievement. The chair of the judges, Mark Lawson, said that this prize, and the Nobel, were won less often by playwrights, perhaps because the examination of whether their work will last is so much more 'brutal', over time, than for novelists or poets. Antonia Fraser made the presentation, because Pinter had been awarded it twenty years before. In his acceptance speech, he spoke – as he had often done before – about having had 'a charmed life'. His father had been killed; his mother's family had been murdered: how could he say this? Yet that was what he felt. He had had a happy childhood. He had been lucky. He felt blest to have been young where and when he was – for instance, to have seen *The Birthday Party* in Bristol in 1962. '*I was there!*' The award was 'very meaningful' to him – especially as it had been awarded to friends such as Pinter, Tony Harrison and Julian Barnes – and he would try not to take it too much to heart that it was for a 'lifetime's achievement'.

He took care, too, with the honouring of other people who were celebrating 'lifetime' achievements in old age, illness or retirement, or who were being memorialised. In March 2017, he spoke at the memorial for Peter Shaffer at the National. In April 2018, he went all the way to San Francisco especially to be the 'surprise' guest at Carey Perloff's retirement party after her twenty-five years at A.C.T., to be greeted with amazement and joy. Closer to home, in September 2018, he took a chartered bus from the Finchley Road to Cambridge, with a group of writers including John Carey and Julian Barnes, to celebrate the publication of *The River in the*

Sky, a new long poem by Clive James, who had leukaemia and was too ill to leave his house. The little party turned into a joking exchange of reminiscences between writer-friends. Clive James had written about and known Stoppard since the 1970s. Stoppard remembered reading his first book, *The Metropolitan Critic*, before he knew James, and thinking that it was the first time he had read literary criticism that seemed to be in 'a real voice'. He decided to write this fellow a congratulatory postcard – but turned the page to find himself being praised. So then he thought that sending a postcard would be like saying 'Thanks for the plug!' Julian Barnes thought this typically modest and funny.

All these markings of lifetime achievements – and of his eightieth year – naturally brought mortality to mind. And, as naturally, there were some signs of physical decay: his knees hurt, he got breathless going up to his study, he felt more tired. But he still smoked his three puffs of every cig-arette, all day long, and was generally robust and stoic. Interviewed on his eightieth birthday, he said drily: 'I didn't mind being *seventy-nine*,' but added that eighty as an idea was older than eighty as a fact. Asked whether he thought he had exceptional energy, he demurred: he simply followed through his commitments. Asked whether he thought much about death, or feared it, he replied, somewhat sarcastically: 'I *note* that many people die in their eighties and more people die in their nineties. And I also *note* my deteriorating physical body . . . but I don't give it more than its due.' He feared pain, but he didn't fear death. Nor did he think about it obsessively; he thought of it, calmly, as something one should consider. He was much more preoccupied with the need to write a new play than with being an octogenarian.

On 1 July 2017, two days before his eightieth birthday, he had his party in the Physic Garden. This time it was a co-hosted event, and he and Sabrina were shoulder to shoulder all the day long. His whole life was there in the garden, including his sons and their families, Peter his brother, who had recently been widowed, Fiona and Richard and their children, and his cousin Sarka, the first person to tell him about his mother's family. Miriam came, and Felicity, and Sinéad, and his first love, Isabel Cortan, now in her eighties. His teams were there: Jacky and Dave, the London Library

people, Rose Cobbe and friends from the agency, Dinah Wood and others
from Faber. Mick Jagger held court in one corner, Jerry Hall, with her new
husband (Rupert Murdoch) in another, in among the usual extraordinary
mix of stars, musicians, directors, producers, actors, translators, historians, journalists, playwrights, novelists, biographers, scientists, publishers,
very old friends (including Anthony Smith, up from Bristol) and very new
babies, including Will's. There was a strong feeling of celebration in the air,
and presents and flowers piled up. The sun shone, of course: that was part
of his luck.

35

A Charmed Life

So what's the first thing you can remember?

How is this to end?
. . . With tears and a journey.

Time and again he had talked about his good luck. He told people that he had had a charmed life and a happy childhood, even though he was taken from his home as a baby in wartime, his father was killed and many members of his family, as he later discovered, were murdered by the Nazis. This narrative had become part of his performance, his built-in way of thinking and talking about himself. And that story of a charmed life was profoundly connected to his sense of luck in having become English. A patriotic gratitude, and a pleasure in belonging to his adoptive country, which, in contrast to many other places, was a free country, was the life-long outcome of his childhood luck.

A charmed life seems a highly appropriate phrase for him, too – not that he would put it like this – because of his own charm. 'Charm' is a difficult word. It usually makes a person sound shady: glib, superficial, manipulative. If it's possible to redeem the word, you'd want, in his case, to talk about 'deep' charm: a charm that comes from attention, kindness, intelligence, humour, physical charisma – as well as glamour. And, also, charm as a form of concealment. Stoppard's charm is not a barrier to the extent of the worldly, famous novelist Abravanel in Philip Roth's *The Ghost Writer*, whose 'charm was like a moat so oceanic that you could not even see the great turreted and buttressed thing it had been dug to protect. You couldn't even find the drawbridge.' But it does work as a form of defence and a means of persuasion. He knows what effect he has on people. Charm is also a vital characteristic of his work: the 2017 production of *Travesties* shows that off perfectly. And 'charm' in its sense of spell or enchantment – like the 'charms' that Prospero says goodbye to, having set Ariel free, at the end of *The Tempest* – is the secret of Stoppard's profession, the magical thing that happens in the theatre, hard to say quite how or why: 'It's a mystery.'

But his sense of having had a charmed life has its dark side too. Luck, the fall of a coin, plays a big part in his plays. Some of his characters get away with it, and get lucky. They escape the war to the blessed zone of Swiss neutrality. They visit an oppressed Eastern European country, but are free to go home again. They find the person they love, at the very end of the play, by accident or coincidence. But there are as many characters who don't have any luck. They don't know who they are or what they are supposed to do. They are uncertain and confused, and they never get any answers. They are far from home, in exile with no hope of return. They do not get their heart's desire. They do not escape the worst of history. They die bewildered, or too soon.

As he came into old age, his sense of his 'charmed life' underwent a retrospective shift. Of course there had been profound changes before that. His thoughts about his own history, and the way he used it in his work, had been altered by his friendship with Havel, by finding out the facts of his Jewishness and returning to Czechoslovakia in the 1990s, and by his mother's death. But, in his eighties, the past came back for him in a different way, entailing some pain and self-reproach. He was a person and a writer for whom 'kin' and 'kinship' had always mattered deeply: a family man. And he was thinking more and more about his kin, his family history and the responsibility he owed it. He had rethought, many times, what it meant to be Czech, to be an Eastern European child turned Englishman. Now – as can happen in old age – his history and his family's past became increasingly a preoccupation. What had once been obliterated came back to haunt him.

He reproached himself for having trotted out his line so often over the years, of having had a charmed life. What if you turned it inside out and looked behind the cliché? What was the other side of the story? What of those who did not have the luck, who did not escape the worst of history? Late in the day, he asked himself why he had not thought or written about this, why he had not faced up to it.

It was in March 1993 that he had learnt from Sarka, at the National Theatre, about his Jewish family history, to his mother's distress. It was in November 1994, in Prague, that Alexandr Rosa had shown him the family album. But, even though, after that, he had asked his mother a few more questions, he hadn't pressed her or gone far with it. After her death in 1996, he felt freed up to write autobiographically in the 1999 piece 'On Turning Out to Be Jewish', and to create a version of the Czech life he might have had, in *Rock 'n' Roll*, in 2006. But otherwise he had continued to do what his mother had wanted, to face away from his family's past. He had not gone any deeper into that history or used it as material for a play.

Some time after 2012 he read a novel called *Trieste* by a Croatian writer, Daša Drndić (who died in 2018). It's an extraordinary, harrowing story, in which fiction and fact overlap, of an old Catholic–Jewish Italian woman, Haya, who comes from a Habsburg Empire-era, multilingual Jewish family. She had a son, by a German officer who then became the barbaric commander of the Trieste concentration camp. She has been trying to find her son, who becomes obsessed with the family past. Haya lacerates real historical figures whom she describes as 'bystanders' or 'blind observers'. They include Herbert von Karajan, Madeleine Albright and Tom Stoppard: people who discover their family history, but turn a blind eye to it. Her 'blind observers' are 'ordinary people' who 'play it safe. They live their lives unimpeded.' She tells Stoppard's story (with many inaccuracies). Once escaped to England, his family 'live happily ever after, as if there had never been a family, a war, camps, another language'. 'Until 1999 [*sic*] Tom Stoppard has no clue he is Jewish; then (by chance) he finds out that he is . . .' He learns of his family, she says, in the Czech Republic. 'He learns that his grandfathers and grandmothers, uncles and aunts, all of them disappeared as if they had never lived, which, as far as he is concerned, they had not, and he goes back to his lovely English language and his one and only royal homeland.'

Reading this, Stoppard accepted the charge. She was clearly saying, well, fuck you and your 'charmed life', *good for you*. He thought: yes, actually, she's right. He felt that Drndić was justifiably blaming him for excluding from this 'charmed life' all those others who had 'disappeared'. He took it as an intelligible rebuke. He felt regret and guilt. It was a late echo of his mother's own survivor's guilt. He went back over his family history, and his Jewishness. It began to seem to him that he had been in denial about his own past. He increasingly felt that he should have been rueing his good fortune in escaping from those events, rather than congratulating himself. As a playwright, he needed to inhabit those lives he never lived, in his imagination. He started to think about a play which would answer the rebuke.

His everyday memory was getting worse, his long-term memory was changing. Very early scenes and moments came back ever more clearly, as if he were recovering memories which had always been there. But it was a sadness to him that he had no physical memory of his father. He remembered being on a beach in Singapore when his father must have been there, but he couldn't actually remember him, except from knowing what he looked like from photographs. He disappeared, like all those family members whom he only knew from photographs, and all that remained of him was a scar on a Czech woman's hand. It was only his mother who didn't disappear.

He thought intensely and often about his Jewishness, as he had not done in his twenties, or for that matter his thirties and forties. Three of his aunts, all four of his grandparents and his great-grandmother had been killed in the concentration camps. He had spent his life thinking of these appalling events happening to other people, horrified as any outsider was horrified, not as someone with a personal involvement.

These feelings were not to do with nationhood, or religion, or orthodoxy, or politics. He was unmoved by efforts to make him identify as a 'Jewish writer'. He had always 'bridled' at any attempts to define him in that role. His support for Soviet Jews in the 1980s had been in terms of human rights, not because of religion. He had no interest in travelling regularly to Israel or in making any public identification with the Jewish faith. He didn't know much about the Jewish faith, in fact, just as he couldn't speak Czech. As a boy he hadn't thought of himself as Jewish. He had 'colluded' with his identity as an Englishman 'with great enthusiasm'; if he thought of himself as Jewish, it was just as an 'exotic fact' which he felt made him more attractive and interesting than being Anglo-Saxon, but which he hadn't thought seriously about. He went to Sunday services at school. Being Christian was like being English. He grew up in a Christian culture, trying not to be an outsider. He had got married, the first time, in a church. And his mother hadn't made a distinction between being a religious Jew and racially Jewish: to her, Jewishness meant religion, and she was a complete atheist. This was in sharp contrast to Miriam's parents, who had lived with them at Iver, her father an observant Jew and, in Stoppard's view, a very good man; her mother, a convert, much more devout. They were in his mind as he worked on his new play.

Unlike his mother, he was not an atheist – though he recoiled from all extreme expressions of religiosity. 'I think about God a lot,' he said in 2020. 'Suddenly, out of the woodwork, out he pops.' He believed in prayer, however foolish one might feel in doing so. His 'prayer' had nothing to do with organised religion: it came out of a sense of something beyond our knowledge, beyond the material world. And his sense of his Jewishness had nothing to do with Jewry or Yahweh. Somewhere he'd read that you can stop being a Jew outwardly, but the inner man never stops being Jewish. He began to think that was true of himself. What would being 'Jewish' mean? For him it had to do with a strong sense of family, and the valuing of the intellectual life.

He set himself to read about the Jews in Europe and about the Holocaust, though this wasn't entirely new reading. Some of these books had been on his shelves for years. Rather as books on Byron had been in his library for ages before they came in useful for *Arcadia*, or as he had collected large amounts of materials about the Fourth Estate in case he ever wrote about it again, it felt as if he had stored up this reading against the possibility of a future play, like a squirrel for when winter comes.

His reading on the Holocaust, including Martin Amis's grotesque, sardonic 2014 novel about Auschwitz, *The Zone of Interest*, which he admired, and Nikolaus Wachsmann's meticulous and horrifying 2015 history of Nazi concentration camps, *K.L.*, came to a head in the summer of 2018, when he started writing his play. He was having sleepless nights, and nightmares about the Holocaust. He couldn't stop thinking about what happened, when he was a child, to his family and to millions of others.

He also had a particular interest in the history of Jews in Vienna. This went back to his Schnitzler plays, and connected to his friendships with Marjorie Perloff and Daniel Kehlmann. He had long ago read Gregor von Rezzori's 1969 novel *Memoirs of an Anti-Semite*, and George Clare's classic, *Last Waltz in Vienna: The Destruction of a Family (1842–1942)*, about the extermination of an Austrian Jewish family and the return of the boy who had escaped to England, to his family home after the war. He had read Joseph Roth's great epic of farewell to the Habsburg Empire, spread over three generations of the Trotta family, *The Radetzky March*. He knew the work of the novelist Stefan Zweig, child of the Habsburg Empire, Viennese Jew, pacifist and exile, who committed suicide in 1942, the day after finishing his memoir, *The World of Yesterday*, and whose fiction often evokes the world of assimilated Jews in late-nineteenth-century Vienna. He read Edmund de Waal's *The Hare with Amber Eyes*, the story of what happened to his Jewish-Viennese family and their possessions. He read Marjorie Perloff's autobiographical memoir, *The Vienna Paradox*, and talked to her about the fate of her 'wholly assimilated' Austro-Viennese family. He read Michael Goldfarb's *Emancipation*, on the European history of the Jews coming out of the ghettos.

In 2011, he saw Daniel Kehlmann's play *Ghosts in Princeton*, which told the story of the mathematician Gödel and his path into insanity, driven out of Vienna by the Nazis, and living in Princeton alongside Einstein. In 2018, he had some long conversations with Kehlmann about Jewish-Viennese history. Kehlmann told Stoppard the story of his grandfather, who ensured that his wife survived the war by paying a non-Jew to claim (falsely) that he was her father. There were many similar stories of life-saving, false claims of illegitimacy or mixed parentage, which Stoppard would use as a crucial plot device. Kehlmann recommended a post-war Austrian family novel, Ernst Lothar's *The Angel with the Trumpet*, in which real historical figures appear, including Hitler as a failed art student. Kehlmann was one of the first readers of and advisers on the new play, and he felt as though Stoppard were telling his, Kehlmann's, own family history.

The reading spread wider. It included histories of Austria, books on the Evian Conference, on Klimt, on anti-Semitism and culture in Vienna, on Seder, on British policy in Palestine, on Herzl, on expropriation and restitution – and on his lifelong interest, mathematics. He read up on the Riemann Hypothesis, and on the game of cat's cradle and its application to mathematical 'dynamical systems', which was to be one of the strings pulled through the play.

He pillaged from everywhere, without covering his tracks: he *wanted* the play to show up the historical testimonies it had emerged from. He used names and family stories, lines and scenes and cultural details from many sources. Two young Viennese army officers are called Theo and Fritz, just as in Schnitzler's *Dalliance*. One of the stories which most affected him was from Alexander Waugh's *The House of Wittgenstein: A Family at War*. One morning in late March 1938, just after the *Anschluss*, Hitler's annexation of Austria into Nazi Germany, Paul Wittgenstein comes into the room where his sister Hermine is sitting, 'his face white with horror', and says to her, '*Wir gelten als Juden*': 'We count as Jews!' 'Both he and his sister and his siblings', Waugh continues, 'suddenly and unexpectedly found themselves subject to all the anti-Semitic restrictions and prohibitions of the National Socialist regime.' And this was a wealthy, art-loving, intellectual, bourgeois family who had been Catholics for two generations and who considered themselves part of Viennese society, as influential and socially central to the community as the Rothschilds.

That moment is at the heart of the new play, *Leopoldstadt*, which starts in turn-of-the-century Vienna, most cultured of all European cities, where Jews, a tenth of the population, had, a generation before, 'been granted full civil rights by the Emperor Franz Josef, and had fled from the Pale and the pogroms in the East, many of them to the tenements of Vienna's old Jewish quarter, Leopoldstadt', and from there to the luxurious homes of the Viennese middle classes. He was fascinated by that history of the assimilated Viennese Jews of the nineteenth century, families like the Wittgensteins, or the Perloffs, or the de Waals, or the Clares/Klaars, who thought they were Austrians, protected by their wealth, property, social class, professions and social standing, but who, in 1938, as far as the Nazis were concerned, turned out to 'count as Jews'.

The family in *Leopoldstadt* is typical, and he created them out of an amalgam of all the family stories he had been reading. They have left the ghetto behind them. They don't live in Leopoldstadt any more, but on the Ringstrasse. They have converted and intermarried. They are Jewish *and* Protestant *and* Catholic. Their children are baptised and circumcised ('in the same week'). They celebrate Christmas *and* Seder. They are part of the class that run the city and the culture: industrialists, businessmen, factory owners, lawyers, doctors, academics, professional musicians, psychoanalysts. They go to the opera and the best clubs, their wives have their portraits done by society painters and have affairs with dashing Viennese officers. ('You seem to think becoming a Catholic is like joining the Jockey Club,' the head of the family, Hermann Merz, says to his brother-in-law Ludwig. 'It's not unlike, except that anyone can become a Catholic,' he replies.) They still believe in fighting duels as a way of settling matters of honour, and they are willing to go to war and die for Austria.

Hermann and Ludwig have one of the key historical arguments of the play, in its first scene. Hermann has put the life of the Jewish ghetto – the life of his grandparents – behind him. He'd rather go on holiday to the Italian lakes than to Galicia, he has no interest in celebrating Passover, and he defines himself as a Christian. For Hermann, as for many rich bourgeois Viennese Jews, Theodor Herzl's Zionist vision of a promised land for the Jews outside Europe is entirely alien. He doesn't want to leave 'his' city. 'We're Austrians. Viennese,' Hermann says. He averts his eyes from the signs of anti-Semitism in the culture and society he feels he belongs to. But Ludwig reads the signs – signs which are there to be read long before the rise of Hitler. He has a different attitude to assimilation. 'Assimilation doesn't mean to stop being a Jew,' he tells Hermann. 'Assimilation means to carry on being a Jew without insult.'

When the catastrophe comes for these 'assimilated' Viennese Jews, many of them – as in this family – are taken completely unawares. Suddenly they are forced to 'rediscover what it means to be Jewish in the first half of the twentieth century'.

Leopoldstadt is set in one place, the main room of the Merz apartment, and has four time zones. It starts at the turn of the century, the longest section; then jumps to 1924, then to 1938 (after the *Anschluss* and at the time of the Evian Conference on the issue of Jewish refugees) and then to 1955. The transitions are startlingly done through music and movement. The stage, at every date, is full of family. Hermann Merz, wealthy textile manufacturer and Catholic convert, full of pride at having risen up from the ghetto, has married a beautiful Gentile, Gretl, and their only son, Jacob, is meant to inherit the business. Hermann's sister Eva has married a mathematician, Ludwig Jakobovicz, descendant of an orthodox Jewish family living in the Bukovina, in the provinces. Ludwig's sister Wilma has married a Protestant doctor, Ernst Kloster. Ernst and Wilma's grandson, Nathan, who is an offstage baby about to be circumcised when we first hear of him, will also become a mathematician. Ludwig's younger sister Hanna will be a professional pianist. Ludwig and Eva's daughter, Nellie Jakobovicz, will marry an Austrian-Jewish socialist, Aaron Rosenbaum, who is killed in 1934. In 1938, she will make a second marriage to an Englishman, Percy Chamberlain (that name again!) in order to get out of Austria with her little boy. That boy, Leopold Rosenbaum, will take his stepfather's name, and will grow up an Englishman, Leo Chamberlain.

During the play we see different permutations of the big, intermarried Merz–Jakobovicz family: wives, husbands, lovers, grandparents, servants, children and grandchildren. This is above all a play about family. It's not something Stoppard had done much before, certainly not in his early plays, though families do matter in *Arcadia, Coast* and *Rock 'n' Roll*. But here, 'family' is at the heart of everything. As Granny Merz says: 'Family! Jew-hatred is about nothing but blood and kin.' And it is about the lives of children, and their vulnerability, something he had often written about before. We see the children in the play occupied with their children's business – playing, dancing, competing, learning, asking questions, rushing about, making a noise – and, in the end, we will find out what happens to them.

The first scenes show us the *fin-de-siècle* Vienna of Schnitzler and Klimt, Mahler and Johann Strauss, Freud and Herzl. Stoppard made an early decision not to bring any of these characters onto the stage: this is not *Travesties*, and he didn't want it to feel like a *Monty Python* sketch. Instead, Hermann and Ludwig discuss Freud and Herzl, 'a man with a beehive in his bonnet'. Gretl's portrait is painted, offstage, by Klimt. Mahler is discussed: he is taking his Second Symphony to Paris 'to annoy the French'. Hanna's piano-playing brings Viennese music into our ears. Gretl's brief affair invokes the world of Schnitzler's plays, which Stoppard knew so well, and Schnitzler's daring, erotic play *Reigen* (*La Ronde*) plays a small, vital part in the plot. This story of sexual betrayal – an involving piece of human drama – is a turning point for Hermann. Insulted by the young cavalry officer, even before Hermann knows he is Gretl's lover, who tells him that he can't fight a duel with a Jew because a Jew is 'devoid of honour', Hermann bursts out bitterly: 'God forgive me that I should dine with men like you and think myself raised up in the world!' But he will put this mortification to shrewd use, many years later, when he is trying to protect his business and his son's inheritance. Hermann's mixture of vanity, canny ambition, passion and ruthlessness makes him one of Stoppard's most powerful characters.

At the start of *Leopoldstadt*, as in the opening scene of *The Coast of Utopia*, there is a strong sense of the flow and chatter of family life, in a thickly furnished, comfortable setting. The mix of religions makes for comedy: a child puts a Star of David on top of the Christmas tree, the Jewish granny finds Easter challenging: 'I don't mind Christmas because baby Jesus had no idea what was going on, but I feel funny about Easter eggs.' In the 1924 scene, there are some very good jokes about circumcision. You can do low comedy in a serious play, Stoppard notes: after all, Shakespeare does. But religion is also a source of beauty. The first part of the play ends with a family Seder (complete with translation, for the converts and Gentiles at the table), which turns into a dance. It feels as if we are in a historical family epic – as in a Chekhov play, or *The Leopard*, or *The Radetzky March*. With the sudden shift into 1924, there is a sense of loss, which intensifies through the play. 1924 opens in confusion, with new characters – the next generation – rushing in and out. The audience may struggle to work out who they are. We are in the modernist era, and this is turning into a modern play, awkwardly absurd, with people misunderstanding each other, harsh political speeches and a shell-shocked veteran of the First World War, Hermann and Gretl's son Jacob (in the first act a bright, promising little boy), speaking bitterly of the fate of the Jews.

But the past is never left behind. There are recurrences all through, in Stoppardian fashion. A woman serves cake to her family, at the start and at the end. A piano is played, echoing through the scenes. A family album (the play's first working title) is looked at by different characters at different dates. The sad voice of the grandmother, showing the album to a younger in-law in the first scene, and unable to identify some of the faces, echoes through the play: 'Here's a couple waving goodbye from the train, but who are they? No idea! That's why they're waving goodbye. It's like a second death, to lose your name in a family album.'

One of the recurrences through time is mathematics. Asked, while writing it, if the play would be read autobiographically, he responded crossly: It's about a Viennese mathematician, for god's sake! He originally intended the boy, Leo, to be the mathematician. He ended up changing that, but the talent for maths criss-crosses the generations – like knots in a cat's cradle. Ludwig attends the 1900 world conference of mathematicians in Paris, where David Hilbert, an eminent German mathematician, spoke on 'The Problems of Mathematics'. Among those problems was the mathematical genius Bernhard Riemann's famous and as yet unsolved hypothesis on the probability distribution of prime numbers. Ludwig is obsessed, for the rest of his life, long after his brains become befuddled, with Riemann's formula (as many mathematicians have been), rather as Thomasina sets herself to solve Fermat's Last Theorem in *Arcadia*. Riemann's hypothesis only gets an occasional mention in the play, enough to tell us that it has to do with primes, and that it hasn't been solved, and not enough for it to become any kind of metaphor for historical events.

But it's worth noting that links have been made by number theorists between Riemann's hypothesis and probability theory – links which invoke physics, Pascal and the question of how to predict the fall of a coin. The Riemann Hypothesis is about what happens if you replace 'heads' by 'primes'. So you could trace a faint line of connection between Rosencrantz and Guildenstern tossing coins and the Viennese mathematician in this play, over half a century on in Stoppard's lifetime of thinking about probability, uncertainty and chance.

Ludwig also brings in the image of the cat's cradle, a game we watch him teaching his grandson and grand-nephew. Cat's cradle suggests an underlying pattern in what appears to be random and arbitrary, and a closed circle which involves returning to one's starting point. A cat's cradle is a 'dynamical system' which could be read as a metaphor for historical events: 'Each state came out of the previous one.' The game sets us thinking about whether there is order under apparent randomness – as chaos theory did in *Arcadia*. But the maths in *Leopoldstadt* isn't meant as a parallel for what happens to the characters. The point is more that theoretical mathematics is something pure, beautiful and harmless, set against the harmfulness of history.

> Ludwig: If I went to sleep for a hundred years, the first thing I'd ask
>   when I woke up is, 'Has Riemann been proved?'
> Hermann: Why?
> Ludwig: Because if it has, I can state with certainty how many prime
>   numbers exist below a given number *however high*; and if it hasn't, I
>   can't. Not with certainty.
> Hermann: That is a very annoying answer.
> Ludwig: Yes, but it has the saving grace that a number theorist,
>   however great, is innocent of usefulness.

When harm comes to this cultured, assimilated family of mathematicians, doctors, industrialists and pianists, it comes shatteringly, and all at once. The 1938 scene, when the family home is entered and taken over by the brutal figure of the Nazi 'Civilian', is profoundly shocking. The terror is like the Inspector breaking into the home where *Macbeth* is being secretly put on, in *Cahoot's Macbeth*, or like the invasion of Goldberg and McCann in *The Birthday Party*. But this is worse. 'You're not at home now,' the Nazi official shouts at them. We see, all at once, how the stories of home and kin, the tender, complicated, particular human stories, are going to be violently swept away. An inherited gift for theoretical maths; a husband's anguish at his wife's infidelity, and, later, at her illness; a talent for playing the piano; a doctor's skills; a sister's mourning for a brother killed in war; a young girl's sweet flirtatiousness: all these individual goods and ills are to be obliterated. What remains are the terrible choices of extremity: a doctor who has to kill his sick wife rather than let her be taken, a daughter who has to leave her parents behind to die in order to save her son, abandoning them as if she had 'drawn the lucky lottery ticket'.

The big historical stories – the Nazi expropriation of Jewish family possessions, the strategies of intermarried families to prove their offspring were Gentiles, the post-war campaigns for the restitution of stolen property, the suicides, years after, of those who survived, the eventual returns from exile – are brought to us through the one family story. A china cup crushed to bits in a child's bloodied hand invokes Kristallnacht. We don't see the camps and the killings: we don't need to. The shocks and outrages within this one family stand in for millions of others.

As he did his research on the history of Viennese Jews, he had to call, with some embarrassment, on experts (like Rabbi Julia Neuberger), to ask what actually happens at a circumcision, or what the Haggadah was, or whether a woman could sit at the head of the Seder table, or indeed how to pronounce the word 'Seder'. It was as if, he thought, he had *worked* at not being Jewish. And the explanations he needed are all in the play. In this mixed family, there is always someone who has to have Haggadah or Passover explained to them.

The character in need of the most explanations is Leo, the boy who escapes the Holocaust, becomes an Englishman and has a 'charmed life'. In 1938, when the Nazis come for them, Leo is eight. As the shocking scene relentlessly plays out, he is holding a china cup in his hands, which he crushes in his fright, cutting himself. His great-uncle Ernst, the doctor, sews the cut: five stitches.

The play cuts to 1955. The crowded, realistic late-nineteenth-century room of the first act has become a modern set, bare floors and a packing case clashing incongruously with a leftover grand piano. The richly populated family saga has become a fragmentary modern three-hander of trauma, hurtful laughter, howls of anguish, forgetting and memory.

Three members of the family have survived the past, and have come together in a much diminished family reunion: Leo, his cousin Nathan and his aunt Rosa. (In Marber's production, brilliantly, this is the first time we hear an Austrian accent, alongside a British and an American accent: all three of these people are 'foreigners' in their different ways.) All are grieving: Leo for the loss of his mother, Nellie (Ludwig's daughter), killed in the Blitz when he was thirteen. Rosa, now a New York Freudian analyst in her sixties, carries the unbearable guilt of not having been able to get the family out in time. Nathan, who in 1924 was the baby who was about to be circumcised, and in 1938 the boy playing cat's cradle with his great-uncle, is a survivor of Auschwitz. Almost every other member of his family, we are now to learn, was exterminated.

Leo Chamberlain is now a rather smug, unthinking young Englishman of twenty-five, in Vienna for a literary festival (he writes funny books). His mother didn't want him to remember the past, she wanted him to be an assimilated English boy. 'She didn't want me to have Jewish relatives in case Hitler won . . . I loved being English . . . Mother and I only spoke English.'

His aunt Rosa survived because she was in New York; now, in her sixties, once more in Vienna, she has bought back the family apartment and is fighting for the restitution of the Klimt portrait of Gretl Merz. Nathan is a mathematician, now in his thirties, who has decided to come back to Vienna even though, as he says bitterly, 'Austria is officially innocent,' and 'Anti-Semitism is a political fact.' 'It can't happen again, Nathan!' Leo assures him confidently. He asks them some ignorant questions about the past, and makes some blithe remarks about his 'charmed life' as a cricket-playing English boy. He is proud to be British: 'You know . . . fair play and parliament and freedom of everything, asylum for exiles and refugees, the Royal Navy, the royal family.' 'Oh, I forgot Shakespeare,' he adds. They laugh at him: 'I don't think he's Jewish.' So does the audience. When he wrote the lines, Stoppard knew ('alas') that they would get a laugh. It's impossible to make a speech in a play like that, now, and be taken seriously. But Leo Chamberlain meant all that seriously in 1955 – and so did Tom Stoppard. This is, in dramatic form, the theme of his 2013 lecture 'Circumspice', with its memories of his sense of 'comfortable national superiority' from when he became English at the age of eight, to his present sense that 'we are selling the family silver', and that we may need to write 'obsequies for the England we have mislaid'.

Nathan calls Leo an 'accident of history', and turns on him after he has talked about his charmed life and his lack of memory of his Jewish past: 'No one is born eight years old. Leonard Chamberlain's life is Leo Rosenbaum's life continued. His family is your family. But you live as if without history, as if you throw no shadow behind you.'

The whole play was written, Stoppard says, in order for this speech to be made. And then the past comes back, to us, and to Leo. He starts to remember, because of what he is being told. Nathan reminds him of how he got the scar on his hand. Leo remembers, at last and for the first time, his cut being sewn up by his great-uncle the doctor: five stitches. He remembers the game of cat's cradle played with Ludwig and Nathan. The moment at which Leo utters the words 'cat's cradle' is the moment at which the play's grief pours down on his head. He weeps. His aunt comes back into the room, carrying the family tree she has drawn for him. She asks him: 'So what's the first thing you can remember, Leo?' He asks her to forgive him. She says she too must be forgiven, and tells the story of her failure to rescue the family. Suddenly, all the lost dead flood back into the room, just as they were in the Seder scene, while Leo, looking at the family tree, is asking what happened to them all. His aunt and his cousin tell him their fates, in single words, like the tolling of a bell: cancer, suicide, death march, the camps where they died. The list ends with the name of the smallest child, killed at Auschwitz. That is the play's last word. We see the family, stilled as in a family album, standing behind the survivors in silence, as the stage darkens.

It is not Tom Stoppard's, or Tomáš Sträussler's, story; and it is. He went back to the piece he wrote in 1999, 'On Turning Out to Be Jewish', and took from it, almost word for word, his exchange with his cousin Sarka in 1993 when she drew him a family tree and told him the story of his family. (He told the cast, in rehearsal, to read this piece.) He used the 'family album' which his second cousin showed him in Prague in 1994. He returned to his mother's story. He echoed Jan's words in *Rock 'n' Roll* about his childhood love of England, in Leo's speech. He gave Leo the scar he had touched on the woman's hand, left by his lost father. He wrote into *Leopoldstadt* his remorse and guilt at not having thought enough about his family's past, in a play which concerns far more than one life, but comes out of that life. Something of what is lost is returned to the grown-up boy: it is memory. One of the themes of the play is restitution; and the play could be described, in the story of Stoppard's life as a writer, as an act of restitution.

He started writing the play in the summer of 2018. In the autumn he had to go to New York for *The Hard Problem*. At the end of the year he went to Moscow to rehearse the Russian version of that play. He was homesick and sleepless: his head was full of *Leopoldstadt*. Back in Dorset, he finished writing it in April 2019. He showed it to Patrick Marber and Sonia Friedman – it was to be a commercial West End production – and they started in on it together. Marber noted that he had learnt from the Royal Court a mantra which went: 'You treat a new play like a classic and a classic like a new play.' Through the summer of 2019 they worked on the text, on casting, on the design (by Richard Hudson) and the lighting (by Neil Austin). They were mulling over tricky questions. Should there be an interval? (Stoppard had wanted it to run straight through at two hours, but eventually accepted that there should be a break.) Could anyone as dazzling as Felicity Kendal in her thirties (he wondered) be found to play Gretl? In a cast of over forty, which parts could be doubled? Were any of the characters redundant? Should they economise with fewer children? – since every part played by someone under twelve, by Equity law, must entail three sets of child actors. Would audiences be confused by the number of characters and the new people appearing in every scene?

These problems, and the rewriting they entailed, went through into the autumn of 2019, and then rehearsals began. Patrick Marber wanted a few things explained more clearly; Stoppard sometimes demurred: 'I like them to sit with their backs to the engine, and only later to find out where they were going,' he said of his audiences. He did make some tweaks, but not every one of them got into the published text. The cast were encouraged by Marber to read up on history, and to give short lectures to each other at the start of rehearsals on some aspect of the play's background. Maps of Vienna plastered the walls of the rehearsal room. Most of the actors in the first cast – apart from Ed Stoppard, playing Ludwig – hadn't known much about Stoppard's history. The play made them think not only about that but about their own families' pasts. For Ed Stoppard, the 'resonances' with his own family history were powerful: 'Doing this play,' he said, 'I've never felt more connected to my heritage.' The company were moved by the play, and there were often tears in rehearsal. Stoppard, listening to the first read-through, said to them: 'Is it okay for me to cry at my own play?' Every time he watched it, he was afraid he might make 'a public spectacle' of himself, weeping at his own work. But the note he gave Marber for the cast was: however funny the play is and however moving it is, it needs to be done with sharp, ironical discipline – sharp, hard and tough. They should get on with it, and keep up the pace. Not too much crying, he warned. Let us do the crying.

Performances began to sell out seven months in advance, as soon as the play was advertised at the end of June 2019. News items ran with titles like: 'Tom Stoppard's Most Jewish Play to Run at Wyndham's Theatre', 'Will Tom Stoppard's Latest Play Be His Most Personal Yet?' In interviews, he was asked whether the play had been written in reaction to current expressions of anti-Semitism in Britain. No, he replied, he did not 'sniff the air' and decide that now was the time to write a play about the cost of being a Jew. The play had converged with what was going on. He was asked repeatedly about his family history and his Jewishness. It was not an autobiographical play, he kept saying, but it was 'about a part of myself'.

He was asked, too, if this was his last play. Seeming to admit that it might be, he talked about how much energy it had taken to write it, and how hard it would be to write anything else 'after that', and that he might be eighty-six or eighty-seven by the time another play emerged. But then, at once retracting, he added: 'I don't have plans to stop thinking.' 'What else would I be doing?' 'While I'm thinking I'm potentially writing.' And he noted that he had just done a new piece for radio, which would be aired in May 2020. This was another Jewish story, an adaptation of Daniel

Kehlmann's play *The Voyage of the St Louis*, about the shipload of Jewish refugees turned back from Cuba in 1939 and forced to return to Germany, where many of them perished.

Leopoldstadt (which was to have a six-month run) had its first preview on 25 January 2020, in the week of the seventy-fifth anniversary of the liberation of Auschwitz. Marber's beautiful, intelligent production embedded the play firmly in its historical context, with a gauze on which the date of each scene was projected, and photographs and film shots of Vienna and its inhabitants from 1899 to 1955. Neil Austin's lighting bathed the first scene in golden sepia, like an old photograph, changing by the end to bare brightness and deep darkness. Eloquent music thickened the atmosphere – some historical, like Schoenberg's *Verklärte Nacht* and Sibelius's 'Valse Triste', and some, including a 1950s-style jazz piece, composed for the play by Adam Cork. The big cast, young and old, worked together to tell the play's painful story with extraordinary strength and deftness – in particular Adrian Scarborough's very powerful Hermann, Faye Castelow, enchanting as Gretl, Sebastian Armesto doubling as their son Jacob and as the anguished survivor Nathan, Ed Stoppard as a saintly, gentle Ludwig, Luke Thallon equally magnetic as Fritz and as Leo, and Jenna Augen as Rosa, who must carry the weight of the play's ending.

Some early viewers felt confused by the number of characters; some Jewish members of the audience felt the play assumed too much ignorance about Judaism; others were moved to talk about their own family histories. Most audiences became intensely involved, especially with Hermann and Gretl, laughed at the jokes, held their breaths at the family's destruction, and came out tearful and overcome.

Reviewers picked up eagerly on Stoppard's suggestion that this might be his last play, talking (perhaps prematurely?) of his 'swan song'. One, sounding almost like an obituarist, called it 'the last great play of the last great writer of the twentieth century'. Not all the critics rose to this sense of a momentous theatrical event. There was a good deal of grumbling – as anticipated – about the large number of characters making it 'baffling' and 'hard to follow who's who', the 'voluminous research' not translating into 'engaging conversation', and the 'expositional history lessons' being 'leaden' or 'admonitory' or 'stiff'. The word 'static' was used more than once. But even those who resorted to the old line, that Stoppard had always been accused of being 'too clever by half', 'a cerebral gymnast', 'lacking the power to move us beyond words', acknowledged that *Leopoldstadt* was 'irrefutable evidence to the contrary'.

Reviewers who cavilled at the talkiness of the earlier scenes found themselves overwhelmed by '1938' and '1955', and, at the play's end, left 'bereft at history'. The *New York Times* critic – the pointer towards the play's possible transfer to the States – praised its 'emotional power', its 'gravity and eloquence'. The reviewers' key quotes, uniquely in the history of his plays, were all about emotion: 'Deeply, achingly moving' . . . 'devastatingly moving' . . . 'powerful and moving' . . . 'achingly poignant' . . . 'I defy anyone to sit through the final scene dry-eyed' . . . 'a late master-work, by turns wise, witty, and devastatingly sad'.

All the reviewers noted the connections to his own life: '*Leopoldstadt* feels like an act of personal reckoning for its creator.' 'Raising the emotional voltage, Stoppard puts a version of himself on stage.' 'A personal play of a most unusual and generous kind . . . a masterpiece.' One critic, acutely, was surprised at how much 'scorn' and 'self-laceration' Leo ('who could be Stoppard himself') feels at his own ignorance of his past. Above all, wrote another, it is a play about 'memory and the act of remembering'.

Leopoldstadt's press night was on 12 February 2020. Just over a month later, due to the Covid-19 pandemic, all theatres went dark, and *Leopoldstadt* – for the time being – ended its run, on 14 March.

I asked Stoppard, in the summer of 2019, as he finished the play, whether writing it had appeased the emotions which went into it. No, he replied.

That exchange was the last of many conversations, stretching over several years, which I have had with him since he asked me to write his biography. In our opening conversation, I asked him what the first thing was he could remember – and that's how this book starts. The question is one of the jokes in *Rosencrantz and Guildenstern*. ('What's the first thing you remember?' . . . 'No, it's no good, it's gone. It was a long time ago.') I didn't know, then, that in *Leopoldstadt*, over fifty years after *Rosencrantz*, the question would return with deeply serious meaning: 'So what's the first thing you can remember, Leo?'

While I've been writing about Stoppard, his life, and his feelings about his own life, have been changing. He told me that he imagined the process of my writing his biography would be like leading parallel lives. He would be living his life, and I would be writing about his life, and occasionally the lines would intersect. That's exactly how it has been. While I've been working in his archives, talking to people who know him and writing this book, he's been getting on with being Tom Stoppard. Every so often I catch up with him: in conversation, in rehearsal rooms, at his public appearances and parties, occasionally on a platform with him in London or Oxford or New York. At such events, he teases me about biography. On one occasion he turned to the audience, before I got out my first question, and said: 'You know the writer who said, "Biography adds a new terror to death?" Well, here she is!'

Anyone writing a life of Stoppard would know that he has always had mixed feelings about biography. You can't go far in his work without running up against remarks like that of Mrs Swan to the would-be biographer Mr Pike in *Indian Ink*: '*Biography* is the worst possible excuse for getting people wrong.' One of the pleasures of *Arcadia* is the comeuppance of the predatory, dishonest biographical sleuth Bernard, of whom it is said: 'I don't care to be rubbished by the dustbin man.' Oscar Wilde is quoted, creatively, in *The Invention of Love*, with this epigram: 'Biography is the mesh through which our real life escapes.' It's Wilde who also says (but Stoppard wrote his lines for him): 'It's only fact. Truth is quite another thing and is the work of the imagination.' Often, in his talks, he's compared the relative merits of biographical fiction or biographical plays with biography and history, insisted on other ways at getting at 'the truth of a person' than hard facts, and suggested that historical facts may have a more unstable relation to the truth than fiction. For all these mixed feelings, he has been patient, accessible and generous to his biographer. I tell him what Beckett said to his first biographer: 'I will neither help nor hinder.' On the whole, Stoppard has helped and not hindered. But his line to me is: 'I'm not supposed to be helping you, you're on your own.'

There have been moments when he clearly regretted setting this book in motion, and would have preferred me not to be asking personal questions about him of his friends, or reading his archive, or asking him about his past. For all that he is a public and highly visible personage, he is also a reserved, shy and embarrassable private man, protective of himself and of his family. Sometimes he has been baffled by the whole process and by the questions I've asked him. This can't be any use to you, can it? he has often asked, in mid-conversation. But he is also intrigued by how the process works. He once said that it must be like making an ordnance survey map, *and* a plan of the house, *and* a map of the world.

If I had tried to make a map of his whole world, and talked to every person he has ever known or worked with, I would have spent many more years interviewing most of the theatre, media and literary profession. Beyond his friends and family and close working colleagues, I have had to take a representative slice. But in well over a hundred interviews, there has been remarkable consistency about him. In the land of showbiz, which is not free of spite, he has an exceptionally good reputation. Malicious gossip doesn't seem to attach to him, perhaps because he doesn't engage in it himself. There is, generally, a powerful sense of love, respect and admiration for him on all sides, even where there may be political differences, or twinges of envy.

I've often asked people to sum him up with three words. They come up with: polymathic, brainy, inspirational, passionate, rigorous, sympathetic, conservative with a small 'c', irresistible, supportive, witty, curious, open, gentle, thoughtful, amatory, daunting, clear-thinking, focused, stimulating, brave, warm-hearted. (And, also, from one theatre designer, 'great hair'.) By far the most frequent adjectives have been: loyal, kind, considerate, glamorous, generous and intelligent. Hardly anyone, oddly enough, says 'funny' – though he is. Nobody says cruel, proud, selfish or inattentive. The people who are giving me these accounts of him are sincere: this is what they feel about him. But, also, they know that he will read their views of him in this book; they want to praise him. When he does read this book, he repeats to me something he has often said before: he is good at performing niceness, but he is not as nice as people think.

And he does come with warning signs, too. One young playwright, who adores him but has witnessed him in critical mode, added to his adjectives: 'And a tiny bit evil.' One grand old woman of the world, an old friend of his, said to me: 'Beware of the charm.' A theatre director noted that he used his politeness to get what he wanted from people. A woman who has often worked with him notes that he is not influenced by anyone when he wants something his way. 'Solitary' and 'private' are frequent adjectives. Many people who know him have said they don't feel they know him well. They don't know who his close friends are and they aren't even sure if he has any. One playwright said, I've known him for forty-five years and I don't know him at all. Another, who after many years can't decide whether he is a friend or not, calls him elusive, paradoxical and difficult to pin down. Another described him as completely, icily alone, a solitary: 'Occasionally the shutter comes down, and you know.' Quite a few people speak of his having a core of steel. One director (echoing Spielberg's view of him as 'intractable') says that, professionally, he would only ever do what he wants to do; he wouldn't change to meet people's expectations. But in all these conversations, I am given the sense that he *matters*. People feel that Stoppard has historical significance, that he will be remembered, and that he has made a difference to our culture. A famous writer, who loves him dearly, said: 'He is one of the most important people in the world.'

One of the pleasures, and challenges, of writing the biography of a living person is that the life is changing as you write about it. There is also the problem of the ending. (He makes wry mortuary jokes occasionally about needing to provide me with a good last line.) But that difficulty is also a perfect illustration of the open-endedness of biography. There is no such thing as a 'definitive' or conclusive Life. The difficulty of finding an ending is a bit like the problem that arose with *Shakespeare in Love*. Will and Lady Viola couldn't go off into the sunset together – there was the small matter of history to consider. Brilliantly, Stoppard wrote the problem into the script. 'How is this to end?' says the furious and bewildered Lord Wessex to Queen Elizabeth. And she replies, with dry, sad realism, that it will end as many love stories do, 'with tears and a journey'.

1998 *Shakespeare in Love* (co-author with Marc Norman, screenplay); *Poodle Springs* (screenplay)
2000 *Vatel* (screenplay)
2001 *Enigma* (screenplay)
2002 *The Coast of Utopia: Voyage, Shipwreck, Salvage*
2003 Brecht's *Galileo* (written as screenplay 1970–1)
2004 Pirandello's *Henry IV*
2005 Sibleyras's *Heroes*
2006 *Rock 'n' Roll*
2007 *On 'Dover Beach'* (radio)
2008 Chekhov's *Ivanov*
2009 Chekhov's *The Cherry Orchard*
2012 Ford's *Parade's End* (TV); *Anna Karenina* (screenplay)
2013 *Darkside* (radio)
2014 Lee Hall's *Shakespeare in Love* (stage)
2015 *The Hard Problem*
2017 *Tulip Fever* (co-author, screenplay)
2019 *Penelope* (libretto)
2020 *Leopoldstadt*

Abbreviations and Bibliography

Individuals

AF: Antonia Fraser, historian, wife of Harold Pinter
AS: Anthony Smith, writer, author of *Wordsmith*
BS: Barnaby (Barny or Barnie) Stoppard, second son of TS and JS
DH: David Hare, playwright
ES: Edmund (Ed) Stoppard, second son of TS and MS
FK: Felicity Kendal, actor
FP: Frank Pike, Faber editor
FS: Fiona Stoppard, half-sister
GD: Gordon Dickerson, PFD agent and KE's partner
HP: Harold Pinter, playwright, cricketer
IC: Isabel Dunjohn, later Cortan, Bristol friend
JM: Jacky Matthews (previously Chamberlain), personal assistant to TS
J O'B: Jack O'Brien, theatre director
JS: Jose Stoppard, née Ingle, first wife
JW: John Wood, actor
KE: Kenneth Ewing, agent at PFD (Peters Fraser and Dunlop)
KS: Kenneth Stoppard, stepfather
KT: Kenneth Tynan, theatre critic, National Theatre artistic adviser
MA: Manny [Emanuel] Azenberg, Broadway producer
MC: Michael Codron, West End producer
MJ: Marigold Johnson, wife of Paul Johnson
MN: Mike Nichols, film and theatre director
MS: Miriam Stoppard, née Stern, medical expert, second wife
M[B]S: Marta (later Bobby) Stoppard, mother
OS: Oliver (Ollie or Olly) Stoppard, first son of TS and JS
PJ: Paul Johnson, journalist, historian
PM: Patrick Marber, writer, director
PPR: Piers Paul Read, novelist
PS: Peter Stoppard, brother, accountant
PW: Peter Wood, theatre director
RE: Richard Eyre, theatre director
SC: Sinéad Cusack, actor
SF: Sonia Friedman, producer
SGS: Sabrina Stoppard, née Guinness, third wife
SS: Steven Spielberg, film director
TN: Trevor Nunn, theatre director
TS: Tom Stoppard
VH: Václav Havel, Czech playwright, dissident, president
WS: William (Will) Stoppard, first son of TS and MS

Archives

BBC Archive: BBC Written Archives Centre, Caversham Park, Reading
Brotherton: Piers Paul Read Archive, Brotherton Library, University of Leeds
Codron archive: Michael Codron office archive, Aldwych Theatre
Faber archive: TS archive at Faber & Faber
HR: Harry Ransom Archive, University of Texas at Austin
IC papers: Isabel Cortan (née Dunjohn), personal papers
JM archive: Jacky Matthews's archive of TS papers (sent to HR, 2020, apart from
    Appointment Diaries)
NT: National Theatre archive
PS archive: Peter Stoppard, personal papers
TS archive: TS's personal archive (including 'Journal for Edmund', JE I and JE II)
TSL: TS's letters to his parents, TS's personal archive
UA: United Agents TS archive

Selected Bibliography of Works Consulted

Other works referred to are given in full in the Notes.

Baker 2013: William Baker and Amanda Smothers, eds, 'The Real Thing': Essays on Tom
    Stoppard in Celebration of his 75th Birthday, Cambridge Scholars Publishing, 2013
Biblio: William Baker and Gerald N. Wachs, Tom Stoppard: A Bibliographical History, The
    British Library, 2010
Billington 1987: Michael Billington, Stoppard the Playwright, Methuen, 1987
Billington 2007: Michael Billington, State of the Nation: British Theatre since 1945, Faber,
    2007
Brassell: Tim Brassell, Tom Stoppard: An Assessment, St Martin's Press, 1985
Cambridge: Katherine E. Kelly, ed., The Cambridge Companion to Tom Stoppard,
    Cambridge University Press, 2001
Codron: Michael Codron with Alan Strachan, Putting It On, Duckworth, 2010
Delaney 1990: Paul Delaney, Tom Stoppard: The Moral Vision of the Major Plays,
    Macmillan, 1990
Delaney 1994: Paul Delaney, ed., Tom Stoppard in Conversation, University of Michigan
    Press, 1994
Demastes: William Demastes, The Cambridge Introduction to Tom Stoppard, Cambridge
    University Press, 2013
Fleming 2001: John Fleming, Stoppard's Theatre: Finding Order amid Chaos, University of
    Texas Press, 2001
Fleming 2008: John Fleming, Tom Stoppard's Arcadia, Continuum, 2008
Gottland: Mariusz Szczygieł, Gottland: Mostly True Stories from Half of Czechoslovakia,
    2006, trans. Antonia Lloyd-Jones, Melville House, Brooklyn & London, 2014
Gussow: Mel Gussow, Conversations with Stoppard, Nick Hern Books, 1995
Hayman 1977: Ronald Hayman, Tom Stoppard, Heinemann, 1977
Hunter 2000: Jim Hunter, Stoppard: A Faber Critical Guide, Faber, 2000
Hunter 2005: Jim Hunter, About Stoppard: The Playwright and the Work, Faber, 2005
Jenkins: Anthony Jenkins, The Theatre of Tom Stoppard, Cambridge University Press, 1987

Nadel: Ira Nadel, *Double Act: A Life of Tom Stoppard*, Methuen, 2002
Sammells: Neil Sammells, *Tom Stoppard: The Artist as Critic*, St Martin's Press, 1988
Wordsmith: A. C. H. Smith, *Wordsmith: A Memoir*, Redcliffe, 2012

Selected Articles, Interviews, Features

Other articles referred to are given in full in the Notes.

Hagerty: *British Journalism Review*, Vol. 16, No. 4, December 2005, ed. Bill Hagerty, 'Tom Stoppard: My Love Affair with Newspapers', 19–30
PR: Shusha Guppy, 'Tom Stoppard: The Art of Theater VII', *Paris Review* 109 (Winter 1988), 25–51. In Delaney 1994
TALK 1999: *Talk* magazine, September 1999, 'On Turning Out to Be Jewish', 190–4, 241–3. Also printed (with other illustrations) in *Sunday Telegraph*, 10 October 1999, as 'Another Country'
Tynan 1977: Kenneth Tynan, 'Withdrawing with Style from the Chaos', *New Yorker*, 19 December 1977; reprinted in *Show People: Profiles in Entertainment*, Weidenfeld & Nicolson, Simon & Schuster, 1979, 44–123; extracts in *Gambit: International Theatre Review*, Tom Stoppard Issue, John Calder 1981, 19–41

Newspapers

BEW: *Bristol Evening World*
S: *Scene*
WDP: *Western Daily Press*

Works by Tom Stoppard

This list gives first performance, broadcast or film release dates, and first UK publisher and publication dates, followed by a list of currently available collected volumes of Stoppard's works, with contents. It does not give details of unpublished screenplays, or of acting editions, translations, or revised editions of each play, except when my quotations are taken from the revised editions. It does not include published essays, lectures, prefaces, reviews, journalism or broadcast interviews. These are referenced, where cited, in the Notes. A *Bibliographical History* of Stoppard's work was published in 2010 (see 'Works Consulted'). There is currently no updated, complete bibliography of his work and no complete standard edition of his Collected Works.

A: *Arcadia*, first performed 1993, Faber, 1993, reprinted with corrections, 1993
AB: *Albert's Bridge*, first broadcast 1967, first performed on stage 1969, Faber, 1969
ADS: *Artist Descending a Staircase*, first broadcast 1972, first performed on stage 1988, Faber, 1973
AM: *After Magritte*, first performed 1970, Faber, 1971
AMCE: *Another Moon Called Earth*, first on TV 1967, Faber, 1969
Anna Karenina, released 2012, Penguin Random House, 2012
The Boundary, with Clive Exton, first on TV 1975, Samuel French, 1995

Brazil, released 1985. Jack Mathews, *The Battle of Brazil*, Crown Publishers, 1987

CO: Chekhov's *The Cherry Orchard*, first performed 2009, Faber, 2009

CU: *The Coast of Utopia*, first performed 2002. Each play in the trilogy, *Voyage,
Shipwreck, Salvage* [V, Sh, S] published separately, Faber, 2002. Revised edition of all
three plays in one volume, Faber, 2008

D: Schnitzler's *Dalliance*, first performed 1986, in *Dalliance* and *Undiscovered Country*,
Faber, 1986

Darkside: *Darkside: A Play for Radio Incorporating* The Dark Side of the Moon *by Pink
Floyd*, first broadcast 2013, Faber, 2013

DHCM: *Dogg's Hamlet, Cahoot's Macbeth*, first performed 1979, Inter-Action, 1979, Faber,
1980

The Dissolution of Dominic Boot, first broadcast 1964, Faber, 1983

DL and NFD: *Dirty Linen* and *New-Found-Land*, first performed 1976, Inter-Action, 1976,
Faber, 1976

DOG: *The Dog It Was That Died*, first broadcast 1982, Faber, 1983

DOP: *Dogg's Our Pet*, first performed 1971, Inter-Action, 1979

EAFM: *Enter a Free Man*, first performed 1968, Faber, 1968

EGBDF&PF: *Every Good Boy Deserves Favour*, first performed 1977, and *Professional
Foul*, first on TV 1977, Faber, 1978

EOTS: *Empire of the Sun*, released 1987, The Movie Script, screenplay, 1987

The (Fifteen-minute) Dogg's Troupe Hamlet, first performed 1976, Inter-Action, 1979

G: *Galileo: A Screenplay*, written 1970–1, *Areté*, Issue 11, Spring–Summer 2003

H: *Hapgood*, first performed 1988, Faber, 1988. Revised, Faber, New York, 1994

HENRY: Pirandello's *Henry IV*, first performed 2004, Faber, 2004

HEROES: Sibleyras's *Le Vent des peupliers*, translated by TS as *Heroes*, first performed
2005, Faber, 2005

HP: *The Hard Problem*, first performed 2015, Faber, 2015

I: Chekhov's *Ivanov*, first performed 2008, Faber, 2008

IL: *The Invention of Love*, first performed 1997, Faber, 1997

INK: *Indian Ink*, first performed 1995, Faber, 1995

Introduction 2: Stories by New Writers ('Reunion', 'Life, Times: Fragments', 'The Story'),
Faber, 1964

ITNS: *In the Native State*, first broadcast 1991, Faber, 1991

IYGIBF: *If You're Glad I'll Be Frank*, first broadcast 1966, Faber, 1969

J: *Jumpers*, first performed 1972, Faber, 1972. Revised, Faber, 1973, 1986

L: *Leopoldstadt*, first performed 2020, Faber, 2020

LD: Havel's *Largo Desolato*, first performed 1986, Faber, 1986. In Václav Havel, *Selected
Plays 1984–1987*, Faber, 1994

LMM: *Lord Malquist & Mr Moon*, Anthony Blond, 1966, Faber, 2005

The Love for Three Oranges, libretto, first performed 1983, Bodley Head, 1984

'M' is for Moon Among Other Things, first broadcast 1964, Faber, 1983

ND: *Night and Day*, first performed 1978, Faber 1978. Revised, Faber, 1979

Neutral Ground, first on TV 1968, Faber, 1983

On 'Dover Beach', first broadcast 2007, *Areté*, Issue 23, Spring–Autumn 2007, Faber, 2012

OTR: Nestroy's *On the Razzle*, first performed 1981, Faber, 1981

PE: Ford Madox Ford's *Parade's End*, adapted by TS, first on TV 2012, Faber, 2012

Penelope: libretto, first performed 2019, MusicSales Classical, G. Schirmer, 2019

PF: *Professional Foul*, first on TV 1977, Faber, 1978
RC: Molnár's *Rough Crossing*, first performed 1984, Faber, 1985
R&G: *Rosencrantz and Guildenstern Are Dead*, first performed 1966, Faber, 1967
Rosencrantz and Guildenstern Are Dead: The Film, released 1990, Faber, 1991
RIH: *The Real Inspector Hound*, first performed 1968, Faber, 1968
RR: *Rock 'n' Roll*, first performed 2006, Faber, 2006
RT: *The Real Thing*, first performed 1982, Faber, 1982. Revised, Faber, 1988
S: Chekhov's *The Seagull*, first performed 1997, Faber, 1997
A Separate Peace, first on TV 1966, Hutchinson Educational 1969, Faber, 1983
SiL: *Shakespeare in Love*, Marc Norman and TS, released 1998, Universal Studios, 1998,
    Faber, 1999
StC: *Squaring the Circle*, first on TV 1984, Faber, 1984
T: *Travesties*, first performed 1974, Faber, 1975. Revised, Faber, 1993, 2017
Teeth, first on TV, 1967, Faber, 1983
UC: Schnitzler's *Undiscovered Country*, first performed 1979, Faber, 1980
WATN?: *Where Are They Now?*, first broadcast 1970, Faber, 1973

COLLECTED VOLUMES

Plays 1: *Tom Stoppard: Plays One*, Faber, 1996 (*The Real Inspector Hound, After Magritte,
    Dirty Linen, New-Found-Land, Dogg's Hamlet, Cahoot's Macbeth*)
Plays 2: *Tom Stoppard: Plays Two*, Faber, 1996 (*The Dissolution of Dominic Boot, 'M' Is
    for Moon Among Other Things, If You're Glad I'll Be Frank, Albert's Bridge, Where Are
    They Now?, Artist Descending a Staircase, The Dog It Was That Died, In the Native State*,
    reissued 2012 with *On 'Dover Beach'*)
Plays 3: *Tom Stoppard: Plays Three*, Faber, 1998 (*A Separate Peace, Teeth, Another Moon
    Called Earth, Neutral Ground, Professional Foul, Squaring the Circle*)
Plays 4: *Tom Stoppard: Plays Four*, Faber, 1999 (*Dalliance, Undiscovered Country, Rough
    Crossing, On the Razzle, The Seagull*)
Plays 5: *Tom Stoppard: Plays Five*, Faber, 1999 (*Arcadia, The Real Thing, Night and Day,
    Indian Ink, Hapgood*)
RADIO: *Stoppard: The Plays for Radio*, Faber, first published as *The Dog It Was That Died
    and Other Plays*, 1983, then as *The Plays for Radio*, 1990, reissued 1994, and in 1996 as
    Plays 2
TELEVISION: *The Television Plays 1965–1984*, Faber, 1993, and in 1998 as Plays 3
Five European Plays, Grove Atlantic, 2018 (*Dalliance, Undiscovered Country, Rough
    Crossing, On the Razzle, Largo Desolato*)

Note on Spellings

Bata: I use the universally known form 'Bata', rather than the spelling of the original family
name, 'Bat'a'.
Sträussler: TS, and some online references and books on TS, give his father's family name
as 'Straussler'. All family records have 'Sträussler', which I use.
Marta: TS's mother's given name was Marta, sometimes written, as by TS, with the 'h', as in
the English spelling. She signed her own letters as 'Marta', which I use.

Acknowledgements

My first and deepest thanks go to the subject of this biography, who asked me if I would write it, gave me access to a wealth of materials and permission to quote from them, put me in touch with many of his colleagues, friends and family, responded to my questions, undertook long conversations about his life and work over several years, read the typescript for factual errors, and, in spite of his reservations about biography as a genre, and his many other commitments, has been, throughout, helpful, generous and philosophical.

I owe a great debt of thanks to members of Tom Stoppard's family: to Sabrina Stoppard for her hospitality, kindness and friendship; to his sons Oliver, Barny, Will and Ed for their willingness to talk to me; to his brother Peter and Peter's late wife Lesley for hosting me in Bristol and for cheerfully providing answers to many questions and crucial materials; to his sister Fiona for her generosity and candour; to his cousin Sarka Gauglitz for lending me her letters from Tom Stoppard's mother; and to Miriam Stoppard for making me welcome and for several invaluable conversations.

I am hugely grateful to Jacky Matthews for her help, friendship and efficiency, and for all the generous hospitality she and her husband Dave gave me in Winchester. It would have been impossible to do the work on this book without Jacky's support.

I thank Tom Stoppard's lawyer, Laura Munro at Blake Capthorne, and his accountant, Diane Ruskell, for their helpful information.

In the Czech Republic, I am very grateful to the following for their help: in Prague, Tom Stoppard's second cousin Alexandr Rosa and his daughter Kveta Smidova; in Zlín, Filip Groschl, Pavel Riha, Vit Štourać, Antonin Bájaja, and the late Emil Máčel. For the history of the Sträusslers and the Gellerts in Zlín, I am extremely grateful to Vera Somen and Andrew Gellert.

For help and materials relating to David West, Peter Jones and 'Classics For All', I am grateful to Rosemary Burton, Catherine Hadshar and Christina West.

For help and materials relating to the Dolphin School and Peter Roach, I am grateful to Jill Broome and Sally Roach.

At Mount Hermon School, Darjeeling, I thank Partha Dey and Neena Mandira West for showing me round the school and telling me its history.

For permission to attend rehearsals of *Rosencrantz and Guildenstern* in 2017, and for his interviews and encouragement, I am grateful to David Leveaux; and for friendly communications during those rehearsals, to Daniel Radcliffe, Joshua McGuire, David Haig and William Chubb. I thank Nicholas Hytner for allowing me sit in on rehearsals of *The Hard Problem* in 2015. I am grateful to Patrick Marber for giving me access to final rehearsals of *Travesties* in 2016 and to rehearsals of *Leopoldstadt* in 2020.

At United Agents, I am extremely grateful to Rose Cobbe and St John Donald for information and materials, and also to Anthony Jones. For help and professional support for my work, I thank, with feeling, my agent Caroline Dawnay, Kat Aitken, and also Sophie Scard.

At Faber, I thank Stephen Page, Mitzi Angel during her time there, Robert Brown, Alex Bowler, Suzanne King, Anne Owen and Sophie Portas. My warmest thanks go to Dinah Wood for her patience, her acute and sympathetic reading, and her impeccable professionalism.

At Chatto & Windus, I thank Clara Farmer for her generous understanding.

Colleagues and students at Wolfson College Oxford, especially at the Oxford Centre for Life-Writing at Wolfson, have been a source of support, inspiration and encouragement.

A large number of people have given me interviews, information, stories, suggestions, translations, hospitality, advice, access, permissions to quote, and help of many kinds. I list them here, with my grateful thanks:

Deke, Jill and Jamie Arlon; Simon Armitage; Emanuel Azenberg; Ed Berman; Michael Billington; André Bishop at the Lincoln Center; Robert Bookman; John Boorman; Michael Brandman and Joanna Miles; the late Helen Brann; Harvey Brown; Robert Carsen; Vera Chok; Glenn Close; Sir Michael Codron and his staff at the Aldwych Theatre; Lottie Cole; Angela Connor; Anna Cooke; David Cornwell; Tim, Hélène and Ben Corrie; Isabel Cortan; Bob Crowley; Rachel Cunningham-Day; Julie Curtis; Sinéad Cusack; Mark Damazer; Gordon Dickerson; Sos Eltis; Michael Fend; Martyn Fletcher; Roy Foster; Lady Antonia Fraser; Sonia Friedman; Paul Gallagher; Jo Glanville; Derek Goldby; Michael Grandage; Victoria Gray; Nicholas Grene; Bill Hagerty; Sue Hales; Henry Hardy; Sir David Hare; Alexandra Harris; Sir Max Hastings; the late Drue Heinz; Sir Nicholas Hytner; the late Clive James; Marigold and Paul Johnson; Peter Jones; Daniel Kehlmann; Felicity Kendal; Kathleen Kennedy; Michael Kitchen; Natalia Koliada of Belarus Free Theatre; the late Benjamin Lee; Elizabeth Leedham Green; David Leveaux; Amanda Lillie; James Loehlin; Tim Luscombe; Alastair Macaulay; Ian McEwan; Jerome McGann; Margaret Macmillan; John Madden; Patrick Marber; David Marks; Deborah Moggach; Trish Montemuro; Kathryn Murphy; the late Peter Nichols; Bill Nighy; Sir Trevor Nunn; Jack O'Brien; Andrew O'Hagan; Arkady Ostrovsky; Ursula Owen; Bridget Patterson; Carey Perloff; Frank Pike; Eric Price; Philip Pullman; Alex Pyz; Diana Quick; Piers Paul Read; Robyn Read; Sir Tim Rice; Dame Diana Rigg; Daniel Rosenthal; Sir Simon Russell Beale; Max Saunders; Diane Sawyer; Bernard Schwartz at the 92nd Street Y; the late Sir Roger Scruton; Graeme Segal; Anthony Smith; John Smith; Andrew Speed; Steven Spielberg; Jean Strouse; Adam Thirlwell; the late John Tydeman; Richard Vinen; Rupert Walters; Janet Watts; Teresa Wells; Susanna White; the late Charles Wood and Valerie Wood; Blanka Zizka.

My warm thanks go to my admirable researcher, Sumaya Partner, and to my friend Vanessa Guignery for her generous assistance while she has been working at the Harry Ransom Center.

I have some very particular, personal debts of gratitude. I thank my good friend, Mark Lawson, a rich fund of knowledge on Tom Stoppard and his work, for his generous help throughout. I thank Richard Eyre, with admiration and gratitude, for his advice, his reading, and his encouragement. I thank Julian Barnes, who from the first to last moments of this book's progress has been a listener, a rigorous and inspiring reader, and an advice centre. I thank my dear friend and reader, the unmatchable biographer Jenny Uglow, who has been at my side all through my work on this book, as with every book, and who has helped it take shape. Above all I thank my husband John Barnard, my life's companion, here and in the dedication.

I am grateful to numerous archivists and librarians for their help. Above all, at the Harry Ransom Center at the University of Austin Texas, I am grateful to Steve Enniss, Eric Colleary, Cristina Meisner, Rick Watson, and to the ever-helpful staff of the Center.

My thanks also to:

Samantha Blake at the BBC Archives

Lincia Daniel at 'Learning on Screen', British Universities and Colleges Film and Video Council
Erik Dix and Charles Lamb, Notre Dame Archives
Angie Edwards, Librarian and Archivist, Pocklington School
Karina Girnyte at the Westminster School of Media, Arts and Design
Hannah Johnson and Melissa Kunz, Special Collections, McFarlin Library, University of Tulsa
Erin Lee, Malcom Mathieson and Frances Horner at the National Theatre Archive
Philip Marshall and Helen O'Neill at the London Library
The staff at the V&A Theatre and Performance Enquiry Service
The staff at the Brotherton Library Special Collections, University of Leeds

Text Permissions

Isaiah Berlin, by permission of the Trustees of the Isaiah Berlin Literary Trust.
Dirk Bogarde, *An Orderly Man*, Bloomsbury, 1983, by permission of United Agents on behalf of The Estate of Dirk Bogarde.
Daša Drndić, *Trieste*, translated by Ellen Elias-Bursac, published by Quercus Editions Limited, 2012, pp. 84–6. Reproduced by permission of the publisher and by permission of Houghton Mifflin Harcourt.
T. S. Eliot, excerpt from 'Mr Mistoffelees' from *Old Possum's Book of Practical Cats* by T. S. Eliot, copyright © 1939 by T. S. Eliot, renewed 1967 by Esme Valerie Eliot. Reprinted by permission of Houghton Mifflin Harcourt Publishing Company and by Faber & Faber Ltd. All rights reserved. Excerpt from 'Burnt Norton' from *Four Quartets*, published by Faber & Faber Ltd, copyright © 1942 by T. S. Eliot, renewed 1970 by Esme Valerie Eliot. Reproduced by permission of the publisher and Houghton Mifflin Harcourt Publishing Company. All rights reserved.
Richard Ellmann, by permission of Special Collections, McFarlin Library, University of Tulsa.
Simon Gray, by permission of Victoria Gray.
Graham Greene, unpublished note on TS's adaptation of *The Human Factor* for Preminger film, reproduced by permission of David Higham Associates.
Václav Havel, copyright © The Estate of Václav Havel, reproduced by permission of Casarotto Ramsey & Associates Ltd. All rights whatsoever in this material are strictly reserved and application for performance etc. must be made before rehearsal to Casarotto Ramsay & Associates Ltd, 3rd Floor, 7 Savoy Court, Strand, London WC2R 0EX (info@casarotto.co.uk). No performance may be given unless a licence has been obtained.
Clive James, by permission of Robert Kirby, United Agents.
The National Theatre, by permission of the National Theatre Archive.
Peter Nichols, *A Piece of My Mind* by Peter Nichols, copyright © Methuen, 1987. Reproduced by permission of Alan Brodie Representation Ltd, www.alanbrodie.com.
Harold Pinter, by permission of Harold Pinter's Estate.
Piers Paul Read, literary papers and correspondence, courtesy of the Brotherton Special Collection, University of Leeds, Piers Paul Read Archive.
The Tom Stoppard Archive, by permission of the Harry Ransom Center, University of Texas at Austin.
Kenneth Tynan, reproduced by kind permission of the Estate of Kenneth Tynan.

Photograph Credits

With the exception of those listed below, photographs are from the Tom Stoppard papers held at the Harry Ransom Center at the University of Texas at Austin.

Page 3: *The Coast of Utopia*, Russian style, 2007 (© RAMT/designed by Andrey Bondarenko). *The Coast of Utopia*, English cartoon, 2002 (© Steve Fricker/Telegraph Media Group Limited, 2002).

Page 4: Tony Award winner, 10 June 2007 (Jason Szenes/EPA/Shutterstock).

Page 5: Cartoon fodder: *Private Eye*, 2017 (reproduced with permission of *Private Eye* magazine and Russel Herneman). Visiting the refugee camp The Jungle at Calais, 23 February 2016 (© Souvid Datta/Guardian News & Media).

Page 6: Photo courtesy of Christopher Simon Sykes.

Page 7: *The Hard Problem* at the Wilma Theatre, Philadelphia, January 2016 (photograph by Alexander Iziliaev). *Leopoldstadt*, Wyndham's Theatre, January 2020 (© Marc Brenner).

Page 8: Stoppard during *Leopoldstadt* rehearsals, 19 January 2020 (Bryan Appleyard/ *Sunday Times*).

Endpapers: original manuscript page of *Rosencrantz and Guildenstern Are Dead* (Tom Stoppard papers, Harry Ransom Center, University of Texas at Austin).

Every effort has been made to trace copyright holders and to obtain permission for the use of copyright material. The publisher would be pleased to rectify any omissions that are brought to its attention at the earliest opportunity.

Notes

1: First Acts

3 *What's the first thing*: R&G, 7.

4 *felt no identification*: TS, interview HL, 28 June 2014. PR.

4 *I grew up*: Speech for Honorary Doctorate, 4 May 2007, Janáček Academy of Music and Art, Brno.

4 *patriotic pride*: Speech, Czech National Theatre, Prague, 30 April 2004.

6 *answering the call-up*: Quoted in Gottland, 8.

6 *Beck family*: HR 34.5, TS to KT, nd [late 1977]. Birthplace of M[B]S: TS gives as Rosice in Brno speech, 4 May 2007. (Family records give Rousinov, near Brno.)

8 *The fact that my mother*: HR 122.4, 122.5, typescript of TALK 1999.

8 *carpets, curtains*: M[B]S, Memories, unpublished, written for TS and PS, 1982.

8 *exactly 193 square feet*: Gottland.

9 *The Firm's policies*: Gottland, 26–7. For Zlín and Bata, see also Burkhard Bilger, 'Sole Survivor', *New Yorker*, 14 and 21 February 2005, 152–67; Anthony Cekota, *The Stormy Years of an Extraordinary Enterprise: Bata 1932–1945*, Universum Sokol, NJ, 1985.

10 *It is important*: Eugen Sträussler, 'On Sleep', *Zlín* (Bata company weekly newspaper), 23 November 1934, translator unknown. *Zlín*, 22 November 1937, on Eugen Sträussler's lectures.

11 *not handsome*: M[B]S, Memories.

11 *The Sträusslers and the Gellerts*: Vera Somen to TS, 24 January 1999. Emil Máčel to TS, 31 October 1999, 16 December 1997, 24 September 1999. Dr F. Albert-Recht to TS, 20 September 1999.

11 *slightly mischievous smile*: Dr I. Friedmann to TS, 27 November 1999.

11 *gave Nelly a ring*: Vera Somen to HL, 6 February 2015.

13 *The Sträusslers, leaving*: Vera Somen to HL, 6 February 2015. Andrew Gellert to HL, 15 February 2015. John Nash, 'Timeline of Dr Jan Antonin Bata', via www.zlin.estranky. cz. Emil Máčel, Document on Bata doctors, 'Letter to Julia' [descendant of Dr Albert], nd. Nadel, 12, on rise of anti-Semitism in Czechoslovakia in 1930s.

13 *my given name*: RR, ix, 13. TS, interview, *Independent*, 8 June 2006.

2: In Transit

14 *Did you ever feel*: Gussow, 132. Tim Adams, 'Writer and Fighter', *Observer*, Human Rights Special Issue, 21 September 2008, 4–5.

15 *somewhere safe*: HR 7.1, Screenplay of *Empire of the Sun*.

16 *St Christopher medallions*: TALK 1999. 'Another Country', *Sunday Telegraph* version of TALK 1999, 10 October 1999. M[B]S to Emil Máčel, 11 March 1995.

16 *the invasion*: TSL, nd [1960]. TS, interview HL, 28 June 2014. PS, interview HL, 31 May 2014. M[B]S, Memories. HR 122.4, 122.5, typescript of TALK 1999. T. N. Dupuy, *Asiatic Land Battles: Expansion of Japan in Asia*, Franklin Watts, 1963. www.cofepow.org.uk:

civilian evacuees from Singapore. Michael Pether, 'S.S. Redang', to TS, 11 September 2015. In a letter from M[B]S to TS, nd, she gives Eugen Sträussler's death date as 12 February.

18 *I learned*: M[B]S, Memories. On Darjeeling: Barun Roy, *Unwritten History of Darjeeling Hills*, BarunRoy.com, 2003; Hazel Innes Craig, *Under the Old School Topee*, BACSA, 1991; FK, *White Cargo*, Penguin, 1999.

19 *Very often*: 'Going Back', *Independent Magazine*, 23 March 1991. Also as 'In Search of Childhood', *Mail on Saturday*, 4 May 1991. For Darjeeling and Mount Hermon, thanks to Neena Mandira West and Partha Pratim Day, Mount Hermon School, 24 October 2019.

19 *It was famous*: 'In Search of Childhood', *Mail on Saturday*, 4 May 1991.

20 *One boy kept them awake*: 'Going Back'.

20 *interestingly naughty*: TS, interview HL, 28 June 2014.

20 *We smallest boys*: 'Going Back'. HR 35.4, Joy Abrahams to TS, 5 April 1983. Her mother Mrs Callow was the housemistress at Mount Hermon School.

21 *initials in the tree*: HR 124.5, TS, 29 May 1984, to Jane Longmore, editing 'Famous Memories of Famous Childhoods' for the Church of England Children's Society.

21 *opening a bookshop*: HR 39.8, Mount Hermon School Report. TS, *Front Row* interview, BBC Radio 4, 14 April 2017.

21 *American soldiers*: HR 1.1. TS, notes for film script 'A.O.P.', July 1981.

22 *familiar and safe*: 'Going Back'. The memory is in WATN?, in RADIO, 106.

22 *I felt the significance*: TALK 1999.

23 *he hoped they would get married*: HR 35.1, George Newton to TS, 22 January 1985.

24 *I had to decide*: M[B]S, Memories; TS, interview HL, 28 June 2014.

24 *the place everybody would want*: TS, interview HL, 28 June 2014.

25 *that had not saved them*: TALK 1999.

25 *Berta Kindová's son Sascha*: Alexandr Rosa, grandson of Berta Kindová, interview HL, Prague, 20 September 2015, email 28 September 2015.

26 *a change of name*: Deed Poll, 11 March 1946, East Retford, signed K. F. Stoppard.

26 *their naturalisation*: TS, Naturalisation Certificate BNA59166, 22 February 1960, the National Archive, Kew. PS to HL, 22 June 2019.

27 *he would remember*: TSL, nd, February 1974.

3: Englishness

28 *Jenkins (to Gale)*: WATN?, in RADIO, 100.

28 *How could I*: M[B]S, Memories. TS, interview HL, 28 June 2014; PS, interview HL, 31 March 2014.

28 *The Dolphin School*: HR, Picture Archive, 5.

29 *At the age of eight*: TS, interview HL, 28 June 2014. TS, Introduction, Deborah Devonshire, *Counting My Chickens and Other Home Thoughts*, ed. Susan Hill, Long Barn Books, 2001.

30 *That boy will go far*: Mark Amory, 'The Joke's the Thing', *Sunday Times*, 9 June 1975, cited Nadel, 44. Jill Broome, daughter of Peter Roach, interview HL, 30 September 2015. TS archive, Mary Stokes, letter to M[B]S, 1 March 1985.

30 *My method*: TS, interview HL, 28 June 2014. *The Pleasure of Reading*, ed. Antonia Fraser, Bloomsbury, 1992, reprinted 2015, 160–6.

30 *precocious*: PS, interview HL, 31 March 2014.
31 *chastened*: Commentary, 'Going to Bat for Britain', *House & Garden*, Condé Nast, November 1987.
31 *Suffering cats*: TSL, nd [1962].
31 *he played a puppet*: TSL, 14 November 1948; TS archive, Mary Stokes to M[B]S, 1 March 1985.
32 *I hope his soul*: TS, interview HL, 28 June 2014. TSL, nd [1962].
32 *Gale: We walked into French*: WATN?, in RADIO, 104.
32 *plum dumplings*: TALK 1999.
33 *Our first house*: TS, Introduction, Devonshire, *Counting My Chickens*.
33 *to fish, to love*: TALK 1999.
34 *No pride*: EAFM, 15.
35 *his mother's favourite*: TS, interview HL, 14 October 2017.
36 *the boys' education*: TS, interview HL, 28 June 2014; PS, interview HL, 31 March 2014; M[B]S, Memories; TALK 1999. Nadel, 45–53, on Pocklington School, gives the classics master Jim Eggleshaw more credit for encouraging TS than TS does.
36 *it was safer*: M[B]S, Memories.
36 *Stoppard would look back*: TSL, nd [1973]. TS, interview HL, 15 October 2017.
37 *That history*: PS, interview HL, 31 March 2014; TS, interviews HL, 28 June 2014, 17 18 June 2019. TALK 1999.
38 *a good student*: The Pocklingtonian, 1953, 1954, with thanks to Angie Edwards, Archivist, Pocklington School. On sciences, HR 121.22, 'Playing with Science', *CALTECH* magazine, 1994.
39 *some criticism*: TS archive, Pocklington School reports, 1951–3. Nadel, 48, on debating.
40 *My first conscious response*: 'Is It True What They Say about Shakespeare?' *International Shakespeare Association*, OUP, 1982, 10–11. TS, abridged *Merchant of Venice*, Shakespeare Schools Festival, BBC Learning Zone, October 2005; Paul Arendt, 'Stoppard Cuts Shakespeare Down to Size', *Guardian*, 11 October 2005.
40 *His private reading*: The Pleasure of Reading.
40 *Suits of armour?*: TSL, letters from Pocklington, nd [early 1950s].
41 *A. J. Wood had bet*: HR 36.3, A. J. Wood to TS, 28 January 1954.

4: The Newcomer

42 *I felt part*: ND, 1999, 316.
42 *I wish I'd known*: Hagerty, 19. TS, interview HL, 1 November 2019.
42 *National Service*: Information on National Service, with thanks to Professor Richard Vinen. PS to HL, 22 June 2019. TS, interview HL, 28 June 2014.
42 *landed a job*: TS, typescript on Bristol journalism, JM archive, 12 May 2008. Wordsmith, 72. HR 146.11, Bristol NUJ membership book. Elected probationary member, 1 November 1955. Paid 5 shillings a month.
44 *the current provision*: Biblio, H 138, 'Hiding Their Talents in the Earth', WDP, 23 October 1961.
44 *Bristol Old Vic*: Charles Wood, interview HL, 13 June 2015.
46 *Not all the arts*: Biblio, H 106, 'They Can't Live on Laurels', WDP, 7 June 1961.
46 *Stoppard covered*: Biblio, H 121, 'Save the Bomb Site', WDP, 10 July 1961, Brennus.
46 *little magazines*: Biblio, H 79, 'Bristol Magazines Reviewed – 2', WDP, 22 February 1961.

46 *what he wanted*: TS, interview HL, 28 June 2014. TS, typescript on Bristol journalism, 12 May 2008.

47 *write to a deadline*: Deadline difficulties often mentioned in interviews, e.g.: HR 122.9, TS, interview John Knight, *Sunday Mirror*, 18 December 1966: His 'old newspaper training makes him write to a deadline'. Kathleen Halton, *Vogue*, 15 October 1967: 'His wife says he's like a Kamikaze pilot, almost incapable of starting until it's too late.'

47 *first day at the office*: HR 34.11, TS replying to invitation to an *Evening World* reunion, 16 April 1987. Hagerty, 20.

47 *The mistake*: 'Life, Time: Fragments'. *Introduction 2: Stories by New Writers*, Faber, 1964, 126. Hagerty, 26.

47 *first signed piece*: Wordsmith, 80. The only report on a caving accident in the Mendips in TS's first years at WDP, on 11 April 1955, has no byline.

47 *Other early signed pieces*: e.g. WDP, 24 June 1958 (new homes), 24 May 1957 (coffee bars).

48 *naive character*: WDP, 31 December 1956, 19 June 1956, 15 January 1957 (caving), 7 March 1957 (Rag Week).

48 *annual Goram Fair*: WDP, 'Goram Comes to the Fair', 27 July 1957.

48 *not a soft job*: Biblio, H 1, 'Saint Nick – the Facts (unsuitable for children)', WDP, 24 December 1957.

48 *motoring correspondent*: Biblio, H 2, 'Too Good to be Guyed', WDP, 9 May 1958.

48 *romantic passion*: Biblio, H 4, 'A Matter of Gender', WDP, 30 May 1958.

48 *considerate drivers*: Biblio, H 3, 'Mind that Cow! Motoring with Tom Stoppard', WDP, 16 May 1958.

48 *being in the know*: Hagerty, 27.

49 *loved the business*: TS, typescript on Bristol journalism, 12 May 2008.

49 *Subbing*: Bill Bomford to IC, 20 May 1998, cited Nadel, 61.

49 *The feeling was catching*: Hagerty, 20–1.

49 *In the real world*: IC, interview HL, 1 June 2015. Bill Bomford to IC, 20 May 1998. HR 34.1, 'In Another Country', *Village Voice*, 3 May 1962.

50 *eulogising my eyes*: HR 43.7, Gwen Watford to TS, 1 December 1992.

50 *A Beauty Queen*: 'Dolores' to TS, 20 April 2011, JM archive.

51 *encounter with Beckett*: TS, interview RE, for RE, *Talking Theatre*, Nick Hern Books, 2009.

51 *first theatre review*: Gussow, 6. Biblio, H 6, 'To Speak of Two Hamlets', WDP, 5 June 1958.

52 *My name was not up*: Biblio, H 10, 'Act II . . . in Which Tom Stoppard Tries Another Profession', WDP, 13 September 1958.

52 *Tyrone Guthrie*: See Robert Sellers, *Peter O'Toole, The Definitive Biography*, Pan Macmillan, 2015.

53 *i think i'm going to write*: TS to IC, nd [spring 1959].

54 *taken a jump*: HR 36.3. Hagerty, 20. Membership of NUJ suspended for two months from 18 December 1959. General Secretary, National Union of Journalists, to TS, 29 January 1960, JM archive. Nadel, 65.

54 *gas main blew up*: John Smith, www.gentlemenranters.com, 11 January 2008. John Smith, interview HL, 9 October 2015. TS has no memory of this: TS, interview HL, 1 November 2019.

54 *I'm literary*: BEW, 16 April 1960.

54 *cool satire*: Biblio, H 18, 'Tom Stoppard treads The Beatnik Track to find a roomful of people all acting as if they were alone', BEW, 8 March 1960.

55 *film-reviewing*: Hilton Timms to IC, 14 May 1998.

55 *stand-ins*: RIH, in Plays 1, 7. For evolution of RIH, see Fleming 2001, 258, n. 8.

55 *covered everything*: Biblio, H 13, BEW, 22 September 1959. Biblio, H 34, BEW, 12 July 1960. Biblio, H 14, BEW, 29 September 1959. Biblio, H 26, BEW, 3 May 1960. Biblio, H 19, BEW, 9 March 1960.

56 *a row of chorus girls*: Biblio, H 20, BEW, 15 March 1960.

56 *breeziness about women*: Biblio, H 39, BEW, 16 August 1960. Biblio, H 30, BEW, 31 May 1960.

56 *witless inanity*: Biblio, H 22, BEW, 5 April 1960.

56 *The sacred cow*: Biblio, H 30, BEW, 31 May 1960.

56 *Huck is Huck*: Biblio, H 37, BEW, 2 August 1960.

56 *What interested him*: Biblio, H 32, BEW, 14 June 1960. Biblio, H 39, BEW, 16 August 1960. Biblio, H 16, BEW, 22 October 1959. Biblio, H 29, BEW, 24 May 1960.

57 *very odd*: TSL, nd, 1973. TS, interview HL, 15 October 2017.

57 *deep shade of red*: HR 35.3, Patricia Hatton to TS, 9 May 1984.

57 *not on his wavelength*: IC, interview HL, 1 June 2015.

58 *book reviews*: Val Lorraine, review of Monique Lange, *The Plane Trees*, WDP, 18 December 1961; review of Marie-Claire Blais, *Tête-Blanche*, WDP, 9 April 1962; review of Martin Esslin, *The Theatre of the Absurd*, WDP, 4 June 1962.

59 *I'd like to be famous*: TSL, nd, April 1961.

59 *easier and more exciting*: TS, interview HL, 28 June 2014.

59 *i told val*: TSL, nd [13 July 1960]. TS to IC, nd [1960].

60 *In sleep we walked*: TS to IC, nd.

60 *Talking it through*: TSL, nd [July 1960]. TS to IC, nd [late summer 1960].

5: Brennus

62 *All in all*: Biblio, H 194, 'It's So Unlike Us', WDP, 27 August 1962. Brennus's farewell to the column.

62 *keep it light*: TSL, nd [March 1961]. Biblio, H 41, 'In Good King Brennus's Golden Days', WDP, 30 August 1960. HR 36.3, 14 December 1960, R. J. W. Hawkins, Director, WDP, to 'My dear Brennus': 4 gns for each article as Brennus. List of Brennus pieces during November 1960, total £29 9s 6d.

62 *Brennus would make fun*: Biblio, H 183, 'Brennus Goes to a Dress Show', WDP, 25 May 1962.

63 *the gift of ignorance*: Biblio, H 64, 'The Crest of the Wave. Films', WDP, 14 December 1960.

63 *Smith and Stoppard*: For AS, Alison and TS, see Wordsmith. TS, AS, IC, interviews HL. TS correspondence with AS and IC. Biblio, H 64, 'The Crest of the Wave. Films', WDP, 14 December 1960. For 'gags', HR 37.1, TS to AS, November 1963: 'The gag-writer . . . just gags with people as we do in conversation, so in fact I merely played "your" part as well as "mine".'

64 *indefatigably facetious*: HR 124.5, TS to David Harrison, 6 March 1986.

64 *looked unhealthy*: Biblio, H 73, 'Tottering from the Sick Bed . . . Brennus at the Orchid Show', WDP, 3 February 1961.

64	*smoked non-stop*: Biblio, H 169, 'Side-light on the Smoking Scare', WDP, 19 March 1962.

64	*a rose is a rose*: Biblio, H 45, 'An Olympic Spirit Prevails among the Rosarians', WDP, 20 September 1960.

64	*could be cynical*: Biblio, H 118, 'Peter Scott', WDP, 30 June 1961. Biblio, H 161, 'Guinness Pays for Poetry', WDP, 2 February 1962. Biblio, H 49, 'Faith, Hope and Enterprise', WDP, 7 October 1960. Biblio, H 166, 'Yokel-like in the Wicked City', WDP, 26 February 1962.

65	*specialist societies*: Biblio, H 62, 'Into Battle', WDP, 2 December 1960.

65	*The average Brennus reader*: Biblio, H 56, 'Three Cheers for Santa', WDP, 8 November 1960.

65	*Chatterton*: Biblio, H 154, 'Two per Hour per Glass Case', WDP, 1 January 1962.

65	*A six-year-old acquaintance*: Biblio, H 41, 'We Approve of the Informal Carrying of Swords', WDP, 30 August 1960.

65	*hilariously useless*: Biblio, H 83, 'For a Cycling Bookmaker', WDP, 2 March 1961.

66	*the sound-word 'bonk'*: Biblio, H 109, 'Delights of Redland', WDP, 16 June 1961.

66	*She never replies*: Biblio, H 125, 'Perhaps, Sir, This Is the End', WDP, 11 August 1961.

66	*an Irish landlady*: Biblio, H 48, 'Mrs McCleary Goes West', WDP, 6 October 1960.

66	*Fritzy laments*: Biblio, H 51, 'I Take Fritzy for a Ride', WDP, 15 October 1960.

67	*maladjusted vegetarian*: Biblio, H 123, 'Sending Up Selwyn', WDP, 28 July 1961.

67	*short ironic pieces*: TSL, nd [March 1961], nd [December 1961].

67	*Battles had constantly to be fought*: Wordsmith, 80, and 76–81 on the WDP Arts page.

68	*Colin Wilson*: Biblio, H 134, 'Scraping the Bottom of the Old Tin Trunk', WDP, 2 October 1961.

68	*experimental fiction*: Biblio, H 162, 'The New Wave Begins at Calais', WDP, 5 February 1962.

68	*La Dolce Vita . . . Shadows*: Biblio, H 115, 'A Bitter Sweet Life', WDP, 28 June 1961. Biblio, H 71, 'The Wrong Door', WDP, 18 January 1961.

68	*The unwritten code*: Biblio, H 150, 'Sugar at Tiffany's', WDP, 18 December 1961.

69	*Albert Finney*: Biblio, H 69, 'Finney; I Have Lost My Personal Life', WDP 11 January 1961.

69	*The anti-hero*: Biblio, H 95, 'Anti-Hero with a Briefcase', WDP, 5 April 1961. Biblio, H 74, 'The New Hero Is Spinning Money', WDP, 8 February 1961.

69	*different kind of rebel*: Biblio, H 58, 'A Fusion of Promise', WDP, 16 November 1960. Biblio, H 171, 'Rebel without a Crusade', WDP, 16 April 1962.

69	*Kenneth Tynan*: TS, Foreword, Kenneth Tynan, *Theatre Writings*, ed. Dominic Shellard, Nick Hern Books, 2007.

70	*noted drily*: Biblio, H 58, 'A Fusion of Promise', WDP, 16 November 1960.

70	*Pinter came to Bristol*: TS, *Circumspice: The PEN/Pinter Lecture 2013*, Faber, 2013, 5.

71	*His report*: Biblio, H 155, 'The Tense Present – Harold Pinter', WDP, 8 January 1962.

72	*honesty*: TS, *Circumspice: The PEN/Pinter Lecture 2013*, Faber, 2013, 9.

73	*Art is not withheld*: Biblio, H. 82, 'What Is There More, Tell Me?', WDP, 1 March 1961. Biblio, H 142, 'Arnold Wesker – Is the Horse So Thirsty?' WDP, 30 October 1961.

73	*not progressive enough*: Biblio, H 157, 'Who's Talking of Jerusalem?' WDP, 15 January 1962.

74	*Arthur Miller*: Biblio, H 110, 'Modern Writers – 8. The Misfits in the Machine', WDP, 21 June 1961.

74 *not uncritically*: Biblio, H 163, 'Enfant Terrible Has Middle-age Spread', WDP, 12 February 1962. Biblio, H 170, 'All-American Activities', WDP, 2 April 1962. Biblio, H 180, 'The Private Eye as Purgative', WDP, 14 May 62. Biblio, H 145, 'Double Focus – the Plight of the Sane Lunatic', WDP, 13 November 1961.

74 *Steinbeck*: Biblio, H 61, 'The Articulate Peasant': A Profile of John Steinbeck. *Men Only and Lilliput*, November 1960.

75 *Mailer*: TS: 'Norman Mailer: Readjustments 1', WDP, 6 March 1963.

75 *New York*: TSL, nd [March 1962]. Biblio, H 175, [Brennus], 'We're Getting Pretty Sick', WDP, 4 May 1962. Wordsmith, 87–9. Nadel, 94–5, on New York visit.

76 *Village Voice*: HR 165.20, TS to Mel Brooks, 16 August [1962]. Biblio, H 187, 'The People of the Voice', WDP, 18 June 1962.

76 *feeling for America*: Biblio, H 175. Brennus complained that all the WDP office staff were going on about New York: 'We're Getting Pretty Sick', WDP, 4 May 1962. Michael Pye, interview with TS, *Daily Telegraph*, 31 March 1995. Biblio, H 173, 'Humour. Death by Satire', WDP, 30 April 1962. Wordsmith, 86–8.

6: Walking on Water

77 *When people ask*: 'Life, Time: Fragments', *Introduction 2: Stories by New Writers*, Faber, 1964, 129.

77 *Hemingway*: HR 34.1, Review of Hemingway biographies, *Village Voice*, 24 May 1962. On EH and Pinter, HR 130.9, TS to John Peter, 'HP: The Poet of No-Man's-Land', *Sunday Times*, 7 October 1990. On being 'bitten', HR 121.25, 'Reflections on EH', 21 May 1982. On his qualities, HR 121.14, 'The Hemingway Hero Is Put to Bed', *Observer*, 8 February 1987. TS, interview HL, 19 July 2018. TSL, nd [July 1961]. Biblio, H 68, 'Dateline Glasgow', WDP, 6 January 1961. Biblio, H 103, [Brennus], 'Novel and Dramatic', WDP, 23 May 1961.

78 *spoof CV*: HR 37.1, TS to AS, nd [early 1963].

78 *into his private writing*: TS to IC, 18 September 1961; TS, card to IC, 8 July 1962, IC papers. Biblio, H 189, 'Brennus – a Sentimentalist at Heart – Says . . . Bravo for the Bullfight!', WDP, 18 July 1962.

79 *half-page of a story*: TS to IC, nd [1962?], IC papers.

79 *three stories*: *Introduction 2: Stories by New Writers*, Faber, 1964.

80 *sun-and-wine woman*: TS to IC, 7 July [early 1980s]; 15 July 1995, IC papers.

81 *television play*: *A Paragraph for Mr Blake*, ITV, 23 October 1965.

82 *John Hale*: HR 36.3, John Hale, Bristol Old Vic, to TS, 14 February 1961. For 'Ol' Riley', Nadel, 86.

82 *liked his other play better*: TSL, nd [January 1962].

83 *J: The neck is the weak point*: HR 67.5, typescript of *The Gamblers*.

84 *writing to Isabel*: TS to IC, nd [early 1960s], IC papers.

84 *an agent*: HR 34.11, KE to TS, 28 February 1962. TS, 'The Definite Maybe', *Author*, Spring 1967, 295, gives this order of events, though in other versions TS remembers sending *Walk* first to KE, as in Nadel, 87–8.

84 *wrote home proudly*: TSL, nd [1962].

85 *all glammed up*: TSL, nd [August 1962].

85 *signed off as Brennus*: Biblio, H 194, 'We've Been Rude to Everyone', WDP, 27 August 1962. TS, interview Mark Lawson, *Front Row*, BBC Radio 4, 13 August 2013.

86 *coda to his Bristol life*: Wordsmith, 129–32. John Boorman, interview HL, 24 October, 3 November 2015. *The Newcomers*, BBC2, May–June 1964.

7: On the Scene

88 *Preston: Funny man*: HR, 67.4. 'Funny Man', unproduced, unpublished TV playscript, November 1964.

88 *'Swinging London'*: coined by *Time* magazine, 15 April 1966. For *Scene*, Humphrey Carpenter, *That Was Satire That Was*, Gollancz, 2000; Harry Thompson, *Peter Cook: A Biography*, Hodder & Stoughton, 1997; Billington 2007, 130.

88 *a new magazine*: Magforum.com/time1.htm

89 *virulently trendy*: Tynan 1977, 25.

89 *weekly cock-ups*: TS to IC, nd [autumn 1962], IC papers. TSL, nd [autumn 1962].

89 *over 130 plays*: Hayman 1977, vii.

89 *critical judgements*: Gussow, 3. TS on KT, 2006, typescript, JM archive.

90 *Boot would get personal*: Biblio, H 206, 'O'Toole of Arabia' by William Boot, *Scene*, 19 October 1962. Biblio, H 219, Interview with Peter O'Toole, *Scene*, 12 December 1962. TS, interview HL, 17 November 2015.

90 *admired Brecht*: Biblio, H 195, 'Bits of Bert', *Scene*, 14 September 1962.

91 *Joan Littlewood*: TS, interview RE, in RE, *Talking Theatre*, Nick Hern Books, 2009. Biblio, H 210, 'Everything but Joan', *Scene*, 8 November 1962.

91 *most exciting*: Biblio, H 208, 'Crying Till You Laugh', *Scene*, 25 October 1962.

92 *an outsider*: TS, interview HL, 16 June 2016.

92 *not so venerating*: Biblio, H 211, 'The Ultimate Distillation', *Scene*, 15 November 1962.

92 *quirkiness and oddity*: Biblio, H 204, 205, 'Author in Agony' by William Boot, and 'Theatre Review', *Scene*, 12 October 1962. Charlotte Higgins, 'A Thoroughly Entertaining Failure', *Guardian*, 9 August 2018.

93 *absurd for its own sake*: Biblio, H 222, 'With Vacant Possession of Course', *Scene*, 27 December 1962.

93 *Pure farce*: Biblio, H 197, 'Twelve Years without Trousers', *Scene*, 21 September 1962.

93 Peer Gynt: Biblio, H 202, 'Peer's Progress', *Scene*, 5 October 1962.

93 *Olivier's bizarre turn*: Biblio, H 221, 'Tom Stoppard on *Semi-Detached*', *Scene*, 12 December 1962.

93 *Scofield's Lear*: Biblio, H 212, 'Waiting for Scofield', *Scene*, 15 November 1962.

93 *interviews with William Boot*: Biblio, H 198, 'Revue? Never Again', *Scene*, 21 September 1962.

93 *anachronistic play*: Biblio, H 207, 'Curtmantle', *Scene*, 19 October 1962.

93 *well-written experiment*: Biblio, H 216, 'Fine Hand at Work', *Scene*, 29 November 1962.

93 *in-between plays*: Biblio, H 224, 'Tom Stoppard on In-between Plays', *Scene*, 16 January 1963.

94 *satire*: Biblio, H 230, 'A Very Satirical Thing Happened to Me on the Way to the Theatre Tonight', *Encore*, March–April 1963.

94 *alternative theatres*: Biblio, H 209, 'Off the Shaftesbury Fringe', *Scene*, 1 November 1962.

94 *the BBC*: Biblio, H 220, 'No Mucking About by Aunty', *Scene*, 12 December 1962.

94 *what made for success*: Biblio, H 199, 'Big Fish, Little Fish', *Scene*, 21 September 1962.

94 *Saunders's play*: Biblio, H 227, 'TS on the Physicists', *Scene*, 19 February 1963.

94 *writing about theatre*: Biblio, H 224, 'Tom Stoppard on In-between Plays', *Scene*, 16 January 1963.

94 *comparative grid*: Biblio, H 233, 'How Much Rubbish?', *Scene*, 21 March 1963.

94 *spoof attack*: Biblio, H 223, 'Who Killed Peter Saunders?', *Scene*, 27 December 1962.

95 *sent in a statement*: HR 36.3, TS to *Scene*, 7 May 1963.

96 *well looked after*: HR 36.2, KE to TS, 7 July 1964, KE to TS, 14 September 1964.

96 *his good angel*: GD, interview HL, 11 October 2014. TS, tribute to KE, *The Times*, 24 April 2008; Patrick Stoddart, KE obituary, *The Times*, 23 April 2008. TS, interview HL, 28 June 2014. Tynan 1977, 25. Delaney 1994, 219. Tim Corrie, interview HL, 1 May 2015.

97 *H. M. Tennent*: Billington 2007, 32.

97 *thespian knights*: HR 36.2, KE to TS, 8 June, 23 August 1962.

97 *began to see*: TSL, nd [1962].

98 *revered Eliot*: TS, conversation with PM, Faber, 11 March 2019. Damian Whitworth, 'Faber Turns 80', *Times Literary Supplement*, 16 May 2009.

98 *Frank Pike*: FP, interview HL, 2 May 2014. TS to FP, 13 February 1963, 14 March [1963], Faber archive.

99 *came to be embarrassed*: Tynan 1977, 23; Delaney 1994, 55 (from 1974). TS, interview HL, 28 June 2014.

99 *George Riley*: EAFM, 15, 34.

100 *told Smith*: HR 37.1, TS to AS, November 1963. HR 67.4, typescript of *Funny Man*.

100 I Can't Give You Anything But Love, Baby: HR 14.10, typescript. Fleming 2001, 20–2.

101 This Way Out with Samuel Boot: Tynan 1977, 26. Fleming 2001, 22–6.

101 *another Boot play*: HR 37.1, TS to AS, [23] November 1963. Wordsmith, 120–4. Fleming 2001, 19–20. HR 66.18, *The Dissolution of Dominic Boot*, BBC Light Programme, 20 February 1964; later a TV play [HR 66.19], *The Engagement*, NBC TV, 8 March 1970. See RADIO.

102 *worked well for him*: HR 37.1, TS to AS, November 1963.

102 *made brilliant use*: Billington 1987, 21.

102 *his first moon-shot*: HR 67.11, *M Is for Moon*, 6 April 1964, Light Programme, 'Just Before Midnight', in RADIO.

103 *told Isabel*: TS to IC [nd], IC papers.

103 *expanded TV version*: *The Explorers* [*A Paragraph for Mr Blake*], HR, Gordon Dickerson papers, 8.7. Aired ATV (much changed by Ted Willis), 23 October 1965. HR 37.1, TS to AS, October 1965.

103 *not a success*: HR 36.3, *Daily Express* to TS, 25 October 1963; BBC to TS, 25 February 1964.

103 *Profumo*: TSL, nd [July 1963].

103 *passing tiff*: B. S. Johnson to AS, 26 June 1963, *The B. S. Johnson–Zulfikar Ghose Correspondence*, ed. Vanessa Guignery, Cambridge Scholars Publishing, 2015, 285, n. 581.

104 *lonely and homesick*: TSL, nd [September 1962].

104 *Derek Marlowe*: TS, 'Before We Were Famous', *Spectator*, 2 May 2015. TS, interview HL, 28 June 2014. KT, *Gambit*, 25.

104 *not highly domesticated*: TS, interview HL, 17 November 2015.

104 *Jose Ingle*: AS, interview HL, 31 May 2014. TS, interview HL, 28 June 2014. BS, interview HL, 6 February 2015.

106   *equally irritably*: TS to IC, nd, IC papers.

106   *rare note of crossness*: TSL, nd [summer 1962].

106   *unconditional admirer*: HR 37.1, TS to AS, May 1962. TS letters to IC, nd, IC papers. FS, interview HL, 7 November 2014.

106   *When you walk*: TS, 'Night Thoughts: Three Weeks Before Provence', to IC, nd [August 1963], IC papers.

107   *The letters*: TS to IC, 23 September 1963, 29 September 1963, nd, March 1963, September 1963, IC papers.

107   *to be best man*: HR 37.3, TS to AS, November 1963.

108   *end of 1963*: HR 37.3, TS to AS, October 1963. TSL, nd [1964]. TSL, nd [early 1964]. [Anonymous], 'Writing School in Berlin', *Times Literary Supplement*, 14 January 1965.

109   *a novel*: HR 36.3, Walter Hasenclever to TS, 24 March 1964. TS to AS, 23 April 1964, July 1964.

109   *a play about Rosencrantz*: Several versions of this story exist, the nearest in time in 'The Definite Maybe', *Author*, 1967, 296, and in Tynan 1977, 26.

109   *wrote home excitedly*: TSL, nd [May 1964].

110   *experimental movie*: George Moorse, *In Side Out*, 1964.

110   *advice from the British Council*: HR 37.1, TS to AS [August 1964].

110   *Berlin*: PPR, interview HL, 30 September 2014; HR 37.1, TS to AS, May–September 1964; Wordsmith; TS, 'Before We Were Famous'. Paul Gallagher, interview with Derek Marlowe, 15 June 1984.

111   *several things at once*: Fleming 2001, 260, note 18.

111   *a false start*: HR 37.1, TS to AS, July 1964. TSL, nd [July 1964].

111   Rosencrantz and Guildenstern at the Court of King Lear: Wordsmith, 134. Fleming 2001, 30–5. HR 231.11, 'R & G Meet King Lear' [1964], typescript.

113   *Ewing read it*: HR 36.3, KE to TS, July 1964.

113   Guildenstern and Rosencrantz: HR 37.1, TS to AS, letters, July–August 1964. 'Writing School in Berlin', *Times Literary Supplement*, 14 January 1965. archive.questors.org.uk/prods/1964/berlinplays/docs/programme.PDF.

8: *Rosencrantz and Guildenstern Are Dead*

114   *G: Who are you?*: HR 23.11, 'R & G Meet King Lear' [1964], typescript.

114   *describing life*: TSL, nd [1964].

115   *Tom would be it*: Paul Gallagher, interview Derek Marlowe, 15 June 1984.

115   *Marlowe*: Tynan 1977. Derek Marlowe to PPR, 9 March 1977, 25 January 1978, Brotherton. Benjie Marlowe, son of Derek Marlowe, to PPR, 21 November 1996, after DM's death, Brotherton.

115   *the odd one out*: PPR, 1960s Diary, with thanks to PPR. IC to TS, nd, IC papers.

116   *going to get married*: TS, interview HL, 28 June 2014. TS to AS, early 1965.

116   *imagined a wedding day*: TS to IC, nd, IC papers.

117   *wrote ruefully*: TSL, nd [26 May 1965].

117   *another year or so*: HR 17.3, TS to Derek Bennett, 15 June 1966, addressed from Vincent Square.

117   *their collaboration*: HR 8.1, *Doctor Masopust, I Presume*.

118   *Gluttony*: HR 67.6, *How Sir Dudley Lost the Empire*.

118   *colonial writing*: HR 36.2, KE to TS, 29 October 1965. HR 37.1, TS to AS, August,

October 1965. 'A Student's Diary', Episodes 1, 42, 61, 81. BBC Archive.

119 *His own prospects*: HR 37.1, TS to AS, October 1965. *A Paragraph for Mr Blake*, 23
     October 1965, ATV.

119 *other things for radio*: *The Dog It Was That Died and Other Plays*, Faber, 1983, dedicated
     to Imison, vii–viii; in RADIO, vii. Delaney 1994, 36 (from 1972). IYGIBF was first
     aired on the BBC on 8 February 1966, on Network Three, with Patsy Rowlands and
     Timothy West. It was staged as a play by OTG in Edinburgh in 1969, and by the Young
     Vic in 1976. Dialling 0203 598 2801 on a UK phone in 2017 gave you the voice of Pat
     Simmons, the Speaking Clock from 1963, who inspired IYGIBF. Plays 2, 36.

121 *a longer life*: AB performed by OTG in Edinburgh, 29 August 1969, then from 18
     October 1976 at the King's Head, Islington.

121 *first aired*: AB, Biblio, A4. Screenplay with AS, Wordsmith, 172. HR 1.8, 66.12, 122.9.

121 *international awards*: HR 32.6, Martin Esslin, head of BBC Radio Drama, to TS, re.
     Czech prize, 24 May 1968.

121 *a would-be 'jumper'*: TS had tried out a procrastinating suicide before in an unused
     sketch, *Higg and Cogg*, which he also called 'I'll Jump Tomorrow'. A man jumps from
     a bridge in radio in DOG. Fleming in Baker 2013, 96, note 120. AB, Plays 2, 54–86.

123 *something to write* about: Delaney 1994, 25.

123 A Separate Peace: Plays 3, 22 August 1966, BBC Thirty Minute Theatre, with Peter
     Jeffrey and Hannah Gordon. Billington 1987, 27.

123 Neutral Ground: Plays 3. HR 17.3, TS to Derek Bennett (Granada TV Manchester) 15
     June 1966. Aired 2 December 1968, Granada TV. Cast: Patrick Magee as Philo, Alan
     Webb as Otis, Nicholas Pennell as Acherson, Polly Adams as Carol.

124 *to his regret*: TSL, nd [December 1968].

124 *post-natal*: HR 37.1, TS to AS, August 1965.

124 *His publisher*: HR 36.2, KE to TS, 15, 16 September 1965. KE to TS, October 1965.
     Nadel, 151.

125 *magpie pickings*: LMM, Introduction (2005), vii.

126 *reactionary dandy*: Tynan 1977, *Show People*, 55.

126 *The whole thing*: LMM, 43.

127 *He could not*: LMM, 29.

127 *I think I'd like*: LMM, 137.

127 *I cannot commit*: LMM, 28, 72, 114.

128 *'Spectator as Hero'*: LMM, Introduction (2005), viii.

129 *spattered with Eliot quotations*: LMM, 23, 47, 119.

129 *of a draft page*: HR 23.11, ms of R&G.

130 *intuition of mortality*: Black Notebook, TS archive, given to HL, 20 March 2018.
     R&G, 51.

131 *told Isabel*: TS to IC, nd [27 February 1966, August 1966]. IC papers.

131 *Blond published*: HR 36.2, Blond to TS, 27 June 1967. HR 36.1, Blond to TS, 13
     February 1973. LMM, Introduction, v. There were 481 home sales and 207 export sales
     by December 1966. Between then and December 1968, there were fourteen copies
     sold in the UK. Panther published a paperback in 1968, and then came Faber's 'gallant
     assumption of responsibility' (LMM, Introduction, v), with reissues in 1974, 1980,
     1985 and 2005.

131 *the Royal Shakespeare Company*: On R&G and RSC: Delaney 1994, 159. Fleming in
     Baker 2013, 96–8. Hunter 2005, 198. HR 37.1, TS to AS, nd [30 August 1962]; May

1965. See Simon Trowbridge, *The Rise and Fall of the Royal Shakespeare Company*, Editions Albert Creed, 2013; Peter Hall, *Making an Exhibition of Myself*, Oberon Books, 1993; Michael Kustow, *Peter Brook: A Biography*, Bloomsbury 2005; Michael Blakemore, *Stage Blood*, Faber, 2013.

132	*the play we know*: R&G, 72, 107, 114. All R&G quotes from Faber, 1967, paperback 1968, reset 2000.

134	*The fall of their coins*: For physics and coin-tossing, citing R&G, e.g.: L. Mahadevan and Ee Hou Yong, 'Probability, Physics and the Coin Toss', *Physics Today*, July 2011; Joe Kissell, 'Coin Tossing', ITOTD.com, 9 September 2018.

134	*All they have is words*: R&G, 89, 62, 48, 29, 66, 111.

135	*The word rings*: Edward Petherbridge, *Slim Chances and Unscheduled Appearances*, Independpress, 2011.

135	*He splits himself*: R&G, 68, 117.

135	*language of passing time*: R&G, 52, 86.

136	*absence of presence*: R&G, 116.

136	*work to be done*: HR 37.1, TS to AS, May 1965, early 1965, July 65. HR 36.2, Jeremy Brooks to TS, 22 June, 22 July 1965. TS, interview HL, 16–17 November 2015.

137	*the baby*: TS to IC, nd [27 February 1966], nd [August 1966], IC papers. HR, OS Box 5, 'Freedom from Pain', *Vogue*, 23 March 1971. HR 37.1, TS to AS, May 1966, June 1966. TSL, nd [May 1966]. Alex Pyz-Szukalska, interview HL, 24 May 2015.

138	*long, wordy and rambling*: Biblio, 2, Nicholas Bethell, BBC report, 7 October 1965.

138	*shattering news*: TN, interviews HL, 1 July, 2 October 2017.

138	Tango: aired on BBC Radio 3 on 22 March 1968. See Sammells, 94–8.

139	*good student cast*: Cast included Julian Roach (Player), David Marks (Rosencrantz), Janet Watts (Ophelia), Walter Merricks (Polonius). For R&G at Edinburgh: David Marks and Janet Watts, interviews HL, 5 May, 3 August 2015; TS, interview Janet Watts, *Guardian*, 21 March 1973, in Delaney 1994, 47. Reviews of R&G, OTG minutes, agendas and programmes, with thanks to David Marks. Fleming in Baker 2013, 49, n. 134, on the OTG contract for R&G. MC, interview HL, 8 January 2015, and *Putting It On*, with Alan Strachan, 2010. Fleming in Baker 2013, 83.

140	*rapid alterations*: 'Beard' exchange slightly revised in R&G, 9. For R&G versions, see Brassell, 270–1; Fleming 2001, 50–65; Nadel, 182, 554. For R&G in Edinburgh, TS, 'Festival Comment', OTR programme, Edinburgh Festival, 13 August 1981, cited Nadel, 173.

141	*vetted*: Lord Chamberlain's Office, 10 August 1966, Biblio, 387.

141	*World Premiere*: Delaney 1994, 17.

142	*some people did like it*: Ronald Bryden, 'Wyndy Excitements', *Observer Weekend Review*, 28 August 1966.

143	*One of his favourite endings*: PR, 51.

143	*He read the piece*: Fleming in Baker 2013, 83–5. Trevor Nunn, quoted in Hunter 2005, 199. Tynan 1977. TSL, nd [August 1966].

143	*deluged with similar requests*: TSL, nd [August 1966]. PR, 37.

144	*Derek Goldby*: Derek Goldby, interview HL, 7 January 2016; PR, 32. TS, Foreword, *Kenneth Tynan: Theatre Writings*, ed. Dominic Shellard, Nick Hern, 2007, xv–xvi.

145	*'Olivier' cigarettes*: TSL, nd [spring 1967].

145	*jitters*: Gussow, 23; Baker 2013, 172; HR 36.2, KT to TS, 9 March 1967. Goldby, interview HL, 7 January 2016; Dickersen, interview HL, 11 October 2015. PR, 32.

145 *Gothic edifice*: Gussow, 23.
145 *the first night*: Terry Coleman, *The Old Vic*, Faber, 2014, 165, 168. Patrick Dillon,
      Concrete Reality: Denys Lasdun and the National Theatre, National Theatre
      Publishing, 2015, 10, 23–30. Fleming in Baker 2013, 85–7, 98, n. 152. HR 37.1, TS to AS,
      September/October 66. HR 36.2, KT to TS, 9 March 1967.

9: Success

149 *Moon: . . . it is hard*: RIH, Plays 1, 32.
149 *hated first nights*: TSL, nd [March 1967]. Peter Lewis, 'Quantum Stoppard',
      Observer, 6 March 1988, cited in Delaney 1994, 13, Baker 2013, 87. Daniel Rosenthal,
      'Rosencrantz and Guildenstern, 50 Years On', *Independent*, 13 March 2017.
149 *A legend*: HR 122.9, *Sun* interview, 13 April 1967.
149 *The reviews*: W. A. Darlington, *Daily Telegraph*, 12 April 1967; Irving Wardle, *The
      Times*, 13 April 1967; Ronald Bryden, *Observer*, 16 April 1967; Alan Brien, *Sunday
      Telegraph*, 16 April 1967; Harold Hobson, *Sunday Times*, 16 April 1967.
150 *might have given up*: TS, interview HL, 28 June 2014, 38. TS, interview, *Meridian*,
      BBC World Service, 7 September 1973.
151 *theorising*: Delaney 1994 (from 1972, 1974, 1977), 32, 58, 95. For interpretations of
      R&G, Fleming 2001, 49.
151 *much-repeated allegory*: TS, 'Something to Declare', *Sunday Times*, 25 February 1968.
151 *The play and its author*: Gussow (from 1979), 35; Delaney 1994, 17, 19 (from 1968).
      Brassell, 62.
152 *the gamble paid off*: HR, Picture Archive, 5. Olivier interview, Gaia Servadio, *Evening
      Standard*, 14 February 1972. Last night of R&G, NT, 8 May 1970. Copies sold, HR 37.2,
      TS to AS, May 1967.
152 *the jacket*: Biblio, 2–5. TS, conversation with PM, Faber, 11 March 2019.
152 *programme note*: HR 83.13, EAFM, programme, St Martin's Theatre, 1968.
152 *Beckett*: TSL, nd [August 1967].
153 *productions worldwide*: Biblio, 14. Delaney 1994, 2. Fleming 2001, 48.
153 *whirlwind*: TSL, nd [August 1967].
153 *Fame*: TS, interview HL, 28 June 2014.
153 *He had work*: TSL, nd [July 1967]. HR 36.2, Michael Redgrave, 5 September 1967.
      Richard Attenborough to Doris Abrahams, 8 June 1967. *Kenneth Tynan Letters*, ed.
      Kathleen Tynan, Random House, 1998.
154 Teeth: broadcast 8 February 1967, BBC2 Thirty Minute Theatre. John Stride as
      George Pollock, John Wood as Harry Dunn, Andrée Melly as the Wife, Alan Gibson,
      director.
154 *John Wood*: TS and JW interview, Gussow, 28. AMCE broadcast 28 June 1967, BBC2
      Thirty Minute Theatre. Diane Cilento as Penelope, John Wood as Bone, John Bennett
      as Albert, Donald Eccles as Crouch, Alan Gibson, director. TS on JW: TS, JE I, 21
      February 1976.
155 *If it's all random*: AMCE, Plays 3, 57, 59.
155 *ProtoJumpers*: HR 122.9, *Vogue*, 15 October 1967. Kathleen Halton interview, 1974, in
      Delaney 1994, 72.
155 *Bone and Penelope*: AMCE, Plays 3, 52–3.
156 *mutual aid*: TSL, nd [early 1967].

156 *a teasing poem*: TS to Alex Pyz [Christmas 1969], with thanks to Alex Pyz-Szukalska.

157 *interviewers descended*: HR 122.9, *Sunday Times*, 13 April 1967.

157 *Jose was not happy*: TS interview HL, 28 June 2014. Alex Pyz-Szukalska, interview
      HL, 24 May 2015. HR 46. TS to AS, 14 July 1967.

157 *problems slipped out*: TSL, nd [July 1967].

157 *moved out*: 5 Queen's Gate Place, and Rosedene, Butlers Cross, near Aylesbury,
      described HR 122.9, William Foster, *Scotsman*, profile of TS, 17 February 1968; Alex
      Pyz-Szukalska, interview HL, 24 May 2015; TS, interview HL, 28 June 2014.

157 *very isolated*: TSL, nd [summer 1967].

158 *New York production*: HR 37.2, TS to AS, 14 July 1967.

158 *a couple of swells*: John Boorman, interview HL, 2 November 2015.

158 *argued*: Derek Goldby, interview HL, 7 January 2016. Fleming 2001, 51.

158 *New York*: Winchell: TS, 'My Love Affair with Newspapers', *British Journalism
      Review*, December 2005, 22–3. *Look*, 26 December 1967. Clive Barnes, *New York
      Times*, 17 October 1967, cited in Delaney 1990. HR 122.9, Walter Kerr, *New York
      Times*, 17 October 1967. Jack Kroll, quoted Biblio, 7. Jerry Tallmer, nd, 1967. Robert
      Brustein, *New Republic*, November 1967, in Cambridge, 49. TSL, nd [October
      1967].

160 *astonishing success*: John Cribbin interview, Edinburgh, 28 August 1969. William
      Glover, Show Page, *New York Evening News*, 21 November 1967. 'Stage News', nd.
      Tynan 1977 and in *Show People*, 1980, 49. TS to PS, 16 January 1969, PS archive.

160 *It's about*: Delaney 1994, 219. Mark Lawson, *Front Row* interview, BBC Radio 4, June
      1999. TS, interview HL, 1 November 2019.

160 *bank balance*: HR, 146, 1–2, Accounts pages.

161 *outgoings*: TS to PS, nd [1965], PS archive.

161 *spending*: TS to PS, 21 January 1969, PS archive.

161 *discipline*: PS, interview HL, 31 May 2014.

161 *real money*: HR 37.2, TS to AS, nd. HR, 146, 1–2, Accounts pages, 13 November 1967.
      TS to PS, nd; TS to PS, 3 March 1969, PS archive.

162 *he bought*: HR 37.2, TS to AS, July 1968; TS to PS, 12 May 1970, PS archive.

163 *described him*: Kathleen Halton, American *Vogue*, 15 October 1967.

163 *peacockery*: MS, interview HL, 8 April 2014. TS, interview HL, June 2014.

164 *relished it*: PR, 43.

164 *lunches*: TS to PS, 3 April 1969, PS archive.

164 *Who's Who*: *Sunday Times*, 18 August 1968.

164 *DIFFERENT*: TSL, nd [October 1967].

164 *style icon*: HR 37.2, TS to AS, 14 July 1967. Kathleen Halton, American *Vogue*, 15
      October 1967.

164 *quote that got stuck*: HR 121.20, 'On the Other Side of *Hamlet*', *Sunday Times*, 25
      February 1968. TS, Letter to *Sunday Times*, 3 March 1968. Stephen Moss, *Guardian*,
      22 June 2002.

165 *space and quiet*: TSL, nd [early 1968].

165 *film script*: HR 119.7, TS, *Three Men in a Boat*, BBC2 TV, 22 November 1974; BBC
      Radio 4, TS notes, 1994–5, aired 29 December 1994.

166 *refer to River Thatch*: *Sunday Times*, 16 May 2008. HR 37.2, letter to AS, nd.

166 *Goodnight, wall*: TS, JE I, 28 December 1978.

167 *marriage wasn't working*: HR 36.2, TN to TS, 14 July 1969; PS, interview HL, 31 May

2015; Tim Corrie, interview HL, 1 May 2015; Wordsmith, 157; Alex Pyz-Szukalska, interview HL, 24 May 2015.

168 Enter a Free Man: KE interview, 5 December 1967, unidentified newspaper; Delaney 1994, 22 (1968), 32 (1972), 56 (1974); TS to FP, 29 January 1969, Faber archive. HR 152.10, TS to Faber, June 2006. HR 155.2, TS to Alla Sirotina, 18 June 2007.

168 *critics agreed*: Reviews of EAFM in Cambridge, 106, and Sammells, 23. Fleming, in Baker 2013, 93, n. 90.

169 *film rights of* Rosencrantz: John Boorman to HL, 3 November 2015. TS, R&G 25th anniversary interview, Michael Brandman, 2015. HR 36.1, John Boorman to TS, 11 November 1970. HR 36.2, TS to John Boorman, 17 April [1968]. TSL, nd [January 1969].

170 *screenplay of* Albert's Bridge: HR 66.12, screenplay of AB, TS and AS. Wordsmith, 172–3.

170 *'Spleen'*: TS archive nd. The competition was won in December 1968 by Angus MacPhee. Thirty-one entries were sent in under pseudonyms by the poet Nicholas Moore, son of the philosopher G. E. Moore.

171 *flights of theoretical fancy*: RIH, Plays 1, 24.

173 *It's Higgs*: RIH, Plays 1, vii, TS, 1993.

173 *doesn't know how to do plots*: Delaney 1994, 60. TS, interview HL, 29 June 2014. RIH, Plays 1, vii.

173 DAZZLING: TSL, nd [July 1967].

174 *to Sheridan's disadvantage*: Codron, 185–6; MC, interview HL, 8 January 2015.

174 *Ronnie Barker*: Richard Webber, *Remembering Ronnie Barker*, Arrow Books, 2011, 135–6.

174 *a bit intellectual*: Webber, *Remembering Ronnie Barker*.

174 *Briers who moved*: Delaney 1994, 119 (*South Bank Show*, 1978).

174 *wish fulfilment*: Delaney 1994, 60.

174 *quite a giggle*: HR 37.2, TS to AS, 14 July 1967. HR 161.4, TS to Nigel Gann, 26 July 1971.

175 *reviewers of* Hound: Shulman, quoted MC, interview HL, 8 January 2015. Hobson, *Sunday Times*, 23 June 1968; Bryden, *Observer*, 23 June 1968; Wardle, *The Times*, 22 June 1968, quoted Sammells 1988, 54, 57. For production history of RIH, A. Kabatchnik, *Blood on the Stage*, Scarecrow Press, 2011. Codron, 185–6.

175 *played up*: Delaney 1994, 258 (Goreau 1992).

175 *love of language*: TS, 'Something to Declare', *Sunday Times*, 25 February 1968.

176 *distanced himself*: TS, interview HL, 29 June 2014. Delaney 1994, 25 ('Our Changing Theatre', BBC Radio 4, 1970). Delaney 1994, 67.

176 *exchange of letters*: HR 37.2, TS to AS, 1968. The correspondence (between AS, TS, Richard Hoggart, David Lodge and Mark Spilka) was published in ALTA 7, *University of Birmingham Review*, Winter 1968/69, 1–10.

177 *anti-apartheid movement*: TS to Ethel de Keyser, 3 May 1968; TS to AS, 4 May 1968, JM archive. TS to PS, 29 June 1968, PS archive.

178 *What repelled me*: TS, 'The Year of the Posturing Rebel', *Sunday Times*, 16 March 2008.

178 *hostility*: DH, interview HL, 26 February 2016.

179 *invited to Prague*: HR 36.2, Miroslav Stuchl, Head of Drama, Czech Radio, to TS, 16 July 1968.

10: Miriam

180 *Donner: No, no*: ADS, Scene Nine.

180 *anger and sadness*: TS to PS, 14 May 1969, PS archive. Alex Pyz-Szukalska, interview HL, 24 May 2015. All personal information in this chapter from: TS, letters to PS, PS archive; HL, interviews with TS, MS, BS, FS, Alex Pyz-Szukalska, Tim and Hélène Corrie, AS.

180 *turbulent teenager*: FS, interview HL, 7 November 2014. TSL, nd [1973].

181 *packed with work*: TSL, 24 April 1969, nd [September 1969]. *The Engagement*, NBC TV, 8 March 1970. For cricket, Nadel, 50.

182 *birth*: Biblio, H 248, 'Childbirth', *Vogue*, HR OS Box 5, proofs 23 March 1971, published May 1971.

182 *Miriam*: MS, interviews HL, 8 April, 2 July, 17 September 2014, 8 January 2015. TS, interview HL, 28 June 2014.

184 *After Barny's birth*: TS to PS, nd [autumn 1970], 31 December 1969. PS to James Crichton, Harbottle and Lewis, 2 October 1970, affidavit re. Mrs Jose Stoppard.

184 *large, expensive house*: TS to PS, 14 April 1970, nd, 'Fri/Sat' [summer 1970].

184 *Looking back*: TS, JE I, 7 December 1976.

184 *opportunities*: AS, interview HL, 31 May 2014; Corries, interview HL, 1 May 2015.

184 *made his mind up*: TS to PS, 'Tuesday' [summer 1970].

186 *divorced Miriam*: HR 146.1, Divorce papers, MS and Peter Moore-Robinson, 2 October 1970.

186 *Plans*: HR 146.1, payments to Jose. HR 146.1, Sale of River Thatch, 27 November 1970.

186 *a statement about himself*: TS to PS, nd, 'Fri/Sat' [summer 1970].

187 *The greatest difficulty*: OS, interview HL, 18 August 2016. MS, interview HL, 2 July 2014; TS, interview HL, 28 June 2014. TS to 'Mum and Dad', 22 August [1970], PS archive; TS to PS, 8 September 1970.

188 *Everything is* really *lovely*: TSL, nd [summer 1970].

188 *application for custody*: TS to PS, nd, 'Tuesday' [summer 1970]. TSL, nd [November 1970].

188 *went in his favour*: HR 39.5, Custody application outcome, 18 March 1971. Wordsmith, 156.

188 *Jose's version*: OS, interview HL, 16 August 2016. JS, letter to MS, nd, JM archive.

189 *He was enjoying*: TS to PS, 16 November 1970, 'Tuesday' [autumn 1970], PS archive.

189 *amethyst*: TS to PS, 14 September 1970, PS archive.

189 Orghast: See Jonathan Bate, *Ted Hughes: The Unauthorised Life*, Collins, 2015, 285–311; AS, *Orghast at Persepolis*, Eyre Methuen, 1972, and Wordsmith, 174–6. TS, 'Commentary on Ted Hughes: Orghast', *Times Literary Supplement*, 10 October 1971, Biblio, H 250. Nadel, 227–8, argues for *Orghast* as an influence on DOP and J. MS, interview HL, 8 April 2014. TS to JS [summer 1971], with thanks to OS.

190 *divorced each other*: HR 122.9, WDP, 1 February 1972. The presiding judge observed that it was the first case he had encountered in which one party, Mrs Stoppard, got her decree under the old divorce law and where the other party got his decree under the new Matrimonial Proceedings and Property Act 1970, which had come into force the year before. *Daily Mirror*, 1 February 1972. HR 39.5, Decree nisi, 8 February 1972.

190 *straight back to work*: OS, interview HL, 18 August 2016. MJ, interview HL, 9 September 2014, HR 122.9, Profile of MS, 'All Work and No Play Makes Miriam a Bright Girl', Colin Barnes, 1975.

191 *many letters*: e.g. JS to TS, Sunday 8 May [1994], JM archive.

191 *bits of journalism*: HR 121.4, TS, *Observer* TV review, 31 May 1970. TS to PS, 16 November 1970; nd, 'Tuesday' [autumn 1970].

192 *exaggerated respect*: HR 122.9, 'Tom Stoppard Pops In on the Cast', Jerry Tallmer, *New York Post*, 26 August 1972.

192 *Fernleigh*: TSL, nd [December 1972]. OS, interview HL, 16 August 2016. WS, interview HL, 10 December 2014.

195 *described the last two years*: HR 122.9, 'Tom Stoppard Pops In on the Cast', Jerry Tallmer, *New York Post*, 26 August 1972.

11: 'Tom Stoppard Doesn't Know'

196 *They never quite* understand: Janet Watts, 'Tom Stoppard', *Guardian*, 21 March 1973, in Delaney 1994, 49.

196 *story, with variants*: 'Tom Stoppard Doesn't Know', BBC 2, *One Pair of Eyes*, 7 July 1972, Gussow, 7. Delaney 1990, 162, n. 21, gives all versions, including Jon Bradshaw, 'Tom Stoppard, Nonstop: Word Games with a Hit Playwright', *New York 10*, 10 January 1977, and Janet Watts, 'Tom Stoppard', *Guardian*, 21 March 1973, 12. At Notre Dame University on 28 March 1971, TS says the story 'made him write a particular play'.

197 *driving past Elsinore*: Transcript of Notre Dame Lecture, 28 March 1971. Delaney 1994, 32.

198 *Inter-Action*: Ed Berman, interview HL, 8 July 2015; TS, interview HL, 18 March 2015; TS, note to DOP, in *Ten of the Best British Short Plays*, ed. Ed Berman, Inter-Action in Print, 1979, 80; TS, Preface (1993), and note to DL (1976), Plays 1, vii, 74; Biblio, 48; Susan Croft, 'Ed Berman', www.unfinishedhistories.com; TS, 'Yes, We Have No Banana', *Guardian*, 10 December 1971; Billington 1987, 80; 2007, 167, 203. HR 36.1, 11 January 1970, Ed Berman thanked TS for agreeing to have his play done by Ambiance in April 1970. HR, GD papers, 8.3.

199 *event*: TS, Preface (1993), Plays 1, vii. TS, interview HL, 18 March 2015. TS, 'The Event and the Text', 1988, Delaney 1994, 204. TS, note to DOP, in *Ten of the Best British Short Plays*, 1979, 80–1. HR, GD papers, 8.3: TS notes it was called 'an Opening Ceremony' because it was written for the opening of the Almost Free Theatre, Rupert Street, first performed on 7 December 1971.

199 *opportunity to wrong-foot*: TS, interview HL, 18 March 2015.

199 *My idea of theatre*: HR 84.15, TS Notebook, 16 November 1971.

199 *rational intentions*: TSL, nd [April 1972].

200 *When I encountered*: TS, interview Joost Kuurman, *Dutch Quarterly Review*, 1980, Biblio, 47.

200 *Surreal*: HR 1.2, first draft AM.

200 *nuts-and-bolts comedy*: Delaney 1994, 59. Nadel, 219, notes the debt to 'The Menaced Assassin'.

200 *nonsense plays*: Ring Lardner, 'I Gaspiri' ('The Upholsterers'), 1922.

200 *incongruous opening scene*: AM, in Plays 1.

201 *Wittgenstein*: HR 37.2, TS to AS, July 1968: 'You should see me trying to work out integral calculus with one hand while following Wittgenstein through "Tractatus Logico-Philosophicus" with the other.' Delaney 1994, 87.

202 *serious joke*: *Arts Guardian*, 10 December 1971. Delaney 1994, 87.

202 *language and logic*: Delaney 1994, 87.

202 *language games*: A. C. Grayling, *Wittgenstein: A Very Short Introduction*, Oxford
   University Press, 1988, 2001, 17, 76, 78–9, 83–4, 94. John Campbell, 'Wittgenstein
   on the Role of Experience in Understanding Language', in *Wittgenstein and the
   Philosophy of Mind*, eds Jonathan Ellis and Daniel Guevara, Oxford University Press,
   2012, 64–6.

202 *thought-experiment*: See Hunter 2005, 55, 71, and for DOP also: Cambridge, 129–30;
   Jenkins, 101–4; Brassell, 235–40; Billington 1987, 80–1, 137.

202 *told Ed Berman*: *Arts Guardian*, 10 December 1971.

203 *a lot of language*: DOP, in Ed Berman, ed., *Ten of the Best British Short Plays*, Inter-
   Action in Print, 1979, 89, 93–4; TS, Introduction to DH, Plays 1, 1980, 142.

203 (Fifteen-minute) Dogg's Troupe Hamlet: Gussow, 37. HR 36.1, EB to TS, 27 January
   1972. EB, interview HL, 8 July 2015. HR, GD papers, 8.3, *Dogg's Troupe Hamlet*, Title
   page, 1976. '"Cat will mew and DOGG will have his day". Copyright T. Stoppard and
   W. Shakespeare.' TS, Plays 1, 1980, 141. Biblio, 103.

204 Goon Show: Delaney 1994, 11, 35.

204 *Boxing Day*: JE I, TS archive, 28 December 1975.

204 *killed at Waterloo*: Delaney 1994, 95, 223.

204 *tremendously silly*: Inter-Action film of *Dogg's Troupe Hamlet*, 24 August 1976.
   Patrick Barlow, one of the actors, took the speeded-up Shakespeare idea on into the
   National Theatre of Brent. TS's *Fifteen-minute Hamlet* was broadcast on Radio 4 on
   1 July 2007.

205 *Americanised version*: HR 127.11, TS to Michael Nowak, Commons Theatre Chicago,
   8 March 1985.

205 *extremely successfully*: HR 36.1, Michael Croft to TS, nd, on amazing box-office
   results from the two plays in February and March 1973.

205 *three Stoppard shows*: HR 18.6, Michael Billington on TS, *Washington Post*, 25
   November 1978.

206 *a 'documentary'*: 'Tom Stoppard Doesn't Know', *One Pair of Eyes*, BBC2, 7 July 1972.
   Director Michael Houldey, with Geoff Hoyle and David Ryall (also in R&G and J)
   as the philosophy dons, Maurice Quick as the peacock man and David De Keyser as
   the interviewer. Biblio, 361, L 49. HR 100.7.

206 *his 1971 lecture*: Notre Dame University, 28 March 1971. RMD001 Archives, Notre
   Dame 1971: Joseph Raymond Collection, Photos 1970–1977. GRMD Collection,
   GRMD 1/47 Images: Sophomore Literary Festival, Tom Stoppard, 1971/0328.

207 *resist categorisation*: John Russell Taylor, 'Our Changing Theatre', Delaney 1994, 25;
   Gussow, 5–6.

208 *these questions*: HR 94.19, J script.

210 *Michael Frayn*: HR 36.1, Michael Frayn to TS, 21 May 1973.

211 *in a lecture*: TS, Weidenfeld Humanitas Lecture, Oxford University, 18 May 2016.

212 *familiar grammar*: RADIO, 89.

212 *early notes*: HR 84.15, notes, November 1969, for WATN.

212 *aired*: HR 12.11, WATN, first broadcast 28 January 1970 in two instalments for Radio
   4 Schools Programmes: Dickon Reed, producer. Broadcast for Radio 3, 18 December
   1970: Carleton Hobbs as Dobson, John Wood as Gale. Biblio, A9, L 32.

213 *against his principles*: RADIO, vii.

213 *John Gale wrote*: HR 36.1, John Gale to TS, 11 February 1970.

213 *Oh no*: RADIO, 105. Billington 1987, 74, Hayman 1977, 89, and Hunter 2005, 236, on the 'emotional intensity' of WATN.

214 *Desolation*: ADS, BBC Radio 3, 14 November 1972. With Stephen Murray, Rolf Lefebvre, Fiona Watson, Carleton Hobbs. Consortium: Jenkins, 105. All quotes from ADS from RADIO.

215 *widely praised*: HR 36.1, FP to TS on ADS, 21 September 1972, 18 April 1984.

216 *claimed this argument*: Delaney 1994, 37. TS, interview Richard Mayne, Radio 3, 10 November 1972.

217 *play of deep feeling*: ADS, 121–2, 116. ADS as stage play directed by Tim Luscombe at the King's Head Theatre, transferred to the Duke of York's theatre, then in 1989 played at the Helen Hayes Theater in New York, and frequently produced after that. Delaney 1994, 231–4.

218 *also a love story*: Delaney 1994, 36, 232–3.

12: Acrobatics

219 *What, in short*: J, 1986, 45. All J quotes from the 1986 edition unless otherwise stated. G, 151.

219 *limits of reason*: G, 151; J, 31. See Fleming 2001, 66–81, comparing G with J.

219 *Stoppard suggested*: Tim Corrie, interview HL, 1 May 2015.

220 *admired Brecht*: Biblio, H, 195, 'Bits of Bert', *Scene*, 14 September 1962.

220 *Why did he*: Frances Hill, 'Quarter-Laughing Assurance', *Times Educational Supplement*, 9 February 1973.

220 *political parable*: Bertolt Brecht, *Life of Galileo*, trans. John Willet, Bloomsbury Methuen Drama, 1980, 2006, 47. Brecht's play was written in exile in 1938–9, first performed in 1943, and first staged in English in 1947 by Joseph Losey, in a version by Brecht and Charles Laughton, who played Galileo.

220 *Berliner Ensemble*: Brecht, *Life of Galileo*, 44.

220 *Galileo's recantation*: Brecht, *Life of Galileo*, 25, 131, 246, 256.

220 *does keep close*: Brecht, *Life of Galileo*, 88.

220 *love, war, and drama*: HR 34.4, AS, interview with TS, 1974.

221 *She might well*: G, 21.

221 *Urban VIII*: G, 88.

221 *most lyrical*: G, 30.

221 *horror*: Brecht, *Life of Galileo*, 155–6.

221 *Your Reverence*: G, 88–9.

222 *they sound like Dotty*: G, 18, 78. J, 65.

222 *I do not understand*: G, 40, 49. See Hunter 2005, 45.

223 *impossible equation*: 'A Note on *Galileo*', April 2003, G, 5–6.

223 *lukewarm*: HR 36.1, John Boorman to TS, 19 April 1971.

223 *scathing letter*: HR 36.1, TS to Peter Bart, Paramount, 18 May 1971.

223 *Planetarium*: HR 85.1, *Kine Weekly*, 4 September 1971. *Today's Cinema*, 17 August 1971. G, 5. HR 36.1, London Planetarium to TS, 12 December 1972. See Fleming 2001, 66–81, 269; Kirsten Shepherd-Barr, *Science on Stage: From* Doctor Faustus *to* Copenhagen, Princeton University Press, 2006. HR 36.1, Laurence Olivier to TS, 2 April 1973.

224 *research*: HR 34.4, AS, interview with TS, 1974. Billington 1987, 82.

224 *single image*: Gussow, 14. For 'pyramid', in interviews, also Frances Hill, 'Quarter-Laughing Assurance', *Times Educational Supplement*, 9 February 1973, and Delaney 1990, 38.

224 *a play about an idea*: Cambridge, 116; Delaney 1994, 157, 44, 86.

227 *Bones: Who are these*: J, 41.

228 *Stoppard describes*: Gussow, 14, 34, 107.

228 *which should occupy*: Hill, 'Quarter-Laughing Assurance', *Times Educational Supplement*, 9 February 1973; Gussow, 16.

228 *G. E. Moore*: J, 57, 58. HR 95.11, TS to Dorothy Moore, 20 February 1972. Mrs Moore's protest had been conveyed to TS by G. E. Moore's biographer Paul Levy. George may also have been inspired by stories of the legendary eccentricities of the theologian and moral philosopher Donald MacKinnon. See Nadel, 558, n. 39.

228 *His career*: J, 26, 26, 41, 63, 54.

229 *rhetorical monologue*: J, 36, 57, 63. Nadel, 225, notes the Havel influence.

229 *George: But when*: J, 17.

230 *like Beckett*: Hayman 1977, 103, on Beckett and Zeno. Clive James noted in 1975, picking up the Zeno reference: 'Here and now in Stoppard is a time and place defined by an infinite number of converging vectors each heading towards it at the speed of light and steadily slowing down to nothing before passing through it and speeding up again.' 'Count Zeno Splits the Infinitive', *Encounter*, November 1975.

230 *logically inferred*: J, 30, 62.

230 *What is honour*: J, 45.

231 *And yet I tell you*: J, 62.

231 *usually says*: Gussow, 5, 35.

231 *Are you religious*: PR 44, Delaney 1994, 188.

231 *Things and actions*: J, 31–2.

231 *Stoppard is not*: Gussow, 16: 'Occasionally, I hardly had to change a thing.'

232 *Skinner*: Gussow, 8.

232 *moral judgments*: Fleming 2001, 88.

232 *attacking a dodo*: PR 43, Delaney 1994, 187.

232 *powerfully influenced*: A. C. Grayling, *Wittgenstein: A Very Short Introduction*, Oxford University Press, 1996, 67–8. Ben Rogers, Introduction, A. J. Ayer, *Language, Truth and Logic*, 1936, Penguin, 2001, 9–10, 26.

232 *a main source*: Freddie Ayer noted the resemblance, with amusement, reviewed J for the *Sunday Times*, and became an acquaintance, exchanging philosophical ideas with TS: 'Indeed, I think I agree with Kant that the notion of a cause outside time is unintelligible', etc. HR 36.1, Ayer to TS, 8 May 1972; Mark Amory, 'The Joke's the Thing', *Sunday Times*, 9 June 1974. Baker 2013, 85, Ayer's review of J.

232 *Ayer argued*: *Language, Truth and Logic*, Penguin, 2001, 51, 224, 235.

232 *George explains*: J, 39. Fleming 2001, 88.

233 *George's comment*: J, 38–9.

233 *As Stoppard says*: PR 44, Delaney 1994, 188.

233 *Penelope*: HR, 66.13, TS note for *Another Moon Called Earth*, June 1967.

234 *put it this way*: FK, interview HL, 7 January 2015.

234 *awkwardly tender*: J, 25, 31, 32.

235 *'Forget Yesterday'*: J, 1972, 90.

235 *grief and love*: TS, interview HL, 18 March 2015.

235 *Apollo 16*: J, 14. Michael Hallifax, memo to Olivier, Tynan et al., 21 April 1972,
National Theatre, with thanks to Daniel Rosenthal.

236 *chat shows*: e.g. *The Eamonn Andrews Show* and *Not So Much a Programme, More a
Way of Life* with Ned Sherrin and John Wells, Billington 1987, 85; Hunter 2005, 64.

236 *not interested in politics*: J, 26, 29.

237 *This moment was cut*: J, 1972, 85. A cut regretted by some TS critics, e.g. Hunter 2000,
80, Fleming 2001, 275, n. 19.

237 *Stoppard argued*: Delaney 1994, 64.

237 *1977 review*: TS, 'But for the Middle Classes', review of PJ, *Enemies of Society*, *Times
Literary Supplement*, 3 June 1977.

238 *revived in 1985*: 'The Stoppard Morality Farce Jumps Back', Mandrake, *Sunday
Telegraph*, 31 March 1985.

238 *support from Kenneth Tynan*: Tynan 1977, *Show People*, 91.

238 *Tynan wrote*: HR, 36.1, KT to TS, 11 February 1970.

239 *very bad idea*: Barry Norman, 'TS and the Contentment of Insecurity', *The Times*, 11
November 1972. HR, 36.1, TS to Kathleen Tynan, 23 January 1987.

239 *Tynan's claim*: Delaney 1990, 172. HR, 42.6, TS to *Financial Times*, responding to a
review of *Arcadia* by Malcolm Rutherford, 20 April 1993. TS, interviews HL, 16–17
November 2015, 29 June 2016. Tynan 1977.

239 *originally intended*: TS, interview HL, 10 September 2014.

239 *Tarzan was reinstated*: J, 75.

240 *revolve*: Delaney 1990, 36.

240 *major early change*: J, 1972, 40, 29. MS, interview HL, 2 July 2014.

240 *what to expect*: TS to FP, 15 December 1971, Faber archive.

240 *authorial warnings*: J, 1972, 11; J, 1973, 11; J, 1986, 5. Philip Gaskell, in *From Reader
to Writer: Studies in Editorial Method*, Clarendon Press, 1978, 245, defines the three
textual stages of a work written for performance as first 'the script, the written
version of what was originally intended to be said', secondly 'the performance text'
('developed not by the author alone but by the director and the actors as well'), and
thirdly the published 'reading text'.

241 *Peter Wood*: Fleming, 273; Hayman 1977, 11; Hunter 2005, 179–90; TS, interviews
HL, 18 March, 15–16 November 2015, 29 June 2016; Obituaries: Michael Coveney,
Guardian, 18 February 2016; *Telegraph*, 17 February 2016; Michael Quinn, *The Stage*,
23 February 2016; Alan Strachan, *Independent*, 24 February 2016; *The Times*, 19
February 2016. Delaney 1994, 172–6, Ronald Hayman, 'Peter Wood: A Partnership',
The Times, 8 June 1974.

243 *kid-glovey*: Delaney 1994, 174.

243 *as they began*: Hunter 2005, 130, 181. Hayman 1977, 11. Hordern, 1976 radio interview.
'Yes, We Have No Banana', *Arts Guardian*, 10 December 1971. Gussow, 23. FK,
interview HL, 7 January 2015.

243 *As the run went on*: TSL, nd [January 1972], 9 July 1973. On Dotty, Alan Strachan,
Peter Wood: Obituary, *Independent*, 24 February 2016.

244 *a huge hit*: Delaney 1990, 36.

244 *Later productions*: Billington 2007, 224. Brassell, 115. Billington 1987, 87, 92.
Gussow 18.

244 *Olivier and Peter Hall wanted*: HR 36.1, Laurence Olivier to TS, 2 April 1973.

.

244 *agony*: HR 36.1, TN to TS, 26 February 1973. TN, interview HL, 2 October 2017.
245 *ambition*: Hunter 2005, 200; Gussow, 24.

13: The Home Team

246 *One tried*: TS, funeral speech for John Wells, 30 April 1998, TS archive.
246 *his new play*: HR 124.5, Ronald Bryden to TS, 26 September 1972. Janet Watts,
      interview, *Guardian*, 21 March 1973, Delaney 1994, 46–50; Gussow, 22.
246 *good-natured baby*: TSL, nd [June 1972].
246 *dedicated*: TS to FP, 8 August 1974; T publication details, Biblio, 66.
246 *Miriam was now*: HR 34.1, 'Welcome to the World', *Evening News*, 29 September
      1974. Colin Barnes, interview with MS, 1975.
247 *have a go*: MS, interview HL, 8 April 2014. Family life descriptions drawn from
      interviews with TS, MS, JM, ES, WS, BS and OS, and TSL. TSL, nd [September 1970,
      November 1971], 12 March 1976. Profile of MS by Adrienne Oates, nd. MS to TS's
      parents, 12 March 1976.
249 *bashing tennis balls*: TS, JE I, 15 July 1979.
249 *noted grimly*: TS, JE I, 8 April 1977.
250 *Know thyself*: TS, JE I, 9 May 1977.
250 *Stoppard writes*: TS, JE I, 12 November 1976.
250 *When he is away*: TS, JE I, 7 May 1977, 29 September 1976.
250 *I miss you*: TS, JE I, 11 October 1979.
251 *took pleasure in noting*: TS, JE I, 20 January 1976, 13 June 1976, 17 December 1976, 20
      July 1977, 7 November 1977, 20 January 1979, 15 March 1979.
251 *not entirely a preparation*: TS, JE II, 23 September 1982.
252 *described the fishing*: TSL, nd [September 1977].
253 *got exasperated*: TS, interview, in Hayman 1977, 141.
254 *her first book*: MS, *Miriam Stoppard's Book of Babycare*, Weidenfeld, 1977, dedicated
      to 'Oliver, Barnaby, William and Edmund'. Re. Weidenfeld, TS, interview HL,
      1 November 2019.
255 *cashflow*: TS to PS, 6 March 1974, 10 December 1975, 22 January 1976, 13 February
      1976, 2 September 1977, 16 September 1973, 25 July 1978, 2 August 1978, 11 February
      1979, PS archive. TS, JE I, 2 February 1978.
255 *The House of Bernarda Alba*: TS, interview HL, 2 December 2016. HR 36.1, FP to TS,
      23 March 1973. Michael Leech, 'The Translators', *Plays & Players*, April 1973. Biblio,
      K 43, N 8. TSL, 5 February 1976.
256 *Born Yesterday*: TS, interview HL, 2 December 2016. TSL, nd [summer 1973].
256 *precious bore*: TSL, nd [spring 1973].
256 *Naked Without a Gun*: Hunter 2005, 127. HR 96.1–4, 96.5–8, 16.2, drafts and
      correspondence. Screenplay, TS archive. Hare called the TS screenplay 'putrid' in a
      letter to his agent Peggy Ramsay, but later withdrew this. DH, *The Blue Touch Paper*,
      Faber, 2015, 221–2; Richard Brooks, *Sunday Times*, 8 August 2010, on Peggy Ramsay's
      letters.
256 *suggestion from a TV company*: HR, 13.10, 'Hendrick's America'.
257 *Another plot*: HR, 85.4, Notes for 'The Grapefruit Millionaire'. TS, interview HL, 14
      October 2017.
257 *quirky or personal*: HR 124.6, Neil Hornick to TS, 5 August 1974. Hornick, ed.,

Forwards! A Phantom Captain Book, Unexpected Developments, Aloes Books, 1977. Biblio, F5. TS, Introduction, Glynn Boyd Harte catalogue, Thumb Gallery, 1976. Biblio, F4.

257 The Romantic Englishwoman: HR 23.10, 107.11, drafts and correspondence. HR 23, 10, French review of *The Romantic Englishwoman*, *Le Point*, 9 June 1975: '*les dialogues, brillants, sinon de Pinter, sont de Tom Stoppard*'.

258 Three Men in a Boat: HR 119.3, 7, 9, drafts and correspondence. Delaney 1994, 161. Stephen Frears, conversation with HL, 1 July 2017.

259 *If my arithmetic*: TS to PS, nd [spring 1974], PS archive.

259 *Jacky*: JM, interview HL, 6 June 2014; JM, email to HL, 16 September 2016. Writing methods: TS, interview, *Huffington Post*, 26 January 2015.

262 *thank-you*: Undated notes and cards from TS to JM, JM archive.

262 *Not bad*: Peter Nichols, interview HL, 29 June 2015.

262 *jovial letter*: TS to Jon [Bradshaw], 29 November 1976.

262 *John Wells*: TS, funeral speech for John Wells, 30 April 1998. Teresa Wells, interview HL, 30 September 2014. TSL, nd [February 1975]. AF, interview HL, 23 September 2014.

264 *described him, privately*: TS, JE I, 27 June 1976.

265 *my gymnasium*: TS, JE I, 25 January 1977.

265 *Paul Johnson*: AF, interview HL, 23 September 2014. PJ to TS, nd [mid-1980s]. MJ to TS, 30 April 1991. PJ to TS, 24 November 1990, 10 February 1990. MJ to TS, nd. MJ and PJ, joint interview HL, 9 September 2014. TS, JE I, 14 July 1977. 'But for the Middle Classes', *Times Literary Supplement*, 3 June 1977, 677. Mark Lawson, interview HL, 26 September 2014. Max Hastings, interview HL, 4 September 2014. *New York Times*, 13 November 1983.

268 *Pinter and Pasta*: HR 35.5, American Express Company request to TS, 22 February 1978.

268 Betrayal: TS, JE I, 17 November 1978.

269 *changed the rules*: TS, interviews HL, July 2014, 10 August 2014, 18 March 2015. TS, PEN Pinter Prize speech, 7 October 2013. 'Harold Pinter, Poet of No-Man's-Land', *Sunday Times*, 7 October 1990.

269 *The angel*: TS, PEN Pinter Prize speech, 7 October 2013.

270 *cricket*: Tim Rice, interview HL, 23 July 2015. AF, interview HL, 23 September 2014. Michael Billington, *The Life and Work of Harold Pinter*, Faber, 1996, 385. John Lahr, ed., *The Diaries of Kenneth Tynan*, Bloomsbury, 2001, 340. Tynan 1977, *Show People*, 51–3.

270 *typical match*: AF, *Must You Go? My Life with Harold Pinter*, Anchor Books, 2010, 98.

271 *Bohemian*: AF, *Must You Go?*, 7.

272 *What a nice man*: AF, interview HL, 23 September 2014.

272 *clerihew*: TS, JE I, 14 July 1977.

272 *Dinner with Tom*: AF, *Must You Go?*, 58.

272 *place-card*: AF, *Must You Go?*, 148.

273 *Stoppard's version*: MS, interview HL, 8 April 2014. TS, JE I, 13 April 1976.

273 *relished the story*: TS, interviews HL, 10 August 2014, 1 November 2019. There are numerous versions of the 'Harold Comedy' joke, e.g.: 'Have you thought, instead, of changing your name to Harold Comedy?' in William Langley, Profile of TS, *Daily Telegraph*, 11 June 2006.

273 TS on HP at the 92nd Street Y, 2014: http://92yondemand.org/75-at-75-tom-
     stoppard-on-harold-pinter-1964-and-1989.
274 *I always sign*: AF, *Must You Go?*, 167.
274 *more right-wing*: AF, interview HL, 23 September 2014.
275 *Belarus*: TS, 'Accidental Tyranny', *Guardian*, 1 October 2005. PEN Pinter Prize
     speech, 7 October 2013. HP to TS, 2 October 2005, JM archive.
275 *Pinter's mantra*: Michael Billington, *Harold Pinter*, Faber, 1996, 79.
276 *Alan Ayckbourn*: http://research.alanayckbourn.net/styled-20/styled-29/index.html.
276 *Sir*: Trish Montemuro, interview HL, 24 September 2014.
276 *retrospective exchange*: DH, interview HL, 26 February 2016. DH, *The Blue Touch
     Paper*, Faber, 2015, 222–3.
276 *powerful riposte*: HP to PW, 30 March 1958, in HP, *Various Voices*, Faber, 1998.
     Michael Billington, *Pinter*, Faber, 1996, 83.
277 *wasted*: MS, interview HL, 8 April 2014.
277 *I've known him*: Ronald Harwood, remark to HL, 7 November 2014.

14: *Travesties*

278 *If there is*: T, 1975, 62; 1993, 41. T is much changed between 1975 and 1993 editions;
     editions cited are identified in notes. Changes made for the 2016 production are in
     T, 2017.
278 *idea for a play*: Delaney 1994, 24 (1970).
279 *'revolutionary' and 'artist'*: AS, interview HL, 31 May 2014. Wordsmith, 59. Delaney
     1994, 32, 81.
279 *final speech*: T, 1975, 99.
279 *commemorate*: Hunter 2005, 113 (1968).
279 *comic swirl*: T, 1975, 24–6.
280 *Leninism and Fascism*: Delaney 1994, 64 (1974).
280 *no time for Tzara*: Delaney 1994, 105.
280 *antics of Tzara*: Gussow 1995, 35. Claude Arnaud, *Jean Cocteau*, trans. Bridget
     Patterson, Gallimard, 2003.
281 *superb biography*: T, 1975, 11.
281 *Joyce*: T, 1975, 50. Richard Ellmann, *James Joyce*, Oxford University Press, 1959, 1966,
     430, 435–9, 460.
282 *absurd little story*: Ellmann, 'The Zealots of Zurich', *Times Literary Supplement*,
     12 July 1974, typescript in Ellmann Papers, Special Collections, McFarlin Library,
     University of Tulsa.
283 *some trousers*: T, 1975, 12.
283 *friendly exchanges*: TS to Richard Ellmann, 6 March 1974, 19 May 1974, Ellmann
     Papers. T, 1975, 12–13. Biblio, 66, 340, 12 September 1993.
284 *Great days*: T, 1975, 41.
284 *Carr's presence*: T, 1975, 12. TS and PM interview, Menier Chocolate Factory, T
     programme, 2016. T, 1993, 11. T, undated typescript, ii.
285 *Carr concocts*: T, 1975, 22.
285 *a memory play*: HR 94.14, 15 February 1994.
285 *Carr and Joyce*: T, 1975, 47.
286 *Henry Carr's second wife*: T, 1975, 'Henry Wilfred Carr, 1894–1962', 13. Ellmann, *James*

Joyce, New and Revised Edition, Oxford University Press, 1983, 459, n. 26, 784.

286 *J. F. Shade*: Hayman 1977, 117. TS, speech at Althorp Literary Festival, June 2015; 'I Invented a Professor and Made Up a Quote, Stoppard Admits', *The Times*, 13 June 2015. John Hinderaker, *Books*, 13 June 2015, spotted the reference to *Pale Fire*.

287 *sleight of hand*: Oscar Wilde, *The Importance of Being Earnest*, Oxford University Press, 1995, 254. T, 1975, 32.

287 *What are your politics*: Wilde, *Earnest*, 266. T, 1975, 94.

288 *Memory*: Wilde, *Earnest*, 273.

288 *said of Wilde*: Delaney 1994, 99.

288 *The pleasure*: TS and PM interview, Menier Chocolate Factory, T programme, 2016.

288 *The passing show*: Gussow 1995, 107.

289 *I was writing*: TS and PM interview, Menier Chocolate Factory, T programme, 2016; TS, *Front Row* interview, BBC Radio 4, 3 October 2016.

289 *Tzara cuts up*: T, 1975, 54.

289 *An artist*: T, 1975, 62.

289 *out of it*: T, 1975, 38.

290 *lucky man*: TS, interview Janet Watts, *Guardian*, 21 March 1973; Delaney 1995, 50.

290 *When I was at school*: T, 1975, 46.

290 *Why don't you*: TN, interview Hunter, 2004, in Hunter 2005, 200. TN, interview HL, 2 October 2017.

291 *big parts*: HR 124.5, Ronald Bryden to TS, 26 September 1972. TS interview, *Evening Standard*, 24 May 1974. TN, interview HL, 2 October 2017.

291 *all about height*: Gussow 1995, 29; Delaney 1994, 32, 86.

291 *interlocking curves*: John Wood, interview Hunter, 2004, 235.

291 *one of the greatest*: Billington 1987, 105; 'Great Performances', *Guardian*, 1 June 2015. TS on JW as Carr, JE I, 21 February 1976.

292 *joked to his mother*: TSL, nd [spring 1976].

292 *enthused*: Delaney 1994, 104. *Time* magazine, Biblio, 71; Delaney 1994, 80. *New York Times*, 19 October 1975, Biblio, K 65, 326. Marowitz, *Confessions of a Counterfeit Critic*, Methuen, 1973, 123–4.

292 *heartless, overloaded*: Robert Cushman, *Observer*, 16 June 1974, John Barber, *Daily Telegraph*, 11 June 1974.

293 *Audiences do think*: Carey Perloff, interview HL, 5 October 2015. Nadel, 250, on falling ticket sales in New York.

293 *biggest difficulties*: HR 124.6, HP to TS, 10 July 1974. Hayman 1977, 125. Fleming 2001, 276. TSL, nd [summer/autumn 1975].

293 *one occasion*: 'Real Books, Real Authors', *Author*, Summer 1984. 'The Event and the Text', 1988, Delaney 1994, 207.

293 *in the script*: T, undated typescript, 71.

294 *timidity*: TS and PM interview, Menier Chocolate Factory, T programme, 2016. TS, interview HL, 10 September 2014.

294 *rewritings*: see Philip Gaskell, *From Writer to Reader*, Clarendon Press, 1978, 245–62, examining changes between script, performance text and first Faber publication of T; PW, interview Hunter, 2005, 184; Fleming 2001, 103–7. T, 2017 edition, incorporates changes in the 2016 Marber production.

294 *changes continued*: T, 1993, 58, 60. 'Leftover from *Travesties*', *Adam International Review*, Nos 431–3, 1980, 11–12.

295 *Tynan comments*: Tynan 1977, *Show People*, 112. Quoted in Delaney 1994, 151.
295 *value of art*: Janet Watts, 'Tom Stoppard', *Guardian*, 21 March 1973, in Delaney 1994, 46–50; Delaney 1994, 67, 69 (1974). Nadel, 259, 263, n. 3.
295 *One can see*: Delaney 1994, 65; TS, *Front Row* interview, BBC Radio 4, 3 October 2016.
296 *I think I enlist*: Gussow 1995, 30.

15: Terra Firma

299 *Right and wrong*: StC, 84.
299 *appraisal*: Hayman 1977, 144. Clive James, 'Count Zeno Splits the Infinitive', *Encounter*, 45, November 1975. Clive James, 'To Tom Stoppard: A Letter from London', *Fan Mail: Seven Verse Letters*, Faber, 1977. TSL, nd [summer 1975].
300 *important truths*: PF, 63. All quotes from PF from EGBDF&PF.
300 *too serious*: TS, JE I, 1 December 1975, 13.
300 Have You Any Washing: A possible influence on DL; Brassell, 284, and Billington 1987, 107.
300 *too Stoppardian*: *The Boundary*, BBC TV, 19 July 1975, with Clive Exton, Samuel French, 1991. See Brassell, 172–7.
301 *speeded-up* Hamlet: 'Fifteen-minute Hamlet', 1976, produced for BBC Radio 4, 30 June, 1 July 2007.
301 *Before being carried*: TS, interview Jon Bradshaw, January 1977, Delaney 1994, 98.
301 *crime passionelle*: TS, JE I, 15 October 1975.
301 Toujours la politesse: DL and NFL, 1976, in Plays 1, 73–137.
302 *close to sexism*: Ed Berman, interview HL, 8 July 2015.
302 *inconsequential adequacy*: TS, JE I, 10 January, 31 January, 17 February 1976.
302 *Brian Rix*: Biblio, H 197, 'Twelve Years without Trousers', *Scene*, 21 September 1962.
302 *Whitehall farces*: Grateful thanks to Mark Lawson for his encyclopaedic knowledge of British sex farces.
303 *Samuel Beckett would never*: TS, interview HL, 28 June 2014.
303 *And her drawers*: *The Boundary*, BBC TV, 19 July 1975, with Clive Exton, Samuel French, 1991, 16.
303 *All my ideas*: TS, JE I, 17 December 1975.
303 *rather more topical*: Interview, BBC *Tonight*, 16 June 1976, in Brassell, 284.
304 *no love lost*: Ed Berman, interview HL, 8 July 2015; FP, interview HL, 2 May 2014.
305 *As Berman had warned*: Ed Berman, interview HL, 8 July 2015. Hunter 2005, 64.
305 *Miss Common Sense*: Hayman 1977, 144.
306 *had to cajole*: Ed Berman, interview HL, 8 July 2015. John Leonard, 'TS Tries On a "Knicker Farce"', *New York Times*, 9 January 1977; 'Stoppard in a Minor Mode', *Boston Phoenix*, 6 November 1979.
307 *proclaiming Socialist principles*: TS, JE I, 21 May 1976.
307 *grisly first night*: TS, JE I, 13 October 1976, 11 January 1977.
308 *Tom, as he does*: Ed Berman, interview HL, 8 July 2015.
308 *endless travelling*: TSL, MS to M[B]S and KS, 12 March 1976. TS, JE I, 7 November 1979.
309 *organisation*: TS, JE I, 9 September 1977, 7 November 1979, 30 September 1976. TSL, nd [autumn 1978].

309 *missed his family*: TS, JE II, 11 May 1977, 5 July 1982.

309 *a credit balance*: TS, JE I, 19 January 1977, 2 June 1978, 19 July 1978, 5 January 1979.

310 *Don't think*: TS, JE I, 29 December 1978.

310 *society*: KT, *The Diary of Kenneth Tynan*, ed. John Lahr, Bloomsbury, 2001, 21 October 1976, Ch. 7; lightly revised in Tynan 1977, and *Show People*, 103. TS, JE I, 19 July 1977, 13 November 1976, 18 August 1976, 1 November 1976, 6 November 1976. 24 July 1977, 16 September 1977, 31 July 1977, 6 March 1978. TSL, nd [September 1977]. TS to Simon Gray, nd [2006], with thanks to Victoria Gray.

311 *In his letters*: TSL, nd [1984; May 1994].

311 *royalty*: TSL, nd [July 1974]. TSL, 14 February 1974, nd [spring 1976], nd [October 1976].

312 *Buckingham Palace*: TS, JE I, 19 November 1977, 9 March 1978, 30 December 1977. TSL, nd [spring 1976], 22 November 1977. TS, interview HL, 14 October 2017.

312 *Success*: TS, JE I, 29 December 1975, 13 November 1976, 2 December 1978.

313 *Worry*: TS, JE I, 25 December 1975, 11 August 1977, 9 September 1977, 29 December 1978, 2 December 1978.

313 *My typical bad dream*: TS, JE I, 2 February 1978.

313 *Today I received*: TS, JE I, 25 August 1976.

314 *the only thing that matters*: TS, JE I, 11 January 1978.

314 *invented epitaph*: TS, JE I, 12 November 1977.

314 *moral accounting*: TS, JE I, 14 February 1978.

314 *Hemingway*: TS, JE I, 1 December 1977.

314 *useful quotations*: TS, JE I, 17 December 1975 (W. H. Auden, *A Certain World, A Commonplace Book*, Faber, 1970), 16 October 1976.

315 *prayer*: TS, JE I, 25 December 1975, 2 November 1975, 23 October 1979, 3 July 1978.

315 *feelings about his mother*: TS, JE I, 21 May 1976, 11 July 1976.

315 *long journal entry*: TS, JE I, 11 July 1976, 28 January 1977, 6, 9 February 1979.

316 *British democracy*: TS, JE I, 21 January 1977.

316 *to write 'politically'*: TS, JE I, 2 November 1975, 9 February 1977.

317 *the acts are ordinary murder*: TS, JE I, 1 April 1979, 5 September 1979.

317 *capital punishment*: TS, JE I, 12 September 1976.

317 *breached the boycott*: HR 34.1. TS to *Hibernia*, 20 January 1978. DL was playing at the Abbey Theatre in Dublin when the *Hibernia* journal published an attack on him headed 'Boycott Breached', accusing him of profiting 'from racism'. TS replied: 'This could be "actionable" . . . I donate the author's royalties from South African productions to Amnesty International and other causes.'

317 *American foreign policy*: HR 37.3, TS, 3 March 1977. TS, interview HL, 18 March 2015.

317 *instincts were conservative*: HR 37.3, TS for 'Dramatists' Sub-Committee for the Society of Authors', 26 May 1977, opposing the Writers' Guild's and Theatre Writers Union's 'closed shop clause'. TS, JE I, 12 December 1978, 9 September 1977, 3, 4 December 1978, 3 May 1979. Cf. PEN speech, 2013, for later views.

318 *always had fears*: TS, JE I, 13 October 1975, 12 November 1975.

318 *argument at dinner*: TS, JE I, 28 December 1975.

16: Prisoners of Conscience

320 *To thine own self*: EGBDF, 36.

320 *no moral dilemmas*: PF, 79. All quotes from PF from EGBDF&PF.

320 *distaste for Marxism*: Mark Hurst, 'Slowing Down the Going-away Process – Tom Stoppard and Soviet Dissent', *Contemporary British History*, Vol. 30, Issue 4, 2016, 485–504. Michael Žantovský, *Havel: A Life*, Atlantic Books, 2014, 103–15.

320 *pronounced insane*: EGBDF&PF, 8. Hurst, 'Slowing Down'. TS, JE I, 19 October 1978. HR 37.3, details on TS's membership of Index, PEN, etc.

321 *Amnesty International asked*: EGBDF&PF, 6–7. TS, interview HL, 8 March 2015. TS, JE I, 26 November, 1 December 1975, 30 March 1976.

321 *Fainberg's essay*: Victor Fainberg, 'My Five Years in Mental Hospitals', *Index on Censorship*, Vol. 4, Issue 2, 1975, 67–71.

322 *publicity*: Straitjacket, CAPA News, 2, Spring 1977.

322 *criminally insular*: TS, JE I, 1 December 1975, 30 March 1976.

322 *his cause*: TS, JE I, 21 April, 7 April, 1 May, 29 December 1976.

323 *saw it as an opportunity*: TN, interview HL, 2 October 2017.

323 *Stoppard now knew*: TS, JE I, 10 January 1977, 31 July 1976.

323 *visit to Moscow*: TS, 'A Meeting with Misha', *Straitjacket* 2, Spring 1977. TS, 'The Face at the Window', *Sunday Times*, 27 February 1977. TS, JE I, 12–27 February 1977. Hurst, 'Slowing Down'. TS, 'Russia Diary', unpublished, 12–19 February 1977, PS archive.

325 *Out of that journey*: TS, JE I, 31 July 1976. EGBDF&PF, 9.

325 *described it*: TS, 'Play of the Week', *Radio Times*, 15 September 1977, quoted in Hurst, 'Slowing Down'.

326 *in rehearsal*: Hurst, 'Slowing Down', n. 47; EGBDF&PF, 8. TS, Introduction to EGBDF, published as 'Nothing in Mind', *London Magazine*, February 1978.

327 *Havel*: VH, *Disturbing the Peace*, ed. and trans. Paul Wilson, Vintage, 1990, 1991, 27, 40, 69, 153, 72.

329 *down-to-earth*: VH, *Open Letters, Selected Writings 1965–1990*, ed. Paul Wilson, Vintage, 1992, 235, 145, 239.

329 *finally released*: TS, 'Czech Human Rights', *New York Times*, 7 February 1977. Delaney 1990, 98, 173. See Žantovský, *Havel*, for VH's story.

329 *his plays*: see Michael Žantovský, *Havel: The Garden Party and Other Plays*, trans. Vera Blackwell and others, Grove Press, 1993, 33, 50, 64; *Selected Plays 1984–1987*, Faber, 1994; *Largo Desolato*, English version by TS, Grove Press, 1985.

330 *immediately warmed*: TS, interview HL, 18 March 2015.

330 *his plays darkened*: TS, interview HL, 18 March 2015. Žantovský, *Havel*, 134, 246–7. HR 36.8, VH to TS, 28 January 1984.

330 *feelings poured out*: TS, JE I, 21, 22 January 1977.

332 *fortunate invitation*: Alain Elkann, interview Robert Silvers, April 2014. https://alainelkanninterviews.com/robert-b-silvers/.

332 *time to stop conceding*: TS, 'Dirty Linen in Prague', *New York Times*, 11 February 1977.

332 *Prague jokes*: TS, 'Prague: The Story of the Chartists', *New York Review of Books*, 24.4, 4 August 1977, 11–15; 'My Friends Fighting for Freedom', *Daily Mail*, 20 October 1977.

332 *taken the rounds*: TS, 'Prague: The Story of the Chartists'; 'Looking Glass World', *New Statesman*, 28 October 1977; TS, interview HL, 18 March 2015; DHCM, Inter-Action, 1979, 3. Žantovský, *Havel*, 244.

333 *When Stoppard got back*: 'Play of the Week', *Radio Times*, 15 September 1977. Hurst, 'Slowing Down', n. 59.

334 *The pressure from below*: TS, 'Prague: The Story of the Chartists'.

334 *what I am not writing*: TS, JE I, 14 July 1977, 21 October 1977. Delaney 1994, 110

(1983). But in an unpublished 1983 interview with John Wells for the *Paris Review*, he maintained that his Czech birth had 'not much to do' with PF: it was more about Russia.

335 *nothing is what it seems*: All quotes from EGBDF from EGBDF&PF.

335 *joke about Russian plays*: TN, interview HL, 2 October 2017. TS, re. South Africa, August 2013, JM archive.

336 *nonsense scenarios*: The early notes for EGBDF, 'The Grapefruit Millionaire', include the words 'Axioms of Euclid' and 'Humpty Dumpty'. HR 85.4.

336 *Don't write an ending*: HR 9.4, notes for EGBDF, 14 May 1976.

337 *Geometry*: All quotes from PF.

340 *he was cross*: TSL, nd [September 1977].

340 *surprised*: TSL, nd [September 1977].

341 *one-night premiere*: TS, JE I, 14 July 1977. Levin, quoted in Tynan 1977, *Show People*, 122.

341 *play was filmed*: EGBDF, BBC2, 14 November 1979. Alan Franks, 'Return of the Iron Curtain', *The Times*, 22 December 2008. HR 36.8, VH to TS, 28 January 1984.

342 *It's as if the system*: All quotes from DHCM.

343 *pointed out these parallels*: Tynan 1977. Reprinted in *Sunday Times Weekly Review* as 'The Man in the Moon', 15 January 1978. *Show People*, 44–123. http://www.newyorker.com/magazine/1977/12/19/withdrawing-with-style-from-the-chaos.

344 *a distorting mirror*: TS, JE I, 1 October 1977.

344 *his family's past*: HR 122.4, 122.5, typescript notes for TALK 1999.

345 *asked Tynan to make some cuts*: HR 34.5, TS to KT, nd. HR 34.5, TS to Mark Boxer, 10 January 1978. TS, JE I, 22 December 1977, 11 January 1978. TSL, nd [January 1978]. TS speech, KT Memorial, 18 September 1980.

346 *feeling rather conscious*: HR 6.8, TS to VH, 28 May 1984.

17: The Fourth Estate

347 *There is nothing*: TS, JE I, 19 November 1977.

347 *as he said*: TS, Review of 'OED Supplement, A–G', *Punch*, 13 December 1972.

347 *definitely ert*: TS, interview Ray Connolly, *Sunday Times*, 20 January 1980.

347 *bad journalism*: TS, JE I, 18 December 1977.

348 *felt so short*: TS to PPR, 2 September 1979, Brotherton.

348 *Over the hill*: TSL, nd [July 1980].

348 *The telephone rang*: HR 122.13, unused material for PR, answers to extra questions from George Plimpton, September 1988.

348 *mixed feelings*: TSL, nd [May 1968], nd [January 1969], 24 February 1976, 27 April 1979, 26 March 1987, 19 February 1980. TS, JE I, 22 June 1976, 19 August 1977.

350 *polished anecdote*: Dirk Bogarde, *An Orderly Man*, Chatto & Windus, 1983, 248.

350 *script conference*: HR, 4.4, TS, note on *Despair*, 25 November 1976.

351 *We sat round*: Bogarde, *An Orderly Man*, 259.

351 *very slow*: TS, JE I, 13 December 1977.

351 *candid letter*: Bogarde, *An Orderly Man*, 264. TSL, 10 December 1977, nd [December 1977]. TS, interview HL, 20 March 2018.

351 *violent temper*: TS, JE I, 2, 20 June 1978. HR, 14.8, TS, interview Tom Buckley, *New York Times*, 14 July 1978.

352 *despairing*: HR 14.9, Graham Greene to TS, 11 April 1979.

352 *awful*: HR 107.4, TS, interview, *Patriot Ledger*, 29 November 1983. TS to Chris
      Fujiwara, 2 June 2006, JM archive.

353 *emotionally truthful*: Fleming 2001, 17; unpublished interview with John Wells, in
      1983, for *Paris Review*, 21–2; TS, JE I, 6 January 1978.

353 *the same play*: TS, JE I, 24 September 1976.

353 *opposed calls for a closed shop clause*: Writers' Guild minutes, 26 May 1977. Calls for
      a closed shop clause for writers for subsidised theatres came from the Writers' Guild
      and the Theatre Writers Union.

354 *journalists' strikes*: Delaney 1994, 122, JE I, 9 September 1977, 3 December 1978.
      TS to *The Times*, 11 August 1977. As a Bristol journalist his NUJ membership was
      temporarily suspended for two months in 1959.

354 *protection racket*: TS, interview Maya Jaggi, 'You Can't Help Being What You Write',
      Guardian, 6 September 2008, Hagerty, 27.

354 *look back critically*: Hagerty, 27.

354 *English social virtues*: TS, JE I, 12 November, 19 July 1977.

354 *Again and again*: HR, 34.1, undated piece [1977?].

354 *fantasy*: Delaney 1994, 53 (1977), Cambridge, 27.

354 *big men of journalism*: TS, JE I, 12 March 1978.

355 *Robert Capa*: Unpublished interview with John Wells, in 1983, for *Paris Review*, 15.

355 *centre of the action*: Delaney 1994, 139.

355 *As he said*: Billington 1987, 130; Cambridge, 120; Gussow, 35.

355 *an everyday tale*: TSL, nd [summer 1978].

357 *We're not here*: ND, 92. ND quotations from the revised 1979 edition. For extensive
      ND revisions, during the UK and US runs, see Billington 1987, 127, Delaney 1994, 139,
      199, Fleming 2001, 139, 147, 150, 281.

357 *I am not*: ND, 38.

357 *The argument*: ND, 48, 60, 83.

358 *Do you know*: ND, 85.

358 *People think*: ND, 61.

359 *A free press*: ND, 58. Delaney 1990, 92.

359 *The PM is impressive*: TS, JE II, 30 October 1982. Hagerty, 15, 27.

359 *militant conservatism*: Cambridge, 118.

359 *faint aroma*: Hagerty, typescript, 15.

360 *scumbags*: TS, interview HL, 16–17 November 2015. Hagerty, 29.

360 *provoked him*: HR, DH to TS, 31 August 1978, DH archive.

360 *bag was stolen*: TS, JE I, 29 September 1978. HR, TS to DH, 12 September [1978], DH
      archive.

361 *Hare replied*: DH to TS, 23 September 1978. HR, TS to DH, 9 October [1978], DH
      archive.

361 *one more go*: DH to TS, 25 October 1978, JM archive.

361 *correcting a rumour*: DH to TS, 25 April 1985, JM archive.

362 *some critics were underwhelmed*: Cambridge, 125; Billington 1987, 123; Benedict
      Nightingale quoted in Brassell, 209; Melvyn Bragg, *South Bank Show* interview with
      TS, 1978, Delaney 1994, 124; Bernard Levin, 'deeply disappointing . . . with some
      horrible clumsy preaching', quoted in Fleming 2001, 281, n.1. Codron, 198. Peter Hall,
      Peter Hall's Diaries: The Story of a Dramatic Battle, 1983, Oberon Books, 2000, 460.

362 *No jeep*: Codron, 196. MC, interview HL, 8 January 2015.
362 *coarse and slow*: TSL, nd [autumn 1978].
362 *a huge medal*: TSL, nd [June 1979], PS archive.
363 *Best Play award*: Brassell, 204.
363 *rousing production*: Delaney 1994, 148, Fleming 2001, 150, n. 7, 282.
363 *I adored it*: Diana Rigg, interview HL, 2 September 2016.
363 *Australia*: TS, JE I, 9–17 February 1979.
363 *felt a bit famous*: TSL, nd [February 1979].
363 *I set foot*: TSL, postcard, 5 February 1979.
363 *Maggie Smith*: Michael Coveney, *Maggie Smith: A Biography*, St Martin's Press, 2015,
     164–5.
364 *Life in the theatre*: TS, JE I, 24 November 1979. Codron, 199; Delaney 1994, 141;
     Biblio, 99; TSL, nd [November 1979]. TS, JE I, 15 July, 24 November 1979.
364 *bursts of pleasure*: TS, JE I, 18 July 1978. JE I, 5 December 1978.
365 *a perfect house*: TS, interview HL, 28 June 2014; MS, interview HL, 2 July 2014.
365 *Iver Grove*: N. Pevsner, E. Williamson, G. Brandwood, *Buckinghamshire*, Yale
     University Press, 1994, 414.
365 *commodious*: Sale notices for Iver Grove, 1865, with thanks to Rachel Cunningham-
     Day for a visit to Iver Grove, 4 May 2018.
367 *major purchase*: TSL, 19 April 1979. JE I, 30 June 1979, 24 August 1979.
367 *satisfaction*: TS, JE I, 30 June, 2, 5 September 1979, 24 August 1979.
367 *Miriam's project*: TS, interview HL, 14 October 2017. WS, interview HL, 10 December
     2014. TSL, June 1979. TS, JE I, 13 August, 5 September, 15 September 1979.
368 *guests*: TS, JE I, 8 September 1979.
369 *doing up the house*: TS, interview HL, 28 June 2014; MS, interview HL, 2 July 2014.
370 *Over time they added*: TS, JE II, 24 March, 14 April 1982, 24 June 1983, 18 January, 4
     February 1984, 2 October 1983. TSL, November 1979, 26 May 1983.
371 *parties*: TSL, nd [August 1980], 22 May 1981.
371–3 *Iver Grove life*: HL interviews: AS, TN, Tim Rice, PPR, Tim, Hélène, Ben Corric,
     Deke, Jill, Jamie, Tim Arlon, MJ and PJ, Diana Rigg, TS, MS, BS, ES, OS, WS, PS.

18: Undiscovered Countries

374 *Haven't you ever*: UC, 144.
374 *trip to the Galapagos*: TSL, 23 February 1981. TS, 'Wildlife Observed: The Galapagos:
     Paradise and Purgatory', *Observer* magazine, 29 November 1981, 38–51.
375 *collecting*: TS, 'Reflections on Ernest Hemingway: The Writer in Context', 21 May
     1982. HR 35.2, Carol Rothkopf, 'Building the House of Books' (on Marguerite Cohn),
     Columbia Library Columns, November 1985. Joan Crane, University of Virginia, and
     Carol Rothkopf (Cohn's niece) to TS, October 1984. Jack Hagstrom to TS, 30 October
     1984.
376 *lecturing*: Joseph Raymond Collection, Notre Dame University, TS, Sophomore
     Literary Festival, 28 March 1971, RMD001 Archives, Notre Dame 1971.
376 *no academic interest*: Lecture on RC, October 1984, TS archive, no title, and HR
     122.3. Notre Dame Sophomore Literary Festival lecture, 28 March 1971.
376 *a brazen pragmatist*: *Newsweek* interview, 16 January 1984. TS and PW, interview
     Ronald Hayman, *Sunday Times*, 2 March 1980, quoted in Philip Gaskell, '*Night and*

Day: The Development of a Play Text', in Jerome McGann, ed., *Textual Criticism and Literary Interpretation*, University of Chicago Press, 1985, 175. Notre Dame Lecture, 28 March 1971. HR 129.7, Speech for PEN, 23 March 1985.

377 *Shakespearean productions*: 'The Event and the Text', Whidden Lecture, McMaster University, Hamilton, Ontario, 24 October 1988, in Delaney 1994, 199–211. 'Is It True What They Say About Shakespeare?'

377 *When we refer*: 'Is It True What They Say About Shakespeare?', lecture, 12 April 1980, *International Shakespeare Association*, Oxford University Press, 1982, 9.

377 *less admiring*: 'The Event and the Text', 1988; 'Is It True What They Say About Shakespeare?'.

378 my *reluctance*: quoted in Gaskell, '*Night and Day*', in McGann, ed., *Textual Criticism*, 177.

378 *My plays*: quoted in Gaskell, '*Night and Day*', 177–8.

379 *When you write*: Whidden Lecture, Delaney 1994, 200.

379 *public commitments*: Delaney 1994, 199. HR 129.5, 129.6, 22 October–8 November 1981, San Diego. 'The Event and the Text' lectures: International Conference on the Fantastic, Boca Raton, Florida, March 1982; Shaw Society lecture, 19 May 1983; Kenyon College, 19 May 1984; Harvard, 13 January 1987; Whidden Lecture, McMaster University, 24 October 1988. Clark Lectures, 1980. 'Reflections on Ernest Hemingway', Kennedy Library, Boston, 21 May 1982. TSL, 28 January 1980.

379 *Wherever he went*: HR, 129.6, Robert Patten to TS, 25 November 1982. Selma Warner, tour schedule, 1982; to TS, 10 November 1982. TS, JE II, 30 October 1982.

380 *honorary degrees*: TSL, nd [December 1979]. HR 142.4, Appointment Diary, 1 December 1984.

380 *vice-president of PEN*: HR 129.7, PEN Dawson-Scott Memorial Lecture, 23 March 1985. HR 130.5, 14 December 1987, Introduction for PEN book of cartoons, published 1988.

380 *a fish to water*: TS, JE I, 30 September 1979.

380 *speaking out*: TS, 'Prague's Wall of Silence', *The Times*, 18 November 1981, also in *Index on Censorship*, 1981, and collected in *They Shoot Writers, Don't They?*, ed. George Theiner, Faber, 1984, alongside pieces by Nadine Gordimer, Milan Kundera, Mario Vargas Llosa, Salman Rushdie and others.

381 *public gestures*: 'Arrests in Prague', Letter to the Editor, *The Times*, 4 October 1986. 'Week's Good Cause', 11 October 1981, BBC Radio 4 appeal for Index on Censorship. For Beckett: Nadel, 355, 572, n. 3, citing NT archive; Emilie Morin, *Beckett's Political Imagination*, Cambridge University Press, 2017, 246; Rachael Jolley, '*Index*: 45 years fighting for writers', *Irish Times*, 13 September 2019.

382 *Everything altered*: TS, interview HL, 14 October 2017.

382 Das weite Land: TS, interviews HL, 16 June, 2 December 2016, 14 October 2017. Delaney 1994, 132.

383 *the title*: See Ritchie Robertson, Introduction, Arthur Schnitzler, *Round Dance and Other Plays*, trans. J. M. Davies, Oxford University Press, 2004.

384 *at least as comedy*: TSL, nd [25 January 1979].

384 *satisfying aphorism*: TS, interview HL, 16 June 2016. TSL, 27 April 1979. UC, Plays 4, 140.

384 *distinctive mark*: TSL, 27 April 1979. UC, Plays 4, 88, 91, 94.

385 *key exchange*: Delaney 1994, 132–3. UC, Plays 4, 144.

385 *a bit too busy*: TSL, nd [June 1979].

386 *piece of stagecraft*: TS, 'The Event and the Text', 1988, Delaney 1994, 203–4. TSL, nd [June 1979].

387 *Stoppard's version*: DH, interview HL, 26 February 2016.

388 *Melchior: What weather*: OTR, Plays 4, 353.

388 *Zangler: I feel*: OTR, Plays 4, 314.

389 *great arias*: FK, interview Hunter, 2004, in Hunter 2005, 249–63. FK, interview HL, 7 January 2015.

390 *unbounded admiration*: Michael Kitchen, interview HL, 3 October 2015.

390 *criticisms*: TSL, 22 February [1981].

391 *ticked off*: TSL, 23 February 1981. James Fenton, 'Mr Stoppard Goes to Town', *Sunday Times*, 4 October 1981. See W. E. Yates, 'Razzle-Dazzling Satire on the Move in Theatre', in *Anglo-German Theatrical Exchange*, ed. Rudolf Weiss, Brill, 2015. Irving Wardle, *The Times*, 23 September 1981. TS, interview HL, 16 June 2016.

392 *wonderfully silly*: John Tydeman, interview HL, 14 December 2016. TSL, nd [August 1982]. TS, JE II, 10 August 1982.

393 The Dog It Was: DOG, RADIO, 166, 182, 190, 165. Aired BBC Radio 3, 9 December 1982, filmed for Granada TV, 1 January 1989. Collected in TS, *Radio Plays*, BBC discs, British Library, 1996. Re-broadcast for TS's seventy-fifth birthday series, 2 July 2012.

393 'A.O.P.': HR 1.1, July 1981, July 1983, May 1984, notes for *A.O.P.* The agent was 'Buck' Lyda.

394–7 *documentary film*: StC, aired Channel 4, 31 May 1984: TSL, 1982–3. TS, JE II, 22 March 1982, 26 February, 24 June, 6 October 1983, 2 June 1984. 'Real Books, Real Authors', *Author*, Summer 1984. 'Lech's Troubles with Chuck, Bruce and Bob', *The Times*, 31 May 1984. Steven Paul Davies and Michael Caine, *Get Carter and Beyond: the Cinema of Mike Hodges*, Batsford, 2002. 'Tom Stoppard TV Film on Shelf after Two Years', *New York Times*, 31 December 1985. StC, 1984, Introduction, 9–18. StC, 1982: typescript of StC dated April 1982. TS, interview HL, 18 March 2015, 16 June 2016, 14 October 2017.

394 *careful notes*: HR, 28.9, notes for StC, 15 September 1983.

395 Rashomon-*style*: TSL, nd [late 1983]. StC, 1984, Introduction, 9–18.

395 *compromise*: HR 36.6, TS to FP, 15 May 1984, FP to TS, 17 May 1984.

397 *essential premise*: StC, 1984, 29.

397 *became deeply involved*: HR 142.1, Appointment Diary, 25 January 1983. TS, 'Freedom: But Thousands Are Still Captive', *Daily Mail*, 12 February 1986. HR 142.1, Appointment Diary, 17 July 1986, Henry Moore award. TS to PPR, 20 January 1986, Brotherton. Manny Azenberg, interview HL, 19 November 2014. Mark Hurst, 'Slowing Down the Going-away Process', *Contemporary British History*, 2016.

399 *declined*: Hurst, 'Slowing Down', quoting Margaret Thatcher to TS, 22 January 1986; HR 135.5, Isaiah Berlin to TS, 27 January 1986, with thanks to Henry Hardy.

399 *did not go down well*: TS, interview Mary Riddell, *New Statesman*, 8 July 2002. TS, interview HL, 28 June 2014. TSL, nd [February 1980].

399 *spelt out his arguments*: TSL, nd [February 1986].

19: *The Real Thing*

402 *To speak of*: UC, Plays 4, 114.

402 *Max, an architect*: Delaney 1994, 170, Baker 2013, 16. RT, Faber 1988, 15, 17, 21, 65, 80. All RT quotes from this edition.

405 *the love play*: Gussow 62, Delaney 1994, Hunter 2005, 73. TS, interview HL, 14
     October 2017.
405 *To write a play*: TSL, 10 February 1982, Baker 2013, 9.
405 *It's going to look*: TS, interview HL, 10 September 2014; TSL, 10 February 1982.
406 *All those people*: RT, 20.
406 *said of Henry*: Gussow, 41, Delaney 1994, 7 (1982), 259 (1992), 229 (1989), Hunter
     2005, 258 (1999).
406 *But there's time*: TSL, 6 October 1982.
406 *musical tastes*: Tim Rice, interview HL, 23 July 2015. Baker 2013, 10.
407 *Here we are*: Gussow, 72.
407 *echoes*: TS told Mark Lawson that he had at one point thought of writing a version of
     Othello. Mark Lawson, interview HL, 26 September 2014.
408 *war is profits*: RT, 53.
408 *lunching*: TSL, nd [9 July 1982].
408 *You're jealous*: RT, 51.
408 *Shut up and listen*: RT, 52.
409 *gestating*: RT, 33, JE I, 25 August 1976, 9 February 1977, Gussow, 40. Nadel identifies
     Auden's source as Ortega y Gasset. Nadel, 323, 569, n. 4.
410 *pretty good*: TS, interview HL, 28 June 2014.
410 *I don't know how*: RT, 40. Gussow, 62.
410 *impetuous and risky*: RT, 28, 78, 77.
411 *There are no commitments*: RT, 65–6.
411 *I've been careless*: RT, 75.
411 *Henry: It was about*: RT, 62.
411 *I love love*: RT, 44, 63.
412 *Happiness is*: RT, 61.
412 *Equilibrium is*: Gussow, 74.
413 *very reluctant*: MS, interview HL, 17 September 2014.
413 *Perhaps he should*: TS, interview HL, 10 September 2014.
413 *powerful after-effect*: UC, Plays 4, 94, HR 129.7, 23 March 1985, TS, notes for PEN
     Dawson-Scott Memorial lecture, 'Direct Experience', chaired by HP.
413 *similar face*: TSL, 11 October 1982.
414 *got upset*: TS, interviews HL, 28 June 2014, 18 March 2015.
414 *left a door open*: RT, 75. MS, interview HL, 8 January 2015.
414 *All concurred*: Delaney 1994, 167, John Russell Taylor, *Plays and Players*, October
     1984, Jenkins, 163, *Patriot Ledger*, Boston, 29 November 1983, Fleming 2001, 284,
     n. 9. *Washington Post*, 12 January 1984, *East Side Express*, 12 January 1984. Benedict
     Nightingale, *New York Times*, 8 December 1982. Codron 2010, 200. FK in Hunter
     2005, 251. DH, interview HL, 26 February 2016.
415 *shedding his protective skin*: TS, interview HL, 18 March 2015.
416 *expensive proposition*: MC to KE, 19 August 1981; TS to MC, 26 August 1981, JM
     archive.
416 *bound copy*: TS, interview HL, 10 October 2014.
416 *right opening cast*: TS, JE II, 9 January, 7 February 1982. TSL, 10 February, 24 March
     1982.
416 *playing Annie*: Simon Horsford, 'On Stage', interview with FK, *The Stage*, 11–17 April
     1985. FK, interview HL, 7 January 2015. Reviews of RT: Michael Billington, *Guardian*,

17 November 1982, Robert Cushman, *Observer*, 21 November 1982, Michael Coveney, *Financial Times*, 20 November 1982.

417   *ideal actor for Stoppard*: Hunter 2005, 252–3. FK, interview HL, 7 January 2015.

417   *problems arose*: TSL, 8 October 1982. Baker 2013, 11, MC, interview HL, 8 January 2015. Gussow, 43, Fleming 2001, 156, 165, 285, n. 18.

418   *constant revision*: FK, interview HL, 7 January 2015, Baker 2013, 11, Gussow, 64.

418   *Grove Press*: HR 124.5, Fred Jordan to George Weidenfeld, 13 January 1988. Grove Press merged with Atlantic Monthly Press to become Grove Atlantic in 1993.

418   *annoyed with Faber*: HR 36.6, TS to FP, 22 September 1982. HR 124.5, FP to TS, 1 February 1984. TS to FP, 8 January 1983. TSL, 27 September 1982.

419   *My name is HUGE*: TSL, 6 October 1982. John Boorman, interview HL, 2 November 2015.

419   *reviews were mixed*: TSL, 19, 24 November 1982. RT reviews, all November 1982: Irving Wardle, *The Times*, Milton Shulman, *Evening Standard*, Robert Cushman, *Observer*, Michael Coveney, *Financial Times*, Michael Billington, *Guardian*. Hunter 2005, 77. Roger Scruton, 'The Real Stoppard', *Encounter*, 60, No. 2, February 1983, 46. David Ian Rabey, *English Drama since 1940*, Routledge, 2003, 94. Billington, *Guardian*, 17 January 2015.

419   *cool, elegant set*: TSL, 27 September 1982. J. Scott Parkinson to Anthony Peek, Strand Theatre, 27 August 1982, Codron. Reviews of RT by Coveney, Shulman, Billington. Fleming 2001, 159. Frank Rich, *New York Times*, 23 June 1983.

420   *qualms*: TS, interview HL, 10 March 2015.

420   *big American opportunity*: MC, interview HL, 8 January 2015; MA, interview HL, 19 November 2014; TS, interview HL, 10 March 2015.

421   *delicate moment*: TS, interview HL, 16 November 2017, MC, interview HL, 8 January 2015, MA, interview HL, 19 November 2014.

421   *first challenge*: HR 39.9, MA, interview, *Irish Times*, 23 April 1987. MA, interview HL, 19 November 2014. Royalties: see Association of Theatrical Press Agents and Managers, http://atpamnmam.tripod.com/Royalty_Pools.PDF. During the 1980s, the system changed to a 'royalty pool' system, where the royalty participants would split the weekly operating profits with the investors.

423   *The cast*: Hunter 2005, 243, Fleming 2001, 160. Glenn Close, interview, *New York Daily News*, 1 January 1984. MA, interview HL, 19 November 2014.

423   *get him Henry*: Jeremy Irons, conversation with HL, 1 July 2017.

423   *Mike Nichols*: TS, interview HL, 16 November 2017. 'Mike Nichols's Life', *Vanity Fair*, 11 September 2015. JFK Center for Performing Arts, TS speech, December 2009.

424   *New York first act*: TSL, nd [early 1984].

424   *rehearsal process*: Diane Sawyer, interview HL, 6 January 2018. TSL, 8 September 1983. TS, interview HL, 16 November 2017. TS, JE II, 25 October 1983. Glenn Close, *Hollywood Reporter*, 24 November 2014. Another version of the 'two chairs' story, as told by film producer Michael Brandman, takes place on the set of MN's film *Working Girl*. Michael Brandman, interview HL, 25 January 2015.

425   *extraordinary*: SC, interview HL, 12 July 2017.

425   *loving friendship*: TS, interview HL, 18 March 2015. Mel Gussow, 'The Real Tom Stoppard', *New York Times*, 1 January 1984. Paley Center for Media, the Tony Awards, CBS TV, 3 June 1984. TS speech, JFK Center for Performing Arts, 7 December 2003. Diane Sawyer, interview HL, 6 January 2018.

426   *enormous success*: TS, JE II, 11 February 1984. Frank Rich, *New York Times*, 6 January 1984. HR 23.1, *New Yorker*, 23 January 1984. HR 39.1, Greg Gatenby to TS, 21 March 1985. Gordon Dickerson re. earnings, interview HL, 11 October 2014. André Bishop re. 'rock star', interview HL, 9 August 2015. Speeding fine report, March 1985, Codron.

426   *Will and Ed*: WS, interview HL, 10 December 2014; ES, interview HL, 8 December 2014; BS, interview HL, 6 February 2015; OS, interview HL, 18 August 2016. TS, JE II, 14 April 1984.

427   *This city*: *New York Times* Calendar, 29 January 1984.

427   *enthusiastic congratulations*: TS, JE II, 14 January 1984. HR 35.4, David Mamet to TS, 8 January 1983. Peter Shaffer to TS, 15 January 1982. Re. *Glengarry*, Michael Brandman, interview HL, 29 September 2015. Nadel, 337, on Bernstein.

427   *Heavens*: TSL, nd [January 1983], 27 January 1984, nd [July 1984].

427   *personal effect*: MA, interview HL, 19 November 2014. HR 35.4, Clive James to TS, nd. TS, interview HL, 18 March 2015. HR 35.3, Gustavus Remak Ramsay to TS, 11 January 1984. TS, interview HL, 14 October 2017. TS, interview Scott Rosenberg, *Boston Phoenix*, 13 December 1983.

428   *One can't complain*: TSL, 16 May 1985, nd [early 1984]. HR, 35.1, TS to Guy Dumur, 10 January 1985.

429   Desert Island Discs: TSL, nd [November 1984]. TS to IC, 10 February 1985, IC papers. *Desert Island Discs*, BBC Radio 4, 12 and 18 January 1985. TS to IC, 21 February 2010.

20: Crossing

431   *In the end*: D, Plays 4, 36.

431   *The meaning of life*: LD, 54. Quotes from LD, Havel, *Selected Plays*, Faber, 1994.

431   *work and family life*: TSL, nd [March 1984]. TS, JE II, 24 March 1984.

432   *sporting triumphs*: TSL, 16 May 1985; nd [January 1983]; 26 May 1983; 11 July 1984; 13 July 1984; nd [July 1984]. TS, JE II, 4 August 1985.

432   *this boy*: TSL, nd [1984].

432   *feeling for words*: ES, interview HL, 8 December 2014.

432   *parents' fame*: WS, interview HL, 10 December 2014.

433   *Barny was more interested*: BS, interview HL, 6 February 2015. Deke and Jill Arlon, interview HL, 5 October 2015. Jamie Arlon, Tim Arlon, interview HL, 12 October 2015.

433   *moral lesson*: ES, interview HL, 8 December 2014.

433   *good cook*: TSL, nd [September 1984].

433   *posh dos*: TSL, 26 March 1985; nd [1985]. HR 35.1, TS to Guy Dumur, nd [January 1985]. John Boorman, interview HL, 2 November 2015.

434   *Anna remembered*: Anna Cooke, interview HL, 15 September 2014.

435   *formidable timetables*: TSL, nd [March 1983], May 1983, 23 May 1983, 18 October 1984. TS, JE II, 21 April 1983, 2 March 1984, 4 August 1984.

435   *Her level of fame*: MC, interview HL, 8 January 2015; Angela Carter, *Love*, Picador, 1971, 1987, 115. John Heilpern, *John Osborne*, Chatto, 2006, 390. Valerie Grove, *A Voyage Round John Mortimer*, 2007, Penguin, 2008, 390. MS, interview HL, 2 July 2014.

436 *desolate and exhausted*: TS, JE II, 20 June 1982, 11 July 1982, 23/24 January 1983, 26 February 1983, 14 September 1983, 2 March, 9 March, 24 March 1984, 21 April 1983.

436 *signs of unease*: Deirdre Fernan, *Sunday Times*, 5 May 1991, quoting Glynn Boyd Harte: 'Miriam was always terribly competitive with Tom – she wanted to be as rich and successful as him.'

437 *'Xanadu'*: TS to PS, 5 March 1990, PS archive. 'This fucking house': Delaney 1994, 213 [1989]. Tim and Hélène Corrie, interview HL, 15 January 2015. Deke and Jill Arlon, interview HL, 5 October 2015. MJ, interview HL, 9 October 2014. OS, interview HL, 18 August 2016.

437 Brazil: TSL, nd [early 1984], [late 1985]. TS, JE II, 16/17 July 1983, 9 December 1984. Cambridge, 94. HR 3.7, *Brazil* correspondence. Charles Alverson and Terry Gilliam, *Brazil: The Evolution of the 54th Best Film Ever Made*, Orion Media, 2001. Jack Mathews, *The Battle of Brazil*, Crown Publishers, 1987. TS interview, *New York Times*, 23 August 1985, Biblio, K 147.

438 *opera*: David Lloyd Jones to HL, 24 September 2014. Robert Carsen, interview HL, 31 July 2015. *The Love for Three Oranges*, Richard Hickox, Australian Opera and Ballet Orchestra, translated by TS, Chandos Records, 2005. English Version by TS, Boosey & Hawkes, 1983; *The Love for Three Oranges: The Glyndebourne Version*, illustrations by Maurice Sendak, Bodley Head, 1984. Robert Carsen, *Opéra et Mise en Scène*, L'Avant-Scène Opéra, No. 269, 2012.

441 *plethora of running gags*: All RC quotes from Plays 4.

442 *In all my born days*: RC, 272.

442 *Strangely enough*: SiL, 23, 134–5.

442 *ought to have worked*: On AP music for RC, TS, Programme notes, *Penelope*, 2019. Billington 1987, 164; John Barber, *Telegraph*, 31 October 1984; Michael Coveney, *Financial Times*, 31 October 1984; Jack Tinker, *Daily Mail*, 31 October 1984. Milton Shulman, *Evening Standard*, 31 October 1984. TSL, nd [August 1984], 10 September, 18 October, 30 October 1984. TS, JE II, 29 October, 9 December 1984. TS to AS, 14 February 1985. Gordon Dickerson, interview HL, 11 October 2014, on Gish and casting of RC.

443 *wicked parody*: Peter Nichols, interview HL, 29 June 2015. *A Piece of My Mind*, Methuen, 1987, 42–3.

445 *Why can't I*: LD, 41, 52, 55.

445 *Havel thanked him*: HR 16.8, TS to KE, 13 December 1984. Žantovský, *Havel*, 246; VH, *Disturbing the Peace*, 65. HR 16.6, VH to TS, 19 March 1985. TS, note to LD, *Bristol Old Vic Magazine*, 29 March 1986.

446 *men are all the same*: D, Plays 4, 36, 49, 69. HR 36.5, TS to FP, 21 April 1986. TSL, 2 June 1986. Billington 1987, 166. Francis King, *Sunday Telegraph*, 1 June 1986. Frank Rich, *New York Times*, 4 June 1986. John Peter, *Sunday Times*, 1 June 1986.

447 *little of which I understand*: HR 37.2, TS to AS, 19 January 1985; TS, JE II, 9 December 1984.

447 *Revivals*: TSL, nd [March 1984]; TS, JE II, 2 March 1984. TSL, 16 May 1985; Russell Davies, 'Stoppard Directs', *Observer*, 8 September 1985. Codron, 186.

448 Jumpers *at the Aldwych*: TSL, nd [late August 1984]. Delaney 1990, 36, citing Billington. HR 37.2, TS to AS, 14 February 1985. TSL, 26 March 1985. Codron, 203.

448 *rough moments*: TSL, 16 March 1985. Sonia Friedman, interview HL, 20 October 2016.

449 *excitement in the papers*: 'Stoppard morality farce jumps back', Mandrake, *Sunday Telegraph*, 31 March 1985. *Daily Mail*, 10 June 1985. Codron, 203–5. HR 35.1, TS to Paul Eddington, 9 April 1985.

449 *in the end not*: TS, interview HL, 28 June 2014.

449 *next new play*: TSL, 4 December 1986, mentions working on H.

450 *he was a great playwright*: SS, interview HL, 5 January 2017.

451 *immediately butted heads*: EOTS, screenplay, 62, https://www.scripts.com/script/empire_of_the_sun_7624. TSL, 27 March 1986, SS, interview HL, 5 January 2017.

451 *never saw eye to eye*: HR 7.3, 8.3, 8.5, TS to SS and Robert Shapiro, 21 July 1986, TS to SS, 18 March, 23 March 1987. TSL, 26 March 1987. HR, 83.10, SS, Kathleen Kennedy and Frank Marshall to TS, 25 August 1987.

452 *like a jumbo jet*: J. G. Ballard, 'Look Back at Empire', *Guardian*, 4 March 2006. TSL, 26 March 1987.

453 *people confused it*: SS, interview HL, 5 January 2017. KK, interview HL, 11 October 2014.

453 *credits*: TS, interview HL, 28 June 2014, 16 June 2016. Kathleen Kennedy, interview HL, 11 October 2014.

453 *displaced person*: EOTS, Screenplay, 17. HR 8.5, TS to Robert Shapiro and SS, 21 July 1986. TSL, 16 May 1985.

21: Doubles

457 *We're all doubles*: H, 62. All H quotes (unless otherwise specified) from Faber, New York, 1994 edition.

457 *Luxor*: postcard from Egypt, May 1987, JM archive. MS, interview HL, 8 January 2015.

458 *old Welsh drunks*: TS to PS, 19 January 1987, PS archive.

459 *his London home*: 44 Chelsea Harbour sales details, 1994, JM archive. In 2012 the asking price was £3.5 million. TSL, nd [December 1987], [1988]. JM, ES, WS, interviews HL. TS, interview HL, 20 March 2018.

459 *separation from Miriam*: MS and TS divorce, decree nisi, 11 February 1992, JM archive.

460 *Felicity Kendal*: TS, interview HL, 18 March 2015. FK, interview HL, 7 January 2015. MS, interview HL, 8 January 2015. FK, *White Cargo*, 1998, Penguin, 1999. William Hickey, *Daily Express*, 28 February 1998.

463 *You tell me*: PR, 50.

463 *letter to his mother*: TSL, 4 December 1986; nd [1986]; nd [1987], 3 July 1987.

464 *For centuries*: TS, JE II, 9 December 1984. PR, 31.

465 *You can be interested*: OS, interview HL, 18 August 2016.

465 *He read*: PR, 31. Richard Feynman, *The Character of Physical Law*, MIT Press, 1965, 1967. For TS reading for H, and for his interest in and use of quantum physics, see H, programme, Aldwych Theatre, 1988; Demastes, 80–4; Hunter 2005, 80–2; Fleming 2001, 176–9; PR; Cambridge, Ch. 10.

465 *We know how electrons*: Feynman, *Character of Physical Law*, 128, 147. On Schrödinger's cat paradox, Jenkins, 199, n. 5, and P. G. W. Davies and J. R. Brown, eds, *The Ghost in the Atom*, Cambridge University Press, 1986, 28–31. On 'common sense rules', Paul Edwards, in Cambridge, 171.

466 *Feynman quotation*: Paul Edwards, in Cambridge, 171. H, programme, 1988.
466 *Uncertainty Principle*: Heisenberg summed up by Fleming 2001, 177. Feynman, 143.
466 *dual nature of light*: For the wave/particle concept, see Hunter 2005, 81. Also
       Delaney 1990, 131.
466 *the mystery*: PR, 31. 'Two hole experiment' summed up by Demastes, 80–1.
467 *Kerner: Every time*: H, 10.
467 *language of espionage*: PR, 30.
467 *double agents*: DOG, Plays 2, 181. H, 10.
468 *I like all that*: H, 1988, 42.
468 *The West is morally superior*: H, 63.
469 *jargon of espionage*: H, 39.
470 *Kerner: The particle world*: H, 40.
470 *Ma'am*: H, 28.
470 *Wates: She calls me*: H, 23.
471 *Who needed God*: H, 41.
472 *variously circumnavigable*: H, 2.
472 *Kerner, originally a citizen*: H, 38.
472 *witty representation*: Patricia Lewis, 'A Quantum Leap in Theatre', *New Scientist*, 7
       April 1988.
472 *as in other plays*: Delaney 1994, 227 (1989). H, 41.
472 *Understanding the plot*: H, 40. PR, 33.
474 *became an irritant*: Fleming 2001, 176. HR 13.6, Hapgood Crib. Fleming 2001, 287,
       n. 8.
474 *the proposition*: Delaney 1994, 194, 216. Delaney 1990, 138, citing BBC TV Review, 13
       March 1988. Gussow, 79.
474 *We all are*: VII, *Garden Party*, 50.
475 *Kerner: We're all doubles*: H, 62.
475 *Once when he was*: H, 16, 63.
476 *a book about himself*: Nadel called his biography of TS *Double Act*. Methuen, 2002.
476 *admitted to other kinds*: TS to Michael Billington, 1988, in Delaney 1994, 195.
       Gussow, 108, 94.
476 *Getting Hapgood ready*: PR, 50.
476 *problems*: Hunter 2005, 188, 255. FK, interview HL, 7 January 2015.
477 *last straw for Hawthorne*: HR 13.6, TS to Nigel Hawthorne and Roger Rees, 1 August
       1988. Nigel Hawthorne to TS, 1 August 1988.
478 *Wood's production*: Delaney 1990, 125, 143, citing William A. Henry, *Time*, 18 July
       1988.
478 *the play's reception*: Irving Wardle, *The Times*, 8 March 1988. Michael Billington,
       Guardian, 8 March 1988, 28 March 1988, in Delaney 1994, 194. Ronald Hayman,
       Kaleidoscope, March 1988. Ros Asquith, *City Limits*, March 1988. MA, interview HL,
       19 November 2014.
479 *A rumour circulated*: Michael Billington, *Guardian*, 28 March 1988, in Delaney
       1994, 194. Mark Lawson, interview HL, 26 September 2014. MA, interview HL, 19
       November 2014.
479 *I'm not trying*: Demastes, 31. Delaney 1994, 222–3 (1989).
480 *American transfer*: Delaney 1994, 224. TS, interview HL, 29 June 2016. HR 12.7,
       H revision, Act One, Scene Two.

480 *in New York*: J O'B, interview HL, 17 November 2014. MA, interview HL, 19
      November 2014. André Bishop, interview HL, 9 August 2015. *The New Theatre
      Review*, Lincoln Center, Fall 1994. Bob Crowley, interview HL, 10 May 2018.
481 *It's not the machinations*: J O'B to TS, 23 July 1993, JM archive.
482 *new-fashioned melodrama*: Gussow, 106.
482 *closely involved*: TS, interview HL, 16 November 2015. TSL, nd [summer 1995], nd
      [January 1996].
483 *one week in 1989*: *The New Theater Review*, Lincoln Center, Fall 1994, 4. Cambridge,
      175, 183, n. 4. H, 1988, 117, 1994, 63.

22: Script Doctor

484 *What country*: SiL, 155. *Twelfth Night*, Act One, Scene Two.
484 *inside any stage play*: TS and Marc Norman, interview Susan Bullington Katz,
      Written By magazine, March 1999.
484–8 *On the film of* R&G: TS, 'To Film or Not to Film', *Premiere*, 2 July 1990. Mervyn
      Rothstein, 'A One-Act Dialogue Starring Tom Stoppard', *New York Times*, 26
      November 1989. George Perry, 'The Man Who Was King', profile of Sean Connery,
      The Times, Saturday Review, 6 October 1990. TS, 'Connery Dispute', *The Times*,
      13 October 1990, 15. Christopher Bray, *Sean Connery: A Biography*, Faber, 2010.
      Delaney 1994, 236 (on casting), 245 (on not defending the play). Cambridge, 90
      (Nadel, on MGM). Michael Brandman, interview HL, 25 January, 28 September
      2015. TSL, 8 December 1987; nd, 6–8 July [1989], nd [September 1989]. TS,
      interviews HL, 15–16 November 2015, 20 March 2018. MA, interview HL, 19
      November 2014. John Boorman, interview HL, 2 November 2015. Both TS and
      Brandman, long after the event, say that filming had begun with Connery in early
      1989; but TS's letter to *The Times* in 1990 makes clear that Connery left the film just
      before filming started.
488 *The film feels theatrical*: Kathleen Kennedy, interview HL, 11 October 2014. Baker
      2013, 134. TS, interview Michael Brandman for Blu-Ray reissue of R&G, 29
      September 2015. Lyn Gardner, 'The Heart in the Closet', *Guardian Weekend*, 16
      January 1999. TS, interview HL, 16–17 November 2015. TS, 'To Film or Not to Film',
      Premiere, 2 July 1990.
490 *Pinter sent*: HR 130.9, HP to TS, 18 August [1990].
490 *Venice Biennale*: Michael Brandman to HL, 15 February 2015; TS, interview Michael
      Brandman, 29 September 2015.
490 *Azenberg put it grimly*: MA, interview HL, 19 November 2014.
491 *different moral universe*: Tim Corrie to HL, 1 June 2015. TS, interview HL, 20 March
      2018. TSL, 17 June 1991, nd [1992]. TS, interview Michael Brandman, 29 September
      2015.
491 *its own rules*: TS, interview Michael Brandman, 29 September 2015. Delaney 1994,
      238, 197, 236. Demastes, 21.
491 *I enjoy doing films*: TS, interview, *New York Times*, 26 November 1989. TS, interview
      HL, 2 December 2016. Bob Bookman, interview HL, 16 September 2014. Rose Cobbe
      and St John Donald, United Agents, interview HL, 8 April 2014.
492 *According to Kennedy*: Kathleen Kennedy, interview HL, 11 October 2014. TS,
      interview HL, 16–17 November 2015.

492 *be authentic*: Kathleen Kennedy, interview HL, 11 September 2014. TS, interview HL, 16–17 November 2015. SS, interview HL, 5 January 2017.

493 *(a) soapy*: HR 69.20, TS to SS, 1989, SS to TS, 21 June 1990.

493 Indiana Jones: HR 94.1, TS to SS, 1988. HR 94.4, Kathleen Kennedy to KE, 17 October 1989. www.dailyscript.com/scripts/indiana-jones-and-the-last-crusade.pdf.

494 *uncredited words*: Kathleen Kennedy, interview HL, 11 September 2014. TSL, 19 January 1994.

495 *range of Universal films*: HR 124.1, TS to *Independent*, 13 April 1999. Glenn Close, introducing TS for PEN/Allen award, 12 May 2015.

495 *the most irritating note*: HR 66.6, TS to Casey Silver, 5 May 1991, 1 September 1991. HR 79.5, notes to Casey Silver on *Charlie*, 11 December [1991].

496 *Boring line*: TS, notes on *Robin Hood* to Ridley Scott [2010], JM archive.

496 *What you've got here*: HR 79.5, TS to Casey Silver, 11 December [1991].

496 *there are at least three*: HR 66.6, TS to Casey Silver, 23 April [1991].

496 *liked a particular director*: TS, interview HL, 2 December 2016.

496 Billy Bathgate: HR 73.13, TS to Jeffrey Katzenberg, 7 March 1990. TS to KE, 17 July 1991. TSL, 17 June 1991.

498 *Galahad of the mean streets*: TS, *Poodle Springs* screenplay (unpublished), typescript, August 1991.

498 *You swore to me*: John Le Carré, *The Russia House*, Hodder & Stoughton, 1989. TS, screenplay, unpublished.

499 *comically awkward meeting*: David Cornwell [John Le Carré], interview HL, 24 February 2017; anecdote also appears in Adam Sisman, *John Le Carré: The Biography*, Bloomsbury, 2015, 471.

499 *not 'cut out'*: HR 117.3, TS to KE, 3 July 1989. TS to FP, 6 September 1989. HR 127.8, TS to FP. David Cornwell, interview HL, 24 February 2017.

500 *message of good will*: HR 117.3, TS, 31 October 1991.

500 *lifelong friendship*: TS, interview HL, 2 December 2016. David Cornwell, interview HL, 24 February 2017. David Cornwell to TS, 7 October 2010, JM archive.

502 *Jagger's global fame*: TS, interviews HL, June 2014, 16 June 2016.

502 *thought of working together*: HR 129.4, TS to Mick Jagger, 5 December 1983, 12 December 1983, 18, 29 June 1984, 6 November 1990.

502 *first discussion*: TSL, nd [November 1995]. Robert Harris, 'Enigma in the Making', *Sunday Times*, 30 September 2001.

503 *Bletchley, codes, convoys*: TSL, 3, 22 February 1996. Harris, 'Enigma in the Making'.

503 *Of course Paramount pay*: TSL, 3, 14 February 1996. HR 159.5, TS letter re. Poles, 29 September 2001. HR 159.7, TS contribution to Bletchley, 28 November 2001. TS, 'No Reason for Polish Concern over Film', letter, *Daily Telegraph*, 4 October 2001. Harris, 'Enigma in the Making'. TS to Prince Charles, 4 October 2001, JM archive.

504 *musicals*: Gussow, 88–9. TSL, nd [March 1994].

505 *decided to do* Cats: HR 59.2, Screenplay of *Cats*, third draft, August 1994. TS to SS, 19 August 1994. TSL, 10 January 1994, April 1994. TS, interview HL, 14 August 2017. Gussow, 88.

506 *The greatest magicians*: Andrew Lloyd Webber, Trevor Nunn and Richard Stilgoe, *Cats: The Book of the Musical*, Really Useful Productions, 1983.

506 Hopeful Monsters: Nicholas Mosley, *Hopeful Monsters*, 1990, Eland, 2009, 62, 449.

507 *Stoppard took notes*: HR 43.8, TS notes on *Hopeful Monsters*, 18 May 1993.

507 *held these ideas*: HR, 43.8–9, 44.2, 61.3–7, notes on *Hopeful Monsters*. TS, interview HL, 16–17 November 2015. Appointment Diary 1995, 12–14 August 1995, JM archive. TSL, nd [summer 1993], 10 January 1994.

507 Shakespeare in Love: John Madden, interview HL, 7 November 2014; TS, interviews HL, 28–29 June 2014, 14 October 2017, 20 March 2018. TS to HL, 2 May 2018.

508 *first remarks*: TSL, nd [July 1992].

508 *not the ampersand team*: TS and Marc Norman, interview Susan Bullington Katz, *Written By*, March 1999.

508 *made up lots of jokes*: HR 117.10, Antony Jones, UA, to TS, 25 September 1998.

508 *nice to be out*: TSL, nd [October 1992].

509 *it had been altered*: For full accounts of the changes in the screenplay of SiL between 1992 and 1996, see Nadel, 416–22, and James Shapiro, *Shakespeare in a Divided America*, Faber, 2020, 201–25.

509 *This strand was abandoned*: See Shapiro, *Shakespeare*, 208, on the changes from Norman's version.

509 *we cannot tell*: SiL, 141.

510 *parallels*: Caryl Brahms and S. J. Simon, *No Bed for Bacon*, 1941, Black Swan, 1999, intro. Ned Sherrin. 'Bard's Beginnings', *Los Angeles Times*, 10 January 1999. John Mortimer, *Will Shakespeare*, BBC TV, 1978, published as *Will Shakespeare: An Entertainment*, Hodder & Stoughton, 1977.

510 *play fast and loose*: HR 117.10, David Parfitt, producer, notes on SiL. For TS and Shakespeare, see Jill Levinson, 'Stoppard's Shakespeare' in Cambridge, 154–68.

511 *Stoppard jokingly*: Ira Nadel, *The Times*, 11 June 2002. SiL, Universal video, TS interview, extra materials. HR 117.15, TS, *Sunday Times*, 2 December 1998.

511 *early pages*: HR 51.6, ms of SiL, on rear of typescript, A, 1992.

512 *Can a play show us*: SiL, 95.

512 *Theatre jokes*: SiL, 67, 106, 23.

513 *Stoppardian morsel*: John Madden, interview HL, 7 November 2014; SiL, Universal video, Sandy Powell interview, extra materials.

513 *How is this to end*: SiL, 150.

514 *against Weinstein*: Weinstein was found guilty in a New York City court of sexual assaults, including rape, on 24 February 2020.

514 *their revenge*: SiL, Universal video, extra materials.

514 *first ending they shot*: HR 51.2, 164.9, ms of SiL.

23: Changing States

516 *All portraits*: ITNS, 72.

516 *was – life*: TS, interview HL, 20 March 2018.

517 *Havel became president*: Tim Luscombe, interview HL, 22 July 2016. HR 144.4, Appointment Diary, 21 March 1990. HR 124.4, VH to TS, 10 October 1989. HR 122.10, TSL, 10 May 1991, describing trip to Prague. HR 144.6, Appointment Diary, 3–5 May 1991, visit to Prague.

518 *Their separation*: TS, MS, BS, ES, OS, PS, WS, interviews HL.

518 *stories*: *Daily Express*, 17 November 1990. *Daily Mail*, 16 November 1990. Appointment Diary, September 1990.

519 *duly reported*: *Daily Express*, 22 November 1990. *Daily Mail*, 21 November 1990.

519 *at pains to explain*: Richard Stoppard to TS, 22 February 1991, JM archive. TSL, nd [March 1991].

520 *Although he will leave*: *Daily Mail*, 21 December 1990.

520 *No, Miriam said*: Anna Cooke, interview HL, 15 September 2014.

520 *It's over*: *Daily Express*, 26 December 1990.

520 *house in Chelsea*: TS to Sandra Lofts, property sales, 30 April 1991, JM archive.

520 *The woman who told us*: Corinna Honan, 'FeMail Interview', *Daily Mail*, 30 April 1993.

521 *For Tom and Miriam*: *Sunday Times*, 5 May 1991.

521 *letters of sympathy*: Derek Marlowe to TS, 31 December 1990, JM archive. IC to TS, July 1991, IC papers. David and Jane Cornwell to TS, 5 December 1991. HR 130.9, AF to TS, 24 November 1990. AF, interview HL, 23 September 2014.

521 *he told his mother*: TSL, nd [27 February 1991].

522 *she did grieve*: MS, interview HL, 8 January 2015.

522 *divorce*: Decree nisi, 11 February 1992, JM archive.

522 *some stranger having it*: TSL, nd [June 1992].

522 *Barny would remember*: BS, interview HL, 6 February 2015.

523 *changes and preoccupations*: TSL, 23 May 1990, nd [spring 1991]. Diane Ruskell, interview HL, 13 June 2016; PS, interview HL, 31 April 2015.

524 *spoke up*: TS, 'What Is to Be Done?' Lecture in support of Rushdie, Stationers' Hall, 14 February 1992, broadcast on *Arena*, BBC2, with Günter Grass, Martin Amis and Salman Rushdie. Published in the *Observer*, 16 February 1992, as 'Let Iran Make Amends on Rushdie', and in *The Rushdie Letters*, ed. Steve MacDonogh, University of Nebraska Press, 1993. Ronald Dworkin in 'A New Map of Censorship', *Index on Censorship*, May 1994. TS to Ronald Dworkin, 5 May 1994, TS archive.

525 *board of the National*: TS, interview HL, 14 October 2017. NT, RE to TS, 16 October 1989. For TS at the National Theatre, see Daniel Rosenthal, ed., *Dramatic Exchanges: The Lives and Letters of the National Theatre*, Profile Books, 2018. RE, Diaries, 11 October 1989; RE, interview HL, 29 January 2018.

525 *difficult issues*: Patrick Dillon, *Concrete Reality: Denys Lasdun and the National Theatre*, National Theatre Publishing, 2015, 82. Rosenthal, ed., *Dramatic Exchanges*, 260–1, 271–2, 285–7. NT, Board Minutes, 23 March 1996. TS, interview HL, 17–18 June 2019.

526 *operational reasons*: NT, Board Minutes, 29 January 1996.

526 *small details*: NT, Board Minutes, 24 June 1991, 27 January 1992, 30 November 1992, 16 December 1993, 24 March 2000.

526 *voice can be heard*: NT, Board Minutes, 20 December 1990, 12 September 1994, 24 May 1993.

527 *dread of biography*: HR 37.2, TS to AS, nd [1993]. HR 122.11, 'A Talk with Tom Stoppard', John Fleming, *Theatre Insight*, Issue 10, Vol. 5, 1 December 1993, 19–27. From Fleming interview with TS, 14 October 1993.

528 *I feed off myself*: Demastes, 154, n. 8. TS, interview Elizabeth Broderson, ACT programme for INK, 20 December 1998.

528 *increasing anxiety*: TSL, nd [December 1992]. Michael Hordern with Patricia England, *A World Elsewhere*, O'Mara Books, 1993. TSL, nd [summer 1993]. Mark Lawson, interview, *Independent*, 10 April 1993.

529 *touches of autobiography*: TS, Introduction, *Not in the Script*, Bristol Old Vic, 1992. Mark Everett to TS, 13 September 1991, TS archive.

529 *in the shop near the Capitol*: In Antonia Fraser, ed., *The Pleasure of Reading*, Bloomsbury, 1992, reprinted 2015, 160–6.

529 *back to India*: HR, OS 8, photo of TS on train, *Mail on Sunday*, 4 May 1991. 'Going Back', *Independent Magazine*, 23 March 1991, *Mail on Sunday*, 4 May 1991. India trip itinerary, JM archive. TSL, postcards from India, nd [January 1991].

531 *Thirty years on*: HL, visit to Mount Hermon, 24 October 2019.

532 *a poet and a painter*: Gussow, 120. HR, 61.7, has many pages of revisions of Flora's poems.

532 Rasa *is juice*: ITNS, 1991, 23.

533 *God of Playwrights*: TS, interview HL, 10 September 2014.

533 *using what I've got*: Gussow, 120.

533 *A woman is writing*: HR 61.7, ITNS notes, 1988/1989.

534 *Flora Crewe*: ITNS, 32, 73, 76.

535 *Flora: While having tiffin*: ITNS, 11.

536 *'theories' become 'opinions'*: ITNS, 35, INK, 1995, 36.

536 *talking about colonialism*: ITNS, 46, 85.

536 *Flora is impatient*: ITNS, 37, 44.

536 *gets an education*: ITNS, 46, 65.

537 *It makes me so cross*: ITNS, 19.

537 *not a particularly* Indian *painter*: ITNS, 3.

538 *We were up to date*: ITNS, 10.

538 *Orchards of apricot*: ITNS, 81.

538 *soppy old thing*: Delaney 1994, 252.

538 *the commentator*: Gussow, 121.

539 *telling you things*: ITNS, 19.

539 *This is why God made*: INK, 4, 3, 50.

539 *worst possible excuse*: INK, 5, 9.

539 *stopped clock*: ITNS, 72.

540 *I'm the only person*: Gussow, 125.

540 *Otherwise, it's hanging over*: Gussow, 125.

540 *criticisms*: Gussow 102, 124. Fleming 2001, 208, 219, 294–5. Delaney 1994, 240–2. Antoinette Burton, *Empire in Question*, Duke University Press, 2011, 250–1.

541 *a little jewel*: Hunter 2005, 256–7.

541 *impeccably tactful*: John Tydeman, interview HL, 14 December 2016, and in Hunter 2005, 191–6. TS, interview HL, 10 September 2014.

541 *It upset him*: TS, interview HL, 10 September 2014. HR 127.8, typescript of Introduction to RADIO, 1994.

541 *It won't do*: TS to Dan Crawford, 15 June 1992, JM archive.

542 *fifty-fifth birthday*: TSL, 22 August 1992. TS, interview HL, 15–16 November 2015. OS, interview HL, 18 August 2016.

542 *holy inspiration*: Gussow, 129.

542 *to be a poet*: Hunter 2005, 189.

543 *He must have – altered*: INK, 79.

543 *having to give explanations*: INK, 73. Gussow, 123, 137.

543 *Anish: Oh yes*: INK, 18.

544 *Forgive my ungilding*: TS to Aldwych Stage Door, 30 May 1995, Codron archive.

544 *came to love the production*: Codron, 206–7; Gussow, 126, 141.

544 *One critic*: Peter Kemp, 'Flinging Mangoes at the Resident's Daimler', *Guardian*, 17 March 1995.

544 *You don't have to think*: Matt Wolf, *Variety*, 12 March 1995. Vince Canby, *New York Times*, 10 April 1995.

544 *one of the happiest experiences*: Codron, 207. Kendal in Hunter 2005, 257.

24: *Arcadia*

545 *Thomasina: Yes*: A, 128, 75, 94. All A quotations, unless otherwise noted, are from the Faber 1993 edition, 'reprinted with corrections'. That edition is used in Plays 5.

545 *Time had always been*: IYGIBF, 1966, Plays 2, 36. HR 231.11, 'R&G Meet King Lear'.

546 *time is the subject*: A, 53. HR 42.1, holograph notes for A.

547 *told Bobby*: TSL, nd [1991].

547 *Arcadia came out*: TS, interview Elizabeth Angel-Perez, Sorbonne, 14 October 2011. TS, interview HL, 20 July 2018.

547 *new systems of thought*: HR 66.7, TS, 30 April 1994 to *Ark*. Typescript of 'Spy Stuff as a Metaphor for the World of Physics', *New York Times*, 27 November 1994; 'Playing with Science', *Engineering and Science*, Caltech, Vol. 58, No. 1, Fall 1994, 3–13.

548 *chaos theory*: Fleming 2008, 48–9. Gussow, 84, 306.

548 *global nature of systems*: James Gleick, *Chaos: Making a New Science*, Heinemann 1988, Vintage 1998 (hereafter 'Gleick'), 5.

548 *Where chaos begins*: Gleick, 5, 3. Fleming 2008, 49. Leonard Smith, *Chaos: A Very Short Introduction*, Oxford University Press, 2007 (hereafter '*Chaos* VSI'), 3.

549 *If you could stop*: A, 9.

549 *the irregular side*: Gleick 3, 41, 7.

549 *The modern study of chaos*: Gleick, 8, 22–3, 306, 42. Fleming 2018, 49.

549 *sensitive dependence*: Fleming 2008, 49; *Chaos* VSI, 16

549 *butterfly effect*: Gleick 8, 67. Fleming 2008, 49. *Chaos* VSI, 6.

550 *nursery rhyme*: *Chaos* VSI, 2.

550 *The unpredictable*: A, 64.

550 *Mandelbrot*: Gleick, 56, 86.

550 *within those random states*. Fleming 2008, 50.

551 *Ada Lovelace*: Fleming 2008, 60. Cambridge, 176. TS on May and Ada, ACT, *Arcadia* programme, 2013, 24.

551 *functional iteration*: Gleick, 61, 166.

551 *She's feeding the solution back*: A, 60, 61.

551 *You do not have to be Einstein*: TS, interview Elizabeth Angel-Perez, Sorbonne, 14 October 2011. TS, interview HL, 20 July 2018.

552 *fractal geometry*: Gleick, 98, 17, 47, 104, 78.

552 *Self-similarity*: Gleick, 103.

552 *a method whereby*: A, 64.

553 *what fascinated him*: TS, interview Robert Osserman, 19 February 1999, typescript, 12 February 2002, 8, 13, JM archive.

553 *entropy explained*: James Gleick, *Time Travel: A History*, Fourth Estate, 2017, 118.

553 *she has become wiser*: A, 8, 19, 128.

553 *foreseen the law of entropy*: Fleming 2008, 50–1. Gleick, 257, 308–11.

554 *noise*: *Chaos* VSI, 166, 157.

554 *bifurcation*: Fleming 2008, 52.

555 *a joke to make you all mad*: A, 10.

555 *Andrew Wiles*: Simon Singh, *Fermat's Last Theorem*, Harper Perennial, 2011.

555 *pure metaphor*: TS, 'Playing with Science', *Engineering and Science*, Caltech, Fall 1994.

556 *what his father was doing*: ES, interview HL, 8 December 2014.

556 *a big* talkfest: TS, interview HL, 14 October 2017.

556 *The new mathematics*: Gleick, 117.

557 *improvements*: A, 19, 15. Mark Girouard, *Life in the English Country House*, Yale University Press, 1978, 8, 210. TS clearly read Girouard and Christopher Hussey, *The Picturesque*, 1927.

557 *the picturesque*: J. R. Watson, *English Poetry of the Romantic Period*, Longman, 1985, 46. Martin Price, 'The Picturesque Moment', in F. H. Hilles and Harold Bloom, eds, *From Sensibility to Romanticism*, Oxford University Press, 1965, 260. A, 25.

557 *Lady Croom is appalled*: A, 16, 18, 39. A, first edition, 28.

558 *What you painted*: A, 117.

559 *what is carnal embrace*: A, 4, 7.

559 *every sensitive young woman*: Girouard, *English Country House*, 215.

559 *hare's breadth*: A, 79.

560 *Thomasina*: A, 1, 5, 14, 85–6.

560 *Paper*: A 50, 66.

561 *the set*: A 1, 15. Nicholas Grene, *Home on the Stage*, Cambridge University Press, 2014, 174, 170.

561 *As Stoppard once explained*: TS to 'Val', 28 February 2003, JM archive.

561 *My father never*: A, 18.

562 *witty*: A, 37, 11.

562 *language of the present*: A, 63. Byatt to Nadel, 13 June 2000, in Nadel, 430, 578, n. 15.

563 *all because of sex*: A, 73, 29, 44, 56, 74, 88.

563 *the whole Romantic sham*: A, 27, 66.

564 *It will make me mad*: A, 92.

564 *Time present*: T. S. Eliot, 'Burnt Norton', *Four Quartets*.

565 *extreme statement*: A, 61–2, 74.

565 *the creative moment*: TS, 'Playing with Science'.

565 *his 'Arcadia'*: TS, interview HL, June 2014.

565 *You have to include*: TS, interview Elizabeth Angel-Perez, 14 October 2011.

566 *quite forgotten*: TS, interview Robert Osserman, 19 February 1999, typescript, 12 February 2002, 16, JM archive. TS misremembers Waugh referring to a first edition of one of his own novels. Evelyn Waugh, *A Little Learning*, 1964, Penguin, 1990, 3.

566 *E'en now*: Byron, *English Bards and Scotch Reviewers*, 1809, lines 955–9, *Byron: Poetical Works*, Oxford University Press, 1970, 125.

566 *fragmentary survival*: TS, interview HL, 18 March 2015. TS, 'Gallus', 26 January 2001, for 'Friends of Classics', JM archive. Gussow, 108.

567 *I had a dream*: Byron, *Poetical Works*, 95–6. See Kirsten Shepherd-Barr, *Science on Stage*, Princeton University Press, 2006, 142, in an excellent account of science in A, on how Byron's poem 'complements Thomasina's prescient use of mathematics'.

568 *We shed*: A, 38.

568 *It matters*: Fleming 2008, 59.

569 *protective*: TSL, nd [April 1992]. Jamie Arlon, interview HL, 12 October 2015.

569 *not asked to direct*: PW in Hunter 2005, 189. TSL, nd [June 1992]. TS, interviews HL,
     16–17 November 2015, 18 March 2015, 14 October 2017. RE, Diary, 17 June, 1 July 1992;
     RE, interview HL, 29 January 2018. Codron, TS to MC, nd [July 1992]. TN, interview
     HL, 2 October 2017. FK, interview HL, 7 January 2015. HR 131.1, TN to TS, 22 June
     1992. See Rosenthal, ed., *Dramatic Exchanges*, 252. TN, email to HL, 4 February
     2020.

570 *Germaine Greer*: TN, interview HL, 2 October 2017. Gussow, 138.

571 *So now the bump*: TSL, nd [February 1993].

571 *the new hot young actor*: TSL, nd. TN, interview HL, 2 October 2017, TS, interview
     HL, 18 March 2015.

571 *in rehearsal*: TN, interview HL, 2 October 2017. Hunter, 208. TS notes for A, revised
     in rehearsals, with thanks to Andrew Speed, National Theatre, who as ASM in
     1993 kept the pages TS threw away and showed them to me twenty years later at
     rehearsals of HP.

571 *put their private life aside*: FK, interview HL, 7 January 2015. RE, interview HL, 29
     January 2018.

572 *props*: Trish Montemuro, archive, and interview HL, 24 September 2014.

572 *rewrites*: HR 40.9, 69.24, A typescript and ms versions, TS notes, 9 June 1992.

573 *they had a hit*: FK, interview HL, 7 January 2015.

573 *Eyre celebrated too*: Hunter, 207. RE, Diary, 14 April 1993.

573 *reviews*: Irving Wardle, 'Best Plays of the Year', *Independent on Sunday*, 19 December
     1993. John Gross, *Sunday Telegraph*, 18 April 1993. Charles Spencer, *Daily Telegraph*,
     14 April 1993. Michael Coveney, *Observer*, 18 April 1993. Sheridan Morley, *Spectator*,
     24 April 1993. Michael Billington, *Guardian*, 14 April 1993. Roger Highfield, *Daily
     Telegraph*, 15 April 1993. John Peter, *Sunday Times*, 18 April 1993. Jack Tinker, *Daily
     Mail*, 14 April 1993. Paul Taylor, *Independent*, 13 April 1993. Fleming 2008, 75–8.
     Mark Lawson, 'TomCat's New Tale', *Independent*, 10 April 1993, interview HL, 26
     September 2014. Lyn Gardner, 'The Heart in the Closet', *Guardian*, 16 January 1999.

574 *fell in love with it*: Roger Scruton, interview HL, 7 November 2014. David Cornwell
     to TS, 21 February 1993, JM archive. MS, interview HL, 2 July 2014.

574 *Theatre-goers could buy*: Delaney 1994, 265. Fleming 2008, 78, HR 127.8, FP to TS, 22
     July 1993. Biblio, 142. TS, interview HL, 20 March 2018.

575 *John Wood*: Mel Gussow, interview with John Wood, 'So Rude, So Complex, So Like
     Oneself', *New York Times*, 13 January 1998.

575 *running concurrently*: Codron, TN to MC, 7 June 1994, MC to TS, nd [December
     1994]. TSL, nd [February 1994], nd [May 1994], 7 November 1994.

576 *lost in translation*: Julian Barnes to TS, 18 October 1997. Daniel Kehlmann, interview
     HL, 29 February 2016. Hunter, 189, Fleming 2008, 83. Robert Carsen, interview HL,
     11 July 2015.

576 *plays overlapping*: Fleming 2008, 80. TSL, 15 March 1995.

576 *not an entirely happy*: André Bishop, interview HL, 9 August 2015. RE, Diary, 3
     March 1995.

577 *A.C.T.*: Carey Perloff, interviews HL, 5 October 2014, 29 November 2016. Carey
     Perloff, *Beautiful Chaos*, City Lights, 2015.

578 *revival of* Rosencrantz: Simon Russell Beale, interview HL, 14 February 2019.

578 *frivolous narrative*: HR, 48.8, *Merry Widow* typescript, January 1993.

579 *kept being asked*: Gordon Dickerson to TS, October 1993. Fleming 2008, 81. A,

BBC3, 26 December 1993. TS archive, A, screenplay, 2015–17. TS, interview HL, 16–17 November 2015.

579 *just fell out*: TS, interview HL, 10 September 2014.

25: Mother and Son

580 *All my life*: TALK 1999.

582 *Fiona was well aware*: FS, interview HL, 7 November 2014.

582 *Bobby felt estranged*: M[B]S to Sarka Gauglitz, 6 May 1993, 20 January 1993, 8 November 1994. Translated from the Czech by Kathryn Murphy. With thanks to Sarka Gauglitz.

582 *her life story*: M[B]S to Sarka Gauglitz, 20 January, 15 March 1993. Sarka Gauglitz, interview HL, 27 June 2018. TALK 1999.

583 *almost willful purblindness*: TALK 1999. TS, interview HL, 19 July 2018; PS, interview HL, 31 April 2015.

583 *PEN conference*: Nadel, 461, 581, n. 23, gives details, citing 'Not Only About Theatre', *Theatre Czech* 9 (1995).

583 *Waiting for him*: TALK 1999. Alexandr Rosa, interview HL, 20 September 2015. TSL, 29 November 1994.

585 *I was glad*: M[B]S to Sarka Gauglitz, 10 June 1995.

585 *Irma*: M[B]S to Sarka Gauglitz, 23 March 1996, 8 October 1993. TSL, 3 April [1996]. TS gives date of Irma's death in TALK 1999 as 1995, but M[B]S to Sarka Gauglitz, 23 March 1996, gives date of death as 6 March 1996.

586 *audience knowledge*: TSL, nd, July 1993, summer 1993, March 1994.

586 *the worst (most silent)*: TSL, 27 May, 6 August 1994.

586 *his 'packed' life*: TSL, 28 November 1994, 15 March 1995, 4 April 1995. HR 154.7, TS to PFD, 2 September 1994.

587 *One shouldn't take much notice*: TSL, 18 March 1994.

587 *work on the new play*: TSL, 10 January 1994, 7 February 1994, 19 May 1994, 28 November 1994, nd [August/September 1995], nd [December 1995], nd [May 1996], 14 July 1996.

588 *a lot about* Indian Ink: TSL, 27 October 1995, nd [December 1995], nd [January 1996], 6 January 1995, 1 June 1995, nd [July 1995].

589 *I look to you*: HR 124.3, J O'B to TS, 16 April 1995.

589 *how on-and-off their relationship was*: TS to IC, nd [1996]. TSL, nd [March 1994], 19 May 1994, 28 September 1994, 3 April, nd [1996]. M[B]S to Sarka Gauglitz, 30 June 1994.

589 *Did they get married*: IL, 13.

590 *rueful and funny*: TSL, nd [April 1994], 3 February 1996, 4 April 1995, 15 March 1996, 28 November 1994. HR 124.3, Miles Kington to Peter [Boizot], 30 March 1995.

590 *his public life*: National Theatre: TSL, January–April 1996. TSL, 21 January 1994, 10 January 1996, 17 May 1996.

590 *He often told her*: TSL, 24 October 1994, 3 February 1996, 22 March 1996, nd [February 1995], nd [summer 1995], 13 April 1996.

591 *descriptions of his travels*: TSL, May 1994, June–July 1994, 6 August 1994, July, August 1995, February 1996, 14 June 1996, August 1996. M[B]S to Sarka Gauglitz, 26 July 1993, 8 October 1993, 29 August 1995.

591 *'posh' events*: TSL, 12 May 1994, nd [February 1996], 19 May 1994, nd [November 1993], 15 March 1996.

591 *Chatsworth*: TSL, 17 June, 25 June 1995. TS, interview HL, 14 October 2017. TS, Introduction, Devonshire, *Counting My Chickens*.

593 *domestic front*: TSL, 15 March 1995, nd [July 1995].

593 *amused her*: TSL, 14 July 1996, nd [13 April 1996], 9 October 1994.

593 *chided her*: TSL, nd [1995], nd [December 1995], 4 April 1995, nd [1995].

594 *her family worries*: M[B]S to TS, 12 March 1994, TS archive. M[B]S to Sarka Gauglitz, 6 May 1993, 26 July 1993, 8 October 1993, 9 December 1993, 30 June 1994. M[B]S to Emil Máčel, 2 September 1995.

594 *she became ill*: TSL, 17 May 1996, 14 July 1996, 29 August 1996, 1 September 1996, 7 October 1996. M[B]S to Sarka Gauglitz, 2 July 1996.

596 *grieving for his mother*: TS to IC, 21 October 1996. TS, interviews HL, 28 June 2014, 16 June 2016. JM, interview HL, 6 June 2014. FS, interview HL, 7 November 2015. PS, interview HL, 31 April 2015.

26: Reinventions

598 *AEH: But it's all true*: IL, 92.

598 *working on two plays*: TSL, 16 May 1996, TS, interview HL, 16–17 November 2016.

598 *Chekhov*: TSL, 16 May 1996, TS to IC, 7 February 1997. S, v–xii. Cambridge, 20, 22. Biblio, 204.

599 *equivalence*: TS, interview HL, 16 November 2017, S, vii.

599 *put his own mark on the translation*: All quotes from S.

600 *reviews*: *Variety*, 15 May 1997, *Independent*, 12 May 1997, *Daily Telegraph*, 17 May 1997. TS, interview HL, 18 March 2015, 16 June 2016.

601 *Romantic/Classicist contrast*: Alastair Macaulay, 'The Man Who Was Two Men', *Financial Times*, 31 October/1 November 1998.

601 *On casting*: Rosenthal, ed., *Dramatic Exchanges*, 281. Mel Gussow, interview with John Wood, 'So Rude, So Complex, So Like Oneself', *New York Times*, 13 January 1998.

602 *Biography*: IL, 93.

602 *Resident: When it comes to love*: INK, 47–8, revised from ITNS, 55.

602 *years of research*: TS, interview HL, 14 October 2017. A. E. Housman, *Classical Papers*, 3 Vols, Cambridge University Press, 1972. The ms of IL, donated by TS to the British Library in 2004, contains letters and notes on his use of sources. See Biblio, Appendix Two, 384–5.

602 *comical despair*: TS to RE, 20 May 1994, in Rosenthal, ed., *Dramatic Exchanges*, 278.

603 *afternoon with a Latin dictionary*: TSL, 17 May 1996. 'Gallus', 26 January 2001, for 'Friends of Classics', JM archive.

603 *textual cruxes*: Correspondence between TS and David West, with thanks to Christina West. DW to TS, 7 April 1998, 2 August 1996; TS to David West, 27 July 1997, 8 January 1996, 23 July 1997. IL, 49. Horace, Odes 4, 1, in *Horace: Odes and Epodes*, trans. David West, Oxford University Press, 1997. DW to TS, 20 May 1997. See Alastair Macaulay, 'Tom Stoppard, A. E. Housman and the Classics', Baker 2013, 150–67, and Charlotte Higgins, 'In Love's Labyrinth', *Guardian*, 6 October 2007, for the accepted theory that 'Catullus invented the love poem'.

604 *looking for a style*: TS to David West, 18 July [1996?], 16 May [1997?], nd [1996]. David West to TS, 20 May 1997, 27 August 1996.

604 *A good sentence*: TS to David West, 10 October 2002, 7 September 2009.

604 *What emotional storms*: IL, 102.

605 *Decadence was a blind alley*: IL, 85.

605 *most famous victim*: See Richard Ellmann, *Oscar Wilde*, Hamish Hamilton, 1969, and Michèle Mendelssohn, *Making Oscar Wilde*, Oxford University Press, 2018, for two of many versions of Wilde's story.

605 *Oh who is that young sinner*: *The Poems of A. E. Housman*, ed. Archie Burnett, Clarendon Press, Oxford, 1997, 'Additional Poems', XVII, 137. IL, 82.

606 *I sit here*: HR 94.15, TS to Paul Naiditch, 21 August 1996.

606 *When he started writing*: Rose Cobbe, interview HL, 8 April 2014, UA. TS, interview HL, 16 June 2016.

606 *Charon: He's late*: IL, 2.

607 *Everyone is here*: IL, 30.

607 *I could teach a dog*: IL, 34. TS, 'The Lad That Loves You True', *Guardian*, 3 June 2006.

607 *One of Stoppard's sources*: J. A. Symonds, 'A Problem in Greek Ethics', written 1873, privately published 1883, reissued under his name 1903, Arno Press, 1975. Macaulay, 'Tom Stoppard, A. E. Housman and the Classics', 154–5. IL, 102.

608 *heroic absurdity*: Elizabeth Brodersen, 'Stoppard's *Invention*', IL programme, ACT, January 2000. TS, 'The Lad That Loves You True'. 'The Invention of Love', *Lincoln Center Theater Review*, Spring 2001.

608 *He would not stay*: *Poems*, ed. Burnett, 'Additional Poems', VII, 152. IL, 78.

608 *They met on the field*: IL, 76.

609 *You think there is an answer*: IL, 41, 44.

609 *Your 'honour'*: IL, 96.

610 *Housman was a public success*: Brodersen, 'Stoppard's *Invention*'. Fleming, 2001, 240. 'Housman in the Age of Wilde', NT IL programme, 1997. 'The Invention of Love': An Exchange', letters between TS and Daniel Mendelsohn, *New York Review of Books*, 21 September–19 October 2000, www.nybooks.com/articles/2000/09/21/the-invention-of-love-an-exchange.

610 *extraordinary ventriloquism*: IL, 38, 81, 96. Housman, 'The Application of Thought to Textual Criticism', *Proceedings of the Classical Association*, Vol. 18, 1921. Edgar Vincent, *A. E. Housman*, Boydell Press, 2018, 84. See Macaulay in Baker 2013, 161: 'What's original?'

610 *strange last speech*: IL, 100–1.

611 *Diffugere Nives*: IL, 95, 39, 5. Brodersen, 'Stoppard's *Invention*'.

612 *rehearsals*: RE, *Diary*, 11 August, 27 September 1997; RE, interview HL, 29 January 2018. TN, interview HL, 2 October 2017.

612 *incredibly dense*: RE, *Diary*, 13 April, 11 July, 15 August, 19 September, 1 October 1997. RE, interview HL, 29 January 2018. Trish Montemuro, interview HL, 24 September 2014. TS, interview HL, 14 October 2017.

613 *In November 1998*: Codron, IL archive.

613 *Blanka Zizka*: TS, Tribute to Blanka Zizka, Wilma Theater, 1 November 2016.

613 *premiere at A.C.T.*: Perloff, *Beautiful Chaos*, 130, 135.

613 *put on by the Lincoln Company*: *Lincoln Center Theater Review*, Spring 2001.

614 *one bad moment*: IL, 49. J O'B and Bob Crowley, interviews HL, 10 May 2018, 17 October 2014. *Lincoln Center Theater Review*, Spring 2001.

614 *reception*: Susannah Clapp, review of IL, *Observer*, 5 October 1997. David Sexton, 'Theatre? I'd Rather Spend the Night in a Dark Cell', *Evening Standard*, 17 February 1998. HR 94.14, TS to J. R. Lucas, 15 February 1999. Adam Phillips, review of IL, *London Review of Books*, 18 June 1998. DH, interview HL, 26 February 2016. TS to DH, nd. *Lincoln Center Theater Review*, Spring 2001.

615 *not biographical*: Tobias Hill, 'The Poet Punts Down the Styx', *Sunday Telegraph*, 28 September 1997. TS, 'Reflections on "Biographical Fiction"', London Library lecture, 29 October 1997. Biblio, I28. IL, 93.

615 *some of the truth*: Macaulay, 'The Man Who Was Two Men'. IL, 71.

616 *which is his favourite*: TS, interviews HL, 18 March 2015, 1 November 2019. Peter Conrad, 'Thomas the Think Engine', *Observer Review*, 1 November 1998. TS, 'The Lad That Loves You True'.

27: The Scar of Time

617 *I have nothing*: TALK 1999.

617 *knighthood*: TS to PS, nd, PS archive. Teresa Wells, interview HL, 30 September 2014. TS, interview HL, 16 June 2015. MC, David Cornwell, KE to TS on knighthood, June–December 1997, in TS. 'Arise, Sir Tom', *Guardian*, third leader, 13 December 1997.

618 *sexy at 60*: Kate Kellaway, 'Tom's Foolery', *Guardian*, 6 July 1997.

618 *they were all there*: French Embassy Guest List, 11 September 1997, JM archive.

618 *more than a job*: Codron. FP, interview HL, 1 May 2014. Dinah Wood, interview HL, summer 2013. UA, interviews HL, 8 April 2014.

620 *miscellaneous requests*: UA files.

620 *all manner of approaches*: JM archive. Andrew Billen, *Evening Standard*, 27 January 1999.

621 *break-up of his relationship*: TS, interview HL, 16–17 November 2015.

622 *gleeful rumours*: The Insider, 21 July 1997. *New York Daily News*, 3 July 1997. *Sydney Morning Herald*, 4 July 1997. Kate Kellaway, 'Tom's Foolery', *Observer*, 6 July 1997. Datalounge, 28 February 2015.

623 *Boorman remembered*: John Boorman, interview HL, 2 November 2015.

623 *Curtains for the Tom and Felicity Show*: Daily Mail, 28 September 1998. Andrew Billen, *Evening Standard*, 27 January 1999.

623 *Marie Helvin*: TS, interview HL, 16–17 November 2015. Helvin relationship referred to as fact in Cambridge, 9, Nadel 524, 586, n. 50.

624 *Lacoste*: TS, interview HL, 20 March 2018. HR 26.10, TS to AS, 9 August [2001]. Arlons, interview HL, 5 September 2015. Carsen, interview HL, 31 July 2015. https://www.homesandproperty.co.uk/property-news/buying/holiday-homes/the-real-provence-the-luberon-30098.html.

625 *One of his many public talks*: 'Technique and Interpretation in the Performing Arts', New York Public Library, 29 March 1999. 'Pragmatic Theater', *New York Review of Books*, 23 September 1999.

627 *War Child*: TS, interview HL, 2 December 2016. David Lister on War Child, *Independent*, 22 December 1997. Ed Vulliamy, 'War Child and the Bosnian War 15

Years On', *Observer*, 4 July 2010. Trish Montemuro, interview HL, 24 September 2014. HR 156.1, TS, for 'War Child', 8 May 1997.

628 *awards*: See Nadel, 519, and Shapiro, *Shakespeare in a Divided America*, 216, 224, both drawing on newspaper reports: George Rush and Joanna Molloy, 'Spielberg, Benigni; a "Beautiful Friendship"', *New York Daily News*, 22 March 1999; Franc DiGiacomo, 'A Tense Best-Picture Victory', *New York Observer*, 28 March 1999.

629 *Oscars*: HR 158.9, Oscars Itinerary, 21 March 1999; WS, interview HL, 10 December 2014; John Madden, interview HL, 7 November 2014. Susan Billington Katz, 'Rhyme and Reason: A Conversation with *Shakespeare in Love*'s Marc Norman and Tom Stoppard', *Written By*, March 1999. Andrew Billen, 'A Play about Myself? It's Not a Subject I Have Any Appetite For', *Evening Standard*, 27 January 1999. Lyn Gardner, 'The Heart in the Closet', *Guardian Weekend*, 16 January 1999.

631 *new production of* The Real Thing: TS, interview HL, 18 March 2015. David Leveaux, interview HL, 12 October 2014. Biblio, K 258, TS and David Leveaux in conversation, Donmar RT programme, May 1999, in Hunter, 156–9.

633 *Praise*: Tony Blair to TS, 13 June 2000; PM to TS, 17 July 1999; Glenn Close to TS, 14 April 2000, JM archive.

633 'On Turning Out to Be Jewish': TALK 1999. Reprinted as 'Another Country', *Sunday Telegraph*, 10 October 1999. Biblio, H 297.

633 *ineradicable*: TS, Czech National Theatre, Prague, 30 April 2004.

634 lacrimae rerum: TS to David West, nd [1998]. TS to Gore Vidal, 26 May [1998], JM archive.

635 *If I understand*: PS, interview HL, 30 April 2015.

636 *I have been visiting*: TS to Gore Vidal, 26 May [1998], JM archive.

636 *wrote it up*: TALK 1999. Biblio, H 297, citing Nadel, 583.

639 *Reactions*: Madeleine Albright, 'Funny, he doesn't . . .' in 'Readers Write Back', *Talk*, September 1999. Alexandr Rosa, interview HL, 20 September 2015. PS, interview HL, 31 April 2015. Steven Spielberg, interview HL, 5 January 2017. Diane Sawyer, interview HL, 6 January 2018. MA, interview HL, 19 November 2014.

28: Sir Tom, OM

643 *He's a free man*: CU, Sh, 183.

643 Rosencrantz *was chosen*: HR 154.8, Nicki Stoddart to TS, 2 October 1998. Nadel, 523.

643 Enigma: HR 155.1, Anthony Jones to TS, 17 April 2000.

643 *Don't resign*: HR 158.9, TS, fax to JM, 4 February 1998.

643 *film approaches*: HR 158.13, TS to Sydney Pollack, 17 July 1998. HR 160.3, TS to Francis Ford Coppola, 21 July 1997. HR 160.3, TS to Harvey Weinstein, 5 November 1999. HR 159.3, Matthew Warchus to TS, 10 April 2001.

644 *many 'no's*: HR 154.8, 5 January 1998, re. Radio 4. HR 155.1, *Nova* magazine to Rose Cobbe, 2 August 2000. HR 155.12, TS to Michael Scammell, American PEN, 9 December 1996. HR 159.3, re. Milan, 27 July 2002. HR 159.4, TS re. Croatia, 2 August 2002. HR 159.4, TS to Homer Swander, 28 June 2002. HR 159.5, TS to AAAL, 11 October 2002.

644 *invitations and queries*: HR 124.1, John Tusa to TS, 7 September 1999. HR 159.5, TS to Pippa Haywood, 14 November 2001. HR 159.3, Chris Hogg to TS, 18 February 2002. HR 159.6, TS re. Tydeman, 15 January 2002. HR, 165.3. Net Book Agreement,

Daily Telegraph, 29 January 1997. HR 160.3, TS re. script-writing, nd. HR 160.7, TS to National Theatre, 17 September 1998.

645 *his responses*: HR 159.4, TS 'Yes-ish', 26 April 2002, to Penguin invitation to a Christopher Hitchens book launch. HR 165.2, Julian Barnes to TS, 26 August 1996. HR 155.2, TS re. Joyce, 26 August 2000. HR 159.7, Todd Louiso to TS, 19 May 1998.

645 *lunched with the Queen*: Martyn Fletcher, interview HL, 26 June 2015.

646 *Other engagements*: Appointment Diary entries, 2000–02, JM archive. Invitation to TS re. Prince's Education Summer School, 26 January 2002, JM archive.

646 *Portraits*: 1970, by Ottilie Tolansky; 1976, by John Bratby; March 1978, double photo portrait of TS and IIP by Arnold Newman, in NPG; 1980, charcoal drawing by Howard Morgan, in NPG; 1998, two portraits by Anthony Fry, see TS in *Anthony Fry*, Umbrage Editions, 2001; 2003, bronze bust by Angela Conner, Chatsworth. HR 35.6, John Bratby to TS, 24 June 1976.

647 *dead theatres*: TS to HP, 11 February 1995. TS, interview HL, 16 June 2016.

647 *catnip*: TS to Michael Kustow and Adrian Mitchell, 14 February 1999, JM archive.

647 *Shadow Arts Council*: Peter Hall to Sponsors of the Shadow Arts Council, 10 March 1999, JM archive.

647 *a fault line in the history of art*: TS, 30 April 2001, speech at the Royal Academy. 'Making It: Is Conceptual Art an Empty Room or a Breakthrough?', *Times Literary Supplement*, 15 June 2001, 'Thinking Is Not Enough: Art Involves Making, Too', *Daily Telegraph*, 15 June 2001; Fleming, 2008, 23. Janet Street-Porter, *Independent*, 5 June 2001. MA, interview HL, 19 November 2014, recalling TS's 1989 speech at Duke.

648 *always contradictions*: PM to TS, 17 July 1999, JM archive. Ed Berman to TS, 26 May 1999, JM archive.

649 *his work for PEN*: PEN reading for Writers in Prison, 11 April 2001; PEN gala, 10 September 2001. JM archive.

649 *reluctant to ask*: HR 155.8, 11 May 1998, re. Amnesty. HR 155.12, 22 May 1997, re. PEN.

649 *all over the world*: HR 154.8, 156.6, 156.4, 158.4 for productions in early 2000s.

649 *I'll explain that*: TS, Reading, 92nd Street Y, New York, 27 March 2001. With thanks to Bernard Schwartz.

650 *youngest son's marriage*: ES, invitation to prenuptial dinner, 30 January 2001, and to wedding, 3 February 2001. Appointment Diaries, Dinner with Stamps, 5 February 2001, JM archive.

651 *Val Lorraine*: Appointment Diary, 18 February 2001, JM archive; Ross Lorraine to TS, 29 October 2001. Wordsmith, 245.

653 *he came up to expectation*: SC, interview HL, 12 July 2017.

654 *sent love to Sinéad*: MN to TS, 15 November 1997, JM archive. Appointment Diary, 29 May 1998.

29: Utopia

657 *Don't look*: CU 2008, Alexander Herzen (AH) to Sasha Herzen, S, 257. Each play of CU, *Voyage*, *Shipwreck*, *Salvage* (V, Sh, S), was published separately by Faber in 2002. A revised edition of CU in one volume was published by Faber in 2008. All quotations from CU 2008, unless otherwise noted.

657 *History is*: Isaiah Berlin, *Russian Thinkers*, eds Henry Hardy and Aileen Kelly, 1978, revised edition, ed. Henry Hardy, Penguin, 2008, reprinted 2013 (hereafter IBRT),

105, 222, citing AH, *From the Other Shore*, 1850, trans. Moura Budberg, Weidenfeld & Nicolson, 1956.

658 *Utopia is not*: TS, interview Anne Cattaneo, *Lincoln Center Platform Series*, 14 February 2007.

658 *Perhaps it is the artist*: TS, Introduction, CU 2008, xiii.

658 *Public postures*: RT, 33.

658 *Wit and courage*: TS, Introduction, CU 2008, xii.

659 *no fun at all*: TS, Introduction, CU 2008, xiii.

659 *dedicated their lives*: IBRT, 94.

659 *a moth to the candle*: TS, interview HL, 14 October 2017.

659 *I was interested*: TS, interview HL, 19 July 2018. TS, Introduction, CU 2008, ix. TS, interview Maya Jaggi, 'You Can't Help Being What You Write', *Guardian*, 6 September 2008.

660 *I'm having a great time*: KE to TS, 28 December 2000, UA.

660 *I'm writing three plays*: CU, *Lincoln Center Theatre Review*, Fall/Winter 2006, 5.

660 *infected by Isaiah Berlin*: TS, interview HL, 19 July 2018.

660 *the simplest way*: HR 154.5, TS, typescript for Moscow CU programme notes, April 2007. For sources in CU, see also Herbert Tucker, 'History Played Back: In Defense of Tom Stoppard's *The Coast of Utopia*', *Raritan*, 24:4, Spring 2005, 149–69.

660 *He admired Berlin*: Geordie Greig, 'The Play's the Thing', *Tatler*, May 2004. TS, interview HL, 16 June 2016.

661 *Westernised intellectual*: Aileen Kelly, Introduction, IBRT, xxvii.

661 *the arch-enemy*: IBRT, 12, 134, 1. Edward Acton, *Russia: The Tsarist and Soviet Legacy*, Longman, 1986, 1995, Ch. 3.

661 *were reduced*: IBRT, 134, 172, 214. Aileen Kelly, Introduction, IBRT, xxviii.

662 *intelligentsia*: IBRT, 133.

662 *burning moralist*: IBRT 132, 177–8, 304–5.

662 *In the heat*: IBRT, 175.

663 *idolised him*: IBRT, 161.

663 *intellectually irresponsible*: IBRT, 122, 126, 129, 164–5.

663 *cynical indifference*: IBRT, 117.

663 *vast unitary system*: Isaiah Berlin, 'The March of History', in *Political Ideas in the Romantic Age*, ed. Henry Hardy, 2006, 2nd edition, Princeton University Press, 2014, 296 ff.

663 *great despotic vision*: IBRT, 224–5.

663 *If progress is the goal*: AH, *From the Other Shore*, trans. Budberg, 36.

664 *nature obeys no plan*: Isaiah Berlin, Introduction to AH, *From the Other Shore*, xii; IBRT, 98–9, 104–5. TS, *Lincoln Center Theatre Review*, Fall/Winter 2006, 7.

664 *the events which were to transform*: TS, *Lincoln Center Theater Review*, Fall/Winter 2006, 6.

664 *worth speaking to*: IBRT, 314, on Dobrolyubov's rebuff to Turgenev: 'Ivan Sergeevich, do not let us go on talking to each other: it bores me.' TS gives this sentence to Turgenev, CU, S, 288.

664 *dilemma of the liberals*: IBRT, 343–4.

665 *every form of enslavement*: IBRT, 308.

665 *never committing himself*: IBRT, 310–11, 315, 334, 338, 340.

665 *For Turgenev*: IBRT, 168.

666 *He identifies*: Jaggi, 'You Can't Help Being What You Write', *Guardian*, 6 September 2008.

666 Romantic Exiles: American Theatre Wing broadcast, 'Working in the Theatre', #352, discussion of *Coast* with Jennifer Ehle, Ethan Hawke, Amy Irving and Josh Hamilton.

666 *Carr begins his story*: E. H. Carr, *The Romantic Exiles*, 1933, Serif Books, 1998 (hereafter Carr), 25, 112, 39, 121, 181, 228, 184.

667 *a man's political convictions*: Carr, 184.

667 *story of Herzen's personal life*: Carr, 23, 43, 62, 103, 240.

667 *Bedlam*: Carr, 174, 329.

668 *making smart remarks*: TS, interview HL, 16–17 November 2015.

668 *Chekhovian feel*: CU, V, 46. For Gorky and Chekhov in CU, see Nadel, 'Chekhov's Stoppard', Baker 2013, 17–36. ES, interview HL, 8 December 2014.

670 *the Moloch*: CU, V, 110.

670 *after much struggling*: TS to J O'B, 15 March 2001, JM archive.

670 *Grown-upness has caught up*: CU, Sh, 128, 139, 137.

671 *Into exile*: CU, Sh, 145, 166.

671 *the public look to writers*: CU, Sh, 176, 152, 157, 167, 173, 175.

672 *apathy*: CU, Sh, 181.

672 *I'm beginning to understand*: CU, Sh, 183.

673 *It's not just liberty*: CU, S, 298.

674 *theatre of political exile*: CU, S, 240.

674 *They don't give asylum*: CU, S, 238.

674 *It's all downhill*: CU, S, 266.

674 *the romantics*: CU, S, 296, 288.

675 *Herzen: There's no such thing*: CU, S, 299.

675 *Turgenev: You don't believe*: CU, S, 307.

676 *history has no purpose*: CU, S, 335.

676 *a touching speech*: CU, S, 257.

676 *To go on*: CU, S, 336.

676 *Herzen's dedication*: AH, *From the Other Shore*, 3–4.

677 *straight from his sources*: egs drawn from Carr (e.g. 91, 325, 121).

677 *no consolation*: CU, S, 335. Isaiah Berlin, 'Herzen and His Memoirs', *Against the Current: Essays in the History of Ideas*, ed. Henry Hardy, 1979, 2nd edition, Princeton University Press, 2013, 266.

677 *seven Bakunins*: TS, *Lincoln Center Theater Review*, Fall/Winter 2006, 7.

677 *the best lines*: TS, interview Anne Cattaneo, *Lincoln Center Platform Series*, 14 February 2007.

677 *No, not at all*: CU, Sh, 216.

678 *Life pours*: AH, *From the Other Shore*, 34–5.

678 *We believe*: AH, *From the Other Shore*, 107.

678 *Who will find fault*: IBRT, 223–4.

679 *whether we're good*: TS, interview Anne Cattaneo, *Lincoln Center Platform Series*, 14 February 2007; TS, interview Marshall Brickman, 15 January 2007, published in *On Writing*, Writers' Guild of America, July 2007, 9.

679 *indignantly objected*: DH, interview HL, 26 February 2016; Bob Crowley, interview HL, 10 May 2018.

680 *But don't you ever*: CU, Sh, 126.

680 *All those people*: TS, interview Anne Cattaneo, *Lincoln Center Platform Series*, 14 February 2007.

681 *What kind of madman*: HR 155.2, TS to *New York Times*, 25 November 2006, in response to Bill Grimes's review of CU.

681 *a lot of laughs*: KE to TS, 28 December 2000, UA.

681 *Russian absurdities*: CU, Sh, 136, Sh, 132, S, 322.

681 *Turgenev: I'm agreeing*: CU, S, 319.

681 *Don't scream*: CU, S, 231.

681 *one-liners*: CU, V, 74. CU, S, 279. CU, S, 232, CU, Sh, 161.

682 *give me Mackenzie's*: CU, S, 307.

682 *find the key*: ES, interview HL, 8 December 2014. CU, Sh, 140, 157. TS, interview Anne Cattaneo, *Lincoln Center Platform Series*, 14 February 2007.

682 *links to his past work*: TS, 'Something to Declare', *Sunday Times*, 25 February 1968.

682 *the English welcome refugees*: CU, S, 238.

683 *A poem can't be*: CU, V, 43.

683 *Perotkin: And what was*: CU, S, 315–16.

683 *by far the most arduous*: TS, interview Dominic Cavendish, *Daily Telegraph*, 29 June 2002. HR 160.7, TN to TS, 18 December 2000, TS to TN, 20 December 2000. See Rosenthal, ed., *Dramatic Exchanges*, 302–3. TN, interview HL, 2 October 2017.

684 *The delay*: Simon Russell Beale, interview HL, 14 February 2019. Michael Billington, *Guardian*, 20 December 2002. TN, interview HL, 2 October 2017.

684 *9/11*: TS, interview HL, 14 October 2017; TN, interview HL, 2 October 2017.

685 *cinematic feel*: TN, interview HL, 2 October 2017. TS, 'The Forgotten Revolutionary', *Guardian*, 2 June 2002. TS, interview Dominic Cavendish, *Daily Telegraph*, 29 June 2002.

685 *strong cast*: Patrick Marmion, 'West End Girls', *Daily Mail*, 20 June 2002. 'Tom's Secret Weapon', 'This London', *Evening Standard*, 21–27 June 2002. TS, interview HL, 1 November 2019.

686 *reviews*: Benedict Nightingale, *The Times*, 5 August 2002. Charles Spencer, *Daily Telegraph*, 5 August 2002. *Guardian* round-up of reviews, 10 August 2002. Nicholas de Jongh, *Evening Standard*, 5 August 2002. Michael Billington, *Guardian*, 5 August 2002. *Sunday Times*, 11 August 2002. John Lahr, *New Yorker*, 23 September 2002. Aleks Sierz, *Tribune*, 16 August 2002. NT, CU, reviews and features, 2002. For CU at the National, see also Jonathan Croall, *Buzz Buzz! Playwrights, Actors and Directors at the National Theatre*, Methuen Drama, 2008.

686 *right-wing appropriation*: Paul Goodman, 'The Police Used to Carry Gazetteers Rather than Guns', *Daily Telegraph*, 5 August 2002.

687 *to take away freedom*: TS, 'The Question Is: Why Should Anyone Obey Anyone Else?', *Daily Telegraph*, 2 May 2002.

687 *Personal responses*: HR 159.2, Michael Herzen to TS, 29 November 2002. HR 159.1, Simon Gray to TS, nd. Michael Frayn to TS, 27 September 2003, in Rosenthal, ed., *Dramatic Exchanges*, 311. David Leveaux, interview HL, 12 October 2014.

687 *staging it at the Lincoln Center*: Bob Crowley, interview HL, 10 May 2018, J O'B, interview HL, 17 September 2014. André Bishop, interview HL, 9 August 2015.

688 *O'Brien and Crowley made*: HR 150.5–7, CU, 'Blocking Master', Lincoln Center production.

688 *particularly savage note*: J O'B, interview HL, 17 September 2014.
688 *I'm not laying down*: HR 154.5, TS, rehearsal notes for CU, Lincoln Center production.
689 *wasn't a polemic*: HR 150.9, TS, interview Cathleen McGuigan, 'One Brit vs. the Utopians', *Newsweek*, 4 December 2006.
689 *find their characters*: American Theatre Wing broadcast, 'Working in the Theatre', #352.
689 *I find his calm*: Simon Gray, *The Smoking Diaries*, Vol. 3, *The Last Cigarette*, Granta, 2008, 219–20.
689 *critics enthused*: Ben Brantley, 'Those Storm Tossed Revolutionaries Reach Port', *New York Times*, 19 February 2007. *New York Times* feature, 30 November 2006.
690 *In New York*: HR 155.5, TS, interview Marshall Brickman, 15 January 2007, published in *On Writing*, Writers' Guild of America, July 2007, 9.
690 *rethinking*: TS, Introduction to Grove edition of CU, July 2007. CU, S, 262.
690 *extremely different*: Biblio, A 26, on variant editions of CU.

30: Commitments and Engagements

692 *I think it's also*: TS to Aleks Sierz, in 'Sir Tom in the Doghouse', *Daily Telegraph*, 10 October 2005.
692 *lost to the winds*: BS, interview HL, 6 February 2016.
692 *unceasing ticktock*: TS, 'Here's Looking at You, Syd', *Vanity Fair*, 5 November 2007.
693 *pragmatists, political managers*: Žantovský, *Havel*, 498.
693 *to congratulate you*: TS to VH, 29 January 2003. TS, JE I, 22 January 1977.
693 *mysterious twelve-minute exchange*: TS, screenplay *Ohio Impromptu*, 25 February 2000, JM archive. The 1981 play was a commission for a Beckett expert at Columbus, Ohio. Pat Nason, 'While Waiting for Godot', UPI, 13 September 2002. All nineteen plays were aired in the UK and USA in September 2002. https://en.wikipedia.org/wiki/Beckett_on_Film.
694 *Iraq War*: TS to David Wilson, Stop the War Coalition, 30 August 2005. TS, interview Adam Thirlwell, *Believer Magazine*, 1 September 2005, https://believermag.com/an-interview-with-tom-stoppard.
694 *completely drained*: TS, interview John Tusa, BBC Radio 3, 20 August 2003. TS, interview Hunter, 2003, in Hunter 2005, 170, 177–8.
695 *revival of* Jumpers: Patricia England to TS, 7 August 2003, JM archive. Sam Leith, interview with TS, *Independent*, 8 November 2003. TS, interview John Tusa, BBC Radio 3, 20 August 2003. ML, interview HL, 26 September 2014. Michael Billington, *Guardian*, 19 June 2003. Matt Wolf, *Variety*, 24 June 2003. Paul Taylor, *Independent*, 25 November 2003. David Leveaux, interview HL, 12 October 2014. Simon Russell Beale, in Hunter 2005, 238, and interview HL, 14 February 2019.
696 *Sonia Friedman*: TS, interviews HL, 16 June 2016, 1 November 2019. SF, interview HL, 20 October 2016.
698 *I gave a party*: HR 158.12, TS, 'Stalking Chandler', *Sunday Telegraph*, 2 August 1998.
700 *I might die before*: TS to A. S. Byatt, 12 May 2003, JM archive.
700 *the party's openness*: AF, interview HL, 23 September 2014. TS, interview HL, June 2014. Invoice, 4 June 2013, JM archive. FP, interview HL, 2 May 2014. Thank-you cards for parties, JM archive, e.g. Hytner to TS, 7 September 2011. Teresa Wells to

TS, 6 September 2011. AS to TS, 7 July 2003. Tom Hollander to TS, 9 November 2011. Michael Blakemore to TS, 9 September 2011. Bamber Gascoigne to TS, 12 July 2007. Rose Cobbe to TS, 9 July 2007. Martyn Fletcher, interview HL, 26 June 2015.

701–4 *London Library* [LL]: Max Hastings, interview HL, 4 September 2014. TS to LL donors, 23 January 2009, 22 July 2008, 30 June 2008. LL to TS, 12 May 2004. Lottie Cole to TS, 1 March 2011. TS to David Attenborough, 16 July 2007. TS, public interview HL, 'Words in the Square', LL, 6 May 2016. TS, interview HL, 16 June 2016, 14 October 2017. Sebastian Shakespeare, 'The Player', *Tatler*, June 2010. TS, LL speech, nd. Jan Dalley, *Financial Times*, 19 April 2005. Geraldine Bedell, 'Shelf Stocker', *Guardian*, 17 July 2005. Lottie Cole, interview HL, 17 September 2014. Teresa Wells, interview HL, 30 September 2014. Correspondence re. LL subscription charges, 2007, in JM archive. Complaints re. subscription in *Times Literary Supplement*, *Spectator*, *Evening Standard*, November–December 2007.

705 *social self*: J O'B, interview HL, 17 October 2014. TS in conversation with HL, 'Words in the Square', LL, 6 May 2016. TS, interview HL, 16 June 2016.

705 *All understood*: Debo, Duchess of Devonshire, to TS, 23 June 2004, JM archive.

706 *When Manny Azenberg*: TS to Karen Azenberg Mericola, nd [November 2003]. Appointment Diary, September 2002. TS, interview re. Previn, *Today*, BBC Radio 4, 1 March 2019.

706 *Mike Nichols*: TS, Kennedy Center Awards, 7 December 2003. MN to TS, 9 December 2003, JM archive. TS, Mike Nichols Tribute, 7 December 2003, available on YouTube.

707 *Australia*: TS, interview Bob Carr, Sydney Town Hall, 15 January 2004. Bob Carr to TS, 6 September 2002. Lissa Twomey, Sydney Festival, to JM, 15 January 2004.

707 *Isaiah Berlin Lecture*: Gareth Roberts to TS, 4 November 2002. TS to Gareth Roberts, 26 November 2002. TS, Berlin lecture, JM archive. Henry Hardy, summary of lecture, *Wolfson College Record*, 2003–4. TS to Mr Cooper, 12 January 2005. Speeding fine and speed awareness course correspondence, 10 June 2004, 7 September 2004, JM archive.

709 His Dark Materials [HDM]: Anthony Jones to TS, 5 June 2002. Screenplays: *The Golden Compass*, Second Draft Revisions, September 2003; HDM, Part 2 and Part 3, March 2004. Hunter 2008, 176 (May 2003). TS to Philip Pullman [PP], January–February 2003. PP to TS, 22, 26, 28 December 2002, 2, 14 February 2003. TS to PP, nd [February 2003]. *Golden Compass* typescript, 110, 125, cf. *Northern Lights*, Scholastic Books, 1995, 1998, 310, 374. TS to Deborah Forte, New Line, 11 August 2003. TS to Chris Weitz, 27 November 2004. PP to TS, 23 November 2004. 'Fate of the Cosmos (and of a Studio) Hangs in the Balance', *New York Times*, 30 August 2017. PP, interview Jeanette Winterson, *Harper's and Queen*, 10 December 2004. 'Dark Material', *Empire*, 29 September 2006. Anthony Jones to TS, 9 August 2005. Writers Guild to TS, 10 August 2007. PP, interview HL, 6 February 2019. In 2019 a successful TV series of *His Dark Materials* was made by Jack Thorne.

713 *Emily: Don't go away*: Darkside, 2013, 48.

713 Tulip Fever [TF]: TS, interviews HL, June 2014, 16–17 November 2015, 16 June 2016, 7 December 2016, 14 October 2017. John Madden, interview HL, 7 November 2014. Deborah Moggach, interview HL, 1 February 2019. Dreamworks to TS, 20 February 2004. 'British Films Wiped Out by Tax Bombshell', *Observer*, 22 February 2004. 'Closing Loophole May Crush UK Film Industry', *Observer*, 15 February 2004. TF screenplay, final draft, 24 March 2003. Screenplay by TS, revisions by Peter Chelsom

and Tinker Lindsay, current revisions by Moira Buffini, 27 April 2014, Ruby Films and the Weinstein Company. JM archive.

715 *short version of Shakespeare*: Paul Arendt, 'Tom Stoppard Cuts Shakespeare Down to Size', *Guardian*, 11 October 2005. TS, Appointment Diary, 20 November 2003. Cherie Blair to TS, nd [2003], JM archive. TS to Sean Lennon (mentioning *Merchant*), 2 September 2004, JM archive. BBC documentary of production, October 2005, available via https://learningonscreen.ac.uk/ondemand, with thanks to Lincia Daniel.

716 *Pirandello's Henry IV*: HENRY, 63, 48, 36, 44, 52. Cf. *Henry IV* in *Pirandello: Collected Plays*, ed. Robert Rietty, Vol. 1, John Calder, 1987. Victoria Segal, 'Just Mad about Harry', *Sunday Times*, 9 May 2004. Geordie Greig, 'The Play's the Thing', *Tatler*, May 2004. William Hickey, *Daily Express*, 8 April 2004. TS, *Times Book Section*, 3 May 2004. TS to Eric Price, Grove Atlantic, 14 March 2005. Michael Grandage, interview HL, 14 February 2019.

717 *another European play*: HEROES, 68, 32, *passim*. HR 151.3, TS to Gérald Sibleyras, nd. Lizzie Loveridge, *Curtain Up*, 21 October 2005. Sierz, 'Sir Tom in the Doghouse'. Rose Cobbe and St John Donald, interview HL, 20 May 2015. Typescript HEROES, JM archive.

719 *His work had been banned*: Nadel, 527, 587, n. 57. Nadel notes that Joseph Brodsky translated R&G in 1970 and that the translation was rediscovered in the 1980s.

719–22 *Russia*: Arkady Ostrovsky, 'The Estate Russia's In', *FT Magazine*, 6 September 2003. 'The Man Who Glimpsed Utopia', *Intelligent Life*, Winter 2007. Ostrovsky, interview HL, 10 July 2017. Hunter 2008, 174–5. 'Stoppard's Russians Come Home', *Wall Street Journal*, 11 October 2007. Nina Raine, 'Tom Stoppard in Moscow', *Guardian*, 23 June 2007, *Areté*, 22, Winter 2006–Spring 2007. TS, programme note for CU in Moscow, April 2007. TS to Bolshoi Drama Theatre, 29 October 2002. Arkady Ostrovsky to TS, 22 October 2002. Marina Dmitrevskaya to Nicki Stoddart, 25 October 2002. Riga Theatre to Nicki Stoddart, 24 October 2002, TS archive.

723 *Belarus Free Theatre*: *Human Rights House Foundation*, April, June 2017. TS to Natalia Kaliada, 2 March 2005, JM archive. *Granta* 119 (2012). Arkady Ostrovsky, 'Just Imagine', *Economist*, 23 July 2010. TS, interview HL, 2 December 2016. DH, interview HL, 25 February 2016.

723 *Minsk*: TS, Introduction, February 2012, 'Theatre of Fortune', Nikolai Khalezin and Natalia Kaliada, *Granta*, 119, 2012. Arkady Ostrovsky, 'Just Imagine', *Economist*, 23 July 2010.

724 *he was practical*: TS to Natalia Kaliada, 5 September 2005, JM archive. Mark Ravenhill, 'Welcome to Theatreland', *Guardian*, 13 February 2008. TS, 'Accidental Tyranny', *Guardian*, 30 September/1 October 2005. Natalia Kaliada, interview HL, 12 March 2019.

725 *My mother*: TS to Aksana Kazakova, 1 November 2005, JM archive.

725 *support for the Belarusians*: TS to Alessandro Martinez, Premio Europa, 29 January 2007, JM archive.

725 *performed it at Leeds*: On TS and HP in Leeds, Alfred Hickling, 'Being Harold Pinter', *Guardian*, 16 September 2007.

726 *Stoppard calmed everyone down*: TS to H2o lawyers and Belarus campaigners, 30 March 2011, JM archive.

726 *You could be forgiven*: TS, 'We Must Not Be Distracted from This Brutality', *Independent*, 8 March 2011.

726 *took over his life*: TS, Appointment Diary, 2011. Carole Cadwalladr, 'The Battle for a Free Belarus', *Guardian*, 4 April 2011. TS, interview HL, 20 March 2018. Larry Rohter, 'Escaped from Belarus, Actors Raise Voices', *New York Times*, 4 January 2011.

727 *third father*: Natalia Kaliada, interview HL, 12 March 2019.

727 *The necessity of freedom*: TS, Foreword, *On Freedom: Powerful Polemics by Supporters of Belarus Free Theatre*, Oberon Books, 2015.

31: *Rock 'n' Roll*

728 *We have to begin again*: RR, 99, 13.

728 *He had a habit*: Delaney, 213.

729 *He was born*: RR, ix.

729 *in a way this play is*: Carey Perloff, *Words on Plays*, A.C.T., 2008, 11.

729 *I've often thought*: Paul Taylor, 'Soundtrack to a Revolution', *Independent*, 9 June 2006. Also RR, ix.

729 *alternative lives*: TS, JE I, 22 January 1977.

729 *Would he have spoken out*: TS, interview HL, 19 July 2018.

729 *self-referential conceit*: TS, interview Mark Lawson, *Front Row*, BBC Radio 4, 2 July 2007.

729 *read back into the history*: RR, xv. TS to Jaroslav Reidel, nd [2005].

730 *essays by Havel*: VH, *Open Letters*, ed. and trans. Paul Wilson, Vintage, 1992, 269. VH, *Disturbing the Peace*, ed. and trans. Paul Wilson, Vintage, 1990, 1991, 127–8. TS, interview Melvyn Bragg, LWT, *South Bank Show*, 18 March 2008. RR, xviii–ix, 73.

731 *pseudo-history*: VH, *Open Letters*, 331ff.

731 *people's civic backbone*: VH, *Disturbing the Peace*, 172–5. RR, 30, xiii.

732 *Words mean*: RR, 27, 99.

732 *champagne liberals*: Arkady Ostrovsky, interview HL, 10 July 2017.

732 *slogans and postures*: TS, 'The Year of the Posturing Rebel', *Sunday Times*, 16 March 2008; TS, interview Melvyn Bragg, *South Bank Show*, 18 March 2008.

732 *Freedom of speech*: TS, 'My Love Affair with Newspapers', *British Journalism Review*, ed. Bill Hagerty, December 2005. Meeting with Bill Hagerty, Appointment Diary, 2 November 2004.

733 *I was proud to be British*: TS, 'Is There Ever a Time and a Place for Censorship?', *Index on Censorship*, 2005, revised 2006.

733 *at least two subjects*: Adam Thirlwell, 'An Interview with Tom Stoppard', *Believer Magazine*, September 2005. (Interview carried out on 18 July and 23 November 2004; information from Adam Thirlwell, 14 January 2019.) TS, interview Mark Lawson, BBC Radio 4, *Front Row*, 2 July 2007.

734 *I don't know how*: TS, 'Tom Stoppard Interviews Sir Tom Stoppard', 'Reading Matters', *Royal Society of Literature Magazine*, March 2005. TS invited to be CL at RSL, 11 March 2004; accepted 18 March 2004.

734 *keywords and topics*: TS, ms notes for RR, 16 January, 29 April 2005, TS archive.

735 *turned into a recluse*: Syd Barrett photo, 'Roger' in 2001, Geoff Robinson/Rex USA, in *Words on Plays*, A.C.T., 2008.

735 *the shimmer of a play*: TS, 'Here's Looking at You, Syd', *Vanity Fair*, 5 November 2007; TS, interview HL, 14 October 2017.

736 *like a box of cornflakes*: Taylor, 'Soundtrack to a Revolution', *Independent*, 9 June 2006.

737 *what he is really interested in*: Carey Perloff, *Words on Plays*, A.C.T., 2008. TS, ms notes for RR, TS archive.

737 *absolutely sensational*: TN to TS, 1 August 2005, TS archive.

737 *his Czechness*: TS, interview Mark Lawson, *Front Row*, BBC Radio 4, 2 July 2007.

738 *Was there anything*: ms notes for RR; RR, 24, 50.

738 *so many neuron-firings*: RR, 46, 51.

739 *I love England*: RR, 26, 27.

741 *bleak, dark playfulness*: RR, 15, 21, 79, 24.

742 *who was using who*: RR, 93.

742 *They're unbribable*: RR, 37.

743 *How bourgeois*: RR, 49.

743 *The working-class vote*: RR, 81.

744 *It was like opening*: RR, 95.

744 *Childhood is a lost country*: RR, 94, 103.

744 *congenital Anglophilia*: TS, interview Mark Lawson, *Front Row*, BBC Radio 4, 2 July 2007.

745 *that's the best thing*: TS, interviews HL, 28 June 2014, 19 July 2018. Carey Perloff, *Words on Plays*, A.C.T., 2008.

745 *something worthwhile*: TS, interview HL, 16–17 November 2015. TN, interview HL, 2 October 2017.

746 *Alice: What are you doing*: RR, 58.

746 *She was rather pleased*: SC, interview HL, 12 July 2017.

746 *wanted it to be done at the Royal Court*: SF, interview HL, 20 October 2016. TN, interview HL, 2 October 2017. Michael Grandage, interview HL, 14 February 2019.

747 *others were not so delighted*: Tom Teodorczuk, 'Rebellion at the Royal Court over Stoppard Play', *Evening Standard*, 22 December 2005. Taylor, 'Soundtrack to a Revolution'. 'Trevor Nunn's Passion Play', *Evening Standard*, 14 March 2006. Dan Rebellato, ed., *Modern British Playwriting 2000–2009: Voices, Documents, New Interpretations*, Bloomsbury, 2013. Louise Jury, 'Stoppard's New Play Opens: And It's More than Rock 'n' Roll', *Independent*, 15 June 2006. Paul Taylor, 'The Royal Court: Caught in the Spotlights', *Independent*, 13 January 2006. DH, interview HL, 26 February 2016. SF, interview HL, 20 October 2016. Ruth Little and Emily McLaughlin, *The Royal Court Theatre Inside Out*, Bloomsbury, 2007, 440–2.

748 *hottest ticket*: Louise Jury, *Independent*, 15 June, 2006. John Walsh, 'Václav Havel: Artist. Dissident. President. Icon', *Independent*, 30 June 2006. Linda Maštalíř, 'Tom Stoppard's *Rock 'n' Roll*', Radio Prague, 28 June 2006.

749 *Almost every day*: VH to TS, 26 June 2006, JM archive.

749 *rave reviews*: Charles Spencer, *Daily Telegraph*, 15 June; Michael Billington, *Guardian*, 15 June; John Peter, *Sunday Times*, 18 June; Paul Taylor, *Independent*, 15 June; Judith Flanders, *Times Literary Supplement*, 23 June 2006. TS, Appointment Diary, 31 July 2006, Stones in Amsterdam.

750 *critical notes to the cast*: TS, notes to TN and RR company, nd, JM archive.

751 *published*: Biblio, A 30 e, 167.

751 *Broadway transfer*: Ben Brantley, review of *Rock 'n' Roll*, *New York Times*, 5 November 2007. On the Broadway strike, wikipedia.org/wiki/2007_Broadway_stagehand_strike. SF, interview HL, 20 October 2016. SC, interview HL, 12 July 2017.

751 *Cusack, true to her politics*: SC, interview HL, 17 July 2017. SF, interview HL, 20 October 2016.

752 *the floor of the stage rose*: TS, 'Why I'm with the Band', *The Times*, 19 December 2009. TS to Alexei Borodin and Natasha Nikolaeva, 18 March 2012, JM archive.

752 *tried to persuade him*: HR 155.2, Mark Damazer to TS, 31 May 2007. TS to Mark Damazer, 31 May 2007, with thanks to Mark Damazer.

753 *he wasn't resting*: TS, interview HL, 17–18 June 2019. Micky Rapkin, 'Tom Stoppard', *Time Out New York*, 18 October 2007. TS, 'On "Dover Beach"', BBC Radio 4, 15 October 2007, published in *Areté*, Spring/Summer 2013. Marion Botsford Fraser to TS, for Necessary Angel Theatre Company, Toronto, 2 October 2007. Plays put on 3 March 2008. JM archive.

754 *what his agents were dealing with*: Rose Cobbe to JM, 7 August 2007, UA.

754 *I am here, honoured*: TS, Speech for Honorary Doctorate, 4 May 2007, Janáček Academy of Music and Art, Brno.

755 *I don't ever quite understand*: Dan David Prize, Tel Aviv University, 19 May 2008.

755 *well-received revivals*: TS, interview Brian Logan, *The Times*, 7 April 2008; Alan Franks, 'Return of the Iron Curtain', *The Times*, 22 December 2008.

755 *personal life altered*: SC, interview HL, 12 July 2017. TS, interview HL, 16–17 November 2015, Bob Crowley, interview HL, 10 May 2018. TS to IC, 12 March 2008. Appointment Diary, first entry for Richard Boyd Barrett, 23 April 2007.

756 *Kenneth Ewing*: TS, address, Service for KE, 19 June 2008.

757 *I won't deny*: TS to Caroline Michel, 25 January 2008, JM archive.

757 *Lunch*: Julian Barnes to HL, 24 July 2016; Diary entry, for Friday 16 July 2010, by kind permission of Julian Barnes.

758 *mischievous story*: Mark Lawson, interview HL, 26 September 2014.

758 *the William test*: TS to Christopher Hitchens, 9 December 2005, TS archive.

759 *I hardly understood*: TS to AF, 26 December [2008], by kind permission of AF.

760 *'Another Time'*: *Areté*, 28, Spring/Summer 2009.

760 *laughter and lament*: Nina Raine, 'Tom Stoppard in Moscow', *Guardian*, 23 June 2007, *Areté*, 22, Winter 2006/Spring 2007.

761 Ivanov: Reviews by Charles Spencer, *Telegraph*, Benedict Nightingale, *The Times*, and Paul Taylor, *Independent*, 18 September 2008.

762 *in rehearsal*: I, Faber, 2008. TS, interview HL, 16 June 2016. TS to Michael Grandage, nd. Michael Grandage, interview HL, 14 February 2019. Thanks to Mark Lawson for Pinter details.

762 Cherry Orchard: SC, interview HL, 12 July 2017. TS to IC, 18 March [2008]. TS, interviews HL, 16–17 November 2016, 17–18 June 2019.

763 *so close in tone*: HR 166.7, literal translation and notes on CO, Helen Rappaport, 2000, 2008.

763 *the most cruel, unfeeling Chekhov*: Simon Russell Beale, interview HL, 14 February 2019. CO, 35, 12, 56, 64.

764 *Gaev: The orchard*: CO, 20–1.

32: *Parade's End*

765 *The only thing*: PE, 70, 275.

766 *quotations about fishing*: OS, birthday card to TS, nd. Quotes by 'Sparse Grey Hackle'

and Izaak Walton from Nick Lyons, ed., *The Quotable Fisherman*, Sterling, 1998, 2004.

766 *I worry about them*: TS, interview Maya Jaggi, 'You Can't Help Being What You Write', *Guardian*, 6 September 2008.

766 *Sometimes there were tensions*: ES, interview HL, 8 December 2014. WS, interview HL, 10 December 2014. BS, 6 February 2015.

766 *Ed's successful career*: ES, interview HL, 8 December 2014. Maureen Paton, 'Ed Stoppard: A Testing Inheritance', *Independent*, 15 September 2005. ES, interview Dominic Cavendish, *Daily Telegraph*, 19 May 2009.

768 *They had fun*: David Leveaux, interview HL, 12 October 2014. ES, interview HL, 8 December 2014. TS, interview HL, 2 December 2016. TS, notes on *Robin Hood* to Ridley Scott, Scott to TS, nd [2009], JM archive.

768 *The reviewers agreed*: Michael Billington, *Guardian*, 5 June 2009; Emma John, *Observer*, 6 June 2009; Charles Spencer, *Daily Telegraph*, 6 June 2009.

769 *ten-minute two-hander*: 'Pizza/Torture', for *The Laws of War*, 'Cries from the Heart', Royal Court Theatre, 16 May 2010.

769 *'craving' a new play*: Mark Lawson, 'Tom Stoppard: "I'm the Crank in the Bus Queue"', *Guardian*, 14 April 2010.

769 *possible ideas*: Mark Lawson, 'Tom Stoppard'. TS to Alastair Macaulay, 1 August 2013.

770 *country retreat*: Tobias Grey, 'Between the Lines', profile of TS, *Town and Country Magazine*, March 2013.

770 *How are you to know*: TS to Teaching Institute, 30 July 2009.

771 *Stoppard would adapt*: Daniel Kehlmann, interview HL, 29 February 2016. *The Voyage of the St Louis* (*Die Reise der Verlorenen*), adapted by TS for BBC Radio 4, 2020.

771 *being overloaded*: TS to Gerardo Vero, March 2010.

772 *alarmingly formal*: Gary McKeone, Invitation to Windsor, 2 December 2010, annotated by TS to TM. St George's House Lecture, 3 June 2011.

772 *make a thought-experiment*: TS, 'The Privilege of Artists', St George's House Annual Lecture, 3 June 2011.

772 *saying no*: TS to Silvia Corsi, 2010. TS to Jitka Sloupová, 26 March 2012. TS to Daniel Kehlmann, nd.

773 *'Delight'*: TS, May 2009, *Modern Delight*, Faber, 2010.

773 *embarked on one major project*: Grey, 'Between the Lines'. TS, interview John Preston, *Daily Telegraph*, 24 August 2012. Information re. PE: TS, interviews HL, 28 June 2014, 19 July 2018, 17–18 June 2019; Susanna White to HL, 7 November 2017. TS, Introduction, PE, v–xiii. 'Behind the Scenes', PE, BBC DVD, 2012.

774 *Ford*: For life and work, see Max Saunders, *Ford Madox Ford: A Dual Life*, Oxford University Press, 2 vols, 1996, 2012. TS also consulted one of Ford's many other biographers, Alan Judd.

774 *lonely buffalo*: Saunders, *Ford Madox Ford*, I, 470, II, 68.

775 *Consciousness*: Saunders, *Ford Madox Ford*, I, 5.

775 *eighteenth-century English mind*: Quoted in Saunders, *Ford Madox Ford*, I, 208.

777 *with the intention*: Saunders, *Ford Madox Ford*, II, 199. Ford Madox Ford, Letter to William Bird, in *No More Parades*, 1925, Penguin, 1948.

777 *I did have to unravel*: TS, interview John Preston, *Daily Telegraph*, 24 August 2012.

778 *pulling the strings*: PE, 126, 240, 334.

778 *piled on the comedy*: PE, 106, 222, 136.

779 *We've seen the last*: PE, 197, 274–5.

779 *long, frustrating process*: DH, interview HL, 26 February 2016. TS to Piers Wenger and Damien Timmer, 'not sent'; TS to Timmer and Wenger, 11 October 2010.

782 *as involved in film*: Rose Cobbe, interview HL, 8 April 2014. PE, xi.

782 *godsend*: Rebecca Hall to TS, 5 December 2011.

782 *arguing against over-signalling*: TS, post-production notes to Susanna White, 6 April 2012. TS to Kary Antholis, 13 June 2012. TS to Lucy Richer, 20 February 2012. TS to Damien Timmer and Piers Wenger, 11 October 2010, JM archive.

783 *The motor-plough*: PE, xi. SDN, 15. PE, 33. TS re. PE, interviews HL, June 2014, 2 December 2016, 14 October 2017, 19 July 2018.

783 *critical success*: Ben Bryant, *Daily Telegraph*, 28 August 2012; Ben Laurence, *Daily Telegraph*, 7 September 2012; John Preston, *Daily Telegraph*, 24 August 2012; Serena Davies, *Daily Telegraph*, 24 August 2012; Ben Dowell, *Guardian*, 20 September 2012; David Robson, *Daily Telegraph*, 31 August 2012; Laura Donnelly, *Daily Telegraph*, 2 September 2012; Gerard Gilbert, *Independent*, 25 August 2012.

784 *pleased to get approval*: TS to Julian Barnes, 11 September 2012, with thanks to Julian Barnes. Saunders, *Ford Madox Ford*, I, vi, II, vii. TS to Max Saunders, 11 January 2010.

785 *horrid surprise*: TS interview at Séries Mania, Paris, *Expatica*, 27 April 2013. TS to Ben Stephenson, Controller, BBC Drama, nd.

786 *feminist sympathies*: Quotations from *Anna Karenina: The Screenplay by Tom Stoppard*, Vintage Books, 2012.

786 *I wrote it 'straight'*: TS to Alastair Macaulay, 1 August 2013.

786 *bold and rewarding*: TS to Alastair Macaulay, 1 August 2013. TS, interview HL, 2 December 2016. TS, interview Robert McCrum, *Guardian*, 2 September 2012. Peter Bradshaw, *Guardian*, 5 September 2012. Richard Brody, *New Yorker*, 16 November 2012. Philip French, *Observer*, 9 September 2012. TS, Introduction, *Anna Karenina: The Screenplay*, Vintage Books, 2012. *Anna Karenina*, 23, 98, 174.

787 *memorial*: Michael Coveney, 'Remembering John Wood', *WhatsOnStage*, 5 July 2012.

787 *Havel*: Žantovský, *Havel*, 10–11. 'Remembering Václav Havel', Programme, 29 February 2012. Dagmar Havel to TS, 3 April 2012.

33: *Circumspice*

789 *What is the Good*: Darkside, 28.

789–92 *Sabrina Guinness*: SGS to TS, nd. Charles Handy, *The New Alchemists*, Hutchinson, 2004, on SGS and YCTV. SGS, interviews HL, 28 September 2015, 14 October 2017. Heather Hodson, 'The Guinness Who Got Away', profile of Hugo Guinness, *Tatler*, August 2015. News items on SGS mentioned her links to Warren Beatty, Jack Nicholson, Rod Stewart, Michael Douglas, Bryan Ferry and Robert Powell, among others. Re. SGS and Paul McCartney: newspaper items, March 2007.

792 *Piers Paul Read observed*: PPR, Diary, 5 September, 5 December 2011, with thanks to PPR.

793 *a public couple*: HL interviews with SF, PS, Diane Sawyer, Tim Rice, DH, John Boorman, David Cornwell, Teresa Wells, AF, MJ, PPR, JM, Bob Bookman, Lottie Cole; TS, interviews HL, 16 June 2016, 14 October 2017, 20 March 2018.

794 *his public life*: TS and Rolling Stones, MOMA, 14 November 2012. TS, interview
     HL, 17–18 June 2019. Edward Helmore, 'The World's Oldest Schoolboys', *Wall Street
     Journal*, 15 November 2012. Tobias Grey, 'Between the Lines', *Town and Country
     Magazine*, March 2013. *Anna Karenina* premiere, 4 September 2012.
795 *You know, Sabrina*: John Boorman, interview HL, 2 November 2015.
795 *a Grade II listed 1790s house*: John Newman and Nikolaus Pevsner, *The Buildings of
     England: Dorset*, 1972.
796 *relative instability*: TS, 'Live Theatre and Dead People', Chalke Valley History
     Festival, 30 June 2013.
797 *enchanting*: David Cornwell, interview HL, 24 February 2017.
797 *papers reacted predictably*: 'It Girl and the Egghead', *Daily Express*, 2 December 2013.
797 *wanted to get on with the next play*: Mark Lawson, 'Tom Stoppard: "I'm the Crank in
     the Bus Queue"', *Guardian*, 14 April 2010. TS, interview HL, 17–18 June 2019.
798 *anxious watchfulness*: TS, *Circumspice: The PEN Pinter Lecture*, Faber, 2013. On
     Leveson: TS, *Independent*, 17 March 2013. TS, interview HL, 29 June 2016. Bill
     Hagerty, interview HL, 3 August 2016, re. TS at BJR Conference, Westminster
     University, 14 June 2016. Max Hastings, interview HL, 2 December 2016.
798–9 *Leveson*: Roy Greenslade, 'Big Names Back Press Regulation', *Guardian*, 18 March
     2014. TS, 'Leveson's Legal Backstop Is Aimed at a Rogue Press – Not a Free Press',
     Independent, 17 March 2013. Steve Barnett, 'Six Myths Surrounding Leveson', *Political
     Quarterly* and Hacked Off, 22 October 2013. Wikipedia entries on Leveson, the Royal
     Charter, the PRP and IPSO. TS re. Richard Bean's *Great Britain*, in Rosenthal, ed.,
     Dramatic Exchanges, 356.
799 *you were in deep trouble*: TS, Letter to *Guardian*, 21 July 2018.
801 *tolerance, fair play*: TS, *Circumspice: The PEN/Pinter Lecture*, Faber, 2013.
802 *gratuitous swipe*: TS, interview Erica Wagner, *New Statesman*, 5 February 2015. TS,
     interview HL, 20 March 2018.
803 *This discussion*: Homa Khaleeli, 'This Seems Like a Solvable Problem', *Guardian*, 22
     February 2016. TS, interview HL, 2 December 2016. DH, interview HL, 26 February
     2016, Natalia Kaliada, interview HL, 12 March 2019.
803 *world events were too monstrous*: TS, interview Erica Wagner, *New Statesman*, 5
     February 2015.
803 *a long conversation*: TS, interview HL, 2 December 2016. Arkady Ostrovsky,
     interview HL, 10 July 2017.
804 *horrifying*: TS, interview Mark Lawson, *Front Row*, BBC Radio 4, 19 August 2013.
804 *national treasure*: TS to Mark Damazer, 31 March 2010, with thanks to Mark
     Damazer.
805–6 Darkside: TS, interview Mark Lawson, *Front Row*, BBC Radio 4, 19 August 2013.
     TS to Alastair Macaulay, 1 August 2013. TS to James Robinson, 21 September 2012, 24
     January 2013, JM archive.
806 *Scene 1: A billion years ago*: TS, Richard Hillary Lecture, Trinity College, May 2011.
807 *The earth is a common*: *Darkside*, 28.
807 *more to us*: TS, interview Mark Lawson, *Front Row*, BBC Radio 4, 19 August 2013. TS
     to Alastair Macaulay, 1 August 2013. Reviews: Robin Hilton, *National Public Radio*,
     26 August 2013. Gillian Reynolds, *Daily Telegraph*, 28 August 2013. Larry Rohter,
     New York Times, 26 November 2013. Nosheen Iqbal, *Guardian*, 30 August 2013.

34: The Eightieth Year

809 *We're dealing in mind stuff*: HP, 37.

809 *turning* Shakespeare in Love *into a play*: TS to Lee Hall, 13 February 2012, Lee Hall to TS, 17 May 2013, JM archive. SF, interview HL, 20 October 2016.

810 *He was my hero*: Tributes to MN, BBC News, Entertainment and Arts, 21 November 2014; Sam Kashner, 'Mike Nichols's Life and Career', *Vanity Fair*, 11 September 2015.

810 *Those unwritten plays*: TS, interview HL, 28 June 2014. (Two plays were written about Price, in 2010 and 2016.) TS, interview Simon Hodgson, *Words on Plays: The Hard Problem*, A.C.T., 2016–17 season.

811 *told the National Theatre cast*: HL notes, TS in rehearsal, HP at the National Theatre, 8 December 2014.

811 *The 'hard problem'*: David Chalmers, *The Conscious Mind*, Oxford University Press, 1996. Jonathan Shear, ed., *Explaining Consciousness: The Hard Problem*, MIT Press, 1999. TS, 'First Person', HP programme, National Theatre, January 2015. Elspeth Sweatman, 'Bananas Don't Think', and Shannon Stockwell, 'The Strange Phenomenon of Kindness', *Words on Plays: The Hard Problem*, A.C.T., 2016–17 season. Shannon Stockwell, interview David Chalmers, 1 August 2016. 'The Hard Problem: What Is Consciousness?', *Economist*, 12 September 2015. 'The Problem of Perception', 'Phenomenal Intentionality', in *The Stanford Encyclopedia of Philosophy*.

812 *summed up in an argument*: HP, 23–4.

813 *another version of the argument*: HP, 11.

813 *the most important problem*: John R. Searle, 'The Mystery of Consciousness', *New York Review of Books*, 6 and 16 November 1995. The essay is referred to by TS in interview with Alexis Soloski, 'A Story as Complex as the Playwright', *New York Times International Edition*, 19 October 2018.

814 *Prisoner's Dilemma*: TS, interview HL, 28 June 2014. Ken Binmore, *The Origins of Fair Play*, Max Planck Institute, 2006, 9. Robert Trivers, 'The Evolution of Reciprocal Altruism', *Quarterly Review of Biology*, 1971, cited in https://en.wikipedia.org/wiki/Prisoner's_dilemma. TS, 'First Person', HP programme, National Theatre, January 2015. 'Evolutionary Game Theory', 'Biological Altruism', *Stanford Encyclopedia of Philosophy*,

815 *competitive altruism*: *Darkside*, 34.

815 *Who is the you*: HP, 15. HL notes, TS in rehearsal, HP at the National Theatre, 8 December 2014.

815 *hard to learn*: TS, interview HL, 28 June 2014.

816 *selfless behaviour*: 'The Playwright and the Scientist', TS in conversation with David Sloan Wilson, *The Evolution Institute*, evolution-institute.org, 14 April 2015. Short version in Stuart Jeffries, 'The Hard Problem: TS on the Limits of What Science Can Explain', *Guardian*, 22 May 2015. TS, interview Alain Elkann, conducted 14 January 2015, https://www.alainelkanninterviews.com/tom-stoppard/, 26 February 2017. Experts consulted for HP also included John Chalmers, John Searle, Thomas Nagel, Ken Binmore, Colin Blakemore and Roger Penrose.

816 *a dualist*: David Sloan Wilson, *Does Altruism Exist?* Yale University Press, 2015. TS also read David Sloan Wilson and Elliott Sober, *Unto Others: The Evolution and Psychology of Unselfish Behaviour*, Harvard University Press, 1999. Armand Leroi to TS, 2 March 2012, JM archive. TS to John Searle, 11 June 2013. 'The Playwright and the Scientist'.

817 *allow for outliers*: Malcolm Gladwell, *Outliers: The Story of Success*, Little Brown, 2008, 7, defines an outlier as 'a statistical observation that is markedly different in value from the others of the sample', or 'a place where normal rules don't apply'. Simon Hodgson, 'Credit Crunch', *Words on Plays: The Hard Problem*, A.C.T., 2016–17 season. HP, 68.

818 *Everyone should say a prayer*: HP, 44, 50, 51.

818 *Hilary: You know it's a miracle*: HP, 75.

818 *Some values haven't changed*: 'The Playwright and the Scientist'.

819 *For want of a better word*: TS and Nicholas Hytner, National Theatre Platform on HP, 6 February 2015.

819 *It's about evolutionary biology*: TS and Hytner, National Theatre Platform on HP, 6 February 2015. TS, interview HL, 28 June 2014. Hytner in rehearsal, HP at the National Theatre, 8 December 2014.

819 *In rehearsal*: Vera Chok, emails to HL, September 2015.

820 *writer's nest*: HL notes, HP rehearsals, 8 December 2014–8 January 2015.

821 *mainly negative*: Dominic Maxwell, *The Times*, 29 January 2015; Quentin Letts, *Daily Mail*, 28 January 2015; Matt Wolf, *Arts Desk*, 29 January 2015; Michael Billington, *Guardian*, 29 January 2015; Paul Taylor, *Independent*, 29 January 2015; Dominic Cavendish, *Daily Telegraph*, 29 January 2015; Susannah Clapp, *Observer*, 1 February 2105; Mark Lawson, *New Statesman*, 19 February 2015.

821 *And I really resent it*: TS and Nick Hytner, National Theatre Platform on HP, 6 February 2015. TS, interview HL, 18 March 2015. Terence Blacker, *Independent*, 8 February 2015; Camilla Turner, *Daily Telegraph*, 7 February 2015; Michael Billington, *Guardian*, 9 February 2015; Matt Rudd, *Sunday Times*, 8 February 2015; 'Pass Notes', *Guardian*, 10 February 2015; TS, 'The Hard Rewrite', Letter to *Independent*, 10 February 2015.

822 *successful afterlife*: TS, interview HL, 14 October 2017; TS, Cameron Mackintosh Lecture, Oxford, 11 October 2017; TS with David Chalmers, HowlRound Theatre TV, 15 December 2015. HP reviewed Toby Zinman, *Philadelphia Inquirer*, 14 January 2016.

823 *airport paperback science*: TS with Carey Perloff and Robert Semper, 'Ways of Knowing', 14 October 2016, The Exploratorium, San Francisco.

824 *much more emotional*: J O'B, interview HL, 27 September 2018.

824 *moved from America to Russia*: Arkady Ostrovsky, interview HL, 27 June 2019. TS in Moscow with HP, Irina Razumovskaya, 6 December 2018, Julie Curtis's translation.

824 *play about artificial intelligence*: TS, unfinished play (*Galatea*), 2018, TS archive.

825 *new production of* Hapgood: TS, interview HL, 29 June 2016. TS, video presentation on H, Hampstead Theatre, December 2015.

825 *screenplay of* Arcadia: TS, interviews HL, 16–17 November 2015, 14 October 2017. TS, A, Screenplay, working draft, 18 August 2017, TS archive. TS, interview Michael Brandman, 29 September 2015.

826 *screenplay of* A Christmas Carol: TS, interview HL, 6 December 2016. TS, *A Christmas Carol*, draft screenplay, 20 April 2016, TS archive. Cf. Charles Dickens, *A Christmas Carol*, Stave Three, 1843. Ben Child, 'Bennett Miller and Tom Stoppard Team Up', *Guardian*, 3 March 2016.

827 Penelope: TS, interview HL, 2 December 2016, 14 October 2017. *Penelope*, draft libretto, 30 June 2017, TS archive. www.wgbh.org, 25 July 2019; www.masslive.com, 25 July 2019; *Berkshire Eagle*, 25 July 2019; www.wbur.org, 24 July 2019; *Boston Musical*

Intelligencer, 26 July 2019. Programme of concert, Florence Gould Auditorium, Seiji Ozawa Hall, Tanglewood, 24 July 2019, includes final libretto of *Penelope*. https://www.nytimes.com/2018/11/15/arts/music/tanglewood-summer-2019.html.

828 *bestsellers*: Rose Cobbe to HL, 4 July 2019.

829 *This is why*: PM to TS, 7 December 2002, 17 July 1999, JM archive. All quotes re. PM's T: TS, conversation with PM, Faber, 11 March 2019. PM and TS, interview Rupert Christiansen, *Daily Telegraph*, 4 October 2016. TS and PM interview, Menier Chocolate Factory, T programme, 2016. TS, interview HL, 29 June 2016. TS, Preface, T, 2017. TS, interview Samira Ahmed, *Front Row*, BBC Radio 4, 3 October 2016. PM, *WhatsOnStage*, 1 March 2017.

830 *new solutions*: T, 47, T, 2017, 37. TS to HL, T rehearsal, September 2016.

832 *Audiences and critics alike adored it*: Reviews of T, 4–5 October 2016, by Dominic Cavendish, *Daily Telegraph*, Michael Billington, *Guardian*, Ann Treneman, *The Times*, Paul Taylor, *Independent*, Kate Kellaway, *Observer*.

832 *A playtext is not*: TS, Preface, T, 2017.

832 *resisted attempts to be drawn*: TS, interview Michael Brandman for Blu-Ray reissue of R&G, 29 September 2015.

833 *In 2017*: HL notes, R&G in rehearsal, National Theatre, January–February 2017; TS, interview HL, 14 October 2017; David Leveaux, interview HL, 4 February 2017. R&G programme, National Theatre, 2017. David Leveaux, *WhatsOnStage*, March 2017. TS, interview Andrew Dickson, *Guardian*, 11 February 2017. R&G, revised edition, Faber, 2017.

834 *rewrites*: R&G, 1967, 48; 2017, 58; R&G, rehearsal text, 2017, 45.

835 *Ah mine own Lord*: R&G, rehearsal text, 2017, 78.

836 *I'm sitting in a room*: TS, interview Andrew Dickson, *Guardian*, 11 February 2017.

837 *the question isn't*: PEN/Allen Foundation Literary Service Award, Natural History Museum, New York, 12 May 2015.

837 *The idea that the writer*: TS, Weidenfeld Humanitas Lecture, Oxford University, 18 May 2016.

838 *'Professing'*: TS, Cameron Mackintosh Lecture, St Catherine's College, Oxford, introduced by Roger Ainsworth, 11 October 2017. Previous holders of the Chair included Ian McKellen, RE, Diana Rigg, Nicholas Hytner, PM, Michael Frayn, TN and Simon Russell Beale.

839 *public celebrations*: BA Honorary Fellowship, Annual General Meeting, 21 July 2017. Mark Lawson, AF and TS speeches, David Cohen Prize for Literature, 8 November 2017.

839 *He took care*: Carey Perloff retirement party, San Francisco, 9 April 2018. Clive James publication party, Cambridge, 14 September 2018. Julian Barnes to HL, September 2018. Tom Gatti, 'I've Got a Few of These Stories: An Afternoon with Clive James, Tom Stoppard and Julian Barnes', *New Statesman*, 3 October 2018.

840 *brought mortality to mind*: TS, interview HL, 2 December 2016. TS, *Today*, BBC Radio 4, 1 July 2017.

35: A Charmed Life

842 *So what's the first thing*: L, Scene Nine.

842 *How is this*: SiL, 149–50.

842 *charm was like a moat*: Philip Roth, *The Ghost Writer*, Cape, 1979, 58. TS in conversation with HL, 'Words in the Square', London Library, 6 May 2016. SiL, 23.

844 *She tells Stoppard's story*: Daša Drndić, *Trieste*, trans. Ellen Elias-Bursac, Maclehose Press, 2012, Houghton Mifflin, 2014, 84–6. TS, interviews HL, 20 March, 19 July 2018.

845 *memory was changing*: TS, interviews HL, 2 December 2016, 20 March, 19 July 2018.

845 *bridled*: Bryan Appleyard on TS, 'But What Else Will I Be Doing?', *Sunday Times*, 19 January 2020.

845 *colluded*: TS, interview John Wilson, *Front Row*, BBC Radio 4, 11 February 2020.

846 *I think about God*: Appleyard, 'But What Else Will I Be Doing?'.

846 *believed in prayer*: TS, interview HL, 29 June 2016.

846 *set himself to read*: TS, interview HL, 17–18 June 2019. 'Author's Note', L, Faber, 2020.

846 *His reading on the Holocaust*: Selected reading: Martin Amis, *The Zone of Interest*, Cape, 2014. Nikolaus Wachsmann, *K.L.: A History of Nazi Concentration Camps*, Little, Brown, 2015; George Clare, *Last Waltz in Vienna: The Destruction of a Family (1842–1942)*, Macmillan, 1982, Pan, 2007; Marjorie Perloff, *The Vienna Paradox*, New Directions, 2003; Daniel Kehlmann, *Geister in Princeton*, 2011, trans. 2012 by Carol Brown Janeway as *Ghosts in Princeton* (unpublished), collected (in German) in Daniel Kehlmann, *Vier Stücke*, Hamburg: Rowohlt, 2019; Ernst Lothar, *The Angel with the Trumpet*, 1942, trans. Elizabeth Reynolds Hapgood, Harrap & Co., 1946; Stefan Zweig, *The World of Yesterday*, 1943, trans. B. W. Huebsch, University of Nebraska, 1961; Arthur Schnitzler, *The Road into the Open*, 1908, trans. Roger Byers, University of California, 1992; Alexander Waugh, *The House of Wittgenstein: A Family at War*, Bloomsbury, 2008; Saul Friedländer, *When Memory Comes*, trans. Helen Lane, University of Wisconsin, 1978, 1979; Gregor von Rezzori, *Memoirs of an Anti-Semite*, 1868, trans. J. Neugroschel and G. von Rezzori, New York Review of Books, 2008; Theodor Herzl, *The Jewish State*, 1896, trans. Sylvie D'Avigdor, Dover, 1988; Edmund de Waal, *The Hare with Amber Eyes*, Chatto & Windus, 2010; Karl Sabbagh, *Dr Riemann's Zeros*, Atlantic Books, 2003.

848 *We count as Jews*: Waugh, *House of Wittgenstein*, 216.

848 *been granted full civil rights*: L, press release, June 2019; Mark Brown, 'Stoppard Returns to West End', *Guardian*, 26 June 2019.

849 *The family in* Leopoldstadt: All quotations from L, Faber, first edition, published 6 February 2020.

849 *rediscover what it means*: Brown, 'Stoppard Returns to the West End'.

852 *It's about a Viennese mathematician*: TS, interview HL, 19 July 2018.

852 *Riemann's hypothesis*: Grateful thanks to Graeme Segal, James Maynard and Harvey Brown for information. Markus Shepherd, 'Tossing the Prime Coin', http://www.riemannhypothesis.info/2014/10/tossing-the-prime-coin, 12 October 2014.

854 *as if he had worked*: TS, interview HL, 17/18 June 2019.

855 *comfortable national superiority*: TS, *Circumspice: The PEN/Pinter Lecture*, Faber, 2013.

857 *I like them to sit*: TS to HL, January 2020.

858 *resonances*: ES, interview David Jays, 'My Surname Was an Albatross', *Guardian*, 29 January 2020.

858 *often tears*: HL, notes, TS in L rehearsals, 14, 16, 17 January 2020. TS, interview John Wilson, *Front Row*, BBC Radio 4, 11 February 2020.

858 *News items*: Mark Brown, 'Stoppard Returns to West End with His Most Personal Play', *Guardian*, 26 June 2019; Nicholas Daniels, 'Tom Stoppard's First Jewish Play

Leopoldstadt to Run at Wyndham's Theatre', *Londontheatre*, 27 June 2019; Dominic Cavendish, 'Will Tom Stoppard's Latest Play Be His Most Personal Yet?', *Daily Telegraph*, 27 June 2019. Appleyard, 'But What Else Will I Be Doing?'. Douglas Murray on TS, 'I Aspire to Write for Posterity', *Spectator*, 21 December 2019. TS, interview John Wilson, *Front Row*, BBC Radio 4, 11 February 2020.

858 *another Jewish story*: TS, adaptation of Daniel Kehlmann, *The Voyage of the St Louis*, produced by Sasha Yevtushenko, BBC Radio 4, 9 May 2020.

859 *assumed too much ignorance*: Mark Lawson, 'Honour and Courage', *Standpoint*, March 2020.

859 *Reviewers*: Dominic Cavendish, *Daily Telegraph*, 12 February 2020. Andrzej Lukowski, *Time Out*, 12 February 2020. Clive Davis, *The Times*, 13 February 2020. David Benedict, *Variety*, 12 February 2020. Arifa Akbar, *Guardian*, 12 February 2020. Ben Brantley, *New York Times*, 12 February 2020. Sarah Hemming, *Financial Times*, 13 February 2020. John Nathan, *Jewish Chronicle*, 12 February 2020. Susannah Clapp, *Observer*, 16 February 2020.

860 *Deeply, achingly moving*: Inna Rogatchi, '*Leopoldstadt*: Tom Stoppard's Kaddish', *Times of Israel*, 9 February 2020. Michael Billington, *World at One*, BBC 4, 13 February 2020.

860 *noted the connections*: Ben Brantley, *New York Times*, 12 February 2020. Tim Bano, *The Stage*, 12 February 2020. Sarah Hemming, *Financial Times*, 13 February 2020.

861 *You know the writer who said*: TS and HL, platform interview, 92nd Street Y, September 2018.

861 *mixed feelings about biography*: TS, London Library Lecture, 29 October 1997; 'Live Theatre and Dead People', Chalke Valley History Festival, 30 June 2013. TS, interview HL, 14 October 2017.

864 *a story Stoppard has often told*: Delaney 1994, 200. Revised by TS, interview HL, 1 November 2019.

Index

P: ~~We can't look at ~~each other~~ in~~
~~humiliation of it, to be tricked out~~
~~and ludicrous in~~

P: We can't look at each other
humiliation of it — to be trie
which makes ~~us~~ our profession w
The plot was two corpses gone b
stripped naked in the middle of ~~noth~~
bottomless well.

Ros: Ooh! (

P: There we were — ~~the~~ ~~present~~
in fancy dress, swearing love,
with wooden swords, ~~&~~ spear
~~&~~ of faith ~~and promises~~ hum
gestures, every pose vanishing
postured for the clouds, ~~and~~
don't you see? We've ne